THE ENGLISH NOVEL IN THE MAGAZINES

1740–1815

The First Known Magazine Illustration of a Work of Fiction
(From "Sir Launcelot Greaves," Chapter II, in the *British Magazine*)

THE ENGLISH NOVEL IN THE MAGAZINES 1740-1815

WITH A CATALOGUE OF 1375 MAGAZINE NOVELS AND NOVELETTES

BY

ROBERT D. MAYO

NORTHWESTERN UNIVERSITY PRESS
EVANSTON
LONDON: OXFORD UNIVERSITY PRESS
1962

Open access edition funded by the National Endowment for the Humanities/Andrew W. Mellon Foundation Humanities Open Book Program.

Robert D. Mayo. The English Novel in the Magazines, 1740-1815. Evanston, Ill.: Northwestern University Press, 1962.

ISBN 978-0-8101-3856-8 (paper)
ISBN 978-0-8101-3857-5 (ebook)

Printed in the Netherlands

Original edition LCCN 62-11619

TABLE OF CONTENTS

ILLUSTRATIONS

ACKNOWLEDGMENTS

The contents of this book were collected with the kind assistance of a great many librarians on both sides of the Atlantic. In the United States I have traded on the good will of numerous private and public institutions, but chiefly the Widener and Houghton Libraries, the Athenaeum, the Yale University Library, the New York Public Library, the Library of Congress, the University of Chicago Library, the Newberry Library, the Huntington Library, and the Northwestern University Library. This distinguished and disinterested service I shall acknowledge collectively, making particular mention only of Ben C. Bowman of the Newberry Library, Marjorie G. Wynne of the Rare Book Room at Yale, Winifred Ver Nooy of the University of Chicago Library, and Marjorie L. Carpenter of Northwestern. Needless to say, without the facilities and full cooperation of the Northwestern University Library staff as well as the excellent collections of eighteenth-century periodicals at the Newberry and the University of Chicago, I could not have written this book. I am grateful also to Northwestern for supplying me with photographs of the *Mirror* and the *Monthly Review*; the Yale University Library for photographs of the *British Magazine* and *Mist's Weekly Journal;* and the University of Chicago for those of the *Gentleman's Journal,* the *Rambler,* the *London Magazine,* the *Lady's Magazine,* and the *New Lady's Magazine.*

In Great Britain and the Irish Free State, in the summer of 1955, I was received with unfailing courtesy and good nature in literally dozens of libraries great and small, including the Library of the British Museum; the London University Library; the London Library; the Bodleian; the Oxford Public Library; the University Library, Cambridge; the John Rylands Library, Manchester; the Manchester University Library; the Birmingham Public Library; the Ipswich Public Library; the Bath Municipal Library; the Bristol Public Library; the National Library of Scotland and the Signet Library; the Edinburgh University Library; the Edinburgh Public Library; the Mitchell Library, Glasgow; the King's College Library, Aberdeen; the Dundee Public Libraries; the Queen's College Library,

Dundee; the Dumfries Public Library; the Berwick Public Library; the Queen's University Library, Belfast; the Linen Hall Library, Belfast; the National Library of Ireland; the Trinity College Library; the King's Inn Law Library, Dublin; and the Public Library, Kevin Street, Dublin. Upon my return to this country, I felt that I could write almost as pleasurably upon the subject of English, Scottish, and Irish libraries as upon their holdings in eighteenth-century periodicals.

A great many friends generously assisted me in collecting materials at home and abroad, among whom I should single out for mention Ruth P. Hagstrum, Carlene E. Prior, Mme. C. Jouhannaud-Raynal, Gaylord and Eileen Haas, David V. Erdman, Nicholas Joost, Marilyn Schoenbaum, Martin Wine, and Ned Edgington. Professors Jean H. Hagstrum and Richard Ellmann of the Northwestern English Department and Dean Moody E. Prior of the Northwestern Graduate School willingly undertook the painful task of reading my manuscript at various stages of completion and gave me much excellent criticism. My wife has been of constant service to me at every step, collecting materials at the Library of Congress, Widener Library, and Yale, reading and improving the text, and correcting proof. Her mother, Mary D. Maris, lent a hand in the thankless labors of preparing the indexes, and Mrs. Thomas J. McNichols ably typed almost the entire manuscript.

To Dean Moody E. Prior and Assistant Dean Robert E. Baker of the Graduate School I am indebted for generous financial assistance. The Northwestern Graduate School shared much of the cost of my trip abroad and afterwards offered a generous grant to assist publication.

I hope that my numerous debts to English and American scholars are all acknowledged in the notes, but every student of eighteenth-century magazines feels special sense of obligation to Walter Graham, Ronald S. Crane, F. B. Kaye, Richmond P. Bond, and their students, for their able pioneer work in British periodicals during the last thirty-five years.

R. D. M.

INTRODUCTION

The following pages represent a new chapter in the lesser history of the English novel. They bring to the attention of students of prose fiction over 1300 novels and long short stories published in British magazines between 1740 and 1815, most of them hitherto unlisted. They attempt to characterize these works as a body of fiction, to separate them into intelligible categories, and to define some of the conditions under which they were produced. By *magazines* is meant all types of eighteenth-century periodicals exclusive of newspapers—not only miscellanies like the *Gentleman's Magazine* and the *Lady's Monthly Museum*, but essay-serials, essay-miscellanies, weekly journals, reviews, abstract serials and learned repositories, and specialized periodicals of every kind, except those primarily concerned with conveying intelligence.

Previously, historians of the novel have written as if the stream of prose fiction that flows between *Pamela* and *Waverley* were fully reflected in the publishers' lists and registers of new books—that is, by the works cited in the *London Catalogue* and elsewhere, or noticed in the *Monthly*, the *Critical*, and other reviews. The general audience for fiction has been imagined as borrowing novels from lending libraries, buying them from book-sellers, and passing them from hand to hand. In this manner, it has been assumed, works of fiction were circulated, and the notices given them in the reviews are a rough index to the fiction with which the reading public was occupied. This is the view which underlies such admirable works on the eighteenth-century novel as J. M. S. Tompkins's *The Popular Novel in England, 1770–1800,* and James R. Foster's *History of the Pre-Romantic Novel in England.*

This view is not incorrect, except for its lack of inclusiveness. The fact is that there is a considerable repository of prose fiction which seldom figured in the publishers' lists and which was rarely mentioned in the reviews, but which nevertheless enjoyed a wide currency in eighteenth-century England, and was both "pre-romantic" and "popular". The 1,375 titles listed in the appended Catalogue represent less than one-tenth of the stories published in British magazines during three-quarters of a century—only the longer and on the whole more interesting items. Prose fiction in one form or another had begun to figure in English serial publications from the last years of the seventeenth century, and by the second half of the eighteenth, with a marked increase after 1770, there were few popular magazines of the many published in Great Britain and Ireland that did not attempt to satisfy the growing appetite for "tales" and "histories". Moreover, many of the more serious publications followed suit. Fiction of some sort was found in four hundred and seventy different periodicals published between 1740 and 1815. Some, it is true, published only an occasional story, or the summary of a new novel, but others devoted as much as one-half of their contents to fiction, at the same time that they enjoyed circulations of anything from one hundred copies to fifteen thousand monthly. Much of this fiction was borrowed from books and other outside sources, but about half was original, and was never reprinted in volume form.

Admittedly the original fiction of the magazines is very uneven in quality. For reasons which will be developed during the course of this survey most new magazine fiction published between 1740 and 1815 was lacking in vigor and permanent value. Some of it was written by hacks, some by amateurs. But some was also written by Dr. Johnson, Hawkesworth, Goldsmith, Eliza Haywood, Smollett, Mackenzie, and James Hogg. Much of it was considered not worth publishing in separate form. But it seems to have satisfied readers of the miscellanies, which, as time went on, increased in size and circulation more or less in proportion to the amount of prose fiction that they offered. The fact that there was so much fiction published in eighteenth-century magazines, at the same time that it was so bloodless, is a phenomenon in the history of taste. It is largely the result of the rapid growth of a new reading audience which was naive, sentimental, and eager for the airs of gentility. The new novel-reading public of the eighteenth century has usually been viewed as entering through the doorways of the circulating libraries. Actually, the stationers, news-carriers, and book-sellers' shops, where magazines were obtainable, were more numerous and more accessible. They were found all over England, and they offered a wide variety of serial publications at anything from a penny to a shilling a copy. The number of magazine readers in the last quarter of the eighteenth century is a highly speculative figure, but it must have included nearly everyone who could read. Even the circulating libraries offered magazines to subscribers.

We should not, as we have sometimes been invited to do, oversimplify the eighteenth-century "reading public." To a considerable degree it defies analysis. There were both vertical and horizontal lines of separation between readers that greatly complicate the picture of the general audience—which was monolithic in size but not in character. The various types of magazines are themselves testimony to the heterogeneity of the public taste, and the appeals to reader interests and prejudices, sometimes within the same periodical, were extremely diversified, if not contradictory. The picture which emerges from this survey is one that seriously qualifies the elegiac view of the eighteenth-century common reader. In the very years when the critics of mass culture celebrate the union of popular and cultivated taste, new magazines, addressed to the sentimental tastes and genteel aspirations of a numerous class of readers, were already circulating on a large scale. Few of these readers, if the common miscellany is any evidence, showed much interest in the novels of Defoe or Smollett, or any acquaintance with the works of the Abbé Prévost.

Even in the seventeenth century the magazines had begun to specialize, directing their appeal to readers of widely different tastes and sensibilities, and the tendency towards the fragmentation of the reading audience was greatly enhanced in the eighteenth. For a brief period the *Tatler* and *Spectator* managed to unite some of the divergent arms of the Augustan reading public, but after their time English magazines tended increasingly to separate into definite types and species, each with its own level of taste and its own class of readers. The chief value of periodicals for the study of prose fiction lies precisely in this fact—that they provide a more accurate picture of the amorphous character of the eighteenth-century reading audience, and therefore help us to appraise an extremely complicated literary situation. A new form of writing that aroused controversy, the novel made its advance only slowly and uncertainly, on a front which was extremely fluid in some sectors and very firm in others. The total situation cannot be accurately reconstructed from lists of eighteenth-century novels, which were often printed in unknown quantities, and were read by nobody knows whom; but it is reflected in the magazines, with their enormous range of titles and their various specialized appeals.

At the same time, in spite of their differences, eighteenth-century magazines do constitute a definite class of publication with unmistakable affinities.

Diversified as they were in the kinds of interest which they satisfied, the essay-serials, the different types of miscellanies, the reviews, the weekly journals, and the specialized periodicals were interrelated in important ways. If they did not always compete for the same readers, they may be said to have issued from adjoining shops in Grub Street and Paternoster Row. They borrowed shamelessly from one another, attacked and supplemented one another, and followed parallel procedures. The mere fact that they were all serial publications associated them in various ways. They were very often assembled and printed in the same shops, and circulated through the same agencies. As a result the stories of Johnson's *Rambler*, the *Town and Country Magazine*, and the *Lady's Monthly Museum* bear a certain family resemblance. In manner and technique they belong to a tradition in British magazine fiction which is not in all respects the tradition of *Moll Flanders*, *Pamela*, *Tom Jones*, and *Peregrine Pickle*. The novelette, or story of medium length, as we shall see, though far from common outside, is a familiar ingredient of both the essay-serial and the popular miscellany, and it had its approved subject matter, methods, and narrative devices. Moreover, writers of original magazine fiction in the eighteenth century tended to imitate one another more than they did the English novelists.

In this book attention is focussed upon the longer pieces of magazine fiction, that is, upon stories in excess of five thousand words. Such a separation is somewhat artificial for two reasons. In the first place, the shorter pieces enjoyed a vast preponderance. Outside the magazines, of course, it was otherwise. In the "Registers of New Books" and "Monthly Catalogues" the long stories noticed outnumber collections like Marmontel's *Moral Tales* and Charlotte and Sophia Lee's *Canterbury Tales* by at least ten to one. But within the periodicals that published fiction this ratio was exactly reversed, and the novels and novelettes, numerous as they are, are only the larger islands in an archipelago of anecdotes, short "histories," and apologues. The century is usually thought of as belonging in a large part to the novel, but approached through the magazines it is an age of tiny tales and diminutive narrative sketches, a principal legacy of the *Tatler* and *Spectator*. In fact, many of the so-called novelettes of the magazines are merely short stories that have strayed, so to speak, into a higher bracket. For this reason it will be necessary to say nearly as much about short fiction as long.

In the second place, the separation of short and long is unnatural because there is no very definite point at which the long story may be said to come into being. There were no established orders of magnitude in eighteenth-century magazine fiction, which ranged unmethodically and by imperceptible degrees from fables and anecdotes of less than one hundred words to full-length novels of over two hundred thousand.

One might expect that installment publication itself would provide a reasonable criterion for length, and that serial fiction could be set apart as a definite class of magazine story. Unfortunately, however, except in the single-essay periodical, serialization was so irregular and accidental a feature of eighteenth-century magazine stories that it affords no fixed standard of any kind. Some magazines printed unbroken narratives of ten to fifteen thousand words, whereas others divided stories of a thousand words or less into several parts. Sometimes the same story was printed both ways. Outside the magazines, novelists tended to think in terms of "chapters" and "volumes" of conventional magnitude. But in the magazines, chapter divisions had little meaning, and installments were often mere mechanical divisions made by the editor's pencil or the printer's rule.

The term *installment*, therefore, has little significance in discussions of eighteenth-century periodical fiction, even though length was increasingly a factor in the changing situation, and long stories became far more numerous as time went on. In order to provide a scale against which to measure the progress of magazine fiction, the line of demarcation in this study between short stories and novelettes has been set somewhat arbitrarily at five thousand words. This leads to a few absurdities in classification, but it has the excuse that stories below this limit were often printed as wholes, and those above were usually divided into two or more parts. In other words, in this neighborhood, somewhat more than in any other, authors and editors tended to be confronted with the fact of installment publication, and the serial novelette (such as it was) came into being. Typically a magazine *novelette* is a story of five to twelve thousand words, divided into two to six parts, and completed within the course of a few weeks or months, or within the compass of a single annual or semi-annual volume. If this length seems closer to what modern readers would call a short story, it should be remembered that in the magazines of the earlier period all normal proportions were greatly reduced in scale. A primary aim of the miscellanies was *multum in parvo*, and in this endeavor most of them were so successful that they are really a mishmash of snippets and slivers among which a story of ten or fifteen pages seems to possess almost massive proportions.

A magazine *novel*, on the other hand, is defined as a story in excess of twelve thousand words, usually (but not always) divided into many parts, and parceled out for publication over the course of a year or more. It should again be emphasized, however, that few authors, before the end of the century, made any serious effort to adopt a special strategy for serial publication. One surprising difference between the eighteenth and the nineteenth centuries, in the realm of magazine fiction, is the relative indifference of the earlier period to the art of serialization.

The boundaries selected for this study, particularly the division between Chapter I and the later chapters, may also seem to be somewhat arbitrarily fixed, but they conform conveniently to familiar landmarks in the history of the novel, and are supported by conditions in the magazines themselves. Although most of the forms and procedures of eighteenth-century magazine fiction were established before 1740, and a good deal of long fiction had already been reprinted in the weekly journals and in the miscellanies, only a handful of *original* stories in excess of five thousand words were actually published in the magazines before that date. The history of magazine fiction, in other words, begins with the *Athenian Mercury*, the *Gentleman's Journal*, the satirical journals of the late seventeenth century, and the *Tatler* and *Spectator*, but the account of the magazine novel proper, that is, the long story written expressly for magazine publication, really begins much later with the "Travels of George Drake" in the *Universal Spectator* of 1740, and the more concentrated efforts of Mrs. Haywood in the *Female Spectator* of a few years later. It is in Mrs. Haywood's "Triumph of Fortitude and Patience" (1745), incidentally, that Richardson's influence upon periodical writers was first decisively felt. Moreover, during the same decade the popular miscellanies returned to the field in greater numbers than ever before, and after 1739 they largely gave over the practice of reprinting the classics of the English novel, and began to make room for original fiction.

The terminal date of 1815 is similarly supported by historical conditions, not merely because the emergence of Scott signaled a major change in the status of the English novel—actually *Waverley* and *Guy Mannering* had no immediate effect upon magazine writers—but because, in the early years of the nineteenth century, the traditional alignments of serial publications underwent a series of drastic revisions. After a hundred years of more or less sustained activity, the essay-serial at length dropped out of view. More important, the new type of review represented by the *Edinburgh* (1802) and the *Quarterly* (1809), and revived weekly journals like the *Literary Journal* (1803) and the *Examiner* (1808), invaded areas which had long been the preserve of the old-type reviews and miscellanies. By 1815 the *Edinburgh* alone had achieved a circulation of about twelve thousand copies a month.

It was with the *Edinburgh Monthly Magazine* of 1817, however, that the new era of popular magazines and magazine fiction really began. From the first issue of Blackwood's periodical, the "Original Communications" greatly outnumbered the "Select Extracts." Furthermore, like the new reviews, it was prepared to pay for what it received, and pay well. As magazine writing became more lucrative, a new class of professional authors entered the picture. John Galt's *Ayrshire Legatees*, which began its run in *Blackwood's* in 1820, was the first serial novel of real merit written expressly for publication in a popular miscellany since Smollett's *Sir Launcelot Greaves* (1760–61). There were also mechanical changes that spelled out the new age. The first printing machine in England is said to have gone into operation in 1811 or 1812 with the printing of the *Annual Register*, and steam began to be used in 1814.[1] Many of the old-type miscellanies, of course, continued to survive far into the nineteenth century, particularly among the women's magazines, but after 1815 they breathed a kind of antique air.

The Catalogue of magazine novels and novelettes appended to this study represents a serious attempt to be exhaustive. All of the major holdings in the United States, Great Britain, and the Irish Free State have been examined, and although a few items may have been overlooked, it can safely be claimed that it includes all the larger and more influential magazines published between 1740 and 1815, in addition to the great majority of lesser-known ones. There are, of course, reasons why such a list can never be complete. A number of eighteenth-century serials have not survived; others exist only in broken runs; and a few are inaccessible. But the listings are as full as present circumstances permit. Many of them are based upon fragments scattered through several libraries.

The Catalogue should be useful to readers interested in trends and influences in eighteenth-century fiction, the relative popularity of different narrative kinds, and the divagations of the common taste. The miscellanies were especially responsive to the fluctuations of literary fashion, and provide a kind of running chronicle of eighteenth-century taste on a month-by-month basis. Oddly enough, considering their neglect, most of these stories are more readily available to students in the United States than are the more elusive productions of the circulating libraries—and some of them were far more widely read. In addition, this material throws a good deal of light on publishing conditions in the eighteenth century, the labyrinthine relations between various magazines, and the character of the reading and writing audience. It also provides a valuable index to continental influences, since the amount of translated fiction is rather large, and some of it never appeared in separate form—at least not in comparable proportions. Certain writers like Marmontel, Arnaud, Florian, and Mme. de Genlis are discovered to have enjoyed an unsuspected popularity, while others—usually reckoned more influential—never found their way into the magazines at all, and were seldom even mentioned by commentators.

Since in this work I have been obliged to reconnoiter an extensive new terrain in the history of the novel, I have in general adhered to the familiar contours of magazine history, concentrating on the leading types of serial publications and the kinds of fiction and the attitudes towards fiction associated with each.

In Chapter I, I have traced the origins of magazine fiction in England in the seventeenth century and followed the development of different narrative traditions in the miscellany, the single-essay periodical, and the weekly journal. This chapter embraces a crowded half-century from 1690 to 1740, during which most of the practices of the succeeding seventy-five years were established. Almost all of the fiction discussed is very short, but it is out of such particles that a great deal of later novelistic substance was created.

In Chapter II, I have followed the fluctuations of the long magazine story in the single-essay periodical from the *Female Spectator* of Eliza Haywood to the *Spy* of James Hogg. The essay-serial made only fugitive contributions to the literature of the novel, but it was to attract almost all the really gifted authors who wrote for the magazines between 1740 and 1815. Some of this material is already familiar, but the close attention given it here has this justification—that the long fiction of the single-essay periodical has not hitherto been viewed in terms of a separate journalistic tradition. Moreover, the stories of Mrs. Haywood, Hawkesworth, Mackenzie, and others were so widely reprinted in the miscellanies and so influential that the total picture would be incomplete without them. There was also in the essay-serial a great deal of comment on the novel by critics in the school of Johnson, Hawkesworth, and Mackenzie, which I have attempted to place in a different critical tradition from that of the monthly reviewers.

Chapter III attempts to define the relation of the *Gentleman's Magazine* and other "historical"-type miscellanies to the English novel and the magazine tradition in prose fiction. The *Gentleman's* was the first important eighteenth-century miscellany in the field, and for at least twenty-five years the most successful magazine of any kind in England. It made a few early experiments with serial fiction, but like other miscellanies of the same type, until 1750 gave only casual attention to the novel. What later happened to the *Gentleman's*, the *London*, and the *Universal*, however, bears striking witness to changing conditions in British journalism, in which magazine fiction played an increasingly important role. In this chapter, which also covers the reviews, I have sought to separate the critical tradition of the *Monthly* and *Critical* from that of the single-essay periodicals, and to consider "reviews" of novels as a species of magazine fiction.

In Chapter IV and Chapter V, I have attempted to reduce to some kind of order the promiscuous and mongrel fiction of all types of miscellanies, and to formulate some of the special conditions that governed its publication. In the general anarchy that prevailed in the eighteenth-century magazine world, it was impossible for the miscellanies to produce a literature which was anything but amorphous, fragmentary, and highly derivative. Because of its abundance and immediacy, however (much of it was written by readers themselves), this material is of considerable interest in the history of taste, and it provides important evidence of the differing kinds of popularity enjoyed by the classical English novelists and others in the pantheon of eighteenth-century periodicals. Chapter IV covers the various kinds of reprinted fiction found in British magazines, and reviews the criticism of the novel in the common miscellanies, In general, this criticism represents an uneasy compromise between the didactic bias of the essay-serials and the more permissive attitude of the monthly reviews. Chapter V gives separate attention to the original fiction of the miscellanies, describing the contributions of Smollett, Mrs. Lennox, and Goldsmith to the history of magazine fiction, and the subsequent retreat of competent professional writers from a field increasingly dominated by amateurs and anonymous hacks.

The three appendices that follow Chapter V are really a series of extensive footnotes on interesting or important aspects of magazine fiction that could not be fitted easily into the main scheme: the fiction of the religious magazines, beginning with Wesley's *Arminian*; the magazines specializing in prose fiction, of which the *Novelist's* was the leading representative; and foreign fiction in translation, chiefly the French novelists, with whom magazine writers showed a marked tendency to consort from the days of the *Gentleman's Journal.*

Addressing himself in 1895 to the question of whether Smollett's *Sir Launcelot Greaves* was the first magazine story ever published in parts, Saintsbury wrote that "it would require a very long ransacking of the dustiest of dustbins to be quite certain of this."[2] The deferred housecleaning has at last taken place, and although only a few abandoned treasures have been restored to light, a great many new facts have been uncovered, and some curious old relics brought down from the attic. The facts have the advantage of all new facts. They call for a healthy re-examination of some existing formulations, and in this case they help us to a better understanding of Defoe, Johnson, Hawkesworth, Smollett, and Goldsmith by illuminating some of the conditions under which they wrote.

The contents of the dustbin, on the other hand, will remind us of what we have sometimes been tempted to forget—that if there has been no progress in popular taste since the days of Fielding, Smollett, and Sterne, there has been no great decline either.

CHAPTER I

The Magazine Tradition in Prose Fiction

In January, 1860, the firm of Smith, Elder, and Company in London launched a new shilling magazine edited by W. M. Thackeray. Intended to compete with long-established miscellanies like *Blackwood's*, *Fraser's*, and *Bentley's*, the *Cornhill* was designed to combine the quality of the best literary periodicals with serial fiction, yet sell at the modest price usually associated with novels issued in monthly parts. The new enterprise was lavishly financed. "No pains and no cost were spared," the publisher later wrote, "to make the new magazine the best periodical yet known to English literature."[1] The illustrious author of *Vanity Fair* and *The Newcomes* was offered £ 1000 a year to lend his name as editor to the new periodical, and £ 350 in addition for each installment of a new novel, still unwritten, to be published serially in the magazine. Besides Chapter I of "Lovel the Widower," the first number of the *Cornhill* included the first installment of a new Barchester novel written expressly for the magazine, for which Trollope was paid "more than double" what he had received thus far for a three-volume novel.[2] Succeeding issues of the magazine published for the first time other now-celebrated works of Victorian fiction in installment form, including Thackeray's *Philip*, Trollope's *The Claverings* and *The Small House at Allington*, Mrs. Gaskell's *Wives and Daughters*, Reade's *Put Yourself in His Place*, Meredith's *Adventures of George Richmond*, and George Eliot's *Romola*. For the privilege of printing the latter novel in his magazine George Smith offered the prodigious sum of £ 10,000.

The extraordinary position of eminence occupied by serial fiction in the *Cornhill* was not achieved overnight. On the contrary, it was only the consummation of a prolonged period of evolution that began in the seventeenth-century and advanced by such slow and uncertain stages that even the modest innovations of Smollett's *British Magazine* in 1760 were too far in advance of their time. Between "Sir Launcelot Greaves" in the *British* and

"Framley Parsonage" in the *Cornhill* lie a hundred years of reaction, compromise, and timid experimentation before important works of new fiction, commissioned for the magazines and illustrated by leading contemporary artists, were to be granted equal status with the best poetry, criticism, and painting of the day.

The phenomenal success of the *Cornhill*, of which the first number sold 120,000 copies, was possible only because of a gradual shift in reader sensibility during the previous century and a half, and a radical revision of serious critical opinion concerning the English novel. The new fiction of the 1740's had won an extraordinary audience within a very short period, so that Millar could offer Fielding £ 600 for *Tom Jones* in 1748, and later £ 1000 for *Amelia*. But though greeted with surprise and interest in some quarters, Richardson and Fielding won anything but universal approval. Many readers remained hostile to the novel in general; others simply indifferent. And the progress of fiction was impeded further by the inertia of a prepotent journalistic tradition. The eager response to *Pamela* and *Joseph Andrews* by the novel-reading public and the deep interest taken in the successive volumes of *Clarissa* was answered in the magazines by relative silence. All the brilliant achievements of the 1740's set up only a ripple in the literary periodicals of the day, and it was still a whole generation before the magazines themselves were to respond with original fiction on a comparable scale.

The conservatism of the magazines in the face of the novel is the more striking since in principle they were dedicated to keeping in touch with the times and were traditionally occupied with new thought and new writing. Unlike the newspapers, where the literary features were largely supplementary and always subject to curtailment in times of public excitement, the various types of magazines tended to give important and regular attention to literary subjects. The twin aims of the miscellanies, the most numerous class of magazines after 1750, were "Knowledge and Pleasure," in the pursuit of which they filled their columns with essays, poems, and short fiction along with accounts of new inventions, historical and antiquarian discoveries, and articles on philosophy, history, geography, mathematics, travel, art, biography, and contemporary life. The single-essay periodical considered manners and belles-lettres its special province; and other types of magazines, also, even when they did not directly concern themselves with literature, by their emphasis upon the arts and sciences, domestic life, learning, and the cultivated use of leisure, tended to foster a climate where literary pursuits could flourish.

In general, therefore, the magazines of the eighteenth century were favorably disposed towards belles-lettres. But towards the different *kinds* of literary endeavor there were sharp differences of opinion, and various types of magazines tended to reflect the tastes and prejudices of different classes of readers. Because of the precedents established by Addison and Steele, the informal essay was generally approved (although not yet fully recognized as a literary genre). Poetry likewise enjoyed universal favor. It is one of the striking features of the period, as both the magazines and newspapers make abundantly clear, that lyric and narrative poetry were fully accepted in nearly every rank and condition of eighteenth-century life. There were few serial publications, if they did not already possess a "Parnassian Corner" or "Temple of the Muses," that could not find a place for a song, an ode, or a ballad, a set of verses by the poet laureate, or the prologue and epilogue of a new play. There was little need to justify poetry as a means of literary expression, even to the most puritanical readers. The drama, on the other hand, was less widely approved, though lent powerful support by the example of Shakespeare and Dryden. Many essay-serials, miscellanies, and reviews ignored the theatre, and some attacked it. But others devoted themselves almost exclusively to the London stage, and popular magazines after 1770 were filled with accounts of new plays and operas, anecdotes of the theatre, essays on the drama, and the lives of favorite actors and actresses. Both the *Critical* and the *Monthly Review* gave sympathetic attention to new plays and operas, once they appeared in print.

The status of prose fiction, however, was more confused. From the beginning, readers on various levels and in various compartments of eighteenth-century life were uncertain whether they should sanction "novels and romances." The problem became one of the moot questions of the age. As a literary form the novel has traditionally been associated with middle-class tastes and aspirations. In its accessibility, its concreteness, and its concern with problems of practical morality and everyday life, it was eminently suited to appeal to readers with only a superficial commitment to neoclassical doctrine. Undoubtedly the development of the new prose fiction and the rise of a new reading public are closely related. At the same time, however, there is danger of over-simplifying this relationship, since, except for fables, allegories, apologues, and tales of a very trivial character, prose fiction was clearly viewed with suspicion by important segments of the bourgeois reading audience. For most of the eighteenth century the novel was under intermittent attack in the magazines, where these classes found a kind of open forum. The objections raised were both aesthetic and ethical, but the latter were more urgently voiced. The novel was a literary form of doubtful origin and dubious literary associations. It violated "truth and nature," it propagated false taste, false feeling, and false morality, and it corrupted the young and the uninformed. The charges rung upon these themes were endless, and they were urged with increasing frequency as the century unrolled. Furthermore, these charges were pressed not only in the essay-serials and the reviews, which were traditionally conservative, but in the popular miscellanies themselves, which published quantities of "tales" and "histories," and where prose fiction would presumably find a more favorable reception.

Viewed from the long range of history, therefore, the English novel was unquestionably the creature of the middle-classes, but for more than a century it was considered an unwelcome intruder by powerful spokesmen in the same circles. Its full acceptance was impeded by pious prejudice, ignorance, and snobbery; and the development of magazine fiction was correspondingly marked by hesitations, subterfuges, and half-hearted surrenders that suggest some of the tensions that this form of diversion tended to create. As the literature of the novel increased in richness and authority in the second half of the century, the pressures to publish and not to publish magazine novels, and to approve and disapprove the new fiction, increased, and magazine editors accommodated themselves in varying ways to the conflicting public demands. The nature of these accommodations varied widely from periodical to periodical, depending upon the type of reader to which the magazine was addressed, and the literary forms and methods with which it was traditionally associated. In order to understand the development of magazine fiction from 1740 to 1815, therefore, it will be necessary to follow the general outlines of magazine history from the time of William III, observing the gradual advance of the English novel in public favor and the critical disapproval with which it was received.

The Abstract Serials and Learned Repositories

The oldest literary periodicals, the learned journals and abstract serials of the seventeenth century and their eighteenth-century successors, need not detain us long, since they flatly disregarded most works of entertainment. Although their principal function was to notice new books, neither the *Philosophical Collections* of 1679–1682 nor the *Weekly Memorials for the Ingenious* of 1682 paid the slightest attention to fiction, or to imaginative writing in general, except classical and foreign literature. In the *Works of the Learned* (1691–1692) La Crose asked authors and booksellers who sent him books to

> remember that this is the *Works of the Learned*, and that I cannot mention *Plays*, *Satyrs*, Romances and the like, which are fitter to corrupt men's morals, and to shake the grounds of Natural Religion, than to promote Learning and Piety.[3]

Dunton's *Compleat Library* a year later promised an "Historical Account of the Choicest Books, Printed in all Languages,"[4] but it meant of course the choicest books in the world of *learning*, and like La Roche's *Memoirs of Literature* (1710–1714, 1717), the *New Memoirs of Literature* (1725–1727), the *Present State of the Republic of Letters* (1728–1736), and other publications in the same lofty line, it was largely devoted to essays in natural philosophy and extracts and summaries of new books of an historical, antiquarian, or scientific character. La Roche published in 1722 the names of eighty-eight of the subscribers to his second edition.[5] They were anything but common readers, the procession being headed by Her Royal Highness the Princess of Wales, shepherded in turn by the Archbishop of Canterbury, the Bishops of Durham and Hereford, the Duke and Duchess of Kent, the Earls of Sunderland and Halifax, numerous other grandees, and members of the two universities. Whatever the private literary vices of this august procession, it is not surprising that the *Memoirs of Literature* should publicly exclude every kind of ephemeral literature, and that later journals in the same tradition should pursue an Olympian policy towards prose fiction. The abstract serials, the learned repositories, and the associated political and historical registers of the eighteenth century are an imposing community of periodical publications, but in the lesser history of the English novel, they count for nothing and may henceforth be dismissed from view.

It was only when the register of new books, or literary chronicle, separated itself from the learned periodical and became a specialized magazine in its own right, although addressed to a more general audience, that prose fiction achieved any recognition at all. Lintot's and Wilford's *Monthly Catalogue* of 1714–1715 and 1723–1730, and the *Monthly Chronicle* of 1728–1732, included some novels among the other books they listed, though without comment. One of the first genuine reviews of a novel in an English periodical is that in the *Literary Magazine* of 1735–1736, which noticed briefly a few miscellaneous works of foreign fiction in its "Literary News," and then published in April, 1736, one five-page summary of Crébillon's *Les Égaremens du cœur et de l'esprit*, at the same time remarking that

> Romances are commonly monstrous compositions of extravagant characters, and surprising events. For which reason they are justly treated with contempt by men of sense.[6]

Later *Pamela* did receive one notice as "a sort of novel" in the *History of the Works of the Learned*[7]—a tribute no doubt to Richardson's personal reputation in publishing circles, since the journal did not ordinarily review narrative works. With the establishment of the *Monthly Review* in 1749, however, prose fiction finally began to win the attention of critics—not because of any very favorable opinion of the genre, but because of the encyclopedic program of the journal. The *Critical* adopted a similar policy in 1756, and henceforth the novel as a form of literary expression was granted serious, though sometimes grudging, recognition by eighteenth-century reviewers, about which something will be said in a later chapter.

The ATHENIAN MERCURY

Among the learned periodicals of the seventeenth century, Dunton's *Athenian* (1691–1697) represents an important new departure and a definite displacement in the direction of a more popular reading audience. Its expressed purpose was to answer

> *all manner* of Nice and Curious Questions in *Divinity*, *Physick*, *Law*, *Philosophy*, *History*, *Trade*, *Mathematick* &c. and all other Questions whatever proposed by *Either SEX*, or in any Language, fit for a Resolution.[8]

In its supplements it also published "Accounts of the most considerable Books printed in England, or transmitted to us from Foreign Parts," so that it was also a kind of abstract journal, although obviously intended for less learned readers. Some of its answers were in verse, and it occasionally engaged in other kinds of facetiousness. Nevertheless the intention of Dunton's journal was fundamentally serious, being to satisfy the miscellaneous inquiries of an audience eager for learning, instruction, and practical advice.

The *Athenian* published no formal fiction, and is deserving of attention here on only one account—namely, the interest that it took in problems of conduct and representative cases, set forth in concrete terms that every reader could understand, and fortified with homilies on everyday morality. One writer, for example, may be involved in "an unlawful amour," another inquires about the validity of a promise made to a highwayman, still others present strange dreams for interpretation, or invite the opinion of the *Athenian* upon an extraordinary piece of deception. The concrete lower and middle-class world of *Mrs. Veal* and *Moll Flanders* impinges directly on nearly every page of the magazine. Almost all such cases are brief (100 to 150 words), although the replies are often much longer. But others occasionally run to four or five hundred words, like the one presented in October, 1691, which speaks almost in the language of Defoe:

> About twelve years ago a Tradesman in this Town, who was newly set up, married a young Woman who was about seventeen years of age, her Relations were dead, her Fortunes were 600 l. which was paid him down on the day of Marriage. The Woman quickly found that her Husband neglected his Trade, which made her the more careful to get an insight into it her self, and being a quick and industrious Woman, in a little time she understood and managed the Trade as well as any Man cou'd do; thus for eight years they lived together creditably, quietly and comfortably, as any couple in the World, she being the fondest and best Wife (as he used to say) that ever Man had; in that eight years they had six Children, three of them are still living.[9]

Now (we are informed) the husband has "fallen to Gaming, Drinking, &c." He has wasted all their substance, her portion included, and is threatened with debtor's prison. Moreover, he has lapsed into impotence. Meanwhile a neighbor of the pair, a single man of good health and with a free estate of

£ 300 per annum, has seriously offered "marriage" to the wife—including a solid settlement on her and the children, and a separate maintenance of £ 20 a year for the husband. Would she be justified in entering into such a relationship, which on his part her legitimate husband is eager for her to embrace, but about which she has some serious scruples? "I'le assure you (declared the same correspondent) the whole Relation is true to a Tittle"—whereupon the *Athenian* delivered a stern lecture upon adultery.

The "cases" of Dunton's *Athenian* all profess to be "true," although they conceal the names of the parties, and many of the circumstances, if not the whole story, must sometimes have been imaginary. But invented or not, they represent a pre-typical form of magazine fiction and point the way toward a great deal of later writing in essay-serials and weekly journals, stories with quasi-real characters and situations (many of them presented by "correspondents"), combined with a strong element of ethical exhortation. Historically they lead directly into the numerous "portraits" and "instances" presented in the *Tatler* and *Spectator* and Defoe's "letters" in *Mist's* and *Applebee's*, and ultimately into the "histories" and "pictures of life" in the *Female Spectator*, the *Rambler*, and the *Adventurer*, although by the time of Mrs. Haywood, Dr. Johnson, and Hawkesworth, as we shall observe, they have drifted away from their original anchorage in common life.

The *Athenian* was a highly successful venture, running for six years and filling several folio volumes. Some readers found fault with it for "meddling with things too *trifling* and *low*," others with "things *too high*," that is, too abstruse. It aimed to satisfy both parties, as it said, being designed "to lye for common Chatt and Entertainment on a Coffee-house-Board."[10] Judging from the naïveté of many of the questions, and their incongruous mixture of pedantry, piety, and practical concerns, its audience was chiefly drawn from the middle ranks of life—tradesmen, literate artisans, and small professional people—although it seems to have attracted other readers also. In his *Life and Errors* Dunton proudly wrote:

> Our Athenian Project did not only obtain among the populace, but was well received by the politer sort of mankind.[11]

The success of the *Athenian* naturally inspired imitators during the next twenty years, differing from one another in tone and emphasis, but none of the later question-and-answer sheets—the *Lacedemonian Mercury*, the *Ladies*

Mercury, the *British Apollo*, the *Athenian News*, and so on—produced any genuine fiction; and with the development of new types of magazines, this species of periodical gradually disappeared from view, although question-and-answer departments are frequently encountered in magazines and newspapers until the end of the century.

Defoe's *Review* (1704–1713) was primarily a weekly journal debating questions of public interest, but its supplements, the "Mercure Scandale" of 1704–1705, and the *Little Review* of 1705, belong to the *Athenian* tradition, "consisting in answers of questions and doubts, remarks, observation and reflection."[12] Except for short letters presenting "cases" and incidental anecdotes and illustrations, however, neither the *Review* nor its supplements published any prose fiction, although in manner and tone, of course, they anticipate the author's later novels. Defoe had also written for the *Athenian*, and therefore Dunton's periodical probably deserves more attention than it has hitherto received in histories of the English novel. Certainly it employs to a very striking degree those basic methods of the new fiction which Ian Watt embraces in the term "Formal Realism," and which Defoe is often credited with inventing.[13] In turning his back upon the romantic tradition in the novel and in winning a new audience for fiction, Defoe was unquestionably a pioneer, but his novels are not so much a new mutation as the protracted extension of a journalistic convention that was already thirty years old. It is a long step from *Oroonoko* and *Incognita* to *Robinson Crusoe* and *Moll Flanders*, but an easy one from the old cases and instances of the *Athenian Mercury* and the *Review*—with their concern for "real" people and events, their pious exhortation, their passion for practical problems of the here and now, their referential language, and their convincing air of authenticity.

The GENTLEMAN'S JOURNAL

The prose fiction of the *Athenian Mercury* is purely embryonic. But in a very different type of periodical, genuine magazine fiction was to enter very early upon the scene. The *Gentleman's Journal, or the Monthly Miscellany*, as a matter of fact, followed the first number of the *Athenian* by only nine months. The first issue of Motteux's miscellany for January, 1692, was a sixty-four-page melange of letters, essays, occasional poems, informative articles, reviews of new books and plays, gossip, news, and enigmatical verse, designed to appeal to a variety of tastes within the "town." It also contained two satirical stories, "The Vain-Glorious Citt, or the Stock-Jobber," and "The Noble Statuary." During the next thirty-four months the *Journal* appeared thirty-one times and published about thirty other "Novels" and "New-Town Adventures, for the Amorous and Gayer Sort of Readers."[14] In addition it included a stream of fables, anecdotes, dreams, *jeux d'esprit*, and tales in verse, so that the quantity of fiction is conspicuous. None of the "novels" is long (by modern standards they are really *short* short-stories), and none was extended beyond a single number. In fact, brevity was to be the general rule for magazine fiction for the next fifty years. The longest story of the *Gentleman's Journal* is "Love's Alchymy, or a Wife Got out of the Fire" (less than 4000 words), published in March, 1692. It concerns a trick played on "a covetous old Don" by a pretended alchemist named Sprightly, who won the Don's daughter by his ingenuity and saved her from an unworthy marriage.

Motteux collected the contents of his miscellany from every available source, at the same time that he tried to coax readers into writing for him. The first number expressed the hope that "Authors of the Learned, witty and diverting things, which are made every day, would oblige the world with them," by offering them to the *Journal*. But he was far less successful in enlisting prose writers than in securing verse, and only two of the thirty-some "novels" are attributed to outside correspondents—one of them to "a Lady." The rest seem to have been adapted from the French, Spanish, or Italian, or written by the editor himself after continental models, in his own mannered, somewhat "literary" English.

The tales of the *Gentleman's Journal* are mostly satirical adventure stories, amorous histories, or tales of intrigue and gallantry in keeping with fashionable taste in the last years of the seventeenth century. A few of them, like "The Treacherous Guardian," have a slight sentimental bias, presenting "the Principles of true Virtue" in a favorable light,[15] but more often they are cynical if not ribald in their treatment of love. The protagonist of "Hypocrisy Out-done," for example, Will Snapmore, "a very handsom, gay Spark, of most pernicious Principles, and a damnable deluding Tongue to Womankind," is treated with cavalier complacency.[16] His successive rogueries, from which he escapes scot-free in the end, are errant gallantry of the sort that the *Tatler* and *Spectator* were soon to be treating with irony and

May e're obtain access, with pleas'd surprise,
Still list'ning to her Tongue, still gazing on her Eyes!
Who catch each Glance that from those Eyes *is sent,*
And, with it, give your Numbers ornament!
Each Glance *she casts can make our Numbers shine,*
Each Word she speaks can point the bluntest Line;
Thus, only thus our Songs can be divine.

Now, for a Novel. I am sometimes much put to it, to discover Adventures worth relating: Take that which follows for a Fable if you please; however, I am credibly inform'd, that most of the Particulars are true.

Hypocrisy Out-done: Or, The Imperfect Widow.

WILL *Snapmore* was a very handsom, gay Spark, of most pernicious Principles, and a damnable deluding Tongue to Womankind: He had had however a generous Education, and an indifferent Estate of his own, which he had almost wasted e're he married the unfortunate *Arabella*, a Lady much above his deserts in every respect. Her miseries began on her Wedding-day; which was about the sixteenth Year of her then departing Happiness. At 17 *Snapmore* quitted *her's* for the *Bed* of *Honor*, and went over to *Flanders* as a Voluntier, where he was wounded. His vicious appetite of variety had made him loath the chast Embraces of his Wife, whose Fortune he had more than half consumed, before he left her; which he did (it seems) with a design never to see her more. For upon the cure of his wound, he quitted the Camp, and retir'd to a Town in the *Netherlands*, where he took upon him the Name of *Beaugard*; while, in the mean time, he caused to be writ Letters to his Lady and Friends, with a certain account of his being kill'd in that Action The News of it had surely dispatch'd his poor afflicted Wife too, had not her excellent piety supported her in this her imaginary misfortune. About a Twelve month after, he married a young Widow of that Town, who fell passionately in love with him; when he chang'd his Religion, as well as his Name. It had been happier for him, could he have chang'd his Nature. With this second Wife he liv'd near a year and half, at a most profuse Rate: When finding that her means wou'd not long support his Extravagancy, he bethought himself of a Retreat from her: In order to which, he pretended he would go to one of the Confede-

An Early "Novel" in the *Gentleman's Journal* (1693)

amused contempt. Moreover, the first story of the *Gentleman's Journal,* "The Vain-Glorious Citt," sneers at tradesmen and merchants and describes the humiliation of a presumptuous citizen, "Mr. Venture," who married his housemaid and yet dared to raise his eyes towards fashionable society. "The Quaker's Gambols" of a few months later is a sarcastic account of a couple of non-conformist buffoons. Whatever audience Motteux was addressing, it was certainly not the dissenting and commercial classes. He claimed for "Hypocrisy Out-done" that he was "credibly inform'd, that most of the Particulars are true,"[17] and like the later authors of secret histories, he seems to have worked into his stories a certain amount of gossip and scandal from high life. The settings of nearly all are contemporary. Contemporaneity joined with brevity and raciness, in fact, is what Motteux meant by *novel.* But even if authentic, the narrative situations have been so embroidered in accordance with polite taste, and so charged with the atmosphere of gallantry and intrigue, that it is hard to imagine that they are exactly contemporary with the *Athenian,* where, as we have seen, the "cases" drawn from middle and lower-class life also purport to be true.

Questions of "audience" are difficult to resolve, since so little has actually been done on this difficult aspect of literary study. Histories of magazines, like those of the novel, are sometimes written as if these productions had no audience at all, or (what amounts to the same thing) as if they were all competing for the same kinds and classes of readers. Yet the subsequent course of magazine fiction demonstrates that eighteenth-century taste was anything but homogeneous, that serial novels and romances, though highly acceptable in some quarters, were proscribed in others, and that even the major novelists enjoyed popularities of different kinds as well as different degrees. If the readers of the *Athenian* were largely drawn (as Dunton declared) from the London "populace," augmented by a few of "the politer sort of mankind," those of the *Gentleman's Journal* would seem to be, in Motteux's words, "the Pretenders to Wit and Gallantry" and "the Amorous and Gayer Sort of Readers"—presumably, the beaux and belles of the town and of the court of St. James, the patrons of the theatres, the smarter habitués of the coffee-houses, and the admirers of Dryden, Congreve, Nahum Tate, and Mrs. Behn. The first collected volume of the *Journal* was dedicated to William, Earl of Devonshire, one of the celebrated sports and poetasters of the day, to whom Motteux wrote:

> My *Journals* aspire no higher, than to attend your *Lordship* when you enter into your *Closet*, to disingage your Thoughts from the daily pressure of Business; or when you retire to that *New Wonder of the Peak*, your beautiful Seat...[18]

But it is not necessary to embark in the social history of the late seventeenth century to discriminate sharply between the literary modes of the *Gentleman's Journal* and the *Athenian* or the tastes and sensibilities implied by each, though both may have lain side by side on the same coffee-house tables and shared some of the same readers. On the one hand, during the three years of its existence the *Gentleman's Journal* not only published quantities of "Novels" and "New-Town Adventures", but presumed a serious interest in polite literature, plus a considerable acquaintance with the various *kinds* of poetry, as well as of prose fiction.[19] The manner of Motteux's miscellany, in short, is both modish and "literary." Moreover, it is frankly entertaining. Its acknowledged model was the *Mercure galant*, a magazine for the fashionable world in Paris.

On the other hand, in order to enjoy a very considerable popularity within its own sphere, the *Athenian* published no prose fiction at all, contenting itself with informative answers on hundreds of topics of both erudite and practical interest, with concrete "cases" and "instances" from middle-class life, and with facetiousness of an obvious sort. Except for the occasional verses of the "Poetical Mercury," mostly doggerel, and its abstracts of a few foreign books, the *Athenian* has no "literary" quality at all and no air of fashion or politeness, although it occasionally answered literary questions. On one occasion, when asked "Whether 'tis lawful to read Romances," the editors replied that in their opinion it was *lawful* and that they might

> have some *Convenience* too, as to forming of the *Minds* of *Persons of Quality*; yet we think 'em not at all *Convenient* for the *Vulgar*, because they give 'em extravagant Ideas of *practice*, and before they have *Judgment* to byass their *Fancies*, generally make 'em think themselves some King or Queen, or other...[20]

Added to this (they declared) is "the softning of the Mind by *Love*" and "the fooling away so many *hours*, and *days*, and *years*, which might be better employ'd," so that in the *Athenian's* considered opinion young people would do better not to read them at all, or at best sparingly. All these socio-ethical charges against romances (later extended to include prose fiction in general) were to be endlessly repeated in later eighteenth-century magazines, few of which were ever to accept novel-reading as casually as did the editor of the *Gentleman's Journal.*

The Comic Journals

The impression of sharp disparities in the taste for fiction in the late seventeenth century between "Persons of Quality" and the "Vulgar," and between "town" and "city," is strongly confirmed if we bring into the picture other serial publications of roughly the same period. Most newspapers, of course, were fairly neutral in character, and were presumably read by all literate classes. But the various comic journals, allegorical serials, and satirical weeklies in the line of the *Mercurius Democritus* (1659), the *Mercurius Fumigosus* (1660), *News from Parnassus* (1681), the *Heraclitus Ridens* (1681–1682), the *Hippocrates Ridens* (1686), and *Momus Ridens* (1690–1691), were obviously designed for a fairly popular, or uncultivated, audience. Some were vaguely political in bias; others were intended to be informative; but most of them were more frankly diverting than the *Athenian.* Once again, however, the literary resonance is very thin, compared with that of the *Gentleman's Journal.* The level of taste and sensibility is very low, and the emphasis is typically upon the palpable everyday world, jocosely viewed, and upon subjects drawn from politics, or from lower and middle-class life rather than from the polite world. There is no "New-Town" quality at all in the comic journals, and in spite of their freedom of expression, no "Wit and Gallantry." At the same time, however, they do contain a variety of narrative and marginal-narrative species very different from those found in the *Gentleman's Journal,* in the form of dialogues, moral and political allegories, dreams, fantastic adventures, mock histories, satirical reports from the moon or mythical countries, and jocose news of the London streets and the magistrate's court—forms, like the "cases" and "instances" of the *Athenian,* that look towards some of the later narrative devices of the *Tatler* and *Spectator.*

The most interesting, but the most exceptional, of the comic journals, from the point of view of magazine fiction, is *News, from the Land of Chivalry,* a weekly half-sheet, which appeared in three numbers in February, 1681, and offered the Pleasant and Delectable History: And, the Wonderful and Strange Adventures of Don Rugero de Strangemento, Kt. of the Squeaking Fidle-Stick: And, of several other Pagan Knights and Ladies.

The first number, consisting of two "Chapters," gives the story of the mock hero's birth, and the various prodigies with which it was accompanied (Chapter I), followed by a farcical account of his childhood, and the way in which he acquired his mighty "Fidle-Stick" and other "implements" that were to make him famous through all the "Land of Chivalry" (Chapter II). The manner of these episodes is coarsely and grotesquely satirical.

In the succeeding number Don Rugero (sometimes spelled "Rugiero") was sent to school of "a very Learned and Sage Magician" to learn "lying," "railing," and necromancy (Chapter III). He stole his master's conjuring cap and wand, and made a fantastic voyage to the moon, from which he had a bad fall, impairing forever his sense of judgment (Chapter IV). The third number (Chapters V and VI) chronicles his triumph over his old master, his attendance at the university, and the burning of his library by his father—whereupon the story breaks off. These six chapters are the sole contents of the journal, which contains no actual news except, in the second number, jocular intelligence concerning a new and "very puissant Gyant" in the "Land of Chivalry", named *Heraclitus Ridens. Heraclitus Ridens*, a dialogue journal of the Tory persuasion, published between February, 1681, and August of the following year, is described in the *News* as a ravenous monster with a "Head as big as a Tun of Heidelburgh, being full of fume and smoak," and "a great forked Tongue that speaks Dialoguish or Pagan Pro and Con"—thus confirming what of course was obvious to every contemporary reader of the journal from the outset, namely, that the "Land of Chivalry" is really the England of Charles II, that "Don Rugero de Strangemento, Kt.," is Sir Roger L'Estrange, for eighteen years the detested Surveyor of the Press, and a special object of odium to the Whig and Protestant interests in 1681 because of his counter-moves in the Titus Oakes affair.

"Don Rugero" has considerable interest as the first serial novel published in a British periodical publication, but it had no imitators and established no tradition for works of this character. Probably its readers were ill prepared to enjoy sustained works of prose fiction. It was obviously addressed to an audience well informed in political matters, but possessing a very low order of literary sensibility, its range of allusiveness in this respect being even less than that of the *Athenian Mercury*. There is a single reference in Chapter II to *Don Quixote*, the "Knight of the Windmill," than whom (it is prophesied) Don Rugero shall be "more famous"; but otherwise the *News* presumes no knowledge of English, French, or Spanish fiction, only a taste for scurrility and fantastic vituperation. The author proposed, if encouraged, to extend his story through twenty-four numbers in all, and therefore, presumably, to provide a continuous narrative of forty-eight "chapters." Such encouragement, however, was not forthcoming. The whole venture was abandoned after only three numbers, and surviving copies of these are extremely rare. Viewed in terms of magazine history, therefore, "Don Rugero" is a literary sport, and it was many years before a comparable effort was made to achieve sustained narrative effects in an English periodical publication.[21]

The *London Spy* of Ned Ward likewise belongs to the satirical tradition in seventeenth-century journalism, and since it won a genuine popularity, it offers a more important precedent than *News, from the Land of Chivalry*. The *Spy*, published in eighteen monthly numbers between 1698 and 1700, is a satirical progress through the seamy side of contemporary London. The idea was not completely original. "Rambles" of one kind or another were a popular species of moral slumming in the late seventeenth century, of which the excursions of Moll Flanders may be considered a still later blossom.[22] The "Spy" is a country scholar, who, growing restive with his studies, comes up to London to "Expose the Vanities and Vices of the Town." He keeps a journal of his visit for his colleagues, recording with a mixture of relish and horrified fascination the sights, sounds, and smells of the metropolis. An old school-fellow takes him to dine at a tavern. They visit Aldgate, Billingsgate, the Custom House, and the wharves, and then slowly continue their eighteen-month's peregrination from one quarter to another, viewing the life of the city and its suburbs through the eyes of an original.

Because it provided jocular intelligence, the *London Spy* is something of a comic journal. It is also a species of anti-romance, like "Don Rugero," though it is less a work of genuine fiction since the Spy himself is so little involved in the crowded events which he mirrors. This difference itself may help to account for its greater popularity. Like the De Coverley papers, which it anticipates, the book has characters, scenes, episodes, and a degree of continuity (a journey), but no sustained narrative action. In later numbers the travels of the Spy are interrupted with descriptions of newsworthy events, essays, satirical portraits ("an Irishman," "a Beau," "a Stock-jobber"), and verses written en route—so that Ward's journal is something of a disguised miscellany also, although the polite readers of the *Gentleman's Journal* must have found it excessively fantastic and devoid of true wit. The real audience of the *Spy* is hard to visualize with any degree of wholeness, though the magazine was certainly a successful venture ("the Publick Snapping at it," Ward wrote, "with as much Greediness as a News-monger at a Gazett").[23] On the one hand, it concerns itself, like the cases of the *Athenian*, with unvarnished aspects of lower and middle-class life, and on the other hand, Ward wrote a highly figurative and self-conscious vernacular which (like that of *News, from the Land of Chivalry*) would be comprehensible only to a fairly literate reader. In any case, the *London Spy* seems to represent a literary mode more closely associated with "popular" literature than with "polite." The *Wandering Spy* of 1705 adopted a similar formula, except that its episodes involve dreams and allegories.[24]

Successors of the GENTLEMAN'S JOURNAL

The *Gentleman's Journal* attracted other imitators, besides the *London Spy*. The years from 1692–1710 are a kind of experimental period in which various attempts were made to find the formula for a successful magazine. For some reason, however, none of Motteux's successors for a number of years seemed willing fully to adopt the miscellany principle—that is, to produce a flexible combination of informal articles, poems, essays, short stories, and other diverting pieces, some original, some collected from various outside sources, or translated from foreign literature. Most writers on Motteux have emphasized the revolutionary features of his journal, and there is no question that it was prophetic in many important respects. But the striking fact about Motteux's influence is not that it operated immediately, but that it failed to do so—the long period of delay before a similar miscellany appeared, with a full measure of prose fiction. Some of his successors, like the *Miscellanies over Claret* (1697), the *Diverting Post* (1704–1706), and the *Muses Mercury* (1707–1708), specialized in poetry, which already enjoyed almost universal favor. Others combined with other species of periodicals, like the *British Apollo* (1708–1711) with the question-and-answer sheet; the *Monthly Miscellany, or Memoirs for the Curious* (1707–1710) with the abstract journal; and the *Ladies' Diary* with the almanac. But none of these magazines, except the last, significantly, published any prose fiction beyond cases, anecdotes, and *jeux d'esprit.*[25] Dunton's *Post Angel* (1701–1702), for example, offered a combination of news and providential events, obituary articles, questions and answers, accounts of new books, poetry, and essays—but no stories. The degree to which British serials before 1709 eschewed the models of prose fiction afforded by the *Gentleman's Journal* is indicative of the indifference with which "novels" and "histories" were regarded outside those limited circles which read and enjoyed the stories of Cervantes and Scarron, *Oroonoko*, *Incognita*, *Lindamira*, and other tales of love and gallantry, and to which Ozell in 1709 addressed his *Monthly Amusement.*[26]

The literature of the novel in 1700 was already considerably diversified, extending in a broad arc from heroic and arcadian romances in reprint, collections of *novelle* from the French, Spanish, and Italian (and English imitations), pseudo-memoirs and "historical" novels through comical romances and rogue stories, marvellous voyages, pious allegories and allegorical satires, to criminal biographies, chapbook romances, and vulgar redactions of older works of fiction. But except for the extreme ends of this spectrum not much is known about the kinds of works read and approved by various classes of readers. The periodical publications of the period from 1690–1700 indicate a sharp cleavage in the public taste between "popular" and "polite" literature, in addition to a number of subsidiary fissures spreading out in other directions. But the sociology of literary taste in the late seventeenth and the early eighteenth centuries is still somewhat obscure. One thing is clear, however: during the half century from 1690 to 1740, though polite taste as represented by the *Gentleman's Journal* and the novels of Aphra Behn, Mrs. Haywood, and Mrs. Manley, remained relatively constant, or slightly retreated from prose fiction as it became more widely disseminated, there were far-reaching adjustments in the common taste. As a result novels and romances began to be regarded as acceptable entertainment by segments of the reading audience which had previously ignored them or viewed them with disfavor. This revolution in taste was a social phenomenon of considerable magnitude, in which periodical publications necessarily played only an accessory role. But as far as it is reflected in the history of journalism, it seems to have been accomplished by the various periodicals for women, chiefly the essay-serials under the leadership of the

Tatler, and (to a lesser degree) by the weekly journals and newspapers of the period from 1720 to 1740. First, however, something should be said about the feminine audience.

Periodicals for Women

Although the *Gentleman's Journal* was somewhat limited in its range of appeal, it broke new ground by enlarging its circle of readers in one important area. Possibly taking his cue from the *Athenian*, which had begun devoting occasional numbers to queries from women (chiefly on the problems of courtship, marriage, and domestic life) Motteux declared in his first issue that "this is no less the *Ladies Journal* than the *Gentlemens*," and one later number actually appeared under that title in token of the editor's esteem.[27] A good deal of the fiction in the new miscellany, as well as a number of its other features, was frankly designed to attract feminine readers. Dunton's and Motteux's magazines, therefore, are to be reckoned as the first English periodicals for women. The feminine audience was (so to speak) their invention, and it should be included among other momentous discoveries of the seventeenth century. Further periodicals intended partly or exclusively for women followed within a few years.[28] In 1704 John Tipper, a Coventry schoolmaster, brought out the *Ladies' Diary*, an "Almanack designed for the Sole Use of the Female Sex," which was also a kind of *Ladies' Journal*, since it offered in addition to the usual paraphernalia of almanacs, a miscellany of recipes, medicaments, female biographies, advice on marriage and family life, mathematical questions, poems, and stories. Here appeared between 1705 and 1709, a dozen years after the *Gentleman's Journal*, the first serial story in a British miscellany, the "Comical Adventures" of a poltroon in love, called "The Unfortunate Courtier," continued in several annual installments.[29]

The circulation of the *Ladies' Diary* was of portentous magnitude (four thousand copies of the first number were sold). Moreover, Tipper's readers were more eager to write for him than were Motteux's—suggesting that occasional writing was already beginning to be regarded as a genteel avocation for women. This is precisely the period when the feminine novelists were moving prominently into public view, and they were attended in the *Ladies' Diary* by a company of eager volunteers which in later years became so great an army that it drove talented professional writers from the field. In the 1706 volume the editor of the *Ladies' Diary* made known to the "Charming Fair" his readiness to receive from his readers "any *Eni[g]mas*, Copies of *Verses*, Pleasant *Stories*, or any other thing proper for *Ladies' Diary*," and met with so eager a response "from all Parts of the Kingdom" that he declared he could not "insert a Tenth Part" of what he received.[30] Encouraged by these signs, Tipper undertook to publish in 1711 "a *Monthly Book* of the same *Bigness and Price*" as the *Ladies' Diary*, devoted exclusively to diversions of this kind, entitled *Delights for the Ingenious, or a Monthly Entertainment for the Curious of Both Sexes*, and containing

> a vast Variety of Pleasant Aenigma's, Delightful Arithmetical Questions, Curious Stories, Witty Epigrams, Surprizing Adventures; with Songs, Anagrams, Dialogues, Emblems, Elegies, Epitaphs, and other Useful and Diverting Subjects both in Prose and Verse.[31]

At the same time the *Ladies' Diary* was allowed to revert to its original function as an almanac.

Tipper's new enterprise was a fairly close approximation of the old *Gentleman's Journal*, including among its other delights several sentimental and satirical tales from one to two thousand words in length, although none were in serial form. After only eight numbers, however, it was extinguished by the new tax on pamphlets. But already, even before the *Ladies' Diary* had divided, a new miscellany entitled the *Records of Love, or Monthly Amusement for the Fair* (1710) had appeared, where for the first time in eighteen years, in a magazine frankly addressed to women and young people, we find a full-blown miscellany in the tradition of the old *Gentleman's Journal*. In the *Records of Love*, however, there was one important change of focus. The new magazine emphasized not only prose fiction and love, but virtue and propriety, and favored sentimental over satirical subjects.

> Each Paper will contain [the prospectus promised] something new and diverting, according to the example of the first Novel, without any Personal Reflections [i.e., without scandal] or Immodest Obscenities, it being chiefly design'd to promote a Love of Virtue in our Youth, by insinuating Examples, and diverting Passages.[32]

In conformity with this moderated program, each number of the magazine offered one or more novels, not in the notorious manner of "The Quaker's Gambols," "Hypocrisy Out-done," or even "The Unfortunate Courtier" (which also contained a good deal of coarseness), but genteel histories "Done out of the French," facetious sketches and entertaining episodes, and tales of love, courtship, and marriage, in the more romantic mode of Motteux's "Treacherous Guardian." In "The Gentleman Gardiner" a marquis assumes the disguise of a gardener in order to court Angelica, "the most Beautiful Lady in Paris." He wins her heart, but encounters a formidable obstacle to their union in the pretensions of another suitor, of superior station, the Count de Bluteaux. The Count, however, is led to withdraw his claims, and the gratified lovers are united in "a Deluge of Tears." In *Fiction and the Reading Public* Mrs. Leavis credits Richardson with discovering the Tears of Sensibility thirty years later. (In her eyes, in fact, this is "his chief contribution to the novel.") But in the *Records of Love* they are already beginning to flow. Moreover, "The Gentleman Gardiner" displays some of the same "romantic idealism," the "easy responses," the quality of "daydream," and other deleterious signs of popular fiction which she lays at the door of much-later novelists.[33]

In "The Generous Heiress" of the *Records of Love*, there are definite Richardsonian notes. The happiness of a rich and beautiful orphan is threatened by the designs of a selfish guardian, who intends to marry her to his oafish son (a species of Soames). Obtaining permission to visit London for a month, she marries a handsome and worthy husband of her own choosing, thus thwarting her persecutor's designs. The magazine also offered some serial fiction. The circumstances of "The Generous Heiress" proved "so numerous and surprising" that it was "continued in the next Paper," and later "The Wandering Dancing Master" similarly appeared in three installments. Both, however, are very short, and neither seems to have been written with a view to serialization.[34]

Just who were the four thousand purchasers of the *Ladies' Diary*, and to what extent they were the same readers as those of the more genteel *Records of Love*, is a difficult problem in social history. It is safe to say, however, that with new leisure and prosperity and with improved educational opportunities, particularly in the middle ranks of society, the number of young readers and feminine readers was sharply on the increase, and that henceforth essay-serials and miscellanies alike tended to pay special attention to the supposed predilections of both. These predilections may have been painful to self-appointed censors of manners and morals, but they are hardly surprising. In the seventeenth century, no doubt, women readers were chiefly drawn from cultivated society, but as others were added from the middle ranks, it is only natural that they should not rebel against fashionable modes but embrace them, and that they should incline more towards the graces of the old *Gentleman's Journal* (once the "Personal Reflections" and "Immodest Obscenities" were expunged) than towards the pious pedantries of the *Athenian* and the *Post Angel* and the crudities of the comic journals. We would expect women readers to show some interest in mathematics and astronomy, which were regarded as blue-stocking accomplishments and therefore in vogue, but not in trade, in politics and public affairs, in unglossed pictures of middle and lower-class life, or in jocular intelligence of any kind. Their eyes were inevitably turned in an opposite direction. Moreover, they were not averse to novel-reading as a pastime, in spite of the disapproval of the pious, for it was a diversion with an air of elegance and ease. The *Records of Love* gravely assured its purchasers that the magazine enjoyed the "Encouragement" of "many Honourable Persons of the First Quality."[35] Such claims would not be urged upon readers already in the highest spheres.

The surprising fact about the *Records of Love* is not its genteel bias, therefore, but the degree to which it anticipates the popular miscellanies of fifty to a hundred years later. It is a distant harbinger of the new age in English magazines. The tiny magazine survived for only twelve numbers, but in manner and tone it belongs to the future far more than do the ponderous pseudo-miscellanies of the same period. In the face of the sweeping political and social changes of the eighteenth century, there was a remarkable consistency in feminine taste from first to last—from the *Records of Love* of the early eighteenth century to the *Lady's Monthly Museum* and *Belle Assemblée* of the early nineteenth. Allowing for surface changes in fashion and manner, it is one of the constants of eighteenth-century life, operating as a kind of magnetic influence of increasing force upon periodical publications that aspired to a degree of general acceptance. The same predilections, of course, were shared by thousands of male readers, but they are always found in their purest form in those magazines intended wholly or in part for women.

In general it may be said that this mode is sentimental, rather than satirical; "romantic" rather than anti-romantic; optimistic, genteel, and moral. It is interested in high life, rather than low, in virtue rather than vice, in perfection, in social success rather than social failure; in the problems of love, courtship, and marriage; in manners and propriety; in poetry, prose fiction, and the arts; in the life and pursuits of "Persons of the First Quality"; and in the preciosities of literary fashion. The eighteenth-century novelists themselves were to gain admittance to the popular miscellanies to the extent that they met these requirements. But in the early years of the century, the most satisfactory accommodation was made by the essay-serials under the leadership of the *Tatler*, the pivotal importance of which in the history of magazine fiction can hardly be exaggerated.

The TATLER

The numerous prototypes of the *Tatler* have been fully explored, and do not need to be reviewed. The most striking fact about Steele's periodical, however, is not that it was a kind of journalistic pastische, but that it succeeded in combining several divergent modes in contemporary taste. The *Tatler* achieved a kind of reconciliation of opposites by the ingenuity of its methods and by Steele's ability to assume a strategic position between different kinds and classes of readers. It not only made a strong appeal to fashionable circles and the literary elite; it was also a considerable popular success—attracting a following from the old audience of Ned Ward and the satirical journals, the question and answer sheets, and serials like Defoe's *Little Review*, in addition to finding a new audience in city, town, and country for whom other journals were in one way or another too dull, too ribald, too pious, too learned, too naive, too unsophisticated, too partisan, too fantastic, too cynical, too sentimental, or too crudely written. Very important also, was its appeal to feminine readers. The degree to which such an audience was in the front of Steele's mind is shown by his special deference to the "Fair Sex" in the first number, in honor of whom he declared (with some irony, of course) the new periodical was named, and to whom a regular part of the contents was to be directed.

Moreover, prose fiction was unquestionably an important factor in the success of the *Tatler* at a time when fiction was still considered by many readers a dubious, trivial, or at best an unfamiliar form of entertainment. The *Tatler* published more fiction than any magazine that preceded it, the *Gentle-*

man's Journal perhaps excepted. There is narrative in some form in nearly every issue, though much of it was disguised. It usually appears not in the form of "novels," "histories," and scandalous "adventures," but as little visions and allegories, inquiries from readers presenting cases and instances, anecdotes, episodes in the life of Mr. Bickerstaff, and jocular intelligence of high life—narrative forms which were by long usage familiar to many readers in the middle and lower ranks of life. By his Whiggish compromises in the realm of belles-lettres, in other words, as well as by his moral and didactic emphasis, Steele was able to make fiction palatable to many readers who on principle tended to disapprove of it, at the same time that he brought within the range of polite taste some of the marginal and submarginal narrative species of the old comic journals. His narrative devices, in particular, deserve a close scrutiny, since they were to become the basic coinage of magazine fiction for the next hundred years.

The first issue of the *Tatler*, for example, after outlining the program which the editor intended to follow, proceeds directly to sketch the satirical "history" of Cynthio, "a very pretty gentleman" who fell hopelessly in love while brushing his teeth. This news was issued from White's Chocolate House, from which Steele promised to send his "accounts of gallantry, pleasure, and entertainment," and he concluded:

> The reader is desired to take notice of the article from this place from time to time, for I design to be very exact in the progress this unhappy gentleman makes, which may be of great instruction to all who actually are, or who ever shall be, in love.

From the very first number, therefore, the *Tatler*, like the old *Gentleman's Journal*, showed a considerable interest in love and gallantry, as well as in high life, but in Steele's periodical these subjects were treated with amused raillery and thus brought within the arm of morality, decency, and good sense that would make them acceptable to a numerous class of readers in the city and elsewhere. For the same reasons, probably, Steele gave his characters romantic names like Flavia, Delamira, Chloe, and Clarissa, names familiar to readers of novels, romances, and secret memoirs. But the nomenclature was practically his only other concession to the modes of contemporary fiction.

Intelligence concerning Cynthio is heard from time to time, sometimes indirectly. Between the fourth number of the *Tatler* where Clarissa, the recipient of Cynthio's abject devotion, is presented and the eighty-fifth number, when his death and entombment are chronicled, he appears or figures in the background in half a dozen papers.[36] His progress, therefore, makes a kind of mock serial romance in essay form, in which the attention of readers is casually sustained for over six months. It is the earliest example in the essay-serial of one of the indigenous forms of continued story, the *cumulative episode*, in which the narrative is always being added to, at the same time that it is always complete.

Meanwhile there had also been appearing in the *Tatler* a flood of shorter pieces of a fictional or semi-fictional character. A very few of Steele's stories in the *Tatler* were given formal titles, like "The Civil Husband" (No. 53), "The History of Tom Varnish" (No. 136), and "The History of Caelia" (No. 198), in the manner of the *Gentleman's Journal* and the *Records of Love*, but the great majority were submerged in the running commentary on manners and morals, appearing in the form of anecdotes, illustrative episodes, "portraits," autobiographical letters from readers, or the adventures of Mr. Bickerstaff and his familiar. The discursive and narrative modes are so deeply intertwined in what Steele called in No. 172 his "libertine manner of writing by way of essay" that the reader is often uncertain whether he is engaged with one or the other. The De Coverley papers and the Lizard family chronicle in the *Spectator* and *Guardian*, of course, were to bring the narrative episode to a still higher degree of development, so that little remained but to unite sketches of this kind with a single theme and narrative action, thus creating genuine novels and novelettes of manners. Encouraged by the new literature of the novel, a few later writers ventured to take this step.

Occasionally one of the stories of the *Tatler* involves an antique subject (like the redaction of the *Iliad* in No. 6, or of the "beautiful romance" from *Fénelon* in No. 156), but nearly all of them are contemporary in setting and present characters and situations more or less within the range of familiar experience. In this respect they strike a kind of balance between the "cases" of the *Athenian* and Defoe's *Little Review*, and the "novels" of the *Gentleman's Journal*. Steele's didactic intention is set forth in No. 172. The "unhappy catastrophes" of "princes, and persons who act in high spheres" are moving to all of us, but their effects are somewhat transient since they "pass through our imagination, as incidents in which our fortunes are too humble to be concerned," and therefore tend not to create "new habits" of thought.

> Instead of such high passages [Steele wrote], I was thinking it would be of great use (if anybody could hit it) to lay before the world such adventures as befall persons not exalted above the common level. This, methought, would better prevail upon the ordinary race of men; who are so prepossessed with outward appearances, that they mistake fortune for nature, and believe nothing can relate to them, that does not happen to such as live and look like themselves. (No. 172.)

By "persons not exalted above the common level," however, Steele did not mean the subjects of the *London Spy* and the comic journals, nor even those of the *Athenian Mercury*. Neither the *Tatler* nor the *Spectator* normally projected its themes on the level of lower or middle-class life. A few of the stories, like "Will Rosin" and "Tom Varnish," were drawn from the trading and small professional classes, or from even lower social strata. But more often they depicted genteel society somewhat below the highest spheres—and thus began that drift towards polite subjects and high life which was henceforth to characterize most writing in the essay-serials. Steele's stories usually involve "ladies of quality," gentlemen of "great estate" and "ancient descent," "wealthy heiresses," "young lords," "fops," "fortune-hunters," "town-ladies," "beaux," and "belles." They were intended, of course, as object lessons for the polite world, but at the same time they helped to inform readers in other ranks of life concerning the manners and ideals of cultivated society. It has long been recognized that both the *Tatler* and the *Spectator* were a species of courtesy book in periodical form. Those members of Steele's middle-class audience (particularly the women) who aspired to lives of fashion and leisure, would hardly be repelled by his preoccupation with good breeding and good manners, especially if he called for the extension of the middle-class virtues of piety, simplicty, and good sense into the upper levels of English society. The ultimate effect of Steele's example, however, was to lend the prestige of the *Tatler* and *Spectator* in support of those later critics among whom Richardson was a leader who called for pictures of genteel life in the English novel, and opposed the "low subjects" of Fielding and Smollett.

Interspersed with the stories of high life and genteel society in the *Tatler* are little domestic tragedies and tragi-comedies of a sentimental turn. Many of these are also love stories, in which Steele attacked the inhumanity of man, the harshness of parents, buying and selling in marriage, and the evils of jointures and settlements, and set forth the advantages of mutual love and trust, unselfishness, and prudence among the middle and upper middle-classes. Some of Steele's domestic tales are purely sentimental; in others irony and humor, satire and pathos, are blended in equal parts. There are certainly ironic overtones, for example, though they may have escaped some readers, in the sentimental presentation of Tom Trueman in No. 213, one of the "heroes of domestic life" by reason of his having relinquished £ 30,000 in order to marry his master's daughter.

Domestic apologues, together with sketches of high life and manners, were among the chief legacies of the *Tatler* and *Spectator* to the eighteenth-century magazines, and writers in the essay-serials and miscellanies for a century to come were to emphasize now one, now the other, at varying points on the scale of satire and sentiment. The ingenuity and flexibility of Steele's narrative methods almost defy classification, but there were several other narrative species of the *Tatler* and *Spectator* which aroused the particular admiration of later generations of writers, and by this means came to found families in magazine fiction. Among these were (1) the *mock-heroic* or *mock-sentimental tale*, (2) the *satirical adventure story*, (3) the *dream narrative*, and (4) the *allegory*. The first two were minority species in the *Tatler* and *Spectator*, important chiefly as precedents enlarged upon by later writers in the magazines. The third and the fourth (which were often combined) were themselves given special emphasis by Addison and Steele.

The "Progress of Cynthio," already mentioned, is a series of episodes in the mock-sentimental vein, but "The History of Orlando the Fair" in Nos. 50–51 has an added interest because it was frankly presented as a serial novel, like "Don Rugero" and "The Unfortunate Courtier." The story, attributed to Addison, is divided into two parts of unequal length (twelve hundred, and four hundred words). The first installment offers an ironic panegyric on the marital exploits of Orlando, a paragon of masculine beauty and "an enthusiast in love," and presents an episode illustrative of his regal sense of his own importance. The "Continuation" in the succeeding number describes the disaster that overtakes him after an "unlucky accident" discloses his bigamy. The satire of "Orlando the Fair" is double-edged. It is first of all directed against the silliness of women who make heroes of such worthless gallants (Orlando is described as "the universal flame of all the fair sex"), and secondly against the sentimental "histories" of love and gallantry then enjoying a vogue in polite circles. At the end of the second part, a promise is made to reprint from time to time Orlando's "soliloquies in verse and prose," so that the whole may have been projected as a running parody of novels like the celebrated *Portugese Letters* (1678) and Mrs. Behn's *Philander and Sylvia* (1683), both of which had since been versified wholly or in part. The fact that Orlando's story, like the "Progress of Cynthio," was partly based upon real events gave it also the character of a "secret history," and thus made contact with another facet of contemporary taste.[37]

The *satirical adventure story* belongs to a somewhat different class of fiction. Here the attempt is made to ridicule human vices and follies from an odd or somewhat impersonal point of view—usually through the imaginary experiences of some inanimate object. "The Adventures of a Shilling" in No. 249 is an example of this type of story. Mr. Bickerstaff falls asleep after a conversation with a friend, and dreams that a shilling on the table turns up on its edge and gives an account of its life and adventures, beginning with its "birth" on a mountain in Peru. The whole chronicle is intended to provide an amusing picture of human levity and cupidity. The various adventures of Pacolet, Mr. Bickerstaff's guardian angel, and of "the Author when Invisible,"[38] have much the same purpose, exposing to view normally inaccessible truths about human behavior. Such stories were introduced quite casually in the *Tatler*, but they were to have a very numerous progeny in later essay-serials and miscellanies in the form of the satirical or sentimental adventures of wigs, bank-notes, pens, pocket handkerchiefs, and quires of paper. The writers of such stories, of course, were partly inspired by the popularity of novels like Coventry's *Pompey the Little* (1751), Mrs. Haywood's *Invisible Spy* (1755), and Johnstone's *Chrysal* (1760–1765), but it is important to remember that in the periodicals there was a much-older tradition for satirical adventure stories, dating back at least to 1710.

Steele's "Adventures of a Shilling" is also presented in the form of a dream, and therefore it can be classified among the numerous dream narratives of the *Tatler* and *Spectator*. In this type of story the author usually falls asleep over his reading, or after some memorable experience, and has a dream that unfolds an object lesson or discovers some deeper truth. There are about nine such dreams in the *Tatler*, and at least twice as many in the *Spectator*. Most of them are moral or philosophical in character, but sometimes they have political overtones, as when Mr. Bickerstaff falls into a slumber after reading

Book VI of the *Aeneid* in No. 8, and has an apocalyptic vision of the present state of England. Later writers in the political serials were to find in dreams of this kind a safe and effective method of satire. "The Vision of the Golden Rump," published in *Common Sense* in 1737 (to name one of many) was a scurrilous attack on the Walpole administration, about which the Government could do nothing except push through the Licensing Act of 1737, when a dramatized version was in prospect.[39]

Most dream visions in eighteenth-century magazines are also *allegories*, involving symbolic landscapes, personifications of various kinds, and a sustained narrative situation. As a matter of fact, the hybrid form of vision-cum-allegory was so much commoner than either of the component species that it is unnatural to insist upon a separation. Steele and Addison were not the first to introduce visions and allegories into periodical publication, but their presence in the *Tatler* and *Spectator* did much to develop an interest in these forms and to give them approved status. For modern readers they are likely to seem one of the more insipid forms of early magazine fiction, but in the eighteenth century they unquestionably fascinated readers and writers alike. Even before the *Spectator* had materialized, an essay-serial appeared that specialized in narratives of this type, the *Visions of Sir Heister Ryley*. Povey's magazine is a witless imitation of the *Tatler*, deservedly forgotten, but one of his visions, "The Inchanted Palace" (in four parts), is notable as an early example of serial fiction as well as of Gothic supernaturalism.[40]

The SPECTATOR

Most of what has been said about the narrative devices of the *Tatler* is equally applicable to the *Spectator*. The two periodicals followed such similar methods and policies with respect to prose fiction that it is unnecessary to discriminate between their impacts upon later writers, who tended to regard them as merely successive phases of the same phenomenon. On the whole the *Spectator* published less fiction than the *Tatler*, perhaps because it gave increased emphasis to literary criticism, perhaps because it was less conspicuously addressed to women. However, the stories of the *Spectator* include some of its most celebrated pieces ("The Vision of Mirza," "The Letter from a Monkey," "Inkle and Yarico," and "The Story of Hilpa"), and their presence along with many other tales and narrative sketches did a great deal to strengthen the precedents established by the *Tatler*. Again, the precise amount of fiction is difficult to measure, since the boundaries of prose fiction are so fluid, but by almost any count the *Spectator* published at least a hundred stories, including fables and extended anecdotes, domestic apologues, sketches of high life and manners, and "cases," "portraits," and "instances" with a definite narrative element. It also published one mock-sentimental tale, several satirical adventure stories, and a great many dream narratives and allegories. The special emphasis upon the latter in the *Spectator* may be the result of Addison's predilection for this species of writing, but they proved so acceptable to readers of the periodical that Mr. Spectator declared with some irony in No. 524 that it would be possible to make his speculations "little else but a book of visions" produced entirely by his correspondents.

Nevertheless the *Spectator* did make one new and significant addition to the repertory of eighteenth-century magazine fiction, the oriental tale. There are, in the *Spectator*, perhaps a dozen stories in this manner, in addition to other pieces with some degree of eastern coloring. Galland's *Arabian Nights*, which had begun appearing in English translation in 1704, had made a deep impression in cultivated circles, and the *Turkish Tales* of 1708 and *Pilpay's Fables* of 1711 had further intensified the same interest—so that Addison was less an innovator than a mirror of his readers' tastes and interests. All of the so-called oriental tales of the *Spectator*, however, are introduced casually, without emphasis, usually in connection with something else. Most of them are little more than anecdotes drawn from one of the popular collections and used to reinforce a moral or to underline some idea in a diverting manner. The "two pretty stories" from the *Turkish Tales* in No. 94, for example, are simply illustrations in a larger essay on the proper use of time. The longer pieces, on the other hand, "The Vision of Mirza," "The Letter from a Monkey," and "The Story of Hilpa," though "writ (as Addison described it) after the Eastern Manner," technically represent different narrative species. The first is a philosophical vision, the second a satirical adventure story, the last a kind of mock-heroic romance. Despite their fugitive and miscellaneous character, however, Addison's oriental narratives are important, if for no other reason than that he lent the tremendous prestige of the *Spectator* to fiction in this mode. It is largely owing to his example, supported by the later stories of Johnson, Goldsmith, and Hawkesworth, that the long procession of sultans, dervishes, hermits, caliphs, and viziers winds its way through eighteenth-century magazines. Furthermore, the popularity of oriental subjects in the *Spectator* helped to *un*domesticate other tales and apologues so that exotic settings became a familiar feature of magazine tales from the time of the *Guardian* on, thus marking one further stage in the essay-serial's retreat from common life.

The oriental pieces in the *Spectator* have been separated by Miss Conant into four different types: the *imaginative*, the *moralistic*, the *philosophical*, and the *satirical*.[41] But her categories, however appropriate for describing the oriental tradition in prose fiction in general, have little relevance to the practice of writers in the literary serials after Addison, who were less "philosophical," "satirical," and "imaginative" than merely didactic and sentimental. In the *Guardian* this drift is already visible. There are five so-called oriental tales in the *Guardian*, of anything from two hundred to two thousand words. Four of them are really moral apologues; the fifth, the "Story of Helim and Abdallah" in No. 167, is a little romance in which virtuous love is fulfilled in the face of many obstacles. In the polemical serials, on the other hand, the oriental tale, like the dream vision, became a specialized instrument for political satire.

Serial Fiction in the TATLER *and* SPECTATOR

The serial fiction of the *Tatler* and *Spectator* is relatively slight in quantity, but, again, methods and devices somewhat casually introduced were seized upon as important precedents by later writers. Actually, only five or six stories in the *Tatler* and *Spectator* (and none in the *Guardian*) are formally extended into a second number.[42] But there is, in addition to these, a good deal of unacknowledged serial fiction, which later writers were also to emulate. In general, the continued stories of the *Tatler* and *Spectator* fall into one of two categories, or show two divergent tendencies. First we find the *serial tale*, in which a story with a single intrigue or narrative action is simply divided into several installments, and published (usually) in successive numbers until completed. Examples are "The Story of Hilpa" and the "History of Orlando the Fair." The serial tales of the *Tatler* and *Spectator* were all confined to two parts, but one of their early imitators, the *Daily Tatler* of 1715, offered the "History of Marmaduke the Amorous," a sentimental novella, in four.

Very different in method is what may be termed the *episodic narrative*, which was much more loosely organized than the serial tale and could presumably be resumed or abandoned by the author at will. Striking examples of this class of story are the "Progress of Cynthio" (already mentioned) and the several "Adventures" of Pacolet, Mr. Bickerstaff's guardian angel in the *Tatler*. The unhappy passion of Cynthio, of course, is pursued to its quietus in the tomb, which is the comic consummation of all that preceded, and we therefore call these episodes *cumulative*, but either series could have been terminated at any point without breaking faith with the reader. In general, the episodic narrative was better adapted than the serial tale to the genius of the essay-serial, where improvisation was a basic principle, and where emphasis was traditionally placed upon the unity of the individual number. The De Coverley papers possess some of the features of the episodic type of narrative, and they tended to stimulate later efforts in this direction, although as a whole they lack genuine narrative continuity. All the characters of the *Tatler* and *Spectator* were imagined with such vividness that in their successive appearances in the periodical they tended to create a kind of episodic story.

In addition to these two types or polar tendencies in the serial fiction of the *Tatler* and *Spectator*, we find a related means by which a story was sometimes carried beyond the limits of a single number, what we may call the *letter-series*. The epistolary methods of the two periodicals were extremely fluid, and they are not always concerned with "cases" and "histories." Letters, both discursive and narrative, singly and in combination with others, were one of the earliest and most characteristic resources employed to give dramatic interest to the periodical. Usually such efforts were confined to a single number, but occasionally one or another was answered or continued in a subsequent essay, in such a way as to develop a kind of narrative situation. On February 4, 1712, for example, a letter from John Trott was printed in the *Spectator* seeking advice on whether to give up dancing, at which he cut a somewhat ridiculous figure. In a reply from Mr. Spectator in the same issue, he was advised to continue his capers, assuming that he could keep time. Several weeks later a complaint was published from "Eliz. Sweepstakes," one of John Trott's acquaintances in Yorkshire, blaming Mr. Spectator for seeming to authorize her partner's recent excesses in the minuet. In a second letter from Mr. Spectator, therefore, Mr. Trott was enjoined to "confine himself to country-dances." A week later a further development was reported: Mr. Trott had pranced his way out of favor with his lady.[43] Later when we come to Defoe, where letters received still greater emphasis, it will be necessary to discriminate between this and other types of stories in epistolary form, but for the present the various *letter-series* of the *Tatler* and *Spectator* may merely be recognized as a potential class of serial fiction, associated with but somewhat separate from the *episodic narrative*.[44]

Other Essay-Serials, 1715–1740

The extraordinary impact made by the *Tatler* and *Spectator* upon contemporary journalists is familiar history. The *Tatler* had run only a few months when (as Steele declared in No. 229) "small Wits and Scribblers" began nibbling at his lucubrations; and the phenomenal success of the *Spectator* only redoubled the efforts of imitators, with the result that from 1712 on there flowed from the presses of London (and later Dublin, Edinburgh, and the provincial towns) a stream of single-essay periodicals in the manner of the great collaborators. A complete register of the essay-serials of the eighteenth century has never been made, but there must have been more than a hundred published in the quarter century from 1715–1740, and the succeeding seventy-five years brought only a slight reduction in numbers. Writers for more than a century after the *Spectator* were seemingly haunted by the memory of a literary periodical which at the peak of its popularity sold twenty thousand copies a week, and was, as Gay said in the *Present State of Wit*, "in every ones Hand, and a constant Topick for our Morning Conversation at Tea-Tables, and Coffee-Houses." The fact that none of the followers of Addison and Steele, in the direct line of succession, enjoyed a comparable circulation, even though the over-all number of English readers was steadily increasing, resulted not from a dearth of talent (since the species was to attract writers of the stature of Johnson, Goldsmith, and Mackenzie) but from the changing conditions of eighteenth-century life, which gradually forced writers and publishers to specialize in various ways. The partial union of popular and cultivated taste achieved by the *Tatler* and *Spectator* was never equalled by any subsequent eighteenth-century periodical. In comparison, even the prodigiously successful *Gentleman's Magazine* had a more specialized appeal.

The tendency of the single-essay periodical to restrict itself to various subjects or areas of interest, and thus to appeal to special classes of readers, began in the first days of the *Tatler*, and continued through the eighteenth century. Broadly viewed, however, there were two main traditions in the essay-serial, stemming from a very early period and following more or less parallel paths. On the one hand we find the more "literary" tradition of the *Guardian*, the *Lay Monk*, the *Grumbler*, the *Free-Thinker*, the *Plain Dealer*, and other serials devoted to discussions of men, manners, and morality; and on the other hand, the "polemical" line, which used the single-essay periodical as a forum for political, religious, or other controversy. This second line, though stimulated by the success of the *Spectator*, really derives from Defoe's *Review*, Swift and Bolingbroke's *Examiner*, and Addison's *Whig Examiner* and *Freeholder*. A few of the single-essay periodicals of the later period embraced both traditions, but in general the "literary" and the "polemical" represent divergent tendencies. In addition, the Spectatorial essay was quickly embodied in the English newspaper, where in the weekly journal in particular, it flourished once-removed from the others in the form of essay-series and introductory letters. Each of these different types of periodicals followed slightly different policies with respect to prose fiction. All three survived into the period from 1740–1815, and therefore something should be said about each.

The polemical serials of the early eighteenth century were the more numerous breed, and some of them enjoyed circulations in the thousands, in proportion to public interest in the issues with which they were occupied. But they have little importance in the history of magazine fiction, since they tended to make only slight use of narrative. In the direct pursuit of partisan ends, essay-serials like *Pasquin* (1722–1724), the *Briton* (1723–1724), the *True Briton* (1723–1724), and the *Monitor* (1724)—to cite four appearing in a single year— disregarded much of the machinery developed by Addison and Steele to give variety and dramatic interest to their lucubrations. In them the assumptive character was usually dissolved into a mere point of view, which was usually presented in argumentative rather than imaginative terms. Not infrequently the writers of polemical serials had recourse to letters from imaginary readers presenting "cases" and instances, and sometimes dream visions and allegories, "histories", and satirical fables, but these imaginative excursions were always tentative and brief. During the whole eighteenth century the polemical series produced only a sprinkling of political novelettes.

In the literary serials, on the other hand, fiction continued to be a basic ingredient. In these periodicals all of the familiar paraphernalia of the *Tatler* and *Spectator*, the narrative devices included, tended to re-appear—with so very little change, however, that it will be unnecessary to traverse this familiar ground. Few writers in the literary line, for a generation after Addison and Steele, ventured to introduce new narrative forms or to extend the boundaries of the old ones beyond the limits of a single number, or perhaps two. Two of the more distinguished successors of the *Tatler* and *Spectator* in this period, however, deserve mention for marking slight changes in the status of prose fiction in the essay-serial. The first is the *Free-Thinker* of 1718–1721; the second is the *Plain Dealer* of 1724–1725. Both, incidentally, made a serious effort to attract women readers.[45]

The avowed purpose of the *Free-Thinker*, a bi-weekly essay-serial conducted by Ambrose Philips, was to lead Englishmen "out of the Depths of false Learning, the Labyrinths of Sophistry, and the Enticement of vulgar Prejudices."[46] Its tacit aim was to lend independent support to the Whig Ministry. To these ends Philips was assisted by a formidable array of clerical talent, including Gilbert Burnet, then Prebend of Salisbury Cathedral and Chaplain to George I. Richard Steele, also, may have contributed to the journal. The appeal of the numerous philosophical and speculative essays, like those of the *Rambler* thirty years later, was to a narrow circle of sophisticated, if not learned, readers, but because the periodical was also allegedly addressed to women, it contained a good deal of prose fiction, much of it translated from Fénelon.

Several features of the *Free-Thinker* are new. One is the tendency of the tales to detach themselves from the tissue of commentary, and achieve a kind of independent status. The *Tatler* and *Spectator* had provided precedents for this, by giving a few of their stories typographical autonomy. But in the *Free-Thinker* this tendency was greatly enhanced. Instead of pretending to subdue its major fiction to the essay principle, the *Free-Thinker* frankly offered a series of "Winter-Evening Tales," designed "to entice young Ladies to delight in Reading, and to lead them insensibly into the Paths of Philosophy."[47] This practice was to find increasing acceptance in the essay-serials henceforth, which as time went on seemed to feel it less necessary to apologize for their prose fiction by offering it as something else.

A second innovation in the *Free-Thinker* is the degree to which serialization has openly entered the picture. In addition to the usual complement of shorter pieces in the traditional manner, the magazine offered seven continued stories altogether. Of these, four are *serial tales* of two to four parts and three are *episodic narratives*, one of which occupies parts of seven numbers. The "tales"—all part of the "Winter-Evening" series—were adapted without acknowledgment from Fénelon's *Fables* and *Télémaque*,[48] and were usually published in successive numbers until completed. The "narratives" consist, first, of a series of "Philosophical Adventures," drawn from a Spanish novel by Don Juan de Velasco, and resumed at intervals; second, a continuing allegory entitled "Psychostaticks"; and third, the "Story of Miranda," a *cumulative episode* in the line of Steele's "Progress of Cynthio." The first two are not extraordinary, but the last is worth a closer scrutiny since it attracted the attention of Defoe and several later writers, possibly among them, Dr. Johnson.

In No. 95 of the *Free-Thinker*, for February 16, 1718, the editor printed a fictitious letter from Miranda, a young lady with a fortune of £ 1500, who was seeking a husband of good character and orthodox principles. Such letters of inquiry, of course, were a familiar gambit of the single-essay periodical, being designed to invite comment and discussion. The surprising feature of the *Free-Thinker*'s offering is the manner in which the situation was developed in succeeding numbers. Four weeks later, in March, the editor transmitted to his readers a number of eager replies to Miranda's letters, and published some verses on the subject of the model wife. A month later Miranda acknowledged his good offices, declaring that she intended soon to reach a decision and inquiring whether there were any further applications from "Bachelor-candidates." A month later, in May, she was still hesitating between them. At length, in July, she announced her impending marriage to a member of her circle of acquaintance who had discovered her identity. Subsequently the *Free-Thinker* published an "Epithalamium" written by an unsuccessful suitor, and finally, half a year later, a letter from Miranda's bridegroom, extolling her connubial charms.[49] Both the letters and the commentary are an amusing satire on the motives and manners of middle-class courtship, and a continuing homily on matrimony. The separate parts are discrete, and the narrative is therefore complete at any given point. At the same time, however, the series progresses towards a final end, the successful marriage of Miranda, and thus achieves a kind of integrated effect. The "Story of Miranda" thus reflects an increased interest in more elaborate narrative structures, to which the weekly journals were also beginning to respond.

The *Plain Dealer* of Aaron Hill and William Bond represents a slight extension of the new tendencies of the essay-serial in still another direction. The manner of the new periodical, which was launched in 1724, closely approximates that of the *Spectator*, and it therefore contains the usual paraphernalia of illustrative anecdotes, dream visions, and narrative cases. The special interest of the *Plain Dealer* is not in these stereotypes, however, nor in its serial tales (of which there is only one), but the manner in which the series as a whole has been enclosed in a framework of narrative. The assumptive character of the *Plain Dealer* is "a talkative *Old Batchelor*, in [his] grand Climacterick, of a sanguine Complexion; well-limb'd, strong and hearty." The subject of his essays is "the Passions, the Humours, the Follies, the Disquiets, the Pleasures, and the Graces of Human Life." Being "naturally disposed to Quiet, and affected to think calmly," he has always obstinately resisted matrimony. Early in the series, however, his steady purpose is blunted by an incorrigible coquette named Patty Amble, who kisses him once in a fit of raillery. To the Plain Dealer she represents the polar opposite of himself—a person "born in a fit of Laughter; and never a Thought of Gravity." He quickly becomes engrossed by her charms. She figures prominently in four or five of the early papers, and is frequently mentioned thereafter. Finally, in the 117th number, he suddenly announces his determination to marry the girl. This decision abruptly terminates the series, since Patty's sole proviso is that her new husband cease to be a "Plain Dealer"—"the aversion (he declares) of every Wife in Christendom."[50]

The story of the old bachelor and Patty Amble is only the lightest scaffolding within which the more serious essays on good breeding, love, gallantry, poetry, and painting are, as it were, suspended. But it is a move in the direction of the English novel, since technically the essays now "illustrate" the story, rather than vice versa. The *Plain Dealer* affords the first genuine example in the single-essay periodical of what may be termed the *supporting narrative*, or background intrigue, a device later employed with much greater ingenuity in Goldsmith's "Chinese Letters."

So much for the single-essay periodicals during the thirty years from 1710 to 1740. The political serials produced almost no fiction, and the literary (the *Free-Thinker* and the *Plain Dealer* aside) were more or less content to exploit, without extending, the literary possibilities discovered by the *Tatler* and *Spectator*. With them the methods of Addison and Steele, originally so flexible, gradually congealed into a journalistic convention which adjusted itself only slightly to the changing conditions of eighteenth-century life. As a result, the literary serials tended to slip from the position of popular eminence which they had earlier enjoyed, and to address themselves increasingly to a cultivated minority of readers who could appreciate their special methods and point of view and enjoy the new changes being rung upon the time-worn themes of the *Tatler* and *Spectator*. In combination with the weekly journal, however, the essay-serial was for a time greatly to enlarge its range of subjects, and to attract a much more general audience of readers.

Defoe and the Weekly Journals

The weekly journal was a phenomenon largely resulting from the special conditions created by the Stamp Tax of 1712. Alarmed by the outspokenness of the press, the Government in 1712 took steps to curtail its influence. Cap. XVIII of an Act passed in the tenth year of the reign of Queen Anne, therefore, imposed a tax of ½d per half sheet, and 1d per whole sheet on "every printed copy" of such publications, and graduated taxes on pamphlets at the rate of two shillings for every sheet "contained in one printed copy thereof." New taxes were also imposed on paper, and upon advertisements, which constituted a main source of revenue for serial publications.

The immediate effect of this crushing piece of legislation, which took effect on August 1, 1712, was to double the price of most newspapers and essay-serials, and so greatly to curtail their circulations that some of them immediately suspended publication. To this extent the Act of 1712 succeeded in its purpose. Within a short time, however, enterprising publishers discovered a method of circumventing the law by increasing the size of periodical publications beyond a single sheet and thus qualifying as a pamphlet, which paid a two-shilling tax on every *impression* rather than on every copy. The result was the six-page weekly journal. Under this interpretation of the law, all that was necessary to evade the heaviest tax was to overcome the paucity of news by changing from daily, twice, or thrice-weekly publication, introduce a few typographical changes designed to fill up space, and close up the gaps with some sort of extraneous material. The first of the new journals, *Mawson's*, founded in December, 1713, supplemented the foreign and domestic news with commercial data of various kinds, and abstracts of new books and pamphlets for the benefit of "Traders, Merchants, and other Gentlemen in particular, who are delighted with Works of Learning and Ingenuity."[51] Other sheets of the same class, like *Mist's*, *Applebee's*, and *Read's*, which sprang into being in 1715–1716, introduced other kinds of supplementary material, much of it partisan, naturally, but some of it informative and some purely entertaining. From this time the weekly journals became in effect both news-sheets and miscellanies for the amusement and instruction of the newspaper-reading audience.

A more subtle and significant change resulted from the union of the weekly journal with the essay-serial. This marriage was consummated in 1718 when *Mist's* began to publish essays in the form of "letters introductory" to the editor. Defoe has been credited with this invention, which other journals quickly copied, and which worked a gradual transformation in the weekly news-miscellanies, turning them into genuine journals of opinion. From the beginning, *Mist's* had been printing occasional letters from correspondents, both real and imaginary, in the section following the domestic and foreign news. By strategically moving one such letter to the front page, and eventually dropping the pretense of an outside correspondent, Defoe in effect inaugurated the leading article. As a result of this technical innovation, the larger journals achieved a character and an identity quite different from that of other purveyors of news. The weekly essay became the soul of the weekly journal.

Defoe was the most distinguished of the writers for the weekly journals and the presiding genius during their formative period. For nearly ten years, through his inexhaustible energy and fertility of mind, he managed to project his manifold tastes and interests on a kind of national scale. The introductory letter was but one of several methods he devised to mitigate the high-flying toryism of *Mist's Journal*. With one hand he toned down the most violent attacks on the Government, while with the other he flooded the paper with a variety of essays and news-reports on matters of topical interest to which the partisan politics of the paper had no particular relevance—subjects like the plague, the lottery, the laws of divorcement, innoculation, the divinity of Christ, journalistic ethics, dreams and omens, the plight of debtors, and penal reform. Defoe's engagement with every aspect of contemporary affairs is one of his most striking traits. Under his competent direction *Mist's Weekly Journal* became (as he wrote to the editor in a self-gratulatory mood)

> an agreeable Miscellany of Subjects, out of which every Person may pick something wherewith to entertain himself. The Tories read you because they take you to be their Friend. The Whigs read you, because they believe you to be a more just Mirror than they can expect from the Flattery and Forgeries of their own Party. Nay, all People read you, because you have something to please all Tastes, in the several Letters sent to you:—Some Historical, some Philosophical, some Moral, some Monitory, some Serious, some Humourous, &c.[52]

In his endeavour to "please all Tastes" Defoe was a phenomenal success. Chiefly owing to his beguilements *Mist's* became for a number of years the most successful journal in England, with a circulation of eleven thousand copies a week. Professor J. R. Sutherland has declared that the audience of *Mist's* largely consisted of the "small shop-keepers and artisans, the publicans, the footmen and servant wenches, the soldiers and sailors, those who could read, but who had neither the time nor the inclination to read very much.[53] But this is too narrow a view since a good deal of the contents of the journal could be of interest only to readers of some greater degree of literacy. Some of Defoe's letters are obviously intended for persons (as he said) of "Historical" and "Philosophical" tastes; others are of literary interest; a great many, of course, occupy themselves with serious debate of public questions. No doubt, as the *Weekly Medley* scornfully said, *Mist's* was "mightily spread about among the vulgar," but it must have had a great many other readers also, particularly among the Tory interest in the country; and its success, joined with that of its chief competitors, probably impeded the further development of the popular miscellany for a number of years. Some of Mr. Mist's "correspondents" present the familiar inhabitants of the Spectatorial world—that is, old maids, fortune-hunters, neglected wives, jealous husbands, and the fops and fools of elite society. But they also conjure up *Tory* husbands and *Whig* wives, pettifogging lawyers, stock-jobbers and speculators, bankrupts and debtors, news-writers, pick-pockets, Quakers, bigamists, half-pay officers, and village gossips, who seem to crowd the pages from the alleys and by-ways of eighteenth-century life.

In the several hundred pieces written by Defoe to Mr. Mist and Mr. App between 1718 and 1726, fiction played a recognized, but quite subordinate role. Week after week, in addition to strictly political essays and analyses of the news, Defoe produced a stream of frothy letters on various subjects of topical interest, but only occasionally had recourse to narrative forms—even the familiar species of the *Tatler* and *Spectator*. His inhibition on this score is surprising, since the years from 1719–1724 are precisely the period of Defoe's intense activity as a popular novelist. The explanation may lie in the fact that he felt more or less committed in his essays to the epistolary form, where the narrative outlines usually tended to dissolve into some other shape. It may be also that the news-hungry and somewhat politically minded readers of the journals were primarily men—the "Traders, Merchants, and other Gentlemen in particular," addressed by *Mawson's*—for whom prose fiction had fewer allurements, if it was not actually disapproved.

One sign that novel-reading by women was now regarded by many readers of *Mist's* as a folly worth serious attention is the communication from a Female Quixote on March 19, 1720. The letter is an absurd appeal for help in finding a husband on the part of an old maid whose head has been turned by reading "Novels and Romances." "Arina Donna Quixota," as she calls herself, is a person of little beauty and less fortune, whose normal opportunities for marriage, with some "Tradesman" or "Mechanick," she regards with aversion.[54] She is a comic fulfillment of the dangers of romance-reading for the "Vulgar," as outlined by the *Athenian Mercury* a quarter of a century before. Defoe's letter, of course, is a piece of persiflage, presented partly in doggerel, yet he would hardly have bothered to attack a pastime which had no relevance to his readers' tastes and interests. In eschewing narrative forms, therefore, he may have been submitting to the prejudice of his readers. In any case, prose fiction is only a minor ingredient of Defoe's writings in *Mist's* and *Applebee's*, although the surprising manner in which *Moll Flanders* mushroomed out of an earlier letter in *Applebee's*, and the casual way in which he engrafted upon the novel two later letters from "Betty Blewskin" in the same journal show how closely associated in his mind were the methods and aims of the novelist and the weekly journalist.

Some of Defoe's magazine fiction is simply anecdote or diverting intelligence of one kind or another, but the longer pieces are typically little histories or narrative portraits in epistolary form, in the tradition of the *Tatler* and

Spectator. Almost all of them are confined to a single number—like the letter from Arina Donna Quixota referred to above, or the celebrated communication from the precursor of Moll Flanders, on July 16, 1720. Such letters are often little autobiographies by way of self-introduction, asking for counsel or help, or posing questions in a manner reminiscent of the old *Athenian Mercury.* A few, however, carry over into a second or third number, or develop into epistolary exchanges in which interest is suspended for several months. There are three letters, for example, on the mysterious bandbox of Nicholas Boggle; three on the "Platonic" love-affair of Leonard Love-wit; two on the misfortunes of a village scold; three from Nancy, the girl who feared to be an old maid, in addition to a rejected letter of proposal; two from Betty Blewskin, the niece of Moll Flanders (a shrewd piece of advertising); and two from Tom Manywife, a matrimonial adventurer.[55] Most of these stories touch upon problems of love and marriage, but in an atmosphere uninfected by either gallantry or sentimentality. They are a far cry from the narratives of *Gentleman's Journal* and the *Records of Love,* or even the *Tatler.* The manner is heavily facetious rather than urbane, and the subjects are chiefly drawn, not from high life, but from the middle and lower ranks of society.

Although Defoe seems to have felt committed to the epistolary form for his serial stories, he did display some ingenuity in adapting and extending the letter devices of the *Tatler* and *Spectator.* His seven serial stories within this convention follow at least four different methods, all of which were incorporated in the *Rambler,* the *Adventurer,* and later essay-serials. First, there is the *simple letter-series,* in which a chronicle of past events is recorded in consecutive communications. The two letters on "Village Love" in 1724 belong to this class of narrative. They are really a form of "serial tale," the separation into parts being purely perfunctory. On June 13 the nameless correspondent begins his story, which, "being too long for this Letter," is resumed in a second letter on June 20. Both are retrospective.

A more sophisticated use of the epistolary form is the *intermittent letter-series,* which chronicles events as they occur. Tom Manywife and Betty Blewskin give accounts of themselves in their initial communications, and the following week unfold some intervening events. Here the effect is that of periodic reports on a developing situation.

In addition to these two rudimentary types of epistolary narrative, there is the *dynamic letter-series*, in which a narrative situation is presented successively from more than one point of view, or in which two or more correspondents react to one another. This is the method of the John Trott sequence of the *Spectator*, already described. It is also the method that Aphra Behn had employed in *Love-Letters between a Nobleman and His Sister* (1683). By 1725 the novelists were already old hands at projecting stories in epistolary form. Thus *Lindamira* (1702) had adopted the simple letter-series, and the Countess d'Aulnoy's *Travels in Spain* (1691) the intermittent. But there was in the periodicals a separate tradition for fiction in the form of letters arising out of the special methods and devices employed by Steele, Addison, Defoe, and others, and the special conditions attached to journalistic writing. The strategy of the essay-serial and the weekly journal was different from that of the novel, because in the latter there was almost unlimited space, and a story in letter form could unfold without any of the restrictions on prolixity which inevitably existed in periodical publications. The pace of the magazine writer was necessarily far less leisurely, and, compared with the novelist's, his letter-series were therefore extremely sketchy and fragmentary. The separate parts, also, achieved a much greater independence, and some doubt always existed (except in the case of simple letter-series) whether a continuation was to be forthcoming. In the magazines the end of the story was (so to speak) always open. These were, no doubt, disadvantages in achieving cumulative effects. On the other hand, they gave a special feeling of immediacy to the intermittent and dynamic series of the magazines that was usually lacking in the epistolary novel. For one thing, there was a genuine lapse of time between the parts for both readers and writers. Events were described as they occurred from week to week, or month to month, by correspondents who claimed to be, and no doubt sometimes *were*, actual persons.

The periodic pleasures of reading "John Trott" in the *Spectator*, therefore, or the "Story of Miranda" in the *Free-Thinker* (in part, at least, epistolary), were not only different in degree, but different in kind from the more sustained pleasures of reading *Lindamira* or *Pamela*. Later writers in the miscellanies came strongly under the influence of both traditions, and they displayed a good deal of capriciousness and irregularity in their epistolary methods, but the early efforts in the essay-serials and weekly journals were all in the separate journalistic tradition. To this tradition Defoe made important contributions.

Defoe produced three *dynamic series* of letters in *Mist's* and *Applebee's*, of which Mr. Boggle's comic adventures are representative. In March, 1720, Mr. Boggle reports to the editor the receipt of a mysterious box of fine linen. This surprising event, obviously intended as a compliment from some unknown admirer, places him under the deep suspicion of the parish officers. Two months later his difficulties over the bandbox still continue, and he describes several ludicrous errors into which he has been led by his untoward speculations. Five months later Defoe suddenly returned to the same subject in a third letter signed "Berinda," the real dispatcher of the bandbox, who describes with some exasperation Mr. Boggle's failure to penetrate her broad hints and incriminating behavior. At this point the story was suddenly abandoned, although there is apparently no reason why the situation could not have been allowed to develop further.

Defoe also affords one example of the *cumulative episode*, "Miranda Desires a Husband," in which both letters and commentary are blended to create a developing narrative situation—in the manner of the "Progress of Cynthio" in the *Tatler* and the "Story of Miranda" in the *Free-Thinker*. Mr. Free-Thinker's Miranda and Defoe's, as a matter of fact, are the same person. On February 21, 1718, Defoe reprinted in *Mist's* a version of Miranda's first letter in Philips's periodical, a few days after its first appearance. He made no acknowledgement of the source, but this is not surprising, since the *Free-Thinker*, being Whiggish in tendency, was a special object of odium to *Mist's*. Defoe's preliminary comment merely stated that the letter was published at the instance of several readers. Proceeding independently from this point, he developed his own sequence of five or six weekly papers, which had almost run its full course before Mr. Free-Thinker published his first replies.

It is interesting to compare the two series, which are exactly contemporary, and which provide a measure of the difference between the essay-serials and the weekly journals. Defoe's intention was likewise to make sport of the matrimonial market. In this endeavor he lacked Mr. Free-Thinker's suavity. Like the old comic journalists his manner was more facetious than witty. His version of the story, however, is remarkable for its proliferation in terms of the concrete everyday world of 1718. In this he also recalls Ned Ward. Like Philips he printed various replies to Miranda's application, but he summarized many more, citing in one issue alone twenty specific letters

85 No 15

THE WEEKLY JOURNAL: OR, SATURDAY'S-POST. With freshest Advices Foreign and Domestick.

SATURDAY, *March* 15. 1719.

Mr. Mist,

I Have seen the two Letters published in your last Journal, and have perused part of the great Number you have given your self the Trouble to convey to me last Night; I am sorry Gentlemen who at the same time confess they are not within the Terms demanded, should give themselves the Trouble of importuning, and me of denying. I desire you will give the Answers I have herewith sent you to such of them to whom they relate; but I enjoin you to speak in your own Name, for I shall enter into no Debates on this Subject with those to whom I am obliged by my Proposals to send a Negative; I understand you have many more, and some that you think worth publishing; when I see them you shall hear farther, and when this Tide of Folly is ebbed out, I shall not fail to give my Answer and Resolution to be made as publick as my Proposal, in which I shall not fail to give my Answer to your self, Mr. Mist, as well as to the rest of the Gentlemen.

Yours,

MIRANDA MEANWELL.

Mr. Mist, as above, being obliged to give Madam Meanwell's Answers in this manner, speaking of her only in the third Person, desires the Gentlemens Pardon, if he gives the Answer in the very Terms he received them; for tho' they may think Mr. Mist their Rival he is resolved to do them Justice in this Case; if they do not like the Answers, they must blame the Lady and their ill Fortune.

Mr. Pope, near Paul's Wharf, says he has all the Qualifications the Lady expects; but she answers, that is too general, and he don't explain himself.

Mr. Fortune Hunter of Oxford is to be told the Character he gives of himself was agreeable enough, and would have gone a great Way; but the Lady takes it for an Affront that he doubts her Veracity about her Fortune, and questions when she says 1500 Pounds, whether she means Pounds Sterling.

Mr. Moses Soldiery's Letter is come to Hand, but as he owns he has not above half the Qualifications expected, the Lady says she can hear nothing.

Jemmy Meanwell of Manchester's Letter is come to Hand; the Lady says she has many Relations of the same Name, and she does not know but he may be too near-kin to her; besides she cannot like to live in Lancashire.

As for Jack Parchment, he is to take notice, that he does not say in his Letter he has any of the Accomplishments the Lady expects; but that he merits all the Accomplishments she expects; the Lady [illegible] he does not understand him, and we profess we do not know how she [illegible].

Mr. Robert Steers, a Stationer in Newgate Street, is to be told, that a Letter is received under such a Name and Position, wherein he claims all the Qualifications; but the Lady craves Leave on his Account to add one Article to her former Letter, (viz.) That the Gentleman she aims at must know how to Spell English.

Mr. S. W. of Ironmonger-Lane is desired to be satisfied with this answer, that whereas he is sensible of his own Merit, the Lady says when she is sensible of it too he may hear farther.

Mr. Polisarchus is desired to take Notice, the Lady rejects him for Courting an Anabaptist, seeing he owns by his Letter the Anabaptist Lady refused him for his being a Churchman, but he did not refuse her for being an Anabaptist.

To Mr. Samuel Orthodox, with his four Vouchers, from the Rainbow Coffee-House in Ironmonger-Lane, we are ordered to answer; the Lady has put his Name down in her Prayer Book.

As to Don Ferdinando in Yorkshire, who has fell out with his Landlord, Miranda says his Case is to be pitied, and tho' the Landlord is a meer Stranger to her she thinks he must needs be a damned scurvy Fellow, and no doubt sooner or later will come to the Gallows; as for Ferdinando himself, the Lady says his Affair shall lye under consideration.

As to Mr. [illegible] Millis, to be heard of at the three Golden Keys near Aldgate, we have only this to say borrowing from his own Letter, that it is a mistake Sir, you are not [illegible].

Mr. T. D's Letter is received; the Lady answers, she did not intend say any thing of the Stature of the Person she would accept of, so he need not have mentioned it; but since he has done it for her, she answers he is two Inches too short for her.

Mr. K. to be heard of at Lloyd's Coffee-house, Lombard-street, Miranda bids us tell him in few Words, she has heard of him, and don't like him.

Mr. J. Cockshead's Letter is also received from Fenchurch-street; but the Lady says, Cockshead is so near a-kin to Cockscomb, that she is afraid of him.

The Lady is very angry with Bob Harnless of Bridgewater, who pretends to all the Qualifications, and yet (as Miranda has been informed) is a Stranger to every one of them; she has ordered us to tell Bob his Assurance had almost given her the Vapours; besides, it seems he is a [illegible] of a half [illegible], which is such a Mongrel Cut as no Woman would care to be troubled with.

Mr. Tim. Lovewell's Letter is writ so passionately that though the Lady began to like him, yet finding at last the real Cause of his Passion, she ordered us to undeceive him, and desire him to read her Proposal over again, where he will find that her Fortune is not 1500 l. but 1500, and she knows that alters the Case mightily in such hungry Lovers.

Mr

Defoe Summarizes "Miranda Meanwell's" Correspondence

from nineteen candidates, dispatched from half a dozen different coffee and ale-houses in London, from addresses in Newgate Street, Ironmonger Lane, Fenchurch Street, and Paul's Wharf, and from Oxford, Manchester, Bridgewater, Yorkshire, and Totteridge in Herfordshire. Characteristically, Defoe's story of Miranda was never really completed, but trailed off into a series of satirical letters on the subject of an "Office of Matrimony" for the benefit of apprentices, younger sons, and old maids (a favorite subject of derision in the weekly journals).[56]

Thus far we have spoken of the weekly journals principally as modified essay-serials, that is, in their primary function as organs of opinion and as commentators through letters, leading articles, and essay-series on myriad aspects of the social and political scene; and we have tended to disregard the fact that they also functioned as weekly miscellanies, providing readers with an intermittent stream of fugitive odes and epistles, epigrams, verse tales, dialogues, scenes from new plays, accounts of celebrated criminals, and extracts and abridgments of pamphlets and new books, designed to occupy space and to amuse and edify a large and heterogeneous audience. There was, of course, a good deal of difference between weekly journals in this respect, and no doubt, if the truth were known, they would be shown to be not only divided in their politics, but also stratified in terms of the heterogeneous reading audience. On their miscellaneous side, fiction sometimes played a more prominent role, but not on the whole in the larger London journals. Editors were not averse to throwing in an occasional "novel" or short serial tale, but long prose fiction was not a normal ingredient of the better known and more influential papers, which presumably offered their readers something more attractive. *Mist's* seems to have published no serial fiction, apart from the kinds already cited; and during their varying periods of survival *Fog's*, *Read's*, the *British Journal*, the *London Journal*, the *Craftsman*, *Common Sense*, the *Grub-Street Journal*, and the *Weekly Miscellany*—to name some of the more celebrated journals of opinion—published a good many short pieces in the Spectatorial tradition, but only rarely continued stories of more than two or three parts.

Applebee's is an outstanding exception. In 1728, two years after Defoe retired from the paper, it offered its readers a spurious continuation of *Gulliver's Travels* and attacked the increasing preoccupation of its contemporaries with partisan politics, re-affirming its intention of offering the

"Publick" a "delicious Variety of Entertainments fit for all Palates." It laid a particular claim upon feminine readers ("...let the Ladies share in the Entertainment," Mr. App's correspondent declared),[57] and for this reason no doubt commenced a weekly serialization of Gueullette's *Mogul Tales* that occupied two whole years. The *Tales* were followed by a series of English, French, and Spanish "Novels" running intermittently until the magazine expired in 1737. But during the same ten years (that is, 1728–1737), the *Universal Spectator*, another weekly journal that addressed itself in part to women, though it frequently livened its weekly essays with narrative letters and short diverting histories, published only a few stories that extended into two or three parts. One of these, incidentally, was a belated imitation of the *Free-Thinker's* "Story of Miranda."[58]

In the light of the conservative policy of most weekly journals respecting prose fiction, the outspoken disapproval of "Novels and Romances" set forth in No. 91 of the *Universal Spectator* (July 4, 1730) may be significant. It shows the increased tension that the growing taste for prose fiction, particularly among women readers, was creating in the give-and-take world of the weekly journals and the manner in which the private foibles of Addison's "Leonora" and Defoe's "Donna Quixota" were now regarded, by some writers at least, as a public scandal. This essay, published in the period when *Applebee's* was devoting many of its columns to fiction and new popular miscellanies were beginning to creep into public favor, is one of several lucubrations in the *Universal Spectator* recommending reading to the fair sex, and advancing the view that women have natural capacities equal to men's and should therefore make some effort to improve their minds. It is presented in the form of "A Letter to a Lady, concerning Books of *Piety* and *Romances*," submitted by an unnamed correspondent, possibly the Author of the *Universal Spectator* himself, Henry Baker.

In the letter both kinds of books come under attack—pious works for their unreasonable regard for "Enthusiastic Regulations," and their tendency "rather to confound than increase our Knowledge," and romances for their egregious offenses against virtue and good sense. There are a few works of fiction, like Fénelon's *Télémaque,* which the writer will allow to be "very instructive and entertaining," but such works since they "require some Degree of good Sense to relish them" are generally neglected; whereas "every *Footman* and *Chambermaid* are fond of the lewd inventions of H——d or M——l——y." Romances, the writer charges, "ruin more Virgins than *Masquerades* or *Brothels*" because "They strike at the very Root of all Virtue, by corrupting the Mind" and by "raising People's Passions, and encouraging their vicious Inclinations." "I leave you to judge," he adds, "what an excellent Housewife any Damsel is likely to make, who has read the *Persian Tales* [of Ambrose Philips], 'till she fancies herself a *Sultana*."[59]

On the question of romances, therefore, the *Universal Spectator* sharply divided with *Applebee's*, currently completing its two-year's serialization of Gueullette's *Mogul Tales* and about to embark upon its series of French and Spanish "Novels." Mr. Stonecastle, of course, was more conservative in all respects than his rival, Mr. App, the result of his more traditional orientation towards the *Spectator* and his inherited role of censor of manners and morals. But the fact is that the tendency of all the leading journals, *Applebee's* excepted, was to occupy themselves only casually with short tales and histories, and not at all with longer pieces.

Newspaper Fiction

Between 1720 and 1740, however, there were a number of lesser newspapers and journals, in addition to *Applebee's*, which gave particular emphasis to prose fiction in the later manner of the popular miscellanies, and of these some account should now be given. Since the late seventeenth century, newspapers had shown a readiness to include entertaining material of a fugitive character—chiefly, poems, letters, jocular intelligence, and diverting news articles. But they had published almost nothing that can properly be described as fiction, and all of this material was strictly supplementary to the principal function of the news-sheets, namely, to disseminate intelligence and to comment upon it. Defoe's *Weekly Review* had introduced some pioneer literary features, but it was primarily a journal of opinion rather than a newspaper. Besides its fiction was inconsequential. The appearance, therefore, of three serial stories in a twice-weekly English newspaper in 1712–1714 is surprising, especially since two of the stories seem to be more "polite" than "popular" in their literary orientation. During this two-year period the *British Mercury* offered its readers "A Voyage into Another World" (in seven parts) and "A Letter from Madrid" (in five), followed by "The Rover" (in twelve). The last-named is a picaresque novel of over twenty thousand words, unknown earlier in English, but obviously not written for newspaper publication, since it clumsily divided seven chapters into twelve installments.[60]

These three serial stories are important "firsts" for newspaper fiction, though the *Mercury* was hardly a typical news-sheet. It was, in fact, a kind of "house organ" of the Sun Fire Insurance Company, distributed to policy-holders at a supplementary charge of only 6d per quarter. Presumably its readers were householders and the more prosperous members of the commercial classes for whom polite literature might be expected to have some interest. "The Rover" was preceded in the *Mercury* by a brief history of the world "from the Creation, to this Present Time" in seventy-five installments, and succeeded by a fairly extensive "Abridgement of Geography" and a "Short Account of Several Countries"—indicating that even in the *Mercury* fiction was only a minor diversion.

A more significant trend began five years later when the *Original London Post, or Heathcote's Intelligence*, a thrice-weekly newspaper, commenced to print "The Life and Strange Adventures of Robinson Crusoe" in regular installments. The first part of Defoe's novel in volume form had appeared on April 25, 1719. The book was a sensational success, three further editions being called for within the first four months, and Part II quickly followed. Within six months of the first date of publication of the novel, while both parts were still enjoying a brisk sale, Heathcote began his serialization of the novel, in a slightly abridged version. The precise status of this newspaper edition is still somewhat in doubt. It is possible that Defoe or his publisher Taylor conspired in this extraordinary undertaking, which could be considered a form of advertising.[61] No objection, at least, is known to have been made by either author or publisher, although the printer of a similar abridgment in volume form a few months earlier had been immediately threatened with prosecution. On the other hand, under the permissive copyright legislation of 1710, newspapers and magazines had begun to assume a good deal of liberty with respect to literary property, and Taylor may have felt it futile to attempt any legal action.

Heathcote's serialization of *Robinson Crusoe* ran for a little more than a year, and it must have been counted as a success in some publishers' eyes, since in time several other newspapers and journals adopted the same practice. On May 14, 1720, while *Robinson Crusoe* was still running in the *Original*

London Post, a new journal called the *Churchman's Last Shift* appeared which supplemented the news, not with the usual introductory letter or leading article, but with "The Voyages of Sinbad the Sailor" in weekly installments. This collection of tales engaged readers of the journal for over twenty weeks, and it was followed by a second excerpt from the *Arabian Nights*. During the same period the Exeter *Postmaster* offered a condensed version of Defoe's *Captain Singleton* (which had just appeared) in fifty-four installments, succeeded in the following year by "The Tryal of Honesty" from *Robinson Crusoe's Serious Reflections*. It was only in 1723, however, more than three years after *Robinson Crusoe* began its run in the *Original London Post*, that a second London newspaper embarked on a long serial novel. On January 6 of that year Parker's *London News*, a thrice-weekly news-sheet and competitor of Heathcote's paper, commenced a serialization of the *Arabian Nights*, which occupied three years and four hundred and forty-five installments, and was sufficiently popular with readers to lead the paper (even before the *Nights* was completed) to undertake a new series of reprints of various classics of English and foreign fiction, sometimes running two novels simultaneously. Meanwhile, in the *Original London Post*, Heathcote continued from time to time to offer readers reprints or adaptations of Mary Hearne, Mrs. Haywood, and Defoe, accompanied by other serial pieces of a non-fictional character.

The number of serial novels and novelettes, long extracts, and abridgments of works of fiction thus published by British periodicals from 1720–1740 is a highly speculative figure, owing to the great abundance of newspapers and journals circulated during that period and the extremely ephemeral character of most of them. The surviving papers indicate a certain literary activity of this kind, extending roughly over a quarter of a century, but it can easily be exaggerated (as it has been, unintentionally, by Graham and others)[62] by citing titles out of context, and therefore making a major enterprise of what was really a series of peripheral events, or the regular practice of a special few.

R. M. Wiles's recent book on *Serial Publications in England before 1745*, and his earlier Harvard dissertation upon which it was partly based, help us to view this activity in better perspective.[63] The known works of prose fiction of any length (those in excess, say, of three installments), published in journals and newspapers during the twenty-one-year period after *Robin-*

son Crusoe, including those already mentioned, in *Applebee's Weekly Journal*, Heathcote's and Parker's papers, the *Churchman's Last Shift*, and the Exeter *Postmaster*, amount to forty-four items in all.[64] Moreover, they are limited to a small minority of the periodical press, and chiefly to those lesser journals and newspapers that seem to have regarded it as an easy means of padding the news and meeting the competition of more prosperous rivals with entertaining features of a more topical character. During 1724, the busiest year among the purveyors of newspaper fiction, there were four journals and news sheets (one of them published in Exeter) offering long serial stories. During the same year, the "Chronological Index" of *Crane and Kaye* indicates that there were sixty-two daily, weekly, twice-weekly, and thrice-weekly papers published in Great Britain and Ireland, excluding essay-serials. We know little about the provincial papers, but twenty-two of the sixty-two were published in London, and of these twenty-two (as far as we know) only three trifled with serial fiction; Parker's *London News*, the *Original London Post*, and the *Half-Penny London Journal*, papers which served only a small fraction of the newspaper reading audience. Later, during the six-year slack period from 1730–1735, *Applebee's* is the only recorded periodical within this class that published long serial fiction, except for one four-part story in the *Weekly Register* in 1734. There may have been others, of course, but only in the now-evaporated fringes of the periodical press.

Nevertheless, these forty-four surviving titles of serial novels and novelettes have some interest in the history of taste, since they suggest something of the mentality of newspaper editors, and perhaps something of the taste of their reading public. In the first place they are mostly reprinted pieces. *Applebee's* excepted, almost no publisher was willing to expend time or effort upon genuine originals or new translations. On the contrary, it was primarily as an economy measure that these periodicals seem to have resorted to serial fiction at all. The reprinted pieces are in lieu of introductory letters and leading articles.

In the second place these titles consist of either a few old favorites or more recent works of some reputation. On the one hand we find books like *Oroonoko*, the *Arabian Nights*, the Countess d'Aulnoy's *Travels in Spain*, Montemayor's *Diana*, *Cynthia* (with eight trade editions between 1687 and 1726), and various *novelle* by Cervantes, Lope de Vega, and Bandello, all works of proved merit or long-time popularity. Such stories presumably would be welcomed by a new audience of fiction-readers, many of whom were still unacquainted with the classics of prose fiction. On the other hand, we find a few important works of new fiction, either novels written by authors with a considerable following, or works which were enjoying an extraordinary success, like *Robinson Crusoe*, *Captain Singleton*, the *Chinese Tales* and *Mogul Tales* of Gueullette in translation, and *Gulliver's Travels*. With the freedom provided by the Copyright Act of 1710, predatory editors naturally displayed a partiality for the most valuable literary property. There are more reprints of Defoe than of any other single novelist—a further sign of his powerful hold upon the taste of the newspaper-reading public. In addition to and including some of the above-mentioned works, there is an outstanding emphasis upon travel books of all kinds, pseudo-memoirs, "voyages," "shipwrecks," and stories of piratical adventure—rudimentary and informative works of fiction that make an elaborate pretense of being "true," like the *Voyages and Adventures of Captain Richard Falconer Round the World*, the *Four Years Voyages of Captain George Roberts*, the *Distresses and Adventures of John Cockburne, Esq.*, and *Charles Johnson's General History of the Pyrates*. It is the last-named work of fiction, masquerading as history, that Defoe (writing anonymously, of course) particularly recommended to the readers of *Mist's Journal* on May 23, 1724, saying

> If I were to be ask'd what Sort of Books I would recommend to a Man, who has nothing to do? I should answer, those which have a Mixture of the profitable and pleasant, such I count History, and also Voyages, and Travels... Books of this Kind give a prodigious Pleasure, when they are writ by Men of Sense, who understand the Business of a Travellor, and are judicious in their Observations and Remarks, and do not endeavour to abuse their Readers with fabulous and idle Stories.[65]

Such a book, he declared, was the *History of the Pyrates*, a work so agreeable that "I scarce had Power to lay it by, before I had gone thro' it." Defoe's predilection for this particular work, to which he conspicuously returned in two subsequent numbers of the journal, may result from the fact that Mist seems to have been concerned in its publication,[66] or (as Professor Moore believes) that Defoe himself was the unacknowledged author. So well did he gauge the taste of the audience of the weekly journals, however, that the *History of the Pyrates* was itself pirated at least four times in newspapers and weekly journals during the ensuing two years—beginning within two days of each other in the *Original London Post* and Parker's *London News* in September, 1724, and a year later in two Exeter rivals, Brice's and Farley's journals.[67]

It is difficult to generalize further about evidence which is so scattered and inconclusive, and for this survey unnecessary, since by 1744, except in a few miserable half-sheets, serial fiction of this kind had largely disappeared from the newspapers.[68] We have no means of knowing, for example, whether the purchasers of *Heathcote's* and *Parker's* were simply average newspaper-readers for whom fiction—*any* fiction—was beginning to be of interest;[69] or whether they were special classes of readers, with an already-formed taste for certain kinds of novels, who sought out these papers as a means of obtaining cheap editions of celebrated works of which they had already heard. It could be either, or both, and the implications are not the same. Wiles's "Catalogue of Books Published in Fascicules before 1750" is useful to us, since it provides a rough scale against which we can measure the degree of interest in fiction among purchasers of inexpensive books. Of ninety-seven serial books listed as published in the quarter of a century from 1710–1734, only four are definitely works of fiction (and one of the four is the *History of the Pyrates*, a work of pseudo-history; another is a verse translation of *Don Quixote*). Of the one hundred and seven published during the next five years, 1735–1739, about a dozen are novels or collections of stories. In other words, though works of fiction gained added popularity after 1735 and still more after 1740, in both periods they were far less attractive to economy-minded buyers than histories, biographies, geographies, travel books, pious works, collections of famous trials, dictionaries, and technical publications of various kinds.

In view of this striking disproportion, and the failure of the more prosperous and influential journals to offer much prose fiction beyond essay-type stories and short "histories" of two or three parts, we cannot safely presume that a large general appetite for novels and romances existed between 1720 and 1740. We can merely say that the slight, but unmistakable movement towards prose fiction which is observable in periodicals for women, in essay-serials like the *Free-Thinker* and the *Plain Dealer*, and in the introductory letters and occasional essay-series in *Mist's*, *Read's*, the *London Journal*, and other important weeklies, seems to be strongly supported by the activity of this contemporary minority of newspapers and journals as well. All four classes of periodicals indicate a more widespread interest in the novel as a medium of literary expression than had existed in the days of the *British Apollo*, the *Post Angel*, Defoe's *Review*, and other more or less popular magazines of an earlier period. Thanks partly to the powerful example set by the *Tatler* and *Spectator*, and partly, of course, to a busy generation of novelists and translators working outside the periodicals, within fifteen or twenty years the growing magazine and newspaper-reading audience had appreciably altered its literary taste and was now prepared to allow prose fiction a more conspicuous place among its other diversions.[69]

In 1725 the Walpole Government finally acted to close the loopholes in the Stamp Tax of 1712 by requiring the use of stamped paper in *all* journals and newspapers of whatever size, at the rate of ½d per half-sheet. But the new duty did little to dampen the energies of the weekly journals, most of which merely made a few typographical changes designed to save space, reduced their size from six pages to four, and raised their price to 2d. As a matter of fact, the major portion of the supplementary material in newspapers and weekly journals which has just been described was published subsequent to the Act of 1725. In reality, the emergence of the *Craftsman* after 1726, under the powerful patronage of Bolingbroke, did more to alter the course of events in British journalism. The *Craftsman* was heavily subsidized, and became the leading opposition newspaper. Its inevitable effect upon other journals was to intensify their own political activities, and thus to curtail their entertaining features. The *Craftsman* adopted a number of Spectatorial features,[70] as did a great many other weekly journals in the same period, and it not infrequently published visions and allegories, fables, oriental apologues, narrative letters and "cases"—mostly of a political character. But with the exception of one political novelette, "The History of the Norfolk Steward" (allegedly written by Alexander Pope), all of the prose fiction of the *Craftsman* is brief and strictly routine.[71]

One may speculate what the effect upon the novel would have been had the weekly journal of Defoe and his contemporaries survived as a vehicle for narrative essays and letters into a period when magazine fiction was more widely accepted as a medium of literary expression. It would possibly have had a salutary influence upon writers in both the miscellanies and the essay-serials to have had a continuing tradition of topical fiction, conspicuously unsentimental and unromantic, occupied with subjects drawn from the middle and lower ranks of society, and touching at many points the social, political, and economic realities of eighteenth-century life, in opposition to the genteel fatuities of the popular miscellanies and the sterile didacticism of the essay-serials. Unfortunately, however, the movement among the weekly journals in the second quarter of the eighteenth century was gradually away from the species of "agreeable miscellany" that Defoe had initiated. Through the *Champion* and *Jacobite's Journal* the journalistic tradition of Defoe made direct contact with Fielding, and thus served to water the soil that produced *Joseph Andrews* and *Tom Jones*—both of which, as opposed to *Pamela* and *Clarissa*, had their topical side. But by Fielding's time the weekly journal had largely surrendered its many-sided miscellaneous character, and become a much more specialized instrument for satire and partisan polemics. Though the audience for prose fiction had since greatly increased, Fielding contributed even less than Defoe to the development of the magazine story.

Later Miscellanies, 1731–1739

A further serious blow against the old type of weekly journal with entertaining features was struck by the *Gentleman's Magazine* of 1731. Cave's new periodical was a resounding success, partly owing to his enterprise and ingenuity, partly owing to the copyright situation which permitted him to prey mercilessly upon journals and newspapers, epitomizing their leading articles and robbing them of their wittiest pieces. The small but important family of magazines, of which the *Gentleman's* stands at the head, occupies a special enclave in the realm of magazine fiction, which will be explored in a later chapter. At this point, it may merely be remarked that the *historical* miscellanies provided "entertainment" of a different order from that of more popular magazines, and adopted correspondingly different policies with respect to prose fiction. With two exceptions the *Gentleman's* published no stories of novel or novelette length before 1750.

The gradual specialization of the weekly journal for partisan purposes, and the failure of the *Gentleman's* and the *London Magazine* to purvey much light entertainment, quickened the revival of the common or "non-historical" type of miscellany in the 1730's. After an interval of more than twenty years, during which only a few isolated and unsuccessful attempts were made to establish entertaining magazines on the miscellany principle, at least five new periodicals of this class suddenly appeared within the space of as many years—the *Weekly Amusement* of 1734–1736, the *Oxford Magazine* of 1736, the *Lady's Curiosity* of 1738, the *Lady's Magazine* of 1738–1739, and the *Universal Spy* of 1739. These new miscellanies were far from homogeneous in manner or content, but they are all recognizable progeny of the old *Gentleman's Journal*, the *Records of Love*, and the *Delights for the Ingenious.* Three of them, significantly, were directed wholly or in part to women, and most of them came freighted with prose fiction only a few years after Mr. Stonecastle's correspondent had denounced novels and romances as the corrupters of footmen and chambermaids, and the ruiners of virgins.

The Lady's Curiosity, or Weekly Apollo, conducted by "Nestor Druid, Gent.," an imaginary editor of ancient family and genteel connections, was a monthly compilation of short stories, poems, and tiny essays on such edifying subjects as "Extravagance in Dress," "How to Govern Husbands," and the "Duties of a Married Life." Among other feminine fripperies it also offered answers to questions on the problems of love and courtship. Its monthly issues were numbered, but undated, and dealt with subjects of such timeless interest to women that it was re-issued fourteen years later, ostensibly as a new compilation.[72] The *Lady's Magazine, or the Compleat Library* of 1738–1739 also invited the particular patronage of feminine readers, but did not disdain to raise its eyes towards others as well. It described itself as

> a very curious Collection of Histories, Travels, Novels, Poems, Songs, Letters, &c.... Calculated for the Benefit of Persons in all Ranks and Conditions; but in a particular Manner, with a view to the Improvement of the Fair Sex (that noble Part of Creation) and as an Amusement for their vacant Hours.[73]

To this end it offered the Countess d'Aulnoy's *Travels in Spain* in serial form, along with a number of shorter narrative pieces.

The *Weekly Amusement, or the Universal Magazine,* was a still more ambitious enterprise, laying claim to an even greater diversity of interest. Like the *Gentleman's Magazine,* from which it copied several of its features, it boasted on its title page that it offered in its twenty-four weekly pages "more in Quantity, and greater in Variety, than any Book of the Kind or Price."

> The design of the *Weekly Amusement*, &c. is to instruct and entertain the world with what is serious, satyrical, humorous, and jocose; nor shall any thing be inserted but what may be understood by persons of the meanest capacities, and yet pen'd in a style not distasteful to men of polite literature: And in hopes of encouragement in general, no pains or cost shall be spared to render it acceptable, though sold at the low price of TWO PENCE [*i.e.*, the current price of most four-page weekly journals].[74]

In its effort to interest "persons of the meanest capacities" as well as "men of polite literature" the *Weekly Amusement* seems to have been more successful than its rivals, since in its first issue it flatly asserted that "Upwards of seventeen hundred are already become Subscribers," and this number was later raised to two thousand. The claim may well have been true, since the magazine was supported by a dozen book-sellers, but it is hard to reconcile with its short term of survival and the scarcity of surviving copies. More than any of the other miscellanies of this period, the *Weekly Amusement* gave special emphasis to long fiction, offering in the course of its sixty-one numbers, in addition to numerous shorter pieces, "The Letters of Eloise and Abelard" (in six parts), "Letters of a Portuguese Nun" (in seven), and "Tanzai and Neadarne, a Japonese History," translated from Crébillon, and left uncompleted by the magazine's extinction. None of the three stories, however, was written for publication in a magazine. Similarly, the *Oxford Magazine, or Family Companion*, a weekly published the following year (with no surviving copies), offered Aphra Behn's *Oroonoko* in installment form.[75]

The *Universal Spy, or the London Weekly Magazine*, conducted by "Timothy Truepenny, Gent.", the fifth in this cluster of miscellanies, is a ten-page weekly of a quite different stripe, although it also was "calculated for the Entertainment of Persons of all Degrees." It purported to mingle "Facts and Amusement," "Morality and Diversion," "Truth and Profit"—and made the now-familiar boast of being "more Instructive and Entertaining than any Thing of the Kind yet publish'd."[76] Compared with the *Lady's Curiosity*, the *Lady's Magazine*, and the *Weekly Amusement*, however, it is a crude and artless undertaking, being printed on cheap paper and lacking all their contrived elegances. Without doubt intended chiefly for masculine readers, the *Universal Spy* was largely composed of serializations of Robert Drury's *History of Madagascar* and the writings of "the facetious Mr. Ward." The regular editions of Ward's *Voyage to Jamaica*, *A Trip to Newfoundland*, and

The Rise and Fall of Madam Coming-Sir, all reprinted here, had long since gone out of print; but, as Wiles's study of serial books shows, there were a number of efforts in the 1730's to revive interest in Ward's books among readers of limited means.[77] Both the title and the contents of the *Universal Spy* are part of this movement, which is opposed in all respects to the emphasis in other popular miscellanies on the elegant and genteel. But the author of the *London Spy* was too crude and too fantastical for the popular audience of the new age (more than half of which were women, if this spate of magazines is any index). These reprints of his works in the *Universal Spy* of 1739 are Ned Ward's last known appearance in a British magazine, and his name does not figure in Wiles's list of serial books after 1738.

The vogue for Defoe's novels and his type of "voyage" and pseudo-history, on the other hand, survived longer than Ward's, but by 1739 this had also undergone some diminution. The current interests among novel-readers in this period were extremely varied, if not contradictory. Judging from the monthly "Register of New Books" in the *Gentleman's Magazine*, which listed about fifty works of fiction during the years 1738–1740, the greatest demand was for "historical" novels, oriental tales, *novelle*, fables, satirical "lives and adventures," scandalous memoirs, and stories of high life. In this melange, "histories," "voyages," and "travels," of the kind Defoe recommended to the readers of *Mist's* fifteen years before, continued to be represented, but a growing emphasis was on the "pomp and parade of romance-writing" that was even then beginning to alarm the author of *Pamela*. It was the eager spectators of this growing procession that the *Universal Spectator* was scolding in its "Letter to a Lady," and that the *Weekly Amusement* was trying to attract with its townish airs, its trivial essays and modish "fables", its little tales of gallantry and intrigue, its songs and dances, excerpts from new plays, and sentimental novels from the French. For this audience, we may surmise, at least for the women readers, Defoe had few charms. Several of his novels (particularly *Robinson Crusoe*) maintained a foothold in popular fancy in the form of new editions after 1740, but if the *History of Madagascar* is really his, as has sometimes been alleged, its reprinting in the *Universal Spy* represents his last appearance in any British magazine for over forty years, during which time his name was seldom invoked by reviewers and his works were completely ignored by the swarm of amateur scribblers who supplied later miscellanies with much of their original fiction.[78]

By 1740, therefore, as we have observed, there was a well-defined tradition for prose fiction in British serial publications, some forms of which were indigenous to the magazines, although others were drawn from the familiar province of the "English Novel." This tradition, however, was not the same for all periodicals. In the learned journals and abstract serials, heavily weighted in terms of philosophy, science, history, and antiquarian study, and in the political and "historical" repositories, largely devoted to summaries and serious discussions of contemporary affairs, novels and romances were regarded as too inconsequential for notice. But in the new literary chronicles, like the *Monthly Chronicle* and the *Literary Magazine*, devoted almost exclusively to noticing new books of various kinds, works of fiction were beginning to be listed among other "Works of Entertainment," and occasionally received grudging attention.

At the end of the fourth decade of the eighteenth century the principal medium for periodical fiction was still the essay-serial, in the *literary*, however, not the *polemical* line. Twenty-five or thirty years before, the *Tatler* and *Spectator* had been the most important single agency for enfranchising the magazine story, and extending the taste for fiction among classes of readers for whom, except in very rudimentary forms, it had previously been an alien form of entertainment. Addison and Steele were still a dominant influence upon weekly journals and newspapers, many of which felt it mandatory to adopt at least a few Spectatorial features. By 1740, however, the general following of the literary serials had largely evaporated, owing to their increasing emphasis upon traditional methods and devices. As a class of publication, the weekly journals and newspapers, on the other hand, enjoyed very commodious circulations, but after a quarter of a century of fugitive experimentation with serial narratives, mostly essay-type stories, they had gradually begun to relinquish prose fiction, along with some of their other miscellaneous features.

In the 1730's two different kinds of miscellanies emerged—the *historical*, which admitted fiction only casually, and the *common* (or "non-historical") variety, where all forms of popular entertainment tended to receive greater emphasis. The five magazines, just described, were all premature efforts to produce a genuinely popular magazine. Their success was negligible in comparison with the sensational circulations already obtained by the new *Gentleman's* and *its imitators*. The longest-lived and more pretypical in form and content was the *Weekly Amusement*, which survived for a little over a year. But within the next two decades these efforts were to be revived with more conspicuous success.

As a form of serial publication the miscellany was far better adapted than the single-essay periodical to gratify the tastes and interests of a growing audience of undiscriminating readers. Flexibility was its fundamental principle. Unlike most other types of magazines, it could publish poetry, essays, prose fiction, or informative articles, of any kind, in any quantity, old or new, translated or original, whatever it felt its readers might desire. Furthermore, unlike the numerous progeny of the *Tatler* and *Spectator*, it could proceed uninhibited by any inherited obligations as a censor of manners and public morals, and unhaunted by any memory of former excellence. Of all types of serial publication, therefore, the miscellany was the most promising medium for mass entertainment, as later events were to show.

CHAPTER II

The Single-Essay Periodical, 1740-1815

The Essay Tradition

All the periodical essayists who wrote between 1740 and 1815 were not Tatlers and Spectators, but journalistic orthodoxy was their single, most outstanding trait. Many of them were quite content to simulate the language, the intonation, and even the gestures of Isaac Bickerstaff and Mr. Spectator, and others betray a strong family resemblance. The polemical serials, of course, were less mannered than the literary variety, since their historic function was to address themselves vigorously and single-mindedly to public debate. Nevertheless, they had their own rhetorical and typographical traditions, which survived with only a few modifications until the nineteenth century. Some of the more spirited, like the *Monitor* and the *North Briton*, enjoyed very extensive circulations. But typically the polemical serials produced discursive rather than imaginative writing. Alltogether they contributed only three political novelettes to the list appended to this study. Two of these are dream narratives, and one is an allegorical history.[1]

The literary serials, on the other hand, were intently occupied with belles-lettres and traditionally employed a variety of narrative forms. With a few outstanding exceptions, however, they tended increasingly to be addressed to the cultivated minority—academic circles or specialized audiences of *literati* and *cognoscenti*. Many of them were conducted by college and university students, others by old maids and eccentrics, country clergymen with an urge to appear in print, dilettantes, provincial gentlemen for the amusement of the local gentry, or literary societies. Some of the outstanding members of this class, of course, were intended to make their way in the London trade, but aside from the *World*, the *Connoisseur*, the *Adventurer* and a few others, it is doubtful whether any of them achieved circulations in excess of a few hundred copies, at least in their original issue. Nevertheless, the single-essay periodical was a familiar minor feature of eighteenth-century life, never far out of view after 1740, although always overshadowed by the enlarged circulations of the miscellanies, the annuals and reviews, the weekly journals, and the newspapers. The tenacity with which the literary essay-serial maintained its toe-hold in the eighteenth-century consciousness is indicative of the deep impression that the *Spectator* still made upon the imagination of polite readers and others. The number of single-essay periodicals published between 1740 and 1815 amounts to at least one hundred and twenty titles, more than one-half of which must be regarded as "literary."[2] This number is exclusive of the numerous *essay-series* published in newspapers, miscellanies, and elsewhere, which, if added to the others, would swell the total to several hundreds.[3]

The most eminent of the literary serials published in the second half of the eighteenth century, namely the *Rambler*, the *Adventurer*, the *World*, the *Connoisseur*, the *Lounger*, the *Mirror*, and the *Looker-On*, quickly came to be regarded as classics in the genre, and enjoyed circulations in book form far exceeding those of their original issues. These seven were collected, along with the *Tatler*, the *Spectator*, the *Guardian*, and a few other titles in Chalmers's *British Essayists* in 1817. But others omitted by Chalmers earned a certain celebrity, at least when they were gathered into volumes; for example, the *Female Spectator*, the *Microcosm*, *Olla Podrida*, the *Loiterer*, the *Sylph*, *Literary Leisure*, and the *Speculator*. The most eager activity of the essayists occurred in the period from 1750–1760 and in the last twenty years of the century, but the line was never interrupted for long. There were only a few years between 1740 and 1815 when some latter-day *Spectator* or *Guardian* was not politely bowing its way onto the stage in London, Dublin, or Edinburgh, or later in towns like Lincoln, Winchester, or Windsor.

Meanwhile the luster attached to the names of Addison and Steele continued undimmed during the entire century. Their writings were everywhere regarded as models of elegance among those classes increasingly preoccupied with manners and self-realization. The *Tatler*, the *Spectator*, and the *Guardian* went through edition after edition (there were seven each of the *Tatler* and *Guardian* between 1740 and 1800, and twenty-five of the *Spectator*)—and thus the new generation of essayists was always being tested by comparison with the old. It was customary for the author, in inaugurating a new series, to choose a title which would epitomize his particular humor or predilection, at the same time that it would remind readers of his literary lineage. His almost invariable obligation in his first number was to make his obeisances to his distinguished predecessors and thus reassure his audience that he intended to adhere to traditional modes. He was typically a self-appointed censor of manners and morals, a guardian or critic of social institutions, a commentator on contemporary life, a philosopher, and a literary critic. His manner was formal, erudite, familiar, jocular, austere, sentimental, or sententious, according to the special role that he had elected to perform. Sometimes, like the *Rambler* or the *Adventurer*, he was content merely to represent a disembodied point of view, but often he presented himself in terms of some assumptive character, whose life and adventures were made the subject of his various lucubrations. Around him he sometimes gathered a group of secondary characters making up a family or "club," whose diverse humors and sentiments were unfolded during the course of the series. In order to diversify further the contents of his magazine the essayist frequently had recourse to fiction in the form of fables and anecdotes, amusing episodes from his experience, sentimental or satirical histories, parodies, oriental tales, fairy stories, dream visions, and allegories; and in his labors he was usually assisted by a number of "correspondents" who wrote him letters on various subjects, often presenting their own histories or inviting his comment upon striking cases that came within their view.

Not all of the literary serials of the eighteenth century embodied all these possibilities (a certain number of mutations were approved), but such was the *idea* of which later periodicals were admittedly imperfect copies. It is customary to regard the minor essayists of the eighteenth century as hidebound by tradition, as by late eighteenth-century ideas of "originality" they were; but imitation was a possible and widely approved mode of literary expression, which most of these writers tacitly accepted. A completely new or individual literary manner was the last wish of the authors of essay-serials. If they were not Tatlers, Spectators, and Guardians, they were nothing at all.[4]

The orthodoxy of the literary serials was the more remarkable since it survived a number of basic changes in the conditions of publication. Most essay-serials, in the early years of the century, had been printed on two sides of a single half-sheet, in double columns. Within this restricted area, space was allotted for a title, a publisher's inscription, and sometimes advertisements. It was possible to curtail the heading, omit advertisements, and reduce the size of the font, and occasionally this was done in the *Spectator*. But even with the most rigorous compression there was a theoretical limit for the single sheet of approximately three thousand words, and most numbers were about half that length. Typically, single-essays in the *Tatler*, the *Spectator*, and the *Guardian* ran from fifteen hundred to seventeen hundred words, and shorter pieces were much more common than longer pieces, since issues were sometimes divided into several parts.

In the middle years of the century, however, the folio half-sheet gave way generally to a sheet and a half (six numbered pages), single column, and later in the century essay-periodicals were printed in a variety of typographical forms. Yet such was the force of the example set by Addison and Steele that little effort was made to enlarge the physical limits of the essay. The *Female Spectator* of Eliza Haywood is an exception, since hers was a species of monthly publication. But the average *Rambler*, *Adventurer*, and *World* did not exceed the average length of the *Spectator* by more than a few hundred words, and the papers of the *Mirror* and the *Lounger*, twenty-five years later, were no longer. The *Looker-On*, a still-later periodical, was given to essays of three thousand words, but this was exceptional. By what amounted to an almost inviolable precedent the periodical essayists of the eighteenth century, until at least 1790, felt impelled to maneuver within a circumscribed area in which only a limited number of evolutions were possible. The only approved method of exceeding this limit was to do as Addison and Steele had occasionally done—namely, to carry the essay or story over into a succeeding number or, without sacrificing the autonomy of the individual pieces, to resume the subject at intervals.

In the later prose fiction of the essay-serial, both these methods were employed, and the much greater number of serial tales in pairs, triads, and quartets, from the time of the *Free-Thinker* on (in comparison with the total of only five pairs in the *Tatler*, *Spectator*, and *Guardian* combined) is indicative of a growing urge to achieve more sustained effects than were possible in fifteen hundred to seventeen hundred words. But this solution afforded the essayist only a partial escape from his confinement, since two or three papers (that is, three to five thousand words) was still felt to be the proper magnitude for serial fiction of this kind. Furthermore, the force of tradition was such (and it was strongly supported by the method of publication) that emphasis was still placed upon individual papers. Johnson, for example, usually adopted the epistolary form for his serial fiction, and in such cases he always began a new letter when he resumed his narrative, which was technically a separate piece, and which in fact sometimes developed a new theme entirely. The increase in length, therefore, did not necessarily bring a corresponding increase in scale. Until the end of the century most of the serial fiction of the single-essay periodical gave the impression of being essays in miniature.[5] For this reason, in part, the novel and novelette never became thoroughly domesticated in the essay-serial, and their total number over the seventy-five year period comes to only about fifty.

Volumes of Essays in Series

The traditional outlines of the essay-serial and the very precise categories with which it was associated were to survive even more drastic changes than those just described, as a result of its being transplanted to other types of publication where effects in miniature were not a typographical necessity. In the later years of the century, the sale of most essay-serials in their original issue was so small that they were rarely a lucrative venture until gathered into quarto or octavo volumes and sold over the counter as collections of essays. For some reason the better serials always enjoyed a much greater supplementary circulation of this kind—perhaps because this was the aspect which the famous *Spectator* itself now presented to the world. As a matter of fact many serials were undertaken with an eye only to the collected edition, which was speedily offered for sale as each volume was completed.

Given the interest in collections of periodical essays, therefore, we are not surprised to find essay-series appearing directly in book form without any preliminary circulation at all. The last third of the century affords many examples of these simultaneous sequences,[6] of which Cumberland's *Observer* was probably the most popular. Cumberland's series first appeared full-blown in 1785 in forty numbers (later greatly expanded to 153), without any essential change in manner or content from genuine single-essay periodicals. It contained the usual melange of short critical and narrative papers, the lighter pieces alternating with serious essays on religion, morals, and classical learning. In addition it even affected some of the usual paraphernalia of letters from "correspondents," episodes in the recent experience of the author, and the developing by-play associated with weekly or bi-weekly publication. These pretenses seemed to arouse no surprise anywhere. Cumberland's pseudo-serial was greatly admired, and its two novelettes were immediately seized upon by the predatory miscellanies and reprinted paper by paper, alongside those of the *Lounger*, and other genuine essay-serials—thus attaining piratically a kind of authentic periodicity.[7]

Weekly Journals

The peculiar vitality of the Spectatorial tradition is further shown by the degree to which it preserved its identity when combined with other species of periodicals. We have already remarked how, under the leadership of Defoe, the old literary serial was in part incorporated into the weekly journal and how its subjects and methods of expression were adapted to the tastes and interests of the newspaper-reading public. Although this period of captivity lasted for many years and unquestionably had some effect upon the taste of the general audience, it wrought no obvious change in the essay convention, except to strengthen the use of the epistolary form. In both the *Rambler* and the *Adventurer* the emphasis upon "letters" was greatly increased over that of earlier essay-serials. By 1740, however, the weekly journals had largely given themselves over to partisan controversy, and the commentary upon men, manners, and society, the little narrative sketches in the form of letters, and the occasional "novels" were therefore allowed to lapse. The prose fiction of the weekly journals after 1735 or 1740 is negligible in quantity. Some of the weeklies, twice-weeklies and thrice-weeklies in the satirical tradition continued to affect a number of Spectatorial features, but the *Champion*, the *Covent Garden Journal*, the *Spring Garden*, or the *Drury Lane* did not frequently employ narrative devices, or publish serial stories.

The reluctance of the journals to emulate the novel is strikingly illustrated by Fielding's record in the *Champion* (1738–1742). In spite of the author's obvious talent for fiction, the *Champion* published nothing except short essay-type narratives in the course of its run of over four hundred numbers. The "Voyages of Mr. Job Vinegar," which appeared in thirteen installments between March and October, 1740, studiously seems to avoid a narrative structure.[8] Although it is in part an imitation of *Gulliver's Travels*, and invokes at the outset the "Adventures of *Cassandra*," the "Countess *Danois's Fairy Tales*," and *Robinson Crusoe*, the "Voyages" are actually not narrative at all, but a series of satirical fragments without any serious attempt to exploit the imaginative possibilities suggested by these works. The pseudo-travels of "Mr. Job Vinegar" in the *Champion* ran more or less contemporaneously with a similar series in the *Universal Spectator* called "Drake's Travels"—a moral allegory adapted from Bishop Hall's *Mundus alter et idem.* This voyage, however, shows a greater interest than Job's in following a narrative line. But even in this series the voyager-narrator seems to make a conscious effort to keep himself out of the story.[9]

The indifference of the weekly, twice-weekly and thrice-weekly journals after 1740 to the possibilities of prose fiction as a form of entertainment is also underlined by their lack of interest in the theory or the criticism of the novel in a period when the genre was undergoing a phenomenal development. Considering the great number of such serials and the wide range of their commentary on contemporary life, including the usages of polite society, they are conspicuous in their disregard for one of its increasingly prominent features. In this respect, as we shall see, they differ sharply from essay-serials like the *Rambler*, the *Adventurer*, and the *World*, where the advance of the novel in public favor was a matter of serious concern. Fielding's casual remarks on *Clarissa* in the *Jacobite's Journal*, and his review of the *Female Quixote* in the *Covent Garden* were exceptional. With all the ink spilled in the "paper war" over *Amelia*, almost none was spent upon its literary qualities. The *Universal Spectator* was more belleletristic than most contemporary journals. It survived until 1746, supplementing its weekly essays with a good deal of original short fiction, chiefly in the manner of the *Spectator* and the *Free-Thinker*, but including also in 1743–1744 several novelettes from the French.[10] But among the other journals of the highly polemical age of Sir John Hill, Henry Fielding, and Arthur Murphy, the literary bias of the *Universal Spectator* was somewhat anomalous. Though conducted by Fielding at the very zenith of his reputation as a novelist, the *Covent Garden Journal* contains even less narrative than the *Champion*. Like Defoe, Fielding seemed to regard his journalistic writings and his prose fiction as quite disassociated.[11]

Newspapers

Two other legatees of the *Tatler* and *Spectator* after 1740 are the newspapers and the miscellanies, both of which had begun in the middle years of the century to make room for regular or occasional columns of a literary or semi-literary character, more or less in the manner of Addison and Steele. The first of the newspaper columnists seems to have been Sir John Hill, whose "Inspector" appeared daily in the *London Daily Advertiser* between 1751–1753.[12] But Johnson's "Idler" and Goldsmith's "Chinese Letters" achieved a much greater celebrity. The first was published in 104 weekly numbers in Payne's *Universal Chronicle* beginning in 1758; the second in the *Public Ledger* two years later. Because of their outstanding artistic merit, both made something of a splash and thus tended to strengthen the literary tradition in British newspapers.

The fiction of the eighteenth-century newspaper does not come within the range of this study, but its exclusion is more ostensible than real. First, compared with the formidable number of news-sheets published in the second half of the century, the amount of newspaper fiction is minute; and second, the fiction itself is of negligible importance. It may be said to consist of two kinds: short pieces in reprint and extracts from new novels, occasionally continued beyond a single number; and original stories and narrative sketches in the prescribed manner of the essay-serial. The prose fiction of this latter type is nearly always brief. The "Idler," for example, which contains more fiction than most newspaper series, includes only three or four narratives extending into a second paper, and the longest of these is only three thousand words. During 1758–1759, when the "Idler" was running in Payne's newspaper, on the other hand, Owen's *Weekly Chronicle* published no fiction of any kind and no columns of Spectatorial essays or introductory letters, although it offered a good deal of poetry and other entertaining features. A third competitor of Payne's and Owen's, Wilkie's *London Chronicle*, printed in the same two years extracts from the recently published *Voyages of Capt. John Holmesby*, Sarah Fielding's *Countess of Dellwyn*, and Johnson's *Rasselas*, but offered no original fiction of any kind.

Later newspaper series, collected like the "Idler" in volume form and published under such titles as the *Schemer* (1763), the *Visitor* (1764), the *Babler* (1767), the *Batchelor* (1772), and the *Grumbler* (1792), naturally contain a certain amount of essay-type fiction, but only occasional serial pieces.[13] Goldsmith's "Chinese Letters" (republished as the *Citizen of the World* in 1762) is a conspicuous exception, about which something will later be said. As a series of newspaper essays, it employed an elaborate and surprising variety of narrative devices. But the "Chinese Letters" aside, the eighteenth-century newspaper contributed almost nothing to the literature of the novel, as the catalogue of magazine stories appended to this study demonstrates. In their appetite for new fiction, essays, and poems, at no expense of money or effort, the miscellanies regularly preyed upon the newspapers, weekly journals, and essay-serials alike, stripping them of their principal attractions while these papers were still offered for sale in the stationers' shops. Few pieces of an entertaining character ever escaped their vigilance. Yet there are only two stories of novelette or novel length in the whole list of 1375 which are known to have originated in a British newspaper or weekly journal—the *Universal Spectator* excepted.[14]

Miscellany Series

The essay-series of the miscellanies, on the other hand, are a quite different matter, for in them the amount of narrative material was considerable, and practically all of it was "original." They constituted, as a matter of fact, a primary source of *new* fiction for the popular miscellanies. About twenty-five of the long stories listed in the catalogue derive from one or another of the essay-series of the miscellanies, and the amount of short fiction that they published is, of course, vastly greater. In a recent valuable study Melvin R. Watson describes and analyzes no less than 280 essay-series, appearing in fifty-nine different miscellanies over a period of seventy-five years—beginning with Sir John Hill's "Occasional Spectator" in the *British Magazine* for 1746, and extending through the "Book Worm" of the *European Magazine* for 1820.[15] In the "Occasional Spectator," as in the "Inspector" of the *London Daily Advertiser*, however, Hill was some years ahead of his time. The miscellanies, in general, were slower to adopt essay-series on a wide scale, but about 1760 the larger miscellanies suddenly took them up, and for over half a century they became an almost inevitable ingredient of magazines with a broadly popular appeal. The *Lady's Magazine*, where they were most liberally received, published forty-one different series of this kind between 1771 and 1807. The *European* published thirty-four over the course of thirty-nine years; the *Town and Country*, in a shorter space, fifteen; the *Westminster*, thirteen. More than half of these series, it is true, ran for ten numbers or less, but some of them survived for longer periods, and two in the *Lady's*

Magazine and the *Town and Country* enjoyed runs of seventeen years.[16]

The extraordinary popularity of essay-series in the half century from 1760–1810 is a phenomenon in the history of journalism that deserves serious attention, since their influence after 1760 radiated widely through the common miscellanies, and served to strengthen the hegemony of Addison and Steele. While the single-essay periodical during the same period enjoyed no real popularity outside polite circles, only a kind of *succès d'estime*, readers of popular miscellanies with circulations of five, ten, and fifteen thousand a month, showed a deep craving for vulgarized versions of the same thing, published under such fatuous titles as "The Man of Pleasure," "The Matrimonial Preceptor," "Momus the Laughing Philosopher," "The English Marmontel," and "The Female Rambler." Taking 1775 as a representative year, for example, Watson finds twenty-three miscellany series in operation—ten of which were new, thirteen of which were continued from 1774.[17] During the same year (a slack period for the essay-serials) only two single-essay periodicals are known to have existed—both political. With a ratio of more than ten to one, one might expect to find in the popular series some greater degree of vitality, some fresh approach to subject matter, or some new principle animating the old forms. Yet the condition is quite the reverse. The luxuriance of the magazine series is purely vegetative. Most of them are the usual concoctions of moral essays, vignettes of social life, narrative episodes, and "characters," sugared with a few novelties and watered down for popular consumption. In the single-essay periodical during the same three-quarters of a century, a few of the authors were writers of genuine distinction, and many of the others achieved a certain level of literary craftsmanship and (within prescribed limits) a certain freshness of humor or fancy. But the swollen company of amateurs and anonymous hacks who wrote essay-series for the miscellanies (with a few exceptions—Boswell being one) produced only fopperies, oddities, and pious pedantries.

The appetite of the common reader for such insubstantial fare is a fascinating problem in the history of taste. A great deal of this material, of course, was designed to satisfy the pious and sentimental prejudices of a miscellaneous audience, conscious of its inadequacies, and eager to be preached at, improved, and informed with polite learning. But this pre-occupation can hardly explain the special popularity of the essay-series, since many of the other ingredients of the miscellanies were obviously addressed to the same end, the serial novels and novelettes, for example. Watson seeks to account for the phenomenal interest in essays by observing that they were frequently written by amateurs of little talent, many of whom were provincial,[18] but this view leaves still unanswered the question why so many writers felt impelled to concentrate on essay-series, and readers to read them. The miscellanies opened up to amateur writers many other avenues of expression.

The popularity of essay-series was obviously the product of many factors, but an important one was certainly the historical association of the informal essay with manners and good taste, and the air of urbanity and "ton" which it traditionally breathed. After religion and domestic morality, its principal concern was the social virtues, and the accurate representation of men and manners, particularly at the upper levels of society. Johnson declared that a man who wished to achieve a proper style could do no better than give his days and nights to Addison, and many of the writers and readers of the miscellanies obviously took this kind of advice seriously. An ability to write Spectatorial essays in a manner "familiar but not coarse, and elegant but not ostentatious," was a sign of arrival for the amateur scribbler, and among his readers a taste for such essays was the cachet of the achieved "lady" "lady" or "gentleman," especially since the *Spectator* seems to have enjoyed wide favor in the academies as a means to enlarge the mind, perfect the style, and acquaint the uninitiated with the usages of polite society.[19] The endless stream of essay-series in the miscellanies, in other words, was part of the pseudogenteel aspect of the popular magazines, as their particular emphasis in the *Lady's*, the *European*, the *Town and Country*, and the *Westminster* would indicate.

The greatest number of these essays are conspicuously unconcerned with genuine middle-class problems, outside the realm of manners, morals, and the domestic virtues. They are a far cry from Defoe's popular letters to "Mr. Mist" and "Mr. App" of half a century before, with their good-natured but tough-minded discussion of social, economic, and political problems. Since Defoe's days the general audience had greatly increased in size, but it had also radically revised its reading tastes, and the middle ranks of society had acquired a good many obvious social aspirations. Many of the essay-series of the miscellanies were addressed to small professional people and tradesmen, to the wives of artisans, to idle women of the mercantile classes, and to their children in the boarding schools and academies that were springing up all over England. For these readers and others, the problems of enfranchisement and political reform, the American and French Revolutions, India, Deism, and Methodism, seemed pale in comparison with the immediate problems of achieving social acceptance. Addison and Steele had intended in the *Spectator* to bring philosophy out of the academies and into Augustan drawing-rooms. They would have been amazed to discover, more than fifty years later, how much of their familiar furniture had been moved back into the academies.

The prose fiction of the miscellany series is conspicuous because of its quantity, but practically all of the pieces are short. Most of the 280 series catalogued by Watson inevitably included fiction of some kind, but they overwhelmingly accepted the traditional limits of the essay-type story as well as its traditional forms. At the hands of so many popularizers, naturally, the narrative conventions of the *Spectator* underwent a certain amount of erosion, but no new methods or devices emerged around which later practice would crystallize. The typical story of the magazine series is a tale or narrative episode of one thousand to fifteen hundred words, heavily framed with morality and oriented towards domestic life or the institutions and concerns of polite society.[20] The nearly universal emphasis on brevity in these stories is important, since it unquestionably influenced other writers in the miscellanies, and therefore lent powerful support to those forces which conspired for nearly a century to keep the magazine novel from coming of age. Of the more than thirty long stories of the miscellany series which are listed in the Catalogue, most are members of one or another of the traditional species of the single-essay periodical. About half are found in series in the *Lady's Magazine*, the *Ladies' Monthly Museum*, and the *European*, and hence distinguished by their close adherence to traditional forms.[21] Some others are less conventional, but usually in some freakish or amateurish way.

In general, the essay-stories of the miscellanies are more fruitfully approached, not through their family association with the single-essay periodical, but through their interrelationship with the other contents of the popular miscellany. Not only were the essay-serial and the miscellany typically addressed to different classes of readers, with different tastes and interests, and different orders of sensibility, but their conditions of publication were fundamentally different. The single-essay periodical like the *Rambler* or the

Mirror traditionally gave particular emphasis to its single-essay content. It made its way, one issue at a time, usually at weekly or twice-weekly intervals, among a small but fairly homogeneous circle of readers, who were presumably interested in it for its own sake, and prepared (for the time being) to give it sympathetic and undivided attention. The success of such a serial was felt to depend upon many factors—its moral persuasiveness, its critical insights, its humor and sentiment, its urbane portraits of genteel life, and, of course, its ability to provide amusing variations upon the familiar themes of the *Tatler* and *Spectator*. Above all, its success depended upon its ability to achieve cumulative effects, whereby some unity of thought and feeling was imposed upon a variety of narrative and expository materials. In other words, while possessing independent interest, the individual numbers were intended also to be read in terms of the preceding series as a whole. As magazine writing went, in the eighteenth century, the single-essay periodical maintained a high level of achievement. It was rarely a very lucrative enterprise, but its potentialities were such that it was able to attract some of the most talented professional writers, and it offered a continual challenge to gifted amateurs like Chesterfield and Walpole.

The essay-writers of the popular miscellanies, on the other hand, typically addressed a large general public of heterogeneous tastes and interests—a public that purchased the magazine (if the contents are any index) for its miscellaneous character, rather than for any particular feature. Such an audience might give the essay-writer desultory attention, or none at all, so that he could never really assume any collective memory. The individual papers were usually published at monthly intervals, subject to the will of careless and quixotic editors, less interested in quality than in quantity. They were printed in the same issues, and often in adjoining columns, with a rout of novels and short stories, excerpts from new books, essays and informative articles on a hundred subjects of popular interest, anecdotes, recipes, charades and acrostics, occasional verses, and remedies for head-ache and mad-dog bite. Above this babble of voices the essay-writers of the miscellanies somehow had to make themselves heard, and much of the vapidity and jejune mannerism which they displayed represents an attempt to catch the glassy eye of the casual reader.

Many of them failed, of course, but in the mass they succeeded, and the essay-series are an important factor in the popular taste of the period from

1760–1810. For if the essayist was forced to compete with other writers in the miscellanies, they in turn were compelled to meet his competition, and that of the extracts from genuine essay-serials which were constantly being reprinted in the miscellanies, particularly the prose fiction. The result is that *essay-series* as well as *essay-serials* represent a powerful polarizing force in the eighteenth-century miscellany. This is seen in the nearly universal emphasis upon brevity, and in the widespread confusion between narrative and essay forms, which was one of the principal inheritances of Spectatorial tradition. It shows up in many other ways as well—in the excessive didacticism of magazine fiction; in the importance attached to the short epistolary form; in the interest in characters as representative types; and in the various ways in which the narrative action was projected in terms of illustrative scenes and episodes.

Some of these tendencies, of course, existed outside the essay tradition, and conceivably would have emerged independently, had the *Tatler* and *Spectator* never entered the picture at all. But an accurate index of the influence of the essay tradition upon the common miscellany is provided by the universal prevalence of its typical narrative forms. At least half of the original prose fiction of the popular miscellany between 1740 and 1815 may be directly associated with one or another of the familiar species of the *Tatler* and its successors. It may safely be claimed on this basis alone that Addison and Steele are the single most important influence upon magazine fiction in the eighteenth century—Richardson, Sterne, and other popular novelists not excepted. To the extent that the essay-serial and the essay-series included narrative ingredients, they were a force operating in the miscellanies in conjunction with the novelists in creating and satisfying a general taste for prose fiction, but to the very great extent that they concentrated upon short narrative species they acted as a powerful force in opposition to the English novel. The great preponderance of short fiction over longer works in eighteenth-century miscellanies is largely the legacy of Addison and Steele, and the nineteenth-century magazine novel could only appear after the hundred-years spell cast by these two literary wizards had been broken.

These different aspects of the essay tradition having been defined, we may now revert to the main line of the single-essay periodical and observe its response, both creative and critical, to the growing public interest in novels and romances.

The FEMALE SPECTATOR

The first of the new essay-serials after 1740 to be steered into the strong current beginning to run in the direction of prose fiction was itself the work of a successful novelist. By 1744 Mrs. Haywood was already an old hand at the wheel of public taste—as dramatist, journalist, translator, and popular author of romances and secret histories. The first number of the *Female Spectator* was published in April, 1744, and succeeding numbers appeared more or less regularly for the next two years—enough to make, when collected, four octavo volumes. Typographically viewed, Mrs. Haywood's single-essay periodical is quite unorthodox. In appearance it is more a serial-book than an essay-sheet, the single parts being published at monthly intervals (but undated) in the form of "Books" or chapters of fifteen to sixteen thousand words. In manner and substance, however, it is squarely in the tradition of the *Tatler* and *Spectator*.

The "sole aim" of the *Female Spectator*, as the "Author" variously expressed it, was "to reform the faulty and give an innocent amusement to those who are not so," "to refine the public taste," "to promote religion, morality, and good manners," and in general to follow in the footsteps of her "learned brother of ever-precious memory." Some of her "lucubrations" were of interest to readers of both sexes, but she gave special attention to the rectification of female manners, castigating back-biting, gossip, "time-killing," "gadding," and so on, and recommending piety, modesty, and good sense, and vigilant discipline of those softer feelings to which women (in her eyes) were lamentably subject.

The first book of the new *Spectator*, having outlined these aims and described the little society which was to implement them, proceeded at once to a matter of first importance—the false ideals of love to which women so foolishly subscribe. Never leaving this interesting subject for long, the author occasionally touched on ancillary questions—the dangers of excessive parental restriction, the disasters sometimes attending masquerades, and the heady pleasures of Vauxhall, fortifying her exhortations with a fascinating stream of "portraits," anecdotes, events within her personal experience, and little illustrative stories. Some of the succeeding books of the *Female Spectator* develop single themes, like the ideals of true and false taste, the importance of good nature, and the evils of prejudice; but others range casually over a variety of subjects of importance to women readers. There is some irony in the fact that the author whose "lewd inventions" were formerly under attack in another *Spectator* as the "corrupter of virgins"[22] should herself undertake an essay periodical which sought

> To check the enormous growth of luxury, to reform the morals, and improve the manners of an age, by all confessed degenerate and sunk.[23]

There are four members in the little "club" of the *Female Spectator*, chosen presumably to represent various points of view among the readers of the new periodical. The first is an "excellent" wife; the second, "a widow of quality"; and the third, the daughter of a wealthy merchant—all women, we are told, of good sense and sprightly good humor. In addition to these, of course, there is the "Author" of the series, described as "a woman of experience and observation, fine understanding, and extensive genius." Very little is heard of the other three after the early numbers, and they are probably imaginary. The Female Spectator herself carries the burden of the essays, with the aid of several "correspondents," most of whom write suspiciously like the Author herself.

The typical method pursued in the *Female Spectator* is the long essay with intercalated stories, letters, and other diverting materials, of which the didactic tendency is heavily underscored at the beginning and then reviewed in the commentary that follows. There is one lengthy dialogue in Book IX, and an account of "Topsy-Turvy Island" in Books XVI and XIX, but prose fiction is the principal resource of the series, which includes more than fifty stories of one kind or another, in addition to numerous portraits and anecdotes of a marginal character. Some of the narratives are very brief, but in "Books" of fifteen thousand words the author had room to spread herself, and six are of novelette length or longer. One of them occupies a whole number. The amount of fiction fluctuates from volume to volume. Volume I (Books I to VI) largely consists of illustrative stories, but the emphasis on fiction falls off suddenly in Volume II after a correspondent charged the Author with being "an idle, prating, gossiping old woman." For a time thereafter the amount of direct exhortation becomes greater. But readers complained about that also, and in later volumes the tide of prose fiction returns. The fourteenth book of the *Female Spectator*, which contains two of the novelettes of the series, will serve to illustrate both the method and the manner of Mrs. Haywood's serial, as well as hold up to view several of her most popular stories.

The Author begins her "entertainment" for the month with a long letter from a correspondent who signs herself "Claribella" of "Red-Lyon-Square." Claribella entreats the sympathy of the Female Spectator for those unhappy females, otherwise faultless, who incur the condemnation of society for a single breach of decorum, often made under the influence of "ungovernable passion." The case in point is Aliena, a friend of Claribella, whose adventures have been (we are assured) as surprising as any in "the most celebrated romance." Aliena is "the daughter of a gentleman descended of a very ancient family," whose fortunes have greatly declined. As a result, she is dowerless, but is otherwise "one of the most charming creatures in the world"—"the darling of all that knew her"—distinguished by her beauty, her sweetness of character, and her unsullied innocence. Her only weakness is love ("the fatal softness of our sex," as Claribella describes it). One of her suitors, with whom she became infatuated, is the commander of one of His Majesty's ships, "a gentleman of good family, agreeable in person, and handsome in fortune." His intentions were unquestionably honorable, and everyone expected a declaration, but unluckily his ship was commanded to the West Indies for three years, and perhaps considering Aliena's youth (she was only fourteen or fifteen), he departed without proposing a definite engagement.

Aliena loved him with violence, and was prostrate at his departure. At length she desperately assumed the habit of a boy, secretly followed her lover to Gravesend, and engaged herself, without his knowledge, as cabin boy on board his ship. Unluckily her disguise was quickly detected, and she was subjected to various humiliating liberties before her true identity was known. Meanwhile, her absence being discovered at home, her lover was falsely accused of spiriting her off. This led to some coolness between him and her family, and as a result he has definitely allowed the relationship to lapse. Meanwhile, says Claribella, Aliena's reckless escapade is everywhere known, and she has become the unhappy object of derision among her acquaintance.

The Female Spectator is invited to comment upon Aliena's "unhappy story," and she gladly obliges with several pages of analysis and recapitulation. Aliena's "astonishing" breach of decorum is reviewed; the "romantic turn" of her mind; the unfortunate effects of her reading (not prose fiction, it should be observed, but Beaumont and Fletcher); and her fatal error in judgment. "A gentle, generous, tender soul we are ready to allow her," Mrs. Haywood declares, but her conduct is not to be excused, no more than is the Captain's coldness in failing to write to her, although his first reservations and final withdrawal were not without some justice and reason. The harshness of Aliena's family is also hard to exculpate, and there is genuine danger that after this "first wound" to her reputation she may be driven to some new excess. In the future she should be "used with more gentleness," though the "sincerity and good-nature of Claribella can never be too much applauded." Letters like hers and the one that follows, the Author declares, will always be received with pleasure, since they prove that "wit, and the love of virtue, are not altogether banished the realm." Whereupon, without further delay, she embarks upon the second novelette of Book XIV, "The Lady's Revenge," submitted by a correspondent who signs herself "Elismonda" of Kensington.

"The Lady's Revenge" is a feminine rogue story in miniature, displaying considerably more "wit" than "love of virtue." The intrigue turns upon the various retaliations practiced by a lady named Barsina upon a "gay gallant" who has jilted her. As a result of her skillful machinations, the unlucky Ziphranes is made to believe that Barsina, in her desperation, has fatally poisoned them both, and he is nearly killed by the various physicians called in to save his life. He has barely recovered from this illness when he is allowed to encounter Barsina's "ghost," and in the hysterical ravings that ensue he reveals to the whole world his guilty secret. At last:

> Disregarded by his wife, ridiculed by his acquaintance, and uneasy in himself, he lives an example of that vengeance which Heaven seldom fails to take on perjury and ingratitude.[24]

The weight of this surprising moral not being thought sufficient, the Female Spectator supplements it with half a dozen pages of sober reflection upon "the great force of imagination," especially upon guilty hearts. Where there is guilt, there must be fear, as Ziphranes's comic agonies testify. The only remedy against imaginary terrors, she assures the readers of "The Lady's Revenge" (somewhat irrelevantly) is "reason and reflection," and "an absolute resignation to the Divine Will, which can alone support us under that shock." In closing, she acknowledges receipt of the "useful essay" signed "Philo-Nature," which was to occupy a considerable portion of Book XV.

In providing readers with tales of passionate love and gallantry, treachery, adventure, and intrigue, "The Misfortunes of Aliena" and "The Lady's Revenge" are typical of most of the narrative pieces of the *Female Spectator*. Mrs. Haywood divided her attention about equally between exemplary heroines who achieve happiness and well-being through love of virtue, and foolish, proud, and willful damsels like Aliena who fall into traps laid by themselves and others. In her first number, she wrote:

> An instance of shining virtue in any age, can never be too often proposed as a pattern, nor the fatality of misconduct too much impressed on the minds of our youth of both sexes.[25]

The long story of Alithea in Book VI, for example, is part of a general discussion of "Good Nature." The heroine is an eighteenth-century Griselda who reclaims her erring husband by a supreme demonstration of affability and conjugal love. "The Story of Sabina" in Book XI, on the other hand, is "an example of the ill consequences attending on unreasonable prejudice." Sabina is the victim of a blind caprice which makes her reject Luellin, "one of the most handsome and best-bred men of the age," merely because he is a Welshman, and give herself instead to "a common sharper of the town," who makes her truly wretched.

The longest of Mrs. Haywood's tales in the *Female Spectator*, "The Triumph of Fortitude and Patience, over Barbarity and Deceit" (15,000 words), is a prolonged chronicle of persecuted love with a marked Richardsonian inflection. The heroine, Jemina, is a lovely orphan of good family, left destitute by a worthless father. Being "perfectly well turn'd and genteel in all her motions," she engages the attention of Lothario, a gallant of "fine person" and "great estate," who is a visitor in the house of her aunt. Lothario is "an adept in all the arts of intrigue," and he contrives secret opportunities to recommend himself to Jemina, not without some success, for she comes to care for him. What follows is described as "the struggle of a soul divided between love and honour." Like Pamela, Jemima is perfectly upright. She has (she says) "nothing but my virtue and reputation that I can call my own," yet she loves Lothario, and dreads "that in some ungarded moment that love might be the destruction of her virtue." Like Pamela, also, she holds firm, and in the end Lothario can only satisfy "his wild desires" by embarking upon a secret marriage with Jemima, which through his guile she is forced to accept. A long train of distresses ensue for Jemima, which are greatly multiplied by the disingenuousness of her husband, who has no real intention of ever recognizing her as his wife. But heaven, we learn, only tries Jemima "to make her virtue more conspicuous." In due time Lothario falls into a consumption, and in a death-bed repentance publicly acknowledges his wife, who is thus providentially rescued at the very nadir of her fortunes. In this long, involved, and harrowing story,

> Both sexes may indeed find very good lessons for the improvement of their morals!—a just remorse arising from a consciousness of guilt in Lothario, patience and courage under the most shocking of all distresses in Jemima, and hospitality and charity in that worthy lady who relieved her, are all too beautifully painted, not to make the sensible reader deeply affected with them.[26]

The subject matter is more sensational than Hawkesworth's, but the program anticipates that of the *Adventurer*, a few years in the offing.

There are two striking features of the *Female Spectator* from the point of view of the essay tradition—neither before emphasized. The first is the buoyancy and independence of mind with which Mrs. Haywood approached the already time-worn conventions of the essay-serial. She is the most eclectic of the major essayists. Those parts of the tradition that suited her purpose she adapted with discernment and skill; others, including many of the traditional narrative forms, she simply abandoned. There are no animal fables, fairy stories, oriental tales, or allegorical visions in the *Female Spectator*—simply domestic tales, "portraits," "cases," and edifying episodes drawn from high life. She wrote for a feminine audience whose measure she took with shrewdness and intelligence. Her bias was strictly upper-middle-class (though whether all of her readers were from the same level of society is very doubtful). There is hardly one of her heroines who is not rich or well-born, or who does not have some pretentions in polite society. But apart from her tendency to inflate and sentimentalize the world of fashion, Mrs. Haywood was something of an anti-sentimentalist since she occupied herself with the genuine problems of her sex, and debated them with a good deal of common sense and worldly knowledge. Moreover, in a manner somewhat reminiscent of Defoe, she made a serious effort to enlarge the restricted province of her readers' interests, by including serious discussions of subjects like English policy on the continent and the education of women.

Furthermore, Mrs. Haywood, the professional novelist, displayed considerable ingenuity in the way in which she accommodated the methods and subjects of popular fiction to what she called her "Spectatorial function." The fifty-some tales and novelettes of the *Female Spectator* are edifying sermons on prudence and propriety at the same time that they also manage to be, in some way, secret histories, *romans à clef*, novels of sentimental adventure and intrigue, satirical tales of gallantry, and amatory romances. Readers with a taste for contemporary fiction of this kind would find in the *Female Spectator*, if not the genuine article, at least a recognizable facsimile, which they were invited to view by means of a number of alluring gestures. The first book of the Female Spectator, for example, promptly assures her audience that all of her stories "bring real facts upon the stage," and that in order "to secure an eternal fund of intelligence," she has a secret army of "spies" not only in London, but in Bath, Tunbridge, "the Spaw," and elsewhere on the continent, ready to supply her with all the "secrets" of the polite world. Therefore, "nothing curious or worthy remark" can escape her knowledge, and she can penetrate as if invisible "the mysteries of the alcove, cabinet, or field." Lest she be considered a mere scandal-monger, however, she assures her readers that she has artfully "concealed" the real names of the participants, and all persons are enjoined *not* to make "what they call a key to these lucubrations."

Readers of essay-serials since the time of the *Tatler* had been accustomed to the claim that many of the cases and instances were "true," but they had seldom been promised so intriguing a combination of edification and scandal. In Steele, the fashionable taste for secret histories had been treated with some irony; Mrs. Haywood's more "townish" attitude was a partial throw-back to the modes of the *Gentleman's Journal*, which (as we have seen) were now beginning to be revived in compilations like the *Weekly Amusement*.

Equally significant from the point of view of popular taste is the emphasis upon love in the *Female Spectator*. The passion, in fact, is the abiding theme of her discourse—that "fatal softness" of the female nature that has wrought so many follies and wrecked so many lives. Mrs. Haywood begins by deploring the false definition of love which prevails in many "plays, novels, and romances" although, quite understandably, she does not linger over these sources of danger, with all three of which she was herself associated. Her purpose is to bring the light of reason into this dark and damp area, and to ventilate it with the breezes of prudence and common sense. At the same time it is a subject about which she cannot say enough. At least half of the stories of the *Female Spectator* deal with some aspect of love, courtship, or marriage, and even when Mrs. Haywood is led to consider other social and domestic problems, variations on the same themes provide a kind of background music.

> It may be judged [she writes in her final number], that on the business of love I am too serious; but I know nothing more concerns the happiness of mankind than that by which their species is to be propagated, and which by being ill conducted, makes all the miseries of civil life.

She is tireless in warning her readers of the rigid requirements of social decorum, the preciousness of a good reputation, the artifices of men, and the pitfalls which await the young and the unwary in a predatory society (requirements of which she herself no doubt had felt the pinch); and in driving her points home she inevitably has recourse to narrative situations involving gallantry and intrigue, seduction, adultery, rape, loose-living, clandestine relationships of various sorts, and other kinds of libertinage. Clara Reeve, in the *Progress of Romance*, forty years later, paid solemn tribute to Mrs. Haywood for her return to morality in her later years, and her atonement for the "amorous novels" of her youth by her final labors in "the service of virtue."[27] But the reformation was only a matter of emphasis, since it had always been a pious pretense of Mrs. Haywood that her "amorous novels" carried a very useful moral. Moreover, there is more than a breath of scandal in some of the stories of the *Female Spectator*.

Considering its bewitching blend of passion and propriety, fashion, and gossip, it is not surprising that the *Female Spectator* should achieve a very gratifying sale, and that several of its stories (especially "The Lady's Revenge") should re-appear in the miscellanies for a number of years. In addition to these, there were several unacknowledged adaptations in the *Universal Magazine*, which were in turn reprinted. The number of borrowings from the *Female Spectator*, however, is less than one might expect—probably for two reasons. First, with the exception of "The Lady's Revenge" (reprinted six times) and "The Triumph of Fortitude" (reprinted twice), the stories of the *Female Spectator* required some pains to disengage from the essay-medium in which they were suspended—an effort which many editors were unwilling to make. Second, the *Female Spectator* antedated by ten or fifteen years the extensive revival of the popular miscellany, by which time its stories of high life may have seemed a little out-of-date. Mrs. Haywood's greatest following in later years was among the provincial magazines. The decline of her serial from fashion is shown in the record of its collected volumes, which ran rapidly through six editions in about ten years (that is until 1756), and then waited until 1771 for a seventh and last.

The RAMBLER

The *Female Spectator* is only the first of about a dozen so-called revivals of the single-essay periodicals in the period from 1744–1755, but among its successors only the *Rambler* and the *Adventurer* have any genuine interest in the history of magazine fiction. Johnson's magazine published only one story of novelette length. Nevertheless the *Rambler* is important, because of its special emphasis on prose fiction, its pronouncements on the subject of the English novel, and its decisive influence upon the much more popular *Adventurer*.

Approached from the point of view of the essay tradition, the *Rambler* is in many respects a most surprising publication—surprising, of course, for its literary merit, but startling also because of its extraordinary admixture of personal and unconventional elements. Viewed in retrospect, of course, among the other volumes of Chalmers's *British Essayists*, the *Rambler* stands strategically in the center of the great tradition which it confirms and extends in a manner that now seems inevitable. But considered as a journalistic venture, submitted anonymously to the public in the spring of 1750, and intended to make its way among a swarm of other pamphlets and serial publications, it seems a most unlikely combination of tradition and idiosyncrasy. The early numbers of the *Female Spectator* were designed to attract readers and disarm criticism; those of the *Rambler* seem to have been designed to repell them. Its title, certainly, promised a casual approach to human affairs (if not worse),[28] and typographically the paper appears, more than Mrs. Haywood's, to invite readers to enjoy a new set of variations upon the familiar themes of Addison and Steele, Budgell, and Ambrose Philips. Far from gratifying most of these expectations, however, Johnson in his first paper did not even mention the *Spectator*, but looking grandly over the top of Addison's head, invoked the names of Homer, Horace, and Plutarch. Moreover, the succeeding numbers turned out to be a series of somber and magisterial disquisitions in anything but the Spectatorial manner. Considering what we now know of Johnson's opinion of Addison, and the prayerful solemnity with which he embarked upon this enterprise, his loftiness is not surprising. But except to a few serious and discriminating readers the *Rambler* must have seemed a ponderous, proud, and perverse publication.

It is unnecessary to comment on the celebrated style of the *Rambler*, or to linger on most of its contents, which have long occupied the attention of scholars. We may merely re-affirm that, historically viewed, it represents (like the *Female Spectator*) a partial splintering of the essay tradition—in Johnson's case, in favor of its moral, religious, and literary ingredients, and at the expense of those witty, elegant, and lightly satirical sketches of men and manners which a few years later were to become the speciality of the *World*. Johnson, of course, was quite conscious of this displacement of emphasis, as well as the rigorous demands which he made upon readers, and his preoccupation with the problem of popularity and literary reputation in the *Rambler* reflects some of his feelings of uneasiness. In the 23rd paper he frankly admitted his deviation from the norm for essay-serials, and the "tumult of criticism" thus unleashed, but he affirmed that each author

> has a rule of choice peculiar to himself; and selects those subjects which he is best qualified to treat, by the course of his studies, or the accidents of his life[29]

The extent to which Johnson departed from the approved manner of the essay-serial is amusingly underlined by the efforts of his occasional collaborators to pull him back into line. The several "billets" written by Miss Mulso in No. 10, in which the Author of the *Rambler* comments upon his numerous "correspondents," are a brisk exercise in the long-familiar manner of the *Spectator*. Four imaginary letters are excerpted, and three of them directly raise the question of the character of the new publication. The first letter, from a "set of candid readers," acknowledges the superior genius of the Author, but expresses the wish that he might

> condescend to the weakness of minds softened by perpetual amusements, and now and then throw in, like his predecessors, some papers of a gay and humorous turn.

The second, which alludes to Addison for the first time in the series, flatly declares that if he insists upon being "a mere essayist, and troubles not himself with the manners of the age," he will earn nothing but neglect. A third, from "Lady Racket," invites him to find subjects for his "living characters" in the glamorous company which congregates at her house on Sundays. Richardson's letter in No. 97 delicately pursues the same theme. It begins by recalling the impression made upon him by the original *Spectator* papers, of precious memory, and the striking manner in which they focussed upon the "foibles of those times."

> I cannot but wish [he writes] that you would oftener take cognizance of the manners of the better half of the human species, that if your precepts and observations be carried down to posterity, the Spectators may show to the rising generation what were the fashionable follies of their grandmothers, the Rambler of their mothers, and that from both they may draw instruction and warning.

Richardson's letter as a whole is an elegiac comment upon the decline of manners and of the domestic virtues in recent times, and an indirect appeal to the *Rambler* to animadvert upon those follies which it is the historic function of the essayist to expose and correct. His essay won the largest sale of any of the *Rambler* papers.

Considering Johnson's pertinacity and independence one wonders why in the *Rambler* he bothered to employ as much of the paraphernalia of the Spectatorial tradition as he did, and why he did not frankly appear before the world as a "mere essayist," as Miss Mulso's second correspondent scornfully suggested that he had. The sale of the individual numbers of the *Rambler* was not large (according to Murphy it seldom exceeded five hundred copies), so that Johnson would not have sacrificed much, and he might have gained more, by giving up the traditional methods of the *Spectator* and offering readers a series of lay-sermons and literary papers, as some later essayists were to do successfully. The third *Rambler*, for example, is an attack upon the contemptible race of modern critics, and the impediments which they add to the already difficult tasks of authorship. Johnson could have far more effectively developed his theme with a fund of personal anecdotes and historical citations of the kind that distinguished his familiar conversation. Instead he embarked upon an Addisonian allegory on the origin of criticism, "the eldest daughter of Labour and of Truth." This cumbersome flight of fancy was certainly unnecessary to hold the attention of those readers who were willing to follow him through the labyrinthine periods of these and earlier pages. But here, as elsewhere in the *Rambler*, Johnson felt impelled to don the ill-fitting garments of Mr. Spectator and Nestor Ironsides, and to perform many of the usual gyrations. He wrote himself a great many letters in ponderous imitation of the *Spectator*, grandly addressed himself to the problems of his feminine readers (who were largely, one suspects, hypothetical), and adopted many of the approved narrative modes of the essay tradition. The *Rambler* contains ten oriental tales, eight dream visions and allegories, several fables, a mock-sentimental romance, and a great many fictitious cases, tendered in the form of "pictures of life."

Johnson was not unsuccessful as a Spectatorial story-teller, but it is doubtful whether any of the grave and learned readers of the *Rambler* really required this expedient. In the last of his papers he expressed his disdain for the usual arts by which literary favor is obtained, and declared that his efforts had been addressed to those "whose passions left them leisure for abstracted truth, and whom virtue could please by its naked dignity." His ungainly orthodoxies in the single-essay tradition, however, do not entirely conform to this picture of himself. They unquestionably helped to ensure his monumental reputation with later eighteenth-century readers, for whom the *Rambler* became a mine of moral and literary wisdom (the work went through ten collected editions by 1784, and sixteen by 1810), but they probably also helped to invite some of the neglect of posterity, for whom Johnson told himself he was really writing.

Dr. Johnson on the Novel

The literary papers of the *Rambler* were an important part of the undertaking, and once Johnson had made his "ceremonial entrance," expatiated upon the difficulties of his task, and disposed of the tribe of critics, he turned in the fourth paper to a subject of pressing importance—the new English novel. This celebrated paper is the first serious criticial treatment received by

THE

RAMBLER.

NUMB. 4. Price 2 *d.*

SATURDAY, *March* 31, 1750.

To be continued on TUESDAYS *and* SATURDAYS.

Simul et jucunda ct idonea dicere Vitæ HOR.

THE Works of Fiction, with which the preſent Generation ſeems more particularly delighted, are ſuch as exhibit Life in its true State, diverſified only by the Accidents that daily happen in the World, and influenced by thoſe Paſſions and Qualities which are really to be found in converſing with Mankind.

THIS Kind of Writing may be termed not improperly the Comedy of Romance, and is to be conducted nearly by the Rules of Comic Poetry. Its Province is to bring about natural Events by eaſy Means, and to keep up Curioſity without the Help of Wonder; it is therefore precluded from the Machines and Expedients of the Heroic Romance, and can neither employ Giants to ſnatch away a Lady from the nuptial Rites, nor Knights to bring her back from Captivity; it can neither bewilder its Perſonages in Deſarts, nor lodge them in imaginary Caſtles.

I REMEMBER a Remark made by *Scaliger* upon *Pontanus*, that all his Writings are filled with Images, and that

The Celebrated *Rambler* No. 4 on the Novel

the novel in the single-essay periodical, and one of the most influential statements on the subject in the whole of the eighteenth century, for the weight of Johnson's authority and the force of his prejudices were to affect deeply the thinking of all other essay-critics.

The essential feature, in his eyes, that distinguishes "the works of fiction, with which the present generation seems more particularly delighted" from "the fictions of the last age" is the fact that they seek to "exhibit life in its true state, diversified only by accidents that daily happen in the world, and influenced by passions and qualities which are really to be found in conversing with mankind." As a class of writing they represent (he declared) "the comedy of romance," and are therefore more or less subject to "the rules of comick poetry." Being deprived of the "machines and expedients" of the old heroic romance, the modern story-teller seeks to portray *familiar* objects, *real* manners, and *life-like* situations, and "to bring about natural events by easy means, and to keep up curiosity without the help of wonder." The result is that the novelist's works are extremely accessible to unsophisticated readers, a fact that greatly adds to the difficulty of his task, since every reader becomes a potential critic. The writing of novels therefore requires not only "that learning which is to be gained from books," but the kind of experience arising from "general converse and accurate observation of the living world." Thus Fielding had also written in the celebrated first chapter of *Tom Jones*, Book IX—from which Johnson might almost be quoting.

In Fielding's book, however, the "depravation" of public morality caused by "foolish novels" and "monstrous romances" had been given only passing mention. In the *Rambler* it became "the most important concern" of the writer of familiar histories. The great ease with which they are read entails serious obligations to society. The fact is that novels are "written chiefly to the young, the ignorant, and the idle, to whom they serve as lectures of conduct, and introductions into life." In the old romances, people and events were remote from common life, so that readers were less likely to make an immediate application to their own lives. But modern romances are scanned by a multitude of eager and unformed minds, open to every kind of suggestion and erroneous impression. Willy-nilly, therefore, they are object lessons for youth, with momentous potentialities for both good and evil. This being true, the novelist's aim is not to hold the mirror up to nature. On the contrary, there is real danger to the young in exhibiting virtues and vices promiscuously mixed as they are in real life, for by this means good and evil may easily be confused, the sympathy which is aroused for the first being transferred indiscriminately to the second. It is the duty of the novelist to discover in nature what is *deserving* of imitation—to portray true virtue undistorted by ugliness, unworthiness, or evil; to render vice abhorrent; to teach the young prudence; and to strengthen them against temptation.

> In narratives where historical veracity has no place [Johnson declared in concluding], I cannot discover why there should not be exhibited the most perfect ideas of virtue; of virtue not angelical, nor above probability, for what we cannot credit, we shall never imitate, but the highest and purest that humanity can reach, which exercised in such trials as the various revolutions of things shall bring upon it, may, by conquering some calamities, and enduring others, teach us what we may hope, and what we can perform.

Such is Johnson's view of the novel as expressed in the *Rambler*—a view which recognizes some of the difficulties attendant upon the novelist's art, but which submerges that art completely in the more pressing claims of moral efficacy.

Johnson's paper on prose fiction, which is dated March 31, 1750, followed by only thirteen months the first edition of *Tom Jones*, and appeared at the very zenith of that novel's popularity. It can be read, therefore, as a defense of *Clarissa* against its detractors, and a conscious or unconscious rejoinder to Fielding's theory of the novel as expressed in the inital chapters of *Tom Jones*. Both Richardson and Fielding had appealed to "nature" in justification of their works, particularly in the realm of character. Johnson's emphasis upon this concept in his *Rambler* paper represents an attempt to establish Richardson's higher claim to truth, and perhaps to answer Fielding's various satirical references to those "models of perfection" that are commonly introduced into novels but are never encountered in real life. Here, as elsewhere, though without naming him, Johnson seems to be attacking the "mixed" character of Tom Jones, and his paper further supports Richardson's canons of criticism, as expressed in his prefaces and correspondence, by emphasizing ethical rather than technical questions, and by viewing fiction primarily in terms of its effect upon young people. If the world is to be "promiscuously described" (presumably as it is in Fielding's novels), Johnson declared, "I cannot see of what use it can be to read the account." The answer, of course, lies in the realm of "literary pleasure." But however enlarged a view Johnson took elsewhere of the categories of "wit," "fancy," and "imagination,"[30] and of the art of Henry Fielding, in the *Rambler* essay on the novel they receive short shrift—presumably because of the immediate threat posed to society.

In according the novel recognition as a genuine literary genre, Johnson performed a service to the new fiction of his day, but in seeming to reduce it to a mere arm of pedagogy, he was a force for reaction and prejudice. As a result of the gradually increasing eminence of the *Rambler*, these views became henceforth the orthodox position of essay-writers on the English novel, and thus further widened the breach between common taste and the essay-serial, which had in Addison and Steele's time been temporarily closed, and which Mrs. Haywood had made a vigorous effort to bridge.

Fielding's reply to Johnson's strictures in the *Rambler* (not a conscious reply, probably) is found in the celebrated 24th number of the *Covent Garden Journal* two years later in which he reviewed *The Female Quixote*. His generous comments on *Clarissa* earlier, in the *Jacobite's Journal* of 1748, had praised the novel not for its moral purpose (of which, of course, he did not disapprove) but for its artistic excellence—its compelling "Simplicity," its picture of "Manners," its "deep Penetration into Nature," its "Power to raise and alarm the Passions," and to create overpowering suspense—in short, for Richardson's mastery of "all that Art which *Horace* compares to Witchcraft."[31] In the review of Mrs. Lennox's novel in the *Covent Garden* he further developed this point of view in such a way as to underline his differences with Johnson and Richardson. He praised *The Female Quixote* for affording "very useful Lessons to all those young Ladies who will pursue it with proper Attention," but the primary emphasis in Fielding's paper is upon the artistic excellence of the book rather than its moral purpose—its "characters," "incidents," "general design," "originality" of conception, plausibility and probability, unity of action, humor, and so on[32]—practical *literary* considerations, which Johnson had pushed aside entirely in favor of the theoretical question of moral efficacy. Among the critics of the essay-serials, however, Fielding was to collect few disciples (although in the *Monthly Review* his point of view was beginning to receive an airing), whereas the stern voice of Johnson on the English novel was to reverberate through essay-serials and essay-series for the rest of the century.

Johnson's Magazine Fiction

It is doubtful whether Johnson saw any significant relation between the "familiar histories" in which his generation was delighting, and his own narrative pieces in the *Rambler*, yet the fairly large quantity of fiction in the periodical and the unusual number of short serial stories show him bending visibly with the breezes of popular fancy, at the same time that he produced a kind of fiction which conformed to his ideas of empirical and moral "reality." Johnson's best-known narrative pieces in the *Rambler* are his mock-sentimental romance, "Anningait and Ajut" (Nos. 186–187), and the oriental tale, "The History of Seged" (Nos. 204–205)—what he described in his last number as the "excursions of fancy"—but the prevailing species of the *Rambler* is the so-called "picture of life." Johnson was in no way the inventor of this type of story, which is really an extension of the old cases and narrative portraits of the *Tatler* and the *Spectator* (and of Theophrastian tradition), but he gave it such emphasis in his periodical, and charged it with such moral portentousness that it seemed to become the special feature of the *Rambler*. Of the sixty-eight numbers of the serial that are wholly or largely devoted to narrative, fifty-three may be classified as "pictures of life."

The Johnsonian "living picture," as it is also called, is typically a portrait of some representative character, or the account of some person's unhappy experiences in life, offered as an illustration of a moral or social evil, and intended to excite satirical laughter or abhorrence. As Johnson explained in his last paper, its purpose was to lead the reader to "the contemplation of his own manners," and therefore, although "some enlargement may be allowed to declamation, and some exaggeration to burlesque," it was supposed to mirror "reality"—by which he meant, of course, "resemblance" (or verisimilitude) informed by moral truth in such a way that vice and virtue are clearly discriminated.

The *Rambler*'s pictures of life are typically personal histories or confessions cast in letter form, although there are a few third-person narratives, identical in most other respects. The story usually begins with a statement of the theme or lesson to be derived from the events to be described, sketches the narrator's social and family background (usually upper middle-class), and then proceeds to lay his case before Mr. Rambler, or to give an account of his discoveries in the world. The first of the pictures of life in the *Rambler*

(No. 12) is the acrimonious "History of Zosima," Zosima is the daughter of a country clergyman forced by her father's poverty to seek domestic employment. Her letter to the *Rambler* details a long series of humiliating experiences with prospective employers, the theme of which is the cruelty and selfishness of men in their treatment of servants. Zosima is herself a victim of human callousness, but others of Johnson's correspondents, as, for example, Cleora the spoiled beauty in No. 15, themselves display the vanity and folly of mankind. Cleora's satirical observations on the passion for dice and cards in her circle, however justified, have an ironic base, since they are provoked by pique at the loss of attention she herself suffers. Succeeding "pictures of life" in the *Rambler* develop such themes as the visionary delights of wealth, the unhappiness of most marriages, the selfishness of the rich, the ignorance of parents, the irresponsibility of guardians, and the extravagant expectations of youth. Despite his emphasis upon ideal virtue in the fourth paper, Johnson in his own narratives is quite uninterested in pictures of perfection, focussing instead upon the ignorance, viciousness, and folly of mankind. Typically his stories are studies in blasted hopes and expectations, although sometimes his subjects achieve peace of mind, or a qualified satisfaction in life.

Johnson's stubborn adherence to the epistolary form in the *Rambler* is another of the surprising features of the series, considering how ill-prepared he was to exploit its possibilities. There are about seventy letters in the *Rambler*, and most of the "living pictures" are presented in this form. His imagination was more than equal to the task of projecting his themes and ideas in terms of concrete situations, supported by a wealth of significant detail. But he seemed unwilling (or unable) to adopt an epistolary style in conformity with the character of most of his alleged correspondents, who ostensibly represent a wide variety of personality types. With a few of them, particularly the women, he made fugitive efforts to adopt a suitable manner, and even (like Richardson in his novels) to record animated conversations verbatim, but most of the time he merely addressed to himself letters identical in manner and similar in structure to previous communications.

"The History of Hymenaeus's Courtship," the only story actually to attain novelette length in the *Rambler*, illustrates this limitation. It is a dynamic series of four letters on the same theme as the "Miranda" episodes in the *Free-Thinker* and Mist's *Weekly Journal*, and the later imitation in the *Universal Spectator*, with at least one of which (probably the first-named) Johnson would seem to have been acquainted. The first two letters from Hymenaeus, in *Rambler* Nos. 113 and 115, give an account of the long series of disappointments and betrayals which he has suffered at the hands of the female world, and which have banished him, in spite of himself, to a life of "frozen celibacy." Two weeks later Tranquilla comes forward with the story of her own adventures in courtship, "which (she says) the ladies may oppose to the tale of Hymenaeus." Owing to the caprice and selfishness of a long line of lovers and pretended suitors, she has been unable to find a man with whom she "could venture an inseparable union," although "antiquated virginity" is anything but her desire. After an interval of five months in the *Rambler*, during which time these two frustrated lovers are presumably brought together, the marriage of Hymenaeus and Tranquilla is announced in a letter signed by both, in which they describe an exemplary match based upon parity of fortune, similarity of interests, love, and mutual consideration. Typically, Johnson the essayist does not comment upon his "living pictures." Hymenaeus and Tranquilla interpret their own histories, which, not unnaturally, are heavy with disenchantment. But considered as epistolary exercises their letters are undiscriminated. Their solemn indictments against humanity are indistinguishable from each other, or from those made elsewhere by the Author of the *Rambler*, and their joint communication on the felicities of true marriage might as easily have been written by Eubulus, Eumathes, Captator, or any of Johnson's other imaginary correspondents, all of whom tend to write like moral whales. In his eyes, that they should speak to his readers in the first person was a sufficient concession to epistolary decorum.

Johnson carried a few of his other pictures of life into successive numbers as in the "Story of Eubulus," the disappointed author, in Nos. 26 and 27, or the three communications from Eumathes, the tutor of an over-indulged young nobleman, in Nos. 132, 194, and 195. Eight of the *Rambler's* pictures are thus serialized, including "Hymenaeus's Courtship." In addition to these, he offered two two-part serial stories among the "disquisitions of fancy."

The precedents for serial fiction established by Addison and Steele, Defoe, Philips, and other earlier essayists were fairly numerous and were already differentiated into a variety of distinctive types. They included, to run down the list, *serial tales* and *episodic narratives*; various kinds of *letter-series* ("simple," "intermittent," and "dynamic"); *cumulative episodes*; and *supporting narratives* in the general framework of the series. The ten serial stories of the *Rambler* avail themselves of several of these types. They include two serial tales ("Anningait and Ajut" and the "History of Seged"), five simple letter-series (the first being the two communications from Eubulus in Nos. 26–27), two intermittent series (from "Euphelia" and "Eumathes"), and of course the dynamic series of Hymenaeus and Tranquilla. But the emphasis which Johnson placed upon the first two types in the *Rambler* suggests a certain disregard for the ingenious techniques devised by his predecessors for carrying a story from one number to another, since of all the methods available to him these two were the most perfunctory. The only difference between Eubulus, Misocapelus, Victoria, Misella, and Captator, and most of the *Rambler's* other correspondents is that they pour their woeful histories into *two* letters instead of one. In the first they describe their entrance into life and the first stage of their experiences; in the second, they resume their chronicle, which is carried forward to the moment when they first took up their pens. They report on no intervening developments, although the second letter sometimes embarks upon a new theme. They undergo no change of character, or acquire no new insights from their recapitulation of events. They end in the same state of mind in which they began—unhappy, disillusioned, or dismayed.

The story of Euphelia, in Nos. 42 and 46, is an exception, her history being resumed two weeks later, after she has made new discoveries about rural society; and so is that of Eumathes, who picks up his story again after seven months. But apart from these two examples of genuine periodicity, and "Hymenaeus's Courtship," Johnson made no visible effort to exploit the potentialities of periodical publication. All the ingenuity expended by his friend Richardson in *Pamela* and *Clarissa* to make the letter-form a significant and truly functional narrative device were lost on Johnson the practising story-teller. His indifference on this score is important because of his powerful influence on Hawkesworth, one of the most widely admired and imitated magazine writers, and their joint influence upon other essay-writers during the next sixty years.

In time the *Rambler* came to enjoy a very considerable sale in the collected volumes. But the record shows that the essays were not particularly popular with magazine readers for a good many years. Cave gave them marked attention in the *Gentleman's Magazine* (a token of friendship and respect), and "Seged" and "Anningait" are often encountered at the end of the century in collections of magazine classics. "Hymenaeus's Courtship," however, was never reprinted in its entirety, nor, in fact, were most of the other serial pieces on which we have lingered. Judged by the record of the miscellanies, Johnson's only popular fiction (apart from the numerous epitomes and extracts taken from *Rasselas*) was not the stories of the *Rambler*, but the short "Vision of Theodore, the Hermit of Teneriffe" (4700 words), an allegorical vision written for Dodsley's *Preceptor* in 1748, and "The Fountains, a Fairy Tale" (5000 words) contributed to Ann Williams's *Miscellanies in Prose and Verse* in 1766. Both of these pieces, being in approved and long-familiar dress, made a series of phantom reappearances in odd corners of miscellanies for the next fifty years. The real legacy of the *Rambler* to magazine fiction, outside its author's critical opinions, was John Hawkesworth's *Adventurer*.

The ADVENTURER

The *Adventurer* was launched only eight months after the completion of the *Rambler*—with Johnson's encouragement, and, after a few numbers, his active participation. The first issues of the new periodical appeared in November, 1752, printed on folio half-sheets, single column, "for J. Payne, at Pope's Head, in Pater-noster row, where [it was declared] Letters to the *Adventurer* are received."[33] Despite the conventional invitation to readers to contribute and the elaborate pretense that much of the published material was provided by "correspondents," Hawkesworth admitted in the last number that only a very few of the 144 numbers of the *Adventurer* were actually contributed by strangers. It is doubtful whether any readers had been deceived, since Hawkesworth's epistolary methods were nearly as mechanical as Johnson's. The fault is less conspicuous, however, since his style was more simple and rapid.

The "ultimate design" of the new periodical, as Payne, the publisher, declared in a letter to the Reverend Dr. Birch, was

> to promote the practice of piety and virtue upon the principles of Christianity; yet in such a manner that they for whose benefit it is chiefly intended may not be tempted to throw it aside.[34]

Allowance must be made, of course, for Payne's effort to enlist the support of an influential clergyman, but the statement was not inaccurate, since virtue and piety were obviously a major pre-occupation of the new periodical. It has been said that Hawkesworth consciously wrote as a pedagogue, with the young misses of his wife's boarding school in Bromley in view. He declared in the last number that he wrote for "the YOUNG and the GAY." But some of the pieces are too mature to fit this description. Many of them, it it is true, seem to be written for young people. But others are addressed to "ladies," married as well as unmarried, and "gentlemen" of indefinite social status. Hawkins declared that Hawkesworth wrote to establish himself as a man of probity and high principles who might be entrusted with the superintendence of a female seminary.[35] If this is true, he succeeded in an unexpected way for among the many delighted readers of the periodical was Archbishop Herring, who, at its conclusion, made Hawkesworth a Doctor of Canon Law.

The plan of the *Adventurer*, as Johnson explained in a letter to Joseph Warton, called for three ingredients—"pieces of imagination, pictures of life, and disquisitions of literature."[36] The last-named were chiefly to be provided by Warton, who wrote critical essays on *King Lear*, *Paradise Lost*, and kindred subjects; the "pieces of imagination" and "pictures of life" by Hawkesworth, with the assistance of Johnson and a few other writers. Of the 144 papers Hawkesworth wrote seventy, Johnson twenty-nine, and Warton twenty-four. Over fifty are wholly given over to prose fiction, in addition to which there are numerous illustrative anecdotes and stories included in the essays. The fiction is in the usual forms associated with the essay-serial: *satirical adventures stories*, like the "Adventures of a Louse" and "a Halfpenny"; *allegories*, like "The Origin of Cunning"; *dream visions*, like "A Visit to Bedlam"; *fables* and *fairy tales*; and (most important) *eastern stories* and *domestic apologues*. Many of these are in the epistolary form, for which method the author acquired from Johnson a definite taste. As a story-writer Hawkesworth was no great innovator, except in the quantity of prose fiction which he included. In this respect he greatly strengthened the tendencies already displayed in the *Female Spectator* and the *Rambler*. The *Adventurer* contains altogether twelve serial stories of from two to four parts, and, of these, nine reached novelette length (seven by Hawkesworth; one each by Johnson and Mrs. Chapone). This emphasis upon serial fiction was itself something of a novelty, and joined with Hawkesworth's simplicity, optimism, and winning good nature, helps to account for the large sale of the periodical.

Hawkesworth's methods of serialization, however, show that he was as indifferent as Johnson to the problems involved in adapting the long story to the traditional character of the essay-periodical. With one or two unimportant exceptions, not the slightest effort was made in the *Adventurer* to exploit the advantages of periodicity. Of the twelve continued stories in the *Adventurer*, six are serial tales, one or two of the others are simple letter-series, and three or four are *serial letters*—a variant form to which Hawkesworth gave considerable currency, if he did not invent it. The serial letter is a single communication from a "correspondent," divided by the editor into several parts. Instead of formally sub-dividing his long epistolary histories into two or more letters, as Johnson typically did, bowing his way on and off the stage with each new appearance, Hawkesworth simply produced a single long epistle which was then segmented in conformity with the requirements of installment publication. The stories of Opsinous, Fidelia, Desdemona, and (in part) Benevolus all belong to this class of serial fiction, each one occupying two or three successive numbers of the periodical, and beginning and ending with a single salutation and close. Compared with the solemn gyrations of Johnson's letter-series, the serial letters of the *Adventurer* display an engaging directness and freedom from pretense, but like the serial tales with which they are obviously allied, they frankly disregard the autonomy of the individual number, and to that degree subvert the traditional principles upon which essay-serials were supposed to operate. Following Hawkesworth's persuasive example, later writers were to take even greater liberties, and allow their serial letters and serial tales to extend over many numbers.

Hawkesworth's Theory and Practice

If Hawkesworth was indifferent to the special problems presented by the long story in an essay periodical, he was not uninterested in the theory of prose fiction. It is in the realm of psycho-aesthetic principles, and the realization of these principles in terms of his own stories in the *Adventurer*, that he made his real contributions to magazine fiction.

Having presented himself in the first number in his role as "Adventurer"—

that is, as a modern knight-errant in the service of virtue and truth, and having dwelt in the second on the difficulties of his undertaking, he turned, in the fourth paper, to an analysis of the principal weapon at his command—namely, the resources of narrative art. Johnson had remarked upon the possible usefulness to morality of the methods of the English novel; Hawkesworth was prepared to implement this criticism. The fact that no writing affords more general entertainment than the "relation of events" endows the champion of virtue with extraordinary powers, which he was prepared to employ in his battle against error, infidelity, and vice. The kinds and classes of narratives are several, however, and not all are equally potent. The first is that class of narrative events that really happened leave as is —*history*, *voyages and travels*, and *biography*. These all have the advantage that they transcribe directly from the book of "Nature" (Hawkesworth ignores Johnson's distinction between moral and empirical reality). But none of them engages the passions or "gratifies curiosity" to the same degree as do the products of art, that is, the *epic* (including the *old romances*); *dramatic poetry* (especially *tragedy*); the *novel*; and supernatural stories of *genii and fairies*. Epic poetry can command both the feelings and the fancy to a superlative degree, but only at the expense of some truth to life. On the other hand:

> The Novel, though it bears a nearer resemblance to truth, has yet less power of entertainment; for as it is confined within the narrower bounds of probability, the number of incidents is necessarily diminished, and if it deceives us more it surprises us less. The distress is indeed frequently tender, but the narrative often stands still...

In the last analysis the "most generally pleasing of all literary performances," in Hawkesworth's eyes, are tales like those of the *Arabian Nights*, though they too are written in "open violation of the most known and obvious truths." Once he suspends his disbelief, however, the reader is beguiled by the procession of "new scenes" and "unbounded prospects" which open before him. Such tales, Hawkesworth declares, can be read "by almost every taste and capacity with equal eagerness and delight."

The fourth paper of the *Adventurer* is an important one in establishing the artistic theories that animated Hawkesworth at the beginning of his project, and, unlike Johnson's essay on the modern novel, it obviously has a conscious relation to the program of the succeeding numbers. From the prominent position which it occupies near the head of the series, it is clear that he intended to make prose fiction the principal ingredient of his periodical, and his emphasis upon the oriental tale shows that this species of narrative would enjoy his particular attention. In its ultimate fulfillment, however, the *Adventurer* was to follow a slightly different course, giving domestic apologues (*i.e.*, the "pictures of life") a somewhat greater degree of emphasis than the "pieces of imagination." The oriental tales were to achieve the greatest reclame, but, in numbers, the domestic tales were to become Hawkesworth's most important single means of enlisting his young readers in the cause of goodness and piety. Their subjects, like Johnson's, tend to be orphans of good family in temporary distress, the sons of wealthy farmers and country gentlemen, young men of "elegant person" and "large estate," and young ladies "of an eminent boarding school near London"—in other words, persons of a slightly elevated station in life, who either fall from felicity through recklessness, high living, or infidelity to the principles of revealed religion, or (more likely) make a fortune or a great marriage by their prudence and high principles. In Hawkesworth there is much more emphasis than in Johnson upon patterns of excellence.

The domestic tales receive no direct attention in the fourth paper, but if we read Hawkesworth's general remarks on prose fiction with some degree of hindsight, taking into account what he says about the oriental tale, the novel, and other types of narratives, we may extract from his early pages a kind of aesthetic for the magazine story that will accommodate both types of prose fiction. In the first place, although Hawkesworth was to offer his readers more serial fiction than any of his predecessors in the single-essay periodical, he clearly had no intention of emulating the novel. His criticism of the novel is that it lacks economy and speed. Readers (presumably he means *some* readers, or perhaps *magazine* readers) weary of its parade of "trivial circumstances," "languid descriptions," and "impertinent declamations." For this reason a paper like the *Adventurer* should concentrate upon shorter pieces of fairly simple outline, turning upon a single incident or chain of circumstances. The real pleasure from a story comes when events are "produced in regular and connected series," when they "follow in a quick succession," and when they are supported by a few, but not an excess of "discriminating circumstances." If events are "too minutely related, they become tiresome; and if divested of all their circumstances, insipid." The effects of a successful story are indirectly described in his comment upon the limitations of biography:

> ...there have been few among the whole human species, whose lives would furnish a single adventure; I mean such *a complication of circumstances, as hold the mind in an anxious yet pleasing suspense*, and *gradually unfold in the production of some unforeseen and important event*; much less *such a series of facts, as will perpetually vary the scene, and gratify the fancy with new views of life*. [Italics ours.]

Hawkesworth's psychological theories are further developed in the sixteenth paper when he turns his attention to the all-important subject of "instructing by fiction." The powers of enchantment possessed by the literary adventurer impose upon him portentous responsibilities for the moral well-being of society. By reason of the very substance of art, the story-teller is willy-nilly an ethical teacher, deeply involved in the struggle for men's souls. Moreover, since the feelings which motivate human conduct are brought into play not by ideas and admonitions but by "facts," "pictures," and concrete objects, the moral precepts should not merely be stated in the story. In this form they gain only "the cold approbation of reason." The precepts must be implicit in the events themselves, and be animated by every resource at the writer's command.

Thus far in his sixteenth paper Hawkesworth is elaborating the view set forth in the fourth number of the *Rambler*, on the moral efficacy of familiar histories, and the necessity for presenting unmixed virtues and vices. In prose fiction, Johnson had written, vice "should always disgust, nor should the graces of gaiety, or the dignity of courage, be so united with it as to reconcile it to the mind." But Hawkesworth goes on to develop this view further in terms of the actual operations of the human mind and thus to extend Johnson's remarks into the psychological sphere. Man's reason is not only likely to be misled by a mixture of good and evil qualities in the same character. The perversity of human nature is such that it is more deeply stirred by "natural" than by "moral excellence," and would rather suffer from "want of virtue" than from "want of parts." Virtue alone, unfortunately, is not a sufficient recommendation for most readers. If the fatal levity of the human heart is to be overcome, and if piety and goodness are to receive a proper hearing, they must be clothed with every ornament of human nature.

Hawkesworth proceeds to demonstrate human frailty by means of a pair of imaginary portraits. The first exhibit, Florio, is a gilded butterfly, endowed with all the graces of society—a man of parts, polished and educated by travel, witty, liberal, elegant in dress, and splendid in his person. "Among the ladies Florio has made many conquests; and has challenged and killed in a duel an officer, who upbraided him with the breach of a promise of marriage, confirmed by an oath, to a young beauty, whom he kept in great splendor as a mistress." Against this Lovelace, Hawkesworth balances a pedestrian young man called Benevolus, a person without taste or wit, awkward and stiff, "the jest of an assembly, and the aversion of ladies." Florio's only lack is principle; Benevolus's only splendor is his moral rectitude and tender conscience. But he is "a faithful friend, and a kind master," compassionate, wisely generous, and right thinking. "Which of these two characters [Hawkesworth asks] woudst thou chuse for thy own? whom dost thou most honour, and to whom hast thou paid the tribute of involuntary praise?" The answer to this gloomy question is henceforth never long out of the essayist's mind. It informs all of the prose fiction of the *Adventurer*, and in particular the domestic tales, which begin in the seventh number with "Distress Encouraged to Hope: the History of Melissa," a serial tale in two parts, the first of Hawkesworth's magazine novelettes, and the founder of a prolific family of magazine fiction.

Melissa's father was the younger son of a country gentleman. Since the whole of the estate went to his elder brother, it was hoped that he might make his way in trade, and to this end he was apprenticed to a wealthy merchant of Bristol. But the young man foolishly spurned the rewards of "honest industry," dreaming only of adventure. His imagination was fired by the exploits of military heroes, and he enlisted in the army as a common soldier. Nor was this the end of his recklessness. He also imprudently eloped with a girl of good family, who was instantly disinherited by her father. The young wife followed her husband to the wars on the continent. He was killed at the Siege of Namur; she died in premature labor; and Melissa was the blameless victim of this chain of disasters.

At this critical moment, however, the hand of providence first intervened. Melissa was nursed by a sympathetic widow who had lost her own child, and she was afterwards befriended by an English officer, who sent her in time to her maternal grandfather with the certificate of her mother's marriage. The hapless child, however, was turned from her family's door "with menaces and insult," and would certainly have perished but for the kindness of an uncle, "who had been rejected by his father for having married his maid." In his home Melissa found a modest security, and was taught to read and write and to sew. But her aunt and uncle died when she was only thirteen, and for a second time she was thrown upon the world. This time the neighboring squire, struck with her character and "touched with her distress," gave her shelter, and made her the companion of his daughter. Thus ended Part I of Melissa's story, at a moment when her fortunes seemed about to turn for the better. But in Part II, where the story was resumed without further ceremony, there were more trials to come.

Melissa became a favorite in the squire's family. She was "taught dancing and music, introduced to the best company, elegantly dressed," and soon was as happy as she could wish. Unluckily, however, in her eighteenth year, she attracted the attention of the only son of her benefactor, who attempted to win her favor by assiduous attentions. He was otherwise a serious young man, who "reverenced her virtue," but knowing his father's temper he could only entertain hopes of making Melissa his mistress. Melissa stubbornly resisted all his advances, even when he at length offered marriage. Her motive was pure gratitude to her benefactor, but it was misunderstood. The squire could only imagine that Melissa had conspired in this courtship, and for the third time she was cast out upon the world. Returning the £ 50 that her employer had given her in sending her away, she immediately took lodging in a "reputable house" in London, and set to work earning her living with her needle. One day, some time later, by a happy accident, she discovered that she was being sought as heiress to her paternal grandfather's estate, and she successfully claimed her inheritance. One of her first acts in coming into her £ 1500 a year was "to justify her conduct to the squire, whose kindness she still remembered, and whose resentment she had forgiven." Returning in state to her old benefactor, she addressed him as follows:

> When I was a dependant upon your liberality, I would not assert my innocence, because I cannot bear to be suspected of falshood; but I assert it now I am the possessor of a paternal estate, because I cannot bear to be suspected of ingratitude.

Whereupon the old gentleman led her to his son and apologized to them both. Within a few weeks she married the young man, "with whom she shared many years that happiness which is the reward of virtue."

The "History of Melissa" is typical of all of Hawkesworth's domestic apologues, and of a great deal of eighteenth-century magazine fiction. For this reason it is important to observe some of its generic traits. The story is a practical object lesson from first to last, and begins with a direct statement of the principal moral to be derived from it. Hawkesworth obviously does not scorn "the cold approbation of reason." He merely feels that it should be fortified with all the resources of the novelist's art.[37] Melissa's "eventful history" is

> a series of events from which the wretched may derive comfort, and the most forlorn may be encouraged to hope.

The same moral is underlined from time to time during the course of the story, at the same time that it is made inherent in the events themselves. Hawkesworth is nothing if not explicit. In addition to this principal theme, however, there are a number of other precepts folded into the story, which is by no means limited to a single meaning; the folly of Melissa's father, who was the victim of his romantic illusions; the eminent respectability of a mercantile life; the heartlessness of her maternal grandfather; the Christian charity of her various benefactors, and above all the prudent and upright manner in which the virtuous Melissa conducted herself in the successive crises of her life. In her fundamental integrity and in her delicate moral scrupulosity, Melissa is as perfect an "idea of virtue" as Johnson could wish, and the "reality" in which she is enclosed is faultlessly clear in all of its outlines. In his later novel, *Almoran and Hamet*, Hawkesworth was to be criticized for his confused view of providence, but in the domestic tales of the *Adventurer* the Almighty was to operate with uniform propriety in favor of the virtuous. If Melissa was made to endure far more than she deserved, it was only, like Mrs. Haywood's Jemima, to demonstrate her superior qualities of character and the value of hope.

Since the domestic tales of Hawkesworth (as well as his oriental tales) always recount the adventures of a single protagonist, they usually begin, like the story of Melissa, or Johnson's "living pictures," with the subject's family and social origins, and then proceed rapidly through the events of his life in chronological order. His stories contain no mysteries to be unfolded, or interpolated histories, of the kind to which the contemporary novel was so addicted. They require no back-tracking, or oscillation between different scenes or sets of characters. The intrigue unwinds in a single thread, severed at intervals of proper essay length. Part I of "Distress Encouraged to Hope" carries Melissa through a succession of misfortunes; Part II continues her ordeal, and in due time elevates her to fortune. A suitable motto from Virgil is provided for each part, a practice made familiar by the *Spectator*, and eventually extended through the agency of the *Rambler* and the *Adventurer* to a good deal of magazine fiction. The motto of Part II of Melissa's history, translated, is "Endure and conquer, live for better fate." That of Part I is "What I have heard, permit me to relate"—referring to the claim frequently made in the domestic tales of the magazines that these stories are "true," "factual," or "real." Melissa's story in the *Adventurer* is tendered as the life of a lady recently dead, "whose name is known to many." But the claim is purely routine, and would deceive no one, since the story, though simple in outline, is obviously contrived to exhibit the author's professed narrative values.

It is in the realm of the "real" and the "probable" that the domestic tale of Hawkesworth's periodical can be distinguished from the more exotic eastern variety, as the fourth *Adventurer* explains. The one is taken up with familiar experiences; the other transports its readers into the more alluring "regions of fancy." The first confines itself to the "known and obvious truths" of human life; the second admits supernatural beings. The separation, however, is more apparent than genuine. Once the agency of genii and fairies is admitted

> no event which is deemed possible to such agents is rejected as incredible or absurd; the action of the story proceeds with regularity, the persons act upon rational principles, and such events take place as may naturally be expected from the interposition of superior intelligence and power.

In other words, although the oriental tales may run counter to "natural probability" in a single respect, they never violate "moral probability," since the ethical laws and the principles which govern human character will operate throughout with uniform consistency. This minor difference and major similarity is illustrated by the most celebrated of Hawkesworth's oriental pieces in the *Adventurer*, "Amurath, an Eastern Story," offered in Nos. 20, 21, and 22.

The story of Amurath, which is told in the first person, is a kind of allegory of the human conscience. Upon the death of his father the sultan, Amurath succeeded to the throne. Being only eighteen, he was counseled by a benign genius, Syndarac, who gave him a ruby ring of "deep colour and uncommon brightness," the power of which was to remind him of "the nature and tendency of every action." In any deviation from the right, the ring would prick his finger and the stone grow pale. At first there were no warnings, since Amurath was humble and devoted to his noble father's memory. But gradually his fundamental selfishness asserted itself. His first evil act was almost unconscious. He wantonly struck a dog, and on being reminded of his cruelty he felt surprise and regret. Subsequently, however, he was betrayed into more extreme acts of evil, and at length he ceased to pay any attention to the warning of the ring. He oppressed his people, encouraged servility in his court, and surrendered himself to lust and sensuality. He even attempted to violate the chastity of his betrothed, the virtuous princess Selima. But she was rescued by the hand of Syndarac.

In his frustration Amurath threatened her father with death, and dashed the ruby ring to the ground, whereupon his guiding genius suddenly appeared before him and declared,

> "Thou hast now, as far as it is in thy own power, thrown off humanity and degraded thy being: thy form, therefore, shall no longer conceal thy nature, nor thy example render thy vices contagious."

At this moment Amurath found himself transformed into a beast, half-wolf and half-goat, bellowing in the desert. In this unnatural condition he suffered ignominy and privation, and through his suffering as an animal learned what it was to be human. By degrees, as he acquired self-discipline and moral understanding, he was transmogrified into a dog and later a dove, and at last, when his love for Selima became truly virtuous, he was restored to his betrothed, his throne, and his dominions.

As a moral apologue it is obvious that "Amurath" is equivalent in many ways to the story of Melissa. However different their surface aspects, both stories were intended to recommend human kindness and charity, and to demonstrate the evils of vice and egotism. Through suffering, Amurath had to learn the value of goodness, which Melissa never doubted, but once he took the right path he reaped both the material and spiritual rewards of exemplary conduct. In his great distress, at the nadir of his fortunes, Amurath was also encouraged to hope. In addition, Amurath embodies two important themes of the *Adventurer*, which Hawkesworth singled out for particular mention in his last paper and which he felt were especially important for his young readers—namely, the idea that evil is of gradual and easy descent when once the human subject deviates from the level of purity and innocence; and that such a descent can lead only to hopeless misery.

In the "History of Melissa" these ideas are only implicit, but they are the principal theme of the domestic tale of Opsinous, or "The Influence of Infidelity upon Moral Conduct," a serial letter which occupied three issues of the *Adventurer*, a few weeks later. Opsinous was the only child of a wealthy farmer, who placed his son's education in the hands of the curate of the parish, a pious man. Unfortunately, however, the boy's education was thought to have unsuited him for farming, and he was allowed to go to London to study for the law. He was led astray by the easy ways of the city, and seduced by the deistic thinking of the taverns. The libertine principles which he imbibed there led him by degrees to seduction, murder, and self-slaughter. In "Opsinous" these warnings are reinforced by the story's alleged "resemblance to everyday life"; in "Amurath," by an appeal to the fancy involving sultans and seraglios, miraculous visitations, and transformations. Thus Hawkesworth's "moral lectures" converged upon the young and the gay from two directions. The aim of the oriental tales was to "surprize" them into a love of goodness, that of the domestic apologues was to "deceive" them to the same end.[38]

In the last *Adventurer*, its oriental tales were viewed as efforts to "amuse the imagination," although they have been criticized by Miss Conant for being deficient in precisely this quality. Compared with those of Goldsmith, Johnson, Marmontel, and Voltaire, for example, they seem to her to be distinguished by the slightness of their oriental machinery and the thinness of their characterization.[39] By modern standards these criticisms are no doubt justified, and it is an indisputable fact that Hawkesworth has failed to hold his audience beyond the nineteenth century. In his defense, however, we may remark that both of these features were the result of his settled conviction regarding his function as a story-teller, and his conscious efforts to achieve economy and speed. Moreover, they were failings that passed unnoticed by his contemporaries. The *Adventurer* made a considerable impression in its original issue. Its circulation, Hawkins declared, was "more diffuse" than the

Rambler;[40] and four collected editions were called for within ten years. The record of the Catalogue strongly supports the impression of Hawkesworth's popularity. As a group, the novelettes of the *Adventurer* were more widely reprinted during the next fifty years than those of any other essay-serial—and more widely imitated. Seven of the ten were gathered into other magazines, most of them several times. "Amurath" alone, the most popular of his stories, was reprinted six times. Until the early nineteenth century Hawkesworth's name stood next to Addison's as a master of both oriental and domestic fiction. "If *Juvenis* will study the Tales of an *Addison*, a *Hawkesworth*, and a *Johnson*," the editor of the *Universal* wrote in 1781 to one of his young contributors, "he will learn in what consists the peculiar excellency of Eastern composition."[41] As late as 1813 the editor of the *Ladies' Monthly Museum* was still suggesting to his correspondents:

> Without presuming to dictate to our contributors, we beg leave to remark, that *short moral Tales*, after the manner of those in the "*Adventurer*," would be esteemed.[42]

The WORLD

Despite the powerful precedents for magazine fiction established within ten years by the *Female Spectator*, the *Rambler*, and the *Adventurer*, and the positive emphasis provided by Johnson's and Hawkesworth's theoretical papers on the subject, later writers in the single-essay periodical failed for a number of years to respond to this stimulus. With one trifling exception,[43] not a single essay-serial for a quarter of a century between the *Adventurer* of 1752–1754 and the *Mirror* of 1779–1780 published any long fiction at all —neither the *World* (1753–1756), the *Entertainer* (1754), the *Connoisseur* (1754–1756), the *Old Maid* (1756), the *Busy Body* (1759), nor the *Bee* (1759)— to name some better-known titles. Like the earlier *Prater* (1756), the *Busy Body* of 1759, in which Goldsmith had a hand, specialized in a single human foible, and although for a few numbers it seemed as if the life and adventures of the titular character might develop into a continuous narrative, this promise was unfulfilled. Goldsmith's *Bee*, on the other hand, a kind of essay-miscellany with many original pieces, included a story in nearly every number, but all the fiction was extremely short. Goldsmith brought to the magazines the greatest talent for fiction of his generation, Smollett and

Fielding excepted; yet, like Fielding, he gave little impetus to the development of the magazine novel. With the exception of the "Chinese Letters," which will be mentioned later, the drift in Goldsmith was almost entirely in the other direction. Of all familiar works of eighteenth-century fiction, *The Vicar of Wakefield* shows the most pronounced influence of the single-essay periodical.[44]

The period from 1759–1779, it is true, was one of relative poverty for the essay-serial, except for the political journals. Between Goldsmith and Mackenzie it attracted no important novelists or essayists, and the number of literary serials sharply declined. That the absence of long fiction in existing periodicals was not entirely accidental, however, is indicated by the outspoken policies of the *World*, which expressed definite and emphatic views on the novel. Among the numerous eighteenth-century literary serials since the time of the *Spectator*, the *World* unquestionably enjoyed the most sustained public success in its original issue. It survived for four years (209 numbers), during which period it is said to have sold 2500 copies a week. Many conditions conspired in this prosperity. The *World* was floated by an important book-seller, Robert Dodsley; conducted by a popular dramatist, Edward Moore; and supported by a brilliant battery of amateur and professional talent, including Lord Chesterfield, Horace Walpole, the Earls of Bath and Cork, Francis Coventry, Richard Berenger, Sir James Marriott, William Whitehead, Soame Jenyns, Richard Owen Cambridge, and Joseph Warton. The illustrious patronage of the *World* undoubtedly was the most important single factor in its success. When it became known, Chalmers later wrote, "that the *World* was 'the bow of *Ulysses*, in which it was the fashion for men of rank and genius to try their strength,' we may easily suppose that it would excite the curiosity of the public in an uncommon degree."[45] To read the *World* was for several years *de rigueur* for every pretender to fashion and every onlooker of the polite world.

But the large sale of the *World* may also have ensued because it relinquished all obvious intention of being a guardian of public morality, and frankly adopted the role of a witty and ironical commentator upon fashionable follies. The *World* emphasized precisely those polite graces which both Johnson and Hawkesworth had neglected, and which Richardson and the other friendly critics in the *Rambler* had called for in vain. The design of the new periodical, as Moore wrote in the first number, was

> to ridicule, with novelty and good-humour, the fashions, follies, vices, and absurdities of that part of the human species which calls itself the WORLD, and to trace it through all its business, pleasures, and amusements.

That there was some policy in this emphasis is demonstrated by the 104th paper, in which Cambridge reviewed the aims of the periodical, and defended its "innocent mirth and levity" on the score of moral efficacy. He did not deny that every writer should "take care that some useful moral be inculcated," yet unless he can amuse and entertain his readers, they "will sleep over his unenlivened instructions." The first duty of the *World*, in other words, was to divert its readers so that it could perform its second, which was to improve their manners, their morals, and their literary taste.

> I do not mean to reproach the age with having no delight in any thing serious [Cambridge drily declared]; but I cannot help observing, that the demand for moral essays (and the present times have produced many excellent ones) has of late fallen very short of their acknowledged merits.

In a paper thus dedicated to fashion and entertainment, and in a period when a whole edition of Fielding's *Amelia* was sold out in a single day, one might expect to find prose fiction of all kinds, in generous quantities, but the condition is quite the reverse. In Moore's periodical, despite the editor's obvious flair for popular and sentimental writing, prose fiction had to encounter not only the opposition of disguised moralists like Cambridge, but the open hostility of the arbiters of manners and literary taste. The result is that the *World* contains fewer long stories than even the *Tatler* and *Spectator*.

Left to his own devices, Moore would probably have produced a much more popular (which is not to say fashionable) serial, in which prose fiction would have played a more significant role. He wrote sixty-one of the 209 papers in the *World*, and they contain the usual mixture of fables, allegories, parodies, narrative letters and portraits, satirical sketches, and domestic tales. The well-known author of *Fables for the Female Sex* had a definite partiality for domestic apologues somewhat removed from the "business, pleasures, and amusements" of high life promised in his initial number.[46] But his natural tendencies were inhibited by his collaborators, who turned the paper into more satirical and more conservative channels. In the fourth and fifth papers, while Moore was still bearing the full burden of the writing, he published a sentimental history in two parts, very much in the manner of Hawkesworth. The *World* was almost exactly contemporary with the *Adventurer*, and the "Story of Mr. and Mrs. Wilson" followed quickly the stories of "Melissa," "Opsinous," and "Amurath" in Hawkesworth's periodical. It is a study of wifely scrupulousness and forgiveness in which Mrs. Wilson, a model of connubial excellence, wins back a straying husband, and gains a child for herself, by the delicacy and nobility with which she faces the discovery that her partner has a mistress.

In the thirteenth number of the periodical, however, which was devoted to answering letters from correspondents, the story of Mrs. Wilson became a subject of dissension. One reader, "Tom Tell-Truth," bluntly warned Mr. Fitz-Adam against publishing such foolish stories, saying "Take care of novels: the town swarms with them"; whereas another, in this case a feminine reader, praised it as "a lesson of instruction to every woman in the kingdom," and expressed the hope that she might find "the elegant moral tales" of the *Spectator* revived in the *World*. The author of this number (again, Moore) amusingly responded to both these suggestions, promising blandly to "write no more novels," and to devote his future papers "entirely to novels," but the fact is that no more serial stories in this vein found their way into the *World*, although Moore occasionally indulged himself with shorter sentimental and domestic fiction. In the whole of the subsequent series of 196, there are only three narrative papers which extend into a second number—all satirical.

The retreat from serial fiction represented by the *World*, which we find repeated in the historical miscellanies during the same period, but reversed in more popular compilations, was accompanied by a number of direct attacks on the novel which left no doubt about the attitude of at least four of the important writers in the *World* towards fiction in general. The first of these attacks was made by William Whitehead in the nineteenth number, who in a letter exclusively devoted to criticism of the novel charged "modern artists" with "ignorance" and "indecency." The "writers of heroic romances, or the Loves of Philodoxus and Urania," he declared, frankly pitched their works *above nature*. Their writings were inflated and unreal, but they did no serious harm to the young because their pictures of life were too far-fetched. Their models defied imitation. But the "present race of romance-writers" is more dangerous. They write on low subjects and they write in a low manner.

> Romances, judiciously conducted, are a very pleasing way of conveying instruction to all parts of life. But to dwell eternally upon orphan-beggars, and *serving-men of low degree*, is certainly what I have called it, writing *below nature*; and is so far from conveying instruction, that it does not even afford amusement.

Besides, when they attempt to portray "what they call genteel life" they display ignorance of the most obvious essentials. (The intimation is that they are persons of no breeding.) The chief fault of "this sort of trash," is its "extreme indecency." In whatever way it may be disguised, these writers are largely pre-occupied with "fornication and adultery," which are admitted by nearly everyone to be detrimental to an ordered society. For this reason Mr. Fitz-Adam is enjoined to interpose his authority and forbid his readers "to open any novel or romance unlicensed by [him]; unless it should happen to be stamped RICHARDSON or FIELDING." The partial retreat represented by Whitehead's qualification at the close is a grudging admission of some of the achievements of the previous decade, but the effect of this praise is greatly diminished by his scorn for the whole tribe of modern romance-writers, including the author of *Peregrine Pickle*, at whom he seems to be glancing in his animadversions on "low subjects". The attack recalls Mr. Stonecastle's in the *Universal Spectator* twenty years before, except that this one is more exacerbated. It is not women alone, but society at large that is now threatened by the dissemination of the novel.

Only six numbers later, in No. 25, Chesterfield continued the offensive in an imaginary letter from Parthenissa, a clergyman's daughter, which exposes the danger of precisely those works which Whitehead had found relatively harmless, namely,

> those treasures of sublime honour, spotless virtue, and refined sentiment, the voluminous romances of the last century.

Having a taste for reading, and a too-tender heart, Parthenissa founded all her ideas of love upon the inflated idealism of these works, with the result that she fell an easy victim to a perfidious dragoon, who seduced her by addressing her

> sometimes... in the moving words of Varanes, sometimes in the tender accents of Castalio, and sometimes in the warmer language of Juba.

The point of the attack, which is wittily obscured by ironical praise of Parthenissa's exalted character, is the manner in which she had been unsuited for life by her reading; and this is also the burden of the 79th paper, "On the Mischiefs of Romances," by Richard Berenger, who attacked the "error in education" resulting from "putting ROMANCES into the hands of young ladies." These works pervert their imaginations with "chimerical ideas of romantic love" and cheat them with impossible expectations of visionary happiness. Berenger likewise exemplified this danger in a little story of "Clarinda and Antonio." Clarinda was the only child of a wealthy merchant, who spent every available hour

> in the ensnaring practice of reading NOVELS and ROMANCES; of which CLELIA was her favourite, and the hero of it continually in her head.

The result of this avocation was that when a match suitable to her rank and fortune offered itself, she rejected the gentleman for his valet de chambre, Antoine, whose imagination was no less romantic than hers, and who was "almost as conversant with ROMANCES as CLARINDA." The upshot of Clarinda's folly was that she married no one, and her exasperated father "entailed his estate on his next kindred." Like Chesterfield's Parthenissa, Clarinda is another Arabella from Mrs. Lennox's *Female Quixote* published only two years before, but both young ladies have a still older lineage in the magazines, going back at least to Defoe's "Donna Quixota" in Mist's *Weekly Journal* of 1720.

The fourth direct attack on prose fiction, of which there were no defenders in the *World*, was made by Richard Cambridge in the 70th paper, one of a series of discussions on the proper use of leisure time and the advantages of reading. Several correspondents in the *World* had described books as both the "food" and the "physic" of the mind. In Cambridge's opinion, however, contemporary taste could unfortunately "relish nothing but personal character [i.e., scandal], or wanton romance," among which he included oriental fiction.

> Hence arises [he declared] that swarm of memoirs, all filled with abuse or impurity, which, whatever distinctions my present correspondent may make with relation to FOOD and PHYSIC, are the POISON of the MIND.

As in Whitehead's earlier paper, the intensity of Cambridge's attack was slightly mitigated by a highly complimentary allusion (it would seem) to

Fielding—described as "a very eminent wit," who, "to the honour of this nation," has shown himself "incomparably superior in drawing characters" —with the result that there is some uncertainty how far Cambridge's indictment of "romances" is intended to reach. None of the four critics in the *World*, as a matter of fact, was pressing the same charges against the novel, or even pillorying the same kind of work. The only rationale of these charges is reaction. But they spell out on the part of these writers, and presumably many cultivated readers, a deep dissatisfaction with the growing taste for fiction in general, which seems also to be reflected in the long retreat of the single-essay periodical from serial fiction.

Goldsmith's "Chinese Letters"

It was during this relatively unproductive period from 1754 to 1779 that Goldsmith published his surprising series of "Chinese Letters" in the *Public Ledger* (1760–1761). Here, at least, was one work which ran counter to the prevailing current among essay-writers, although it is actually not an essay-serial, but an essay-series, published in a newspaper. The ingenuity of its narrative methods, however, only serves to expose the paucity of contemporary essay-writing in the magazines. The numerous sources of the "Chinese Letters" seem to have been fully recovered. They consist principally of Montesquieu's *Lettres Persanes*, Lyttelton's *Letters from a Persian*, and D'Argens's *Lettres Chinoises*, upon all three of which Goldsmith was quite content to make wholesale drafts. But the extent of his cribbing from these sources has tended to obscure one important difference between him and them, namely that the "Chinese Letters" are a genuine periodical series, appearing not as a full-blown collection of epistolary essays, but at fairly regular intervals in a daily newspaper over the course of eighteen months. They are therefore also an effort in the Spectatorial manner—that is, a developing series of lightly satirical sketches of men, manners, and morality, diversified with episodes drawn from the day-to-day experience of the Author, illustrative cases, anecdotes, fables, diverting histories, domestic apologues, and eastern tales. The series includes also an allegory, a dream, a fairy tale (in two parts), and even attacks in the manner of the *World* on the inanity and obscenity of contemporary fiction. Therefore, in subject, in tone and manner, but above all in the aspect which they first presented to contemporary readers, the "Chinese Letters" are conspicuously in the tradition of the *Tatler* and *Spectator*, even though Goldsmith drew much of their substance from collections of pseudo-letters.

Goldsmith's principal narrative devices, designed to unify and give continuity to the series, were probably also borrowed from Montesquieu, Lyttelton, D'Argens, and others, rather than from Addison and Steele, Defoe, Ambrose Philips, and William Bond. Nevertheless it is worth remarking that there were precedents for all of them in the tradition of the essay-serial; namely, intermittent and dynamic letter-series, cumulative episodes, and supporting narratives, including the general framework of a journey or progress through London by a "spy" or original observer. In Goldsmith's hands these devices were adroitly blended and coordinated into a single scheme in a manner beyond anything yet attempted by his predecessors in the essay-serial. But except in degree they were in no way alien to the essay tradition, and in a period when the novel was daily gaining in prestige and popular favor they might therefore have strengthened the tendency among the essayists to make a more sophisticated use of narrative in their series. The fact that they did not is additional evidence of the seriousness of the retreat from the novel in the single-essay periodical from the time of the *World* on. In neither their original, nor their collected form as *The Citizen of the World*, did the "Chinese Letters" evoke any visible response among the periodical essayists of the late eighteenth century, and although some of the letters reappeared in the *Royal Magazine*, the *Court Miscellany*, the *Weekly Amusement*, and the *British Magazine*, the whole series was never reprinted in the magazines, and therefore a possible source of influence upon other periodical writers was dissipated.

The MIRROR, the LOUNGER, the LOOKER-ON, and Other Essay-Serials, 1779–1815

The revival of the long story in the essay-serial was led by Mackenzie, who wrote for the *Mirror* of 1779–1780, and a few years later for the *Lounger*. He produced several celebrated pieces of magazine fiction—probably the most distinguished since Addison and Steele. In the quarter of a century or more that had elapsed since the *Rambler* and the *World*, the position of the novel in public esteem had been strongly consolidated. A whole new generation of writers led by Sterne had augmented the legacy of the 1740's with a number of brilliant and surprising works of fiction. Whatever the run-of-the-mill novel might be in 1780, novels like *Tristram Shandy*, *A Sentimental Journey*, *The Vicar of Wakefield*, *The Memoirs of Miss Sidney Bidulph*, *The Fool of Quality*, *The Man of Feeling*, and *Evelina* could not simply be stigmatized as "poison of the mind" or dismissed as the diversion of "the young, the ignorant, and the idle." The Author of the *Rambler* himself in 1759 had offered *Rasselas* to the novel-reading public, which embraced it with some eagerness. Five years later, Walpole, one of the leading writers for the *World*, published (and later acknowledged) *The Castle of Otranto*, a work distinguished by some of the very excesses that his colleagues had attacked. Since 1749 and 1756 there had been two eminent reviews giving regular, if somewhat grudging, attention to new fiction. Moreover, the flood of miscellany fiction was now in full tide, and a great number of periodical publications, including even the *London Magazine*, were offering readers original novels and novelettes, new translations from the French and German, extracts and abridgments of recent works of fiction, and popular novels in "review." It is striking testimony of how isolated the world of the essay-serials had become that Mackenzie's very modest efforts in the *Mirror* should appear as innovations and should stimulate belated efforts on the part of essay-writers to make contact with this neglected aspect of contemporary taste.

The *Mirror* was anything but an experimental publication. It was conceived and written by a conservative "society" of Edinburgh intellectuals, mostly young advocates, whose chief concern once the decision to go before the public was made, was to preserve their anonymity. The special interest of Mackenzie's circle was sensibility—viewed as a literary, moral, and psychological phenomenon. Their professed aim in the *Mirror* was "to investigate those passions and affections of the mind which have the chief influence on the happiness of individuals, or of society," and they therefore wrote a good many formal papers on the subject of the feelings, of which the *Mirror* and the later *Lounger* together offered a kind of critique. But the *Mirror* was in other respects a very orthodox periodical, conceived and executed in full deference to Spectatorial tradition. The Author was pictured as a man of solid parts and education, with "a mind habituated to reflection," dividing his time between "study and society," and interesting himself in both "the spring and motives" of human actions and "those approaches to error into which unsuspecting innocence and integrity are too apt to be led."[47] The principal character in his gallery was his friend, Mr. Umphraville, introduced in the sixth paper, an eccentric bachelor and country gentleman with "a considerable knowledge of jurisprudence." Mr. Umphraville's various humors were interspersed with those of other characters, and with moral and philosophical papers, letters from imaginary readers, episodes in the day-to-day life of the Author, satirical sketches, and tales—in the usual manner of the literary serials.

The guiding genius of the *Mirror* and its acknowledged editor was Mackenzie, already the author of three successful novels. Mackenzie wrote about forty of the 110 papers, and assisted with many of the others. The total amount of fiction in the *Mirror* is not large (it is considerably less than that of the *Adventurer*), but the serial narratives begin in the twelfth number, and it is obvious that the author expected to put his talent as a novelist to some use. The letter from "John Homespun" in No. 12 was followed by several others in the same manner, which proved so acceptable to readers that Mackenzie later resumed the story in the *Lounger*—a periodical so similar to the *Mirror* in manner and inspiration that it may properly be regarded as a continuation. The sale of the *Mirror* was small in its original issue, being less than four hundred copies, but it achieved immediate success in its collected editions, of which nine were required in the first twelve years. The *Lounger* had a smaller sale in sets, but compared with other single-essay periodicals in its day was also very well received. Both the *Mirror* and the *Lounger* helped to revive interest in essay-serials and essay-series.

In addition to the usual complement of shorter narratives, these two periodicals together contain nine serial stories, of which five are of novelette length. Once Mackenzie had led the way, other essayists tended to take the same path, and, during the next decade and a half, a number of serials like the *Weekly Mirror* (Edinburgh), the *Selector*, the *Busy Body*, the *Country Spectator*, the *Looker-On*, the *Ranger*, the *Culler*, the *Sylph*, and the *Parlour Window* made efforts to achieve sustained effects in prose fiction. During the thirty-seven year period between 1779 and 1815 eighteen single-essay periodicals altogether, out of a total of perhaps fifty, published more than thirty stories in excess of five thousand words. Apart from the serial stories of the *Mirror*, the *Lounger*, the *Looker-On*, *Literary Leisure*, and the James Hogg's *Spy*, however, most of this fiction is deservedly forgotten, although in the present survey it has some interest, since it displays on the one hand the gradual break-down of the essay tradition, and on the other its timid accommodation to changing tastes and conditions.

Collectively viewed, the thirty-one novels and novelettes of the essay-serial in its final phase are very miscellaneous in character, and do not separate into very precise categories. The late eighteenth-century essay-periodical became a last retreat of literary reactionaries, genial eccentrics, and genteel amateurs, each of whom tended to take a somewhat special view of its character and function. As might be expected, most of their stories are didactic in tendency, but otherwise they are a curious mixture of conventional and "original" features, of satire and excessive sensibility, of formalism and formlessness. Some do not depart in the slightest degree from the usages of the past; others, more experimental, represent an attempt to write the kind of story that answered their authors' outspoken objections to the contemporary novel. Still others make a complete surrender to late eighteenth-century fashions, with hardly a backward look at their venerable ancestors. In short, this fiction shows signs of being written in a period of literary ferment and sharp clashes between old and new. After Addison and Steele, Hawkesworth, and Goldsmith (of the *Bee* and the *Essays*, not *The Citizen of the World*), the principal models are Sterne, Mackenzie, and Marmontel—all three of whom, it should be remarked, were also powerful influences on writers in the miscellanies. The resulting combinations are sometimes daring and ingenious, and sometimes merely bizarre.

In general, however, despite their numerous eccentricities in manner and method, the long stories of the late eighteenth-century essay-serials still tend to divide into one of the two main classes which had long before been defined in the *Tatler* and *Spectator*. That is, they are either serial tales or episodic narratives. In both these categories Mackenzie achieved the only real distinction. In addition to these two main classes, however, there were several outstanding efforts in the *Looker-On* and *Literary Leisure* to develop supporting narratives in a new mode.

The serial tales of the late eighteenth century are the more numerous class (serial letters and simple letter-series having largely fallen out of fashion). From the point of view of strategy, however, they are less interesting than the episodic narratives. Except in length, they show no technical advance over the *Free-Thinker* and the *Adventurer* of half a century before—whose legacy they actually are. They make no effort to introduce "chapters," or otherwise subdivide the narrative action after the manner of the novel. They are merely enlarged apologues, attached to the general series by a single ficelle, or sometimes without the benefit of any formal introduction. The longest of the stories in the *Adventurer*, Miss Mulso's "History of Fidelia," had reached only ten thousand words, and most of the other tales in Hawkesworth's magazine fell between six and seven thousand. Those of the essay periodical in its final phase, however, frequently ran to twice these lengths, without any further accommodation to the conditions of their publication. There is no obvious reason why some of them should have been published in essay-serials at all.

"Caroline of Abbyville, an Instructive Tale," in Mrs. Eustace's *Parlour Window*, for example, is simply a sentimental novel, without chapter divisions, published in segments of uniform length, in company with some of the usual ingredients of essay-serials. The author was so little concerned with achieving discrete effects that the first two installments divide in the middle of a sentence, like some of the early serial fiction of the newspapers, and the *Ladies Magazine* of 1749–1753. Other writers took more pains than this, yet long serial tales like Mrs. Eustace's were obviously prejudicial to the dynamic principles upon which essay-serials were presumably based. They signify the disintegration of the essay tradition, and show the intrusion of an alien, but more vital, literary form.

Many of the serial tales of this period of revival, however, do separate into one or another of the familiar categories of the past—as, for example, "The Empire of Nothing, a Vision," in the *Looker-On*; "The Tablets, an Eastern Allegory," in the *Sylph*; "The Adventures of Emma, a Moral Tale," in the *Ranger*; "The History of a Country Curate," in the *Country Spectator*; "Abadir and Zatima," in *Juvenal*; and "The Dangers of Changing Occupations, Verified in the Life of a Berwickshire Farmer," in the *Spy*. In these visions and allegories, eastern tales, domestic histories and apologues, the increase in length was accomplished by two means—either by extending the story into many installments of the usual length, or by enlarging the separate parts to three or four thousand words, so that the conventional two or three part story might reach ten thousand words or more. "The Affecting Story of a Mendicant," in the *Intruder*, for example, and "The Scotch Tutor" in the *Spy*, are each about eleven thousand words in length; but the first is in only three parts, whereas the second is in seven. In its own way, of course, each represents a break-down of the old tradition in the single-essay periodical of a cumulative series of short pieces in a variety of modes. The separate numbers of Coleridge's *Friend* swelled to sixteen octavo pages, so that his sentimental "Story of Maria Schoning" (5100 words) was easily enclosed within the limits of a single number. The longest of the tales of the essay-serials was "Caroline of Abbyville," already mentioned, which, uncompleted, ran to eighteen thousand words. Another story of novel length was Hogg's "Life of a Profligate Student" (17,000 words) in the *Spy*, offered as a very perfunctory letter-series in four long installments (one of the few pieces of late essay-type fiction in epistolary form).

Henry Mackenzie

Mackenzie wrote three serial tales for the *Mirror* and *Lounger* (in addition, of course, to a larger number of undivided pieces): the "Story of La Roche" in three parts; the "Story of Louisa Veroni" in two; and the "Story of Father Nicholas" in three.[48] All three stories attracted the attention of readers and reviewers as soon as the papers were collected in volume form and came within the notice of the general trade, and all three had long runs in the miscellanies. Only the first and last-named, however, actually achieved novelette length. "Father Nicholas" is the story of a prodigal husband whose "natural feelings of virtue" were corrupted by the "dissipation and extravagance" of Paris, and whose evil infatuation eventually destroyed both his wife and children. It is one of a long line of domestic tales in the essay-serials illustrative of the evils of gambling. But Mackenzie, writing under the powerful influence of Marmontel, was able to charge this stereotype with considerable emotional intensity. Pathos and moral sensibility were Mackenzie's forte, and his formal tales in the *Mirror* and *Lounger* are celebrated studies in this manner. Leigh Hunt was voicing the opinion of his generation when he declared in the "Introduction" to his collection of *Classic Tales* (1806) that "In a simple pathetic story [Mackenzie] is never excelled, perhaps never equalled, by any British writer."

The feeling for tradition was keener in the *Mirror* and *Lounger* than in most contemporary periodicals of the same class, and Mackenzie made a special effort to bring each of his tales within the framework of the series as a whole, both technically and thematically. the "Story of Father Nicholas," for example, written on the theme of "The Power of Corrupt Society and False Shame over the Natural Feelings of Virtue," is related by the protagonist himself, whose acquaintance the Lounger made in a Benedictine convent. Similarly, the Author of the *Mirror* had met the subject of "Louisa Veroni," Sir Edward ———, in Florence, and later learned his whole story—illustrative of the absence of "natural feeling" in the "higher ranks of society." The "Story of La Roche," offered to the editor as a possible "translation from the French" (i.e., from Marmontel), is tendered as an illustration of religion not as a "system" but as a "feeling."[48] All three, are thus directly associated with the major theme of the periodical. Considered as serial fiction, however, none of them represents any advance over the past, being really single configurations subdued to the special requirements of publication in a single-essay periodical. This fact is underlined by the frequent reappearance of "Father Nicholas" and "La Roche" in the miscellanies, where they were variously printed in one installment, in two, and in their original three, without requiring any adjustments in phrasing, except the omission of Mackenzie's prefatory remarks.

Mackenzie's *serial tales* were more widely reprinted than his *episodic narratives* (and were therefore much more influential), owing to the ease with which they could be extracted from the main tissue of the series, but the second are equally distinguished as fiction, and, viewed as stories in installment form, display much more technical ingenuity. The *Mirror* and the *Lounger* include one dynamic series of letters, one intermittent series (ingeniously interlocked with the first), and one cumulative episode. All three are deserving of attention, since they represent the final fulfillment of the long tradition of episodic narratives in the essay-serial.

The story of the Homespuns is begun in the twelfth essay of the *Mirror*, in a letter from John Homespun seeking counsel and comfort. He describes himself as "a plain country-gentleman, with a small fortune and a large family." He has already established some of his children in life, but four of his daughters still remain, all "tolerably handsome," and plainly and sensibly brought up. Unluckily, however, the two eldest were invited for Christmas to the country house of Lady ———, a Scottish noblewoman, and they have come back from the month's holiday with their heads turned, their country complexions ruined, and their simple tastes corrupted by the fashionable

N° 12. SATURDAY, *March* 6, 1779.

To the AUTHOR of the MIRROR.

SIR,

I AM a plain country-gentleman, with a ſmall fortune and a large family. My boys, all except the youngeſt, I have contrived to ſet out into the world in tolerably promiſing ſituations. My two eldeſt girls are married; one to a clergyman, with a very comfortable living, and a reſpectable character; the other to a neighbour of my own, who farms moſt of his own eſtate, and is ſuppoſed to know country-buſineſs as well as any man in this part of the kingdom. I have four other girls at home, whom I wiſh to make fit wives for men of equal rank with their brothers-in-law.

About three months ago, a great lady in our neighbourhood (at leaſt as neighbourhood is reckoned in our quarter) happened to meet the two eldeſt of my unmarried daughters at the houſe of a gentleman, a diſtant relation of mine, and, as well as myſelf, a freeholder in our county. The girls are tolerably handſome, and I have endeavoured to make them underſtand the common rules of good-breed-

ing.

Mackenzie's "History of the Homespuns," from the Seventh Edition of the *Mirror* (1787). The numerous collected editions of the *Mirror* were much more familiar to eighteenth-century readers than were the original sheets. The story of John Homespun, in one of the collected editions, figures in the penultimate chapter of *Northanger Abbey*.

follies which they have witnessed. The letter, which occupies the whole number, is intended as a little homily on plain living and good sense.

John Homespun's comic extremities are further developed in a second communication to the *Mirror* (No. 25), describing a condescending visit of Lady ——— to his home that brings out all the latent snobberies of the older women, and corrupts the younger girls and the servants as well. Mr. Homespun has resolved to be master of his own household, but he begs for Mr. Mirror's own support in his behalf. The Author accedes to this request by offering in the thirtieth number an essay (also by Mackenzie) on the decline of manners—a favorite subject of both the *Mirror* and the *Lounger*, and one of their traditional themes.

Three months later the chronicle of the Homespun family was resumed in the *Mirror* in a third letter, this one written by Elizabeth Homespun, the eldest sister and a leader in these events. She confirms her father's fears, having learned a bitter lesson in "pride and haughtiness." In a visit to Edinburgh she has been badly snubbed by Lady ———, who obviously considers her only a friend for the country. Lady ———'s shallowness and insincerity have brought Elizabeth to her senses and allowed her to entertain a lover suitable to her station in life. This pleasant domestic comedy was suddenly revived in the *Lounger* (No. 17) five years later when John Homespun again took up the "authentic" accounts of his "grievances." Elizabeth has married sensibly, but the other girls remain, and now a "new plague" threatens his peace of mind. A young man, one of his neighbors, has returned from India with a fortune of £ 100,000. His wife, the "little chit" Peg Mushroom, has brought mischief into the whole region, and into the Homespun household in particular, with her fantastic parade of muslins, shawls, feathers, and perfumes, and her tattle of

> Nabobs, Rajahs, and Rajah-Pouts, elephants, palaquins, and processions; so stuck full of gold, diamonds, pearls, and precious stones, with episodes of dancing girls and *otter* of roses.

The Homespun womenfolk have again behaved like fools, and the father now considers moving from the neighborhood.

The story is not yet ended. A year and a half later, there was still another letter from John Homespun. Young Mr. Mushroom has now become a favorite of Lord and Lady ———, who intend that he shall stand for parliament. Mr. Homespun's vote is sought, and he and a neighboring freeholder are invited to visit ——— Lodge, from which, after a very perfunctory reception, they make a precipitant departure. The last letter, like the earlier ones, and like the episode of Colonel Caustic, running currently in the same periodical, develops the contrast between the wholesome goodness of the former age in Scotland, and the ostentation and vulgarity of the new.

Supplementary to this dynamic series of letters from the Homespuns, and adroitly articulated with it, is a second letter series, written by Margery Mushroom, the sister of the nabob. Her chronicle, told in the *Lounger* Nos. 36, 56 and 62, runs parallel to that of the Homespuns, and throws a comic crosslight on theirs. The burden of Margery's complaint is that their new riches have brought them anything but happiness. It is irksome always to be fashionable, yet the pretense must be maintained. In Edinburgh the Mushrooms have enjoyed a dubious social success, and in the country Margery is listless and bored, separated by her new luxuries from the simpler, more wholesome pleasures of the past, after which she really hankers.

The stories of the Homespuns and Mushrooms are now infrequently read or mentioned, but in their day they made an impression upon the numerous readers of the *Mirror* and *Lounger*. It is to the letters of John Homespun that Mrs. Morland had recourse in the penultimate chapter of *Northanger Abbey*, when she was convinced that Catherine's head had been turned by her stay at the Abbey.

> "There is a very clever Essay [she said] in one of the books up stairs upon much such a subject, about young girls, that have been spoilt for home by great acquaintance—'The Mirror,' I think. I will look it out for you some day or other, because I am sure it will do you good."

Then, "anxious to lose no time in attacking so dreadful a malady," she went upstairs to obtain this medicine, and after some trouble in finding it, descended to discover a gentleman caller who effectively removed any need for Volume I of the *Mirror* that day. Another admirer of Mackenzie's magazine fiction was Walter Scott, who wrote in his essay on Mackenzie for the *Novelist's Library*: "The historian of the Homespun family may place his narrative, without fear of shame, by the side of *The Vicar of Wakefield*."[49]

Scott also admired (and imitated in *Waverley*) the cumulative episode in the *Lounger* involving Colonel Caustic and his sister. The assumptive character of the serial is a kind of professional idler and spectator of Scottish life, who offers his readers "transcripts" of what he has "felt or thought" or "records" of what he has "heard or seen" in his intercourse with mankind. The first of the characters which he brings before the public, in the fourth number of the serial, is Colonel Caustic, described in the syllabus of the collected edition as "a fine Gentleman of the last Age, somewhat severe in his remarks on the present." Colonel Caustic, whose acquaintance the Lounger makes at an assembly in Edinburgh, is visiting the city on business after forty years of residence in the country. He finds great changes in the capital, mostly for the worse. In the sixth essay Mr. Lounger accompanies him to the theatre, and eight papers later joins him at a dinner given by a friend. Everywhere they encounter the same rudeness, brashness, and vulgarity, which lead the Colonel to question the alleged improvements of the age.

Saddened and discomfited, Colonel Caustic retreats to the country, where Mr. Lounger visits him in a later series of three papers. Against a background of unspoiled nature the character of the good-hearted but critical colonel is further developed. He and his sister are the soul of breeding, and like their rural seat, examples of "nature in its best state." But even here, at the well-spring of goodness, there are signs of new decay. Their neighbor, the upstart Lord Grubwell, is a canker in the country rose, and a threat to the whole garden. He invites the colonel and his guest to dinner, and in his household they observe the same decline in warmth, refinement, and purity which the Colonel had remarked in the city.

> Instead of the plain, wholesome fare, the sober manners, the filial, the parental, the family virtues, which some of our households possessed [the Colonel sadly declares], these great people will inculcate extravagance, dissipation, and neglect of every relative duty...

Mr. Lounger returns to Edinburgh with the hope of seeing his crusty old friend there again, but in one of the last of the general series, No. 95, the Colonel sends a young relative to say that he will come no more. "I should only find," says he, "the same follies and the same vices; the same coarse or frivolous men, and the same vulgar or giddy women, I saw there two winters ago." Mr. Lounger's ironic defense of the present age, dispatched in reply to Colonel Caustic, is the final chord in this cluster of elegaic sketches.

Like Sir Roger de Coverley, his earliest progenitor, Colonel Caustic was never intended to be separated from the larger tissue of the series of which he constitutes the principal "portrait," and it never occurred to editors of the miscellanies who plundered the collected volumes of the *Lounger* to gather the seven papers in which he prominently figures together. Nevertheless, considered as a group, they possess an essential ingredient for serial fiction lacking in the De Coverley papers (and the Umphraville papers in the *Mirror*), namely a continuous narrative action turning upon a single theme or set of ideas.

Mackenzie's Successors

Mackenzie had several successors among the periodical essayists who made ingenious attempts to develop more elaborate narrative structures, combining serial tales and cumulative episodes. The most interesting of these efforts is the "Story of Eugenio" in the *Looker-On* of 1792–1793. The *Looker-On* was a late eighteenth-century effort by William Roberts, a fellow of Corpus Christi College, to emulate the *Spectator* in a semi-religious mode. The alleged Author is the Reverend Mr. Olive-Branch, A. M., an aging bachelor who occupies a living in a rural parish. The theme of the series is the shallowness and moral decay of the present age, and the need for a return to religion. Mr. Olive-Branch's friend Eugenio is a case in point, a young man now deceased, whose life was marked by failure and defeat. The character of this ill-fated young gentleman—"so different in the frame of his mind from the young men of the present day"—is obliquely introduced in the eighth number of the *Looker-On*, in an essay on the uses of solitude. Eugenio died in Mr. Olive-Branch's arms twenty years ago, leaving his papers, "a little packet" of poems and letters, from which his friend releases excerpts from time to time in the course of his cogitations.

These preliminaries occupy parts of four issues (Nos. 8, 12, 18, and 27); then, in No. 42 of the series, the formal history of Eugenio is begun—a long chronicle marked by melancholy, suffering, and sensibility. The story, much of which is presented in Eugenio's own words, is intended to occupy the "two or three succeeding papers," but it fills eight numbers in all, and extends to 24,500 words, being, even without the supplementary material, one of the longest stories in any essay-serial.

Eugenio's father was a professional soldier in the continental wars. As a boy Eugenio's mind was given too high a pitch by his family's aspirations and by his reading, and he acquired vainglorious ideas of honor and military prowess which unsuited him for university life, where it had been expected that he would take religious orders. Subsequently he had a brief but disillusioning career in journalism, and the same in the military under the king of Prussia. The meaning of Eugenio's woeful history is that "religion should be made the great and leading object in the education of youth." Eugenio himself declared that his fatal defect was an insufficiency of moral philosophy. But his story also expresses a number of other favorite ideas of Mr. Olive-Branch—the evils of war, the present decay of learning and of taste, the infidelity of the times, the degradation of modern journalism, and the dangers of sensibility uncontrolled by the teachings of revealed religion. After the completion of Eugenio's history in No. 49, Mr. Olive-Branch is not done, but continues to draw upon his hero's writings in later papers, and to give further glimpses into his life and his hopeless love for the virtuous Amelia (unluckily promised to another). Of this attenuated story neither the serial tale nor its appendages were ever reprinted in full, except in the several editions of the *Looker-On*.

A similar method of creating a kind of supporting narrative by allowing a serial tale to encroach upon the other members of the series was adopted in *Literary Leisure, or the Recreations of Solomon Saunter, Esquire*, sixty essays published between 1799 and 1800. In this periodical, obviously written under the influence of the *Looker-On*, "The History of Phillip Dellwyn" is presented as a kind of episode once-removed in the life of the author of the serial, who obtained the manuscript from a Quaker friend. The story is told in a series of Mackenzian "fragments," written in the hand of the unhappy victim, and printed in three successive early numbers of the periodical. Phillip, the alleged author of these memoirs, is another Eugenio, an "enthusiastic" young man of proud heart, pale countenance, and "ardent impetuous temper." His history is more romantic, however. A mysterious shadow darkens his name, and after the death of his female "guardian," in defiance of his advisers, he sets out to discover, if possible, his real identity. He becomes a tutor in a noble family, and contracts a "fatal passion" for the lovely Lady Matilda, plighted to his friend, Lord Villars. A number of startling circumstances convince him that he is really the natural son of the haughty

Earl of St. Albans, Lord Villars's father. He confronts the Earl with his suspicions (which are supported by the nobleman's incriminating behavior) —is rejected—retires to Wales—discovers his unhappy mother's grave there—and dies "the slow but sure disease of a broken heart." This tearful story, in its main part, is a serial tale that could be (and was) extracted intact from the general series as a kind of "Story of Father Nicholas" or "La Roche," and thus it appeared in the *Entertaining Magazine*. But the name of the unhappy Dellwyn is frequently invoked in later numbers of *Literary Leisure*, where the essays of Solomon Saunter are interspersed with "several pieces in verse" transcribed from his subject's manuscripts and designed to show the character of his sensibility. In addition, the "wild and marvellous" "German" tale, in Nos. 38, 44, and 45 ("The Story of Seraphina") is offered as Dellwyn's composition.

Eugenio and Phillip Dellwyn, therefore, are not only the subjects of serial tales; they are among the principal "portraits" of the *Looker-On* and *Literary Leisure*, as Colonel Caustic is in the *Lounger*. In this scale of their being, they are, of course, part of the traditional apparatus of both serials. But in them the old humorous type of character represented by Mr. Umphraville and Colonel Caustic, or Mr. Olive-Branch's aging mother, gave way to a new man of feeling along Mackenzian lines. By these means the authors hypostatized their own sentimental tendencies, and thus maintained their traditional outlines as arbiters of manners and morality. They became Mr. Olive-Branch's and Solomon Saunter's *alter egos*, as it were, whose lives and fragmentary literary remains were used to offset their more conventional lucubrations, and give the series a modish quality, and something of the interest of a novel.[50]

The last of the single-essay periodicals in the period from 1740–1815 to include conspicuous quantities of prose fiction was the Edinburgh *Spy* of James Hogg, published in 1810–1811, and described as "a Periodical Paper of Literary Amusement and Instruction." A less likely candidate than Hogg to serve as public censor and *arbiter elegantarium*, it would be hard to imagine. He described himself in the *Spy* as "a common shepherd who never was at school, who went to service at seven years of age, and could neither write nor read with accuracy when twenty." He had been discovered by Laidlaw, who introduced him to Scott and Leyden in 1802, when they were collecting ballads for the *Minstrelsy*. Hogg was self-assured, keen-witted, and ambitious, and not without a certain literary talent. After publishing a few pastorals in the *Scots Magazine*, and enjoying a modest literary success in 1807 with a volume of ballads called *The Mountain Bard*, the profits from which were expended in an ill-fated attempt to establish himself as a tenant farmer, Hogg appeared in Edinburgh with the serious intention of publishing a periodical paper. When Scott twitted him by asking him how he compared himself with Addison, Steele, and Johnson, he replied, "No sae yelegant, maybe, but I'll be mair oreeginal."

As an essay-serial, or better, essay-miscellany partly in the tradition of Goldsmith's *Bee*, the *Spy* was orthodox in many respects. In others, however, it was indeed highly original, and its prose fiction represents a sharp break with the genteel tradition. Hogg's subjects are characteristically not wealthy heiresses, young gentlemen of ancient family, upper middle-class eccentrics, and the spoiled beauties of polite society, but common shepherds like himself, tenant farmers, and misguided originals of humble background, who have a closer affinity with the subjects of the *Lyrical Ballads* than with those of the *Mirror*, the *Lounger*, the *Looker-On*, and *Literary Leisure*. Moreover, Hogg's serial stories, of which six achieved novel or novelette length, are technically extremely rudimentary. The important new precedents for essay-fiction established by Mackenzie, Roberts, and others, were all lost on the Ettrick Shepherd, if he was even aware of their existence. In the *Spy* he returned to the simpler, more naive narrative methods of the *Adventurer* and the *Rambler*. Nevertheless his stories display a refreshing energy and candor. Hogg was bluntly disdainful of the genteel prejudices of his provincial readers. His "Allegorical Survey of Scottish Poets," an episodic narrative occasionally resumed, stepped on so many Scottish toes and raised such a clamor, that he was finally forced to desist. The "Life of a Berwickshire Farmer," a nine-thousand-word homily on "The Dangers of Changing Occupations," presented the sexual lapses of its young ne'er-do-well hero with such frankness, that Hogg lost half of his subscribers in a single swoop. A few years later, Hogg found his true metier and his proper audience writing rural tales and ghost stories for *Blackwood's* and *Fraser's Magazine*.

After fifty-two numbers the *Spy* terminated on a note of disenchantment, the Ettrick Shepherd complaining that "the learned, the enlightened and polite circle of this flourishing metropolis, disdained either to be amused or instructed by the ebullitions of humble genius." No doubt the amused contempt of the Edinburgh elite seriously impeded the success of the *Spy*. But there were other obstacles which Hogg's genteel contemporaries in the single-essay periodical were encountering as well. In the first place, they now had to meet the competition of a great variety of other periodical publications—reviews, miscellanies, and literary journals—many of them also published locally, and all ingeniously designed to engage the attention of a large and heterogeneous audience, increasingly uninterested in eighteenth-century modes of thought and expression. Furthermore, as purveyors of prose fiction to this audience, the *Spy*, and other early nineteenth-century essay-periodicals, had to meet the competition of the novel itself. For if the *Mirror*, the *Lounger*, the *Looker-On*, *Literary Leisure*, and the *Spy* could invade the territory of the English novel, it in turn could invade theirs, and had done so for many years with eminent success. As a flexible medium for expressing miscellaneous opinions on men, manners, and society, supported by a variety of humorous characters, episodes, and subsidiary stories, and subjects drawn from middle and upper-class life, the novel had gradually usurped both the function and the authority of the single-essay periodical. Partly for this reason, partly because of new publishing conditions and changing literary fashions, the essay-serial gradually sank out of view.

When Scott published *Waverley* in 1814, he acted out of more than patriotic whimsey in dedicating the book to Henry Mackenzie, not as the celebrated author of *The Man of Feeling* and other novels of a bygone period, but as the "Scottish Addison"—"the only man in Scotland" who could successfully trace "the evanescent manners of his own country," and "whose sketches of Colonel Caustic and Umphraville are perfectly blended with the finest traits of national character."[51] Colonel Caustic and his sister belong to the period of the '45. They are also the principal progenitors of the Bradwardines in *Waverley*, as Scott's dedication was in part intended graciously to acknowledge. But there are many other points of contact between *Waverley* and the tradition of the *Mirror* and *Lounger*, one of which was the insistence of the author of the Scotch Novels upon his right to anonymity.

The Waverley series enjoyed an unprecedented success in quarters that had hitherto remained cool, if not antagonistic, to the new fiction. There were, of course, many reasons for this. Scott's novels not only had their Caustics and Umphravilles, their Eugenios and Phillip Dellwyns, their Homespuns, and their Scottish rustics in profusion; but they also presented a vast parade of historical and pseudo-historical figures against a background of romantic scenery which satisfied deep urges on the part of early nineteenth-century readers. Equally important, from the point of view of conservative opinion, they combined serious instruction with genteel amusement, and thus conspicuously met many of the social and ethical objections to prose fiction which had been voiced in essay-serials and essay-series since Johnson's day, and which had been renewed with particular emphasis during the last thirty years.

The Essay-Critics

In their traditional roles as moral censors, literary critics, and arbiters of public taste, the essay-writers of the late eighteenth century felt it mandatory, as Johnson and the writers in the *World* had before them, to take some formal notice of the English novel, by this time thoroughly entrenched in public favor. "Novel reading is now the only taste of the day," the author of the *Trifler* exclaimed in 1796. "Volumes upon volumes are heaped up, and the subject through the whole of them is love."[52] He was only giving utterance, however, to the dismay of a long line of periodical essayists in the last twenty years of the eighteenth century when confronted with what Mackenzie himself had called "the common herd of Novels (the wretched offspring of circulating libraries) which are despised for their insignificance, or proscribed for their immorality."[53] Collectively viewed, the essays on prose fiction and on the public taste for fiction published between the *Mirror* of 1779–1780 and the *Miniature* of 1805 are numerous, and they constitute a fairly homogeneous body of critical opinion, being animated by similar principles and predilections and associated by common aims and procedures. The leading voices in this critical school, if we include volumes of Spectatorial essays, were Mackenzie, Richard Cumberland, Anna Seward, and the Reverend Vicesimus Knox, but the tutelary authorities inevitably were Johnson, Addison, and Steele.

The first principle that governed the thinking of the essay-critics, not unnaturally, is the ethical function of literature—the fundamental view that whatever auxiliary functions it might acquire, the ultimate purpose of imaginative writing is to instruct and inform. This conviction, of course, was shared by many other critics of the novel, and (among periodical writers) it deeply informed the opinions of the *Monthly* and *Critical* reviewers, who likewise felt serious concern over the moral and social effects of the new fiction. But there were fundamental differences between the reviewers and the essayists in their approach to the novel to which writers have hitherto given insufficient attention. The reviewers were committed by policy to saying something about every novel that came their way, and they were therefore constantly involved in problems of practical criticism. Misguided as much of the literary opinion of the reviews may have been, it was at least concerned with concrete situations and literary realities. The periodical essayists, however, felt no such compulsion to descend into the market place. They tended rather to inhabit the Olympian heights of general ideas where reaction was still the rule, and where Johnson's effigy was still the commanding figure. Their principal concern was not the merits and deficiencies of each new novel of the month, but the general propositions laid down by the *Rambler* a generation before, and the problems presented by the old opposition between *Tom Jones* and *Clarissa*. Their criticism was in its important outlines theoretical and retrospective.

In addition, reviewers and essayists placed very different degrees of emphasis upon the question of moral efficacy—as had Fielding and Richardson in the past. All reviews were to some extent surrogate miscellanies, intended to entertain as well as inform readers by offering them extracts and summaries of new novels, plays, and books of verse. They were designed for a larger, more miscellaneous audience of readers, who expected critics to consider more than a single aspect of books under serious review. No matter how much importance reviewers might attach to socio-ethical criteria, in dealing with important works of imagination they were expected to move on to other, more purely literary matters. As a matter of fact, except when the drift of the novel was contrary to good morals and good sense, they tended to by-pass questions of this kind and proceed directly to the problems of character, plot, diction, and sentiment. Their general orientation, as we shall see, was more towards Fielding than towards Johnson or Richardson.

By a long and venerable tradition, on the other hand, the periodical essayist was led to view his column as a kind of ethical tribunal, where his first duty, if not his only duty, was to the truths of reason and the laws of principle. In his discussions of prose fiction other questions might sometimes engage his attention, as for example the old problems of the classification of the novel among other literary genres, and the advantages and disadvantages inherent in the novelist's art (both of which had received the attention of Johnson), but by and large these more purely literary problems were laid aside in favor of the overwhelming question of the moral potentialities of works of fiction, particularly their effect upon the young and the inexperienced. Within this restricted area the essayists still found room for some sharp debate, but not for questioning the dicta that the novelist was first and last a species of philosopher, or (as the *Miniature* described him) "an *agreeable* Moralist," illustrating ethical principles in practice as well as stating them in theory; and that the essayist's own role was to keep this function constantly within the public view.

Given this theoretical and didactic bias, the periodical essayists naturally seem undiscriminating in their approach to contemporary fiction, able only to see that collectively it was affected and sentimental, false, trivial, banal, and indecent—in short, a continuing public disaster. For most of them, fiction existed only to be deplored. It was rarely mentioned by title, usually anathematized as a class. Novels encourage the evil propensities of the human heart, the *Sylph* (1795) flatly declared; they "generate and promote a corruption of manners; and, under the pretense of following nature, take off that curb from the passions, which reason and religion would impose."[54] Popular novels offer "false representations of human life," said the *Peeper* (1796), in which "love and lust are made synonymous terms, adultery generally proves the necessary consequence of matrimony, undutifulness to parents, suicide, duelling, &c. &c. are recommended to the practice of all their gentle readers." These are stronger views than some other essay-writers expressed, but not different in kind. For each of the "most excellent pieces in the shape of romance in our language," the *Peeper* wrote (without mentioning any approved titles), "there are twenty of the contrary."[55] The *Busy Body* (1787) was more emphatic: "There is not among every hundred novels of the day, one fit to be read."[56] The *Miniature* went even further (quoting Dryden on a different subject): "There is not in a thousand of them one man or woman of God's own making."[57] Their cautious acknowledgments of past achievements by the English novelist were always heavily overshadowed by his serious offenses in the present day.

The attack on contemporary fiction was usually directed against the form itself, but inevitably spread out against the sources of the nuisance—that is, the "literary locusts" that produced novels and the book-sellers who published them; the agencies by which they were disseminated (the circulating libraries and the boarding schools); and the readers who tolerated such trash, especially women and young girls. By a series of venerable precedents since the days of "Orlando the Fair" in the *Tatler* and "Leonora's Library" in the *Spectator*, the tastes and reading habits of the Fair Sex had been the particular concern of periodical essayists. The authors of the *Universal Spectator*, the *Female Spectator*, the *Rambler*, the *Adventurer*, and the *World* had all busied themselves with idle women. In keeping with this historic function, a correspondent in the *Lounger* proposed in 1784 a satirical "scheme" for "a new Sort of Periodical Publication," concocted to suit feminine tastes, and admitting only female subscribers and female contributors—composed entirely of such special ingredients as gallantry and fashion, scandals of high life, critical notices of new novels and plays, "productions of the Female Muse," and "little affecting histories, [intended] to animate the female world to virtuous and worthy deeds" by fully acquainting them with evil as well as good.[58] The only surprising thing about this proposal is the writer's seeming unawareness that such publications were already in the field—in quantity.

In their efforts to bring the novel's overwhelming lapses against good sense, good morals, and literary decorum within some kind of perspective, the essayists likewise frequently had recourse to parodies and burlesques; ironical tributes to readers, writers, and publishers; satirical recipes for popular romances; and other forms of ridicule familiar to periodical writers from the days of the *Tatler*. The intensity of their feelings as public censors sometimes blinded them to their own literary lapses, inasmuch as a good deal of sentimental fiction since the time of Steele had found a congenial climate in the humorous and whimsical world of the essay-serial. Mackenzie's tales in the *Mirror* and *Lounger* were offered more or less concurrently with his attacks on sentimentalism. The *Looker-On* published a travesty in the mock-sentimental mode called "The Memoirs of Eliza, or the Eleve of Sensibility,"[59] seemingly unmindful of the fact that the literary manner of the Eugenio papers was anything but austere, and that his hero's little verses and tearful letters could easily lend themselves to the same treatment. In their reaction against prose fiction, the essay-critics even pilloried some of the most innocuous species of the essay-serials and miscellanies. *Olla Podrida*, published in Oxford, offered a mock poetic of the sentimental tale.[60] The *Loiterer* of James Austen published a spoofing letter from a correspondent who signed herself "Sophia Sentiment," and who chided him for neglecting the tastes of the ladies, pointing out that there had been

> in eight papers, not one sentimental story about love and honour, and all that.—Not one Eastern Tale full of Bashas and Hermits, Pyramids and Mosques—no, not even an allegory or dream have yet made their appearance in the *Loiterer*.[61]

The Author's reply was that he intended to gratify his feminine readers with something equally interesting, but less trite than "Novels, Eastern Tales, and Dreams."

Attacks on sentimental fiction, however, were epidemic in most periodical publications in the last quarter of the eighteenth century, and except for the higher degree of literacy and sophistication which most of the essay-critics display, theirs are little different from those of other journalistic commentators on the new fiction. The distinctive feature of the essay-critics is not their satires, burlesques, and lampoons, but their continued debate of the theoretical problems raised by Johnson, and their attempt to resolve those problems in conformity with their traditional role as guardians of manners, taste, and morality. The degree to which these considerations tended to overrule all others is strikingly illustrated by Mackenzie's essay in *Lounger* No. 20, written at a time when he was already the successful author of three sentimental novels, and a number of admired magazine stories in the same mode.

Mackenzie begins, as Johnson had before him, by speaking of the favor which prose fiction has found among "the young and the indolent"—largely because of its direct appeal to the imagination without any corresponding "labour of thought." He protests, however, that "the contempt which [the novel] meets from the more respectable class of literary men" is undeserved. Abstractly viewed, as "an interesting relation of events, illustrative of the manners and characters of mankind," it merits more respect than it has received. Certainly, as a literary form, it is hardly less difficult than the epic or the drama.

> The conduct of its fable, the support of its characters, the contrivance of its incidents, and its development of the passions, require a degree of invention, judgment, taste, and feeling, not much, if at all, inferior to those higher departments of writing, for the composition of which a very uncommon portion of genius is supposed to be requisite.

Added to this is the difficulty which Johnson also had underlined, that the novel presents scenes, characters, and situations from everyday life, in which any departure from verisimilitude is immediately obvious. Every novel-reader, however, is not only his own critic; he is also (says Mackenzie) a potential novelist, eager to try his hand at a craft where neither learning nor knowledge seems to be required. Disdainful of competing with the crowd of amateurs and hacks, therefore, "men of genius and knowledge" have left the novel in the hands of inferior practitioners, who have degraded it as a literary form, and perverted its "moral or instructive purpose."

Thus far Mackenzie has cautiously urged the claim of the practising novelist, and he might have been expected to take Fielding's path, and develop his own views on the art of the novel. Instead he suddenly assumes the mantle of the public censor, laying aside all problems of craftsmanship, and making a kind of blanket indictment of modern fiction in general. He assures his readers that he does not mean to proscribe *all* novel-reading; he is even willing to allow that it may promote some good. But the total effect of the essay is one of suspicion and distrust, and ultimately Mackenzie the novelist says nothing about prose fiction of which Johnson the moralist could possibly have disapproved.

For Johnson the chief objection to novels had been simply their failure to make a clear separation between right and wrong—their mixing of vice and virtue. In Mackenzie's eyes this threat is multiple, especially in "that species called the *sentimental.*" In the first place, such novels tend to create a perverted system of ethics, in which the proper hierarchy of virtues and excellences is confused, and lesser duties are exalted over higher. In other words, in sentimental fiction the "virtues of sentiment," like love, friendship, and compassion, are placed in competition with the superior claims of parental duty, justice, and prudence, and the result is a blurring of moral values in their proper scale. (He is, of course, in part thinking of *Clarissa.*) A still greater danger is the tendency to separate ideals from action, and conscience from feeling. Sentimental novels are a form of moral escape. The emphasis upon sensibility leads readers to surrender to "impressions which never have any effect upon their conduct" and thus to "pay in words what they owe in actions." This consequence he calls "a depravity of the most pernicious sort." Furthermore, such works tend to subvert reason and common sense by filling the mind with false and inflated ideas of happiness. A certain amount of refinement of feeling Mackenzie is prepared to allow to his own age, but sentimental novels create a "sickly sort of refinement" in which quite visionary ideals and aspirations are substituted for the real blessings and actual attainments of which life is capable. They unfit readers for living in the everyday world.

Up to this point in his *Lounger* essay, Mackenzie has been attacking *sentimental* fiction (his own novels, presumably, included). In the subsequent pages he reverts to the old problem of "mixed characters" in novels in general, and thus by implication extends his strictures over a much wider area. He is willing, he declares, to grant that pictures of "uniform virtue" are less interesting from the point of view of entertainment than their opposite, "the mingled virtue and vice which is to be found in some of our best novels." Mixed characters, however, unfortunately represent a serious threat to the moral life of every reader, who inevitably tends to compare himself with such personages, and similarly to excuse his own faults by balancing them against his virtues. "It is dangerous," he warns, "thus to bring us into the society of vice, though introduced or accompanied by virtue," and this danger exists not only in the "common herd" of novels, but even in those exemplary works of fiction that are often put into the hands of youth. What novels these are, Mackenzie does not specify, but among others he is clearly alluding to *Tom Jones*, as shown by his defense of the "faultless monsters" of the English novel, a phrase that conjures up the familiar opposition of Richardson versus Fielding. He may also, however, be expressing some reservations about the immortal *Clarissa*, since in his two later essays on modern tragedy (Nos. 27–28) the "bewitching address and captivating manners" of Lovelace come under direct attack. Such reservations are typical of the post-Johnsonian school of essay-critics, who tended to put so fine a point upon their ethical sensibilities that in the whole canon of eighteenth-century fiction, only *Sir Charles Grandison* could pass muster, and that novel, some of them were forced to admit, was dull.

As a critic of the novel Mackenzie's forte was psycho-moralistic analysis, and in the paper just summarized (misleadingly entitled "On Novel Writing") this is his chief claim to distinction. He raised the old spectre of "mixed" characters, but he also anatomized effects upon the moral consciousness that both Johnson and Hawkesworth had ignored. His is the most distinguished critique on the novel among the many by the late eighteenth-century essayists, but, like theirs, it is essentially a contribution to ethical criticism.

In addition to psychology and domestic morality, however, the *Lounger* was likewise concerned with what Mackenzie called, in the same essay, "the science of manners." He is therefore found pressing the further charge that novels subvert reason and good sense by generating feelings and states of mind that alienate readers from daily life. In this he was essentially orthodox, adding nothing to the subject beyond the considerable weight of his own authority. It was a charge which had been made against sentimental fiction in the magazines from the time of the *Athenian Mercury*, and which had been given particular emphasis by Defoe, by the author of the *Universal Spectator*, and by several later writers in the *World*. The effect of novels in the social sphere, however, was equally the concern of the post-Johnsonian school of critics in the essay-serial, whose eyes were always on the academy and the family circle, and who tended again and again to voice alarm at the way prose fiction threatened the well-being and the practical aims of a rational society.

Cumberland's well-known "Remarks on the Novel," published as No. 27 in the *Observer* series, more or less contemporaneously with Mackenzie's *Lounger* essay, is representative of this class of opinion, and in coming from the pen of a popular dramatist (and future novelist) it further demonstrates how the social and ethical bias of the literary essayists tended to override all other considerations.

Like Johnson, Cumberland begins with the old problem of the classification of the novel, which he describes as "in effect, a protracted comedy, not divided into acts." In both he points out, we find "the same natural display of character, the same facetious turn of dialogue and agreeable involution of incidents." Then follow several spacious generalizations on the origins of the novel in English, after which he touches lightly upon Richardson and Fielding, its two most distinguished practitioners, whose success in prose fiction (he declares) "perhaps has never been equalled." In the "tragical" and "epistolary" mode *Clarissa* is the model of excellence; in the "comic," *Tom Jones*—"universally allowed the most perfect work of its sort in ours, or probably any other language."[62]

In these preliminary remarks, which occupy about a quarter of his essay, Cumberland is affecting a certain largeness of view, and he seems, like Mackenzie, to be preparing to expatiate upon the art of the novel—perhaps to dwell on "character," "dialogue," and the "agreeable involution of incidents," about which the popular author of *The West Indian* should be able to speak very persuasively. In view of his particular praise of *Tom Jones*, he also would seem to be an apologist for Fielding rather than Richardson, and therefore especially disposed to interest himself in technical problems. But his preface is only a false start. Instead, he reverts without further delay to the old subject of "young minds"—"so apt to be tinctured by what they read"—and the need for parents and tutors to take proper care in their choice of reading, particularly the reading by girls. Of all the novels "formed upon the most studied plan of morality," and therefore likely to be placed in their hands, *Clarissa* is foremost. Everything in it is calculated to make a powerful impression upon the young. Unfortunately, however, in Cumberland's eyes, Richardson's novel is necessarily "one of the books, which a prudent parent will put under interdiction." It leads young people into affectation and sentimental excesses of all kinds; it causes them to spurn the addresses of worthy suitors; it imparts perverted ideals of filial duty; and it furthers the "idle passion" of females for "eternal scribbling"—a favorite complaint of the essay-critics.

Cumberland, of course, speaks as an adviser to the "prudent parent." *Clarissa* is dangerous only to the inexperienced. But he speaks with such vehemence that, like Mackenzie, he seems to enlarge the sphere of his criticism and impugn the novel itself. *Clarissa*, he says, fails in "this most essential point, as a picture of human nature." Its effect upon young people, in other words, is only the consequence of its fundamental falseness and unreality. "As to the characters of Lovelace, of the heroine herself, and the heroine's parents," he declares, "I take them all to be beings of another world. What Clarissa is made to do, and what she is allowed to omit, are equally out of the regions of nature."

This emphasis upon empirical reality in the novel recalls Fielding's own animadversions on "angelic perfection" in *Tom Jones*, and his insistence that the novelist be conversant with the real world. And in his later novels Cumberland was to show himself an eager disciple of the author of *Tom Jones*. But the fact that nearly all of the attention in *Observer* No. 27 is given to the dangers of prose fiction, rather than its methods and technical resources, tends to remove it from Fielding's discussions of the genre, and places it within the didactic tradition of the single-essay periodical. In the *Jacobite's*

Journal and elsewhere, Fielding had praised Richardson's "deep penetration in Nature," and frankly acknowledged his technical wizardry. In Cumberland's essay, on the other hand, the praise of *Clarissa* is purely perfunctory, and the full weight of his authority is thrown single-mindedly against the novel. In the whole of his critique, and in the remaining 125 essays of the *Observer*, there is no further word to justify *Clarissa* as a "model of excellence" in the "tragical" mode, or *Tom Jones* as "the most perfect work of its sort in any language." Like Johnson, Cumberland the essayist seems only to feel that one cannot be too careful of young people. In the light of this emphatic admonition to parents, his praise of Fielding at the beginning of his essay, therefore, is somewhat irrelevant, and here he fell foul of the Swan of Lichfield, another powerful voice among the essay-critics, who in a volume of Spectatorial papers entitled *Variety*, appearing three years later, rushed to engage with the heedless sponsor of *Tom Jones*, and to bring to book this new violator of *Clarissa*.

Working within the traditional limits of psychological and ethical criticism in the essay-serial, Cumberland had had the temerity to reverse Johnson's relative judgments of Richardson's and Fielding's works. In Nos. 25 and 26 of *Variety* Miss Seward hastened to restore the original proportions, and her several references to Johnson and the *Rambler* leave no doubt who her mentor was. *Tom Jones* is admittedly

> a fascinating performance, whose situations are interesting, whose characters display the hand of a master, whose humour is pointed and natural, whose style is easy, and to whose powers of engaging, the pathetic graces have not been wanting.[63]

These allurements, however, like the hero's engaging qualities of character, are only a "splendid veil" obscuring the fundamental moral deformity of the work, whose tendency is all too patently to "encourage libertinism in our young men" and to invite "our young women" to bestow their love and esteem upon "men of profligate habits." (Thus Johnson also had spoken on numerous occasions.) Upon *Clarissa*, on the other hand, Miss Seward cannot squander too much praise. It is a vessel of every kind of good—a work "calculated to inspire delicacy, and discretion of conduct, purity of morals, tenderness, generosity, and piety of heart" in every reader. It is a work sanctioned by a whole generation of pious spokesmen from the pulpit. It is "a work which Dr. Johnson, (so generally unwilling to praise) has been often heard to pronounce, 'not only the first *novel*, but perhaps the first *work* of our language, splendid in point of genius, and calculated to promote the dearest interests of religion and virtue.'"

These are the basic antitheses of Miss Seward's criticism—moral deformity and moral beauty, social evil and social good, which she is prepared to push to intemperate extremes. The technical felicities of *Tom Jones* are only a snare for the unwary, and are quickly brushed aside as irrelevant; those of *Clarissa*, on the other hand, are a kind of Platonic extension of the novel's essential goodness and truth, and consequently are dwelt upon with glowing appreciation.

> It is no where that Morality is more powerfully enforced; it is no where that Piety is more exquisitely lovely. Every individual in that large Dramatis Personae, is known with such distinctness, such characteristic strength, that not a letter, a single speech in the whole work, but so peculiarly belongs to the nature of that spirit, which is supposed to have dictated it; that it is needless to cast the eye back to the name of the speaker, or to look at the signature.

The two essays of Miss Seward are the most extravagant eulogy of Richardson in the whole literature of the essay periodical, and a kind of swan-song for *Clarissa* against whom the tides of taste outside the essay-serial were already beginning to run.

Since Cumberland had attacked Richardson's novel for failing as a picture of human nature, Miss Seward first addressed herself to questions of empirical reality, the character of the life at Harlowe-Place, the authority of Clarissa's family in the long-debated problem of the marriage articles, the probabilities of the book—questions on which Cumberland had not bothered to animadvert. All of the characters of the book, Clarissa and Lovelace aside, both in what they are and in what they do, Miss Seward insisted, are well within the range of experience of "an accurate observer of life and manners."

Clarissa, of course, is another matter. Her mode of being is supra-human. Like the greatest statues of antiquity she is a form of ideal beauty, an idea of "consummate excellence," rather than a near resemblance to the human form. But if the highest function of art is to generate a love of virtue, and to give substance to exalted principles (and *this* canon for Miss Seward was fundamental) then "the model, from which we copy, cannot be too *perfect.*" Clarissa exists in all her splendor to challenge "the generous credulity, and hoping sensibility of youth," and Lovelace is her complement, necessary in his every particular. *Her* goodness demands *his* evil, and his fiendish attraction exalts her resistance to heroic proportions. In this respect Fielding's and Richardson's novels are polar opposites.

> As the *worst* possible moral results from the character of Tom Jones, so does the *best* result from that of Lovelace.

In Lovelace's case we are taught that "gallant courage and brilliant talents" are no guarantee against a vicious character. Moreover, the fact that every generous reader, at the end of the novel, takes a stern pleasure in the retribution that overtakes Lovelace, places all his glittering graces in the proper moral perspective. Clarissa is a study of human perfection; Lovelace of the consequences of "constitutional vice."

Cumberland had also charged Richardson's novel with being "wire-drawn into prolixity." But in her second essay Miss Seward will not allow even this time-worn criticism to stand. The power of the novel to excite curiosity is so great, she says, that in the first reading everyone is impatient of delay. But upon a second perusal, that curiosity being satisfied, all of the "innumerable beauties" of the book emerge in depth—the "master-strokes of truth and nature" in the unfolding of the characters; the fine discrimination displayed in their various epistolary styles; the flashes of "peerless wit" in the letters of Lovelace; the "striking axioms" of the libertine; the pictures of genteel manners; the moral wisdom; the "power of imagery and description"; and above all the figure of the matchless heroine, "rising amidst her severe trials, her deep distresses, and remorseless injuries, into unrivaled magnanimity, while in its noblest elevation, the charm of female softness is never for a single moment lost."

On *Clarissa,* therefore, Cumberland and Miss Seward disagree at every point, although both are operating within the same restricted area, and ostensibly interesting themselves in the same objective; namely, the proper education of the young, and the promotion of a rational society. It is clearer from Miss Seward's than from Cumberland's essay, however, that there are really two separate, though related, kinds of questions in dispute—the one aesthetic, the other tutelary or pedagogical. Both had also been broached in the *Rambler* and the *Adventurer*, and argued *ad nauseum* ever since, though in many essay-critics the distinction between them tended to be blurred.

First, is the function of prose fiction to present life as it is, or life as it *ought to be*? Considered as art, what is its metaphysical base? Are the characters in a novel to be merely "faithful copies of nature" (in Johnson's disapproving words), or ideal projections of human potentialities, expressive of the moral realities that underlie the confused surface of life?

Second, what are the effects of novels upon young people, and what kind of reading should be approved in a class of literary work so popular and so immediately accessible to them? At an impressionable age, to what kind of "world" should the juvenile novel-reader be admitted.

For Johnson the novel was so recent and so superfluous a literary genre that he was willing to give it over entirely to the uses of moral tuition. In other words he collapsed the (for him) less important first question into the second. The purpose of novels is simply to "serve as lectures of conduct, and introductions into life." They can "convey the knowledge of vice and virtue with more efficacy than axioms and definitions," and therefore should exhibit exemplary characters—"the highest and purest that humanity can reach." This position, which was fully supported by Hawkesworth, had the original justification that it vigorously supported Richardson's own view of his works at a time when they were new and exciting, and serious critical opinion on prose fiction was still unformed. It was a partisan stand on a controversial question, which, having Taken, Johnson stubbornly adhered to for the rest of his life. But it was hopelessly out of line with Fielding's and Smollett's practice in 1750, and (as time went on) with that of other important contemporary novelists—as, for example, Sterne. For a long time, as Blanchard has shown,[64] Johnson and Richardson had their way with many other critics of the novel, and Fielding's reputation as a novelist was darkened by charges of "lowness," immorality, and indecency. Goldsmith himself had written slightingly of *Tom Jones* in the *Bee* (1759), and in the "Chinese Letters" he had attacked both Fielding and Sterne on Johnsonian grounds.

Beginning about 1775, however, there came a turn in Fielding's fortunes, and the general esteem for his novels was fortified with a good deal of informed opinion. With almost complete unanimity, however, the essay-critics set their faces against this change. Their Johnsonian prejudices were, if anything, stiffened by the gradual movement towards Fielding. Although

Spectatorial essay-writers were traditionally supposed to keep abreast of new thought, and follow as well as lead in matters of literary taste, most of the essay-critics refused to unbend. In a time of new and surprising developments in prose fiction, and of a revolution in the reading habits of the general audience, their continuing emphasis upon moral efficacy was oppressive, even though promulgated in the name of youth. A writer like Nathan Drake, who welcomed in the *Speculator* (1790) discussion of the new aesthetics of terror, was a prodigy among his kind.[65] Even Hawkesworth's old discussion of the techniques of magazine fiction seems daring in comparison with the new orthodoxies of Mackenzie and Miss Seward.

Not all of the essay-critics of the late eighteenth century, of course, insisted upon the need for exemplary characters. But thirty-five years after Johnson had spoken and a quarter of a century after Richardson's death, Mackenzie and Miss Seward were still trying to impose the aesthetic of *Clarissa* upon the novel in general. And there were many others. In 1796 a correspondent called "Cato" in the Dublin *Flapper*, for example, attacked the characters of Tom Jones and Charles Surface as "pictures of moral and Christian deformity," and the portraits of Blifil and Joseph Surface as a scandal to pious men. This opinion, he declared,

> might be hypercritical if the object were less important, but it is to no judicious or honest man a trifling concern that, in any popular work, the grossest and most pernicious vices are arrayed in a delusive and artificial splendour, while the very semblance of probity is branded with suspicion and conducted to disgrace.[66]

At the time of "Cato's" writing, *The School for Scandal* was already nineteen years old, and *Tom Jones* nearly fifty. But for the essay-critics, and other spokesman for the conservative literary forces of the day, the hero of Fielding's novel, after half a century, was still a painful issue. He was (one suspects) a kind of test-case for the new-type man. They seemed to sense that the Byronic hero was waiting in the wings.

"Cato" made no pretense of speaking only as an adviser for parents. He frankly offered himself as arbiter of the public taste. It was more usual, however, for the essay-critic to enter first upon the question of the proper reading for young people, and then to emerge with a few rules for the novel in general. The *Adviser* of 1797 illustrates this kind of legerdemain. It begins with the familiar attack on *Tom Jones* as "shocking" and "hurtful" to young people, and ends by declaring that the only safe formula for a hero (presumably *any* hero) is an unmixed character.

> That good may ensue from the perusal of a Novel, let the hero be superior to vice; let benevolence be perceptible in all his actions and let him be distinguished by every human virtue. The hero ought to be above nature; but he must not shock us, by the performance of actions which surpass our credibility.

"It is difficult to point out," the Adviser's correspondent adds, "an author who has succeeded in these particulars; the only work I would recommend is the *Sir Charles Grandison* of Richardson."[67]

We find wide agreement among the essay-critics on the need for exemplary characters, but not unanimity, and a few voices were heard on the other side, or at least in favor of separating artistic questions from the purely pedagogical. By his praise of Fielding, Cumberland had tacitly adopted a more liberal view, inasmuch as it suggested the possibility for more than one kind of prose fiction. His subsequent pronouncements on *Clarissa*, however, tended to merge the two kinds of question once more, since he attacked the novel on both scores. Other writers, on the other hand, sometimes managed to effect a more careful separation. Young Canning in the *Microcosm*, which was published at Eton, wrote that "The paths which a *Fielding* and a *Richardson* have trodden, must be sacred."[68] Tom Jones, as a character, is a faithful copy of Nature, but the book's subtle blending of right and wrong, and propriety and misconduct, "require a more matured judgment, a more accurate penetration," than young people are able to bring to it; therefore it should be denied to such readers.

In his first volume of *Moral and Literary Essays*, described as "juvenile efforts," the Reverend Vicesimus Knox took a relatively open-minded view of the novels of Richardson and Fielding, especially the latter. Richardson's were "written with the purest of intentions of promoting virtue," but suffer from the "lively description of love, and its effects." Fielding's, on the other hand, are classics. "His works exhibit a series of pictures drawn with all the descriptive fidelity of a Hogarth. They are highly entertaining, and will always be read with pleasure"—but like Richardson's novels they "may corrupt a mind unseasoned by experience."[69] In his later volumes, however, the mature pleasures of moral censorship tended to overcome the judgment of the literary critic. Knox's essay "On the Moral Tendency of the Writings of Sterne" (No. 145) makes no distinction between classes of readers, seasoned or unseasoned. Sterne is simply "the grand promoter of adultery, and every species of illicit commerce." His novels are a threat to "public and private morality." ("How much are divorces multiplied since Sterne appeared?") And in a still-later essay (No. 174), devoted in part to choosing books for a "lady's library," Knox gingerly approached the inevitable question of *novels* across a broad plateau of translations of the ancients, Shakespeare, Milton, Pope, the *Spectator*, and the most moral French writers—arriving finally at the dictum: "Novels, it is feared, will not be dispensed with: those then of Richardson and Fielding, are allowed, yet not without reluctance."

In contrast with Knox's *Moral and Literary Essays*, *Olla Podrida*, published by Thomas Monro of Magdalen College in 1787–1788, represents the most liberal wing of the essay-critics on the novel. The fifteenth paper contains the usual attack on sentimental fiction, "those rhapsodies of nonsense which are so liberally poured upon the publick under the title of Sentimental Novels," and which are "utterly subversive of common sense, and not very warm friends to common honesty." It makes the additional point, however, more typical of the monthly reviewers than of the essay-critics, that the writers of such trash have forgotten (or disregarded) the "many admirable models" offered by the past upon which their style might be formed, namely, the "delicate and refined sentiment" of *Grandison* and *Clarissa*, the view of "the world more perhaps as it is, than as it should be" in *Joseph Andrews* and *Tom Jones*, and "the happy mixture of satire and moral tendency in the *Spiritual Quixote* and *Cecilia*." The succeeding paper (written by Henry Headley) goes even further down the road to Fielding. It is an attack on the extravagant machinery of retribution employed in the modern drama—"the bowl and the dagger," "devastation and bloodshed," and consummate villainy. "Nature," this critic wrote, "deals in no such hyperboles," and he proceeds to add:

> With uniform and unexampled characters either of vice or virtue in the extreme, the aggregate of mankind are little affected; as they cannot come under their observation in real Life, they have few claims to their notice, and none of their belief, in fictitious representations. Mixed characters alone come home to the minds of the multitude. The angelic qualities of a

> Grandison, or a Harlowe, are reflected but by the hearts of a few solitary individuals, whilst those of Jones find a never failing mirrour in the greater part of mankind...
>
> The judicious blending of the lights and shades of a character, so as to make the one necessarily result from, and fall into, the other, constitutes one of the most difficult branches of the Art; and in the works of common writers it is in vain we look for an effect of the kind... A character of uninterrupted detestation can scarcely exist; and when it is obtruded upon us, we have a right to question the ability of him who drew it.[70]

Headley's essay on the drama, however, is the only full and explicit defense of Fielding's aesthetic encountered in the whole range of the essay-serial.

The unreal and retrospective character of novelistic criticism in the single-essay periodical and in collections of Spectatorial essays is witnessed by their difficulties in finding works of prose fiction of which as literary arbiters and pedagogues they might with propriety approve, or even praise advisedly. Mackenzie mentioned with approval not a single novel in the whole canon of eighteenth-century fiction. His socio-ethical ideas on prose fiction were so rarified that they led only to a literary vacuum. Cumberland nominated only *Tom Jones* and *Clarissa* (later withdrawn). Miss Seward mentioned with favor *Clarissa, Sir Charles Grandison*, and *The Female Quixote*, while deploying all her powers of invective against *Tom Jones*. Other essay-critics were content to leave it at that, or to venture only a few other titles, usually old and established works like *Don Quixote, The Vicar of Wakefield*, or *Telemachus*. "Candidus" of the *Trifler*, in a cautious "Vindication of Novels" (No. 19), appealed to "Johnson, Hawkesworth, Marmontel, and Fénelon"—and later added Mackenzie's name. The mention of Marmontel was extraordinary, despite his great appeal to readers of all classes; normally French fiction outside of Fénelon was damned in toto. Lady R———, the literary spokesman of the *Adviser*, in the essay cited earlier, could recommend only *Sir Charles Grandison* and Mackenzie's *Man of the World* (an afterthought), but she condemned the hero of *The Man of Feeling* as "too insipid and unnatural" for safe acquaintance. *Literary Leisure* (1800) stigmatized all modern fiction as trash, but made an exception of Fielding, Goldsmith, Fanny Burney, and (the only such tribute discovered) the "mighty Magician of Udolpho."[71] Several writers mentioned Fanny Burney—*Literary Leisure* finding *Camilla* superior to her other novels, *Olla Podrida* approving *Cecilia.*

But Sterne and Smollett were either ignored, or named only to be damned. Smollett, said Knox, had talent, but his humor is coarse. "His *Peregrine Pickle* has, I am convinced, done great mischief, as all books must do, in which wicked characters are painted in captivating colours." Novelists like Sarah Fielding, Henry Brooke, Bage, Cumberland, Mrs. Sheridan, Frances Brooke, Langhorne, Mrs. Inchbald, Holcroft, Dr. Moore, Clara Reeve, Maria Edgeworth, and Charlotte Smith, who were welcomed with at least qualified praise from the reviewers when they appeared, obtained not even a nod of recognition from the haughty circle of essay-critics.

The jejune didacticism of the essayists is worth close attention, for it demonstrates how far, since the time of Addison and Steele, the essay-serial had drifted from its strategic position in the center of contemporary opinion. In failing to discriminate between the good and bad in current fiction, and in refusing to come to terms with literary realities, the essay-critics sacrificed any serious claim upon the attention of novel-readers, whom they greeted only with sneers and exhortations.

We should be mistaken, however, if we were to regard the essay periodicals as representing only themselves. Their numbers, after 1785, were relatively few, and (except for a couple of titles) their circulation was extremely limited. But they enjoyed a large following in the miscellanies, and encouraged an army of letter-writers and essayists in amateur circles. The essay-critics are important because they provide a valuable guide to the tastes and prejudices of those powerful but reactionary forces in English society that on moral, social, and quasi-aesthetic grounds stubbornly resisted the advance of the English novel until at least the time of Scott. It was against die-hard critics of the novel like these that Jane Austen spoke out in Chapter V of *Northanger Abbey*, in a passage that also attacked the *Spectator*. The two were closely associated in the conservative syndrome.

The prose fiction of the essay-serial from the *Female Spectator* to the Edinburgh *Spy* shows the same drift from the main stream. When we consider how flexible were the methods of Addison and Steele, and how shrewdly they took the measure of their audience, we cannot help being struck by the fact that, although the single-essay periodical continued to attract some of the most illustrious authors in the century, many of them practising novelists, its fiction, considered as a whole, is extremely narrow, unimaginative, and overweighted with morality. Many of the stories of the essayists, including most of the longer pieces which we have cited, were reprinted in the miscellanies, and thus obtained a general hearing, but except for the moralized stories of high life in the *Female Spectator*, the domestic and oriental apologues of Hawkesworth, and the sentimental tales and narrative episodes of the *Mirror*, the *Lounger*, the *Looker-On*, and *Literary Leisure*, most of them were out of contact with the real audience for prose fiction between 1740 and 1815. The reason is partly the heavy weight of tradition on this species of periodical, which increasingly inhibited efforts to introduce new, unauthorized narrative forms. But it is also the fact that the genteel and conservative circles where the essay-serial maintained its foothold tended to view the novel as an inferior and socially mischievous form of literary expression.

The critics in the historical miscellanies and the monthly reviews were also conservative, but they were not committed to a policy of total reaction, and they were therefore able to exert a much greater influence upon their readers' tastes and interests.

CHAPTER III

Historical Miscellanies and Associated Periodicals

The GENTLEMAN'S MAGAZINE

The revised stamp tax of 1725 only slightly dampened the energies of the weekly journals and newspapers containing entertaining features, but it struck an indirect blow against them by insuring the success of the *Gentleman's Magazine*, for twenty-five years the leading magazine of any class in England. According to the provisions of the new act (11 George, Cap. 8), a tax was imposed from 25 April, 1725, amounting to one penny "for every Sheet of Paper, on which any Journal, Mercury or other News-Paper whatsoever, shall be printed." The result was that most surviving six-page journals were immediately reduced to four numbered pages, quarto size. Even then the cost of stamped paper alone was one-half penny per copy. After 1725, therefore, weekly journals usually sold for two-pence apiece. The *Gentleman's*, appearing once a month in 1731, offered forty-eight (and later fifty-six) pages octavo at only six-pence, and it contained in addition all the best pieces extracted from the daily and weekly papers. It also summarized the news, but successfully escaped the tax, since it was (as it claimed) really *reprinting* the news, rather than transmitting intelligence. The distinction probably made little difference to provincial readers, who were accustomed to receiving news late anyway, but it gave the *Gentleman's* a considerable economic advantage. At the same time that it published the news and epitomized the leading articles of the journals, it included a good deal of miscellaneous information of the kinds that the genuine news-sheets had customarily conveyed—prices of stocks, notices of births, deaths, and marriages, obituary articles, lists of new books, promotions, and ecclesiastical preferments—so that Cave's monthly compilation was an outstanding bargain.

The *Gentleman's* was not only advantageously situated with respect to the newspaper tax; it was further aided by the anomalous copyright situation.

The parliamentary Act of 1710 had given booksellers in England and Scotland definite copyright protection within certain limits—namely twenty-one years on old books (that is, until 1731), and a maximum of twenty-eight on new (two periods of fourteen years, if the author survived the first). Supported by the powerful interest of the "trade," this legislation was to prove fairly successful in curtailing piracy among English and Scottish publishers. The anomaly of the situation with respect to magazines was that the copyright strictures were generally construed as applying only to publications in *volume* form, and the magazines claimed the right, and were permitted, to abridge or excerpt any literary work, irrespective of copyright, so long as they published less than the whole, and we have already remarked how in the early years of the century they were sometimes ready to assume that prerogative also. Serial publications, on the other hand, were not protected by the law, so that, although there were angry cries to the contrary,[1] original material of any kind published in newspapers and magazines, unless protected by a royal patent (an expensive and cumbersome procedure), was everywhere regarded as being in the public domain and could be freely printed without permission, and without acknowledgment, as was frequently done.

The special privileges enjoyed by serial publications of being more or less outside the copyright law was a fundamental part of Cave's undertaking from the beginning—the purpose of which was (as he defined it in the well-known "Introduction" to Volume I):

> in the *first* place to give Monthly a View of all the Pieces of Wit, Humour, or Intelligence daily offer'd to the Publick in the News-papers, (which of late are so multiply'd, as to render it impossible, unless a man makes it a business, to consult them all) and in the *next* place, we shall join therewith some other matters of Use or Amusement that will be communicated to us.

In other words, Cave's primary intention was to publish a miscellany of cuttings from other serial publications, and further to supplement this with various kinds of original material, presumably to be supplied by readers or professional writers. The heyday of the gratuitous correspondent, however, was still many years in the future, and except for some of the poetry, the amount of original material in the *Gentleman's* during the first ten years was small. The early volumes were chiefly extracts and epitomes, prepared by Cave with the aid of editorial assistants, and a handful of occasional writers.

The method of the *Gentleman's Magazine*, of course, was not new. A kind of legalized piracy had been the principal resource of miscellanies since the days of the *Gentleman's Journal.* The essential difference of Cave's scheme from Motteux's was its fundamental seriousness of purpose, and the emphasis upon "*all* the Pieces." What the *Gentleman's Magazine* aspired to was not casual entertainment for the Duke's closet, but a kind of monthly digest of news and opinion which had pretentions to both impartiality and completeness. It was intended to provide a kind of running record of current affairs and contemporary opinion, and the later summaries of parliamentary proceedings and the extracts from important new books and pamphlets heightened its serious complexion. The *Gentleman's*, in other words, was not only a miscellany but a kind of abstract journal in the tradition of the learned repositories and political and historical monthlies. This seriously qualified its policies regarding prose fiction.

It will be unnecessary to enter here into the dispute concerning the precise ancestry of Cave's magazine. In the history of eighteenth-century periodical publications, the new miscellany was unquestionably a point of conflux upon which several separate lines of development converged. The important fact is that Cave, like Steele, gathered into a single publication a number of already-familiar ingredients previously associated with different classes of periodicals, and thus at the same time consummated the past, and spelled out the future. In form and method the *Gentleman's Magazine* served as a model for all succeeding miscellanies, even those of very different purpose, which were eager to emulate its phenomenal success. Considered as a miscellany, however, it reflects a different order of sensibility from the *Weekly Amusement* of 1734–1736 or the *Lady's Magazine* of 1738–1739. A similar distinction must be made for the more successful imitators of the *Gentleman's*— the *London Magazine*, the *Scots Magazine*, the *Gentleman's and London Magazine* of Dublin, and (to some extent) the *Universal Magazine*, as long as they preserved their original character. All of these magazines, at the outset at least, had serious pretensions of an "historical" character—that is, they aimed to give a comprehensive picture of public affairs, to epitomize current opinion, and to record advances and new discoveries on a broad front. Together with a good many "repositories" and "registers" of the eighteenth century, the "reviews," and the "annuals," all of which had equivalent aims, they show a different emphasis from that found in later, more popular, magazines, which present so similar an appearance. Whether or not the term *historical* is an accurate description of the essential character of the *Gentleman's*, it is a useful term to use in separating it from other miscellanies of a more popular character. [2]It is also a term which is helpful in defining the differing attitudes of the two kinds of magazines towards the novel.

The *Gentleman's*, the *London*, and the *Scots*, of course, were all "popular" in the sense that they enjoyed commodious and more or less constant circulations, joined with exceptional longevity. The *London* survived for fifty-four years, the *Scots* (under the same title) for sixty-five, the *Gentleman's* for nearly one hundred and eighty. Cave's new magazine was an instantaneous success. Five editions of the first number were sold out immediately, and within a short period it became the leading English periodical, with the largest circulation of any monthly magazine.[3] Nevertheless, although it earned the support of a very numerous class of readers, particularly during its first quarter-century, the *Gentleman's* was obviously not written for, nor read by everyone, as even a casual inspection of its contents indicates.

In the first place, unlike the *Weekly Amusement* of 1734–1736, the *Gentleman's* made no special effort to appeal to women. In its annual "Prefaces" it never paid its respects to the ladies (a significant omission). But more important, it typically eschewed all those trivial matters which occupied so considerable a part of the women's magazines—problems of love, marriage, and domestic life, the latest fashions, recipes and specifics, charades and acrostics, patterns and popular songs, new dances, and novels and novelettes. In fact, far from being in real competition with each other, the *Weekly Amusement* and the *Gentleman's* represent divergent tendencies in eighteenth-century magazine history, which a good many later miscellanies (including some "historical" ones) made rather ungainly efforts to compromise.[4]

In the second place, apart from a certain amount of its poetry, the *Gentleman's* made no conspicuous effort to satisfy the taste of the "town"—to cite another mode among eighteenth-century miscellanies for both men and women. It published accounts of new plays, but no gossip of the theatre, no pictures of actors and actresses in celebrated roles, no biographies of rakes, footpads, and sporting men, no scandals of high life, nor (with a couple of exceptions) notorious divorce trials. The *Gentleman's Magazine* was completely uninterested in the *beau monde*, or in the activities of the court. The "Town and Country" of Sylvanus Urban was a quite separate sphere from that of the *Court, City and Country Magazine*, the *Westminster Magazine*, and the numerous other magazines for the "smart set" of a later period. The complexion of periodical publications, of course, had greatly changed since the days of Motteux, but these "townish" publications bore a much more direct resemblance to the old *Gentleman's Journal* than did the *Gentleman's Magazine*. The method of Cave's serial was very similar to that of Motteux's, but its contents had a closer affinity with those of the *Athenian Mercury* and the *Works of the Learned*—which is to say that the magazine was serious, informative, and even erudite. It was a magazine for gentlemen in the enlarged eighteenth-century sense—that is, a magazine for the commercial classes, for professional people, both great and small, and for alert readers with no matter what social connections, possessing an interest in politics and government, history and biography, mathematics, machinery, theology, natural history, antiquities, literature, and geography. Its typographical ugliness was a badge of its fundamental sobriety and practicality. It was crammed with facts and curious information, and offered "amusement" chiefly to persons who, like the readers of *Mist's* under Defoe's leadership, were interested in diverse aspects of the contemporary scene. Its outstanding success for twenty-five years demonstrates that until 1750 or 1755 such readers made up the principal part of the magazine-reading public.

It is important to distinguish also between the modes of the historical miscellany and the single-essay periodical, because, although the two were closely associated and unquestionably enjoyed many of the same readers in the period from 1731 to 1755, they were quite different in their orientation towards prose fiction. Both tended to disregard it, but in different ways and for different reasons. The essay-writers in the literary line were traditionally preoccupied with manners and modes, with art, the theatre, and belles-lettres. As literary critics and censors they sounded a hostile retreat from the novel because of its flagrant offenses against good sense, good taste, and good morals, and its alleged effects upon young people. Their historic function was to rail against fashionable follies and vices, and to quicken their readers' moral sense. The *Gentleman's*, however, was a more disinterested spectator. It was not greatly concerned with the ethical potentialities of literature or with correction of the public taste. Its function was to observe and to record eighteenth-century life in the round, of which belles-lettres formed a small though important segment. It assumed a position of eminence from which even the moral disquisitions of the *Rambler*, like the partisan essays of the *Craftsman*, appeared merely as expressions of contemporary opinion. If the *Gentleman's* tended to slight the English novel during the magazine's early years, it was not because of prejudice or snobbery, but because of the encyclopedic interests of its readers.

Early Fiction in the GENTLEMAN'S

Except for the Parliamentary Debates, which usurped the principal place in the magazine during the period from 1738–1745, the most important part of every issue of the *Gentleman's* during the first ten or twelve years of its existence was the summaries of "Weekly Essays," which sometimes occupied as much as half the entire issue. The essays were drawn from a great number of newspapers, journals, and essay-serials—the *Grub-Street Journal*, the *Free Briton*, the *Old Whig*, the *London Journal*, the *Weekly Miscellany*, the *Universal Spectator*, *Applebee's*, *Fog's*, the *Daily Gazetteer*, and so on. All of the reprinted articles were fairly short to begin with, and most of them were further condensed in the process of review. A great many, naturally, were polemical, but some in the normal course of events were essays on manners, morals, and general ideas in the main tradition of the essay-serial and the weekly journal, and thus were likely to contain fiction in one of the familiar forms. The first story in the *Gentleman's Magazine*, for example, is contained in the first number, in an essay extracted from the *Universal Spectator*, No. 117 (January 2, 1731). The essay consists of a series of portraits illustrative of the type of person who exculpates himself for his lack of consideration for others by pleading his "humour " It concludes with "a merry story" (really an anecdote) of "a certain Colonel," whose footman taught him a rude but effective lesson in thoughtfulness and good manners.

The amount of early fiction in the early *Gentleman's* is considerable, although it is almost entirely of this kind—anecdotes, fables, dream visions, illustrative stories, and little histories in the form of letters, which gain an entrance to the magazine through the "Weekly Essays" under review. The Index of Volume III (1733) lists seventeen items under the heading of "Stories," but actually there are many others that for some reason the tabulator overlooked. All, however, are of this same fugitive character, and all are brief. Of the seventeen indexed stories some are narratives of less than a hundred words; all except one occupy less than a page; the longest (from *Fog's Journal*), giving the account of an itinerant quack, comes to only nineteen hundred words. The *Weekly Amusement* and other popular miscellanies, as we have noted, were soon to be diverting their readers with quantities of prose fiction, including full-length novels and novelettes, but the publication of prose fiction for entertainment's sake obviously did not figure in Cave's original plan.

After seven years of relative indifference to prose fiction, Cave at length undertook to publish a story of novelette length. By this time he was beginning to put less emphasis upon clippings from current periodicals, and was paying more attention to original compositions, usually offered as "Dissertations and Letters from Correspondents." "A Story Strange as True," a novelette in seven short installments, published between April, 1737, and March, 1738, may have been a gratuitous contribution from a reader, as it pretends to be, but more probably it was a calculated experiment on Cave's part with a new kind of magazine material.[5]

The piece, variously titled as "A Story Strange as True," "The Adventures of a Female Correspondent," and "The Lady's Adventures," is presented in the form of a serial letter to Mr. Urban from "Maria," who submits it as the "true history" of her own parents. Even if the assertion were not already a time-honored counter of magazine fiction, it is certain that the story would deceive no one, since it is a highly contrived artifact, in the manner of contemporary *novelle*.

A lady named Arabella (Maria's alleged mother) became enamored of an English clergyman (later Maria's father), who had little interest in women, and least of all in Arabella. With the connivance of his mother and twin sister, Myrtilla, who supported the imposture, she succeeded in convincing the world that they had been secretly married. The claim was carried into the courts, and at length the bewildered clergyman had no choice but to submit to a real marriage. He took revenge, however, by refusing to consummate the union, and by taking flight to France. There he was followed by his inexorable "wife" and sister, who were intent upon renewing their stratagems. These finally led to the innocent clergyman's arrest on the false charge of violating a nun—an accusation which unfortunately placed him under sentence of death. After further involvements, and various changes of costume and identity, all three were happy to extricate him from this dangerous predicament, and the parents of Maria were at last reconciled.

"A Story Strange as True" was a novelty in several respects, quite apart from its unexpected appearance in the *Gentleman's Magazine*. In the first place it was the longest serial story (9500 words) thus far written expressly for publication in a British miscellany, those of the *Weekly Amusement*, the *Oxford Magazine*, and the *Lady's Magazine* being all either old pieces reprinted, or translations from the French. In this early period Cave still regarded all miscellanies of whatever character as direct competitors, crowing in his annual "Prefaces" over their demise and sneering at their efforts (as he believed) to emulate the *Gentleman's Magazine*. In offering his readers an *original* story in serial form, he was, as it were, replying in kind but offering better. The final intrigue of "A Story Strange as True," which turns on the schemes of an amorous French priest and a rapacious "Lady Abbess," involves scenes of clerical skullduggery and conventual license, and thus exploits prejudices against the Roman Church recently renewed in the controversy over Catholic Toleration.[6] But the story as a whole is frankly entertaining without any serious polemical purpose. Moreover, the separate installments, which were evidently published as received, not only show some effort to divide the narrative into effective units for serial publication, but sometimes invite interest in the "wonderful events" to follow. In all these respects Cave's serial story was unusual, if not far in advance of its time.

In the last two installments Maria promised to provide at some later date a further account of "poor Lucia," an unfortunate victim of priestly lust, who helped the lovers to escape. But this engagement was never fulfilled. It may be that Cave's readers were apathetic to this species of entertainment (although the story was still being reprinted in popular miscellanies half a century later), or that the sequel was rejected by Johnson, who assumed important editorial duties in 1738, and would hardly be disposed to interest himself in the confessions of a debauched nun. Possibly Maria herself lost interest in the venture, since she had already allowed five months to lapse between the fifth and sixth installments of her first story; or the continuation may have been crowded out by the increased attention being given to parliamentary questions and events preceding the fall of Walpole. It should be observed, however, that the magazine's preoccupation with public affairs did not prevent it from making room a few months later for a second serial narrative in a more familiar mode, "The Apotheosis of Milton, a Vision."[7]

Because of its surprising length (6900 words) this story is likewise worth closer scrutiny.

The "Vision," like "A Story Strange as True," is presented in the form of a serial letter to Mr. Urban, a positive sign in the *Gentleman's* (though not elsewhere) of its "originality." Again the authorship is uncertain. Accidentally confined in Westminster Abbey after the closing of the gates, the writer was forced to pass the night among the tombs. Pacing the aisles at midnight he was met by an august old man, bearing a gleaming taper, who identified himself as the genius of the place, and who took the visitor in tow. Suddenly they were conveyed to a spacious hall "sacred to the Spirits of the Bards, whose remains are buried, or whose Monuments are erected within this Pile"—at the very moment when "the Great Milton" was about to be admitted to the circle. (A monument to Milton had recently been erected in the Abbey.) The gathering of the elect becomes the occasion for a series of imaginary portraits of ancient and modern poets, beginning with Chaucer, Drayton, and Spenser, and ending with Betterton, Sir Samuel Garth, and "Mr. Stepney." The circle being at length completed, the name of Milton was presented by Chaucer, the "Father of English Poets," who "enlarged, with great Eloquence, upon the fine Qualifications, the Learning, and the Genius of Milton" as a man who had brought the name of England for poetry to a pitch equal to that of Greece and Italy. To this nomination, however, Cowley took violent exception. While admitting Milton's literary genius, he questioned his moral qualifications for a seat in this assembly, accusing the puritan poet of promoting "black Designs against the Dignity, the Character, and the Life of the best of Sovereigns." At this point, at the end of the fifth installment, even before Milton himself had appeared, the story was broken off—perhaps because it had now entered upon a sensitive area of political discussion, perhaps because it had already occupied (with interruptions) nine months, and was only just getting under way. In any case, the promised continuation, like the sequel to "A Story Strange as True," was never forthcoming.

"The Apotheosis of Milton" was a clever piece of topical fiction growing out of a number of recent events: the new monument in Westminster, the popular revival of *Comus* at the Drury Lane in 1738, and Birch's new edition of Milton's *Historical, Political and Miscellaneous Works* published in the same year.[8] In this respect it departed sharply from the practice of miscellanies of a more popular character, where the fiction usually did not comment upon contemporary events. Topicality, however, was the soul of the weekly journals, especially (among works of fiction) their dream visions, the authors of which for many years had been accustomed to find recent events darkly reflected in their dreams. Many of these apocalyptic excursions had found their way into the "Weekly Essays" of the *Gentleman's*, so that both the method and manner of the new piece were familiar.[9] Nevertheless, in point of length as well as in the range of its allusiveness, the "Apotheosis of Milton" was extraordinary, and joined with the "Adventures of a Lady," it seemed to promise further efforts on Cave's part to enlarge the "historical" framework of his magazine to include sustained works of prose fiction. Probably he was more impressed with the allurements of his competitors than he was willing to admit.

For some reason, however, the promise of these two stories was unrealized. Genuine serial fiction, though by this time a recognized ingredient of most popular miscellanies and a few weekly journals and newspapers, made only an abortive beginning in the *Gentleman's*, and twelve years were to elapse before the editor again published a story of comparable length. The continued presence of numerous shorter pieces, however, within as well as without the "Weekly Essays," and the sporadic notices received by new novels in the monthly "Register of New Books," indicate that the magazine was less prejudiced against fiction than it was occupied with more pressing matters, in comparison with which novels and romances seemed inconsequential. In this respect the attitude of the *Gentleman's* resembles that of the weekly journals from which it drew much of its contents.

Other Historical Miscellanies

Meanwhile a number of other historical miscellanies, imitators of the *Gentleman's Magazine*, had appeared on the scene. The *London Magazine* of 1732, the earliest and most formidable rival, was for many years a close equivalent of Cave's publication, offering similar parliamentary news, "Weekly Essays," domestic and foreign intelligence, extracts from books and pamphlets, and miscellaneous data. The *Scots Magazine* of 1739 and Exshaw's *Gentleman's and London* of 1741 were not only imitators, but plagiarists, carrying over into their own columns verbatim any pieces from the two London publications that they felt might be of interest to readers in Edinburgh and Dublin, supplemented with other materials of more regional interest. The *Universal Magazine of Knowledge and Pleasure* of 1747 (to which we shall return) had a slightly more popular cast, but it too declared itself to be an "impartial record of the times." Thus by 1750 there were five important monthlies of this class competing for the attention of readers in the capital cities of Great Britain and Ireland and outlying regions, and of course there was a crowd of shorter-lived imitators also, like Budgell's *Bee* (1733–1735), the *Country Magazine* (1736–1737), the *Publick Register* (1741), the *History of Our Own Times* (1741), and Dodsley's *Museum, or the Literary and Historical Register* (1746–1747). Until 1750, or even later, the *Gentleman's* was the leading London periodical, which most publishers of new miscellanies felt they must emulate, or perish. In time, however, the character of the general audience changed, as large new classes of readers emerged who showed less interest in learning and contemporary affairs. This shift in sensibility, which was marked by increased interest in novels and romances as a form of popular entertainment, is reflected in the vacillating policies of the leading historical miscellanies. Until 1750 the *Gentleman's*, the *London*, the *Scots*, the *Gentleman's and London*, and the *Universal* followed consistent policies with respect to prose fiction, publishing only short tales and apologues, many of them incidental to the weekly essays. But about 1750 all five (to which we shall henceforth limit our view) underwent a change of heart, and more or less simultaneously began to admit a few longer pieces of serial fiction among the usual complement of shorter ones.

The date, of course, is a significant one in the history of the English novel, since it marks the completion of the crowded decade which brought Richardson, Fielding, Smollett, and other new novelists suddenly into public view. The impression made on the general taste by the new literature of the novel had already been reflected in the *Female Spectator* (1744–1746), and was about to be felt in the *Rambler* (1750–1752) and the *Adventurer* (1752–1754). But much more significant from the point of view of the historical miscellanies was the increasing currency of such compilations as the *British Magazine* of 1746–1750, the *Ladies Magazine* of 1749–1753, and the *Royal Magazine* of 1750–1751—all relatively short-lived emissions, but members of a numerous and growing class of periodical. There were ten such magazines in circulation in the year 1750 alone. With their special emphasis upon popular entertainment, the new common (or non-historical) miscellanies offered for the first time a serious threat to the eminence of the historical variety, hitherto so successful in holding the attention of urban and country readers.

For this reason, probably, the *Gentleman's* suddenly offered its readers, in 1751, a long oriental tale in two parts, "Asem and Salned," and a couple of years later the "Story of Alexis and Matilda" (from Mrs. Haywood's novel, *The Invisible Spy*), and "Rosetta and Chamont, a True Story" —all pieces from five thousand to nine thousand words in length. The *London Magazine* countered with a long summary of Fielding's *Amelia*, and "The Adventures of Bertholde," extracted and translated from the *Histoire de Bertholde*; the plagiaristic *Gentleman's and London* of Dublin elected to reprint four of these five pieces; the *Scots* on its part offered "Asem and Salned" reprinted, three novelettes from the *Adventurer*, and "Disinterested Love, or the Triumph of Constancy," attributed to a "French Magazine"; and the *Universal* printed a total of three long stories, "Virtue Triumphant, or the History of Repsima, an Eastern Tale," and two disguised redactions of novelettes from the *Female Spectator*— a grand total of seventeen printings of twelve different items over a five-year period. These assorted stories, scattered and miscellaneous though they be, are worth attention not only for what they are—that is, typical examples of miscellany fiction at the mid-century—but for what they represent, namely, a slight response to gradual changes in the status of the English novel. The subterranean pressures were perhaps imperceptible to casual readers in the period from 1750–1755, but considered seismographically, in relation to the unfolding record of the previous twenty years, these seventeen stories register an unmistakable tremor in the world of Mr. Sylvanus Urban.

Only five of the twelve items are offered as originals, or at least bear no outside attribution. The rest are frankly borrowed or adapted from a variety of sources. In later miscellanies, at least in the leading London publications, the proportion of original fiction was to be much larger, owing in part to the efforts of amateur scribblers; but unlike the *Rambler* and the *Adventurer* of the same period, the English miscellany shared in no tradition of personal craftsmanship. Fiction being called for, the editors of the *Gentleman's* and its competitors simply had recourse to the inevitable methods growing out of the eighteenth-century copyright situation—publishing anonymously such original pieces as conveniently came to hand, but amply supplementing these with extracts from new and old books, epitomizations of popular novels, translations from the French, and narrative pieces lifted from essay-serials and other periodicals—in most cases without acknowledgment. The historical miscellanies, it is true, were usually more scrupulous than other compilations in naming their sources. They could presume some degree of interest on the part of their audience in being informed of the sources of their reading. But in plagiarizing from their competitors, editors were understandably more reticent, lest readers be moved to transfer their allegiance. The *Scots*, it will be observed, admitted its borrowings from the *Adventurer* and a "French Magazine," but not "Asem and Salned." The *Gentleman's and London*, being almost entirely composed out of the London miscellanies, which presumably also circulated in Dublin, admitted nothing.

The practice of the *Universal Magazine* was more egregious, but typical of a good deal of later piratical practice. "Virtue Triumphant" was taken, without any acknowledgment whatever, from Ambrose Philips's translation of *The Thousand and One Days*, published forty years before, and already in its sixth edition. Since oriental tales were in vogue, the editor merely reached for a convenient source, and appropriated the last story in Philips's collection. "The Happy Consequences Which Result from Good Nature" and "The History of Ariana" show an equal disregard for the claims of authorship. Both are disguised versions of stories which had appeared in the *Female Spectator* ten years earlier, "Dorimon and Alithea" and "The Misfortunes of Aliena." In each case the *Universal's* writer, "R. C.," shamelessly plagiarized the originals, condensing the first, enlarging the second, substituting new names for the principal characters, and offering the final product as a new work of fiction. The name of Mrs. Haywood was completely shut out.

By and large, however, the derived fiction of the historical miscellanies, when acknowledged, is less incongruous than these and the other "originals." That is, the reprinting of stories from the *Adventurer* was quite in conformity with the policy of gathering "Pieces of Wit" from current periodicals. Most of the historical miscellanies, we have remarked, took some notice of essay-serials, although they had hitherto tended to pass over the longer narrative pieces. So too with the story in the *Scots* attributed to a "French Magazine," and the epitome of Fielding's *Amelia*. Each was relevant in its way to the usual pursuits of the historical miscellanies, which sought to keep in touch with new publications of all kinds, foreign and domestic. Both the *Gentle-*

man's and the *London* had for some years casually assumed some of the functions of book review journals—hence the long summary of *Amelia*, the new novel by the brilliant author of *Tom Jones* (of which a shorter review had appeared in the *London* in 1749). Similarly, in November, 1754, Mrs. Haywood's *Invisible Spy* had been duly listed by the *Gentleman's* among new works of "Entertainment," and in the following month the magazine returned to the novel, appraising it briefly in a single paragraph followed by a five thousand-word extract and condensation of the "unhappy adventures" of Alexis and Matilda. But the various originals or pseudo-originals of the *Gentleman's*, the *Universal*, and the other periodicals represent nothing but themselves, and being offered as mere entertainment, without comment or attribution, they cut a somewhat curious figure among the usual paraphernalia of the historical miscellanies, and show a blurring of their traditional aims.

"Asem and Salned" of the *Gentleman's*, an unacknowledged translation from the *Mercure de France*, for example, is a highly romantic adventure story in the popular eastern mode. Asem, a young merchant of Basra, marries a beautiful and virtuous maiden of the city, who ardently reciprocates his love. On her wedding night, however, Salned has a slight fall, and to her husband's amazement, and her own, suffers a miscarriage. Asem refuses to accept her passionate protestations of innocence, and divorces her. For the same reason, her father refuses to receive her again in his house, and she becomes an outcast. In the course of her wanderings she befriends another woman, Geraldi, who has been equally unfortunate, having been accused by her husband of unlawful commerce with a young nobleman named Zenoder. The two women disguise themselves as merchants and go to sea. Their ship is attacked by a corsair, and they are taken prisoner and carried to Basra to be sold as slaves. Here they are purchased by Zenoder, Geraldi's supposed lover, who does not recognize her. By a marvellous train of fortuitous circumstances, Geraldi's husband is at last convinced of his wife's innocence, and she is restored to his favor. Afterwards Salned is similarly exculpated, when it is revealed that she was the victim of a designing aunt, who accomplished with drugs what Salned would never have consciously submitted to. Both stories, allegedly, illustrate how heaven justifies the innocent.

"Rosetta and Chamont," a sentimental romance of contemporary setting, is equally contrived, though it claims that the personages involved "are now well known in France," and that "the account is compiled from some letters written by the lady to a particular friend." Rosetta was a beautiful courtesan of loose principles but generous heart. About to retire on a fortune of 20,000 livres, which she had accumulated in her profession, she was moved to befriend an unfortunate young man of good family, who was utterly destitute. Her disinterested act awakened his love, and in the end, despite her generous efforts to escape his grateful importunities, he discovered her whereabouts, and they were married, and "long enjoyed the pure and exalted felicity of that love which is the desire of the soul and the boast of reason."

"Asem and Salned" and the others, of course, were far from being the first stories of a romantic character that had appeared in the historical miscellanies. Short sentimental tales and apologues had been a familiar ingredient in both the weekly journals and the essay-serials since the days of the *Tatler* and *Spectator*, and by these paths had long since found their way into the *Gentleman's* and its principal competitors. But by reason of their greater length these novelettes received a kind of emphasis that was incongruous with the traditional aims of the historical miscellanies. Part I of "Asem and Salned," for example, was sandwiched between a piece "From the Gazetteer" on electoral reform, and an account from France of a recent infestation of wolves near Poitiers. Part II, the following month, was bounded by scientific papers on "Aether" and "Putrifaction." Moreover, unlike "A Story Strange as True" and the "Apotheosis of Milton" of fifteen years before, neither "Asem and Salned" nor "Rosetta and Chamont" was topical in any way. Both, therefore, were quickly transplanted to the congenial climate of more sentimental popular miscellanies, where "Rosetta and Chamont" took up more or less permanent residence.[10] But in the *Gentleman's Magazine* they seem like exotics tenuously rooted in a grimy and irrelevant world.

The GENTLEMAN'S after Cave's Death

The death of Cave in 1754, and the consequent passing of the magazine into the hands of Richard Cave and David Henry, seems to have called for a decision regarding the kind of miscellany which the *Gentleman's* was henceforth to be. Was it to preserve its original character, or was it to move in the direction of more broadly popular compilations, which were everywhere emerging in growing numbers? The question was debated in the "Preface" to the 1755 volume, in which were published seven imaginary letters "exhibiting the various opinions of different classes among our readers concerning their respective contributions."

The first letter was from "Jack Dactyl," who flatly disapproved of all the historical features of the magazine, recommending instead of this "rubbish" four or five more pages of poetry, a fuller account of plays and operas, and "a few more entertaining stories"—precisely the kind of fare identified in 1755 with miscellanies like the now-defunct *Ladies Magazine*. But Jack Dactyl's voice, although heard first, was the only one raised in favor of such diversions—indicating, perhaps, that he was not to be seriously considered. His objections to the "dryness" of the *Gentleman's Magazine* were countered by the remaining six, each one of whom, however, demanded a different kind of emphasis.

"Mr. Tradewell," representing the powerful mercantile interest, took an entirely opposite stand, disapproving the "vain and trifling subjects" to which the *Gentleman's* was sometimes given—the "paltry rhimes," the "frothy merryment" of many of the Weekly Essays, the inconsequential summaries of new plays, and "antiquities," and the "accounts of shells and mushrooms, and old towns"—and urged "a larger and more particular account of publick affairs, the general topics of debate in the great assembly of the nation, a fair state of such political questions as relate to our publick conduct in this remarkable crisis, and some seasonable animadversions on our state pamphleteers." Such had been a primary emphasis of the *Gentleman's* in earlier years.

The third letter was from Jonathan Vertu, who likewise disapproved of "stories that are professedly without truth" and "verses that are altogether without use"; and the other four, Sylvester Polyglot, Jacob Lemma, Dr. Pulse, and Mr. Rus—representing various vocations and avocations—in turn urged greater attention to natural history and antiquities, philosophy, mechanics, astronomy, mathematics, meteorology, biography, and accounts of new books.

The conclusion which Mr. Urban drew from these conflicting demands was that since all of these classes of readers found something in the *Gentleman's Magazine* to suit their tastes, "his present plan ought to be pursued without the least alteration." Actually, however, during the ensuing years the magazine was gradually to drift further away from the predilections of both Jack Dactyl and Mr. Tradewell, and towards the interests of its learned correspondents, an inevitable consequence, no doubt, of the growing size of the reading public and the resulting tendency of periodicals to specialize in one way or another.

Throughout the first twenty years of its existence, the *Gentleman's* had fully served the interests of the commercial classes, as far as they were expressed in the demands of Mr. Tradewell.[11] But for a number of years there had been signs that the general magazine public had begun to weary of the perpetual squabbles of the partisan press, which since the fall of Walpole had lost a good deal of their pertinence. Now, with the period of peace and relative stability that followed the Seven Years War and the Rebellion, Cave's magazine had begun to relax its emphasis upon pressing public affairs. The slight flirtation with prose fiction, represented by the three novelettes published between 1751 and 1755, and the 1755 "Preface," was a sign, so to speak, of the periodical's availability. But the *Gentleman's* was to resist further temptation to go the way of the new popular miscellanies. Under the continued pressure of a large correspondence from scholars and informed amateurs, it gradually transformed itself into a kind of clearing house for historical, scientific, and literary information, and thus won the plaudits of the Polyglots, Pulses, and Lemmas, but inevitably sacrificed its long-held position of leadership among British periodical publications.

In this new phase, prose fiction was destined to play an even more subordinate role, and after "Rosetta and Chamont" it was ten years before the *Gentleman's* was to publish another story of comparable length. In 1765 it suddenly offered "A Story from the French of Voltaire," who had been for several years an object of public interest; "The Trial of Friendship," translated from Marmontel, a new French author of whom the popular miscellanies were making capital;[12] and in the following year (less relevantly) "The Double Mistake, a Tale, from the French," in three parts. "The Life and Adventures of Ambrose Gwinett," on the other hand, published in 1768–1769, was evidently considered by the editor to be a genuine memoir, although it was probably fiction. If these three or four pieces represent a revival of interest in magazine fiction on the part of the *Gentleman's* they were largely ignored by its immediate competitors, all but one of which continued for several years longer to preserve their essentially "historical" character. "Ambrose Gwinett" is the last piece of long fiction published in the *Gentleman's*, and, with time, even the short tales and apologues tended to give way, as the magazine became increasingly a compendium of facts and miscellaneous learning. The extent to which Cave's once-lordly miscellany was displaced by changing conditions in the magazine world is indicated by the respectful but somewhat condescending appraisal of the *Gentleman's* by a correspondent in the *Universal* in 1804:

> As a work of general amusement, it can advance few claims to general approbation; but it may advance claims to something better,—that of being a repository of numerous interesting and important facts; a store-house, from whence, the antiquarian in particular may derive many useful commodities; and though there be seldom any frivolous school-boy essays, amusing tales, pretty fragments, and similar nonsense, yet it often admits disquisitions of general utility, and discussions of useful questions.

But he went on to add that the magazine appeared to be verging "towards a state of decrepitude and empty garrulity," with only occasional flashes of its old vigor, as if "inspired by a transient recollection of what it was."[13]

The GENTLEMAN'S on the Novel

The record of the *Gentleman's Magazine* as a book-review periodical confirms some of the observations which have been made about its relation to the English novel, and its lesser function as a literary periodical. During most of the three-quarters of a century with which this study is concerned, the magazine also operated as a chronicle of new books in which a certain amount of attention was inevitably given to prose fiction. This feature of the magazine began modestly in 1731 as a mere list of "Books publish'd" during the month, set up in imitation of a similar department in the *Monthly Chronicle,* but gradually extended. At first Cave was content merely to list books by title, giving publisher and price. Later he began to group them under such headings as "Historical," "Sermons and Divinity," and "Poetry." Here new works of fiction were cited along with all other publications that came to the attention of the editor, who was sometimes uncertain, however, whether they should be classified under "Miscellaneous," "History," or

"Poetry and Entertainment"—a sign of the dubious status of the English novel at St. John's Gate, as well as elsewhere.

Beginning in 1748, however, the editor began to subjoin brief descriptive comments to a few of the listed items. This was in addition to publishing occasional extracts and summaries of new books in the main body of the magazine—a practice pursued casually from its earliest years. The little notices in Cave's "Register," however, seem to have no particular rationale, unless they merely represent books to which the editor happened to have access. Important new works of learning and imagination were often passed over in favor of fugitive tracts. The first novel to be so noticed, for example, and the only one in 1750, was *The Life of Harriot Stuart* by Charlotte Lennox, which is described in a few words. The reviewer added that no part is "short enough to be detached, nor can it be abridged without great injury to the original," which is "penn'd with the purity of a *Clarissa*."[14] *Harriot Stuart,* of course, was not an inconsequential work in contemporary eyes, and it attracted the special favor of Johnson (who may have himself prompted the above comment), but the casual character of the notices in the "Register" is suggested by the fact that in the following year (1751), three lesser works of new fiction were selected for brief comment (*The Geese in Disgrace, a Tale*; *The Adventures of Lady Frail*; and *The Adventures of General Edwards, a Creole*), whereas *Pompey the Little*, *Peregrine Pickle*, and *Amelia*, although listed, went otherwise unremarked. The next year, however, Mrs. Lennox's *Female Quixote* received a short review of about 200 words—largely devoted to Fielding's commendation of the novel in the *Covent Garden Journal.*

With time, a few of the paragraphs in Cave's "Register of Books" lengthened, and some greater attention was given to reviews in the main body of the magazine. The "unhappy adventure" of "Alexis and Matilda" (1754), already mentioned among the *Gentleman's* longer fiction of the 1750's, was really an illustrative extract following a few remarks on Mrs. Haywood's new novel. Another long piece, "The Trial of Friendship" by Marmontel in 1765, was similarly offered as a sample of Volume III of the *Contes moraux*, which was then being eagerly received in Paris. But marked attention to new novels (Richardson's aside) was never characteristic of the *Gentleman's.* For this reason it would seem that Blanchard has exaggerated the supposed hostility of the magazine to Fielding, whom he regards as conspicuously and intentionally slighted.[15] The *London Magazine* undoubtedly tended to play up the author of *Tom Jones*, whereas the *Gentleman's* favored Richardson, partly because of the rivalry between the two magazines, partly because of Cave's friendship with Richardson. But the fact is that both periodicals at this period paid such slight attention to new fiction that the difference amounted to very little.

In December, 1748, with the publication of the last three volumes of *Clarissa*, Cave inserted in the magazine an alleged letter from Cibber's "Sir Charles Easy," designed to arouse interest in the novel, followed by a two-page letter from Lovelace, extracted from Volume V. But the magazine took no other formal notice of *Clarissa* (except for a Latin epigram in January) until six months later, when it made a striking display of extreme literary partisanship. Among the "Essays" of the month Cave published a highly laudatory review of the French translation of the novel, extracted from "a book lately published at *Amsterdam*." *Clarissa*, the continental critic wrote, is in all respects an advance over *Pamela*, and "all the readers whom we know concur in giving it the first rank among romances." Compared with Marivaux's *Marianne* it is superior in probability and consistency, in "warmth and spirit," in its minute attention to particulars, and (of course) in moral perspicacity. "*Marianne* amuses," the critic declared, "*Clarissa* not only amuses, but instructs; and the more effectually, as the writer paints nature, and nature alone." Taking an inventory of its numerous beauties, he extolled its formidable cast of characters, all precisely delineated, its finely discriminated epistolary styles, its pathetic passages and glowing descriptions, and the "exalted sentiments" uttered by its heroine. Coming to the end, however, and following the usual eighteenth-century method of balancing blemishes against beauties, he brought himself reluctantly to consider some of the possible defects of the novel. ("There never was a book without fault..."). He therefore mentioned Clarissa's inexcusable "assignations" with Lovelace early in the story; her over-scrupulousness and excessive delicacy; the shocking "freedom" of certain scenes and episodes of the book; and some of its improbabilities. It is here that the extraordinary partiality of the *Gentleman's* was revealed. In the text each of the nine objections raised by the foreign critic was numbered, and answered by an elaborate series of "critical annotations" at the bottom of the page, unsigned, and presumably representing therefore the opinion of Sylvanus Urban. The whole is in the typical eulogistic pattern of the Richardsonian school, which would allow no breath of criticism to touch either the novel or its heroine. The so-called "OBJECTIONS ANSWERED," McKillop has shown, were written by the novelist himself, who had used the same method of reply in *Pamela*.[16]

But to praise *Clarissa* was not to disparage *Tom Jones*, and Richardson and perhaps Mrs. Lennox aside, Fielding received more attention in the *Gentleman's* than any other contemporary novelist before Sterne, and much of it was favorable. The fact is that *Pamela, Joseph Andrews, Clarissa*, and *Tom Jones* all appeared a little too early to receive critical notice in the magazine's "Register of Books." For Richardson's party, Volumes I–II and III–IV of *Clarissa*, as they appeared, were important literary events, but they went unremarked in the *Gentleman's*, except for their routine mention among the new books of the month. The publication of the first four volumes of *Sir Charles Grandison* was heralded by a commendatory letter addressed to Mr. Urban (also produced under Richardson's eye),[17] but they received only a quarter of a page in the "Register," about what the *Female Quixote* had received, and the appearance of the later volumes went unsignaled in any way, though duly listed in the "Register of Books" in company with about fifty other new publications of the month.

In general, however, although the attention given to new novels in the *Gentleman's* continued to be perfunctory, they did not receive less emphasis there than did other forms of belles-lettres. In terms of magazine fiction, we have observed, the *Gentleman's* itself made only slight contributions to the literature of the novel, remaining aloof from the tendency of other types of miscellanies to give greater play to fiction of all kinds; but in its function as a book-review periodical it tended to accept the novel as a normal though not-too-important feature of eighteenth-century life, and certainly did little to fan the prejudicial flames that raged on other fronts. Unlike the essay-serials, the *Gentleman's* was uninterested in literary theory, questions of moral efficacy, the state of popular taste, or diatribes against circulating libraries, "literary locusts," and "Lane's Manufactory." Its fingernail reviews of new books tended to be permissive rather than prescriptive, and to display fewer reservations than those in the *Monthly* and *Critical*, the writers of which had many more definite ideas about what a novel should or should not be. For example, the *Gentleman's* took no critical notice of the early volumes of *Tristram Shandy* (that *bête noire* of the monthly reviewers), but immediately excerpted "The Story of Yorick" as a "specimen" of the new novel, and two years later offered "The Story of Le Fever" from the sixth volume, remarking only that this tale is "altogether a master-piece in its kind, and does the Writer great credit"[18]—whereas, though Sterne received much more attention from the *Monthly* and *Critical* reviewers, he was subjected to a constant crossfire on the scores of pruriency and perverse whimsicality.

The UNIVERSAL MAGAZINE

The *Gentleman's* reserved but not hostile attitude towards magazine fiction and novels in general was much more consistently maintained than was that of its principal competitors—all of which ultimately were to surrender to popular pressure. The decision made by the *Gentleman's Magazine* in 1755 not to offer much light entertainment in this form was at first accepted by its chief rivals and imitators. After their tentative experiments with serial novelettes the *London*, the *Scots*, the *Gentleman's and London*, and the *Universal* all seem to have agreed to reaffirm their historical character by confining their narrative pieces to occasional short tales and apologues of a traditional character. During the next fifteen years (that is, until 1770) the first two together published only five stories in excess of five thousand words, and the *Gentleman's and London* of Dublin none at all. Four of the five were epitomes of important new novels. All three magazines also pursued a policy roughly equivalent to the *Gentleman's* in other respects.

This program of renewed austerity, however, although unquestionably approved by the Tradewells, Vertus, and Polyglots among the British reading audience, was manifestly in opposition to a large and growing segment of the public, among which the popular miscellanies were reaping increasing returns in terms of circulation. It was inevitable, therefore, as time went on, that the historical miscellanies would be under mounting pressure to leave their secure, but somewhat confined, haven among the informed minority, and move once again toward the center of the broadening stream of English miscellaneous publications. The *Universal* was the first to leave its traditional moorings. From the beginning it had been somewhat different in tone and character from the others—perhaps because it was a relatively late-comer to the scene, and felt it necessary to assume a slightly variant identity. It was typographically more attractive than the others; its engravings were superior, often being hand-colored; and it placed greater emphasis upon belles-lettres, the arts, and the cultivated use of leisure time. On its title page it specifically addressed itself to "Gentry, Merchants, Farmers, and Tradesmen"—and this diversified orientation is reflected in some of its contents. It also made a direct appeal to feminine readers, offering from the first number a two-page department called "The compleat English HOUSEWIFE," as well as other features of interest to women. In short the *Universal Magazine* from the beginning was a somewhat more popular compilation than the *Gentleman's Magazine*, though in its annual prefaces it continually affirmed its role as the "faithful Chronicle of public Transactions and Events" as well as a "rich Repository of what was most interesting and curious in the various Branches of Science and Literature." It also made perfunctory attempts to include parliamentary news and weekly essays, and for the first thirteen years of its existence it published very little prose fiction.

We have already described the three novelettes which the *Universal* published in 1753. In company with the other historical miscellanies, for a period, it resumed its former conservative policy. But after about ten years the *Universal* seems to have decided that such a policy was unfruitful. Taking the measure of the new interest in Marmontel, it extracted in 1763 "The Connoisseur," from the new translation of Marmontel's *Moral Tales*, and nine months later suddenly embarked upon a full-length novel, "The History of Miss Jenny, translated from the French of Mme. Riccoboni," offered in four installments. After this experiment, instead of reverting to type, it pursued a series of new ventures in serial fiction, which spread into seven of the thirteen issues in 1765: Mme. Riccoboni's "History of Ernestine," "The Fair Adulteress, or the Treacherous Brother, a Novel," and a long abridgment (11,250 words) of the "Gothic Story of the Castle of Otranto," recently published, which the editor offered

> in Hopes that such of our Readers, as delight in Romance and Novel, will find Matter of agreeable Entertainment in it.[19]

(Of this novel, the *Critical* had written only a few months before: "The publication of any work, at this time, in England composed of such rotten materials, is a phoenomenon we cannot account for.") At the same time, these long stories in the *Universal* were accompanied by an increased number of shorter ones in the usual modes, which tended to underline the modified character of the periodical.

Readers of the *Universal* evidently found the new emphasis upon "Romance and Novel" very much to their liking, for, from this time, the magazine entered upon an ambitious program of magazine fiction, which quickly transformed it into a miscellany more closely approximating the *Westminster*, the *Town and Country*, the *Lady's*, and similar compilations of the 1770's and later. In the ensuing forty-five years (that is, from 1766 to 1811) the *Universal* offered its readers exactly a hundred long works of prose fiction, a productive record in the novel exceeded by only a few of the most prosperous and long-lived of the common miscellanies. Most of these stories were in the 5000–12,000 word bracket, but twenty-three of them were of novel-length, the longest being a new translation of Mme. de Genlis's *Adèle et Théodore*, which ran to over 100,000 words.

In its altered role as a purveyor of prose fiction the *Universal* is properly associated with other popular miscellanies, dealt with in two later chapters. But it should be remarked that even in its new phase the *Universal* preserved a certain degree of its original seriousness of purpose, and maintained in the family of popular periodicals a relatively high level of literary taste. It serialized, for example, a long series of extracts from Fénelon, entitled "The Beauties of *Telemachus*," which ran for over three years, and later a prose version of Ariosto's *Orlando Furioso*, which occupied twenty-seven installments. Both of these works would be caviare to the mass of eighteenth-century magazine readers, judging by the record of other miscellanies. The *Universal* also became a clearing center for continental fiction in translation. Twenty-nine of the 112 pieces which it contributed to the Catalogue were offered as works in translation, including novelists of such stature as Fénelon, Marmontel, Arnaud, Montesquieu, Wieland, Kotzebue, Mme. de Genlis, and Rousseau. Owing to the energies and enterprise of the *Universal*, these works, and the names of their authors, were spread into every corner of the land by dozens of lesser miscellanies which drew a regular part of their own offerings from the columns of the *Universal Magazine*. The abridgments and long extracts from new novels offered by the *Universal* also tended to be of a slightly superior grade, including works like *The Castle of Otranto*, Fanny Burney's *Cecilia* and *Camilla*, Mrs. Inchbald's *Simple Story*, and the novels of Charlotte Smith, Henry Brooke, Charlotte Lennox, Frances Brooke, and Dr. Moore. The original novels and novelettes with which the *Universal* occasionally supplemented its extracted and translated pieces were all less than second-rate, but such was the depressed state of practically all new miscellany fiction during the *Universal's* period of operation that they must count as better than most.

Considered, therefore, in terms of the traditional aims and aspirations of historical miscellanies like the *Gentleman's*, the *Universal* made a definite descent in 1763, but considered in relation to its new associates among the popular miscellanies, it was a superior member of its class. Endlessly pilfered itself, it rarely borrowed directly from other miscellanies, and it never stooped to the hypocrisies and vulgarities of the renovated *London Magazine*, which reached its climacteric a few years later.

The Defection of the LONDON MAGAZINE

The defection of the *London* from the ranks of the historical miscellanies is more important than that of the *Universal* because of its close rivalry for many decades with the *Gentleman's*. For the first forty years of their association, as a matter of fact, the two magazines were little differentiated in either method or policy, although there were signs in the 1760's that the *London* was leaning in the direction of a more popular reading public, and a more lucrative market for its commodities. In this period it began paying more marked attention to "correspondents," many of them feminine. In its "Impartial Review of New Publications," it also gave much greater attention to novels than did the equivalent "Review of Books" in the *Gentleman's*. And commencing in April, 1769, the editor of the *London* devoted about four pages in each issue to an essay-series called "The Benevolent Society," designed to "awaken the long-forgotten (or at least long-neglected) dignity of the female character" with the "histories, observations, ideas, and reflections of [a society of] eight not-uninformed females." The qualification for membership was not a serious interest in learning and contemporary affairs, but "*amiable sensibility* of heart."[20]

Nevertheless, the annual "Preface" of 1769 (issued with the collected volume in January, 1770) blandly reaffirmed the intention of the *London* to provide "rational entertainment," as opposed to the levity and triviality of other periodical publications. The proprietors (it was declared) had studiously avoided obtruding "puerilities" into the "closet of the philosopher and the gentleman," or reflections upon private reputations, but had tried to satisfy all the legitimate tastes of their readers in conformity with "reason and morality." In this lofty restatement of principle there was a scornful allusion not only to the magazines for women, which had recently been appearing in increasing numbers, and towards which "The Benevolent Society" was a definite move, but also to the more jaunty *Town and Country Magazine*, a highly successful competitor of the *London*, just established in the previous year.

The *London's* rededication to principle in January, however, did not prevent it from giving special attention in July to the notorious Grosvenor case. Both the *Gentleman's* and the *London* offered their readers full summaries of testimony given at the trial, which had aroused great public interest. But the *London* went on to print thirteen of the sensational love letters which had been introduced as evidence, but were not printed by the *Gentleman's*.[21] That the *London's* interest in this case was more than "historical" is further indicated by the publication of a scurrilous engraving in the September number entitled "A late Unfortunate Adventure at York," showing the royal lover being surprised in Lady Grosvenor's bed-chamber, and the defendant, her bosom exposed, fainting in the arms of her attendants, also in various stages of undress.

The 1770 "Preface," however, betrayed no sign of uneasiness at this bizarre deviation from the magazine's traditional character. On the contrary, it declared that the settled purpose of the *London* was "to give a dispassionate register of events," uncolored by partisan attachments or "popular prejudice." Its parliamentary reports, book-review, and theater departments were vaunted as models of "rigid impartiality," and its various "miscellaneous articles," according to this account, were avidly copied by envious contemporaries. However, the proprietors warned their readers:

> There are some points, indeed, in which they can by no means enter into competition with other Magazines, and in which they would even blush to acquire a superiority; these are in the fictitious histories of amours, or the still more dangerous annals of real gallantry. The *London Magazine* is published to improve, not to corrupt the mind; to inculcate principles of rectitude, not to pandar to the passions of its readers. They are besides honoured with an extensive perusal among the most amiable of the softer sex, and cannot open the unhallowed orgies of the stew, upon a woman of virtue.

In short, they austerely declined to descend to the level of their hated rival, the *Town and Country Magazine*, although their righteous deference to the "softer sex" was a striking sign of the magazine's new *un*-historical tendency.

The following October, however, the cracks in the *London's* facade became a deep fissure, when, in the face of his previous declarations, the editor suddenly embarked upon a sensational new series of narrative sketches entitled "The History of Gallantry," set up in obvious competition with the *Town and Country's* notorious "Histories of the Têtes-à-Têtes annexed," a flagrant chronicle of scandals in high life, the popularity of which had clearly unsettled the editor of the *London*. In an accompanying address "To the Publick" he justified this unexpected right-about-face on the basis of that "love of knowledge, particularly the knowledge of his own species," which is so "natural to man," and the "amusement and instruction" which we must all receive from the "history of living characters," especially when it touches the "grand passion of Love." In exposing to view the secret history of gallantry, the *London* would provide a valuable supplement to the larger history of the times. It would bring "domestick and living examples of virtue and vice... within the reach of the most vulgar and untutored mind," and it would satisfy the laudable human "appetite for truth." Everything in "The History of Gallantry" would be quite "authentick," yet nothing would "shock the ears of the delicate." Other magazines might "excite publick curiosity by vending scandal," whereas the *London* would help to save "young persons" from the "fatal rocks" of indiscretion.

> Let not then the most rigid matron, nor the most prudish old maid dread to peruse this department of our Magazine. We shall never put either to the blush. The former may safely read it aloud to her virgin daughters, and the latter may silently cast her eye over it, without any fever of the blood, and for a moment forget her dogs and monkeys.[22]

How well this laudable intention was fulfilled is shown by the first story of the new series entitled "The Northern Elopement, or the Amours of the Scotch Worthies, Lady Mary Sc——t and Captain Suth——nd," recounting in a satirical manner how General Sc——t, the injured husband, pursued his wife and her lover 400 miles across Scotland and England, at length surprising them *in flagrante delicto* in an inn outside London. This piece is supplemented by an edifying print entitled "A Late Scene at Barnet," showing

Lady Mary's lover escaping through the window of the inn without his breeches. "The Northern Elopement" was succeeded in November by "The Amours of Lord Skinflint, a Scotch Peer," and in December by still another effort in the same raffish vein. Like the *Town and Country*'s "Tête-à-Têtes," each was accorded the leading position in the monthly roster.

The 1771 "Preface," written at the end of the year is a candid confession of venality. "Magazines, if well conducted," the Editor blandly declared, "will always prove barometers of the times, and shew how the spirit of politicks, of religion, of gallantry, and of other pursuits, rises or sinks. The proprietors, meaning to play a winning game, will naturally consult the publick taste; and never mistaking or neglecting it but to their own loss, will thro' necessity soon return into the popular vortex." They intended (he said) to spare "neither industry nor expence" to make their magazine the "completest repository of the learning and genius of the age." Impelled by their need to vouch for the truth of all the recorded facts, they might not be able to publish an amorous history in *every* issue, but they promised that a "Memoir of Gallantry shall be but rarely wanting."

> Some will perhaps blame us here for deviating in some measure from the original plan of this work, and not strictly keeping our word with the publick. But let them not be too hasty in condemning. It is not we but the publick that have made the alterations in the London Magazine. We are in a great measure passive, and act as instruments in the hands of the nation. If it calls for divinity, we give divinity; if it requires politicks, we publish politicks. If love-stories be the mode, we become historians of gallantry; and if antiquities be the fashion, we commence antiquarians. In short, as far as virtue and decorum will permit, we are whatever our readers please. Keeping a publick store-house we must fill it with commodities, for which there is a demand.

Probably, in this surprising recantation, the writer was called upon to justify not only the magazine's humiliating reversal of policy, but its impending retreat from its new position, since "The History of Gallantry," though originally planned to include "the intrigues of all the eminent persons not only in the British empire, but in the neighbouring kingdoms," was abandoned after only one further effort in the same manner.[23] The reason may be that "Amours" and scandalous "Memoirs" offered too grotesque a

THE PREFACE.

MAGAZINES, if well conducted, will always prove barometers of the times, and shew how the spirit of politicks, of religion, of gallantry, and of other pursuits, rises or sinks. The proprietors, meaning to play a winning game, will naturally consult the publick taste; and never mistaking or neglecting it but to their own loss, will thro' necessity soon return into the popular vortex. For want of a due attention to this circumstance, how many rivals has the London Magazine seen perish around it! They have frequently sprung up like an ignis fatuus, blazed for a short time, and sunk at once into the gulph of oblivion. Had not our miscellany been judiciously managed, it could not have preserved its reputation for such a series of years. We cannot pay so bad a compliment to the understanding of the nation as to suppose it capable of an absurd partiality, or of being influenced by any consideration but that of merit. As it is our interest, so it shall be our care, to deserve the continuation of publick favour. Neither industry nor expence shall be spared to render the London Magazine the completest repository of the learning and genius of the age. That we may be able to vouch the truth of the facts recorded in our history of gallantry, we shall not always make a point of having an article of that nature in every number. Hence we shall avoid the errours of precipitation, and the necessity of fiction; two faults with which some of our competitors are universally and justly reproached. We promise, however, that a Memoir of Gallantry shall be but rarely wanting. In our parliamentary Debates we shall adopt a new plan, which will at once secure the graces of novelty, and the charms of perspicuity. A simultaneous view of every question agitated in the senate shall be given by a methodical and historical arrangement of the arguments there advanced on each side. At proper intervals of time the historical facts relative to other countries, which lie scattered and detached in various publications, shall be collected, digested and given in the form of a regular history. Of our miscellaneous articles we need say nothing but that, as usual, we shall select the most instructive and entertaining, that our correspondence and new books afford. The topicks of general conversation and political discussion during the month speak for themselves, and need no other recommendation. Without them no Magazine can be complete. The same observation is applicable to our Review of Books, and to the Reviews contrasted. The want of them would leave our account of literature and literary transactions very imperfect. Some will perhaps blame us here for deviating in some measure from the original plan of this work, and not strictly keeping our word with the publick. But let them not be too hasty in condemning. It is not we but the publick that have made the alterations in the London Magazine. We are in a great measure passive, and act as instruments in the hands of the nation. If it calls for divinity, we give divinity; if it requires politicks, we publish politicks. If love-stories be the mode, we become historians of gallantry; and if antiquities be the fashion, we commence antiquarians. In short, as far as virtue and decorum will permit, we are whatever our readers please. Keeping a publick store-house we must fill it with commodities, for which there is a demand.

The *London Magazine* Descends into the "Popular Vortex" (1771) contrast to the traditional historical features of the *London*, which were not allowed to lapse. More likely, despite the editors assurances to the contrary, they had "shocked the ears of the delicate," into which in recent years the magazine had been assiduously whispering on the side. Between "The History of Gallantry" and "The Benevolent Society" there could be no genuine accommodation of the kind Mrs. Haywood had achieved in the *Female Spectator* twenty-five years before. The rising squeamishness of the age was placing an interdict on "gallantry" for all feminine pretenders to refinement and elegance. Among the popular miscellanies of the same period we find a significant split between what we may call the "townish" and the "genteel." The *Town and Country* and the *Lady's Magazine* after 1770 were the powerful leaders of two divergent tendencies in popular taste—the one increasingly modish, raffish, and satirical; the other predominantly decorous, sentimental, and moral. In the diminishing circle of purely "historical" readers, the *London* obviously had lost out to the *Gentleman's*, and felt itself forced to follow the *Universal* into the "popular vortex." After its crude and ill-timed experiments in the townish mode, it suddenly veered in the direction of virtue and decorum and "amiable sensibility of heart." "The History of Gallantry," abandoned in February, 1772, was followed in the next volume by a new monthly department entitled "The School of Love," consisting of questions and answers on sentimental problems of the heart (the first question posed and answered: "What is love?"), and later by a trashy series of literary sketches called "Court Beauties."[24]

Prose fiction was an essential ingredient of every popular miscellany in 1770, and the tergiversations of the *London* were accompanied, as a matter of course, by greatly increased quantities of narrative material, in which both the "townish" and the "genteel" magazines also specialized. Twice as much space was allotted to fiction in the 1771 volume of the *London* as in the previous two volumes combined. In the fifteen years between 1771 and its demise in 1785 the magazine published a countless number of short tales in the conventional modes of magazine fiction, plus eighteen novels and novelettes. The longest and most representative of these pieces were an imitation of *Pamela* called "Female Virtue and Greatness Displayed in Principle and Refined Improvements," an epistolary novel by an unnamed lady, which ran to a total of twenty-seven installments and 87,000 words; and a highly modish sentimental journey of 57,500 entitled "A Trip to Margate, by Ansegise Clement, Gentleman." Sterne and Richardson were, from 1770, the two principal polarizing forces operating upon writers of magazine novels, and both of these works will find significant mention in a later chapter on original miscellany fiction. On the whole, however, the long fiction of the *London* was inferior to that published by the *Universal* during the same period, partly because the magazine commissioned fewer translations from foreign languages, and depended more upon gratuitous contributions from readers.

The "Impartial Review" of the LONDON

Until 1777 the *London Magazine* was, after the *Monthly* and *Critical*, the leading book-review journal, regularly devoting up to ten pages fine-print monthly to its "Impartial Review." Judged by its relation to the events which we have described, its freedom from partiality was fully demonstrated, inasmuch as during the whole period, the book-reviewer went about his routine tasks as if unaware of the momentous changes which were taking place in his own vehicle. Throughout the brief townish chapter of the *London*'s history, he vigorously attacked the current appetite for scandal, and pilloried the dullness, indecency, and scurrility of such secret histories and scandalous memoirs as came within his notice. In the very month in which the *London* embarked upon its ill-fated "History of Gallantry," he stigmatized a new novel in the same manner, published by Wheble, as "Licentiousness in league with stupidity, attempting to pass a late unhappy affair in high life, as a literary article of importance upon the credulity of the public."[25] By his slashing attacks on the vulgarity and viciousness of the novels published by J. and F. Noble, he involved the magazine in a public squabble with that publishing house, although its own recent excursion into the "popular vortex" put its self-righteous accusations completely out of court. ("Scandal," the editor of the *London* pronounced, "is the property of mean and illiberal minds, and the *Circulating Library* is its Palace.")[26] The monthly reviewer for the *London* also engaged in a continual guerilla war upon sentimental fiction, while other departments of the magazine were spreading before readers a sugared repast of "Pathetic Histories," "Affecting Relations," and little love stories "From the French." He attacked continuously "the common furniture of circulating libraries" and the "literary manufactures" of

Grub Street, and patronized female scribblers during the precise period when the general editor was trying to coax them into writing for him. "In general, the same characters may be given of all modern novels," he began one review. "The same poverty of invention, character and art—the same abundance of nonsense and folly—characterize them all. There is no variation in the style (speak who will) nor in the dullness."[27] Even good fiction he tended to view as amiable nonsense, to be endured only if it did no harm; and he was not propitiated by lofty motives. "We have been disgusted with various kinds of those noxious things called *novels*," he began his review of *The Memoirs of Miss Williams* in 1772, "but this is the first that we have met clothed in a *religious* dress, and it is the most disgusting of all."[28]

Such inconsistencies and such denunciations, however, were characteristic of the popular miscellany, whose audience came to prose fiction with anything but a single mind, and whose editors were constantly compelled to entertain contradictory views respecting the propriety of reading novels and romances. Presumably the eager readers of such early serial stories in the London as "Nancy, or the Village Beauty" (1773) and "The History of Edward and Maria" (1775), not to mention "The Northern Elopement" and "The Amours of Lord Skinflint," were impervious to the jeremiads of the editor of the "Impartial Review of New Books," although his attention to novels in general (however unsympathetic) was a tacit recognition of the larger movements of popular taste. The purely historical miscellanies, of which the *Gentleman's* and the *Scots* (until 1794) were the only important representatives, avoided these bizarre inconsistencies by publishing few magazine stories, except trifles, and giving attention in review to only a few important new works of fiction, leaving to other types of periodicals the task of dealing with the rising tide of vulgar and sentimental fiction.

The Criticism of the Novel in the Monthly Reviews

Closely associated with the historical miscellanies, and addressed presumably to many of the same readers, were the specialized book-review periodicals, chiefly the *Monthly Review* and the *Critical*. In their effort to notice new books of every description, to classify them under various headings, and to assign to each a degree of emphasis commensurate with its contemporary importance, the reviews were also part of the encyclopedic movement in the eighteenth century. Their digests and summaries were an inheritance from the abstract journals of an earlier day, of which, like the *Gentleman's Magazine*, they represented to a certain extent a popularization. Like Cave's journal, also, they addressed themselves to an informed audience of indefinite social status, assuming only a serious interest in learning and contemporary affairs. A small but regular part of their attention was likewise focused on belles-lettres, the rest being devoted to new advances in philosophy, the natural sciences, medicine, political economy, history, archeology, and classical learning. Unlike the historical miscellanies, however, these magazines assigned a more conspicuous role to prose fiction.

The first two numbers of the *Monthly* (for February and March, 1749) noticed no fiction at all, although they gave marked attention to several poetical works. But the third number announced that the journal intended in the future "to register all the new Things in general, without exception to any, on account of their lowness of rank, or price." In conformity with this policy of sufferance, there appeared among the nineteen "Books published in July, 1749," one novel, *Dalinda, or the Double Marriage*, described simply as "the affair betwixt Mr. *Cresswell* and Miss *Scrope*, thrown into the form of a novel," and a small "octavo pamphlet" called *Theosebia, a Vision.* In October, several additional works of fiction were reviewed, one of which, *The Amours of Zeokinizul*, a "secret history," received eleven pages of summary and comment.

The Monthly Review, as we have noted, was not the first journal to notice new works of fiction, and it was still a long time before the novel was to receive full and fair recognition as a medium of literary expression. But Griffiths's policy signaled a momentous change in the status of the English novel, since henceforth the door was regularly open to prose fiction in the principal book-review periodicals, and gradually, under his leadership, novels came to receive a degree of attention roughly proportionate to their merit or general interest. The *Monthly*, for example, gave major attention in 1751 to *Pompey the Little* ($16\frac{1}{2}$ pages), *Amelia* ($5\frac{1}{2}$ pages), and *Peregrine Pickle* (9 pages), works which the *Gentleman's* was content merely to list. The *Critical Review*, established a few years later, accorded prose fiction similar recognition. Although a few later reviews cavalierly refused to notice novels at all, believing with the critic of *Amelia* in the short-lived *Compendious Library* (1752), that "Romances and Novels, in general, have no great right to be in Literary Journals,"[29] most of them fell into line with the more liberal practice of the two most celebrated and widely circulated book-review periodicals.

The criticism of prose fiction in the eighteenth-century reviews has usually been stigmatized as narrow-minded and pedestrian, as by modern standards it unquestionably is. But in its own time it was much less pedantic than the writings of the essay-critics, and it did far more to advance the novel than to impede its progress. In general, the critical canons of reviewers (so far as they had any) were derived not from the precepts of pedagogues and moralists, but from neo-classical theories of the drama and epic poetry, modified by the persuasive achievements of the new English novelists—Fielding in particular, owing to his spirited interest in the theory of the novel, and the numerous "epic" features of his own works.[30] These canons, naturally, underwent a process of erosion over the course of the years, as a result of the rapidly accumulating corpus of new fiction, but by and large we may say that reviewers tended to expect a novel to possess a well-developed "fable", effectively supported with a variety of surprising yet probable incidents, pictures of common life, and interesting characters "drawn from nature." In addition, they felt that the action should be embellished with elegant diction, rational sentiments, lively conversations, just reflections on men and manners, wit, and humor; and that all the parts should converge upon a natural resolution of events which would convey some understanding of the real world and enforce some useful moral.[31]

The attention they gave to the ethical tendencies of works of fiction and their social effects, associates the reviewers with other conservative eighteenth-century critics of the novel, of which Johnson was a leader, and in certain respects they recall the little school of critics in the single-essay periodicals. In fact, they found little in the strictures of Johnson, Hawkesworth, Cambridge, Chesterfield, Mackenzie, and others, with which they could seriously disagree, except in the matter of emphasis; and, in their own criticism, they were given to such dicta as, "Novels, if well written, may be of great use," or "One great aim of novel-writers ought to be, to inculcate sentiments of virtue and honour, and to inspire an abhorrence of vice and immorality."[32] When confronted with the flood of sentimental trash, particularly in the 1770's and 1780's, these critics, also, seemed to regard themselves less as reviewers of new books than as defenders of public morality.

Time and again, in dealing with emissions from the presses of Lane, the brothers Noble, and others, they felt forced to take the offensive, lashing at the ignorance and vulgarity of writers, the deplorable reading habits of young girls, and the evils of circulating libraries. Sometimes erring novelists were roundly spanked by reviewers; other times they were made the object of witty sallies and thrusts of sarcasm and irony. A favorite device was to seize upon some signal ineptitude or silly affectation of the novelist and blast him with his own petard. This method of attack was so common a feature of the "Monthly Catalogue," where lesser works were noticed, that we may presume that it was welcomed by readers of the reviews, who expected to be entertained, and to have their moral and social prejudices flattered, by crisp comments and facetious sallies.

At the same time, however, despite the numerous prejudices they shared, there were fundamental differences in method and emphasis between the monthly reviewers and the essay-critics, of which we have already taken some account. The reviewers were not uninterested in the theory of the novel, a taste for which they had acquired from the prefatory chapters of *Tom Jones*, and many other prefaces written since. They frequently began their notices with a few pronouncements upon the art of the novel, and they were constantly stating and restating the expectations that they held for prose fiction. Inevitably, however, they were practical critics, more concerned with saying something bright or significant about the new novel of the month than with debating the old problems of the classification of the novel, the moral efficacy of unmixed characters, or the relative merits of *Tom Jones* and *Clarissa* as tracts for the young. If anything, they leaned more towards Fielding than towards Richardson. The reviews were strongholds of Fielding's reputation to a degree not sufficiently recognized, and their tacit acceptance of the author of *Tom Jones* and *Joseph Andrews* as the guiding genius of the new English novel represents a sharp break with the canons of the Johnsonian school.

The difference in orientation between the reviews and essay-serials is visible from the earliest serious critiques in the *Monthly*, over which John Cleland and Smollett (to a lesser degree) presided. The first notices of novels were mere comments, as we have remarked, but by 1751 serious attention began to be given to works which were felt to be outstanding in some respect. The reviews of *Peregrine Pickle*, *Amelia*, and *Pompey the Little* in 1751 were by Cleland; and Smollett wrote the shorter piece on Cleland's *Memoirs of a Coxcomb*. In many ways the promise of these critiques failed to be fulfilled in later reviews, but they set the tone and defined the limits for a good deal of later criticism by reviewers, and, conservative as they were, inaugurated a more catholic attitude towards prose fiction than the essay-critics ever showed.

Cleland's review of *Peregrine Pickle*, for example, begins in a manner already familiar in the *Monthly* and elsewhere, by deploring the "flood of novels, tales, romances, and other monsters of the imagination" with which the public is now "drenched and surfeited"—frivolous, lewd, and profligate, works, devoid of either wit or taste; wretched translations from the French; and (what is worse) "depraved" imitations of the same. There is some irony in these remarks flowing from the author of the recent *Fanny Hill*, but of course the reviewer's identity was undisclosed. They probably show a necessary deference to the prejudices of readers of the *Monthly*. After a few clumsy and conventional efforts to differentiate the novel as a literary form, Cleland makes the point that Johnson had made in the fourth *Rambler* only a year before, namely, that this species of writing has a great advantage as a medium of "instruction, under the passport of amusement." Cleland differs in one important respect from Johnson, however: Cleland is obviously interested in the full potentialities of the novel as a form of imaginative literature, rather than as a mere branch of homiletic writing:

> How many readers may be taught to pursue good, and to avoid evil, to refine their morals, and to detest vice, who are profitably decoyed into the perusal of these writings by the pleasure they expect to be paid with for their attention, who would not care to be dragged through a dry, didactic system of morality; or who would, from a love of truth universally impressed on mankind, despise inventions which do not at least pay truth the homage of imitation?

Johnson, at least in his *Rambler* essay, had been willing to relegate prose fiction to the humble service of instructing "the young, the idle, and the ignorant"; Cleland is eager for novels to be read by young and old alike, for whom "they may serve as pilot's charts, or maps to those parts of the world, which every one may chance to travel through." In this light, novels are "public benefits," not to be condemned because they have been abused by "unskilful or treacherous artists," or because they may "bewilder" or "mislead" ignorant travellers, but to be judged by their usefulness to all those who are able to benefit from them. For Cleland the fact that idle women and children are given to novel-reading is no reason to impound the whole art.

> Something in all productions of this sort must be left to judgment: and if fools have not the gift, and are sometimes, in such reading, hurt by the want of it; such a consideration surely says but little against works, from benefiting by which, only fools are excluded, and even that is a misfortune to which nature has made them as insensible as they are incorrigible.

The implications of this enlarged view of the dignity and importance of the novel as a literary form emerge in the course of the rest of the review. Turning at length, as a practical critic, to *Peregrine Pickle*, Cleland epitomizes the novel volume by volume, offering a pastiche of summary, excerpt, and commentary on the work. Judged by the highly finished essays of the *Rambler*, the *Adventurer*, or the *World*, Cleland's is awkwardly, and obviously hastily, written, but it makes the following points, either directly or by broad implication.

First, the novel with which he is concerned belongs to the tradition of *Lazarillo de Tormes*, *Guzman d'Alfarache*, *Gil Blas*, and the comic romances. The pleasures it affords, therefore, are those of Scarron, Aleman, Le Sage, and the like; and what those delicate readers "who call everything *Low* that is not taken from high-life" may stigmatize as ignoble in the subjects of the novel is fully justified in terms of "that humour and drollery which occur in the more familiar walks of common life." Smollett's chamber pots, in other words, justify themselves in the literary sphere. Instead of condemning such subjects outright (as the later writer in the *World* did), Cleland finds it more fitting to ask whether "the author has every where preserved propriety and nature," and whether he has succeeded in "proportioning his style to his subject."

Furthermore, he implies, the varied circumstances of the story, and the numerous "original characters" which it introduces, are to be approved not only because they castigate human arrogance, pedantry, venality, and rancor, but because they have an interest in themselves—as entertaining pictures of life, and as ingenious and self-consistent artifacts that arouse the reader's curiosity and fix his attention over a sustained period of time. In short, they give literary pleasure, and the mixed character of Peregrine Pickle is approved for the same reasons, that is, for both its truth to real life and its consistency. The character of the hero, says Cleland, is maintained through all his vicissitudes "in various spheres of action" with "vivacity" and "uniformity of principle"—

> unbending and fierce in adversity, nosing a prime minister, and refusing for wife a mistress whom he adores; but, tractable and supple in prosperity: a character, in short, too natural to be perfect, but in which the gentle shades serve only to raise the lights of the picture.[33]

In his review of *Peregrine Pickle*, of course, Cleland may be engaged in a piece of special pleading for himself, and back-scratching for Smollett, whom he probably knew as one of the reviewers on the staff (although his essay also praises *Joseph Andrews*, *Tom Jones*, and *David Simple*), but in his notice of *Pompey the Little* a month earlier we find the same emphasis upon the technical felicities of the novel, without disregarding its ethical purpose. The critique of Coventry's novel is given over primarily to long extracts from the book, but the introductory paragraph might have been written by Fielding himself (whose review of *The Female Quixote* in the *Covent Garden* appeared a year later). Cleland praises the novel for its "variety of characters and situations; all painted with great humour, fancy, and wit" and everywhere displaying "a perfect knowledge of the world, through all its ranks, and all its follies"; the "fineness of edge" that distinguishes its satire; the novel's "vein of pleasantry," perfectly sustained from beginning to end; its "natural" characters; and its language "easy and genteel"—in addition to the fact (brought out at the end) that all these features offer a "benevolent correction" of mankind.[34]

The review of *Amelia* in December is equally commendatory, and again it tends to separate, without dissociating, the ethical purpose of the novel from its artistic excellence. In this novel, says Cleland, Fielding

> has interwoven such natural situations, such scenes of trial, taken also from nature, that the attention is for ever kept on the stretch, and one is led on by the attraction of a curiosity artfully provoked, to pursue the *heroine* through all her adventures, and an impatience to know how the married pair will be extricated out of the successive plunges in which they are represented, and in which the writer often successfully presses vice into the service of virtue.

Concerning his ethical purpose (the reviewer says), Fielding "never thought so ill of the public as to make his court of it at the expence of the sacred duties of morality." If his "obligation" to paint the world "*not as it should be, but as it really exists*" sometimes leads his characters from "the paths of virtue and prudence," he always makes examples of them. "Their follies and vices are turned so as to become instructions in the issue of them." But Cleland recognizes also that the cogency of these examples depends upon the degree to which the novelist imbues them with imaginative vitality:

> ...by the attractions of pleasure he puts morality into action; it is alive, and insinuates its greatest truths into the mind, under the colours of amusement and fiction.[35]

In all three of his reviews Cleland gives primacy both qualitatively and quantitatively to the literary qualities of Smollett's, Coventry's and Fielding's novels, and in the only critique of a work of prose fiction that Smollett himself wrote for the *Monthly*, he adopted the same view. In approaching Cleland's *Memoirs of a Coxcomb*, after the usual complaints about the state of the public taste, Smollett makes an attempt first to classify the novel. It is "a narration of adventures, in the world of gallantry, supposed to flow from the pen of the hero who atchieved them." Smollett's summary of the story, which follows, is informed with some feeling, demonstrating that he considers that the ethical tendency of the work is sound—whereupon he turns to observations in which formal questions are paramount.

> The Story [he says] is well connected, and rises in importance from the beginning to the end; the incidents are entertaining and instructing; the reflections judicious and uncommon; the satire nervous, just, and fraught with laudable indignation; the characters well contrasted and sustained, and the stile spirited and correct.

There is perhaps some lack of diversity in the incidents, the reviewer declares, and there are defects of language, but he will pronounce the work "one of those few productions, which, though hastily, nay and carelessly composed, a discerning reader may peruse to an end, without yawning, and even rise from it, with a wish, that the entertainment had been prolonged."[36]

Few of the succeeding reviewers of prose fiction for the *Monthly* and *Critical* during the next sixty-five years were as experienced in the craft of fiction as Cleland and Smollett. Many of them were men of no talent or discernment. For years Griffiths himself handled much of the reviewing of novels for the *Monthly*, which was as a consequence extremely pedestrian. But on the whole these critics displayed a rudimentary respect for the novelist's art when decently practiced, and, however crudely, allowed for a range of literary values ignored by the purely didactic critics. E. A. Baker is mistaken when he declares that the reviewers "uniformly acted" upon Johnsonian principles, "insisting upon the most rigid and indeed the most stilted morality," and "implicitly repudiating" Fielding's views of narrative art.[37] They were merciless in their attacks upon shoddy and vulgar writing, but, with a few egregious exceptions, they welcomed real talent, and in their eagerness to acknowledge distinction sometimes tended to overpraise, rather than underpraise, mediocrity.

The *Critical* reviewer of Mrs. Sheridan's *Memoirs of Miss Sidney Bidulph* in 1761, for example, began with a panegyric of the work, which he felt challenged comparison with *Clarissa* and *Sir Charles*, and then proceeded to eulogize the art of the novel, especially the epistolary species. "Under correction of the critics," he wrote, "we must profess ourselves admirers of this kind of dramatic writing."[38] Later reviewers, on the other hand, grew a little weary of novels written in the form of letters, and they frequently threw up their hands at the polluted stream of fiction that flowed under their window; but, considered as a class, they never completely lost faith in the potentialities of the novel as a literary form.

> We are far from joining in opinion with those who condemn all kinds of Romances, as frivolous, insignificant, uninstructive books [Berkenhout wrote in 1756]: on the contrary, we are convinced, that this imaginary biography, is not only capable of exercising the finest genius, in the writer, but, also, of sewing the seeds of goodness in the heart...[39]

And in the identical issue the same or another reviewer wrote:

> It is amazing, that notwithstanding the vast knowledge of human nature, strength of genius, fecundity of wit, and happiness of expression, which are required in a novel-writer, so many vile romances should, almost daily, crawl from the press.[40]

In dealing with fiction of the lowest grade, the reviewers often invoked moral imperatives, or some other single standard.[41] They disapproved of trash because of its tendency to debauch young girls, or because it was silly or unreadable, and praised other novels, equally bad, for their moral tendency. But with works of greater literary merit they usually raised more than one kind of question. With such works they took account of good craftsmanship, touches of sensibility and taste, interesting characters, and other signs of artistic excellence; and they attacked dullness and triteness, paucity of invention, ignorance of grammar and other defects of style, historical inaccuracies, inconsistencies of character, improbabilities, and "irregularities" of every sort. Of *The Adventures of Miss Beverly*, to which three and a half pages were allocated in 1768, the *Critical* reviewer wrote:

> ...it resembles the separate parts of a polypus; for though each crawls about, they cannot be reduced to a whole. No order, no consistency is observed.[42]

The literary canons of the reviewers, of course, were extremely conservative, if not antiquated, and showed an excessive concern for such categories as "consistency," "propriety," "decorum," and "elegance." They also tended to demand a too-strict adherence to verisimilitude, and to regard imaginative flights as showing defects of judgment. For this they have been properly pilloried in the past. But when faced with real talent, they often allowed the novel to be what it was intended to be, and, equally important, let the novelist speak for himself. Moreover, as time went on they tended increasingly to outgrow the rules. Discussing *The Fool of Quality*, of which he generally approved, though it lacked verisimilitude, the *Critical* reviewer wrote in 1766: "To criticize in the terms of art upon this novel would be as absurd as to condemn a Chinese landscape for not being drawn according to the principles of architecture and perspective."[43] In 1769 he wrote again: "Whether novel-writing ought to observe epic or dramatic rules, is of very little consequence to the public. Like the modern taste in gardening, it is often most pleasing when it appears to be the result of nature."[44] "Nature" as a norm was frequently invoked in the reviews, but in the Author of *Tom Jones*'s rather than the Rambler's sense.

Both Richardson and Fielding were venerated by reviewers as classical writers in the new literary form—Richardson for his "mastery of the human heart" and his "pathetic powers," Fielding for his "humour and originality," his inimitable characters, and the consummate craftsmanship of *Tom Jones.* The "art of taking off characters and manners," said the *Monthly*, descended from "Mr. Fielding," and what, "from his example, was supposed to require the greatest powers of wit, humour, and genius, is now become common to Writers of ordinary capacities."[45] In *Fielding the Novelist* F. T. Blanchard would seem to have exaggerated the depression of Fielding's mid-eighteenth-century reputation by disregarding the numerous signs of his pervasive influence in the reviews, which operated even when the novelist was not mentioned by name. In this important segment of literary opinion, Richardson never gained the ascendancy that he enjoyed in the essay-serials. Reviewers appealed to both, but more often to Fielding.

In time, other English names were added to their list of the approved novelists: Smollett and Sterne (with due reservations about the "lowness" of the first and the "indecency" of the second), Mrs. Lennox, Hawkesworth, Mrs. Brooke, Mrs. Sheridan, Mackenzie, Fanny Burney, and Mrs. Radcliffe. In general, however, reviewers dealt more harshly with the sentimental than with the realist school, and they frequently attacked the followers of Richardson (indirectly, therefore, impugning the master) for their sentimental excesses, particularly their abiding preoccupation with love, their absurd predilection for the epistolary form, and their infatuation with faultless characters. One of the paths from Clarissa's door, critics came to recognize, led directly to the circulating library. They were particularly exacerbated by universal goodness. "Perfection is not the lot of humanity," wrote the *Critical* reviewer of *The History of Sir George Ellison* (1766), "and frail nature can only contemplate, with astonishment, such ideal greatness, such imaginary goodness." A year later the hero and heroine of *The Force of Nature* (1767) were sneered at as "two faultless monsters," while another character in the novel was stigmatized as "one of those notable bits of all-perfection stuff, whom we have so often described." Of *The Woman of Honour* (1768) it was said:

> The same dull round again, of perfect, and therefore insipid and uninteresting, characters; the civil wars of love, duty, pride, resentment, and interest, in one mind... and all carried on, as usual, in the epistolary manner.[46]

In other words, in spite of their insensitivity, their high-handedness, and their egregious lack of imagination, reviewers found the question of whether a novel was entertaining fully as important a test of its merit as whether it was edifying.

We cannot doubt that the formal recognition accorded to prose fiction by the major reviews, however grudging it sometimes was, actively assisted in breaking down prejudice against novels in precisely those quarters where they were viewed with the greatest reserve. The fact that busy, learned and cultivated readers of the *Monthly* and *Critical* should be asked to give a small but fairly regular part of their attention to new fiction season after season, year after year, for more than half a century was no small advantage to the genre as a late-comer on the literary scene. It helped beyond any other single agency (outside the obvious merits of the better novels themselves) to ensure for prose fiction a recognized place in the total eighteenth-century consciousness. It was also a guarantee of ultimate respectability from which the nineteenth-century novelists vastly benefited. The minor revival of long fiction in the essay-serial after 1779 which we have already described is a sign that informed opinion was beginning to be reconciled to the novel, just as the moral and literary essays of the same periodicals are a measure of how deeply suspicion and prejudice still informed the thinking in conservative circles. Nor is this all that the reviews helped to accomplish. The fact is that they themselves operated in some degree as purveyors of novels and romances, and served to cultivate indirectly a taste for magazine fiction.

There was some flexibility in the methods of eighteenth-century reviewers, but the formal arrangement of most book-review periodicals varied very little between 1750 and 1815. The individual numbers were typically divided into two parts—the first consisting of leading articles on the dozen or fifteen most important books of the month, the second consisting of brief notices of the others, in the supplement. By 1770, for example, the *Monthly* was noticing about five hundred English books a year, of which perhaps a third received major consideration. The rest were dealt with summarily in the "Monthly Catalogue." About fifty, or ten per cent, of the annual total of five hundred were prose fiction—novels or collections of short stories. Of these fifty the greater part were given only brief notice at the back, but three or four narrative works a year, more or less, received full-dress reviews of four, six, eight or more pages in the first part of the magazines. In 1769, for example, the *Monthly* thus gave attention to *Tales, Translated from the Persian of Inatulla* (11 pages), *The History and Adventures of an Atom* (14 pages), *The Exemplary Mother* (3½), and *The Loves of Othniel and Achsah* (6). During the same twelve months the *Critical* (which always gave a greater spread to prose fiction) thus reviewed eighteen novels, devoting about ninety pages in two volumes to what it felt were major works of fiction.

The short notices in the "Catalogue" to which lesser works were relegated were often scornful or facetious, but the leading articles were more sympathetic than otherwise, since they dealt with novels that were for some reason considered important, and even when they were hostile, traditional procedures tended to work in the author's behalf. The aim of reviewers, as defined in the 1756 "Preface" of the *Critical Review*, was four-fold:

> to exhibit a succinct plan of every performance; to point out the most striking beauties and glaring defects; to illustrate their remarks with proper quotations; and to *convey these remarks in such a manner, as might conduce to the entertainment of the public.* [Italics ours.]

This program, which was already in operation in the *Monthly*, involved in the case of non-imaginative works a précis of the whole book, an effort to place it encyclopedically in the stream of history, or in relation to previous works of the same class, and to evaluate its contribution to learning or modern thought. Applied somewhat mechanically to novels, it involved a few critical remarks of a general nature, intended to give the reader some kind of perspective on the book; a summary of the story or "fable" in full or in part; and an attempt to develop this outline by quotations, called "specimens of the author's work." The extracts, of course, as the *Critical* had proposed, sometimes illustrated "glaring defects" as well as "striking beauties," but more often they exhibited the latter, as being more conducive to "entertainment." They tended to present memorable episodes or telling portraits, lively conversations, effective passages of description, or touches of humor or pathos, and usually they were accompanied by explanatory material connecting them with the main story. Sometimes summary and extract were combined in a continuous narrative. In any case, more than half of most "reviews" of major works of fiction, and sometimes all except a few sentences, was typically devoted to summary and direct quotation. The framework of such pieces, in other words, was expository, but there was little in the picture itself that was not some form of narrative, and even when the tenor of the views expressed was hostile, the novelist, through the extracts, was permitted to speak for himself.

For example, in the account of *The History and Adventures of an Atom*, the longest review of a novel given in the *Monthly* during 1769, the anonymous critic, who happened to be Hawkesworth, deferred all expression of opinion until the very end of his review. He began at once with the "history" of the book "in substance." The brief outline of the story occupied less than a page, and then, since "Nothing... could bear less resemblance to [the novel], than a concise epitome of the events, taken out of the terms in which they are related," he had recourse to the usual "extracts." First the critic selected a two-page satirical character of the Japanese as a body politic (1000 words), and a similar "description of a late king of Japan and his minister" (500 words). Further details from the story connected these with still another Japanese portrait, and so on. The method of intercalated summary and excerpt (chiefly the latter) was pursued for ten more pages in a straightforward manner without comment, prejudicial or otherwise, gradually building up a picture of the work as a whole. At the end two short paragraphs of criticism were introduced, of which the first, in its entirety, runs as follows:

> There is much spirit, humour, and satire in this piece; but there is also much nastiness and obscenity: of that kind, however, which is disgusting, and consequently not pernicious. There are also some inconsistencies, to which works of fiction are very liable; but which the best of writers have been extremely careful to avoid.

The second (and last) paragraph reported one such "inconsistency" in the work, and then in closing the reviewer said: "There are many inaccuracies of style and expression; but it would be treating a hasty performance of this kind too severely to point them out."[47]

Hawkesworth's critique of *The Adventures of an Atom* (which in the end he clearly did not greatly relish) is timid and superficial. Like much eighteenth-century reviewing of the novel it is extremely perfunctory, and itself displays signs of haste. Partly for reasons like these the literary criticism of the *Monthly* and *Critical* counts for very little in modern eyes. But it is worth observing how different a face the author of the *Adventurer* presents to the world as an anonymous reviewer. He raises no questions here, as in his 4th and 16th papers of "mixed characters," of "moral probability," or of the effects of novels upon young people. He shows no disposition to insist that the novelist should above all teach virtue, and labor constantly "to remove the bias which inclines the mind rather to prefer natural than moral endowments." Praise and blame are quickly dispensed in this anonymous piece of hack writing. The charge of "nastiness and obscenity" is made in half a dozen words, but immediately withdrawn with respect to any vicious effects. The rest of Hawkesworth's critical effort is expended upon the purely formal question of consistency, which the 7000-word epitomization had hardly prepared readers of the *Monthly* to appreciate. For them the real, as opposed to the ostensible, interest of the review was the fact that it presented *in parvo* a fair "resemblance" to the novel, which they could enjoy more or less as a piece of autonomous magazine fiction.

A conservative estimate is that between 1749 and 1815 at least 200 different works of fiction, including most of those that are remembered today, were given major attention of this kind in the *Monthly* and *Critical* alone (not to mention other magazines), and thus enjoyed shadow circulations of which the figures for volume publication take no account. Moreover, since some canons of taste, however rudimentary, did prevail in these reviews, and critics were interested in merit, their weight was generally thrown in favor of superior rather than inferior productions.

During the thirteen years between 1776 and 1788, the intention of the two leading reviews to give a fair proportion of their attention to new fiction, wavered slightly. Both tended to drop novels from the first part of the magazine, and give them fuller attention in the "Monthly Catalogue." But this retreat was only temporary, and by the 1790's the epitomizers and extracters of new fiction were back at their old stand, on an only slightly reduced schedule. The number of new books had increased by at least fifty per cent since 1769. The *Monthly* and *Critical* now noticed about 750 books annually, instead of five hundred and had augmented the number of their major reviews in about the same proportion. Their effort to meet the onslaught of new publications involved retrenchments, from which prose fiction suffered. These were high-water years for the novel, but in the "Catalogue of New Books" the number of short notices actually decreased, indicating that both reviews had seriously compromised their intention to

THE MONTHLY REVIEW,

For JUNE, 1769.

The History and Adventures of an Atom. In Two Volumes. 12mo. 5 s. fewed. Robertfon and Roberts.

THE hiftory is in fubftance as follows: The atom, after having paffed through feveral viciffitudes in the ifland of Japan, was enclofed in a grain of rice, eaten by a Dutch mariner at Ferandó, brought as a particle of his body to the Cape of Good Hope, difcharged there in a fcorbutic dyfentery, taken up in a heap of foil to manure a garden, raifed to vegetation in a fallad, devoured by an Englifh fupercargo, brought to London, amputated with a difeafed part of his body, thrown upon a dunghill, gobbled up by a duck, of which one Ephraim Peacock having eaten plentifully at a feaft of the cordwainers, it was mixed with his circulating juices, and fixed in the principal part of that animalcule, which in procefs of time expanded itfelf into a fon of Ephraim called Nathaniel Peacock. Nathaniel became at length a haberdafher in St. Giles's: the atom was lodged in his pineal gland; and one night, as he was mufing in his garret, called him three times by his name. Nathaniel anfwered with great fear and aftonifhment, and the atom, having difcovered its nature and fituation, told him, that, for the inftruction of Britifh minifters, it would communicate fome political anecdotes, of which it became confcious in Japan. Nathaniel, having recovered from his fright, became amanuenfis to the atom, and the political anecdotes which were thus dictated and recorded, make the fubftance of this work.

Nothing, however, could bear lefs refemblance to it, than a concife epitome of the events, taken out of the terms in which they are related; our account therefore muft of neceffity confift chiefly of extracts, which we fhall felect as judicioufly as we can.

 The

Hawkesworth's Review of *The History and Adventures of an Atom* in the *Monthly* notice every new publication, irrespective of merit. On the other hand, the number of major notices of prose fiction in the two reviews now averaged about five a year. Between 1789 and 1793 (that is, five years) the *Monthly* gave important attention to twenty-eight new novels, and the *Critical* to twenty-three. The excerpts quoted were now a little shorter, and reviewers often refrained from summarizing the whole story, but the method was typically the same—a few general remarks of an *a priori* character, a partial or full outline of the fable, followed by (or including) "specimens of the writer's manner."

During 1794, for example, the *Critical* gave marked attention to ten new novels. The most important of these, *The Mysteries of Udolpho*, received ten pages. Although the reviewer (once thought to be Coleridge) declined to "analyse the story," lest he destroy curiosity over the outcome, he quoted in its entirety the climactic 3500-word episode in which Emily finds her way into the torture-chamber at Udolpho and discovers the effigy of the bleeding corpse. The tenor of the critical commentary was highly favorable, beginning with a graceful comparison to Shakespeare, but, like other monthly reviewers of the 1790's, he allowed a memory of the old categories to haunt his visit to the castle. "Four volumes," he demurred, "cannot depend entirely on terrific incidents and intricacy of story. They require character, unity of design, a delineation of the scenes of real life, and the variety of well supported contrast." For uttering this mild dissent he was quickly brought to book by an outraged admirer of Mrs. Radcliffe, and forced to confess publicly in a later number that he had found *The Mysteries of Udolpho* "the most interesting novel in the English Language."[48]

If, in order to cope with the flood of new books in this later period, the *Monthly* and *Critical* gave diminished attention to new fiction, the loss was compensated by the presence in the field of four other reviews in 1794 (not to mention review-miscellanies like the *European Magazine*)—all more or less pursuing the same methods and policies with respect to prose fiction: the *Analytical Review* (1788–1799), the *British Critic* (1793–1843), the *English Review* (1783–1796), and the *Literary Review* (1794–1795). On its part the *Analytical* allotted only five pages to *The Mysteries of Udolpho*, and the *Monthly* four-and-a-half, but the *British Critic* gave more than eleven, and the *Literary Review* twenty-two.

Most reviews of novels between 1750 and 1815 offered (so to speak) "short story" versions, of anything from a few hundred to a few thousand words, but "novelettes" like Hawkesworth's review of *The Adventures of an Atom* or the *Literary Review's* summary of *Udolpho* were not uncommon. The *Monthly*, in particular, was addicted to elephantine reviews, perhaps because it gave major attention to fewer novels than the *Critical*, perhaps because of Griffiths's personal interest in this species of literature. The *Critical's* notices of *Memoirs of Miss Sidney Bidulph*, Marmontel's *Belisarius*, and *The Spiritual Quixote* all exceeded five thousand words.[49] In the *Monthly*, however, works of comparable importance were sometimes allotted twice as much space. The reviews of *Almoran and Hamet*, *A Sentimental Journey*, and *The Fool of Quality* reached 9000, 9500, and 10,000 words respectively.[50] Furthermore, the *Monthly*, more often than the *Critical*, published serial reviews, in which the story was continued in successive numbers. (This practice, of course, was also employed with non-fictional works.) The first serial review of a novel in the *Monthly* was Cleland's notice of Coventry's *Pompey the Little*, already described, which appeared in three sections in 1751. Volumes I and II of Rousseau's *Eloisa* (viewed by both journals as an important work) received over eight pages in the *Monthly* for April, 1761, and then in September and October, when the other volumes appeared, Griffiths gave them forty additional pages. These accounts of Rousseau's novel, which were mostly excerpts, total 21,000 words.[51]

The *Critical* reviewers, always more discriminating than those of the *Monthly*, received *John Buncle* with reserve. To Volume I in 1756 they allotted slightly more than eight pages, indicating that in their eyes it was an original work of some interest to magazine-readers, but they arraigned the novelist for his many narrative crudities. Volume II they later dismissed contemptuously, saying merely, "This is an irreviewable performance, because the nonsense we encounter in perusing it, is insufferable."[52] In the *Monthly*, however, Griffiths was completely engrossed by Amory's novel. Of Volume I he produced a two-part review of thirty-three pages, given over to a step-by-step summary of the story with extensive extracts, praising the author for his vast learning, prodigious powers of invention, elevated imagination, and pious intentions. Ten years later, when the second volume appeared, the publisher's enthusiasm was still undimmed. Picking up where he had left off a decade before, Griffiths regaled his readers with two further installments of the same length. The total review of *John Buncle*, the longest ever accorded a single work of fiction in the *Monthly*, amounted to 35,000 words.[53] The five notices of *Tristram Shandy* that appeared in the same magazine between 1760 and 1766 also constitute a kind of serial version of the novel totalling 28,000 words. In comparison, the combined notices of the *Critical*, which professed to be bored with Sterne's vogue after only two volumes, amounted to only 4000.[54]

Whether long reviews like Griffiths's helped, or subverted, the sale of novels is a moot question. The complaints made by authors on this score suggest the latter. But the book-sellers, who should know better, thought otherwise, and some of them actually encouraged newspapers and magazines to make extracts from their new publications as a form of advertising. Probably the system worked both ways. Reviewers sometimes did tear the heart out of a novel, and spoil it for later readers by summarizing the intrigue, and quoting the most memorable passages. After Griffiths had done his work, there was little need for anyone to purchase *John Buncle*. On the other hand, the signal attention given to new fiction in the *Monthly* and *Critical*, and other reviews and review-type miscellanies, unquestionably helped to spread the author's name, and a certain acquaintance with his writings, among a much larger audience than he otherwise might have reached, and thus tended to advance his reputation. Furthermore, each novelist in turn probably benefited from the spoliation of all the others, inasmuch as the methods of the monthly reviewers served to cultivate a general taste for novels and romances, and intensify popular interest in new fiction.

The historical miscellanies, as we have seen, functioned as more or less neutral observers in the struggle of the English novel for recognition in the eighteenth century. But the book-review periodicals, forced to enter the field because of their encyclopedic programs, soon found themselves lending aid and comfort to both sides, and in the long run helped to disarm opposition to the novel by offering in their own columns a kind of surrogate fiction that tended to by-pass the various prejudices of conservative readers and lay many of their scruples to rest.

CHAPTER IV

Miscellanies and Miscellany Fiction: Reprinted Pieces

The Rise of the Common Miscellany

The prolonged success of the *Gentleman's Magazine* lent plausibility to Cave's claim to be the father of the British miscellany. Dr. Johnson said that his friend never looked out the window but with a view to the *Gentleman's Magazine*, and the early volumes of the periodical breathe an excited air of self-gratulation. For a number of years its annual prefaces denounced all "magazines" of whatever breed as imitations and plagiarisms; later they became too numerous to mention. Cave's pretensions to being the first in the field were true to the extent that his was the first miscellany of any kind to attract a large audience of English readers; but false in viewing all other magazines in the same class as descents or departures from his own. In the larger perspective of magazine history, the "historical" is only one of several different types of miscellanies, some of which were already current in the 1730's and were to become much more common later on. Furthermore, the basic principles on which the *Gentleman's* operated as a periodical were established long before Cave opened his shop in St. John's Gate. The *Gentleman's Journal*, the *Post Angel*, and *Delights for the Ingenious* all represent much earlier efforts to create a serialized melange of poems, stories, essays, and news, intended to amuse and inform a general audience of readers.

The dissemination of *non*-historical types of miscellanies (which, for convenience, we call "common"), however, had been impeded in the 1720's by the success of the weekly journal and later by the advent of the *Gentleman's* and the *London*; but eventually such magazines were to outrank all other types of periodicals, newspapers excepted, both in numbers of titles and in numbers of readers. Of approximately seventy-five serials published in the year 1740, two-thirds may be classified as news-sheets.[1] Among the remaining twenty-five we discover a number of eminent weekly journals and essay-serials, including the *Craftsman*, *Common Sense*, the

Universal Spectator, the *Hyp-Doctor*, and the *Weekly Miscellany*, and about a dozen specialized serials of various kinds—almanacs, financial papers, abstract journals, academic transactions, and so on. But three historical miscellanies, the *Gentleman's Magazine*, the *London*, and the *Scots*, lead the field, with a combined circulation of perhaps 10,000, and we find only two of a non-historical character—the *Curiosity, or Gentlemen and Ladies Repository*, published at Lynn Regis, and consisting almost entirely of poetry; and the *Christian's Amusement*, a weekly compilation of evangelical poems and sermons. Both are unimportant, except as representing a species of magazine that was soon to overrun England. Their combined circulations certainly did not exceed a few hundred copies. Only a first number of the *Curiosity* has survived.

During the next ten years, however, about twenty new miscellanies appeared which struck out less tentatively in the direction of the *Weekly Amusement* and the *Lady's Magazine* of a decade earlier, among them the *Agreeable Companion* (1745), the *British Magazine* (1746–1751), the *British Magazine* of Edinburgh (1747–1748), the *Newcastle General Magazine* (1747–1760), and the *Ladies Magazine* of "Jasper Goodwill" (1749–1753). Most of the common miscellanies of the 1740's, naturally, were still under the spell of "Sylvanus Urban," until 1755, at least, the most commanding figure in the magazine world. But they really represent a different breed of periodical, in which "Knowledge" tends to give way to "Pleasure," and in which poems, diverting essays, and stories receive a greater degree of emphasis than historical and scientific articles, and summaries of public affairs, although a few miscellanies, like the *Universal*, tried to combine features of both.

The persuasive example set by Cave's magazine in this early period is reflected in the contents of the *Ladies Magazine, or the Universal Entertainer* of 1749–1753. Compared with later magazines for women, for example, this periodical is still heavily burdened with informative essays ("A Dissertation on Royal Societies," "The Theory of Earthquakes," "The Cause of Apoplexies," and so on). The *Ladies* was obviously trying to be of interest to gentlemen as well—while eagerly signaling also to the young people of both sexes. It purported to be

> a most agreeable Amusement, either in the Parlour, the Shop, or the Compting-House, and a delightful Companion in Retirement; as it will

> contain an agreeable Variety of Subjects in the Circle of Wit, Gallantry, Love, History, Trade, Science and News: And will be a most innocent, diverting, and profitable Entertainment for young Masters and Misses, by giving them an early View of the polite and busy World.[2]

Later, the triple role of "Universal Entertainer" not being deemed sufficient to sustain the magazine, the proprietors offered it also as a species of "Weekly Journal"—at the cost of only a penny a week, since by appearing fortnightly, it avoided the tax on newspapers.[3] In this supplementary role, however, "Jasper Goodwill" (the alleged author) was more in the tradition of "Mr. App" than that of "Henry Stonecastle" of the *Universal Spectator*, since he specialized in trials and executions, and in "Confessions and Dying Words."

At the same time, however, the *Ladies Magazine* published a quantity of material which the historical miscellanies and the weekly journals typically avoided, and which was to be the hallmark of popular compilations for the rest of the century—namely, riddles, acrostics, rebuses, and enigmas; fugitive pieces written by readers; collections of "witty sayings"; rules for card games, recipes and specifics—and long prose fiction. In addition to the usual quota of fables, anecdotes, verse tales, allegories, and diminutive histories, also found in the historical miscellanies of the same period, the *Ladies Magazine*, in the course of four annual volumes, offered six stories of 5000–12,000 words, plus a full-length serialization of Aphra Behn's *The Royal Slave* (about 30,000), published (the editor declared) at the urgent request of "many of his female Correspondents."[4] This is the same work of fiction, incidentally, that the *Oxford Magazine* had revived seventeen years earlier, possibly for the same reasons.

The long prose fiction of the *Ladies Magazine* is entirely piratical. Besides Mrs. Behn, it includes "Asem and Salned" from the *Gentleman's*; "The Misfortunes of Aliena" from the *Female Spectator,* the epitome of *Amelia* and "The Adventures of Bertholde" from the *London*; and "A Short Account of the Life of Patty Saunders, Lately Published" [*i.e.*, in book or pamphlet form]. The sixth, "Innocence Preserved, Being the Adventures of Miss Arabella R——y, a Narrative Founded on Some Late Extraordinary Matters of Fact," was taken without acknowledgement from *The Temple Rakes* (1735), published fifteen years before. "Jasper Goodwill," in other words, though he felt impelled to gratify his readers with novels and novelettes, was no more willing than the editors of the historical miscellanies to commission original pieces. The already established procedure in the early 1750's was for all types of miscellanies to obtain their major fiction, as far as possible, gratuitously, from a variety of outside sources. Later Smollett attempted to alter this practice—without success. *The Royal Slave* of Mrs. Behn was only the first of a projected series of reprinted novels in the *Ladies Magazine*, to be drawn from "some of the best Writers of that Class." But this program was terminated by the alleged death of "Jasper Goodwill" from a lingering consumption, and the consequent extinction of the magazine.

During the ensuing half century, however, the magazines devoted to "Universal Entertainment" of this kind greatly increased in number. Moreover, some of them also attracted much larger circles of readers and acquired greater longevity. By 1750, the year in which Johnson's *Rambler* began its run, there were ten common miscellanies in the field, eight of them published in London. No doubt the consciousness of this fact helped to condition the surprising emphasis upon narrative in Johnson's periodical. In 1760 the number of current titles had increased to at least fifteen; in 1770, there were eighteen, including now the famous *Universal Magazine* and the *Town and Country*. In this year Coote inaugurated the *Lady's Magazine*, which was to become the most successful publishing venture of its kind in the century, and the *London Magazine* commenced its precipitant descent into the "popular vortex." By 1790 the number of common miscellanies then in circulation had increased to nearly thirty, including by this time not only the *Town and Country*, the *Lady's*, and the *Universal*, but the *Edinburgh Magazine*, the *General Magazine*, the *New Lady's Magazine*, the *European*, and Walker's *Hibernian Magazine* (Dublin)—all heavily freighted with prose fiction. These eight alone enjoyed a circulation of at least thirty-five thousand. In this decade the common miscellanies seem to crowd all other magazines out of view, except the *Gentleman's*, the *Scots*, the three or four principal reviews, and the two *Annual Registers*; and if, after the turn of the century, their number seems to level off it is only because the field was increasingly preempted by the larger London, Edinburgh, and Dublin magazines, produced by new types of machinery and circulated by more modern methods. By that time the day of the nineteenth-century popular magazines, with their astronomical circulations, was already at hand.

Many of the more than 400 common miscellanies of the eighteenth century were extremely ephemeral, existing only for a few numbers, published by some country printer during the slack season, and eked out to make a single volume for later sale over the counter as a "collection of miscellanies." Some, like the *Curiosity* of 1740, expired after only a single number. But others survived for twenty-five, fifty, or seventy-five years, and in their longevity challenge comparison with the *Gentleman's*, the *London*, and the two celebrated reviews. In general, the provincial publications, which were extremely numerous after about 1780, were shorter-lived, owing to their more restricted circle of readers and their limited financing, whereas those of the capital cities, floated by publishers like Newbery, Coote, Harrison, and the Robinsons, enjoyed a much larger and relatively stable reading public. Such magazines were important publishing enterprises, with formidable lists of subscribers, and comparable profits. The sale of the *Town and Country* and the *Lady's Magazine* in their heyday was reported to be fifteen and sixteen thousand copies a month.[5]

Kinds and Classes of Miscellanies

It is a mistake, of course, to regard the non-historical miscellanies as constituting a homogeneous class of publication. Actually, when closely viewed, they separate into numerous species and sub-species which reflect the amorphous character of the eighteenth-century reading public. This fact is particularly true after 1770, when specialization became the rule. The divergent tendencies in popular taste represented by the *Town and Country* and the *Lady's Magazine* in 1770 were considerably extended during the succeeding twenty years. The more "townish" mode of the former was shared by a numerous family of magazines including the earlier *Court Magazine* (1761–1765), the *Court and City Magazine* (1770–1771), the *Covent Garden Magazine* (1772–1774), the *Westminster* (1772–1785), the *Matrimonial Magazine* (1775), the *Rambler's Magazine* (1783–1790), the *Bon Ton Magazine* (1791–1796), and the *Carlton House* (1792–1797). But even these were further differentiated in the amount of emphasis which they placed upon love and gallantry, scandalous histories, sensational divorce trials, and cases of rape and seduction. Except for its featured "Tête-à-Têtes," for example, the *Town and Country* was a species of *general magazine*, like the *Universal*, uncommitted to any great extent to smartness or raffishness. The *Covent Garden* and the *Rambler's Magazine*, on the other hand, were thoroughgoing "amorous repositories" with stories, poems, essays, and news of the *beau monde* and *demi-monde* which exploited the interest in libertinage and bawdry.[6]

The more polite mode of the *Lady's Magazine*, on the other side, was adopted by a large number of magazines which were attracted by the profits accruing from "virtue" and "decorum." Judging from its enormous circulation the *Lady's* was particularly successful in attracting readers from various quarters, not all of whom were women by any means. Its gratuitous "correspondents" included doctors and clergymen, college and university students, and a large circle of anonymous scribblers many of whom were obviously male. Other outstanding miscellanies in the "genteel" line were the *Sentimental Magazine* (1773–1777), the *New Lady's Magazine* (1786–1795), the *General Magazine* (1787–1792), the *Sentimental and Masonic Magazine* (Dublin, 1792–1795), the *Lady's Monthly Museum* (1798 +), and the *Belle Assemblée* (1806 +). In these magazines propriety was the rule, and every breath of scandal was avoided in deference to that vast, delicate, but undiscriminating audience of readers often referred to as the "British Fair."

Viewed in mass, the feminine audience indubitably operated as a kind of polar force in eighteenth-century journalism from the time of the *Tatler* and the *Records of Love*, but even among the women's magazines there were different emphases and varying shades of editorial address that warn us not to put too fine a point upon the tastes and interests of women readers. The *Matrimonial Magazine, or Monthly Anecdotes of Love and Marriage for the Court, the City, and the Country* (1775), for example, despite its innocuous title, was more "townish" than "genteel." The "Anecdotes" with which it regaled its largely feminine audience were chiefly gossip and gallantry, predicated on the pleasures as well as the dangers of impropriety. Its subjects and manner would obviously be offensive to most readers of the contemporary *Sentimental Magazine*, who were promised in every number "A Sentimental Journey through Life," plus

> A sentimental History, which, at the same Time that it forces the Tears of Sensibility from the Eye, shall inspire the Heart with the Love of Virtue.[7]

Both the *Sentimental* and the *Matrimonial*, furthermore, were very different in their reader-orientation from the earlier *Royal Female Magazine* (1760) or Goldsmith's *Lady's Magazine* (1759–1763)—the first somewhat "historical," the second more dilettantish and "literary"—or from the later, extremely prosperous *Lady's Monthly Museum.* The last-named was received in numerous boarding schools and academies for girls, and therefore sedulously harped upon the theme of the "corruption" and "degradation" in the modern "Female Character," two deplorable signs of which were impropriety and excessive sensibility. Because so many readers of the *Museum* were school girls, its contents were carefully adjusted to the prejudices of parents, teachers, and guardians. The contemporary *Belle Assemblée, or Bell's Court and Fashionable Magazine* (1806 +), on the other hand, avoided the numerous puerilities of the *Museum*, adopting a more dashing approach to high life and pretending to a larger sphere of interest. It was allegedly addressed to older women who sought a more intimate acquaintance with London society, with new fashions, travel, polite literature, the theater, and chitchat of the *bon ton.* The *Beau Monde, or Literary and Fashionable Magazine* (1806–1809), offered the same elegances to readers of both sexes, again without any townish grimaces. There was, in fact, among the miscellanies in the genteel line, a still further separation into the "fashionable" and the "domestic" varieties, to the second of which Robinson's *Lady's Magazine* properly belonged, with its marked attention to patterns and embroidery, and its specifics for head-ache and mad-dog bite.

Several important sub-species of miscellanies should be mentioned, however, in order to supplement this somewhat confused picture: the *review-miscellany*, the *provincial repository*, and the *specialized magazine*, all three of which were very common, and pursued differing policies with respect to prose fiction. We have already mentioned in the last chapter the *general magazine*, of which the *Universal*, after about 1761, became the leading exemplar. Other miscellanies in the same class were the *Newcastle General Magazine* (1747–1760), the *Royal Magazine* (1759–1771), and the *British Magazine* (after 1763). Such miscellanies made a more or less serious effort to adjust to both the "historical" and the "popular" tendencies in contemporary periodicals; and in this respect they were closely associated with the *review-miscellany*, which was similarly intended for urban and fairly sophisticated reading audiences. The chief difference between the general magazine and the review-miscellany was the presence in the latter of a special book-review department, as a result of which the magazine tended to acquire a slightly more bookish cast. Smollett's *British Magazine*, which will receive special attention later on, began as an early review-miscellany, devoting a page or more every month to "An Account of New Books, Pamphlets, &c.," but dropped this feature in 1763 when Smollett left the magazine, and assumed a more "general" character. Between 1767 and 1785, when it at length expired, the *London Magazine* more or less found its way into the class of review-miscellanies. During this period its "Impartial Review of New Books" provided an important precedent for similar magazines. But the *European Magazine and London Review* of 1782–1826, founded by James Perry, was the most distinguished and successful of the review-miscellanies. It regularly devoted ten to twenty pages in each number, in fine print, to its "London Review and Literary Journal," in which serious attention was given to about ten books monthly, including novels. The approach, like that of the *Monthly* and *Critical* was "full" and "impartial," and usually involved a "sketch of the story" along with "specimens" of the author's manner. Most notices of novels in the *European* and other review-miscellanies were short, but some of them ran to five or six thousand words, or even longer. The "reviews" of *The Mysteries of Udolpho* and Dr. Moore's *Zeluco* in the *European* totaled 6000 and 6600 words respectively.[8]

Like the general magazines and like other review-miscellanies the *European* also possessed a number of features traditionally associated with the historical miscellanies, including "Parliamentary Proceedings," obituary notices, serious articles on history, geography, medicine, politics, and trade, and fairly complete summaries of the news. It aimed to keep abreast of the times. Readers of the *Gentleman's*, the *Annual Register*, the *Monthly Review*, and the *Critical*, in other words, would find in the *European* a good deal to satisfy their interest in learning and belles-lettres, science, and public affairs. On the other hand, it was also a frankly entertaining compilation, and published in addition to the "London Review" a considerable amount of prose fiction, including (between 1782 and 1815) thirty-five stories of 5000 to 135,000 words. Many of these were originals, but others, like those of its principal competitors, the *London* and the *Universal*, were translations from the French and lengthy extracts from new novels and collections of short stories.

The review-miscellany formula of the *European* and the *London* was widely adopted by other magazines which hoped to attract readers of some cultivation and literary taste who were not averse to lighter entertainment.

As a result, though they published less fiction than the women's magazines, it was of higher literary quality. In general the word *review* joined with the word *magazine* in a title (as the *British Magazine and Review*, or the *Edinburgh Monthly Magazine and Review*) denoted a certain seriousness of purpose which might or might not exclude fiction, but a lesser degree of austerity than that attached to the word *register* as in Phillips' *Monthly Magazine, and British Register* (1796 +), a review-miscellany which avoided fiction and reviews of new novels altogether, but gave special attention to other kinds of books, and published a good deal of "new" poetry. Similarly, Dodsley's *Annual Register*, founded in 1758, gave regular attention to belles-lettres, but in fifty-seven volumes published only one story of novelette length.[9]

The *Newcastle General Magazine* is properly classified as a "general magazine," but in view of its place of origin it could also be considered as an early and very successful *provincial repository*. The provincial presses were extremely active in the eighteenth century, especially after 1780 or 1785, and literally scores of "miscellanies," "museums," "magazines," and "repositories" appeared designed to exploit the regional market. A few other examples from the north of England and Scotland alone are the *Perth Magazine of Knowledge and Pleasure* (1772–1773), the *Dumfries Weekly Magazine* (1773–1777), the *Cumberland Magazine, or Whitehaven Monthly Miscellany* (1778–1781), the *Berwick Museum, or Monthly Literary Intelligencer* (1785–1787), the *Yorkshire Magazine, or Universal Repository* (1786), the *Caledonian Magazine, or Aberdeen Repository* (1788–1790), the *Dundee Repository of Political and Miscellaneous Information* (1793–1794), the *Arbroath Magazine* (1799–1800), and the *Alston Miscellany, or Gentleman's Magazine* (1799–1801). The same species of publication in Ireland and in the south of England was nearly as numerous.

The editors of such magazines were usually country printers who subscribed to one or more London or Edinburgh publications from which they extracted pieces designed to keep their readers in touch with urban and national affairs, but supplemented their selections with materials of more regional interest, and with original contributions from local scribblers. The longest-lived of these repositories was the *Weekly Entertainer, or Agreeable and Instructive Repository* (Sherborne, 1783–1825), which published the first signed poems of Coleridge, and an early letter from Wordsworth.[10] The provincial repositories tended to be somewhat old-fashioned—that is to say, sober, conservative, avoiding the grosser excesses and affectations of the London magazines. They were essentially family magazines designed to offer something of interest to everyone. They typically combined a certain amount of "historical" material with more popular essay-series, short stories, and novelettes, most of them borrowed from outside, but some of them of local composition. The provincial repositories, like the provincial essay-serials, deserve more serious attention than they have thus far received from students, as guides to some of the striking discrepancies in late eighteenth-century taste. In some respects they were twenty or more years behind the times, and kept alive a great deal of earlier poetry and fiction—the magazine stories of Mrs. Haywood, Dr. Johnson, and Hawkesworth, for example.

Of all the sub-species of miscellanies, however, the *specialized magazine* is probably the most numerous. This was typically a compilation addressed to a single class of readers, or to persons with some special area of interest or point of view. Judging by their quantities, there was a lucrative and growing market in the later eighteenth century for periodicals intended for Baptists, Quakers, Arminians, Calvinists, Roman Catholics, and Freemasons; young people, apprentices, shop-keepers, and merchants; mariners, farmers, and artisans; servants, lawyers, clergymen, college and university students; travellers, prisoners, Sunday-school teachers, and the humble poor—or for readers in any rank or condition of life with a special interest in agriculture, biography, music, art and "antiquities," sports, mathematics, politics, landscape and landscape painting, commerce, prose fiction, the theater, marvels and prodigies, fashions, philosophy, or the occult.

A great many specialized periodicals, of course, were not miscellanies at all, but trade journals, serial manuals, encyclopedias, and "transactions" of one kind or another; but an equal number were genuine miscellanies—that is, collections of original and reprinted pieces, derived from a variety of sources, and intended in some degree to divert as well as instruct their readers. Editors of such periodicals found that they could increase their circulation by offering a certain amount of material of general interest, and consequently many specialized magazines contain poetry, prose fiction, essays, and articles on topics one or more degrees removed from the particular bias of the magazine. Examples of the many specialized magazines displaying some enlargement of purpose are the *Theatrical Review, or Annals of the Drama* (1763), *Freemason's Magazine, or the Constitutional Repository* (Newcastle,

1774), *Arminian Magazine* (1778–1797), *Juvenile Magazine* (1788), *Bellamy's Picturesque Magazine* (1793), *Agricultural Magazine* (1799–1807), *Glasgow Theatrical Register* (1803–1805), *Irish Farmers' Journal* (1812–1826), *Catholic Magazine* (1812), and *Sunday School Repository, or Teacher's Magazine* (1813–1816). But there were scores of others.

The religious miscellanies were particularly numerous in the eighteenth century. Between the *Christian's Amusement* of 1740–1741 (with no fiction at all) and the *Christian Herald* of 1814–1823 (with both long and short stories) there were sixty or seventy-five such periodicals designed to win the favor of the faithful. Many of these magazines had a broadly popular base, and enjoyed enormous circulations. By its seventh year (1784) Wesley's *Arminian Magazine* was adding six hundred subscribers annually to its already extensive list of readers. The *Evangelical Magazine* claimed 20,000 readers by 1808.[11] There had been keen rivalry between Toplady's *Gospel Magazine* (1774–1784), which was Calvinist, and the *Arminian* (1778–1797). The former, which was given to abuse of Wesley, expired after eleven years, but was revived in the *Evangelical Magazine* of 1793, which declared that "Thousands read a Magazine, who have neither money to purchase, nor leisure to peruse, large volumes." Thus convinced of the spiritual magnitude of his enterprise, the editor returned to the arena with twenty-four ministers of a Calvinist persuasion, who engaged to help him do battle with the *Arminian*, which for nine years had monopolized the field, and (he said) had "done more mischief to the cause of religion, than all the folios of Socinus, or the laboured productions of his followers" [i.e., the Deists].[12] The subsequent profits from the *Evangelical* were so great (£ 1000 in three years alone) that they helped to support eighty widows of faithful "Gospel Ministers," not to mention various foreign missions.

Between the various partisan miscellanies, both theological and political, and other magazines organized in terms of some special interest or point of view, there are (so to speak) vertical lines of separation, but between others the boundaries are horizontal, and the specialized magazines, like other types of miscellanies, are highly stratified in terms of the kinds and degrees of sensibility which they imply. They range from crude anthologies of facetiae, ballads, and political songs, marvels and prodigies for the vulgar, and (later) chapbook romances for barely literate readers, to learned compilations for cognoscenti; and ultimately all species shade off by numerous gradations into other types of miscellanies, annuals and repositories, reviews, essay-serials, and weekly journals, so that there is actually no precise method of classification. The only rule is rankness.

The Prevalence of Magazine Fiction

In this jungle of competing and parasitical periodicals that overran the world of Sylvanus Urban during the second half of the eighteenth century, fiction played a significant, but highly variable role. It was never, of course, as widely accepted as poetry, which won nearly universal favor, but it was common in most types of miscellanies in the 1740's, and still more common later on. Of the twenty-eight periodicals roughly classifiable as common miscellanies in 1790, twenty-seven were examined, and twenty-four were found to contain prose fiction in varying amounts (the three that did not were religious magazines). There are no principles governing the prevalence of fiction except in the extremes. Beginning about 1760, magazines that sought to reach a large, unspecialized audience of readers, especially in the middle ranks of life, nearly always offered fiction, sometimes a great deal of it; whereas the more vulgar compilations showed considerably less interest in tales and romances. Until about 1800, it seems certain, the novel held as little fascination for the barely literate as it had in Defoe's day. Judging only from the record of the magazines, one would seriously doubt whether *Pamela* was ever read aloud by the light of the blacksmith's forge,[13] or *Tom Jones* and *Roderick Random* stuck upon bacon racks in many country cottages. But in the magazines for the large and rapidly expanding class of general readers with some greater degree of literacy, particularly those with some social aspirations and leisure, fiction, after 1760, was almost a requirement. On the whole, the more successful the miscellany in the later years of the century—judged in terms of circulation and longevity—the greater the range and variety of its narrative pieces.

Fiction, of course, is almost invariably found in the women's magazines and in miscellanies which described themselves as "universal" or "compleat," which claimed to provide "elegant amusement" or to combine "knowledge and pleasure," or which offered themselves as "entertaining companions" or as annalists of "taste, fashion, and politeness." The essay-critics and the monthly reviewers often spoke contemptuously of novel-reading in the late eighteenth century as if its real centers were the circulating libraries and the girls' academies, but in the opinion of magazine readers themselves, if titles are any index, it was always associated with fashionable society, and the life of elegance and achieved gentility. There were at least seven "Royal" or "St. James's" magazines appearing between 1750 and 1788, and a much greater number that included the words "Court" or "Beau Monde" in their titles. Most of them gave marked attention to prose fiction, although even here one frequently encounters letters denouncing novels and romances. According to Dr. John Moore, it was common in the eighteenth century to indulge in novels in private and denounce them in public.[14] The testimony of the magazines strongly supports this observation, where jeremiads against prose fiction are often found wreathed with vines bearing the forbidden fruit.

At the other end of the scale, fiction tended to be avoided by miscellanies with an encyclopedic or "historical" orientation, by learned repositories, by commercial, academic, or professional magazines, and miscellanies devoted to some particular interest remote from belles-lettres—like theology, politics, mathematics, natural science, commerce, or agriculture. Some of these periodicals were so specialized that they simply by-passed all forms of popular entertainment. Their only visible objection to fiction was its irrelevance. But even in these quarters there was anything but uniformity, and fiction sometimes crept into surprising places. The Catalogue discloses the presence of one or more stories of novel or novelette length in such unlikely publications as the *Freeholder's Magazine, or Monthly Chronicle of Liberty, by a Patriotic Society* (1769–1771), the *Political Magazine, and Parliamentary, Naval, Military and Literary Journal* (1780–1791), the *Historical Magazine, or Classical Library of Public Events* (1789–1792), the *Conjuror's Magazine* (1791–1793), the *Freemason's Magazine, or General and Complete Library* (1793–1798), the *Protestant Dissenter's Magazine* (1794–1799), the *Moral and Political Magazine* (1796), *Recreations in Agriculture, Natural History, the Arts, and Miscellaneous Literature* (1799–1802), the *Sentinel, or British Miscellany and Review* (1804), the *Tradesman, or Commercial Magazine* (1808–1815), and the *Watchman, or Theological Inspector* (1809–1810).

Considered as a class of fiction, the stories of the miscellanies are not an imposing body of literature—being a hodgepodge of odds and ends, fragments and completed pieces, tiny tales and serial novels, originals, translations, abridgments, and extracts, presenting a bewildering variety with respect both to length and to kinds. The range extends from anecdotes of a few lines, and tales of less than a page—scarcely more than stories in outline—to narratives of full novel-length, continued in monthly installments over the course of a number of years. One story ran in the *Lady's*, with interruptions, for eleven years; another for ten. Again, there was no rule regarding length, and individual magazines often followed an irregular policy in this respect. But, in general, short fiction was much more common than long, and novels of twenty, thirty, or forty installments, although frequently found, were a familiar feature of only a minority of magazines. A great many periodicals that offered fiction in quantity flatly refused to publish serial stories at all, and others limited themselves to tales of only two or three parts, as magazines had in the days of the *Tatler* and *Spectator*, the *Rambler*, and the *Adventurer*.

There were several reasons for this policy beyond mere inertia. It was partly a response to readers' wishes, some of whom objected to long stories parceled out in slivers; partly the result of editorial caution—many pieces being left unfinished by their writers, some of whom were volunteers. But the most important reason was probably economic. Most miscellanies were bound and sold in collected editions at annual or semi-annual intervals, and these volumes were usually kept in print and offered for sale separately or in sets as part of the book-seller's permanent stock, sometimes for twenty-five years or more. Under these conditions the sale value of individual volumes was greater if they were self-contained. After several half-hearted attempts to adopt a policy opposed to long serial novels, the *Lady's Magazine* at length threw caution to the winds and gave their writers free rein. But such abandon was unusual. Most magazines concentrated on short fiction. Until 1800, at least, apologues or tiny moral tales outnumbered all kinds of serial stories in the miscellanies by eight or ten to one. Their brevity was well adapted to the ideal of *multum in parvo*, and their didactic purpose accorded well with the claims of *dulce et utile* which were forever being advanced on title pages, in "Addresses to the Public," and in editorial commentary. There was an endless procession through the miscellanies of diminutive "histories," "stories," "fables," "novels," "tales," "dreams," "visions," "fragments," "narratives," and "fictions," framed in some useful moral, from the middle of the century to the end, and their numbers were greatly augmented by translations from the French, where the vogue for sentimental bagatelles seems to have been as intense as it was in England.

Between 1770 and 1815 the *Lady's Magazine* published untold quantities of such trivia, together with 205 stories of novel or novelette length—"histories," "memoirs," philosophical and educational novels, personal chronicles, journals, "series of letters," fictitious voyages, "sentimental journeys" and adventure stories, "historical," "Gothic," and "eastern" romances. Because of its long life, its enormous circulation, and its primary emphasis upon original pieces and new translations, it was by all odds the principal purveyor of magazine fiction in the eighteenth century. But the *Lady's* was only the leader among a very considerable group of periodicals that gave marked attention to prose fiction, both short and long. During the same forty-five years, for periods of varying length, the *Hibernian Magazine* published 132 long stories; the *Universal Magazine*, 112; the *Lady's Monthly Museum*, 81; the *Belle Assemblée*, 80; the *Weekly Entertainer*, 78; the *Edinburgh Magazine*, 59; the *New Lady's Magazine*, 40; the *Weekly Miscellany* of Sherborne, 37. All together, more than two hundred different common miscellanies during the three-quarters of a century from 1740–1815 are represented in the Catalogue of magazine novels and novelettes, and seventy-one of them figure at least five times—most of these longer pieces being floated on a broad, albeit shallow, stream of short narratives of doubtful or unspecified origin.

The boundaries of prose fiction itself are difficult to draw, since the purely narrative works shade off by imperceptible degrees into pseudo-biographies of real people, historical anecdotes, stories actually "founded on fact," "dramatic novels," Ossianic prose poems, moral essays with long illustrative stories, travel books and "tours" with a slight fictive element, "characters" and "scenes" extracted from new novels, "reviews," summaries of plays and operas, collections of short stories disguised as essay-series, and essay-series divided into "chapters"—so that with magazines like the *Lady's*, the *General Magazine*, the *Lady's Monthly Museum*, and the *Belle Assemblée*, it is often hard to judge whether one-fourth or one-half of the contents should properly be classified as fiction. The only certainty is its profusion.

The specialized magazines naturally tended to offer a program of pieces in conformity with their particular rationale. In their prose fiction, in other words, the *Court, City and Country Magazine* concentrated on "Secret Histories of the Court," the *Juvenile Magazine* and *Children's Magazine* on stories of childhood and animal life; the *Family Magazine* on edifying tales of domestic life; the *Wonderful Magazine and Marvellous Chronicle* on accounts of strange voyages and extraordinary lives; the *Cheap Magazine* on the heroic achievements of virtuous artisans; the *Sporting Magazine* on the alleged memoirs of sporting men and gamblers; the *Evangelical Magazine* (so far as it included fiction) on apocalyptic visions, allegories, and the inspired lives of Calvinist saints. Special attention has been given in Appendix I to the stories of the religious magazines, as one form of prismatic response in the specialized magazines to the growing emphasis upon narrative forms.

The differences in manner and subject between the various specialized serials and others, however, should not be overstressed, since many editors appreciated the advantages of maintaining a certain general character. Thomas Dutton's *Bon Ton Magazine*, for example, was an extremely "townish" publication, calling itself the "Microscope of Fashion and Folly" and accenting scandal and ribaldry. As such, it published numerous stories about gallantry in high life and low ("Double Cuckoldom," the "Adventures and Amours of a Bar-Maid," the "Life of a Modern Man of Fashion," and so on). But it also provided a fund of innocuous tales and romances for readers with considerably broader tastes and interests. It printed, for example, a good deal of Gothic fiction, including the fragment of "Sir Gawen" from Nathan Drake's *Speculator*, the most distinguished of the numerous imitations in the magazines of the "Sir Bertrand" of Miss Aikin. It published also a translation of the Chevalier de Florian's "Claudine," snatched from the August, 1792, issue of the *European Magazine*, and printed over the same date. Restricted as the *Bon Ton* was in some respects, in other words, there was in it a kind of common where the general reader might also graze. The same thing is true of many other specialized miscellanies of the late eighteenth century, the editors of which often foraged for fiction among books and magazines of an "universal" character. It is possible, therefore, without greatly over-simplifying the picture, to consider the stories of both the specialized and the more general types of miscellanies as belonging to a single, though heterogeneous, family of narrative works.

Most miscellanies of whatever kind prided themselves on their original pieces, though all of them were in some degree parasitical. Novelty was a highly publicized commodity in the late eighteenth century, and the more prosperous magazines repeatedly proclaimed that they did not borrow from "other periodical publications"—by which they usually meant other publications of the same class, since they all kept an eye upon newspapers, monthly reviews, essay-serials, and other likely sources of entertaining materials. At least half the contents of even the most independent and enterprising of the miscellanies consisted of stories, essays, poems, letters, anecdotes, biographies, and other miscellanea, extracted by the editor from various sources, or collected by interested readers. The provenience of these derived pieces was often named, but frequently it was not, and one of the problems in classifying magazine fiction is differentiating between genuine originals and stories that had already appeared in book form or in another magazine, or which had been adapted or translated from some foreign language, perhaps under a new title. A safe rule to follow is that, unless a story was definitely claimed as such, that is, unless it was explicitly described as written "For the *Westminster Magazine*" or addressed "To the Editor of the *Monthly Mirror*," it was not an original.[15] But the picture is greatly confused by the plagiaristic practices of correspondents, who frequently submitted to editors as their own compositions, essays, stories, and poems which had already appeared in some other book or magazine during the last fifty years. The editor of the *Town and Country*, for example, offered his readers in 1781 "The History of the Count de Comminge" in nine installments, apologizing, however, for a five-month's delay between the second and the third parts, owing to the indisposition of the author.[16] He seemed quite unaware that the story had been written by Mme. de Tencin in 1726, and that it had first appeared in English dress in Charlotte Lennox's *Lady's Museum* twenty years before—whence it was being transcribed for the *Town and Country* by the new "author." Publishers of eighteenth-century magazines were constantly being deceived by their correspondents in this manner. As late as 1815 the editor of the *European Magazine* (to take an extreme case) graciously thanked a reader, and announced three times the forthcoming serialization in the magazine of a new Gothic romance entitled "The Champion of Virtue." Just before its scheduled appearance, he discovered that it had really been written by Clara Reeve, and published nearly forty years before.[17]

Plagiaristic Practices

We should not be surprised, however, if readers were casual about literary property, since editors themselves were so negligent about attributions, often failing to identify borrowed pieces, and permitting translators and adapters to take any liberty with original texts. The historical miscellanies, as we have said, were somewhat more scrupulous in this respect, but even they excerpted and epitomized at will, and from this common practice it was only one step to the manipulations of the *Universal Magazine*, which recast and published as new pieces, addressed to the Editor of the *Universal*, stories from the *Female Spectator* while that popular work was going through its fourth edition. Even Goldsmith in the *Bee* pursued a policy of partial plagiarism in failing to acknowledge his sources. The ethics of the situation were greatly confused, since the nature of literary property was still in debate, and miscellanies were, by long sufferance, a predatory species of publication. When a reader named "Waldensis" complained of a plagiarism in the *London Magazine* of 1779, the editor loftily replied:

> Magazines are repositories for meritorious papers, though they have appeared elsewhere in print. This was the original plan of those miscellanies; therefore they cannot be charged with plagiarism. They have since been improved by the addition of new pieces, through the favour of their correspondents, and thus they furnish to the publick an agreeable variety. This is the history in brief of all Magazines, for the satisfaction of Waldensis.[18]

In general, however, when larger miscellanies like the *Universal* or the *Lady's Magazine* published extracts from recent books or essay-serials, if the publication was a new one, they frankly acknowledged their borrowing, since this information flattered readers' desire to keep in touch with new books and periodicals. But later editors, reprinting at second and third hand, tended to disregard the now-distant origins of their pieces, often assigning them new titles, and abridging and revising as suited their convenience. The list of magazine novels and novelettes appended to this study reveals for the first time some of the devious relations between periodicals, the degree to which the lesser miscellanies preyed upon the greater, and the jealous manner in which even the most independent scanned the columns of their principal competitors. The big London proprietors themselves, too cautious to steal openly from their rivals (for which they would have been publicly exposed), were not averse to following them to the same sources.[19]

For example, "The Adventures of Emma, a Moral Tale," which first appeared in four successive numbers of a single-essay periodical called the *Ranger*, in the spring of 1794, was discovered in the collected edition by the watchful Editor of the *Lady's Magazine*, and reprinted under that title and with a full attribution. Several months later, while it was still running in the *Lady's* (and probably *because* it was running there) the same story was also discovered by the *Universal*, which ran it in *three* parts under the new title of "Albert and Emma, an Interesting History," from the *Ranger*. At this time there were at least four other editors of miscellanies who were feeding on the *Universal*. During the next eight months, therefore, "Albert and Emma" was picked up and carried into the columns of the *Hibernian Magazine* (Dublin), the *Edinburgh Magazine*, the *Scots Magazine* (Edinburgh), and the *Weekly Entertainer* (Sherborne), none of which, naturally, mentioned the *Universal*—and in the first two, the *Ranger* itself went unnamed. In them, to all appearances, "Albert and Emma" was an original piece, except that no claim was made that it was written *for* the magazine. From this point, in its magazine history, the origin of the story in the *Ranger* drops completely out of view. In 1800 the forgetful (or perhaps indifferent) editor of the *Lady's* offered the story a second time, now as "Albert and Emma, a Tale," in *two* installments. Except for the change in form and title, the text is practically identical with that of "The Adventures of Emma," published in the same magazine five years before. On this occasion, however, he made no attribution. It is possible that he was ignorant of its real source, having found the story in an old volume of the *Edinburgh* while foraging for likely materials, or that he felt that the association with the *Ranger*, now six years old, was obsolete.

Meanwhile the editor of the *Britannic Magazine*, who also read old copies of magazines, appropriated the story for his running series entitled "Memoirs of Love and Gallantry," where, with some abridgment and a few superficial changes, it reappeared as "Clairville and Emma." Sometime later "Albert and Emma" was also gathered, as an unbroken narrative, into the *New Magazine of Choice Pieces*, a collection of magazine classics. Thus, although it was reprinted a total of nine times in sixteen years, in eight different magazines, under three different titles, and in several different forms, its origin in the *Ranger* was mentioned in only five.

Humphry Repton's "Friar's Tale," a Gothic novelette of about five thousand words, enjoyed an even more devious history in the magazines, although all of these practices were perfectly normal in the eighteenth century. Originally part of a tissue of essays intended for serial publication, the story was included in the volume called *Variety, a Collection of Essays, Written in the Year 1787*, where it occupied three successive numbers. (It was in this same volume that Repton published Miss Seward's two essays on *Clarissa*, summarized in an earlier chapter.) As soon as *Variety* appeared, "The Friar's Tale" was reprinted by Bellamy in his *General Magazine*, where it now figured, with the necessary changes in the text, as a tale in *two* parts. Because of its convenient brevity, and its modish combination of alpine scenery, Gothic melodrama, and romantic love, it enjoyed an extraordinary popularity in the magazines, and during the next four years was reprinted seven more times—in the *Hibernian Magazine* (1788), the *Aberdeen Magazine* (1788), the *Weekly Miscellany* (Glasgow, 1791), the *Lady's Magazine* (1792), the *Edinburgh Magazine* (1792), the *Sentimental and Masonic Magazine* (Dublin, 1792), and the *Universal Magazine and Review* (Dublin, 1792), sometimes in two parts, other times in three. In none of these miscellanies except the *General*, the *Lady's*, and the *Universal Magazine and Review*, however, was the source of the story in *Variety* named; and in the *Edinburgh*, for no reason perhaps except to give it the appearance of novelty, the story was retitled "The Friar and His Dog."

Meanwhile, "The Friar's Tale" had also caught the eye of a writer for the *Universal*, which published in February, 1789, an abridged version of the story, entitled "Albert and Matilda, an Affecting Tale" (2400 words), without any attribution to *Variety*. The shortened version, naturally, went the rounds of a number of other miscellanies that regularly rifled the columns of the *Universal*. The *Hibernian*, for example, gathered in "Albert and Matilda" automatically, without being aware, evidently, that only seven months before it had also printed "The Friar's Tale" from the *General Magazine*. To add to this confusion, the editor of the *Britannic*, in 1799, included the original "Friar's Tale" among his "Memoirs of Love and Gallantry," but under the title of the shorter version, so that the same story in two forms, both entitled "Albert and Matilda," was available to readers of popular magazines. Later "The Friar's Tale" also found its way into a catch-all compilation called the *Gleaner*. Out of a total of ten reprintings of the original between 1788 and 1806, under three quite different titles (plus an uncounted number of appearances of the shorter version), *Variety* was mentioned only four times.

Repertory Pieces

As a result of perennial and partial resurrections like these, there grew up in the eighteenth century a kind of repertory of miscellaneous poems, sketches, essays, and narrative pieces, once of known origin, but now largely forgotten, upon which lazy and indifferent editors could make unlimited drafts. The *Spectator*, the *Rambler*, the *Adventurer*, the *Female Spectator*, the *Lounger*, and the *Mirror* all made heavy contributions to this shadowy reservoir in the public domain, but it was, of course, augmented by hundreds of pieces from other essay-serials, old miscellanies, newspapers, reviews, books of travel, and collections of stories like the *Arabian Nights*, the *Persian Tales*, the *Chinese Tales*, the *Mogul Tales*, and the *Thousand and One Hours*. No piece, seemingly, was too antiquated to bear another reprinting in some provincial repository, or to fill up an odd corner in the larger London magazines. The "Vision of Mirza" or "Inkle and Yarico" was always good for another fling. Even stories from the old *Gentleman's Journal* enjoyed this kind of disembodied circulation. In January, 1735, Mr. Stonecastle printed in the *Universal Spectator* a new "novel" by a lady, at the same time complaining of the importunities of his "Correspondents," who were eager to see their contributions in print. The editor of the *Gentleman's Magazine*, who regularly summarized essays from the *Universal Spectator*, declared that he would "make very short of it," however, because it had been "before printed in the Dublin Papers." Cave little suspected, however, how old the new "novel" really was. It was "Hypocrisy Out-done" of the *Gentleman's Journal* of 1693. In the same way Motteux's "Treacherous Guardian" turned up anonymously in the *Ladies Magazine* of 1750, and "Embellished with an elegant Engraving," in the *Lady's Magazine* of 1791, and probably in numerous other miscellanies published between 1740 and 1815.[20] Ghostly revisitations like these were everyday occurrences under prevailing conditions in Paternoster Row.

The lesser miscellanies, with their restricted circulations and limited financing, were largely composed of such repertory pieces, being compiled, usually, by a single editor-printer with the aid of a pair of shears and a pot of paste. The provincial repositories, before 1800, placed very little emphasis upon "originality," since they were typically addressed to new and unsophisticated readers among whom "Asem and Salned" or "The Lady's Revenge" might still pass for a novelty. The *Weekly Entertainer*, for example, offered as a magazine supplement (at a reduced price) to readers of the *Sherborne Mercury*, ultimately drew much of its early fiction from the *Female Spectator* and the *New Novelist's Magazine* of 1786–1787, a gallery of old magazine favorites. But the record shows that the editor also took in the *Universal Magazine* for twenty-five years, from which he extracted about half of his offerings, after varying delays of a few weeks to several years. Of the seventy-eight stories of novel and novelette length which he published between 1783 and 1811, only one was described as written "For the *Weekly Entertainer*," and only a small fraction before 1800 had not already appeared in some earlier miscellany. About the turn of the century, however, he began to forage in a wider field—thus indicating that his regional audience had come of age, and was beginning to become restive under a regimen of extracts from the London magazines and repertory pieces. Much the same situation prevailed in eighteenth-century serials like the *Aberdeen Repository*, the *Berwick Museum*, the *Caledonian Magazine*, the *Cumberland Magazine*, and the *Phoenix* of Glasgow. They were at least half anthologies of old pieces of proved merit and popularity, of which the author's name or the source was no longer a matter of consequence.

In London, and to some extent Edinburgh and Dublin, on the other hand, novelty was considered to be a basic condition for survival. The larger magazines, at least, all emphasized the number of their original pieces or new translations and their lesser contemporaries in the same cities, unless they were frankly collections of classics, like the *Gleaner* or the *Entertainer*, were forced to follow suit—either by resorting to extracts from new books of all kinds, or by preying upon their peers, sometimes reprinting pieces with such speed that both the original and the copy appeared in magazines bearing the same date.[21] Some London magazines like the *Weekly Miscellany* and the *New London* contain no more that was genuinely original than the provincial repositories; their pilfering was merely more up-to-the-minute. But the leading miscellanies, which operated as radiating centers for the others, liked to preserve a distinction between what was new and what was old, in some cases carefully separating them in the table of contents into "Original Communications" and "Miscellanies." About a third to a half of the prose fiction found in such magazines was actually being published for the first time, and therefore may be considered genuine miscellany fiction.

In our subsequent survey of the long stories of the miscellanies, it will be useful to preserve this distinction, considering in this chapter those numerous pieces gathered from various outside sources under the permissive copyright legislation of 1710 (but reserving foreign fiction for separate treatment in Appendix III); and considering in Chapter V those novels and novelettes that were actually written for, or at least first appeared in the *Lady's Magazine*, the *New Lady's*, the *London*, the *Universal*, the *European*, the *Belle Assemblée*, the *Lady's Monthly Museum*, the *General Magazine*, the *Town and Country*, the *Monthly Mirror*, and other leading purveyors of "original" fiction.

Reprinted Fiction: Works of Novel Length

Editors of miscellanies enjoyed numerous liberties under the prevailing interpretation of the copyright laws, but they possessed something less than perfect freedom. In twentieth-century eyes their plagiaristic practices may seem boundless, but the fact is, that although many magazines were not averse to publishing full-length works of fiction, they almost never reprinted new novels in their entirety. The Dublin periodicals, being outside the law, were governed only by what the market would bear, but the record shows that English and Scottish editors universally respected the copyright laws, with the usual proviso, of course, about "parts" instead of "wholes." In other words, there was a distinct change in journalistic practice since the early privateering days of the *Original London Post* and *Parker's London News*, when valuable literary property like *Robinson Crusoe* or the *General History of the Pyrates* might be fully invaded within months or days after its first publication. Of the hundreds of long stories reprinted in the common miscellanies between 1740 and 1815, only a very few are full-length reprints of novels, and these occasional exceptions only serve to confirm the rule.

In February, 1804, for example, the *Lady's Magazine* commenced the serialization of Catherine Cuthbertson's *Romance of the Pyrenees*, a Gothic romance in the manner of Mrs. Radcliffe and Charlotte Smith, which had recently been published in four volumes by G. and J. Robinson. But the *Lady's Magazine* also issued from the same publishing house, so that the booksellers were really assuming this privilege with respect to their own property. Moreover, the situation was extraordinary. As a note in the *Lady's Magazine* explained, nearly the whole impression of the novel had recently been destroyed in a warehouse fire "after only a few copies had been sold." Not wishing to reprint the work, probably because the expected second sale did not warrant the cost, the booksellers decided to offer readers of the magazine this "new edition" of *The Romance of the Pyrenees*, "no longer to be procured but in the *Lady's Magazine*."[22] It is significant that no other magazine except the *Hibernian* in Dublin, among the many which regularly filled their columns at Robinson's end of the public trough, ventured to reprint *The Romance of the Pyrenees*, despite its attractive subject matter. In editors' eyes, evidently, the appearance of the novel in the *Lady's* was an accident which in no way altered its status as a copyrighted work. The Robinsons followed the same procedure with respect to their novel *The Algerian Captive*, which likewise remained inviolate, except for a brief extract in the *Entertaining Magazine*.

The whole copyright question was in a ferment for most of the eighteenth century, and piracies by book publishers were common even in England, but the wholesale looting of popular novels in their entirety by magazines was obviously not tolerated. The larger miscellanies were usually in the hands of substantial booksellers, who had every reason to respect literary property, and, under the threat of an injunction, the lesser miscellanies tended to fall into line. The seeming exceptions to this rule, when closely scrutinized, are usually discovered to be long abridgments (parts, that is, rather than wholes), printed in some provincial repository where infringements could easily escape the attention of metropolitan publishers—as, for example, the *Berwick Museum*, which offered slightly reduced versions of *The Champion of Virtue* and *Reginald Du Bray*, or the Glasgow *Asylum*, which reprinted *The Necromancer* (1793), within only a few months of its first publication, under the title of "The Conjurer, a Tale," but cut the story to about one-half its original length.

That the policy of the miscellanies with respect to copyrighted works was not entirely a matter of legality, however, is shown by the practice of the Dublin printing houses, which lay outside the law and enjoyed all the heady privileges of literary license. Despite the existence of a thriving periodical press in Dublin, Cork, Limerick, and Belfast, however, there is not a single example in the Catalogue of a well-known novel reprinted in its entirety—no installment publications of *The Recess*, *Cecilia*, or *The Mysteries of Udolpho*.[23] The fact is that the pace of such novels, written for volume publication, was much too leisurely for serialization in miscellanies under the rule of *multum in parvo*. The division into chapters was cumbersome, since they were usually twice or three times as long as the typical installment. Moreover, to complete a three or four-volume novel in the *Hibernian*, in regular monthly parts of a thousand or fifteen hundred words, would have required at least four years. Even *The Romance of the Pyrenees* had required three, and the editor of the *Lady's Magazine* (and his Hibernian shadow) had been forced to double and triple the usual stint in order to bring it to a close in a reasonable term. It is the longest novel ever published in an eighteenth-century miscellany, with the single exception of *Pamela*, noted below.

There is still another reason why copyrights were respected. Some novelty was a *sine qua non* for periodical publications, even in Dublin, and a popular novel like *The Mysteries of Udolpho*, already available in volumes at a circulating library, or in a cheap Dublin reprint, so that impatient readers could finish it several years before it was scheduled for completion in installment form, would only be a drag on the magazine. *The Romance of the Pyrenees* and a few other works aside, therefore, the longest novels published in British miscellanies were all originals.

For very much the same reason, no doubt, older works of fiction were seldom reprinted in either English or Irish magazines after their copyrights had expired. Harrison's *Novelist's Magazine* (actually a serial anthology) is an outstanding exception; it specialized in cheap reprints of the classics. But the miscellanies almost never had recourse to this easy method of filling their columns. This is another respect in which policy had changed in the second half of the century. In the earlier period, we have remarked, among a first generation of novel-readers, a few newspapers and journals had found it profitable to reprint works of proved popularity, like the Countess d'Aulnoy's *Travels into Spain* or the *Arabian Nights*. During the period from 1734–1739 some of the new miscellanies had continued the same policy. As late as 1753, the *Ladies Magazine* had also offered "The History of the Royal Slave," and had contemplated a whole series of reprinted classics in the genre. But public taste had veered in another direction, perhaps because readers were by this time sufficiently acquainted with old favorites to spoil the game, perhaps because recent achievements in the novel under Richardson's and Fielding's leadership made these pieces seem mannered and out-of-date. In any case, the reprinting of the classics of prose fiction fell out of fashion.

There may have been other exceptions to this policy, especially in the form of supplements, but only two or three show up in the Catalogue. In 1793–1794 the *Wonderful Magazine and Marvellous Chronicle*, which specialized in curiosities and prodigies of all kinds, serialized "The Wonderful Travels and Adventures of Mr. Lemuel Gulliver." Reprinted in its entirety, this work occupied forty-five installments. The *Wonderful Magazine*, however, was a low-grade non-literary publication, designed for readers of meagre background and education, to whom it was necessary to explain that the travels were not the genuine memoirs of Lemuel Gulliver at all, but were "in Reality Written by the Celebrated Dean Swift."[24] Other "marvellous chronicles" in the same magazine were provided in the form of abridgments of *The Castle of Otranto* (taken from an old copy of the *Universal Magazine*), and "The Most Particular Fortunes and Misfortunes of the Famous Moll Flanders, Extracted from Her Own Life"—the first Defoe to appear in a British miscellany in over half a century. In the latter case, however, readers of the magazines were left to believe that the story was real biography. The author's name was never mentioned.

The reprint of *Pamela*, offered by Hogg's *New Lady's Magazine*, is a more important exception, since this periodical offered itself as a serious rival of the *Lady's*. Hogg was an aggressive and unscrupulous purveyor of cheap books, a former journeyman of Cooke, the bookseller who had led the battle in the courts against perpetual copyright. Hogg was involved in numerous magazine enterprises, many of them designed to trade upon the reputations of already-established periodicals. His usual method (not exclusive with him, of course) was to fix upon some magazine with a large circulation, and issue another periodical as much like it in content and appearance as possible, appending the word *New* to the title in a transparent effort to lead purchasers into believing that a familiar publication had entered a new series. In this manner he published a series of miscellanies from 1782 including the *New Christian's Magazine* (1782–1785), the *New London Magazine* (1785–1793), the *New Lady's Magazine* (1786–1795), the *New Town and Country Magazine* (1787–1788), and the *New Wonderful Museum* (1802–1808). The *New Lady's* was the most successful and long-lived of these ventures, and it published no less than forty pieces of novel and novelette length, a record for this ten-year period exceeded only by one or two other miscellanies.

The final offering of Hogg's *New Lady's Magazine* was *Pamela*, submitted in the form of monthly supplements of sixteen octavo pages "for the Entertainment and Gratification of our Subscribers and numerous Female Readers, who with much Reason, indeed, lament the sinking State of modern Novels." In the course of this run, which occupied eighteen months, Hogg boasted that the publication of *Pamela*, "the most valuable and entertaining Novel ever written," was meeting with "universal applause" and was accompanied by a "considerable Increase of Subscribers"; and (like "Jasper Goodwill," now forty years deceased) he promised that another "Product of similar Excellence" would follow.[25] But this intention was never fulfilled for the obvious reason that the *New Lady's Magazine*—Hogg's trumpetings to the contrary—was itself in a sinking state, and did not survive the tenth volume. Hogg's *Pamela*, therefore, is really a serial book, offered as a premium to readers of the magazine, and as an easy means of eking out the thinning contents of a faltering publishing venture. It was also a move in connection with *Hogg's New Novelist's Magazine*, found advertised earlier in the *New Lady's*.[26] The number following that in which Richardson's novel was completed was the last of the *New Lady's Magazine*, and no other publishers of late eighteenth-century miscellanies were moved to adopt the same device, although some of them offered other premiums to purchasers in the form of copper-plate engravings, silver medals, and lottery tickets.

With these few exceptions, therefore, no book-length novels, neither older nor more recent works, were ever reprinted in the miscellanies after 1753. But "*reviews*," *epitomes*, *abridgments*, and *detached episodes* were widely recognized as effective substitutes that avoided the practical, as well as the legal, obstacles in the way of wholesale piracy. They are encountered everywhere in a great variety of hybrid forms, and they represent an important class of magazine fiction. In order to give an accurate picture of editorial strategy in the second half of the eighteenth century, it will be necessary to discriminate between all four of these various methods of exploitation, although in practice editors themselves were little accustomed to distinguish between them, and even in the same magazine pursued inconsistent policies.

"Reviews" and Epitomes

In considering the eighteenth-century *review* as a form of surrogate fiction, we have already observed that the critical methods of the *Monthly* and

Critical were also adopted in miscellanies like the *London*, the *European*, and the *Universal* which gave special attention to new books. In the review-miscellanies, naturally, notices of novels were usually confined to the literary department. But in other types of miscellanies they were often included among the "miscellanies" of the month, where they competed for the attention of readers with short stories, essays, and other forms of popular diversion. Since in the magazines there always was a good deal of activity centered on the publication of new books—including foreign and domestic literary news, advertisements in the form of extracts, and epistolary puffs of the kind with which Defoe and Richardson liked to herald new works—it is useful to confine the term *review* strictly to those articles prefaced by a bibliographical citation, that is, by a heading or a prefatory note giving the title of the work, the authorship (if acknowledged), the name of the publisher, the number of volumes, and so on. Such citations in the miscellanies were usually followed by that melange of summary, "specimen," and *obiter dictum* that in the eighteenth century passed for literary reviewing.

A notable early review in the *London Magazine*, offered no doubt as a counter-move to the first number of the new *Monthly Review*, was the "Plan of a Late Celebrated Novel," appearing as the leading article in February, 1749, and consisting chiefly of a 2500-word outline of *Tom Jones*, enclosed in a few critical remarks.[27] But scores of similar articles were published in the *London* and other miscellanies, both historical and non-historical, during the ensuing sixty-five years—usually short, but sometimes quite long. Other examples of "reviews", taken at random from miscellanies widely separated in time, are the notices of *Peregrine Pickle* in the *Royal Magazine* (1751), *Almoran and Hamet* in the *Scots* (1761), *The Spiritual Quixote* in the *Literary Register* (1773), Mrs. Inchbald's *Nature and Art* in the *Moral and Political Magazine* (1796), and *Waverley* in the *Monthly Museum and Dublin Literary Repository* (1814)—all of which were in excess of five thousand words. The last-named, which reached a total of eleven thousand words, and appeared in four monthly installments, was in effect a serial version of the novel, greatly abridged, of course.

Formal reviewing in the miscellanies, however, outside book-review departments, was less common than certain other methods of exploitation closely associated with it and designed to accomplish very much the same purpose—namely epitomes, abridgments, and extracts or detached episodes.

An epitome was a highly condensed summary of a new work of fiction, intended primarily to acquaint magazine readers with the "fable" of the book. It was so common and so stereotyped a species of writing that it constituted a kind of sub-literary form. The historical miscellanies in particular were given to abstracting works of fiction, as part of their encyclopedic function, but actually epitomes may be encountered anywhere, in newspapers as well as magazines, and those in the *Gentleman's*, the *London*, and the *Universal* were widely reprinted. Three examples, taken at random, from a two-year span (1761–1762), when the interest in new fiction was becoming epidemic, are the "Story of Rousseau's *New Eloisa*" (1000 words) and the "Story of Solyman and Almena, An Eastern Tale... by Mr. John Langhorne" (3900 words) in the *Gentleman's*, and an "Account of Sophia, a Novel, by Mrs. Charlotte Lennox" (1800 words) in the *London Magazine*.[28] In these, as in most epitomes, contemporaneity was their *raison d'être*. Rousseau's novel had just been issued in France, and was expected soon in English dress. *Solyman and Almena* (similarly noticed, incidentally, in the *Scots*)[29] was an important new work of fiction just off the press. Mrs. Lennox's *Sophia* was not yet out, but expected. In this case the *London* had stolen the march on its competitors by turning back for its "Account" to the *Lady's Museum*, where the novel had appeared serially during the previous year.

Another popular novel appearing in 1761, and receiving widespread attention in the miscellanies, was Hawkesworth's *Almoran and Hamet*, of which the *Gentleman's*, the *London*, the *Scots*, and the *Universal* within a month all ran competing epitomes (the last two in the form of "reviews").[30] That in the *Scots* was taken verbatim from the notice in the *Monthly Review* of the previous month. The *Gentleman's* was in turn extracted from Newbery's *Public Ledger*, a daily newspaper with some literary features, in which Goldsmith's "Chinese Letters" were currently appearing. The traffic in epitomes seems to have been general. Having devoted a short leading article to *Tom Jones* in 1749, the *London* gave 7400 words to "An Account of a Novel Lately Published, Intitled *Amelia*," in 1751, allowing it to spread into two installments, and this piece was reprinted the following year in "Jasper Goodwill's" *Ladies Magazine* in five—without acknowledgment, of course. The only virtue in all these pieces (the *Monthly Review*'s alone excepted) was expository. Except as abstracts of works in the public eye, they were nothing at all, being merely perfunctory summaries of the story, in which little or no effort was made to achieve imaginative effects.

Not all epitomes, however, were mere summaries. Some were more ambitious, like "The History of Lady Julia Mandeville" in the *London* (1763), and "The History of Nourjahad" in the *Universal* (1767), both of which were of novelette length. The *Monthly's* summary of *Almoran and Hamet*, just mentioned, although technically a review, ran to 7500 words in the narrative part alone, and attempted to tell the story in such a way as to arouse a kind of total response, not merely to satisfy the reader's curiosity. In other words, the character and function of magazine epitomes, as well as their length, varied a good deal with the occasion. Some were offered as book reviews, others were not. Some remained strictly abstracts, others contrived to give the same pleasures as the original, in capsule form. The "Account of *Amelia*" in the *London*, despite its length, was simply a cut-and-dried résumé of events, volume by volume, until the last few paragraphs, when the epitomist suddenly assumed the mantle of critic, pointing out several "imperfections" in the novel, and taking exception to Fielding's political views. But most long epitomes tended naturally to transcend their critical and expository functions, and to achieve a kind of separate identity as works of fiction. "The History of Nourjahad" in the *Universal*, for example, did not bother to mention the novel's authorship or even to associate it with an original, although the book had just been published and some readers would make the connection. It is in effect an autonomous piece of magazine fiction in the popular oriental mode of the *Adventurer*, distinguished in no way from original "histories" and "novels" already published in the *Universal*. The epitome of Mrs. Inchbald's *A Simple Story* in the same magazine, on the other hand, though equally self-sustaining in interest, was offered as a "review" of the novel, and was immediately reprinted as such in the *Weekly Entertainer* (Sherborne) and the *Universal Magazine and Review* (Dublin)—although in the latter, by a cunning change of venue, it served as a notice not for the London, but for the "Dublin-printed" edition. Being a form of miscellany fiction, these long epitomes have been listed in the Catalogue.

The popularity of both epitomes and reviews in the miscellanies indicates that they were read and discussed by hundreds of readers who probably never came within reach of the original novels. Like the "specimens" and abstracts of the monthly reviews, they provided a kind of shadow circulation for works considerably in excess of their actual sale, and thus extend our total picture of their reputation and "popularity." Despite the inferior literary standards of the miscellanies, curiously, the system tended to operate in favor of the first and second-rate. With the whole world of new novels from which to choose, both epitomizers and reviewers were disposed to take their cues from the monthly reviews and other journals of literary opinion, as well as the larger publishing houses, where some canons of taste prevailed, and they therefore tended to bring before readers the writings of novelists like Hawkesworth, Langhorne, Mrs. Lennox, Rousseau, Mrs. Sheridan, and Mrs. Inchbald, rather than the mawkish manufactures for the circulating libraries. The same thing is true of abridgments and (to a certain extent) extracts from new novels, of which we have yet to speak.

Abridgments

Some epitomes swelled to such proportions that they are really abridgments—that is to say, condensed versions of originals, presented more or less in the author's own words, and attempting to afford the same pleasures as the originals but somewhat reduced in scale. Abridgments were always intended to have interest in themselves, as imaginative works, at the same time that they also figured as condensations of new books. In both these aspects of their being, novelty was an important consideration. There were no abridgments of *Tom Jones, Clarissa,* or *Roderick Random* in eighteenth-century magazines, although, after 1800, a good many condensed Gothic romances and sentimental adventure stories were revived for vulgar readers in compilations specializing in chapbook romances.[31] Editors of eighteenth-century miscellanies, however, were primarily interested in *new* fiction—in works just off the press in London or Paris, and particularly fiction already making or likely to make, something of a splash. Like the publishers of early newspapers and weekly journals, they had a nose for the most valuable literary property.

Taking the measure of contemporary interest in Voltaire, for example, *Lloyd's Evening Post and British Chronicle* presented its readers with a long abridgment (16,000 words) of the first part of *Candide*, recently published in Paris. This striking novelty was immediately reprinted by Thomas Kinnersley in his *Grand Magazine of Magazines*—in three monthly installments.

Kinnersley described this version of the novel, which (he said) had already "run through several editions in French" and was "now translating into English," as "a general view of the author's plan," thus presenting it in terms usually used to describe epitomes. But it is really a free translation and condensation, running to about one-third the length of the two new English versions, published by Scott and Nourse, the first of which had already appeared.[32]

A shorter, but much more famous abridgment, one initiated by Kinnersley himself, is that of *Rasselas*, which was to become a *cause célèbre* in the struggle over literary property. This version of Johnson's novel, published in the *Grand Magazine of Magazines* within a few weeks of the first appearance of the book, was the most daring plagiarism of a copyrighted work of fiction thus far published in an English miscellany. "The History of Rasselas, Prince of Abissinia," offered in April and May, 1759, is a continuous condensation in Johnson's own words, omitting a number of episodes and many of the important conversations, disregarding (in keeping with magazine tradition) the regular chapter divisions, but preserving the main outlines of the original story. This abridgment was sufficiently interesting to readers to impell the *London Magazine* in May to present a competing version of the novel of about the same length, much more hastily done, however, and omitting a good deal of the main story. Beginning in the same month, but proceeding at a more leisurely pace, a series of articulated selections from *Rasselas* totaling 12,000 words was also offered by the *Universal*.

Publishers of novels obviously could not remain indifferent to the increasing encroachments made upon their lucrative copyrights by abridgments like these, which were advertised as drawing cards for the magazines, and for which not a penny of royalties was paid. In 1761, therefore, Dodsley took legal steps intended to curtail this form of piracy, by seeking an injunction in the courts ordering Kinnersley to refrain from violating his copyright of *Rasselas*. The delay of two years between the offense and the complaint indicates that Dodsley was interested only in establishing a precedent. Actually the *Grand Magazine* had ceased publication in December, 1759. The fact that he proceeded against this publisher and not the publishers of the *London* and the *Universal*, who were both still very active, may also result from the fact that their versions, though as long or longer than Kinnersley's, had been less frankly plagiaristic. That of the *London* had been disguised as a "review," and prefaced with a puff which would have seriously qualified Dodsley's claim that the abridgment of the novel had prejudiced its sale. That of the *Universal* had professed to be a series of discrete extracts—and after five months had been left uncompleted.

Sir Thomas Clarke, who rendered the opinion in the case of *Dodsley v. Kinnersley*, denied the injunction to the plaintiff, first because of the brevity of the précis (which amounted to less than a fourth the length of the original); second, because it concerned itself primarily with the *story* of the novel, and not with the moral sentiments, presumably its most precious ingredient. But he also laid weight upon the striking fact (to which we shall return later) that Dodsley, as a means of drawing attention to the novel, had himself caused to be published in the *London Chronicle*, a twice-weekly newspaper, a series of excerpts from *Rasselas* totalling 9000 words, a day or two after its first publication. If this series, begun two weeks before Kinnersley's "History of Rasselas" appeared, was not prejudicial to the interests of the publisher, he argued, how then could Kinnersley's version be? Sir Thomas declared:

> I cannot enter into the goodness or badness of the [Kinnersley] abstract. It may serve the end of an advertisement. In general, it tends to the advantage of an author if the composition be good; if it be not, it cannot be libelled. What I materially rely upon is that it could not tend to prejudice the plaintiffs when they had before published an abstract of the work in the 'London Chronicle.' If I were to determine this to be elusory, I must hold every abridgment so.[33]

Sir Thomas Clarke's opinion reflects a good deal of the feeling in the courts and in Parliament in the eighteenth century that the booksellers, in spite of their pious representations, were operating not so much in the public interest as in their own, and that they were prepared to assume absurd and even contradictory postures if it worked to their material advantage.[34]

The effect of Dodsley's failure to obtain an injunction against Kinnersley, naturally, was to invite magazine publishers to exploit further this legal advantage. From this time (1761), therefore, a good many abridgments of novels begin to appear in the larger miscellanies cheek-by-jowl with long and short epitomes. From about the same time, as we shall see, long extracts also begin to appear, like those of *Rasselas* in the *London Chronicle*. The *Universal Magazine*, in particular, specialized in all these forms of parasitical publication. We have already mentioned in an earlier chapter the 11,000-word abridgment of *The Castle of Otranto* offered in 1765 (four years after *Dodsley v. Kinnersley*), which ran to over a third the length of the original. Another, of *The Fair Adulteress*, appeared later in the same year. During the next eighteen years the *Universal* published a number of still-longer condensations of new novels within a short period after their first publication: "The Adventures of Charles Villers, an Unfortunate Court Dependant" (1766; 17,100 words)—carried over incidentally into three other miscellanies which mentioned neither the original novel nor the *Universal*; "The Excursion, by Mrs. Brooke, Author of *Lady Julia Mandeville* and *Emily Montague*" (1777; 15,500 words): and "Cecilia, or Memoirs of an Heiress" (1783; 23,000 words). The editorial remarks prefaced to the last two provide clues to the magazine's methods and intentions. Of Mrs. Brooke's *Excursion* the editor wrote:

> The present Performance is just published, and greatly admired for the Instruction and Entertainment it contains. From this Circumstance, we have taken the Liberty to select such Parts of it as we apprehended would be most agreeable to our Readers, still keeping in View the great Out-line of the Narrative, and only rejecting such Parts as contained either the fair Author's Reflections, or as were not absolutely connected with the Simplicity of the Fable.

Of Fanny Burney's *Cecilia* he said:

> To present all the Characters that are so admirably purtrayed throughout, would neither be within our Power, nor an Act of Justice to the Writer. But we may be allowed to give an Outline of the Story, with such striking Passages, as have a more forcible Tendency to inculcate the best Lessons of Benevolence and Virtue.[35]

The abridgment of *Cecilia* consists largely of direct quotation, but the interstices have been so adroitly managed that the whole makes an unbroken narrative. Through long experience, dating from its early adaptations from the *Female Spectator* and its "Account of *The History of Rasselas*," the editors of the *Universal* had turned plagiarism into a fine art. Each of the four extracts from *Cecilia* was preceded by comments which called attention to the beauties of the episodes that followed, and flattered the reader's interest in problems of practical morality. The abridgment of Dr. Moore's *Edward* in the same magazine thirteen years later consisted of three long episodes from the book, totaling 11,000 words, each installment skilfully introduced by a thread of narrative connecting it with the last, and given a catchy title like "The Excellent Wife" or "Lessons of Humanity, a Conversation." The inventing of new labels for selections like these, in order to underline their autonomous character and point up their special interest to magazine readers, became *de rigueur* in the larger miscellanies of this later period.

Detached Episodes

A number of other miscellanies between 1761 and 1800 (when this practice tended to die out) offered abridgments of equal or greater length. We have already called attention to the swollen versions of Clara Reeve's *Champion of Virtue* in the *Berwick Museum* and *The Necromancer* in the Glasgow *Asylum*, two provincial repositories. The condensation of Helen Maria Williams's translation of *Paul and Virginia* in the *Weekly Entertainer* also came to more than half the length of the English version, that of *The Adventures of John of Gaunt*, one third. But although other miscellanies were glad to reprint efforts like these, they did not typically initiate such pieces themselves for the simple reason that abridgments, like epitomes and reviews, required an expense of time and labor which many editors were unwilling to make, particularly since there lay at hand an allied resource, equally palatable to magazine readers, and requiring no effort at composition whatsoever, except the labor of transcription—if (as seems likely) the printed original was not sent directly to the type-setter. More than half the citations in the Catalogue are simply extracts from books, pamphlets, newspapers, reviews, single-essay periodicals, and other extramural sources that found their way into at least one miscellany, and sometimes into as many as ten or a dozen; and about sixty different stories are taken directly from full-length works of English fiction. Some of these, also, were reprinted many times so that the grand total for excerpts from novels (that is, with repeats) comes to about 200. This number includes, of course, only the longer pieces. A similar total for unlisted shorter extracts of the same kind scattered through the miscellanies from 1740 to 1815 would be reckoned in the thousands. Those from *Tristram Shandy* and *A Sentimental Journey* alone would probably come to a hundred, and by the force of their example helped to establish a new literary genre, the sentimental "fragment."[36]

The little snippets from new novels with which editors liked to garnish their monthly offerings, or fill up an odd corner, like the "specimens" of the monthly reviews (from which, in fact, they were often taken), were typically a surprising incident, a scrap of conversation, an arresting piece of description or characterization, or a passage of practical morality. They were frankly fragments, intended to be of only passing interest to readers. The longer extracts, on the other hand, which for convenience may be called *detached episodes*, were invariably complete stories or discrete parts, which in the original served some auxiliary function, but which taken out of context achieved a separate identity, as serial novels or novelettes. Unlike the undiscriminated shorter extracts from novels, the detached episodes represent a well-defined class of magazine story, very attractive to readers for several reasons, and no less so to editors, seeing that such pieces brought major talent in prose fiction into their columns without the inconvenience of royalties and author's fees.

The typical novel of the eighteenth century invited this species of exploitation, since it abounded in digressions in the form of personal histories and memoirs, in-set stories, and semi-autonomous episodes, intended to provide a pleasing interlude from the larger movement of the book, introduce a new character, or bring readers up to date on the adventures of a long-absent one. Frequently these pieces were also used to enlarge upon secondary themes, or to present in separate but equivalent terms some animating idea of the central intrigue. Seeking a fuller knowledge of that greater world to which he is denied access, for example, Rasselas commands Imlac the poet to tell him the story of his life—which is a self-contained oriental tale spelling out his disenchantment with the world and his reasons for entering the happy valley. Or Mr. Primrose, in *The Vicar of Wakefield*, returning home from the pursuit of his daughter Olivia, attends a performance by some strolling players, finds his eldest son among the company, and receives an account of his adventures during the last three years. These two are early examples of detached episodes, which acquired independent existence in the miscellanies as "The Adventures of Imlac" and "The History of a Philosophical Vagabond, Pursuing Novelty, but Losing Content."

The gathering of extracts from new books and pamphlets, as well as from essay-serials and weekly journals, of course, was one of the oldest functions of the miscellanies. Cave's magazine in 1731 had been founded on this piratical principle, which for prose fiction had received further sanction from the methods of the *Monthly* and *Critical* reviewers. In the words of the *London* in 1771, magazines were "repositories of meritorious papers" from whatever source, and they could not therefore be "charged with plagiarism." But for some reason, before 1759 or even later, the miscellanies were reluctant to exploit the full possibilities afforded by the detached episode. In 1743 Cave had published a long extract (5300 words) from Annesley's *Memoirs* (which he obviously did not regard as a novel), and in 1754 he supplemented the review of Mrs. Haywood's *Invisible Spy* in the *Gentleman's* with the "Story of Alexis and Matilda" (5750 words). Both selections, however, were accompanied by summaries intended to place the story in relation to the book as a whole, and the "Story of Alexis" was considerably condensed. This was true also of other early extracts in the *London* and the *Ladies Magazine*. None was an imposing attempt to take full advantage of the principle of parts instead of wholes. It may be that at this early period the interest of the miscellany audience in long prose fiction was still inchoate (as the slight number of reprintings from the *Adventurer* before 1764 suggests), or that editors only came in time to realize the enormous flexibility of the Copyright Act. But the striking fact is that, however common later, there is no record of any effort in the 1740's or early 1750's to extract such likely episodes (to name only three) as the "History of Leonora, or the Unfortunate Jilt" from *Joseph Andrews* (1742); the "History of Miss Williams" from *Roderick Random* (1748); or the story of the "Man of the Hill" from *Tom Jones*—although all three, in view of later practice, offered very tempting possibilities for this form of exploitation. It is hard to understand, for instance, why "Jasper Goodwill" of the *Ladies Magazine*, who showed an unmistakable interest in long prose fiction, should have chosen to serialize *Oroonoko* and "A Short Account of the Life of Patty Saunders" in 1752–1753, instead of reprinting the recent sensational "Memoirs of a Lady of Quality" from *Peregrine Pickle*, unless he was inhibited by the powerful auspices under which Smollett's novel had been published. In any case, although extracts of all kinds were a basic commodity of the miscellanies from the beginning, and epitomes and "reviews" were common after 1749, the age of the detached episode, like that of the abridgment, did not really begin until some years later, and the first steps, curiously, seem to have been taken not by the miscellanies, but by the newspapers and at the instance of the book-sellers themselves.

We have already observed that Dodsley, the publisher of *Rasselas*, had caused to be printed in the *London Chronicle* in 1759, as a form of advertisement, three separate excerpts from that novel, totaling 9000 words. The first and longest of these was "The History of Imlac." A few weeks earlier the same newspaper had run as a serial story in two parts, "The Adventures of Mrs. Bilson," an 8100-word episode from Sarah Fielding's *History of the Countess of Dellwyn*—certainly also with the publisher's blessing, since, like "The History of Imlac," it was accompanied by advertisements elsewhere in the paper—in this case, Millar's. Publishers' patronage in this form was a major source of revenue for the *Chronicle*, and it is unlikely that the editor would have acted in opposition to their wishes. He had previously shown only a very slight interest in new novels.[37] Presumably it was the book-sellers themselves (Millar first, then Dodsley) who decided that fiction was now sufficiently interesting to readers of the *London Chronicle* to warrant this extraordinary attention. Both episodes were picked up by miscellanies within a month, the first by the *Edinburgh Magazine*, the second by the *Newcastle General*. Except for the isolated and imperfect cases in the *Gentleman's*, the *London*, and the *Ladies*, already mentioned, these are the earliest detached episodes to find a place in the Catalogue of long magazine fiction.

Even then miscellany editors seemed unwilling to forage for themselves, and although the *Grand Magazine*, the *London*, and the *Universal* were now prepared to embark upon a cautious program of abridgments, it was seven years before other magazines followed the *Chronicle's* lead in publishing long extracts from important new novels. First came "The History of a Philosophical Vagabond" from *The Vicar of Wakefield* (1766); next, "The History of a Reprobate" and "The History of an Englishman's Slavery in Algiers" from Volume III of Brooke's *Fool of Quality* (1768); and then "The Memoirs of Mrs. Williams" from *Letters between an English Lady and Her Friend at Paris* (1770); "The Officious Friend, a Tale," from *The Man of Nature* (1773); "The History of Valvais" (reprinted five times within the space of a few months) from Brooke's *Juliet Grenville* (1774); "The Travels of Himilco" from Johnstone's *History of Arsaces* (1774); "The Story of Old Edwards" from *The Man of Feeling* (1778)—and later others, with increasing frequency, until by 1790 long extracts from new novels became a principal means by which editors of the London miscellanies and their satellites filled their columns with prose fiction. In 1791–1792 a specialized magazine called the *Monthly Extracts* appeared which was devoted exclusively to the "Beauties of Modern Authors," and which published within a fourteen-month's span, among selections of other kinds, ten detached episodes from 5500 to 32,000 words in length. During the same period, these or similar extracts from new novels were also appearing in the *Lady's Magazine*, the *Universal*, the *General*, the *European*, the *Hibernian*, the *Edinburgh*, the *Caledonian Magazine*, the *Weekly Entertainer*, and other miscellanies that gave signal attention to prose fiction. The gradual extension of the detached episode as a form of literary entertainment after 1766 indicates a policy of increasing license on the part of magazine publishers. It also suggests an ever-expanding circle of novel-readers which, by 1790, encompassed even provincial publications.

We shall find it difficult to reduce to any intelligible order so miscellaneous a phenomenon as the detached episodes of the common miscellanies. Though somewhat delayed in their general acceptance, they were eventually far more numerous than either long epitomes or abridgments in the magazines, reflecting probably the greater ease with which they were accomplished. They are also drawn from a somewhat broader range of popular fiction. Even so, it is worth noticing that they are markedly superior in quality to most of the "original" fiction published in the same magazines (of which we shall speak in the next chapter), and that the high incidence among them of works written by Johnson, Goldsmith, Sarah Fielding, Clara Reeve, Ann Radcliffe, Henry Brooke, Charlotte Smith, Mackenzie, and Dr. Moore, suggests that editors, particularly before 1800, were governed not merely by what came to hand, but also by the example, feeble as it was, of the main organs of literary opinion. Many such extracts, on the other hand, are not from the hand of celebrated authors, but from now-forgotten novels like Thomson's *Man in the Moon* (1783), *Memoirs of a Scots Heiress* (1791), Rowson's *Charlotte, a Tale of Truth* (1791), Martin's *Helen of Glenross* (1802), *The Idiot Heiress* (1805), Surr's *A Winter in London* (1806), and *The Metropolis* (1811)—some of which even in their own day attracted only slight attention from reviewers. These works seem to have been chosen at random by miscellany editors without respect to either merit or authorship.

Still another factor was at work among the extractors of new fiction, however, which demonstrates the continuity of later practice with that of Dodsley and Millar in 1759, namely, the principle of publicity. To what extent this motive was operating in miscellanies like the *Universal* and the *European* is difficult to measure, since so little is known of the real relations between booksellers and the proprietors of these powerful periodicals. But it is clear from the record of the *Lady's Magazine* that the house of Robinson, which published numerous works of prose fiction as well as periodicals, was itself occasionally inclined to employ extracts as a form of advertising. Of the eleven detached tales and episodes published in the *Lady's Magazine* between 1790 and 1810 (disregarding numerous shorter pieces and extracts from non-narrative works), at least eight were from novels and other works in which Robinsons had a financial interest.[38] Six of the eight were printed soon after the first appearance of the books, and were obviously intended to draw favorable attention to them—as, for example, "The Negro" (1790), described as "an Extract from a Beautiful Novel of That Name Just Published in Three Volumes by Messrs. Robinsons," or the two "histories" from James White's *Adventures of John of Gaunt* (1790), described as "an Entertaining Novel Just Published." The two long extracts from the *Arabian Tales* (1792), on the other hand, did not appear in the *Lady's* until 1795–1796, and may have been intended to help dispose of remainders, or to revive interest in a fading enterprise.

But though the Robinsons were willing to puff their own wares in this manner, and incidentally enliven the columns of the highly lucrative *Lady's Magazine*, they would hardly have approved of the freedom assumed by the *Weekly Entertainer* (Sherborne), which obtained a copy of one of the same novels, *The Adventures of John of Gaunt*, and printed extracts totaling 30,000 words; or the *Monthly Extracts*, whose own two selections from the *Arabian Tales* in 1792 amounted to 52,000 words. It was extreme "pilfering practices" like these against which Clara Reeve, speaking as an author, had bitterly protested in the *Progress of Romance* (1785), and from which she was herself to suffer in the *Monthly Extracts* a few years later.[39]

The detached episodes published in the larger miscellanies, particularly those of the *Universal*, were naturally widely reprinted by their lesser contemporaries, and some of these pieces, like the more popular stories of the *Mirror*, the *Lounger*, the *Observer*, and the *Ranger*, attained extraordinary circulations of this kind. In the earlier period we find Johnson, Goldsmith,

Henry Brooke, and Mackenzie attracting the special favor of magazine editors; in the later, Charlotte Smith and Dr. John Moore—partly because they happened to be writing at a time when extracts from new novels were in great vogue, partly because they were two of the most widely approved novelists of the day. Miscellany editors made generous drafts in particular upon Charlotte Smith's *Romance of Real Life* (1787), *Ethelinde* (1789), *Celestina* (1791), and *Desmond* (1792), and upon all three of Dr. Moore's novels, *Zeluco* (1789), *Edward* (1796), and *Mordaunt* (1800). The publisher of *The Romance of Real Life*, *Ethelinde*, and *Celestina* was Cadell; Dr. Moore's *Zeluco* and *Edward* appeared over the joined names of Strahan and Cadell; *Desmond* and *Mordaunt* were published by the Robinsons (who, incidentally, did not excerpt either in the *Lady's*). All seven, therefore, came before the public under powerful auspices, and won wide and sympathetic attention from the reviews and review-miscellanies of the time. The extracts from *Zeluco* alone, in the *Universal*, totaled 22,000 words, being spread through seven issues of the magazine. The first six were mere fragments, each given a separate title, but placed also in some intelligible relation to the novel as a whole. The seventh, entitled "The Man of Principle, a Character," is a discrete episode (slightly abridged) of 6700 words. Several of these extracts from *Zeluco*, including the last, were immediately reprinted in the *Weekly Entertainer* and the *Caledonian Magazine*, with acknowledgments of the original, though not of the *Universal*, the real intermediary. In Sherborne and Aberdeen, presumably, Moore's novel was better known through these agencies than through the published volumes, which cost, incidentally, twelve shillings.

The most widely reprinted of any of the sixty or more detached episodes listed in the Catalogue, however, was "The Affecting History of Caroline Montgomery," taken in 1789 from Charlotte Smith's *Ethelinde, or the Recluse of the Lake*. The novel was a literary event for some reason ignored by the *Critical* until October, 1791, but given prompt attention by both the *Analytical* and the *Monthly*. In the latter it received the longest review of any of the fifty-eight novels noticed by the magazine between *Zeluco* (July, 1789) and the English continuation of Le Sage's *Le Diable Boiteux* (August, 1790). The reviewer welcomed *Ethelinde* as a work of great merit by an author "so firmly established, that our commendation, at the present time, may be thought unnecessary,"[40] but devoted four pages to praising the novel. This review appeared in June, but in the previous December, the tireless editor of the *Universal* had discovered the novel on his own and extracted from it the "History of Caroline Montgomery," an in-set story which had already gone the rounds of the *New London Magazine*, the *Hibernian*, the *Caledonian*, the *Scots*, the *European*, and the *Weekly Entertainer*, before the *Monthly* got round to uttering its superfluous eulogy. A few months later the same story was also to appear in the *Edinburgh Magazine*.

Because of its surprising circulation through the medium of the miscellanies, this story may serve as a type of detached episode, and perhaps disclose some of the reasons for its extraordinary success as a piece of magazine fiction—though for this purpose "The Interesting History of the Count de Bellegarde" from *Celestina*, "The History of Valvais" from *Juliet Grenville*, "The Pilgrim, a Tale," from Mrs. Robinson's *Vancenza*, or any of the other popular extracts from contemporary novels would serve equally well.

The novel from which "The Affecting History of Caroline Montgomery" derives begins "on the borders of the small but beautiful lake called Grasmere Waters." Ethelinde Chesterville, a virtuous girl of no fortune but "winning manners, and lovely person," is spending the season on the Newenden Estate as companion to her cousin, the haughty Lady Newenden. Here, among the unruffled waters and imposing mountains of the Lake Country, she meets a handsome young solitary named Charles Montgomery, whose genteel excellences and true manliness shine in comparison with the selfishness and vapidity of Lady Newenden's circle. Ethelinde visits the cottage of the Recluse of the Lake, and meets Charles's mother, who unfolds to Ethelinde her unhappy story. All these preliminaries are waived, however, in the magazine extract, which begins directly with the interpolated "History of Caroline Montgomery."

Mrs. Montgomery belongs to a branch of the Douglas family impoverished by the Rebellion. Her father fell at Culloden, and she and her mother, a woman of acute sensibility, passed to the grudging care of her uncle, an uncharitable man of business. In London Mrs. Douglas fell in the way of a young, rich, and truly generous nobleman, Lord Pevensy, hopelessly chained to an imbecile wife. His tenderness and genuine devotion to Mrs. Douglas, added to her own family's coldness and insensibility, led her to accept his "protection," and in time she bore him two illegitimate sons. After some years, the sudden death of Lord Pevensy from a fever left her again friendless, and harshly thrust aside by the new claimant to the title, who refused to recognize his brother's will unless Caroline became his mistress —a proposal which both mother and daughter, of course, indignantly refused. Mrs. Douglas did not long survive these humiliations, but Caroline married Mr. Montgomery, a Scotch officer in the service of the French, and a trusted friend of the former Lord Pevensy. This marriage was a perfect union of hearts, "where only love presides." She bore Montgomery one son, Charles, the hero of *Ethelinde*. Her husband fell on the field at Minden and was given up for dead, but was saved by the ministrations of an English major (later in the novel discovered to be Ethelinde's father). Some time after, following the decease of her husband, Mrs. Montgomery retired to this lonely cottage in the north, where Charles might cultivate his understanding by reading and contemplation, temper his "too warm" and high-spirited nature, and preserve the virtues of his heart against the vices of the fashionable world.

> I have no wish [she says in closing her story] for any other enjoyment than that I have found: indulging in this remote hermitage the tears which the memory of Montgomery renders sacred; and fulfilling, at least as well as I am able, through not so well as I wish, my duty towards our beloved Charles.

Thus ends the extract in the *Universal Magazine*.[41]

The intrigue of *Ethelinde* has only barely begun when Caroline Montgomery confides to the heroine the "mournful story" of her life. Later, in a desperate effort to win a fortune that will permit him to marry as he desires, Charles will sail to India, be shipwrecked, and return to find he has become his lost uncle's heir. In the interim Ethelinde will herself suffer trials and temptations that fill the better part of several volumes, and of which the "History of Caroline Montgomery" is but the prolegomenon. The in-set story occupies only about 9600 words in a novel that totals 250,000. The themes of both are very similar—the chicanery and rapaciousness of much of mankind, the transcendent goodness and sensibility of a few others, and the providential manner in which virtue is strengthened by true love and a life of solitude and country pleasures. But in its brevity and its simple outlines, the "History of Caroline Montgomery" contrasts sharply with the more involved and pretentious fable in which it is enclosed. In these respects, it is typical of most interpolated histories in the eighteenth-century novel, and in these respects also, so it happens, it strikingly conforms to the indigenous tradition of magazine novelettes since the days of the *Female Spectator* and the *Adventurer.* In other words, viewed in detached form, as it was by readers of the *Universal Magazine* and seven other miscellanies, the "History of Caroline Montgomery" is more like "The Triumph of Fortitude and Patience over Barbarity and Deceit" and "Distress Encouraged to Hope" than it is like *Tom Jones, Clarissa, The Vicar of Wakefield,* or even *Ethelinde* itself. The intervening years, of course, had wrought some changes in taste. Caroline Montgomery is more genteel than Mrs. Haywood's Jemima or Hawkesworth's Melissa, more elevated, at least, in her misfortunes, and her family connections and final withdrawal from the world are more picturesque. Her whole life shows a greater emphasis upon tears. Both her person and her story have a quality of "romantic enthusiasm" which the earlier essay-writers would have disallowed. (This, in fact, had been Aliena's precise fault in the *Female Spectator.*) But her history is otherwise very close to the models afforded by a long line of magazine precedents, being a case history or edifying "picture of life" presented in the form of a first-person chronicle. In conformity with Hawkesworth's aesthetic, also, it follows a single narrative line, beginning with the subject's family and social origins, and proceeding with economy and speed through a series of unforeseen trials and discoveries, the whole being designed to "gratify the fancy," arouse "pleasing suspense," and generate a love of goodness.

Some of the detached episodes of the magazines illustrate the effects of folly or vice or expose common human failings or social evils, like the stories of Imlac and of Goldsmith's "Philosophical Vagabond," but usually they exhibit the struggles of virtue and the rewards of love. Like Jemima and Melissa, Mrs. Montgomery is a type of suffering goodness, as are also, for example, the titular characters of "Old Edwards" from Mackenzie's *Man of Feeling,* Henry Brooke's "Valvais," and "Madame la Marquise de ———," taken from Dr. Moore's *Mordaunt.* In the last-named story the counters have the color of novelty, since the Marquise's persecutions are a consequence of the French Revolution. Suffering émigrées were very much in vogue from 1789. But the archetypal manner in which she survives her tribulations, and wins well-deserved happiness and domestic felicity, also associates her with the growing community of magazine heroines from Jemima to Mrs. Montgomery.

Though originally designed for another purpose, therefore, most detached episodes, divested of their chapter headings and redivided for installment publication, presented an aspect to magazine readers more like that of serial tales than fragments of English novels. Viewed in association with similar stories from essay-serials and collections of literary essays, and various "original" pieces written in imitation of the same, they seemed to be anything but intrusions from an alien world. Though one might expect to find the standard two-or-three-volume novel of the eighteenth century working at cross purposes with the prevailing current in the miscellanies, as to some extent it did in long abridgments and in the full-length works of fiction written or translated for magazine consumption, the actual effect of detached episodes, like that of "reviews" and epitomes, was further to reinforce the indigenous journalistic tradition, and thus to strengthen the general taste for magazine fiction. No doubt this tendency benefited the proprietors of miscellanies at the expense of novelists and their publishers, but the movement was not entirely in one direction, since the practices of the miscellanies in turn, like those of the monthly reviews, helped to swell the large and growing audience of novel-readers. Many magazine-readers, of course, already read novels on their own, but others certainly were lured in that direction by the increasing emphasis in the miscellanies upon fiction of all kinds, not all of which was drawn from the province of the English novel. For in their eagerness to answer the growing public demand for prose fiction, editors had recourse also to collections of short stories, essay-serials and volumes of literary essays, popular histories, travel books, and other non-narrative or extra-literary works.

Fiction Derived from Collections of Short Stories

One of the striking features of the publishing situation in the late eighteenth century is the fact that miscellany editors were able to find a much-greater fund of usable fiction in novels themselves than in native collections of short stories. Outside the magazines, the short story in the eighteenth century enjoyed a very meager existence, and attracted almost no major talent. Across the channel, the situation was very different. But in England, despite the overwhelming emphasis upon brevity in all types of periodicals, and the extraordinary popularity of collections like the *Arabian Nights* and the

Persian Tales, new volumes of short stories and collections of novelettes of strictly English origin were relatively uncommon, and greatly overshadowed by full-length works of fiction. Of the approximately 110 narrative works noticed in the *Monthly Review* in the two years between January, 1789, and December, 1790, for example, only six may be classified as collections of short stories, and two of these are translations from the French. This ratio of nearly twenty to one between novels and short fiction was already beginning to alter. Between 1791–1793, for instance, the *Critical Review* felt impelled to give *major* attention to seven new collections of short stories, more than it had thus recognized in the previous twenty-five years. But, again, six of the seven were translations.[42] In the nineteenth century, English fiction-writers were to find an eager audience for original collections of tales, but in the eighteenth, obviously, their principal energies were either devoted to producing works of novel-length, in the approved manner of Richardson, Fielding, Mrs. Sheridan, Mme. D'Arblay, and Mrs. Radcliffe, or diverted into the quite separate channel of essay-type fiction.

Among collections of short stories, the principal sources for long magazine fiction before 1815, more or less in descending order of frequency, were Marmontel's *Moral Tales* (1764–1766) and the three volumes of his new *Tales* (1792); Mrs. Haywood's *Belle Assemblée* (1724–1726), translated from Mme. de Gomez; Keate's *Sketches from Nature* (1779); *Tales, Romances, Apologues, and Novels from the French of the Abbé Blanchet, M. Bret, M. de la Place, M. Imbert, M. Saint Lambert and the Chevalier de Florian* (1786); *New Tales from the French of M. Florian* (1792); Harriet and Sophia Lee's *Canterbury Tales* (1797); Kotzebue's *Novelettes* (1807); Isaac Brandon's *Fragments, in the Manner of Sterne* (1797); Murdoch's *Pictures of the Heart, Sentimentally Delineated* (1783); and Holcroft's *Tales of the Castle* (1785), translated from Mme. de Genlis. Of these eleven, only the *Sketches from Nature*, the *Canterbury Tales*, Brandon's *Fragments*, and *Pictures of the Heart* were purely English in origin. Eight reprintings are listed in the Catalogue from the first, seven from the second, six from the third, and five from the fourth; as compared with thirty-three from the collection of Marmontel published by Becket and De Hondt in 1764–1766, and eighteen from the three volumes offered by Bew in 1792.

The full force of these discrepancies is not apparent from these figures alone, since they do not include other translations of the *Contes moraux* and the *Nouveaux contes moraux* published in British miscellanies, which, if taken into account, would more than double the incidence of both. What is true of Marmontel is also true of Florian, Mme. de Genlis, and Kotzebue. The great interest in continental fiction in eighteenth-century English magazines, especially short stories and novelettes, is more fully explored in Appendix III. It was partly a matter of literary fashion—things French (and later German) being very much in vogue in genteel circles. The *Lady's Magazine* even published some of its fiction in French.[43] But it was also a reflection of the anarchical copyright situation. The increasing willingness of eighteenth-century editors after 1760–1761 to prey upon one another and upon new publications in volume form, and their extreme reluctance to provide a lucrative market for original fiction of real merit drove talented writers from the miscellanies, leaving them in the possession of understrappers and hacks. The result was that, outside the essay-serial, there were no abundant sources of magazine fiction worth collecting in volume form, no sources equivalent to the *Mercure de France*, for which Marmontel and others wrote. The paucity of tales and novelettes of English origin in eighteenth-century collections, therefore, is a partial feedback from the miscellanies themselves.

The failure of short fiction to flourish on its own in the eighteenth century is strikingly underlined by Leigh Hunt's *Classic Tales*, published in 1806–1807. This important collection, which was intended to contain the best short fiction of the previous age, was almost entirely compounded of short novels and detached episodes, stories from essay-serials and essay-series, and translations of Voltaire and Marmontel. Of the fifty-seven "classics" which it included, nineteen are French, thirty-eight are English. The latter consist of *Rasselas* and *Almoran and Hamet*; four extracts from novels (one from *The Fool of Quality* and *Tristram Shandy*, and two from the *Sentimental Journey*); seven pieces from the *Rambler*, fourteen from the *Adventurer*, two from the *Mirror* and *Lounger*, and nine from Goldsmith's *Essays* and *The Citizen of the World*. Of the thirty-eight English pieces that Hunt thought worth anthologizing, in other words, not a single one was first published in a volume of tales or novelettes, or was ever gathered by the author himself into an exclusive collection of the same kind. Furthermore, only three of the thirty-eight, all by Goldsmith, originated in a British miscellany, and these the author eventually collected, not in a volume of short stories, but in his

Essays of 1764, which completely caught the tone of the essay-serial. In France, under different publishing conditions, and in a different literary climate, the prevailing practice was otherwise, and writers like Voltaire, Marmontel, Florian, Arnaud, and Mme. de Genlis found it profitable both to write short narratives, and to collect them in volumes of *contes* and *nouvelles*, adding new pieces in succeeding editions, and ultimately making a place for such fiction in separate volumes of their collected works. But this practice was relatively unfamiliar in England until the nineteenth century.[44]

Stories from Essay-Serials, Essay-Series, and Volumes of Literary Essays

Thirty-two of the pieces in Hunt's *Classic Tales* are drawn from essay-serials and collections of essays. In this quarter, miscellany editors for more than half a century found a rich quarry for magazine fiction. We have already dwelt at length, in Chapters II and III, upon the close association between the miscellanies and the essay-serials. It began with the first number of the *Gentleman's Magazine*, and continued without interruption for at least eighty years. It is one of the most consistent factors in the shifting and multitudinous world of magazines. Until at least 1810 or 1815, readers of common miscellanies expected to find in them new or extracted essays on manners and morals, diatribes against fashionable follies and vices, and narratives in the long-familiar manner of the *Female Spectator*, the *Rambler*, the *Adventurer*, and the *Mirror*. Most of the approximately fifty long stories mentioned in our second chapter (together with a vastly greater number of shorter ones) eventually found their way into the miscellanies, some of them many times. A few were reprinted from their first appearance in weekly or twice-weekly numbers; more often they were taken from the collected volumes that quickly followed. Many of them achieved a kind of faceless immortality as repertory pieces.

Though the *Female Spectator* (1744–1746) and the *Adventurer* (1752–1753) appeared a little too early for their fiction to win the immediate attention of literary pirates, by the time the *Mirror* and *Lounger* appeared, editors were very eager to avail themselves of such long fiction as they could acquire, and Mackenzie's serial tales enjoyed an extraordinary popularity in the miscellanies, challenging comparison with that of his novels outside. This popularity was preceded, and therefore supported, by the rage for Marmontel, under whose influence he was himself writing, but several of Mackenzie's stories won as wide a currency as the most admired of the *Moral Tales*. His "Story of La Roche" was reprinted eight times; his "Father Nicholas" ten; shorter pieces like "Albert Bane" and "Louisa Veroni" probably even more. Along with the "Adventures of Emma" from the *Ranger*, whose complicated migration through the miscellanies we have already charted, and "Sir Gawen" from Nathan Drake's *Speculator* (1791), Mackenzie's stories are among the most frequently encountered serial novelettes from eighteenth-century single-essay periodicals. Their heavily underscored moral intentions, their sentimental themes, and their tendency to follow a single narrative line made them popular with a whole generation of magazine readers who paid them the additional homage of imitation. Editors, also, appreciated the brevity of these stories, and the ease with which their diminutive essay-parts could be transferred to their own columns.

Since stories like these were usually reprinted from the collected editions of essay-serials (if they were not picked up from another miscellany), we should not discriminate too closely between them and narratives originating in volumes of literary essays and collections of sketches and fugitive pieces, which presented so similar a face to magazine readers, and were closely associated in method and intention. The great number of works like Cumberland's *Observer*, Repton's *Variety*, Drake's *Literary Hours*, Pratt's *Gleanings*, William Jackson's *Four Ages*, and Hayley's *Essay on Old Maids* in the late eighteenth century—to name only a few of the most popular—is a further sign of the continuing authority of the old essay tradition, qualified, of course, by changing tastes and conditions. Such collections, even when not Spectatorial in manner, were frequently diversified with domestic apologues, episodes from genteel life, and (a more recent legacy from Sterne) sentimental sketches and "fragments." Hayley's long *Essay on Old Maids*, with three editions between 1785 and 1793, for example, although ostensibly a "Philosophical, Historical, and Moral" treatise, is really a diverting series of informal essays on such subjects as the "Curiosity of Old Maids," their "Credulity," and their "Affectation," interlarded with anecdotes and personal experiences, narrative portraits, dreams, and edifying "histories" which sometimes fill almost the whole "chapter." The novelettes of Hayley's *Essay* enjoyed a considerable magazine run. The two most popular, "The Affecting History of Miss Amelia Nevil" and "Constantia, or Unexampled Magnanimity," were reprinted seven and six times respectively, under a total of ten different titles.

A few other widely circulated stories from this large general class of literary publication are Dr. Johnson's "The Fountains," from Anna Williams's *Miscellanies in Prose and Verse* (1766); Mrs. Barbauld's "Sir Bertrand," from *Miscellaneous Pieces in Prose* (1773), a Gothic fragment many times reprinted and copied, but too short to be included in the Catalogue;[45] "The Abbey of Clunedale" from Drake's *Literary Hours* (1798); "The Friar's Tale," from *Variety* (1788), already mentioned; and Cumberland's "Ned Drowsy" and "Nicolas Pedrosa," from the *Observer* (1785–1790). The last-named story, originating in three "numbers" of the fifth volume of the *Observer*, is the humorous account of a little Spanish Jew, a "man mid-wife," who through his practice became the innocent possessor of a dangerous secret, and was forced to flee the insidious power of the Inquisition. After surprising adventures at sea, he found a happy refuge in England. This sentimental, patriotic, anti-clerical tale, gathered first into the *Universal Magazine* in 1790, was reprinted in eleven other magazines in the next twenty-five years, including the *Town and Country*, the *Edinburgh*, the *Hibernian*, the *Attic Miscellany*, the *Universal Magazine and Review*, and the *Weekly Entertainer* (where it appeared twice).

Extra-Literary Sources of Magazine Fiction

Besides the numerous sources for derived fiction which have already been described, the proprietors of miscellanies possessed still another source, namely, popular works of history and biography, voyages and books of travel, accounts of life in foreign countries, collections of letters on various subjects, and other works largely discursive in character, that included one or more incidental pieces of prose fiction. The increasing incidence of tales and histories in volumes of this general class, especially after 1785 or 1790, is an indication of how far a taste for fiction had spread among all classes of readers. Some unexpected sources of long magazine fiction are Mrs. Thicknesse's *Sketches of the Lives and Writings of the Ladies of France* (1778), James Murphy's *General View of the State of Portugal* (1798), the Rev. W. Hughes's *Tour through Several of the Midland and Western Departments of France* (1803), Pinckard's *Notes on the West Indies* (1806), and Helen Maria Williams's various books on French life and politics. The stories derived from so miscellaneous a class of writing are naturally diversified in subject and theme, but like the detached episodes from the novels, they tend to be unpretentious narratives of fairly simple outline—apologues, pseudo-biographies, accounts of personal experiences or events witnessed by the writer's acquaintance, and stories about historical personages or representative people. The documentary and didactic intention of most of this fiction tended to dictate an uncomplicated structure, and this tendency was re-inforced by the growing emphasis on naturalness and "simplicity" in the last years of the century.

As magazine fiction, some of these stories achieved amazing circulations, probably ten or twenty times that of the original volumes from which they were drawn. "The Tale of Geneura" from Ariosto, included in Volume III of Mrs. Lennox's *Shakespear Illustrated* (1754), which went through only one eighteenth-century edition, found a place in seven miscellanies, beginning with Mrs. Lennox's own *Lady's Museum* in 1760. A single story by Mlle. Bernard, anthologized in Mrs. Thicknesse's biographical *Sketches*, was reprinted nine times between 1781 and 1808. Beginning in 1790, however, the overwhelming favorite among writers of popular history and biography was Helen Maria Williams, who, thanks to the labors of piratical miscellany editors, became perhaps the best-known contemporary author to the maga-zine-readers of her generation. Almost unknown to the popular audience before her *Letters Written in France in the Summer of 1790*, Miss Williams afterwards became something of a rage, and remained for more than ten years the principal interpreter and popular spokesman for political changes in the neighboring republic.

Miss Williams's connection with France really began in 1785 when, living with her mother and sisters in London, she made the acquaintance of a French woman working as a teacher in England. Several years later Mme. Du Fosse returned to France, and at her invitation Miss Williams herself crossed the Channel, arriving in Paris during the first anniversary of the fall of the Bastille.[46] She was keenly in sympathy with the principles of the Revolution (though not with the later bloodshed), and greatly attracted to the new climate of thought and feeling, which she described in a little duo-decimo volume of twenty-six "letters," published directly after her return to England in the autumn of 1790. Like her later books in the same vein, the

Letters Written in France is an animated medley of anecdote, gossip and hearsay, personal impressions, reports published in the papers, and summaries of political events, the whole presented in the form of an epistolary chronicle. It is also a "Tour", in the then-fashionable manner of such works. In it Miss Williams visited churches, abbeys, and theatres, attended meetings of the National Assembly, and, as the grand climax of her journey, described her trip to Rouen, where she met Mme. Du Fosse's husband. Seven of the twenty-six letters in the volume are given over to the "Memoirs of Mons. and Madame Du F———," a story intended to illustrate the intolerable tyrannies of the old regime, and to justify the bright promise of the new.

M. Du F———, whose accumulated misfortunes were destined to become as familiar to magazine readers as those of Caroline Montgomery, published a year earlier, was the eldest son of a despotic nobleman living near Rouen. Marrying, against his father's wishes, the virtuous daughter of a Normandy farmer, the young heir became the victim of numerous threats and persecutions designed to separate him from his wife and child. At length, like Nicolas Pedrosa, a still-earlier contemporary, he found a haven in England, whither he was pursued by false promises of forgiveness. Deceived by his father into returning to Normandy, he languished for two years in an ecclesiastical dungeon under the sanction of an insidious *lettre de cachet*, unable to communicate his situation to his frightened and unhappy wife. After many sufferings he escaped, and found his way back to England. When his father died a year or two later the young baron renounced his title, and returned to France on the very day that the Bastille fell, confident that he was at last secure from the encroachments of arbitrary power.

This political apologue, which is probably authentic in its general outlines, but in which all the real colors are those of romance, was quickly discovered by the editor of the *European* when the *Letters* came under his eye, divested of its epistolary apparatus, and published as a two-part serial story in the December number and Supplement for 1790. Within the next thirteen months it re-appeared seven times in other miscellanies as "The Affecting History of Monsieur and Madame Du F———," "The History of Monsieur du F———," and "Family Pridé and Parental Cruelty"—a striking sign of public interest in the momentous events then taking place in France, but also of Miss Williams's ability to project these changes in terms that every magazine reader could understand.

A year or two later she took up permanent residence in France, from which there emanated during the next ten or fifteen years a stream of similar "letters," "memoirs," and "tours," designed to take advantage of popular interest in French (and later Swiss) affairs, and enlivened with anecdotes, narrative episodes, and personal chronicles in the manner of the "Memoirs of Mons. and Madame Du F———." Most of Miss Williams's apologues, being short, do not show up in the Catalogue, though they were widely reprinted. Two others, however, were of novelette length—the "History of an Emigrant Family," from *A Tour in Switzerland* (1798); and "Perourou the Bellows-Mender," included in *Sketches of the State of Manners and Opinions in the French Republic* (1801). The first of these described the sufferings of Mme. C———, a virtuous émigrée, deserted by her husband, and forced to live by her needle and pen. Later, when her prodigal partner returned, impoverished by his excesses and weakened by fever, she received him without a murmur of reproach. Together the couple found health and happiness in a Swiss cottage, "amid the salubrious breezes from the hills" and "the simple beauties of unadorned nature." Like most of Miss Williams's stories, this one was allegedly genuine, and perhaps did possess a shadow of truth, but the single-minded, long-suffering character of Mme. C———'s goodness suggests that her real connections were not social, but literary.

The "History of an Emigrant Family," after its first appearance in 1798, was reprinted in six miscellanies within the course of seven months. Miss Williams's outstanding success as a short-story writer, however, was "The History of Perourou the Bellows-Mender, Written by Himself," a tale included in her 1801 volume of *Sketches*, and offered as an illustration of "the humble revolutions of domestic life."[47] Actually "Perourou" is a little bourgeois comedy about a haughty Lyonnaise, who had earned the enmity of a large circle of rejected suitors. Intending to humiliate her, they chose a handsome young artisan, brought him forward as a rich marquis, and succeeded in marrying him to the girl. As soon as the truth became known, Perourou was rejected by his outraged bride, and abandoned by the company of conspirators. But by shrewdly exploiting the funds still remaining in his hands from this mischievous enterprise, he made a large fortune as a banker, and in the end won his wife's love and forgiveness.

It is usual for writers on Helen Maria Williams to declare that "The story of Perourou" achieved posthumous fame through Bulwer's later comedy based on the same story, *The Lady of Lyons*.[48] But it is hard to believe that "Perourou" was more widely known in 1838 than in its own day, since, in addition to its circulation in several editions of the original *Sketches*, it was reprinted in ten different miscellanies within a very short term. It provides still another instance, among the many already cited, of stories that once enjoyed an extraordinary currency in popular periodicals but have since dropped out of view, leaving gaps in the total picture of popular literary culture in the late eighteenth century.

The Criticism of Prose Fiction in the Miscellanies

Besides reprinting stories from novels, collections of essays, and other literary and extra-literary sources, most miscellanies also operated in some degree as journals of opinion, directly or indirectly entering the great controversy over the status of the new English novel. The criticism of prose fiction in the miscellanies, however, though very abundant, is on the whole stereotyped and inconclusive, and has little distinctive character. Unlike the monthly reviewers and the essay-critics, the miscellaneous writers on the novel tend to congregate into no critical school. There is no corpus of criticism in the *Lady's Magazine*, the *Lady's Monthly Museum*, the *European*, and the *Edinburgh*—only many voices expressing divergent views, and revealing a deeply divided mind on the subject of prose fiction.

A great deal of opinion was hostile, of course, and much of it derived, naturally, from Spectatorial tradition. Many of the writings of the essay-critics cited in Chapter II found their way also into the miscellanies, in company with the other contents of essay-serials and volumes of literary essays. Cumberland's strictures on *Clarissa* in the *Observer*, for instance, were widely reprinted, along with his stories of "Ned Drowsy" and "Nicolas Pedrosa." But this was only one of many such extracted pieces found in the miscellanies, warning against the dangers of excessive sensibility and deploring the pernicious effects of fiction-reading upon the young. The authors of essay-series in magazines like the *Lady's* and the *European*, as might be expected, adopted the same attitudes, and to their voices were added those of other self-appointed censors of manners and morals, and literary arbiters, who found the conventional letter to the editor an irresistible opportunity to deplore changes in modern life, including the dissemination of the novel. As prose fiction was taken up by the general reader, it became increasingly the fashion in genteel circles to decry its vulgarity. Even in the strongholds of magazine fiction, one frequently encounters essays and letters on "Novels and Romances" that raise all the time-worn objections of Johnson, the critics of the *World*, Mackenzie, Cumberland, and Knox. "Novels and romances are vehicles of pernicious vices" and the corrupters of public taste. They are "the great incendiaries of the juvenile mind." They "sap the foundation of virtuous dispositions and bring up the rear of vicious inclinations." "Novels not only pollute the imagination of young women, but likewise give them false ideas of life"—and so on.[49] These routine animadversions are taken from the *University Magazine*, the *New Lady's*, and the later *London*, but they could be supplemented by others from the *Monthly Mirror*, the *Town and Country*, the *Universal*, the *Edinburgh*, the *Hibernian*, the *Monthly Visitor*, the *Lady's*, or almost any other popular miscellany published after 1760.

In its 1780 volume, for example, the *Lady's Magazine* published two direct attacks on prose fiction. The first, and more moderate, was offered in a letter signed "A Pastor and Parent," expressing serious alarm over the effect of the "everyday novel tribe" upon his female charges, and enclosing part of a chapter from Pratt's *Emma Corbett* that gave (it was alleged) "masterly" utterance to the same view. This attack, since it praised Richardson at the expense of Rousseau, and quoted with approval an extract from a work of fiction, at least tacitly admitted that there were benign as well as vicious agencies within the community of English novelists.

The second attack, however, called "Cursory Thoughts on the Modern Novel," repudiated contemporary fiction *in toto*, including presumably that of the *Lady's Magazine* itself, stigmatizing it as "the literary opium, that lulls every sense into delicious rapture," and "the powerful engines with which the seducer attacks the female heart."[50] This piece was unsigned, and would seem therefore to represent the editor's own "thoughts" on the subject, were he not found elsewhere in the same issue busying himself with five serial novels, arranging for continuations of still others, and promising a fresh supply of narcotics in the forthcoming volume. Such discrepancies were characteristic of late eighteenth-century miscellanies, which not only failed to discriminate between subject matter of greater or lesser importance, making a hodgepodge of their contents without any consistent perspective;

but were also accustomed to offer wares shrewdly designed to satisfy opposite tastes—mixing *tête-à-têtes* and saccharine love poetry, Shandean fragments and travesties of the same, and stern warnings against seduction along with tear-drenched apologies for fallen women and prostitutes. The average reader, therefore, was unlikely to be disturbed by finding jeremiads on novel-reading printed in adjoining columns with his favorite fiction. Probably he simply disregarded them, or assumed that they were not addressed to him. Most magazine stories, it is true, were too innocuous to come directly under the critics' eye, at least on the familiar score of "lewdness" and "debauchery," although a few censors turned their guns directly on the contents of periodicals, and others left no doubt that they were attacking all sentimental fiction of whatever origin.[51]

Occasionally editors took sides in the general outcry over the degeneracy of the age, of which the novel was considered a principal agency. The publisher of the *Monthly Preceptor, or Juvenile Library,* invited prize essays on the loaded subject: "Whether such a love of Novels as excludes all other reading, or no reading at all, is most to be condemned." The winning essay by "Miss Elizabeth Parker, Aged 14," naturally chose total ignorance in preference to "prejudice and error."[52] At the end of his second, and final, volume, the editor of the *Strabane Magazines* wrote an elegaic farewell to a public that had disregarded his efforts to provide "rational amusements" and had gone whoring after novels.[53] But other editors, including those of juvenile magazines, were usually willing to give the reader precisely what he wanted, even when it forced them into assuming contradictory postures. When the program of Gothic fiction in the *Lady's Monthly Museum* came under angry attack from the principal of a leading female academy, the editor demurred only slightly, and then turned suddenly on a schoolgirl who had innocently submitted a "Midnight Tale" to the magazine, sharply reminding her of the dangers of "impressing young imaginations with gross improbabilities, unnatural horrors, and mysterious nonsense." In the following number, however, the "Author of 'Schabraco'" (an offending story) was permitted to undertake her own defense.[54] Subsequently the program was judiciously curtailed, but not abandoned entirely, since the *Lady's Monthly Museum* was forced to please school-misses as well as mistresses.

A few of the critics of the novel themselves risked damnation in order to show in fictional form exactly how the insidious poison worked. Lydia

Languish in *The Rivals* was only one of a whole generation of imaginary young people corrupted by novel-reading, except that they were usually treated seriously. In the miscellanies the pens were all in the hand of Sir Anthony Absolute. Fulvia, in the *Edinburgh Weekly Magazine* of 1780, suffered the misfortune to "live next door to a circulating library," and acquired an avid taste for the forbidden fruit. "In every moment of listlessness," she dispatched her maid for "a handful of novels, no matter by whom they were written, or what they were in themselves, provided they were sentimental." The result was that she became "too tender, too susceptible, too pure, too elevated," and in an evil hour "ran away with a corporal quartered in town," becoming permanently lost to polite society.[55] In the *Edinburgh Weekly* Fulvia's loss of social, status was considered a sufficient warning to young readers, but in the *Monthly Mirror* (itself an emanating center for sentimental fiction), sterner measures were considered necessary. The young man in "The Novelist, a Fragment," suffered an accumulation of misfortunes. As a result of his reading, he married a milliner and was disowned by his family. Persevering in his folly, he wrote a novel himself, "confessed to abound with sentiment and sensibility," "interlarded with obscenity," and incorporating "the most infamous doctrines of the new philosophy." At length, even his wife deserted him, and his only recourse was suicide.

So poisonous were the vapors of the new fiction, in some writers' eyes, that they could penetrate through an intermediary. Julia, the subject of another piece in the *Monthly Mirror*, was turned from the proper path by casually reading the magazine review of a new novel praised for its moral tendency. Her guardian unheedingly allowed her to send for the work, which proved so alluring that she gave herself over to "one long dream of love," and fell a too-easy victim to the lurking seducer.[56] The miscellanies also printed many stories showing how scribbling for the magazines could precipitate a similar train of disasters.

Pitted against the endless tirades of the reformers, and pictures like these of the evils of novels and novel-writing, were a few essays in favor of fiction. As in the essay-serials, writers occasionally raised their voices in praise of the novel, disregarding its worst excesses and emphasizing its admirable features. But in the face of an embittered and uncompromising opposition, spokesmen for the novel usually tended to adopt a policy of conciliation. Frankly admitting the excesses of circulating-library fiction, and deploring the reading habits of young people, they took their stand on the exceptional value of a few outstanding works of fiction, works like *Sir Charles Grandison*, *Evelina*, *A Simple Story*, *Zeluco*, and Mrs. Lennox's *Euphemia*, of which it could be more safely affirmed they they were "drawn from real life" and were at the same time "pleasant preceptors and safe guardians of morality." The overt defenders of the novel in the popular miscellanies almost always took their stand on the score of moral efficacy; they seldom raised the question of literary pleasure. For this reason their criticism seems more dehydrated than that of the monthly reviewers.

Approaching Mrs. Inchbald's *A Simple Story* armed with all the clichés of the enemy, the critic in the *European* effectually took up a position from which he could survey the ethical eminence of the new novel.

> Accustomed, under the head Novel, to encounter every kind of disgust which inanity can inspire; inured to meet with the gleanings of memory, raked together by ignorant misses or their maukish sentimental mammas, instead of a knowledge of the human heart, its foibles, affections, and struggles; and repeatedly, as we are, the melancholy midwives of such abortions of the mind, how happy are we to have an opportunity to proclaim a more fortunate birth; a child of vigour, health, and energy. Such is our present pleasure.[57]

This comment is extracted from a book-review, but the same position was adopted by many writers of general essays on the novel, or of letters like that of "A Pastor and Father." A two-part piece in the *Lady's Magazine* in 1789 called "Hints on Reading," for instance, readily agreed that there were many books published "whose direct tendency is to seduce the heart, and to pervert the understanding," but insisted that good reading was a prime necessity in "an age of mental cultivation" and that a few solid works of fiction deserved a permanent place on the library shelf.

> *Tom Jones*, *Amelia*, and *Joseph Andrews*, are classics, suited to every age and nation, to every capacity and understanding... Few men can say they read *Tom Jones* only once in their lives, and when they say so, they ought to be ashamed.[58]

But again, though the writer classified *Tom Jones* as a work of entertainment, he felt that its real value lay in its truth to life and its moral efficacy.

Qualified defenses of the novel, expressed in terms like these, and emphasizing the edifying features of the writings of Richardson, Fielding, Goldsmith, Fanny Burney, Mrs. Lennox, and even lesser novelists were a very common feature of eighteenth-century miscellanies. Such essays alternated for years in magazines like the *Lady's* with fulminations against the species in general, creating, in spite of the resulting tension, a much more receptive atmosphere than was encountered in the essay-serials. In this respect the miscellanies closely resembled the monthly reviews, though their criticism was generally less literary and more rigidly ethical in bias. Even in the squeamish women's magazines, *Tom Jones* fared much better than it did in the essay-serials. Writers frequently cited it as a classic without denouncing it in the next breath, or removing it from general circulation. One would expect to find the novel warmly praised in "A Short View of the Celebrated Mr. Fielding's Moral Romances" in the *Town and Country Magazine* for 1777. But in 1803 the *Lady's* published a very remarkable series of "Critical Observations on the Novel of *Tom Jones*", descanting upon its ethical truth, its wit and humor, and its numerous technical felicities, in fifteen successive "Letters from an Uncle to his Niece."[59]

The overt defenders of the English novel, however, were far less numerous than its indirect spokesmen, who vegetated everywhere in the miscellanies with a force and a tenacity that must have filled the reformers with dismay. Actually, prose fiction needed few defenders, supported as it was by a multitude of silent partners. First among these were the story-writers themselves, not only the writers of serial novels, but the industrious scribblers of tiny tales and apologues. Their incessant labors were a kind of continual answer to the critics of the novel, especially since most of their fiction scrupulously observed the proprieties and loudly advertised its didactic intention. Very few original magazine stories were frankly entertaining. The first duty of even the Gothic novelists was to be edifying. The avowed aim of "Grasville Abbey," which ran for more than four years in the *Lady's*, was to show that "vice and virtue are their own rewards"; "The Monks and the Robbers," similarly, professed to be a ten-years' sermon on the solid rewards of goodness — with the text taken from Hawkesworth:

> As the dust is to the mountain, so is all that the storms of life can take from virtue to the sum of good which the Omnipotent has appointed for its reward.[60]

Editors themselves frequently called attention to these lofty aims, and ostentatiously refused to admit stories which did not bear an obvious moral.[61] Such pretenses, naturally, could never satisfy the most zealous moralist, but unquestionably they laid to rest some of the uneasiness generated by critics like "A Pastor and Father" and the author of "Cursory Thoughts on the Modern Novel."

In addition to the story-writers, the editors of most miscellanies were themselves deeply involved in the indirect defense of the English novel by virtue of the emphasis that they placed upon new works of fiction of all kinds. Certainly magazine readers would find it hard to accept at face value the blanket denunciations of reformers in periodicals like the *London*, the *European*, the *General*, the *Monthly Mirror*, and the *New Lady's*, when they were invited regularly, in book-review departments, to interest themselves in the latest fiction, and when the notices of new novels were generously supplemented by extracts, epitomes, and abridgments of the same books in the "Selected Prose" and "Miscellanies" of the month. As we have seen, not all reviewers were sympathetic. Those in the *New Lady's* and the *Monthly Mirror* gave about half their attention to new fiction and were very liberal in their praise. Those in the *London* and the *European* were much more conservative, adhering closely to the standards maintained by the *Monthly* and *Critical*. In other words, they frequently deplored the worst fiction, and occasionally welcomed the best. But the final effect of even highly qualified approval was to impugn the position of the extremists, who wanted fiction put out of court entirely. The *Lady's Magazine* seldom published reviews of new books, except to print numerous extracts, but when Mrs. Inchbald's novel appeared in 1791 it broke its rule, and devoted its leading article in February to a highly laudatory notice of *A Simple Story*, followed in March by a three-page excerpt. Readers could draw their own conclusions about the traffic in "literary opium."

The air of qualified approval that prevailed in the miscellanies was also greatly strengthened by numerous obituary notices, "memoirs," "characters," and "anecdotes" concerning the great fiction-writers of the age. Novelists were public figures in the eighteenth century about whom readers were eager to be informed, and editors responded with a variety of articles of a generally biographical character. Some of these were genuine originals, some were reprinted from other magazines, a great many were drawn, with or without acknowledgment, from works like Arthur Murphy's disquisition on Fielding's "Life and Genius" (1762), Mme. Medalle's memoir of her father, published in the 1778 collection of Sterne's *Letters*, and Anderson's and Moore's essays on Smollett in the editions of 1796 and 1797. But, new or old, their effect upon readers was all one. Collectively they did much to enhance the public image of novelists as eminent ethical teachers, artists, and men of letters. In the 1760's and 1770's these articles typically dealt with major figures like Richardson, Fielding, Voltaire, and Rousseau, but later, as the literature of the novel increased in scope, and the interest in fiction became epidemic, they focused also on writers of lesser magnitude. Examples of such pieces, taken at random from various miscellanies before 1790, are: "Some Account of the late Henry Fielding, Esquire" (1762) in the *Edinburgh Magazine*; "Character of the Life and Writings of the Late Mr. Samuel Richardson" (1775) in the *Westminster*; "Memoirs of Mrs. Lennox, the Celebrated Author of the *Female Quixote* and Other Works," (1783) and "Memoirs of the Life of Mrs. Brooke, the Celebrated Writer" (1783) in the *Edinburgh Weekly*; "Memoirs of the Life and Writings of the Late Dr. Smollett" (1785) in the *Universal*; "Anecdotes of the Late Celebrated Mr. Richardson, Author of *Pamela*, *Clarissa*, and *Sir Charles Grandison*" (1787) in the Sherborne *Weekly Entertainer*; "Anecdotes of Mrs. Frances Brooke" (1789) and "Anecdotes of Thomas Amory, Esq." (1789), in the *European*.[62] A full bibliography of articles like these, published in British miscellanies from 1740–1815 would extend into the hundreds, and some were reprinted many times.

The women's magazines in particular liked to dwell upon the lives of the female novelists from Aphra Behn to Mrs. Robinson, the popularity of whose writings with generations of readers bore striking witness to the advances made by the Sex into public life. Beginning in 1807, for example, the *Lady's Monthly Museum* printed short biographies of Clara Reeve, Maria Edgeworth, Mrs. Brooke, and Mrs. Lennox, while a column called "The Literary Spy" in the same magazine gave sympathetic attention to over thirty modern novelists, many of them women. Similarly, a "Cursory Review of the Literary Ladies of Great-Britain" in the *Belle Assemblée* a year or two earlier included notices of Fanny Burney, Mrs. Inchbald, Charlotte Smith, Mrs. Radcliffe, and Mrs. Robinson.[63] Biographical sketches of novelists almost always contained appreciative comments on the novels as well.

The "Cursory Review" and the "Literary Spy," just mentioned, may likewise be classified among the literary surveys or encyclopedic essays on belles lettres, a related form of oblique defense of prose fiction. Such surveys, in which the novel was increasingly accorded full literary honors, were a familiar feature of late eighteenth- and early nineteenth-century miscellanies. They were popular for several reasons. They satisfied the common reader's desire for self-cultivation by acquainting him with the approved literature of his own day and the past. And they sanctioned his special predilection for fiction by giving the novel a recognized status among more venerable literary forms. The "Introduction to the Study of Belles-Lettres" in Smollett's *British Magazine* for 1761–1762, an imposing series of essays on literary taste, had ignored prose fiction entirely, drawing its principal substance from the writings of antiquity. But later efforts of a kindred nature, encouraged by new books and essays on the "Progress of Romance," tended to adopt a more liberal policy. Some typical belletristic surveys of the 1780's, giving marked attention to prose fiction, are "A View of French Literature for the Present Century" (1782–1784), "On the Literature, Wit, and Taste of Some European Nations" (1784), both printed in the *European*, and "The Lady's Librarian" (1787–1789) of the *New Lady's Magazine*.[64] These encyclopedic essays, and others like them published during the last years of the eighteenth century, are themselves signs of the Progress of Romance, and demonstrate how much more closely the common miscellany was in touch with the progressive literary forces of the period than was the contemporary essay-serial.

An arresting picture of the very different views of the novel adopted by essay-critics and miscellaneous writers at the end of the eighteenth century is provided by the separate "lady's libraries" recommended by the Reverend Vicesimus Knox and Hogg's *New Lady's Magazine*. Knox's views are set forth in a larger essay "On the Choice of Books" in Volume III of his *Essays, Moral and Literary* (with nine editions between 1783 and 1787). Entering the contested area of feminine reading via periodical publications written "on the model of the *Spectator*," Knox demonstrated his basic solidarity with them. He gave first attention to "Rollins Works" [on history and education], Plutarch, Shakespeare, Milton, Pope, "the most esteemed historians," Pope's *Homer*, Dryden's *Virgil*, and Melmoth's *Pliny*, coming at the end to the thorny question of "novels" only because, "it is feared, [they] will not be dispensed with." Bowing to the inevitable, therefore, he reluctantly espoused Richardson and Fielding, although earlier in the same collection he had attacked both novelists as likely to "corrupt a mind unseasoned by experience."[65]

The author of "The Lady's Librarian" in the *New Lady's* suffered from no such inhibitions. Like Knox, he assumed a strong predilection for fiction on the part of his readers, but hastened to give it literary status. Vaulting lightly over "religious works and moral essays" on the fair assumption that his audience had probably already entered into such reading, if it ever intended to do so, he proposed to divide his time equally between "novels, poems, and plays." He began first, like Knox, with periodical papers, although they lay outside his scheme. (To read the *Spectator*, the *Rambler*, and the *Adventurer* was widely viewed as a first step towards self-improvement.) But in the second number he quickly arrived at his principal subject, mentioning particularly *The Vicar of Wakefield*, *Pamela*, *Sir Charles Grandison*, and, "for perusal on Sundays," a little French romance entitled *The Triumph of Truth*. The third and fourth numbers of the *New Lady's* "Librarian" were given to Shakespeare, Dryden, and Pope, but the fifth found him back at his old stand, without any visible show of reluctance, praising Marmontel's *Tales*, Keate's *Sketches from Nature*, Jenner's *Placid Man*, and *The Recess*; and in later columns he expatiated on the beauties of Mackenzie, Fanny Burney, Mrs. Brooke, Mrs. Lennox, Hugh Kelly, Mme. de Montolieu, Mrs. Griffith, and others. At length, in his fifteenth paper, taking final leave of his charges, the librarian led them to a recommended shelf of thirty books which he promised would make them "both wiser and better." Of these, eleven were works of French and English fiction.[66]

The marked favoritism shown to prose fiction in "The Lady's Librarian" of 1787–1789, which was strongly fortified by the presence of ten serial novels and novelettes elsewhere in the *New Lady's* during the same eighteen months, did not prevent the editor from reprinting Cumberland's attack on *Clarissa* in 1789, and publishing in the following year an essay entitled "Remarks on the Dangerous Tendency of Novels," which flatly declared that if the whole species were abolished it would militate a long-desired reformation of manners and morality.[67]

The criticism of prose fiction in the miscellanies, therefore, appears to be based not on compromise, but on contradiction. Motivated by an obvious desire to please the greatest number of potential readers, editors, directly or by implication, embraced all opinions on the English novel without worrying too much about consistency. The new fiction, they conceded, was a serious threat to ordered society, and an evergreen tree of diabolical knowledge; it was also a delightful and profitable companion in idle hours, a useful guide to the social virtues, and part of the necessary equipment of a person of parts. Although editors of essay-serials, historical miscellanies, and the book-review journals expected their readers to disagree on many questions, towards prose fiction they were able to pursue more or less homogeneous policies. But magazines like the *Lady's*, the *New Lady's*, and the *Monthly Mirror* could safely presume no consistent point of view on the part of their readers, only a naive insistence on all points of view.

The amorphous character of the large and growing miscellany audience may be deduced from the opinions that we have cited and from the program of reprinted pieces that editors spread before it for its entertainment. Its character is more fully revealed by the original fiction published in the same miscellanies over three quarters of a century, much of which was written by readers themselves.

CHAPTER V

Original Fiction in the Miscellanies

Most of the long fiction in eighteenth-century magazines was published after 1770, but there were numerous earlier signs that the public appetite for prose fiction was maturing, and that editors were finding it expedient to concentrate on long stories as well as short. Only about fifty of the nearly 1400 novels and novelettes listed in the appended Catalogue were published in the period from 1740–1759, and of these more than half appeared first in essay-serials and weekly journals. About 1760, however, a kind of vacuum seems to have developed in the common taste which tiny tales and apologues would no longer fill, nor would repertory pieces like *Oroonoko*, "The Lady's Revenge," or "Amurath" completely serve, since in the metropolitan centers the new shibboleth for success was "novelty." The early magazine translations of Voltaire, Marmontel, and Mme. de Grafigny were one means of satisfying this craving; the increased attention given to reviews of new novels, epitomes, abridgments, and extracts, to which the historical miscellanies, monthly reviews, and newspapers also contributed, was a second; a third recourse was original magazine fiction, of which we have yet to speak.

In all of these efforts, 1759 was a kind of inaugural year, since it introduced to magazine and newspaper readers the long abridgment of *Candide* (Part I), the three different versions of *Rasselas* of which we have already given some account, and the long extracts from that novel and Sarah Fielding's *History of the Countess of Dellwyn* in the *London Chronicle*, the *Edinburgh Magazine*, and the *Newcastle General Magazine*. 1759 was an auspicious year, also, because it brought before the public, as a miscellany writer and editor, the first major talent to enter the field, Oliver Goldsmith, quickly followed in 1760 by two professional novelists of then-greater reputation, Tobias Smollett and Charlotte Lennox. The descent of these three authors into the "popular vortex" is an event in the history of magazine fiction. Their presence at the same time in Paternoster Row lent a kind of luster to this quarter, as had Johnson's and Hawkesworth's ten years earlier. But the brilliance, unfortunately, was only transient. Not one of these writers enjoyed the kind of success in the miscellanies to which he aspired. All three (the record indicates) found their labors disprized, and by 1762–1763 had deserted the field for others more promising, leaving it largely in the hands of extractors, abridgers, and translators, professional and semi-professional writers of less than mediocre talent, and callow amateurs endowed only with a desire to see their writings in print. The years from 1759 to 1762, in short, are a pivotal point upon which events failed to turn, and the withdrawal of Smollett, Goldsmith, and Mrs. Lennox from magazine writing is a portentous sign of the fate of miscellanies and miscellany fiction for the next half century.

Smollett and the BRITISH MAGAZINE

The leading member of this triumvirate was Smollett, since he had actually been the first to enter journalism and made the most imposing effort to elevate the state of magazine fiction. Smollett was an ingenious innovator and literary entrepreneur, and had the times supported him, he might, in the realm of the serial novel, have single-handed ushered in the nineteenth century. In 1756, at only thirty-five years of age, he had founded the *Critical Review*, which, though not yet, in its fourth year, a very lucrative undertaking, was certainly a public success. Like its projector, the magazine was quixotic and truculent, but always more interesting than the *Monthly* and more sophisticated in its literary judgments. By December, 1759, when the *British* was announced as forthcoming in the London newspapers, Smollett was everywhere known as the presiding genius of the *Critical*. He was also a brilliant luminary in the booksellers' world, familiar to publishers and readers alike as a highly successful compiler of encyclopedic histories and collections of voyages; the translator of *Gil Blas* and *Don Quixote*; and the author of *Roderick Random* (1748), *Peregrine Pickle* (1751) and *Count Fathom* (1753), the first of which had sold 6500 copies in its first two years and was about to go into its fifth English edition. It would have been difficult to find in 1760 a more promising editor for a new periodical publication, or an author whose touch was more likely to bring it immediate success.

Of the dozen or so miscellanies published in London in 1759, the leading three were still of the historical variety, with a fairly stable audience of readers totaling, perhaps, ten or twelve thousand. (The *Universal*'s defection was still four years in the future, and the *London*'s, a dozen.) The other nine miscellanies were, on the whole, flat and pedestrian enterprises, a fact which one would like to believe accounts for the uncertain tenure of most of them, although the failure of Goldsmith's *Bee* in November suggests other reasons. Four of the twelve expired during 1759, but 1760 brought at least five new ones, of which the most important were Smollett's and (two months later) Mrs. Lennox's.

The chief competitor of the new *British Magazine, or Monthly Repository for Gentlemen and Ladies*, in January, 1760, apart from the *Gentleman's*, the *London*, the *Universal*, and the two reviews, was Coote's *Royal Magazine, or Gentleman's Monthly Companion*, which had been launched only six months before with numerous signs that it was intended to be a major publishing enterprise. The *British* was to survive for eight years, the *Royal* for over twelve. Although more frankly entertaining than the historical miscellanies and the reviews, the *Royal* was obviously projected in terms of a fairly literate reading audience; and it anticipated in other respects Smollett's miscellany. That is to say, it was a species of general magazine, emphasizing not only "moral pieces" and "Poetical Essays," but natural history and geography, biography, history, travel, mathematics, antiquities, and (to a lesser degree) "political and other transactions." It also boasted a good deal of original material, presumably provided by the editor and his staff. This material, which, like that of the *British*, the proprietors thought important enough to protect with a royal license, included a number of serial features, consisting in 1759 of "A Compendium of Natural History," "The History of the Present War," "The Modern Traveller," and "The Rise and Progress of the Arts and Sciences"—all strictly *informative* in character. To the casual eye the only important difference, in fact, between the new *Royal* of July, 1759, and the new *British* of January, 1760, was the slightly more literary cast of the latter, joined with a marked emphasis upon prose fiction.

With regard to fiction the *Royal* followed very closely the policies of the historical miscellanies. It had published in its first half year, including the supplement, only three short narratives, one of them a fable of less than a page. Furthermore, seven years were to elapse before the *Royal* printed a story of novelette length. In its equivalent first seven numbers, on the other hand, the *British* offered eight works of fiction, of which one was "Sir Launcelot Greaves" in regular monthly installments of over 3000 words, and two others were serial stories of 8900 and 5500 words. Obviously Smollett intended from the beginning to make prose fiction a major ingredient of his new "Repository for Gentlemen and Ladies." This was, in fact, its principal novelty. The January, 1760, issue led off with Part I of "The History of Omrah," a novelette in the popular oriental mode, followed only a page later by "Chapter I" of a new novel by the author of *Roderick Random*—his first effort in prose fiction since *Count Fathom* seven years before.

"*Sir Launcelot Greaves*"

The claim that has frequently been advanced for "Sir Launcelot Greaves" as "one of the first, if not the first, story published in parts in a periodical" is, of course, mistaken.[1] It is an error based upon ignorance of facts that have required (as Saintsbury said) "a very long ransacking of the dustiest of dustbins" to establish. It overlooks a stream of serial tales, serial letters, letter-series, and cumulative episodes through the essay-serials and weekly journals from the time of the *Tatler* to the *Rambler* and *Adventurer*; it overlooks *Robinson Crusoe*, the *Arabian Nights*, and numerous other works of fiction reprinted in newspapers and weekly journals from 1719 to 1742; and it overlooks, also, "A Story Strange as True" and "The Apotheosis of Milton" in the *Gentleman's Magazine* of 1737–1739; "Asem and Salned", "Rosetta and Chamont," and other serial pieces, translated, and adapted, published in the historical miscellanies in the period from 1750–1755. Even if we disregard these numerous precedents and limit our view strictly to popular magazines, the claim is still greatly exaggerated, since it ignores the early miscellany fiction of the *Ladies' Diary* and the *Records of Love*, the several serial novels and novelettes of the *Weekly Amusement*, the *Oxford Magazine*, and the *Universal Spy* in the period from 1734–1739, and the various long stories ranging upwards of five thousand words listed in the Catalogue and printed in the *Penny Medley* of 1746, the two earlier *British Magazines*, the *Edinburgh Magazine*, the *Newcastle General Magazine*, the *Ladies Magazine*, the *Royal Magazine* of 1750–1751, the *Magazine of Magazines* (Limerick), the *Grand Magazine of Universal Intelligence*, and Kinnersley's *Grand Magazine of Magazines*—all published before 1760. The abridgments of *Rasselas* and *Candide* in the last-named both preceded "Sir Launcelot Greaves" by a number of months, and even the *Royal Magazine* had published one tiny tale in two parts in July-August, 1759.

Far from being anything like the first serial story in a British periodical, therefore, Smollett's novel comes at the end of a complicated process of development extending over more than fifty years. Nevertheless "Sir Launcelot Greaves" did sharply break with precedent in a number of ways, which must have been plain to every purchaser of the *British Magazine* in 1760. It is these forgotten innovations which underlie the excessive and too-simple claims which were later made for Smollett's story as a magazine novel.

In the first place, Smollett's book broke new ground in being a long piece of original fiction written expressly for publication in a British magazine.[2] To find important antecedents for "Sir Launcelot" simply within the same range of magnitude (85,000 words), we find it necessary to turn back more than twenty years to the long translations of Montemayor, Lope de Vega, and others in *Applebee's* of the 1730's, Crébillon's "Tanzai and Neadarne" in the *Weekly Amusement*, the "History of Madagascar" in the *Universal Spy*, and "Oroonoko" in the *Oxford Magazine*—all published before 1740, and none of them genuine originals. The only intervening story of comparable length was Mrs. Behn's novel in the *Ladies Magazine* of 1753 (30,500 words). Judged by the record, therefore, not of the whole century, but of the previous two decades, the two-volume length of "Sir Launcelot" was a startling innovation, its nearest equivalent, after "The History of the Royal Slave," being "Candide" (15,800 words) in the *Grand Magazine*, Crébillon's "Letters of the Marchioness de M———" (left uncompleted at 13,500) in the *Weekly Magazine*, and Mrs. Haywood's "Triumph of Fortitude and Patience" (13,500) in the *Female Spectator*. Moreover, of these three pieces only the last-named was a *new* work of fiction. The other two are both translations.

In addition to its ambitious scale, Smollett's book was extraordinary in being conceived and written for installment publication, and (like the famous serial novels of the nineteenth century, which it anticipates) being already half in print before the end was even in sight. According to the well-known account given by Sir Walter Scott,

> Smollett appears to have executed his task with very little premeditation. During a part of the time he was residing at Paxton, in Berwickshire, on

> a visit to the late George Home, Esq., and when post-time drew near, he used to retire for half an hour, to prepare the necessary quantity of *copy*, as it is technically called in the printing-house, which he never gave himself the trouble to correct, or even to read over.[3]

Lewis M. Knapp has exploded the possibility of Smollett's residence at Paxton in 1760–1761, but he believes that Scott's account may be true in part—that is, that Home may have observed Smollett writing in this manner at Scotston or in Edinburgh,[4] Certainly the novel does display signs of hasty composition, and the contents of Chapters XIX and XX indicate that they were written during or after the novelist's confinement in the King's Bench Prison in the late autumn and winter of 1760, a year after the story had begun its run in the *British*. "Sir Launcelot Greaves," therefore, was planned as well as printed as a serial story, like the letter-series and cumulative episodes of the old essay-serials and weekly journals, and like the two early experiments in the *Gentleman's Magazine* of 1737–1739. In the intervening twenty years, it is true, a good deal of genuine serial fiction had been written expressly for the magazines, but all of it was much shorter than "Sir Launcelot Greaves." For at least a generation before Smollett offered his novel in the *British*, new serial stories even a tenth as long were extremely rare. After 1760–1761 they became much more common—although we are permitted to doubt whether "Sir Launcelot" was the principal factor in this change, which was a phenomenon of much wider implication.

Furthermore, "Sir Launcelot" is unique in being the new work of a novelist of established reputation. The only important exception during the previous twenty years is again Mrs. Haywood, who produced the *Female Spectator* at the zenith of her reputation as a novelist and dramatist. Smollett's move, however, was much more remarkable. Not only was he a writer with a talent greatly superior to hers, but the brilliant new achievements in the novel form since the time of the *Female Spectator* had made novelists public figures to a degree hardly foreseen in 1744. After the *Female Spectator* and a short-lived experiment in 1746 with a different type of essay-serial, called the *Parrot*, Mrs. Haywood had deserted journalism and returned to what must have proved the more lucrative career of a novelist and general author; and Hawkesworth in 1754, having made his reputation in the *Adventurer*, had moved in the same direction. In attempting to reverse Hawkesworth's movement, Smollett was taking a bold step, predicated on a new reading of the contemporary situation. In the *British Magazine* he assumed what earlier miscellany editors had not, namely, that readers would be attracted to the magazine in large numbers by the presence of full-length works of original fiction, and, furthermore, that the name of an established novelist like himself and the assistance of a man of Goldsmith's gifts would make his new periodical particularly acceptable to those literate circles for which its other serial features were designed, "The History of Canada," "The History of the Present War," "The Study of Belles Lettres," and so on. Smollett's last novel, published in 1753, had been a financial disappointment. This was probably a factor in his decision to attempt a long work of magazine fiction, but the number of other imposing features with which the *British* was freighted, works which the proprietors went to considerable expense to obtain and protect, shows that they had expectations of a good profit from the *British Magazine*. It was a capital enterprise in which Smollett's reputation as novelist was a major investment.

Strictly speaking, of course, "The Life and Adventures of Sir Launcelot Greaves" was an anonymous work of fiction. As with his earlier fiction, Smollett did not lend his name directly to the book, and (for some reason) did not even identify it in the *British* as written by the "Author of *Roderick Random*," as he had *Count Fathom* in volume form, and as he later labeled the trade edition of "Sir Launcelot." It is difficult to account for this apparent negligence, except to observe that the tradition for original miscellany fiction (strongly supported by venerable precedents in the essay-serials and weekly journals) was overwhelmingly in favor of anonymity, and that none of the other serial features of the *British* were signed—one of which, at least, is believed by Louis Martz to be by Smollett.[5] Nevertheless, the magazine as a whole was advertised as "By T. Smollett, M.D." (except for the early abstract serials, an unprecedented step),[6] and readers were evidently expected to draw their own conclusions about "Sir Launcelot" and its other contents, or to learn the news by hearsay of the kind represented by Goldsmith's puff in the *Public Ledger* of February 16, 1760.

In this sketch, entitled "Description of a Wow-wow," which followed by two weeks the appearance of the second number of the new magazine, the essayist (who was also anonymous, of course) described how, tired of village life and of himself, he took refuge in a country town hoping to find there a happy "mean between London and the country." Unfortunately, however, the only diversion the place afforded was the so-called "Wow, wow," that is a monthly gathering of townspeople at a public house "to read the newspapers and to hear the tittle-tattle of the day." Here he found the present war being heatedly discussed (note "The History of the Present War" in the *British*), and other public questions so bitterly mooted that a local outbreak was threatened—whereupon

> an Oxford scholar, led there by curiosity, pulled a new magazine out of his pocket, in which he said there were some pieces extremely curious and that deserved their attention. He then read the "Adventures of Sir Launcelot Greaves," to the entire satisfaction of the audience, which being finished, he threw the pamphlet on the table: "That piece, gentlemen," says he, "is written in the very spirit and manner of Cervantes; there is great knowledge of human nature, and evident marks of the master in almost every sentence; and from the plan, the humor, and the execution, I can venture to say that it dropped from the pen of the ingenious Dr. ———." Everyone was pleased with the performance, and I was particularly gratified in hearing all the sensible part of the company give orders for the *British Magazine*.[7]

If "Sir Launcelot Greaves," however, was a new departure because it dropped from the pen of an ingenious celebrity, it is even more surprising in point of merit. Here Smollett took his most sanguine view of the magazine audience. The novel has never been a favorite in the Smollett canon, but in the pedestrian and highly derivative world of miscellany fiction from 1740 to 1760, to say nothing of the succeeding sixty years, it represents a pinnacle of achievement, outstanding for its range of interest and allusiveness, its multiple relevance to contemporary life, and, however fluctuating, the maturity of its literary craftsmanship—especially the marked attention which it paid to the requirements of serial publication. Smollett, for example, divided his novel into twenty-five "chapters." This was itself in 1760 a striking importation from the alien world of the English novel. Furthermore, he gave particular meaning to this typographical innovation by making every installment of his novel at least full chapter-length. All of the traditional diminutive effects of magazine fiction were jettisoned in a work of serial fiction in which the average installment was 3400 words, rather than 2000 (or as was more usual, 1000 to 1500). Moreover, what is doubly surprising about "Sir Launcelot" is the fact that the chapters are lengthy even for Smollett. Those of *Roderick Random*, for instance, average 2500 words; those of *Peregrine Pickle* and *Count Fathom* (excluding the several interpolated "memoirs") run only a shade more or less than this average. In writing "Sir Launcelot" in monthly parts for the *British*, however, instead of maintaining his usual scale or reducing it further in order to meet conventional expectations, Smollett actually extended his normal limits by nearly forty per cent. This was hardly the result of someone else's appetite for copy, since Smollett was his own editor. We may presume, therefore, that it represents a voluntary decision on his part to make the installments of "Sir Launcelot" count for more than the usual "chapter" in a Smollett novel.

The chapters of *Roderick Random*, *Peregrine Pickle*, and *Count Fathom*, unlike those of *Joseph Andrews* and *Tom Jones*, are on the whole fairly perfunctory divisions of the story. Typically they represent merely superparagraphs or larger segments of a narrative line which advances steadily with little or no concern for typographical amenities. They received, in fact, such slight recognition from the story-teller that it would be easy to believe that they were actually inserted in the printer's copy, or at some final stage. In "Sir Launcelot Greaves," however, we discover numerous signs of Fielding's influence, and one is the author's recognition of the integrity of the chapter unit, which was often opened and closed with a formal flourish, and (what is more important) was normally viewed as the natural limits of an episode or a series of related incidents. At the beginning of his novel, Smollett failed to maintain a perfect balance between the monthly parts, which range irregularly from 5000 words (Chapter III) to 1850 (Chapter VI). Such discrepancies were also typical of the chapter lengths in the novels. But commencing with Chapter VII he seems to have found his stride, and thereafter the monthly parts seldom varied more than a page from the archetypal length of 3400 words, now firmly fixed in his mind.

But though Smollett was at first somewhat uncertain in managing the physical limits of his installments, he was never in doubt about what a magazine "chapter" ought to represent in imaginative terms. From the very beginning of the book a kind of episodic principle prevailed. Although the novelist often wrote in haste, and may never even have read over his copy, he seems in general to have felt in "Sir Launcelot" that his purpose *ought* to be to produce a story, the single parts of which, like those of the cumulative episodes and letter-series of the old essay-serials, would achieve a degree of autonomy, and in which the reader would be led to anticipate what was to come without experiencing undue frustration over the necessary interruptions in the story. This balance in "Sir Launcelot" between discrete and cumulative effects was fairly consistently maintained throughout.

Chapter I, for example, sets the famous scene in the Black Lion Inn on the great north road, and introduces with a good deal of animation several important characters. The humors of this scene, very pleasant in its own right, are terminated by loud screams outside and a violent knocking at the door —the reason for which readers are asked good-naturedly to await until the following month.

In Chapter II "the hero of these adventures makes his first appearance on the stage of action." His startling "equipage" is described, and he is moved to explain his mission as knight-errant in the cause of justice and benevolence. This apology invites an interest in his "Story", with which Tom Clarke happens to be acquainted, and of "which the reader, if he be so minded, may partake in the next chapter."

The interpolated history of Sir Launcelot is a long one—longer by several thousand words than either "The History of Mrs. Bilson" or "The Adventures of Imlac," recently reprinted in the *London Chronicle*. It occupies three full installments in the *British Magazine*. But instead of being simply segmented as a serial tale, as contemporary practice authorized, Smollett's story (like the inset stories of Fielding's *Tom Jones* and *Joseph Andrews*) is interrupted with comments by listeners and byplay that give to each chapter something of the quality of an episode. Chapter VI resumes the present action of the novel, which thereafter unfolds scene by scene, event by event, sometimes haphazardly, no doubt, but never disregarding for long the episodic principle.

The tediousness of some of Smollett's "chapters," and the obvious discontinuities of *Sir Launcelot Greaves*, the two-volume novel, have tended to obscure the definite merits of "Sir Launcelot Greaves," the magazine story —in which respect the book was many years ahead of its time. One wonders what conventional miscellany readers were able to make, in 1760, of a serial novel that was at the same time episodic and cumulative, and that demanded so unexpected an interest in so many aspects of eighteenth-century life. The story of Sir Launcelot involves not only a love story in which two well-born lovers are at last united after prolonged separation and suffering (a genteel

THE

BRITISH MAGAZINE,

For FEBRUARY, 1760.

THE

LIFE AND ADVENTURES OF SIR LAUNCELOT GREAVES.

CHAP. II.

In which the hero of these adventures makes his first appearance on the stage of action.

THE outward door of the Black Lion had already sustained two dreadful shocks; but at the third it flew open, and in stalked an apparition, that smote the hearts of our travellers with fear and trepidation. It was the figure of a man armed cap-a-pie, bearing on his shoulder a bundle dropping with water, which afterwards appeared to be the body of a man that seemed to have been drowned, and fished up from the bottom of the neighbouring river. Having deposited his burthen carefully on the floor, he addressed himself to the company in these words: "Be not surprised, good people, at this unusual appearance, which I shall take an opportunity to explain; and forgive the rude and boisterous manner in which I have demanded, and indeed forced admittance. The violence of my intrusion was the effect of necessity. In crossing the river, my squire and his horse were swept away by the stream; and

An Installment of Smollett's "Sir Launcelot Greaves"

stereotype for which readers were amply prepared), but crowded scenes in market-towns and villages, country houses, jails, and inns along the London road. Like *Joseph Andrews* and *Tom Jones*, which had as yet no following whatsoever among magazine writers, "Sir Launcelot" is a species of topical novel, which draws serious attention to the workings of country justice, the absurdities of parliamentary elections, the quality of life in the new King's Bench Prison, and the abuses of private madhouses. The tiny dream visions and allegories of the weekly journals and essay-serials, of course, had often had an immediate relevance to some aspect of the contemporary situation, usually a political or moral one, but not since the time of Defoe (and then only in short pieces) had magazine fiction reflected eighteenth-century life in such diversity, and never (outside the essay-serials, and *there* in a very different manner) had it been so sophisticated in its literary methods.

Far too much has been made of Smollett's alleged failure in judgment in adopting a plan calling for the use of armor in eighteenth-century England. It is an objection, so far as is known, that was never raised in the author's own time, though the novel was ill-received. First uttered by Scott in 1817, this criticism is understandable in an antiquarian and historical novelist always disposed to take armor very seriously, but less so in later critics, including Saintsbury, who have allowed this doubtful prepossession to blunt their full understanding of Smollett's satirical purpose.

In the first place, this time-worn objection places far too great an emphasis upon helmets and breastplates, fighting, and jousting, which are not really the mainspring of the action, but auxiliary features of the novel. Sir Launcelot's armor figures only sporadically in the main intrigue, and drops completely out of view after Chapter XIX. Secondly, it fails to recognize that this device is a satirical donnée of the story, which once accepted (and, as Smollett presents it, it requires no impossible effort of the imagination to do so) permits a wide range of artistic effects, effects which would not have been possible had Smollett written the kind of novel that Scott and Saintsbury proposed. Captain Crowe's seizure is grotesque. Its lack of motivation is no doubt a calculated incongruity. It is a lunatic obsession whose real purpose is to underline Sir Launcelot's more serious mission. As Beattie noted as early as 1764, Sir Launcelot though a type of Don Quixote is not himself a ludicrous figure[8]. On the contrary he is handsome and manly, and, armed cap-à-pie, a figure designed to command our respect and admiration, as well as to startle us.

> I am neither an affected imitator of Don Quixote [Sir Launcelot declares in his apology], nor, as I trust in heaven, visited by that spirit of lunacy so admirably displayed in the fictitious character exhibited by the inimitable Cervantes. I have not yet encountered a windmill for a giant; nor mistaken this public house for a magnificent castle... I see and distinguish objects as they are discerned and described by other men. I reason without prejudice, can endure contradiction, and, as the company perceives, even bear impertinent censure without passion or resentment. I quarrel with none but the foes of virtue and decorum, against whom I have declared perpetual war, and them I will every where attack as the natural enemies of mankind.[9]

This note of super-sanity is the dominant one of the book, in which Sir Launcelot is only occasionally viewed as the crazed lover of Miss Darnel. Most of the time he is (as Tom Clarke says) "the best-natured, worthy, generous gentleman," and the champion of inspired ideals which excite the sympathy of every reader.

> I do purpose... to act as a coadjutor to the law, and even to remedy evils which the law cannot reach; to detect fraud and treason, abase insolence, mortify pride, discourage slander, disgrace immodesty, and stigmatize ingratitude...

Furthermore, Sir Launcelot's armor (unlike Captain Crowe's and Sycamore's) is presented as having a multi-level reference to his heroic mission. First of all, since he rides alone, except for his incompetent squire, it is a defense against criminal violence and the frenzy of mobs—a precaution that is amply warranted by events in the novel. Second, it is a self-imposed discipline on the part of a sensitive man badly shaken by perverse circumstances; and third, it is an amiable caprice, which falls far short of lunacy and self-delusion.

> Some ride with blunderbusses [Sir Launcelot explains], some with pistols, some with swords, according to their various inclinations. Mine is to wear the armour of my forefathers: perhaps I use them to exercise, in order to accustom myself to fatigue, and strengthen my constitution: perhaps I assume them for a frolick.

Finally, Sir Launcelot's armor also serves a ceremonial function in connection with his role as a "general redresser of grievances" outside the political arena. Sir Launcelot (as it were) girds himself with truth, and wears the breastplate of righteousness in the social sphere. His armor is a badge of his "truly British principles"—that is, of a patriotism which in the parliamentary election rejects both the venal whiggery of Vanderpelft and the ignorant and debased Jacobitism of Quickset. It calls, symbolically, for a return to the enlarged ideals of a former age, shorn of its romantic absurdities.[10] When Sir Launcelot is in armor he is always heroic, and the prime mover in numerous acts of justice and benevolence that win our full approbation. His romantic posture everywhere arouses amazement in the book, but excites the contempt only of people like the ignoble Ferret, whose opinion of Sir Launcelot, taken out of context, is for some reason always cited by critics of the novel.

The influence of "Sir Launcelot Greaves" on other magazine writers bears no relation to its extraordinary merits as a serial novel or as a work of creative imagination. Judged by the record of the Catalogue it came to almost nothing. Though it ran without interruption for two years in an important new miscellany, figuring frequently as the leading article, and was several times enhanced with engraved illustrations (another unprecedented mark of attention for a work of magazine fiction), it evoked almost no contemporary comment except Goldsmith's, had no visible impact upon the public taste, and attracted at best two imitators, unless we count Mrs. Lennox's "Harriot and Sophia" as a third. The first of these was "The Fortune-Hunter," a satirical-sentimental novel of six "chapters," inaugurated in the rival *Royal Female Magazine* in July, 1760, the monthly installments of which were constructed upon identical episodic principles. The startling novelty of Smollett's methods in 1760 is indicated by the extravagant claims made on behalf of "The Fortune-Hunter" by the editor of the magazine, at a time when "Sir Launcelot Greaves" was already six months under way. Describing the new work of fiction scheduled to begin its run in the same number, he wrote:

> To heighten the variety even of so various a scene [i.e., the magazine as a whole], in this volume will be given a novel, divided in such a manner, that the portion, in each number, shall make a complete story, in itself, without torturing curiosity, by abruptly breaking off, in the most affecting parts, (the design of which conduct is too plain) at the same time, that such a connection shall be preserved, as shall interest the Mind

to unravel the complicated account of the whole: to every division of which novel, shall be prefixed a print of the most striking scene, in it, executed by the most eminent hands.[11]

But though obviously motivated by the example of "Sir Launcelot Greaves," "The Fortune-Hunter" only feebly fulfills the promise of this program, which was also adopted in "The Disasters of Tantarobobus," a coarsely facetious novel in parts, offered in the *Universal Museum* in 1762, and written (it would seem) under the joint influences of Smollett and Sterne. Here again the "chapters" were regarded as narrative units. Both these works of fiction, however, dropped stillborn into the world. Neither, as far as is known, was ever claimed by any author. Neither was ever imitated in turn, nor (though given major emphasis in its own periodical) was ever thought worth pirzting in its entirety.[12] From this period, other original novels of some length gradually began to find their way into British miscellanies, some of them divided into "chapters." But usually they were modeled, not upon "Sir Launcelot Greaves," but upon the growing corpus of sentimental fiction for which Richardson, Sterne, and Mackenzie provided the principal models. Moreover, almost all were written by amateurs, or by obscure professionals whose identity was never made known to readers. When "Sir Launcelot" completed its run in December, 1761, no other novelist of reputation came forward in the *British* or in any other miscellany (Mrs. Lennox excepted) with a comparable piece of serial fiction, and when Smollett retired from the magazine for reasons of health in 1763, he was replaced by an editor whose name was never revealed.

The original emphasis on fiction in the *British* was more or less maintained after Smollett's departure. During 1763, for example, the magazine published nine short tales and apologues (mostly essay-type fiction), and one novelette, "The Triumph of Virtue," lifted without acknowledgement from the *Universal Magazine* of 1759. Two years later, in 1765, it published fourteen short stories and two longer pieces (taken from Smollett's edition of Voltaire, and the *Moral Tales* of Marmontel). From this time, the principal fiction of the *British*, with the exception of one amateur effort in 1768, was all extracted from other periodicals, new novels, or already published collections. In other words, the magazine, once its distinguished editor withdrew, immediately relapsed into the ways of its leading competitors, the *Universal*, the *Royal*, the *Court, City and Country Magazine*, and the new *Weekly*

Amusement, not one of which showed the slightest disposition to follow Smollett's lead. The last-named, a popular new miscellany that gave considerable attention to prose fiction, subsisted almost entirely during its first years on Mme. de Grafigny's *Lettres d'une Péruvienne* in translation, and extracts from the *Adventurer* and Marmontel's *Moral Tales*. Of the twenty-four long stories printed during its four-year period of tenure, only five do not derive from some recognized outside source, and these five are all of doubtful originality.

The LADY'S MUSEUM of Mrs. Lennox

The record of advance and precipitant retreat in the *British* is to a degree paralleled by that of the *Lady's Museum* of 1760–1761, another highly original compilation, the short life of which tends to support the impression that Smollett's efforts to animate the common miscellany with new fiction of literary quality were premature. The *Lady's Museum*, published by Newbury and Coote, and advertised in the *London Chronicle* only two months after the appearance of the *British Magazine*, may have been stimulated by the promise of Smollett's new venture. More likely it was a spontaneous effort, predicated on similar assumptions regarding the now-advanced state of the general taste.

Like Smollett, Mrs. Lennox already had in 1760 a considerable public following as a novelist and miscellaneous writer. Her first work of fiction, *Harriot Stuart* (1750), had made a very favorable impression on the *Monthly* reviewer, who called it "the best in the novel way that has lately been published." The *Gentleman's*, also, had received it with an air of consequence although today it is remembered only for its American scenes, and Dr. Johnson's famous night-long celebration on the eve of its publication. In the following year, however, *The Female Quixote* had met with universal approbation, and elevated Mrs. Lennox at once into the brilliant inner circle of new English novelists. The book was eulogized by Johnson in the *Gentleman's Magazine*, won an extraordinary notice from Fielding in the *Covent Garden Journal*, and was praised and imitated by the critics of the *World*, who (as we have seen) tended to disapprove of novels and romances on principle. In addition to this, her greatest success in a long writing life Mrs. Lennox had published several popular biographical and historical works, and in 1758 a third novel, *Henrietta* (described by the *Monthly* as "the best novel that has appeared since *Pompey the Little*"—i.e., since 1751). By this industry she had earned little money, but acquired sufficient celebrity to have the *Lady's Museum* printed and advertised over the name of "the Author of the *Female Quixote*."[13]

Like Goldsmith's *Lady's*, published by J. Wilkie, and Kearsley's new *Royal Female Magazine*, its principal London competitors, the *Lady's Museum* represented an attempt to invade the large and growing market for women's magazines. As a somewhat specialized magazine, therefore, it was very different from the *British*, except in being conducted by a well-known novelist, and in placing particular emphasis upon serial fiction. In form and method it is much closer to Goldsmith's *Bee*, which had expired only three months before. In other words, it was a species of essay-miscellany, offering a medley of original and derived pieces on which the personal stamp of the editor was very marked. The first number, published on March 1, 1760, led off with No. 1 of an essay-series called "The Trifler," designed to descant upon problems of feminine interest, followed by an essay on "Studies Proper to Women." This was succeeded by the major feature of this and each succeeding issue, a long installment of the new "Story of Harriot and Sophia," written, readers were indirectly reminded, "by the same moral pen that has given us so beautiful a picture of female virtue, in the history of Henrietta."[14] In addition, the first number of the *Museum* offered a song from Mrs. Lennox's *Philander*, a "Dramatic Pastoral" produced in 1757; three pages of verses; and the first part of "The History of the Dutchess of Beaufort," reprinted from the author's earlier translation of Sully's *Memoirs*. Later numbers of the magazine, which usually ran to about eighty pages, contained a similar blend of spectatorial essays, history and biography, natural history, "Geography" and "Philosophy for the Ladies," poetry, and prose fiction. The stories included "The History of the Count de Comminge" in eight parts, translated from Mme. de Tencin; "The History of Bianca Capello" in three; and "The Tale of Geneura" from Ariosto—all three very popular with later magazine readers, and presumably therefore with the more restricted audience of the *Lady's Museum*. Mrs. Lennox's new novel in monthly parts, however, was obviously viewed as the main attraction of the new magazine, which, with the completion of the story in the eleventh number, suddenly terminated.

"Harriot and Sophia" is the history of two sisters, the elder (Harriot) shallow and vain, the younger (Sophia) truly genteel, and wise as she is good. Upon the death of their improvident father they are left in the care of a silly mother, completely under the domination of her selfish elder daughter. In order to escape the addresses of an importunate Baronet, Sir Charles Stanley, who has made a serious impression upon her heart, but who is evidently not disposed to offer her marriage, Sophia takes refuge in a clergyman's house in the country. By her kind offices there she brings about the union of two deserving lovers, but (as she believes) destroys her own chance for happiness by her apparent involvement with the young man. Sir Charles, who is on the brink of making her an honorable proposal, withdraws, under the impression that her heart is already engaged, and goes abroad. Harriot, definitely slated for a bad end because of her vanities, becomes the mistress of a nobleman, and Sophia retires with her mother to an obscure cottage in the country, where she earns an honest living working with her needle. At last, Sir Charles, who has been unable to forget Sophia, returns and discovers his mistake; explanations follow; and the two are happily united. Sir Charles's dubious character is redeemed, in sceptical readers' eyes, by an imposing display of benevolent enterprises.

As a piece of serial fiction, "The Story of Harriot and Sophia" aroused no public comment, and in collected form, in 1762, it passed through only a single London edition. Miriam Small, Mrs. Lennox's principal biographer, calls it "the most conventional and least original" of her novels[15]—though in its day, as a magazine story, it was nearly as surprising as "Sir Launcelot Greaves." Unlike Smollett, Mrs. Lennox made no effort to adapt her work to the special conditions of serial publication. It is (one imagines) simply her latest novel, written without benefit of chapter divisions, and parcelled out in accordance with her needs as editor of an eighty-page essay-miscellany. On the other hand, she broke sharply with precedent in the length of her monthly installments—which greatly exceeded those of even "Sir Launcelot Greaves," and were among the longest ever published in an eighteenth-century miscellany (3500–7000 words). Their length, in fact, was such that in preparing the two-volume trade-edition of the same novel in 1762, Mrs. Lennox felt it necessary to subdivide the original eleven parts into forty-one conventional chapters.

The relatively short life of the *Lady's Museum*, as well as the absence of any obvious imitations, indicates that the magazine was a publishing failure, although why it should have languished is difficult to determine at this distance. The periodical unquestionably made many fewer demands upon readers than either Smollett's *British* or Goldsmith's *Bee*, and its complement of prose fiction was relatively greater. Moreover, some of its pieces, like "The Count de Comminge" and "The Tale of Geneura," were later to enjoy a considerable popularity as repertory pieces. "Harriot and Sophia" itself was never pirated, probably because, like "Sir Launcelot," it was protected by a royal license, but as a didactic romance with important features borrowed from both *Pamela* and *Clarissa*, it was obviously much more in line with the common taste in magazine fiction than either "Sir Launcelot Greaves" or Goldsmith's stories in the *Royal* and the *British* magazines. It was in very much the same manner and in the same vein, in fact, in which miscellany readers were themselves disposed to write, as the "History of Philander and Clarinda" in the *British Magazine* of 1767 demonstrates. In this crude amateur effort, signed "J. Burton, Baker's Buildings, Bishopsgate," the artless Clarinda, "adorned with native simplicity of soul, and every other female perfection," unhappily falls a victim to her lover's libertine principles on the very eve of her expected marriage, and is abandoned for another. Filled with remorse she takes refuge in an obscure village in the North, where she rears her hapless child in solitude, instilling in her mind the maxim: "Beware of the seductions of men."

In both "Harriot and Sophia" and "Philander and Clarinda" there are the same heavy burden of morality, the same conventional characters and situations drawn from genteel life, the same preoccupation with the problems of love and courtship, and the same emphasis upon ideal goodness—except that as a picture of English society, Mrs. Lennox's novel is immeasurably more mature and much more skillfully executed. It may be, however, that she gave too little attention to the ecstasies of the tender passion, on which J. Burton was inclined to linger, or (more likely) that the magazine as a whole was too elevated for the common reader's tastes and interests. In any case, though ostensibly pitched at a more popular level than the *British*, the *Lady's Museum* aroused only a meager response. The profits accruing from the venture were insufficient to warrant retaining a novelist of Mrs. Lennox's talent and reputation. The new ground which the magazine broke was ignored by other writers and publishers, and apart from Goldsmith's *Lady's Magazine* (soon also to lose its editor), the *Lady's Museum* was the last magazine for women conducted by an author of talent or reputation until the nineteenth century.

Goldsmith and the Miscellanies

The failure of Goldsmith in the miscellanies, the third of this triumvirate of author-editors, is equally illuminating though his is solely a case of disprized merit, uncomplicated by the factor of reputation. Like Smollett, Goldsmith found his way into journalism through the *Monthly Review*. He worked for the Griffiths for about five months in 1757, and evidently tiring of their hegemony, became a kind of free-lance writer. Until March, 1758, he still hoped for a medical appointment in the colonies. In the meantime, he set about translating Marteilhe for Griffiths and Dilly, and contracted to write the *Inquiry* for Dodsley. He also did some further reviewing for the *Monthly*, but in January, 1759, transferred his services to the *Critical*. *The Memoirs of a Protestant* was published in February, and *An Enquiry into the Present State of Polite Learning* in April, by which time Goldsmith had acquired a reputation among the booksellers (though not with the general public) as a man of wide reading and a facile pen. Within the next few months he was invited to write the *Bee* for Wilkie, edit his new *Lady's Magazine*, and to contribute to several other periodicals, among them the *Busy Body*, the *Royal Magazine*, and Smollett's new *British*. Of all of these the *Bee* expresses most completely Goldsmith's idiom.

The *Bee* (1759) was far from being a typical miscellany, except for its accent on tinyness. It was a weekly essay-magazine of thirty-two pages, containing reviews of new plays, diverting stories, poems, essays, and miscellaneous articles—about half written by Goldsmith, the rest selected and adapted from various sources with a good deal of taste and discrimination. In the *Enquiry*, Goldsmith had stigmatized the "Monthly Reviews and Magazines" as being "dull and dronish." He had cited their lack of taste and imagination as a sign of the present decay of polite learning. In the *Bee* he made a serious effort to arrest this tendency. The magazine was informative, witty, and urbane. In the newspaper advertisements that accompanied its appearance, Goldsmith invited readers to compare it "with other periodical publications which more pompously solicit their attention." (He could be thinking of Kinnersley's *Grand Magazine* or the new *Royal*.)

If upon perusal it be found deficient either in humor, elegance, or variety, the author will readily acquiesce in their censure.[16]

Such public self-gratulation was, of course, a journalistic convention, but as an appraisal of the *Bee*, it happened to be true. It was the first genuinely distinguished eighteenth-century miscellany of a non-historical character. It was also the last—the only one of some three or four hundred titles worth reading in its entirety today. Its very merit made it a kind of literary sport.

The *Bee* and the *Busy Body* were both short-lived. Afterwards, in rapid succession Goldsmith tried his hand writing for the *Weekly Magazine*, the *Royal*, Smollett's *British*, and perhaps the *Christian's Magazine*. In addition, from September, 1759, to December, 1761, he seems to have been editor and a leading contributor to Wilkie's *Lady's Magazine*, where as "Mrs. Stanhope," a supposititious matron of breeding and parts, he served as "Polite Companion for the Fair Sex" and presided over their leisure reading. There is something ludicrous about Goldsmith's posture in the *Lady's Magazine*, but he gave at least one sign that he was not unaware of the humor of the situation.[17]

Despite his considerable labors over a three-year period as miscellany writer and editor, however, Goldsmith, like Smollett and Mrs. Lennox, never made any real headway in this species of periodical. The *Bee*, his major venture, expired after only eight numbers—accompanied by a certain amount of public soul-searching on the part of the editor, and energetic efforts to make contact with some kind of solid reading audience. The *Lady's Magazine*, on the other hand, managed to survive for several years. We have no circulation figures for the magazine, but the extreme rarity of surviving copies suggests that it had almost no readers at all. Like the *Lady's Museum*, it was a failure in the very period when magazines for women enjoyed every promise of success. The fact is that Goldsmith, even more than Mrs. Lennox, lacked the vulgar touch. His sweetness was totally wasted on the desert air of Paternoster Row. His real genius was for the urbane, humorous, and lightly satirical modes of the "Chinese Letters" and the *Essays*. Given the occasion and the proper auspices, he would surely have conducted a very successful single-essay periodical, like the *World* or the *Connoisseur*, addressed to the world of fashion and polite learning.

Goldsmith's review of the collected volumes of the *Connoisseur* in the

Monthly for May, 1757, is a glowing tribute to the unique value of the essayist in the Bickerstaff tradition.

> The writer [of these pieces] may be styled the friend of society, in the most agreeable acceptation of the term; for he rather converses with all the ease of a cheerful companion than dictates, as other writers in this class have done, with the affected superiority of an author. He is... perfectly satirical yet perfectly good-natured; and... never, for the sake of declamation, represents simple folly as absolutely criminal. He has solidity to please the grave, and humour and wit to allure the gay...[18]

Such a "friend of society" was Goldsmith himself, and as such, it is clear, he was seriously out of his proper element in the popular magazines of his day. In the *Public Ledger*, the "Chinese Letters" earned him a considerable renown, and in time they were moved to a leading position in the newspaper. As Johnson's "Idler" also demonstrates, the newspaper-reading audience at this period could absorb more sophisticated literature than that of the miscellanies. In the magazines, however, Goldsmith's efforts created no ripple of public interest. He had many plagiarists but no imitators, and, poor as he was, he must have felt in the end that the rewards of writing for the *Lady's Magazine*, the *Bee*, the *Royal*, the *British* and the *Weekly Magazine* (which, with his earnest ministrations, survived for only four numbers), were hardly worth the effort. Certainly his animadversions on the subject of the miscellanies, written at the close of this period in his life, spell out an indictment of the whole species with which Smollett and Mrs. Lennox could not seriously have disagreed.

In No. 3 of "The Indigent Philosopher," a short essay-series published in *Lloyd's Evening Post* in 1762, he uttered an ironical eulogy on the "very flourishing appearance" which the Republic of Letters had presented during the past two years, when "more than ten agreeable Magazines in a month, came flying all abroad fraught with instruction and entertainment." He mentioned the *Gentleman's*, the *London*, the *Universal*, the *Royal*, the *Imperial*, the *British*, the *Christian's*, the *Library*, the *Court*, and the *Lady's Magazine* (the latter, he remarked wryly, conducted "by a Lady of very high quality")

> all serious, chaste, temperate compilations, calculated to instruct mankind in the changes of the weather, and to amuse them with eastern tales, replete with grave essays upon wit and humour, and humorous essays upon the cultivation of madder and hemp.[19]

In the succeeding essay of the series, called "Specimen of a Magazine in Miniature," he returned to the attack by dwelling on the trifling and undiscriminating character of the typical miscellany:

> If a magaziner be dull upon the Spanish war, he soon has us up again with the Ghost in Cock Lane; if the reader begins to doze upon that, he is quickly roused by an Eastern tale; tales prepare us for poetry, and poetry for the meteorological history of the weather. It is the life and soul of a magazine never to be long dull upon one subject; and the reader, like the sailor's horse, when he begins to tire, has at least the comfortable refreshment of having the spur changed.[20]

Following this amiable sneer, in which he included himself, he projected in his essay a kind of mock miscellany called the "Infernal Magazine," consisting of a hypothetical "Address to the Public," a "Dedication to the Tripoline Ambassador," and a witty assortment of representative "specimens." This last essay was collected in the *Essays* of 1765, the well-known "Preface" of which breathes the same benign contempt for the miscellanies—their egregious piratical practices, their fatuous pursuit of novelty, their lack of genuine originality, and the shallowness of their efforts to inform and amuse the public. The whole "Preface," in fact, may be viewed as an oblique repudiation of the miscellanies as a vehicle for genuine literary talent, which the record of the next fifty years was strongly to confirm.

During his three-year term as editor of the *Lady's Magazine* Goldsmith made a genuine effort to fulfill the magazine's professed aim—"to amuse the wise, and instruct the ignorant." It was, of course, far inferior to both the *Bee* and the *British* in literary quality, but as an eighteenth-century women's magazine it was, like Mrs. Lennox's, outstanding for sobriety, good sense, and good taste. "Mrs. Stanhope" obviously took her preceptorial office seriously. She avoided many of the usual fripperies, emphasized history, biography, and natural science, and included generous quantities of domestic and foreign news. Compared with "Jasper Goodwill's" *Ladies Magazine* of ten years earlier, or Robinson's *Lady's* ten years later, both far more successful enterprises, Goldsmith's compilation is distinguished, first, by its more serious concern with contemporary life and belles-lettres (of which the serialized "Memoirs of M. de Voltaire" and Feyjoo's "Defence of Women" are representative); second, by its relative disregard for prose fiction. In both earlier and later women's magazines, fiction was a conspicuous commodity, and even Mrs. Lennox's *Lady's Museum* offered far more fiction than Goldsmith's *Lady's* did, although its presence alone did not insure her success. Within the compass of only eleven numbers, Mrs. Lennox published four long stories, including a new novel of over 50,000 words. In contrast, "Mrs. Stanhope," during Goldsmith's three years, offered her readers two serial stories (one in two parts; the other in six, but continued irregularly) and only a modicum of tiny histories, apologues, and oriental tales, all more or less in the manner of the single-essay periodical.

The narrative ingredients of the "Chinese Letters" aside, therefore, Goldsmith the journalist was conspicuously uninterested in emulating the English novelists. Despite his outstanding talent for fiction, and the fact that a much greater emphasis upon fiction might have strengthened his hand in both the *Bee* and the *Lady's*, he was almost as indifferent to its possibilities as if he had been writing for the *World* or the *Connoisseur*. In his critical writings, he rarely expressed anything but disesteem for the novel. Notwithstanding his encomium of Smollett's fiction in the *Bee* and "Sir Launcelot Greaves" in the *Public Ledger*, neither wholly disinterested perhaps, his prevailing views were staunchly Johnsonian. He attacked Fielding and Sterne in the name of youth, sneered at the taste for "modern romance"—particularly in feminine circles—and stigmatized novels as "instruments of debauchery" and the "delusive" and "destructive" misleaders of youth.[21] In his magazine writings, it is true, he frequently had recourse to narrative forms, but his efforts were almost exclusively within the range and manner of the old essay convention, the brief, fanciful, and lightly satirical modes of the *Tatler* and *Spectator*, the *World*, and the *Connoisseur*, rather than those of the *Female Spectator* or the *Adventurer*. Only one of the known stories he wrote for the miscellanies achieved sufficient length to be included in the Catalogue, "A Reverie at the Boar's-Head-Tavern in Eastcheap," a serial tale about as long as one of Hawkesworth's, published in three successive numbers of Smollett's *British Magazine* in 1760.

"The Reverie" is a satirical dream narrative in which Mr. Rigmarole, a man who sentimentalizes the past, falls asleep over his wine at the Boar's-Head, is visited by Dame Quickly, and enlightened on the subsequent history of the tavern from Sir John Falstaff's time to the present day. It is a long, unedifying story of human brutality, chicanery, and heedless self-indulgence ("a tavern is a true picture of human infirmity")—the whole history being designed to prove to Mr. Rigmarole the truth of one of Goldsmith's ideas, namely, that all ages are "equally absurd and equally vicious." At every stage in Dame Quickly's chronicle (which is amusingly punctured by signs of Mr. Rigmarole's exasperation with her theme)

> It is the same vanity, the same folly, and the same vice, only appearing different, as viewed through the glass of fashion.[22]

This fundamentally serious theme was gracefully elaborated in the "Reverie" with a good deal of humor and fancy, in the manner of Isaac Bickerstaff and Mr. Spectator. Everything in his story was "perfectly satirical yet perfectly good natured," as Goldsmith had written in his review of the *Connoisseur*. But despite the renewed taste for Spectatorial essays in the popular miscellanies of this period, it is hard to believe that Goldsmith's dream narrative could have held much interest for the general reader. In the first place, it conspicuously attacked the sentimental view of love, as well as the romantic view of the past, which informed most magazine tales and histories allegedly set in ancient times. Furthermore, it presumed a high level of reader sensibility—demanding not only a familiarity with the comic characters of Shakespeare's *Henry IV* cycle, but an interest in the life and manners of the past three centuries. The "Reverie" was by no means an erudite work, but its range of allusiveness far exceeded that of other miscellany fiction, "Sir Launcelot Greaves," of course, excepted. The fact that it was accorded a place in the *British* at all is a striking sign of Smollett's serious interest in 1760 in producing a miscellany possessing some degree of literary sophistication.

Goldsmith's serial story was never reprinted in any other magazine during the next fifty-five years, possibly because of its satirical flavor, possibly because of the royal license allegedly protecting the original contents of the *British Magazine*, although this injunction did not prevent the *Edinburgh Museum* from pirating "The History of Omrah" in the same volume. In any case, the "Reverie" never found its way into any other eighteenth-century periodicals, and made no visible impression upon magazine writers and publishers, who in the 1760's were much more taken up with Marmontel's *Tales* and other French fiction, oriental narratives in the manner of Hawkesworth, domestic apologues, genteel stories of high life, and "Secret Histories of the Court." Some of Goldsmith's shorter miscellany pieces, on the other hand, were widely plagiarized, if the "Preface" to the *Essays* is to be believed. Being very brief, they may have seemed to make slighter demands upon their readers, although all show at least a trace of that blandness and urbanity which was the author's special mark. At least four of the five short stories published in the *British Magazine* in 1760, and assigned to Goldsmith by R. S. Crane in the *Cambridge Bibliography*, in some way qualify romantic ideals of conduct, or temper their sentimentality with irony and satire.[23] In these respects, however, they run strongly against the popular current in miscellany fiction.

After Smollett and Goldsmith

The departure of Smollett and Goldsmith from the magazines in 1762–1763, and the extinction of the *Lady's Museum* after only eleven months, signals the end of the only illustrious era that the eighteenth-century common miscellany ever enjoyed. At this moment it stood on the threshold of an extraordinary proliferation, in which prose fiction was to play an increasingly prominent part, but this success was to be accomplished in the conspicuous absence of novelists and short story-writers of any real distinction. For eighteen months between 1762–1764 Robert Lloyd edited the *St. James's Magazine*, to which he managed briefly to attract a few writers of minor talent—Charles Denis, Bonnell Thornton, and George Colman; and here were published some of his first translations of Marmontel, later gathered into the *Moral Tales* of 1764. A few later editors of common miscellanies, like John Thelwall, William Cobbett, Thomas Holcroft, James Anderson the agricultural economist, and James Perry, later the powerful lord of the *Morning Chronicle*, were persons who achieved eminence in some other area. But typically the common miscellanies in the period after 1762 were conducted by industrious non-entities or miscellaneous writers of mediocre ability like William Kenrick (who succeeded Lloyd on the *St. James's*), J. Huddleston Wynne of the early *Lady's Magazine*, Thomas Dutton of the *Bon Ton*, James Sibbald of the *Edinburgh Magazine*, or Thomas Bellamy of the *General Magazine* and the *Monthly Mirror*. Since anonymity was the rule, not only for writers but for editors, and since the large and growing miscellany audience was increasingly indifferent to real literary merit, even some of the largest and most lucrative periodicals were placed in the hands of understrappers and hacks, who for a fee were willing to carry on the pedestrian labors of compilation, augmenting them with translations or original pieces of their own composition. It would be difficult to discover today the names of the successive editors of even important miscellanies like the *Lady's*, the *Town and Country*, and the *Universal*. The Rev. Percivale Stockdale edited the *Universal Magazine* in 1771 for a stipend of seven guineas a month, but found his employers so ignorant and so overbearing that he withdrew after only six months.[24] Smaller enterprises, on the other hand, were often conducted by free-lances, operating on a shoe-string, and sometimes by printers themselves.

It was customary for the larger miscellanies to proclaim that they were presided over by distinguished literati and men of affairs. The *Monthly Mirror*, for example, received "much assistance" and was "promised still more, from several writers of established reputation" regarding the "arrangement" of the magazine. The *Lady's Monthly Museum* assured its readers that "several gentleman of literary eminence have embellished our work with their productions." The *Beau Monde* was professedly "favoured with the correspondence of several literary characters of the first eminence." The *New Universal Magazine*, in the inflated language associated with such periodical enterprises, pronounced that it was

> Conducted by Writers of Established Reputation, who have formed Correspondence for the more perfect Execution of their Work in all the various Countries of Europe, as well as the most capital Cities of Asia, Africa, and America.[25]

But though these and other magazines undoubtedly possessed editors and paid contributors, and may even have maintained staffs, the membership of these illustrious societies was invariably left to the reader's imagination. Furthermore, those writers who did occasionally figure by name as authors of novels and novelettes in the *Lady's Magazine*, the *Lady's Monthly Museum*, the *General*, the *New Lady's*, and the *European*, beginning in the late 1780's and early 1790's, persons like Sophia Troughton, E. Caroline Litchfield, Francis Walsh, Jr., Miss Wyndham Foot James, William Shaw, H. Finn, Eleanor Tatlock, Henry Schroeder, and Anne Blower, unless these names were pseudonyms, were nearly always amateurs or semi-professionals whose identity outside the miscellanies is a matter of pure speculation.

Such, for example, were the Yeames sisters, Catherine and Eliza, the authors of "August and Emily" (1803), "Eliza, or the Hermit's Cell" (1806), "The French Family" (1808), "Andromache Delaine" (1809), "Julia and Palmira" (1816), and numerous shorter signed pieces in the *Lady's Magazine*, of whom we know something only because of a public appeal for their relief in 1814. Their father was Peter Yeames (formerly master of His Majesty's packet, the *Earl of Leicester*), who was captured by Buonaparte in 1803 and held prisoner for many years until he died, leaving a widow and six children. The scribblings of Catherine and Eliza, it is apparent, were not an avocation, but an earnest effort to eke out their paltry income. One may doubt, however, whether they received anything more than a pittance from this kind of piece-work.[26] A similar case of genteel distress is that of Miss D. P. Campbell, who wrote for several years under the name of "Ora" for the *Lady's Monthly Museum*, evidently hoping to acquire some slight reputation which would bring her a little money, but in the end was forced to lay her desperate plight before the public.[27] Such graduate amateurs were more typical of miscellany writers in the period from 1785–1815 than were genuine professionals. Most of them were never heard of again.

Almost the only authors of *signed* novels and novelettes in the magazines of this period, who have any earlier or later record of publication outside, are Clara Reeve, the Rev. George Moore, Mrs. Pilkington, A. Kendall, Joseph Moser, Anna Maria Porter, W. Holloway, James Harrison, Mary Hays, Sarah Wilkinson, Thomas Dutton, and Thomas Bellamy. The presence of the first name on this list is an inadvertence to which we shall presently return; the last three were writer-editors of some reputation but no real talent. For a crowded thirty-year period which includes among its novelists Mrs. Inchbald, Charlotte Smith, Harriet and Sophia Lee, Godwin, Bage, Fanny Burney, Cumberland, Ann Radcliffe, Lewis, Beckford, Maturin, Maria Edgeworth, Jane Austen, Walter Scott, and others, the magazine roster is pitifully meager. A few recognized novelists possibly did contribute to the miscellanies, and may even have maintained lucrative relationships with them. For four months in 1784, for example, Thomas Holcroft was editor of the *Wit's Magazine*, and he later wrote for the *Town and Country* and the *European*. But all of his numerous contributions to these magazines, which include at least three pieces of novelette length, were either unsigned or only initialed, and were therefore enveloped in the prevailing cloud of anonymity. In a later period, of course, this situation was reversed, and many well-known authors earned their first reputation in popular magazines, and many celebrated works of nineteenth-century fiction first saw the light of day in serial form. But in the eighteenth century it may be doubted whether the reputation of any novelist of any stature was ever enhanced by his labors for the miscellanies, Smollett, Goldsmith, and Mrs. Lennox aside. In the Catalogue there are listed only a handful of original works, anonymous or otherwise, that ever graduated from serial publication to volume form. All of these, except for "Sir Launcelot Greaves," "Harriot and Sophia," and the "Reverie at the Boar's-Head-Tavern," are works of unknown authorship, or by writers of very obscure reputation.[28]

Thomas Bellamy and the GENERAL MAGAZINE

As novelist, miscellaneous writer, and author-editor of two popular magazines published between 1787 and 1800, Thomas Bellamy is a representative late eighteenth-century figure who may be profitably compared with Smollett, Goldsmith, and Mrs. Lennox, of an earlier generation. According to the memoir published in the *Monthly Mirror* at the time of his death, he was born in "a very respectable family." His father was steward to Sir Charles Booth, "by whom he was much esteemed." Apprenticed to Mrs. Allen, "an eminent hosier in Newgate Street," Bellamy later operated for many years a very successful wholesale business of his own, until (we are told) "a taste for elegant literature unfortunately intervened." After his failure in business, he was employed as a clerk by Messrs. Harrison the booksellers in Paternoster Row, and publishers from 1780–1789 of the enormously successful *Novelist's Magazine* and several other periodicals, for which Bellamy wrote "a variety of articles, both in prose and poetry." Then in 1787 he struck out on his own with a new periodical called the *General Magazine and Impartial Review*, which, for an independent venture in a highly competitive field, with the support of very little capital, was surprisingly successful. Working for Harrison, as well as Mrs. Allen, Bellamy had obviously learned a good deal about merchandising. He attracted readers o his periodical by offering a premium to each purchaser in the form of a serial book, the *Plays of Shakespeare*, reprinted from the 1773 edition of Johnson and Steevens. The monthly quota of twenty-four pages, which probably cost him little more than the paper and the labor of printing, was quickly raised to thirty-six and later seventy-two, as the magazine caught on and its circulation increased. After six years, unluckily, it was extinguished by the failure of the firm with which it had become associated. But Bellamy was quickly installed as editor of a new and more ambitious periodical called the *Monthly Mirror*, a publication like the *General* in many respects, but oriented more towards the theatre, in which he was likewise interested. The *Mirror* was even more successful than the *General*. It survived for fifteen years, although Bellamy's connection with it was severed by his death in 1800.

Bellamy was an ingenious entrepreneur and a shrewd judge of the popular market. Unlike the earlier editors of the *British*, the *Bee*, "Mrs. Stanhope's" *Lady's Magazine*, and the *Lady's Museum*, he made no serious effort to inform and improve his readers, but gave them precisely the kind of pabulum they wanted. Both the *General* and the *Monthly Mirror* exhibit the same pretentious combination of modishness and propriety which was a principal formula for success in their day, especially among the women's magazines. They display nothing if not "a taste for elegant literature." Bellamy was himself a facile concocter of genteel trifles, and produced for his magazines a regular supply of poetry, moral essays, tales, sketches, and biographies of stage celebrities, both signed and unsigned—in addition to carrying on his numerous editorial duties, overseeing the printing and distribution of the magazine, writing (we presume) the "Impartial Review of New Books," and maintaining a brisk exchange with his magazine correspondents. He had a knack for getting people to write for him for nothing. His "chief talent," however, in the opinion of the *Monthly Mirror*, "lay in the construction of short novels of the sentimental kind, which he put into neat and flowing language, and uniformly devoted to the purposes of moral instruction."[29] Bellamy's program for prose fiction in both his magazines was plainly set forth in that part of the "Preface" to the *Mirror* in 1795 devoted to "NOVELS":

> To this species of literature considerable attention will be paid. Every subject will be *in ipso facto* a MORAL TALE. Regard will be uniformly had to *purity* of SENTIMENT, that nothing may misguide the *heart* or defile the *ear*—the PARENT may read them to his *child*, and the CHILD be instructed—SENSIBILITY shall receive no shock—and MORALITY no injury:—for the great object of the writer will never be forgotten, and that is—to *instigate* to VIRTUE and to *deter* from VICE.[30]

Paying regular lip-service to these principles, Bellamy himself produced for the *General Magazine* and the *Monthly Mirror* eight novelettes and one serial novel, plus a great many shorter pieces, written in a highly affected and platitudinous manner, and spiced with sentimental raptures and Gothic terrors. Feeling, on second thought, that pure morality was probably not too palatable to his readers, the author of "The British Barons," "Caroline Courtney," and "The Hermit of the Cavern" successfully disguised the flavor with a syrupy blend of heart-throbs and hectic melodrama involving fantastic coincidences. In the last-named story the ship on which Alonzo, a young Spanish nobleman, is voyaging takes shelter in the harbor of a lonely island. Disembarking casually to explore the region, he discovers a gloomy cavern buried in "a deep rock valley" between towering cliffs inhabited by a mysterious recluse. The Hermit of the Cavern imparts the story of his guilty life, in expiation of which he has passed thirty years in this remote retreat. At the end there is a flash of recognition. Alonzo falls to his knees and embraces his long-lost father!

Like its principal London competitors in the early 1790's, the *Lady's*, the *New Lady's*, the *Town and Country*, and the *Universal*, the *General Magazine* published quantities of such trashy fiction, including during its six-year term twenty-five works of novel or novelette length. A general break-down of the twenty-five, only part, of course, of a much-larger program in the *General*, displays several features typical of the popular miscellanies of this later period. Like other contemporary editors, Bellamy attempted to achieve a balance between what he called "Selected Prose" (that is, reprinted pieces) and "Original" articles. Eleven of the twenty-five long stories were merely repertory pieces, judiciously extracted from such sure-fire sources as the *Adventurer* (now over forty years old), Repton's *Variety*, Dibdin's *Bystander*, the *Arabian Tales*, and Marmontel and Florian in translation. In making these selections (some of which he had found in other magazines) Bellamy was obviously swimming briskly with the popular current.

It was in the fourteen "originals," however, that the real distinction of the *General* was supposed to reside. It was these stories that caught the eye of contemporary readers, including the piratical editors of the *Gentleman's and London*, the *Hibernian*, and the *Universal Magazine and Review*. (Eleven of the *General's* originals were reprinted in at least one other miscellany, and one of them, Miss Blower's "Maid of Switzerland," was reprinted four times.)

Eight of the fourteen were signed with real names, a somewhat higher proportion than one usually encounters in magazines of Bellamy's day—reflecting the more personal quality of his publication. In this respect he was slightly in advance of his time. During the same six years (1787–1792) the *Town and Country*, the *European*, the *Lady's*, and the *New Lady's* attached very few authors' names to their original stories, although they were already beginning to modify this practice. Until 1815, on the other hand, the *Universal* pursued a fairly rigid policy of anonymity for all its new fiction.

Focusing on the *General's* eight originals of avowed authorship, however, we discover that five were written by the editor himself. As in Smollett's, Mrs. Lennox's, and Goldsmith's day, it was still customary for editors to function also as authors of the magazine—although neither Goldsmith nor Smollett had signed their contributions, nor had Holcroft in the *Wit's Magazine* (1784), except with an initial. The other three originals in the *General* were by a writer of no reputation whatsoever, who called herself "Anne Blower," and of whom nothing is known except that she contributed a great many other pieces to the magazine.[31] In the columns devoted to his "Correspondence" Bellamy several times addressed her as a friend, but this may merely mean that her contributions were gratuitous. Every miscellany editor in the 1790's numbered as many such well-wishers as possible among his poets, story-writers, and essayists, whom he paid with fulsome flattery and public demonstrations of gratitude.[32] The six remaining anonymous and pseudonymous works of the *General*, include one later acknowledged by Bellamy himself, and others signed "G.M." "Clarissa," "Recluse," and "a Lady." The authorship of two of the longest and most pretentious works of fiction published in the magazine, the anonymous 51,000-word imitation of *Tristram Shandy*, which ran for five and a half years, and the pseudonymous 21,000-word "Original Letters" by "G.M.," was not further specified, being evidently considered a matter of no interest to readers. So far as is known, neither was ever acknowledged by any later writer, or ever gathered into volumes for the general trade. The second seems to have been received in installments and published as received. The first may have been written by Bellamy himself, or picked up in Grub Street for a song, being considered too unpromising to risk printing in volume form.

In general, it is worth noting, the authorship of the *poems* and *essays* in Bellamy's magazine is more diversified and more specific. Both forms enjoyed a much greater degree of social acceptability in the late eighteenth century, and writers therefore felt encouraged to acknowledge their contributions. There are poems in the *General* signed W. Hamilton Reid, T. Nicholls, J. H. Colls, Alexander Bicknell, W. P. Carey, and the Hon. Andrew Erskine, for example, as well as "Mr. R———," "a Lady" and "Clarissa." The poet William Cowper himself contributed four poems to the magazine, over his own name. But the story-writers were more cautious. Even though fiction was a principal ingredient of the magazine, and their efforts were far more sustained than the poets', they showed no inclination, Anne Blower aside, to attach their names to their pieces. Certainly there is nothing in the long fiction of the *General* to justify the boast of the memoir that the magazine had been "the means of bringing forward many promising young artists, who are now enjoying the highest reputation with the public." The only novelists that Bellamy ever brought forward by name were himself and Miss Blower, of whom we hear nothing later. The truth is that in neither the *General* nor the *Mirror* did he show the slighest interest in encouraging professional talent. The full weight of his authority, like that of other contemporary editors, was directed towards preserving a condition of perpetual amateurism among his contributors. When an unidentified writer brought to the magazine office, in January, 1791, a new work for which he evidently expected to be remunerated, for example, Bellamy addressed him publicly as follows:

> Mr. ——— who left a Manuscript for Sale, on a subject which would prove very uninteresting to the Readers of the *General Magazine*, is informed that Mr. Luffmann [the author of several prose pieces] and Recluse [the author of an Ossianic narrative] are Volunteers; and that the Contributions of these real Friends to our Work, embellish Space, which the Manuscript we have returned would only occupy.

Furthermore, as if to underscore his meaning, he went on to add:

> In our next Number, the Novel, written by a Lady who forbids us to mention her name, will commence. To this Lady we return our sincerest thanks, and consider her production as a valuable gift.[33]

This novel is probably the 21,000-word "Delights of Benevolence, by a Lady," which began its run in the February, 1791, number, and was appropriated part by part, as it appeared, by the *Universal Magazine and Review* of Dublin—the editor of which was no more anxious than Bellamy to give solid support to promising young novelists.

The Writing Audience

The labor of Bellamy and other late eighteenth-century editors was lightened, and the expense of conducting magazines like the *General*, the *Lady's*, and the *New Lady's* considerably lessened, by the great number of contributions from amateur scribblers like "Clarissa" and "a Lady," who asked for nothing but the pleasure of seeing their pieces in print. No account of long magazine fiction before 1815 should fail to take stock of the reader-writer situation. For a number of historical reasons, the new reading audience was also a writing audience, whose presence tends to be overlooked because of its tacit acceptance of anonymity. At least half of the so-called "original" material printed in the miscellanies from about 1770 to 1815 was produced by industrious amateurs whose names were unknown, often, even to the editors. The handful of learned correspondents and poetasters who addressed letters and verses to Mr. Sylvanus Urban in the 1730's and 1740's became three decades later a legion of eager volunteers, overwhelming grateful magazine publishers with mountains of verses, essays, and sketches, biographical articles, sermons, allegories, news items and extracts from books and other magazines, drawings, musical compositions, recipes and specifics, maxims, riddles, rebuses, charades, acrostics, short stories, and novels—of very dubious literary value, but all strictly gratis. It is no wonder that magazines like Bellamy's could be floated with almost no capital. All that was needed to become an editor, apparently, was an understanding with the printer, a desk, a pair of scissors, and a mailbox to receive the favors of the writing public. More often than not, one suspects, the editor's desk was a mere adjunct of the printing office. "The Printing-Office shall be open to receive Moral Essays in Prose or Verse," announced the first number of the *Microscope* (1799). "For the accommodation of those Correspondents who complain of having to *traverse* the shop of our publisher," said the *Lady's Monthly Museum* (1811) "we have caused a letterbox to be placed in the window." The editor of the *Cottage Magazine* (1811) advised correspondents who particularly wished to have prompt action on their contributions to send them directly to the printer. When the letter-box of the Edinburgh *Weekly Mirror* (1780), which hung "in the stair of the Printing-office," was mischievously stolen, the editor entreated his correspondents to "send their favours to the printing-house" until a new receptacle could be provided.[34]

Unquestionably the editor's letter-box had a deleterious effect upon literary standards, and was a principal reason for the egregious unprofessionalism of most miscellanies. Since, under prevailing copyright conditions, new magazine writing normally enjoyed no protection, and the almost unlimited supplies of piratical material available to editors were amply supplemented by gratuitous contributions from readers, no publisher was willing to waste much money on original stories, poems, and essays, especially since the greater part of the magazine public found the dross as good as real gold. The larger magazines, of course, continued to pay for some contributions, and maintain part or full-time staff writers. Their presence is to be suspected in all magazine stories signed with a single initial.[35] But, in the end, nearly all miscellanies found themselves competing for the amateur loot. Even the new *Monthly Magazine* of 1796, more professional than most of its contemporaries, acknowledged a debt to its reader-correspondents, and in only its second year of publication exclaimed over "the vast accumulation of papers around us"—contributions, that is, from eager volunteers.[36]

The larger magazines, with their more commodious circulations, could command a more extensive writing public than could the smaller, and we therefore expect to find the most imposing amateur efforts in prose fiction, not in little magazines like Bellamy's, but in the columns of the later *London Magazine*, the *Belle Assemblée*, the *Universal*, the *Lady's Monthly Museum*, and particularly the *Lady's Magazine*. If the remarks directed to its "Correspondents" and the annual "Address to the Public" are any index, from a third to a half of all the original fiction published in the *Lady's* from about 1775 to 1815 was contributed by readers of the magazine, mostly female. The exact quantity is hard to define, since amateurism was so completely the order of the day that even commissioned pieces were sometimes disguised as voluntary offerings.[37]

In most miscellanies the regular agency of communication between the editor and his army of scribblers and sub-professionals was the editor's column, usually entitled "Correspondence," "Acknowledgments to Readers," or "To our Correspondents." In this corner of the magazine he acknowledged the receipt of favors; accepted, rejected, or deferred them for later consideration; corrected misprints and misconceptions, apologized for delays, answered inquiries, rendered thanks for readers' "hints," placated the angry, chided the negligent, and firmly reminded his "friends" that they were all volunteers, and that their communications must therefore be *postpaid.* Above all, he employed all his powers of persuasion to insure a continuing flow of reader contributions—as, for example, in the *Monthly Visitor*:

> We here scarcely need repeat what has been often mentioned, that the MONTHLY VISITOR invites ingenious young men to the exercise of their talents, by which means their leisure hours may be dedicated to their own improvement, and to the instruction of the community. The pen is an inexhaustible source of amusement, and the tolerably correct pieces of every youth written in the sacred cause of truth and virtue, shall receive every possible attention.[38]

An editor's first duty, in fact, in launching a new periodical, was to establish immediate contact with the writing public, and to prime the pump with real or manufactured acknowledgments in his very first number.

Almost any editor's column is worth reading for the glimpses it affords into the life of the magazine world, but among the most fruitful is that of the *Lady's Magazine*, the sustained prosperity of which for over half a century was in a large part owing to its ability to coax readers into writing for one another. Appearing in twelve numbers a year, decade after decade, the accumulated columns addressed "To our Correspondents" provide illuminating documentation on the practices of eighteenth-century publishers and the manifold activities of the editor's office. They are themselves a letter-box in the window, where for fifty years literally thousands of nameless amateurs came and went.

For a good many years editors had been leaning on voluntary contributions; and long stories like J. Burton's "History of Philander and Clarinda" in the *British Magazine* for 1768 were an increasingly common feature of the popular miscellanies after Smollett's retirement. But, to all appearances, the *Lady's Magazine* was launched without wasting a single thought on the writing public. The "Address to the Fair Sex" that inaugurated the August, 1770 number seemed to promise strictly a combination of repertory pieces and professional fare. "Every branch of literature will be ransacked to please and instruct the mind," the new editor promised: "Interesting Stories, Novels, Tales, Romances, intended to confirm chastity and recommend virtue... The whole treasure of the Muses will be displayed." An unnamed "lady of some eminence in the literary world" had been commissioned to provide a "sentimental journey" (it transpired later that the editor was speaking of himself).[39] And in addition to this there were said to be "stores in reserve." Surprising as it may seem, the new editor of the *Lady's* went through his paces as if unaware of the mighty company of amateurs waiting in the wings. It is possible that he contemplated publishing a more professional type of magazine, like Smollett's and Mrs. Lennox's. If so, he was quickly forced to change his plans.

The deluge of reader scribblings began with a light sprinkle. In the second number, in a tiny notice near the end of the magazine, the editor acknowledged the "favours and hints" of four correspondents, and others unspecified. In the third, he mentioned six or eight; in the next, about a dozen—and then, as the magazine found favor with the writing audience, the heavens opened up, and two dozen, three dozen, or four would often be named in a single number, plus "more than we can either insert or specify." In response to these increasing demands upon his attention, the editor's replies were gradually extended to half a column, to a third of a page, to half or more in fine print; and finally to a whole page at the beginning of each issue, facing the leading article... Again and again he was moved to express his amazement at the "profusion of Readers' favours," the "immense number of [his] Correspondents," the overwhelming "Mail from Parnassus," "the almost innumerable variety of favours which are pouring upon us from almost every county in England—not to mention Ireland—the European—and the American continent." "We are almost distressed with favours," he confessed in 1772. Two years later the backlog of his commitments became so enormous that he added eight pages to one number of the magazine "in order to balance accounts with [his] Correspondents."

The pen-names of these reader-writers, and the labels applied to them in the editor's column, sometimes give an inkling of the character of the writing public, either real or imagined: *Maria Sprightly*; *Betsy Thoughtless*; *Joan English*; *Maria Teresa*; *E. S. of Geddington*; *A Lincolnshire Lass*; "Cath. Worth, at Mrs. Porter's boarding-school, Launceton, Cornwall"; "a young lady of seventeen"; *Forty-four*; *Almira of Hammersmith*; *Margaret M—h—l, Aged 12 Years*; "a lady of fashion"; *Mrs. Tr——s*; "a young Lady at Miss S. D——'s Boarding School"; "a Lady not Seventeen, in Love"; *Clarissa Harlowe*; "a polite Correspondent from Grosvenor Square"; *A Mother*; and "a female, now abroad, whose husband and herself have figured in high-life." The majority of these scribblers were obviously female, but not all of them by any means. The editor likewise addressed himself to such persons as *Bob Short*; *Juvenis of Sheffield*; *W. Thomas Snow-Rider, aged 9*; *Pedagogue*; "the Rev. Mr. Tasker"; *Dr. Cook*; *Americanus*; "Crutwel, surgeon, at Bath"; *Master Hopkins of the academy, Woodford, Essex*; *William Jones*; "the gentleman who dated from Soho"; "a gentleman of the faculty in Dublin"; "the Gentleman who wrote the poem (signed Aristius) at an Inn," "a choleric Correspondent [who wrote 'a messy letter']"; "a young gentleman of ancient family, and unblemished character," who was "seeking a wife"; *A Country Clergyman*; and a tribe of small fry masquerading under such transparent pseudonyms as *Semai Selwonk* and *Yrneh Yelffo*.

Other magazines, like the *London*, the *European*, the *Universal*, and the *Town and Country*, naturally, had a larger contingent of mature male contributors than the *Lady's*, and normally showed them less deference, but the situation in these magazines was not fundamentally different. The correspondence column of the *London* from about 1769–1785 shows the editor at his receiving window also, checking in a stream of anecdotes, songs, verses, algebraic problems and solutions, advice to the fair sex, "characters," excerpts from books and other magazines, stories, letters, and essays on every conceivable subject, many of which are found printed in the same or later issues of the magazine. Time after time, like other editors, he felt impelled to exclaim publicly over "the Multiplicity of articles" with which he was favored, and the eagerness with which readers of every description took up their pens. The *European*, which had begun in 1782 by establishing *four* "Letter-Boxes" in different parts of London "for the purpose of receiving Essays, Letters, Articles of Intelligence, &c. &c.," was so "overwhelmed" with the flood of reader contributions that it several times disavowed any effort to acknowledge their receipt, and other London miscellanies were forced from time to time to adopt a similar policy, or to render only token thanks for the most outstanding pieces.[40]

There was almost no talk of money for all this labor. Occasionally, illiberal members of the writing audience had the temerity to raise the question of payment, and the proprietors of miscellanies sometimes professed themselves willing to satisfy their reasonable demands, provided, of course, their contributions possessed unusual merit. But they were obviously less interested in raising the literary quality of their magazines by this means than in maintaining a lucrative condition of almost total amateurism. Like Bellamy, after making up half the magazine or more on the basis of "Selected Prose," they were quite content to depend for the greater part of the rest upon whatever they could acquire in the *free* market. The typical "Address to the Public," issued at the end of the year to be bound up in the collected volumes of the *European*, the *Town and Country*, the *London*, and other leading periodicals, always thanked correspondents for their assistance with elaborate courtesy at the same time that it left no doubt in their minds on what basis their continued support was expected. And, as a matter of fact, for most contributors it was sufficient stipend merely to see their favors in print without being asked to pay for the privilege (postage, of course, excepted), and some even offered gratuities to editors. The proprietors of miscellanies always refused these offers of money, with a great show of generosity, but they were also disinclined to encourage a more professional attitude, as the following typical remarks to correspondents, taken from a number of leading London miscellanies over a forty-year period, make abundantly clear:

> *A Montague* may assure himself that we are not so sordidly fond of lucre as to expect any gratification for inserting productions of any of our correspondents; if they pay the postage of their letters it is sufficient, if not [a rare gesture of editorial generosity!], the value of their productions will compensate even for that. (*Lady's Magazine*, 1777).

> The author of the beginning of the Novel [unnamed], is either at liberty to send for his copy to the editor, or favour him with the whole of the narrative, prior to publication; but is desired to advert, that the correspondents of the Lady's Magazine are all *Volunteers*. (*Lady's Magazine*, 1779.)

> In answer to O. X. We are always happy in receiving any Assistance from Correspondents, but should be sorry to offend them by even *offering* a pecuniary Reward. (*Town and Country Magazine*, 1786.)

We before observed to *S. Pure*, that the Proprietor having already been at a great Expence in preparing Materials for this Magazine [at least half were extracted pieces!], no Premium can be given to any Correspondent; but every Communication *freely sent* shall be gratefully acknowledged.

We are again under the Necessity of informing our Correspondents, that no Notice whatever can be taken of any Communication, *unless the Postage be paid*. (*New Lady's Magazine*, 1790.)

T.L.Y. of *Bristol*, is informed that the proprietors would be happy to receive his communications, and to insert them, should they be found fit for the eye of the public. These are the only terms they can offer. (*Monthly Mirror*, 1801.)

A Lady who signs *Clementina*, has expressed a wish to have the '*School of Arts*' revived, which was carried on in some of the former Volumes of this Work. We can have no Objection to devote a Page to such Subjects as that consisted of, if we are furnished with them. (*Lady's Monthly Museum*, 1805.)

Ten chapters of *a novel* have been received from *Miss E. Rooth* with a note, asking 'What the Editor will give.' He *gives* her leave to send for them, when she pleases. (*Monthly Mirror*, 1808.)

On the subject of 'Payment,' in answer to A.B.'s inquiry, we have to observe, that, although the contributions to Magazines are usually gratuitous, we shall feel no objection to allow him a moderate remuneration for his productions, provided that we approve them. (*Lady's Magazine*, 1811.)

M.N.O. is misinformed as to our pecuniary allowance; and our pay list being now complete, his MS. is preserved with care till he reclaims it. (*Belle Assemblée*, 1816.)[41]

Clara Reeve in the LADY'S MAGAZINE

The sharp decline of professional standards in the miscellanies from the days of Smollett and Mrs. Lennox, as a result of the invasion of volunteers, is strikingly revealed by an incident that occurred in the *Lady's Magazine* in the 1770's, more than ten years after the publication of "Sir Launcelot Greaves" and "The Story of Harriot and Sophia."

In October, 1773, the editor had published "A New Song, Set by Mr. Hudson for the *Lady's Magazine*," based on verses by "Miss Clara Reeve, of Colchester," obviously without consulting the author. This freedom (which was perfectly normal for the eighteenth century) evoked a polite reply from Miss Reeve, thanking the editor for this and other attentions, but correcting several grievous errors in the text of the song. At the end of her letter she expressed a willingness to write for the magazine, which she conceded to be "the most *unexceptionable* [italics hers] of any publication of that kind"—an offer that the editor twice acknowledged.[42]

Here the matter rested, however, more than four years. Then, in April, 1778, the magazine published a routine short extract from the "Preface" of Clara Reeve's *Old English Baron*, which novel was one of the literary events of the season just before *Evelina* appeared in the heavens. To this brief selection, which the editor entitled a "Defense of Romances and Novels," he appended some extravagant praise of the author, and announced that in some future number of the magazine he intended to publish a further extract from the novel, which he invited Miss Reeve herself to select. Then he closed his remarks in the following manner:

> We cannot conclude this article without observing, that as she is no stranger to the compiler of this collection, any fugitive or periodical piece from her will be esteemed a favour, and will be sure of insertion.[43]

This extraordinary public invitation to a now-celebrated novelist to contribute to a popular magazine, with a circulation in 1778 of at least 10,000, drew a further reply from the author, to which the editor gave major attention in his June column. The first part of Miss Reeve's letter was critical of the magazine, and this he refrained from printing, protesting, however, that the lady did the magazine honor, "even in her complaints," which were "like the plaintive strains of the nightingale, sweet beyond expression, and amiable to those who are affected by them." But he went on to quote a later extract from her letter wherein she proposed a new translation of Lamarche-Courmont's *Lettres d'Aza* in the following words:

> In the course of my peregrinations, I have met with the *Letters of Aza*, in French, which seem to me the true counterpart of those of Zelia [in Mme. de Grafigny's *Lettres d'une Péruvienne*, 1747]. I translated the two first letters, but other things intervening, I laid them aside and forgot

> them. Your late request suggested a thought, that they may possibly answer your purpose."

This proposal the Editor eagerly and publicly embraced, saying, "We have enriched our collection this month with the *first* [of the letters], we acknowledge the receipt of the *second*, and when it suits this lady's convenience, hope to be favoured with the continuation of the remainder."[44]

In conformity with this plan, the same issue of the *Lady's* offered "Letter I" of the "Letters of Aza, Translated by the Author of *The Old English Baron*," and the following issue, "Letter II," at the end of which a continuation of the series was promised. In the same number the editor again loudly thanked Miss Reeve "for her late condescention," and pointedly reminded her that "her late supply is exhausted, and we wait impatiently for a recruit."

The "recruit," however, was never forthcoming, although further appeals of increasing urgency were uttered in the August, September, October, November, and December issues. The editor also opened the new year with "a friendly jog." In October, he had reported, readers were beginning to "whisper" their impatience at her "silence." (By March their "suspence" was to become "*boisterous*.") The editor therefore begged Miss Clara R—— to give heed to these murmurings, at least by transmitting "the original French" of the *Letters of Aza*, so that he could "perform at [his] *leisure*, what her want of leisure may prevent her from honouring us with." At length, this and still-later appeals in March, April, May, and June proving futile, the editor secured somewhere a copy of the *Lettres d'Aza*, and "Letter III" of the series finally appeared in the July, 1779, number of the magazine, under the new title, "Letters of Aza, But Not by the Author of *The Old English Baron*." Henceforth, the story was pursued regularly to its close in the following February number, though not without public misgivings on the editor's part regarding this usurpation. After a blanket reproach to all his delinquent correspondents in August, among whom the editor now included Miss Clara R——, he was moved to add:

> The last ingenious lady will, we hope, excuse us for continuing the letters of *Aza*, which we are sorry that her own avocations have hitherto prevented; but as soon as she shall condescend to break through the gloom with which we are at present surrounded, we promise her to replace our pen in the ink-stand.[45]

To our CORRESPONDENTS.

WE are under innumerable obligations to *Dr. Cook's* son for his late communications, but are, at the same time, surprised to read an advertisement of those pieces relative to *Diseases incident to Infants*, in a separate pamphlet, this being a kind of invasion of what we esteem *literary property*.

Dr. Richer, we hope, will continue his favours, lest both he and we should be called upon by the public to gratify a curiosity, which we have certainly excited.

Henrietta R——, and the author of *Emilie*, will excuse us for giving them a friendly *jog*, and desire them to continue their several pieces till they are concluded.

Miss Clara Reve, the author of the *Old English Baron*, so justly admired, does us *honour* even in her complaints: they are, like the plaintive strains of the nightingale, sweet beyond expression, and amiable to those who are affected by them. Her criticism on the *Peruvian Letters*, which have been *twice* translated into our language, is, to use her own words, "by a lady, who has completed the story by additions of her own. If we say they make a *pretty novel*, we do them ample justice; but there is not a spark of *fire* which animates the *children of the sun*."

She proceeds thus—" In the course of my peregrinations, I have met with the *Letters of Aza*, in French, which seem to me the true counterpart to those of Zelia. I translated the two first letters, but other things intervening, I laid them aside, and forgot them. Your late request suggested a thought, that they may possibly answer your purpose." We have enriched our collection this month with the *first*, we acknowledge the receipt of the *second*, and when it suits this lady's convenience, hope to be favoured with the continuation of the remainder. Her hint relative to the extracts intended to be made from her *Old English Baron* coincides with our sentiments entirely; and she will excuse us if we should desire her to specify in her next what page or pages she would choose for us to *deposite* in our collection.

We are obliged to *M. B—g—ll* for her ingenuousness, and assure her the piece she recommended is under consideration of the *female committee*.

A. L. J——*s* must be included under the same predicament.

The *Essay on Sensibility*, illustrated in the character of Eliza, by *Academicus*, came too late for this month, as several other ingenious pieces have.

In the poetic line we are honoured with a *Poem on the four Seasons*, by a lady of seventeen. An *Acrostic*, by *S*——. *Another written in a Garden*, by *J. W. The forsaken Maid*, by *G. R*——*y*. *On the untimely Death of a fair Penitent*, by a gentleman of Spitalfields. *Incitement to Praise*, by *W. L*——*by*. *A poetic Version of the Te Deum*, by *Joanna*. *Rebus*, by *A. Z*. *The Choice*, and *on Love*, by *B. T. D*. *Rebus*, by *Anonymous*. *The Wish*, *The first Pair*, an *Elegy to the Memory of an amiable young Lady*, by *Academicus*, alias *Sympathrticus*. *The faithless Fair*, a pastoral, by *W. Hawkins*, and *Cruel Cupid*, which has appeared already in other publications, and is, consequently, inadmissible in this.

As we have not room to specify every favour we have received from our correspondents, our omission must be charged only upon necessity.

The Editor of the *Lady's* Addresses His Correspondents in June, 1778
(Among Them Clara Reeve)

It would be a mistake, of course, to accept at face value the bland interpretation placed upon Miss Reeve's quixotic behavior by the editor of the *Lady's Magazine*. The author of *The Old English Baron* was certainly not so devoid of leisure, or so occupied with "avocations" that she could not finish translating a series of only thirty-five letters, most of which were so brief that, in the substitute translation, the magazine was able to print them at the rate of three or four a month. Nor was the acknowledged author of an admired new novel so difficult of access that she could be addressed only through the columns of a periodical publication. As a matter of fact, the first edition of *The Old English Baron* in 1777 (called *The Champion of Virtue*) had been published by the house of Robinson—hence, perhaps, the assertion in the *Lady's* that Miss Reeve was "no stranger to the compiler of this collection." The second edition had recently been published by Dilly, who would certainly have gladly forwarded a letter to the author at any time. In this respect the editor was somewhat disingenuous.

The stony silence into which Miss Reeve lapsed may have resulted from something much more serious—namely, a realization of what she, as an author of reputation, was being asked to do, which was to write *gratis* for a very lucrative publishing enterprise that had only recently been boasting of its "uncommon, rapid, and increasing sale."[46] She had been publicly invited to contribute to the *Lady's Magazine*. Her reply (it would seem to us) was the prologue to a professional transaction, the two "letters that she enclosed being sample copy, submitted to a bookseller in accordance with established publishing procedures. This reply, however, the wily editor of the *Lady's Magazine* insisted upon transferring to his column for "Correspondents," where he monthly accepted and rejected contributions from his army of volunteers. The name of Clara Reeve was obviously an ornament to the magazine of which he eagerly availed himself, but she quickly discovered that he intended to reimburse her only with sugared compliments and the publication of a few snippets from her novels. His anguished appeals to her in "To our Correspondents," therefore, were something less than genuine. They were an attempt to apply public pressure on her to surrender her professional status. "What must we say to Miss Clara R——?," he wrote in April, 1779, after sending up distress signals for the ninth time. "Let her tell us what she would have us say." But the one thing he could say, and that obviously she had intended him to say at the outset, he was unwilling to say

—namely that the magazine would pay her something like what her labors as an author were worth.

The editor of the *Lady's*, of course, could easily afford to employ an understrapper to complete the translation of the "Letters," if he did not (as he said) do it himself, but, under prevailing conditions in the magazine world, he obviously saw no reason to engage an author of reputation to perform labors that a rout of amateurs were ready to undertake on their own account. This expense the *Lady's* could easily have borne since its profits were enormous. But is was already plentifully supplied with French fiction in translation as well as original novels by reader-writers who were so little motivated by professional ambitions that they frequently did not inform editors of their real names and addresses. In the July, 1779, issue alone, the month in which the "Letters of Aza" were resumed, the magazine in its correspondence column acknowledged the receipt of four new novels, one of which was to begin its run the following month. During the same year, at one time or another, the *Lady's* had twelve other novels and novelettes in the process of serialization, at least half of which were tendered by cringing amateurs.

Amateurism in the Eighteenth Century

It is not difficult to guess, therefore, what must have been the burden of Clara Reeve's "complaints," conveyed to the editor of the *Lady's* at the beginning of this revealing episode. The magazine was one of the fastest-growing and most profitable investments of a prosperous publishing house, and therefore a model for other periodicals of the same class. It was also the very seat of the new amateurism, depending now far more upon gratuitous contributions than did its principal competitors, the *London*, the *Town and Country*, and the *Universal*. The unprofessional character of its contents infected even the editor, who regularly mislaid manuscripts, miscopied titles and authors' names, misnumbered essay-series, printed installments in the wrong order, wrote "To be Continued" at the end of stories already completed, and sometimes published the same story twice. Other eighteenth-century editors were capable of surprising oversights and *lapsus memoriae*, but seldom of so many. Furthermore, if the note appended to the editor's column in November, 1781, is to be believed, the office of the *Lady's* did not even possess a complete file of its earlier issues.[47]

The air of blandness and oily good-nature that the editor affected in his published statements invited the most egregious plagiarisms (sometimes copied from his own magazine), for which he was constantly forced to chide his contributors. Time after time, he allowed himself to be beguiled by writers' promises, publishing serial novels of which he had seen only "specimens" and then finding them broken off by marriage, illness, childbirth, and a variety of other domestic intrusions. Unlike other editors, who usually insisted on having the whole story in hand, the chief of the *Lady's* seemed to learn nothing from experience, permitting his reader-writers again and again to embark upon ambitious enterprises patently beyond their powers to sustain—which they later either brought to a precipitant close, or (more often) simply jettisoned, taking refuge in their anonymity. The columns of the *Lady's Magazine* for more than thirty years are strewn with the wreckage of stories abandoned in transit, with repeated loss of face not only by this miscellany, but by others like the *Hibernian* surreptitiously feeding upon its contents.

Some stories thus abandoned were later resumed by their authors, after the most humiliating public remonstrances by the editor; others were finished by volunteers, who came forward to fill the breach. Several stories in the *Lady's* became successive derelicts. "The History of Captain Herbert and Miss Augusta Nugent," a "Series of Letters" left hanging after eight numbers in 1777, was resumed by another writer two years later, only to be relinquished a second time. "The Treacherous Husband," a story of matrimonial infidelity by "J. L——g, West Lavington, Wilts.," which reads like a parody of itself, foundered and sank in 1781 after seven tiny installments that had already required twenty-one months to produce. A year later, after vigorous protests by the editor, to which were joined "the united clamours of at least fifty of [his] fair correspondents," J. L——g was prevailed upon to revive his story and bring it to a perfunctory close in less than a page. His rather cavalier excuse for this defection: "*bad health* and a multitude of *unexpected incidents*."[48] The only surprising aspect of this episode, which is confirmed by many others, is the naive character of a reading audience able to interest itself in clumsy literary efforts like these, and in diminutive serial stories parceled out in driblets and subjected to appalling lapses of months or even years. "The Fortunate Foundling" (7000 words) in the *Lady's* required ten installments and over two years to complete. "Alcander and Lucinda, a

Moral Tale," was interrupted after only 2250 words and forced to wait more than six years for a conclusion, again of less than a page. The last installments of "Artemisia, or the Happy Conclusion" were suspended forty-five months. In this case the editor of the *Lady's* himself was responsible, having privately decided (without bothering to inform his readers) that the story was a plagiarism.[49]

The curious climate of accommodation and improvisation that prevailed in the columns of this leading London magazine is illustrated by the successive fortunes attending the publication of "The Monks and the Robbers," a Gothic story of priestly villainy. The anonymous author of this highly charged romance suddenly allowed his tale to lapse in 1794 after only three "chapters." The disaster was compounded in the *Hibernian Magazine* of Dublin, which had hopefully embarked upon the same venture. For three and a half years in both magazines Rudolpho rode galloping through the darkness, and Manfredi's infamous brother stood waiting, "with a pale and haggard countenance," at the monastery gate. Finally a new correspondent, "A. Percy," volunteered a continuation. This offer being "willingly received" by the editor of *Lady's*,[50] "The Monks and the Robbers" resumed its course in both magazines with fair regularity. After several years, however, readers became restless, as horror piled on horror, with no sign of relief; and the editor at length began to call for a conclusion. This the writer was able to accomplish, but only after three more years of intensified effort. The total span of attention required for "The Monks and the Robbers," under its successive authorship was nearly eleven years. It is the longest serial story, in point of time, published in the eighteenth century.[51]

The universal urge to break into print, on which the *Lady's* and other eighteenth-century magazines were so willing to lean, was not, of course, a strictly journalistic phenomenon. On the contrary, the feverish activity of the writing audience is obviously part of a much-wider movement existing during the greater part of the century, and deeply involved in the social and intellectual life of the nation as a whole. It reached a kind of grand climax in the 1790's, and was unquestionably a powerful factor in the literary revival of the decade. The new poets were all inveterate scribblers from childhood, for which activity the magazines offered an obvious outlet. Crabbe had written for the *Lady's*; Wordsworth for the *European*; both Wordsworth and Coleridge for the *Weekly Entertainer*. But, equally important for the revival of letters, was the fact that their audience had been preparing in the same way for at least two generations.

As early as 1735, we have already remarked, "Mr. Stonecastle" of the *Universal Spectator* was protesting publicly against the pressures exerted by his amateur contributors:

> As a *Weekly Author*, nothing gives me more Chagrin than the Importunity of my *Correspondents*, who all *eager* to have their Productions appear in *print*, never fail insisting to have them inserted in my *next* journal.[52]

Cave was aware of the same tendency among the learned readers and poetasters of the *Gentleman's* and was already in the 1730's beginning to ride triumphantly with the tide. By 1752 Edward Moore, the author of the *World*, found literary activity so completely the fashion that gifted virtuosos like Chesterfield, Cambridge, and Walpole were willing to write more than half his weekly numbers for him, merely for the pleasure of figuring as authors. In 1753 Johnson devoted a whole number of the *Adventurer* (No. 115) to what he called with some irony the "Age of Authors"—

> for, perhaps, there never was a time, in which men of all degrees of ability, of every kind of education, of every profession and employment, were posting with ardour so general to the press.

In other words, the new professionalism of which Johnson was a leading exemplar had to cope not only with the old-type patronage system, but with the new-type amateurism, in the light of which (he wrote in the same essay) "almost every man is an author, either in act or in purpose." On the one hand, Johnson had to combat Chesterfield the aristocratic distributor of largess, and on the other, Chesterfield the anonymous author of twenty-three papers in the *World*, Cambridge, the author of twenty-one, and Walpole of nine, not to mention more imposing works of learning and imagination.

There is abundant testimony in the remarks of newspaper and magazine writers in the 1760's and 1770's of the same widespread interest in self-expression, the insatiable urge to scribble, the desire to shine as a literary light, which led amateurs of every rank and condition of life to bombard booksellers as well as editors with novels, volumes of verse, collections of essays, sermons, and works of commentary. Johnson's opinion that "nothing excites a man to write but necessity," and that "no man but a blockhead ever wrote, except for money," expressed his own proud feelings as a literary mercenary, but it was certainly not descriptive of contemporary practice. On the contrary, it was a kind of defiant answer to the rising spirit of amateurism sprouting even in his own circle.

Finding Johnson unwilling, in 1776, to consider publishing a "Tour of the Continent" except in terms of the money it would bring him, Boswell characterized Johnson's views as "strange," motivated by indolence, and stubbornly adhered to in the face of "numerous instances" to the contrary.[53] Boswell himself tacitly rebutted them by beginning in 1777, and maintaining for six years, a series of seventy anonymous essays for the *London Magazine*, as far as is known without remuneration. They were also rebutted by Johnson's "Little Burney," whose secret labors on *Evelina* from 1767 to 1777 were anything but extraordinary except in point of merit. There is overwhelming evidence that the effort was being repeated in homes, boarding-schools, and academies all over Britain. "Perhaps the rage of writing was never more epidemical than at present," a writer declared in the *Edinburgh Weekly Magazine* in 1778, the same year in which *Evelina* was published and Clara Reeve's translation of the "Letters of Aza" was interrupted in the *Lady's*. "Every book-seller's window is stuffed with stillborn compositions; and the daily papers, like the bills of mortality, are a continued recital of departed genius and understanding." Across the Irish Channel another, less disenchanted, wrote: "It is, indeed, difficult to be young, and to live in Dublin, without feeling an inclination to scribble."[54] The literary societies springing up everywhere in Britain, at the end of the century, like the ones in Exeter, Sherborne, and Manchester, and the circle of young advocates in Edinburgh who produced the *Mirror* and *Lounger*, all bear witness to the same creative exuberance.

The Effect of the Essay Tradition

The *cacoethes scribendi*, as it was jocularly called, was an infection of epidemic proportions during most of the century, therefore, outside as well as inside the magazines. But, insofar as it may be viewed as a journalistic phenomenon, it was closely associated with the pseudo-genteel aspect of the miscellanies, and derives ultimately, like so much else, from the prepotent tradition of

Addison and Steele. As we have observed, one of the pretenses of the *Tatler* and *Spectator*, the *Free-Thinker*, the *Female Spectator*, the *Rambler*, the *Adventurer*, and other essay-serials time out of mind was that the magazine was really a cooperative undertaking between the author and his readers, who engaged in a kind of public conversation under his leadership. He called attention in his essays to signal instances of vice and folly, goodness, and sensibility, which came under his eye, usually in cultivated society, and his readers supplemented these observations with letters and essays of their own composition, which in turn became the subject of further lucubrations. Thanks to the recent efforts of R. P. Bond we now know in a much more precise way than formerly the extent to which Addison and Steele were occupied with real contributions from readers.[55] With later essayists, however, the use of letters tended to become a mere literary convention. All the correspondence in the *Free-Thinker* growing out of Miranda's offer of herself in marriage is believed to have been contrived. Half of the numbers of the *World* (it is true) were written by volunteers, but practically everything in the *Female Spectator*, *Rambler*, *Adventurer*, *Mirror*, and *Lounger* was composed by the authors themselves or members of their circle. Notwithstanding the emphasis upon letters in all five, their epistolary exchanges were typically playful frauds, and so remained generally, during the continuing life of the essay-serial.

Meanwhile, under the leadership of Defoe and Cave, the letter to the editor had been transplanted to the weekly journal and the monthly miscellany, where it quickly came to enjoy an abundant new life—with this difference in the miscellany, however, that Cave's correspondents tended to be *real* rather than imaginary. To an unprecedented degree, the *Gentleman's Magazine* made contact with a genuine writing audience. The pretense of Cave's and many later eighteenth-century miscellanies was that they too were conducted by hypothetical personages like Sylvanus Urban, Jasper Goodwill, and Mrs. Stanhope, or by societies of ladies or gentlemen engaged in the reform of manners and public morality, or the disinterested pursuit of knowledge, in which enterprise readers themselves were invited to join. This pretense imported into the miscellanies a good deal of the atmosphere of the essay-serial. Most editors, in addressing their readers, adopted the courtly and deferential air associated with the genteel tradition in journalism. The *European Magazine*, allegedly founded in 1782 by "The Philological Society of London," meeting "for the purpose of mutual improvement," solicited the aid of all friends of progress, polite learning, and the arts. A quarter of a century later (1809), the editor was still writing in his annual address:

> We... flatter ourselves, that such as have any useful knowledge to communicate, or any hint that may improve the *mind*, polish the *manners*, refine the *taste*, or mend the *heart*, will be glad for such an opportunity of communicating them to the world.[56]

Thus prompted by generations of miscellany editors, and hypnotized by constant signs of reader-participation in the life of the periodical, it is no wonder that thousands of amateurs came to regard writing for the magazines as a sign of arrival in cultivated society. The eagerness of provincial clergymen, blue-stockings, and college and university students to publish essay-serials and volumes of verses and literary essays, was matched in the miscellanies by a stream of poems, stories, sketches, mathematical demonstrations, characters, and moral disquisitions, designed to exhibit their authors' learning, taste, ingenuity, and knowledge of the proprieties. The degree to which contributors to the miscellanies, amateur and professional alike, continued to write under the shadow of the *Spectator* is indicated by the fact that at least half of the original magazine fiction published in British miscellanies between 1740 and 1815 belongs to one or more of the familiar species of the essay-serials. Most of this fiction was very brief, as tradition prescribed, and therefore does not show up in the Catalogue of Magazine Novels and Novelettes, but some of it spread into the five to twelve thousand word bracket, where it is discovered in the form of serial letters and tales with diminutive parts, episodic narratives, and letter-series of various kinds, bearing such familiar-sounding titles as "The Miseries of Improper Education," "The Danger of Trying Experiments," "The Folly of Precipitate Resentment," "Amyntor and Eudosia, or Polite Friendship," "The Adventures of a Mirror," "The Adventures of a Quire of Paper," "Wisdom and Truth, an Allegory," "Wisdom and Folly, a Vision," and "Abdallah and Almira, or the Constant Couple"—any one of which might have been copied from the Table of Contents of the *Adventurer* or the *Mirror*.

There are scores of such "originals" in the Catalogue, many of them obviously written by readers or graduate amateurs, and showing a pronounced Spectatorial influence. A few of them appeared in essay-series bearing such titles as "The Old Woman," "The Reasoner," "The Contemplatist," and "The Lucubrations of Timothy Hairbrain." But most of them were single works, tendered by well-wishers or constant readers, who adopted names like "Bob Short, Jr.," "Arpasia," "New Correspondent," and "Lucinda," and who offered their stories as edifying pictures of high life, examples of practical morality, and sometimes histories of themselves or of persons who had allegedly come under their observation in cultivated circles. So pervasive was the influence of Addison and Steele, that even writers in the ribald *Covent Garden* and *Rambler's Magazine* frequently felt impelled to adopt the time-worn manner of the *Tatler* and *Spectator* in writing erotic pieces like the "Adventures of a Gold Ring," "The History and Adventures of a Bedstead," "The History of a Hair-Dresser (Found Wrapped up in a Paper with His Curling-Irons)," and the "Adventures of Harry Careless"—the last-named incorporated in a monthly column called "The Rambler."

Until 1800, at least, therefore, Addison and Steele were the single most important formative influence on eighteenth-century miscellany fiction, and their example was continually reinforced not only by repertory pieces and essay-series written in imitation of the *Spectator*, the *Adventurer*, and the *Mirror*, but by the whole syndrome of editor-reader-writer relationships, the inertia of which it is difficult to over-estimate. In addition to the strictly journalistic tradition of essay-type fiction, however, there were a number of other influences operating on story-writers—of which the most important were Richardson and Sterne. There was a babble of many voices in the miscellanies. The rapidly expanding community of eighteenth-century novelists lay very close at hand, and was constantly under view by magazine critics and commentators, by translators, reviewers, extractors, and abridgers, and by compilers of anecdotes and authors of biographical memoirs. On the whole, however, the only story-tellers who deeply penetrated the consciousness of magazine-writers were Richardson and Sterne (and their followers), supplemented by a few French novelists of sensibility and Gothicists under the leadership of Ann Radcliffe. Judged by the record of the Catalogue, the "realist" tradition in English fiction did not win even a minority following in the miscellanies. *Tom Jones* was admired by a great many critics, and was everywhere accepted as a classic. *Joseph*

Andrews, *Amelia*, and *Roderick Random* were among the first works of fiction revived by the *Novelist's Magazine* in 1780. But Defoe, Fielding, and Smollett had almost no imitators among unters. In magazines like the *Lady's*, the *New Lady's*, and the *General* we encounter a great many epistolary romances that recall *Pamela*, *Clarissa*, and *Sir Charles Grandison*, but no "comic epics," picaresque stories, or novels in the satirical tradition. By 1740 the spell of the *London Spy*, with its relish for brute realities, was dissipated in the miscellanies (though it survived for some years in the weekly journals), and simultaneously the old voyages of shipwreck and piratical adventure that had once engrossed the readers of *Mist's* and *Applebee's* dropped out of view, except in those magazines devoted to marvels and prodigies—to be replaced a generation later by sentimental journeys and tours, and vapid imitations of *Tristram Shandy*.

There were many reasons for these preferences, into some of which we shall enter in the following pages. Both Richardson and Sterne were easily accommodated to the already-existing magazine tradition: Richardson because of his emphasis on letters, his close attention to manners and propriety, his preoccupation with the problems of love and courtship, and his didactic bias; Sterne because of his interest in humors and oddities, "characters" and episodes, and significant moments of experience. For magazine readers and writers alike, both seemed very close to home. But the most important reason for their whole-hearted reception in the miscellanies was their sentimental philosophy, for in popular magazines from 1760 or 1765 the spirit of sensibility was completely in the ascendant.

Epistolary Fiction in the Miscellanies

Novels and novelettes in letter form were extremely numerous in the miscellanies after 1770, and fully reflect the popular interest in epistolary fiction. In this regard magazine writers may be viewed as surrendering to a literary fashion of which the accepted leaders were Richardson, Mrs. Sheridan, Fanny Burney, Frances Brooke, and Mackenzie. At the same time, we should not overlook the important precedents for such fiction existing in the journalistic tradition, which made the acclimation of the epistolary novel in the miscellanies very easy to accomplish. Considered in these terms, some magazine stories are *serial letters*, along the lines of "Opsinous" and

"Fidelia" in the *Adventurer*; others are *simple letter-series*, like Johnson's "Story of Misargyrus" (Parts 1–3) and Defoe's "Village Love"; or *intermittent letter-series*, like the letters from "Tom Manywife" and "Betty Blueskin," written by Defoe for *Mist's Weekly Journal*.[57] All three of these rudimentary types of epistolary fiction, as a matter of fact, were much more common in the miscellanies than they were outside, thus demonstrating the persistence of journalistic tradition. Similarly many stories in letter form are found incorporated in essay-series in close association with other Spectatorial paraphernalia.

The *dynamic letter-series*, however, was unquestionably the most approved form of epistolary narrative in the popular miscellanies, both exchanges between two correspondents and those with several correspondents; and although, again, we may find numerous precedents for stories of this class in the *Rambler*, the *Adventurer*, the *Mirror*, and the *Lounger*, most of them were obviously attempting to emulate the English novel. In manner, method, and subject, they spell out the hegemony of the school of Richardson. We may remark this important difference, however—that magazine fiction inevitably tended to make some adjustment to the special requirements of periodical publication. In length alone, the difference is very striking. The best-known and most-admired epistolary novels after *Pamela* tended to be two or three-volume works averaging 150,000 to 200,000 words. *Pamela* (Part I) was 225,000 in round numbers; *Evelina*, 175,000; *Letters from Felicia to Charlotte*, 130,000; *The Memoirs of Miss Sidney Bidulph*, 300,000. The longest magazine originals in the epistolary class were shorter than the shortest of these, and most stories in letter form were less than a tenth as long. At the lower end of the scale they shade off into little exchanges of only a few pages, recalling some of the tiny series of the *Spectator* and other essay-serials. Among those gathered into the Catalogue, however, the typical magazine story in letter form is a novelette of about 10,000 words, or slightly longer, like "A Series of Letters" (9300), "A Series of Letters from Miss Trevors to Miss Roberts" (11,500), or "Female Correspondence" (13,700)—three pieces from the *Lady's Magazine*, any one of which might be considered as highly representative of its kind.

In "A Series of Letters" Miss Harriet Willis is invited to visit her friends the Percies in their new country place, located in a very "genteel" neighborhood. These amenities occupy two letters. In the third and fourth, Miss

Willis arrives at Percy-Place in Captain Percy's "lofty" phaeton, admires the appointments of her room ("elegantly fitted up with chintze") and meets Mrs. Percy's circle of friends, among them Miss Sophia Wallis ("a lovely girl, about eighteen, and very pretty"). The young ladies immediately become inseparable. There is still another visitor at Percy-Place, the extremely eligible Mr. Gordon. To Miss Willis, however, Mr. Gordon remains only a "friend"—though for some time the reason is not clear, since he is young, well-mannered, and "finely made," with very white teeth and "blue and piercing" eyes, and Miss Willis is herself "a very fine elegant woman" who "seldom wants" for beaux. With Miss Wallis, her pretty friend, however, it is otherwise. On being exposed to Mr. Gordon's charms, "her heart received a wound." It was "love at first sight." In her first letter after the encounter she cannot do justice to his person ("he is one of the handsomest men my eyes ever beheld"); in her second, she confides "the pangs of love"; in her third, Mr. Gordon calls at her home while she is "practising some sonatas of Bocchelini's" on the harpsichord, and lays his "hand and fortune" at her feet, ardently declaring "my heart you have long had." This offer Miss Wallis blushingly refers to her parents, who are momentarily expected home.

A ball is given by some friends of the Percies "for all the genteel families in the neighborhood," and it is attended by another eligible bachelor, Sir Edward Ashley. Struck by Miss Willis's "figure," and by "the accomplishments of [her] mind," Sir Edward finds that she has made "an entire conquest of [his] heart" and soon after makes an offer of *his* "hand and fortune." He is refused by Miss Willis, however, who cryptically declares that "[her] heart has long been engaged with the approbation of both [her] parents, to a young man in every way worthy of it." This rejection of so promising a suitor surprises us nearly as much as it does Miss Wallis.

In the next letter, the eleventh in the series, we reach the nub of the intrigue. It appears, when Miss Wallis observes the two in a tender private conversation, that Mr. Gordon has transferred his affections to Miss Willis. Actually, we learn afterwards, he is begging Miss Willis to unfold to him the true state of Miss Wallis's heart, and in the same letter the name of Miss Willis's actual lover, "Mr. Selwin," is first mentioned. All the perplexities of Miss Willis's behavior are now explained (her heart and hand being preempted), and the single impediment to Miss Wallis's happiness being removed by her friend's wise and firm intervention, Miss Willis ends her visit to Percy-Place and returns home. In two final letters, however, she is regaled with a flattering description of Sir Edward's continuing pangs of love, and a glowing account of Miss Wallis's wedding—with Mr. Gordon very handsome in "regimentals," and the bride "in a white lutestring Italian gown; her hat... a white chip with a narrow black velvet edge to it, and trimmed with gauze, &c."

Apart from its numerous fatuities, there are several striking technical features of this epistolary novelette, which it shares with most other members of its class. The first is its diminutive scale. Compared with *Pamela*, *Evelina*, the *Letters from Felicia to Charlotte*, or *The Memoirs of Miss Sidney Bidulph*—with their crowded scenes and myriad episodes—"A Series of Letters" is extremely spare, as a simple letter-count will show. *Evelina*, for instance, contains about ninety letters (including enclosures) from nine different correspondents, most of them much more prolix than either Miss Wallis or Miss Willis. *Argus, the House-Dog at Eadlip* (1789), which Frank G. Black selects as the "typical novel in letters" in the period from 1781–1800, contains "two hundred letters from sixteen pens, set in forty-five different combinations of sender and receiver."[58] In contrast, "A Series of Letters" contains only *eighteen* communications from *three* persons, in *four* combinations of writer and recipient. "Miss Trevors to Miss Roberts," already mentioned, contains fourteen letters, from three writers, in four combinations; "Female Correspondence" fourteen letters, from three correspondents, in only three. A good many longer stories in letter form found their way into the magazines, but nearly all involve a relatively restricted cast of characters and epistolary observers.

A second striking feature of the magazine serials is their accommodation in other respects to the requirements of periodical publication. Again there were exceptions, but epistolary novels and novelettes in the miscellanies were usually printed one letter at a time (or occasionally two) at intervals of at least a month. A story like "A Series of Letters," "Miss Trevors to Miss Roberts," or "Female Correspondence," with fourteen to eighteen parts, therefore required more than a year to complete. The first-named was spread out over a period of twenty months. Thus committed from the outset to an attenuated program of parts, writers inevitably tended to make adjustments of various kinds, avoiding on the one hand the heady prolixities of Richardson, Fanny Burney, and Mrs. Sheridan, and on the other the conventional devices of these and other novelists, designed to give a feeling of greater immediacy to the action and greater animation to the story. Interrupted and resumed letters were fairly common in the magazines, but writers tended to avoid extremes. They employed fewer very long letters (except, of course, serial letters, which are another species), and fewer very short ones, hasty postscripts, letters within letters, or supercharged bulletins scribbled on the scene of action. The magazine serials had their own methods of gaining suspense which tended to exploit, rather than to abridge the normal intervals between communications.

The duration of the narrative action in "A Series of Letters" is indefinite, but it is long enough to encompass a leisurely visit to a country house, a genteel courtship, and a wedding. That of "Miss Trevors to Miss Roberts," in which the heroine traveled to the continent, rejected a frothy French lover of libertine principles, and found a worthy husband of more modest circumstances, occupies at least several months. So also does "Female Correspondence," which turns on the hesitations of a lover modeled on Mackenzie's "Man of Feeling." None of these stories rigidly confined itself to the actual time-lapse involved in serialization. But the discrepancy is not grossly disproportionate. Thus, though their pace must have seemed more measured than that of epistolary novels, it brought concomitant benefits in terms of naturalness and simplicity. The magazine heroines were rarely called upon to perform prodigious feats of epistolary endurance. They wrote less often and were more given to weighing their words. Unlike their cousins in the novel, they kept journals at their peril.

The Problems of Serialization

A third feature that distinguishes the typical epistolary story of the magazines, is its rudimentary technical competence. Viewed in terms of the total edifice of eighteenth-century fiction, of course, "A Series of Letters," "Miss Trevors to Miss Roberts," and "Female Correspondence" are less than trivial. They are the daydreams of school-girls. But compared with other amateur efforts of approximately the same length, like "Philander and Clarinda" and "The Treacherous Husband," they display far greater narrative proficiency, especially at the installment level. In spite of Smollett's leadership in the

British Magazine, most writers of *non*-epistolary serial fiction arrived at no successful accommodation with the rule of *multum in parvo*. Amateurs, sub-professionals, and professionals of the magazines alike, for the next half century, were generally incapable of handling an "episode" along the lines laid down by "Sir Launcelot Greaves." Most of them did not even try. The greater number simply renounced formal narrative divisions entirely, writing instead inflated serial tales, which the editor then sliced into installments of convenient length with the same single-mindedness he displayed in dealing with detached episodes from new English novels.

When magazine writers did attempt chapter divisions, they occasionally made them of conventional novel length, allowing the editor to do his work in the same casual manner—as in "Grasville Abbey," in the *Lady's*, where the editor faithfully preserved the author's twenty "chapters," but subdivided them further into forty-seven monthly parts. Or, driven by the inexorable logic of their situation, writers sometimes tried to produce miniature chapters, modeled on essay tradition, numbered like essay-series, garnished with mottoes, and sometimes even called "Essays"—as in "Essays on Transmigration" (really a serial novelette) in the *Royal Magazine* of 1788. Magazine stories with tiny "chapters" were fairly common after 1800, especially in the *Lady's Monthly Museum* and the *Belle Assemblée*, the new, more professional type of women's magazine, to which the *Lady's* eventually gave place. But practice in this respect was very irregular, and never widely accepted—even by 1815. Outside the essay-serial, most writers for periodicals were incapable of the sustained control necessary to write long stories in effective short installments. It required more mature craftsmanship than they were able (or willing) to command. We encounter many amusing instances in the miscellanies of efforts to achieve and maintain this kind of control. The second author of "The Monks and the Robbers," pursuing the plan laid down by his predecessor, managed to maintain a just distribution of one chapter per installment (about 1500 words) for twenty-one additional parts—thus exhibiting extraordinary dexterity for an amateur (if amateur he was). Then, as he labored to bring his story to a conclusion, "Chapter XXV" dilated into six installments (7000 words). Vacillating wildly between 900 words in "XXVI" and 6750 in "XXVII" he subsequently abandoned all effort at control, allowing his last chapter to mushroom into a monstrous climax of sixteen parts that required three years to bring to a close.

At the other extreme, Miss Eliza Yeames, one of the impoverished semi-professionals for whom the *Lady's* later sponsored a subscription, greatly overcompensated in her initial effort to achieve a proper diminution in scale. The first five "chapters" of "Eliza, or the Hermit's Cell," were so short (about 800 words each) that the editor bundled them all into the first installment. Trying methodically to readjust her sights, the author far overshot her mark in Chapter VI, which ran to over five-thousand words. Then in the succeeding nine she reverted to a scale much closer to that of the first five, except that in Chapter X she introduced an interpolated "history" of four-thousand words. Inset stories and detachable episodes, it should be remarked, like full-length chapters, were another feature borrowed from the contemporary novel that played havoc with effective serialization.

Faced with difficulties like these, which were greatly augmented by the high-handedness and indifference of magazine editors, most writers simply closed their eyes and spun a seamless narrative web—or took refuge in the epistolary form. For in the latter, we may observe, the most serious problems of serialization were simply by-passed. The average magazine installment, though much too short for conventional chapters, very closely approximated in length the typical letter in an epistolary novel. Furthermore, though not an "episode" in the manner of Smollett, the letter was a self-contained narrative unit, with definite boundaries which editors by long usage tended to respect, and even view with favor since it allowed them, if the need arose, to print two or more at the same time. From the writer's point of view, on the other hand, the letter was an easy, natural, and familiar literary form, well within the experience of the unskilled amateur, and presenting (in the separate parts, at least) only rudimentary problems in control. Everyone expected letters to make false starts and have loose ends. Such irregularities were an amiable feature of the epistolary convention, fully justified by the writer's limited view of events, which he was never expected fully to transcend. In a letter-series, once the character and circumstances of the principal personages were imagined, and the story projected in outline, it was a relatively simple matter for the novelist to proceed, one letter at a time, allowing events to unfold episodically, supplemented or not, as desired, by the reactions of other correspondents. The serious problem of point of view, in the face of which "J. Burton, Bishopsgate," and "J. L——g, West Lavington," were helpless, was here rendered disarmingly simple. The glaring inconsistencies of tone in "The Treacherous Husband," which moves with amateur abruptness from one manner to another, and from unqualified praise of Horatio as "a man of the nicest feelings, and the greatest sensibility," to execration of his conduct as "a most vile and detestable husband," were simply side-stepped in the epistolary novel.[59]

It was for reasons like these, no doubt, that magazine authors found stories in letter form highly congenial, as did writers outside, where a good deal of fiction was likewise being attempted by inexperienced amateurs. In spite of the rare talent of its author, *Evelina* would certainly never have succeeded as a first novel, had it been undertaken as a straight-forward narrative in the manner of Fielding. The epistolary form lent itself to improvisation, naiveté, and miscellaneousness of purpose. In "A Series of Letters," for example, the creator of Miss Wallis and Miss Willis would have found it easy to add eight or ten more letters to her series, allowing the mysterious Mr. Selwin to abscond or die of a consumption, and bringing Sir Edward and Miss Willis successfully to the altar. There are, in fact, signs in the story that the unknown author did not entirely rule out this possibility. Though introduced as a principal character in a story where courtship and marriage were the leading motives, Miss Willis was provided with neither a visible lover nor a trousseau. But the author's uncertainty on this score was successfully obscured by the condition of partial disorder and limited omniscience that prevailed in epistolary fiction, and that made it possible on the installment level, at least, for stories within the range of 5000–20,000 words to achieve a degree of technical competence.

Some of the epistolary novels of the magazines, of course, are much more sustained efforts than "A Series of Letters" and "Miss Trevors to Miss Roberts." About twenty originals in the Catalogue are in excess of 20,000 words. These stories approach in magnitude the conventional two or three-volume novel, and in the aspect which they presented to readers are very similar to translations of French epistolary fiction, like Mme. de Grafigny's *Peruvian Letters* and Mme. de Genlis's *Adelaide and Theodore*, which were a familiar ingredient of the popular miscellanies. The longest of these originals were "Harriet Vernon, or Characters from Real Life, a Novel, in a Series of Letters, by a Lady" (113,000 words); "Memoirs of a Young Lady, in a Series of Letters" (96,000); and "Female Greatness and Virtue Displayed," or "The History of Nancy Pelham" (87,000).

Of the three, "Harriet Vernon," though the longest in the number of words, was actually the shortest in its term of serialization—requiring only two years and three months to complete in the *Lady's Magazine*. The reason for this reduced period is that it belongs to a relatively late period (1807–1809), when magazines generally were beginning to lengthen monthly installments in serial fiction, and when the editor of the *Lady's* was willing to favor readers with as many as eight letters at a time. Its twenty-two parts average nearly 4000 words. The publication of "Harriet Vernon" was pursued at forced stages, without interruption from beginning to end, a sign that the complete work was probably in hand from the outset. Beyond the fact that it appeared in the *Lady's*, and that most of the letters ran a little shorter than those of the average epistolary novel, we find no indication that it was projected as a serial novel. One of its letters is 6000 words in length.

In contrast, the "Memoirs of a Young Lady" (1783–1786) displays definite signs of being written for the magazine in which it was published. Only about a third of the novel was in hand before publication was begun, according to the editor's column. Of the forty-four letters in the "Memoirs," several were divided, but most of the rest were printed one or two at a time. Following this leisurely program, the story was forty-two months in the unfolding. The fable, which turns on the sufferings of a young orphan, separated from her true lover by his tyrannical father, and pursued by powerful and unscrupulous enemies, involves a numerous cast of characters, and several subsidiary intrigues. Read in the bound volumes of the *Lady's Magazine*, as no doubt it was by readers who purchased them over the counter, the agonies of Miss Bertie are ingeniously prolonged. But measured out in driblets, over a period of three and a half years, its longueurs must have been unbearable, even for readers with a high threshold of tolerance.

Of the three full-blown epistolary novels already mentioned, "The History of Nancy Pelham" is undoubtedly the most successful, considered as serial fiction. Shorter than the "Memoirs of a Young Lady" by only 9000 words, this story was divided into twenty-seven installments, instead of forty-six, thus requiring of readers a considerably shorter span of attention. Written by a correspondent of the *London Magazine*, of whose name the editor professed himself to be totally ignorant,[60] the novel is a shameless imitation of *Pamela*, elevated, however, to a still-more genteel sphere, and discreetly avoiding those embarrassing freedoms for which Richardson's admirers felt it necessary to apologize. Such squeamishness was very typical of magazine fiction, which in the name of propriety usually suppressed all passages of physical affection. Except in the townish periodicals, writers rarely introduced melting love scenes or episodes implying strong physical desire.

The story was introduced by a letter signed "Arpasia," which offered the work as an antidote to "the direful infection of indecency, lewdness, and vice" spread by other monthly publications (no doubt she had the rival *Town and Country Magazine* in mind), and called attention to its many edifying features. "The History of Nancy Pelham" was addressed "To the Fair Sex of all Ages, Stations, and Ranks," and was intended to exhibit "Female Virtue in Principle and Refined Improvements"—that is to say,

> humility, candour, benevolence, and gratitude, in their agreeable charms, with self-denial and moderation in prosperity.

Having laid down this ambitious program, in a manner more like a three-volume novel than a magazine story, the author next proceeded to spread out in panoply the cast of her "principal Personages," beginning with Sir William Trenchard, the patriarchal sire of Trenchard Manor—"a Gentleman of an ancient family, large landed estates hereditary, besides considerable acquisitions from other sources"—and descending by degree through the major and minor luminaries of the story. Arpasia's model for this feature of her novel, of course, was *Clarissa*, to which Richardson had appended similar fingernail characterizations in connection with his cast of characters. *Clarissa*, however, had included *thirty-two* names, and *Pamela* (I and II), without labels, forty-two; whereas "Nancy Pelham" was provided with only sixteen—indicating that, despite Arpasia's leisurely preamble, she had already commenced the process of scaling down.

The first installment of the novel contains five letters, which display Lady Trenchard's desire for a suitable young companion; bring to her attention Nancy Pelham (daughter of a Church of England clergyman, "Noted for piety, prudence, and integrity"); and successfully install Nancy at Trenchard manor. The most striking difference between this story and "Harriet Vernon" or the "Memoirs of a Young Lady" is the adept use of direct narrative at the end of Part 1, which brings events into focus, signals the passage of several years, and consolidates our impressions of Nancy's extraordinary virtues. In the interest of economy and speed, in other words, the first installment of "Nancy Pelham" abandons a rigid approach to the epistolary method. It is a species of letters-cum-commentary, not unlike the old stories of "Miranda" in the *Free-Thinker* and *Mist's*, though on a much more ambitious scale.

Part 2 brings us seven new letters (after a supposed interval of four years), and Part 5, five others—at the end of which the author again speaks in her own person. The direct method of narration is pursued for several further installments, after which the author once more adopts the flexible combination of letters and summary that enables her to move swiftly over the events of several years. The death of the beloved Lady Trenchard early in the story sends Nancy back to her father and mother, but not before she has attracted the attention of young William Trenchard, the "heir to near 9000 *l. per annum.*" William, a bowdlerized version of Mr. B., makes no secret of his admiration for Nancy, who, like the virtuous Melissa of Hawkesworth, firmly refuses to entertain his addresses, out of gratitude to her employers. After her lover persistently and honorably renews his proposals in her father's house, however, Nancy finally consents to a marriage. This unequal match in point of property is bitterly opposed by the choleric Sir William, who severs all relations with his son, and excludes him as far as possible from his future inheritance.

The inevitable crumbling of Sir William's stubborn pride under the supersonic vibrations of Nancy's "Virtue and Greatness" occupies the larger part of the novel. The process of reconciliation lasts for years, and is imposingly documented with numerous letters from the heroine to her husband, which circulate in the Trenchard family and eventually, of course, come under the eye of Sir William himself. When the crusty baronet at last relents and invites Nancy to Trenchard Manor, the occasion for such letters is removed, and the epistolary method is abandoned entirely. This is the most significant departure from the method of *Pamela*. Richardson, of course, had himself authorized the occasional use of direct narration, and a few later novelists had enlarged this privilege, but in "Nancy Pelham" direct narrative occupies more than half the novel, which is obviously written for installment publication, and which adopts the same protracted time-span we have observed in other magazine stories in letter form. The events of Richardson's

Pamela (Part I) encompass possibly six months, and those of *Clarissa* less than a year;[61] the action of Arpasia's novel is spread over ten years, and at the end of the novel, borrowing another leaf from Richardson, the author promised a sequel on the same generous scale, intending, she said,

> in some future time, to present [Nancy's] conduct to view, as the wise and tender parent forming the minds and manners of a blooming offspring, training them for publick blessings in their several spheres; as the elegant, discreet housekeeper, the faithful, affectionate wife and friend; and lastly, as the charitable, the hospitable, the generous benefactress of the borough and the manor, in her character as LADY TRENCHARD.[62]

The projected "History of Lady Trenchard" never materialized, however, possibly because Arpasia found a more lucrative market for her wares elsewhere in Grub Street, possibly because the tides of taste were already turning against Richardson, and magazine readers and writers were increasingly taken up with imitations of Laurence Sterne, Mackenzie, and (later) Mrs. Radcliffe.

The Imitators of Sterne

The followers of Sterne in the miscellanies are even more numerous than those of Richardson, but they were uniformly less successful. The long parade of Shandean imitations in the miscellanies for more than forty years is one of the dreariest chapters in magazine history. When Volumes I and II of *Tristram Shandy* were published in 1760, they immediately caught the attention of magazine editors, who excerpted passages from these and later volumes, as they appeared, and eagerly pounced on the *Sermons* and *A Sentimental Journey* as well. The *Gentleman's Magazine*, more reserved than most miscellanies in the attention it paid to prose fiction, published extracts from *Tristram Shandy* in 1760 and 1762, and the other leading London magazines all responded in kind—by which means an acquaintance with the novelist's manner and subjects was quickly spread from one end of the kingdom to the other, and strengthened by reiteration.

The reason for these signal marks of attention was partly the general interest in Sterne as a literary celebrity, and partly the ease with which this pilfering was accomplished in works that specialized in interpolations and detachable episodes; but his vogue also resulted from editors' awareness of the fascination that writings in the new manner had for readers of all kinds. The most popular extracts from *Tristram Shandy* were "The History of Yorick" and the "Story of Le Fever," the two pieces reprinted by the *Gentleman's*; from *A Sentimental Journey*, the stories of "La Fleur and the Dead Ass" and "Maria." These and other extracts from the novels quickly became established as repertory pieces, and went the rounds in the town and country magazines. After Sterne's death, when his letters began to find their way into print in magazines like the *Westminster*, the *London*, and the *European*, these also received full piratical honors. As a result, Sterne's letters were more widely circulated in the miscellanies than those of any other eighteenth-century literary figure, and the force of his example was felt also in the epistolary sphere.

The prodigious popularity of Sterne is reflected in these authorized and unauthorized reprintings. It is seen also in numerous anecdotes and memoirs of his life printed in the same magazines, poetical tributes to him and his works, and a stream of jejune imitations both in prose and verse. The sharp attacks upon Sterne's licentiousness and affectation in the monthly reviews and essay-serials, and in works like Goldsmith's "Chinese Letters," made no visible impression upon the general audience, except perhaps to whet its appetite. Readers avidly embraced not only Sterne's originals, but any number of witless imitations at second or third hand. Outside the magazines these took the form of spurious continuations, volume-length essays or stories in the alleged manner of Yorick, or collections of sketches like Isaac Brandon's *Fragments in the Manner of Sterne*—several of which were also widely reprinted in the miscellanies.[63] Among periodical writers, however, the imitations consisted chiefly of little fugitive pieces, often called "fragments," modeled on the tiny extracts from *Tristram Shandy* and *A Sentimental Journey* with which readers were most familiar. This species of magazine fiction no doubt drew some of its sustenance from the old, but still-vital, tradition of dream-visions in the magazines, many of which were also fragmentary in character, but, on the whole, fragments represent a separate and distinct class of literary work, written with a desire to emulate Sterne's "Le Fever," "Maria," and "La Fleur."

The fragment was typically a short literary sketch, lyrical, narrative or dramatic, in verse or prose, in which an attempt was made to achieve a single striking effect or to enlarge a fugitive moment of experience, in an excessively melodramatic or sentimental manner. Sometimes it was a mere soliloquy or rhapsodic expostulation by an unnamed character, sometimes a snatch of dialogue, or a "scene" devoid of context, sometimes a narrative situation of indefinite outline, which explained little, but implied much. Frequently it offered itself as the shred of some much-longer work, entirely imaginary. Many fragments began *in medias res*, and ended abruptly at a moment of great poignancy, or drew the curtain when the full meaning of events was about to be revealed. The "Fragment in the Shandean Stile," signed "Bob Short," and published in the *Edinburgh Weekly Magazine* for 1779 is typical. In this wisp of monologue, only 240 words in length, the unnamed speaker ruminates sadly on the plight of a young girl who was misled by the honeyed words of a "treacherous debauchee"—ruined—abandoned—scorned by the world—and reduced to a state of despair which

> in a few weeks brought her to the grave.—Poor *Amelia*![64]

This is the whole substance of the "Fragment in the Shandean Stile," which is only a moment of sensibility, captured in a phrase. But not all fragments were of this kind. "Henry Somerville, a Fragment," from the *European Magazine* of 1812, was an engraftment on *Tristram Shandy* itself. Less than a page in length, this little episode (which, incidentally, was signed "TRISTRAM"), was offered as a dialogue between Uncle Toby and Mr. Shandy, who tells a sad tale of domestic estrangement, and evokes a characteristic response from his too-feeling brother.[65]

Other sketches in more or less the same manner, taken at random from miscellanies of the intervening thirty-three years are "The Character of a True Philosopher, in the Manner of the Celebrated Mr. Sterne" (1779), "[A Visit to] Sterne's Grave" (1782), "Fragment of a Novel" (1786), "The Bagpiper, a Fragment, Attempted after the Manner of Sterne" (1796), "The Influence of Riches, in Imitation of Sterne" (1803), "The Friseur, Being an Attempt at an Imitation of Sterne" (1805), "The Slippers, a Turkish Tale, Chapter V [no other chapters]" (1805), and "Rambles through Dublin, a Sentimental Fragment, after the Manner of Sterne" (1812).[66] In 1767, when it noticed the last volume of *Tristram Shandy*, the *Gentleman's* pronounced that Sterne's vogue was due for an early extinction. But actually the magazine run was only getting under way. Little whimsical and disjointed

"Shandeans" (as they were sometimes called) were so common by 1771 that one writer in the *Oxford Magazine* attempted an "Imitation of the Imitations of Yorick." Ten years later, magazine editors were still groaning under the deluge of sentimental fragments,[67] and parodies were becoming nearly as common as the ubiquitous originals. But in England the vogue had still twenty years to run, and in Ireland it was to enjoy a still-later summer. In both countries the interest was supported by the rage, from about 1785, of similar pieces in the "Gothic" and "Ossianic" manners.

The popularity of Shandean fragments was to be expected in an age of amateur authorship. We may discover technical reasons for Sterne's vogue as well as for Richardson's, which lent strong support to the sentimental interest of fragments. In the first place, they allowed the inexperienced writer to try his hand at dramatic scenes and portentous episodes without having to face the more difficult problems of integration. He could begin stories at their most interesting point, sustain them as long as desired, and then break them off with a sob, or pass them off as shreds of diaries or ancient manuscripts. Fragments therefore afforded him most of the pleasures, and spared him many of the pains, of literary composition. They were also popular because they offered scribblers a legitimate form of broken contract. The capriciousness that led them to begin formidable literary enterprises in the *Lady's Magazine*, and then abandon them (not without feelings of guilt) when the going became rough, was here viewed in its most amiable light. Under Sterne's aegis such derelictions of duty were not only authorized, they were exalted as signs of moral sensibility. Fragments, therefore, were a form of Shandyism in real life, and became so common and approved a literary mode that magazine editors were sometimes in doubt whether for a given story they should promise a continuation or not.

Most "fragments," naturally, were very short, only a few hundred to a thousand words. But the followers of Sterne were so numerous that some were inevitably led to attempt more sustained efforts—like "The Life and Opinions of Timotheus Randy, Stay-Maker" (5000 words), "The Oxonian's Sentimental Trip to London" (8000), "Sentimental Vagaries, by a Rattler" (7500), "The Sentimental Rambler" (7600), "The Welch Parson" (5800), and "The Woman of Feeling, a Sentimental Fragment" (5000). Among these stories of novelette length a number of sub-species can be distinguished. The first two are complete novels in capsule form—one a scandalous exposé of high life in three "chapters," the other a little journey in seven installments. "The Sentimental Rambler" and "Sentimental Vagaries," on the other hand, are enlarged episodes, extended into several monthly parts. The "Rambler" interprets "sentimentally" the events of a single afternoon's walk "in quest of health and recreation"; "Vagaries" is a long narrative preface to a tale that never is told.

"The Welch Parson" and "The Woman of Feeling," still another subspecies, are fragmentary novels, with a full-flown intrigue suggested in part. The fact that both, albeit greatly taken up with virtue and benevolence, were first published in the *Town and Country Magazine* in bizarre conjunction with its notorious "Tête-à-têtes," shows how general and undiscriminating was the surrender to Shandyism. The "Welch Parson" begins with seven diminutive chapters, skips suddenly to the fifteenth, and then breaks off abruptly. The hero, a handsome solitary, rescues a lovely castaway from the breakers off Wales, but the fate of her daughter Charlotte remains in doubt. Upon leaving the parsonage, the lady invites Charles to visit her in London, so that "his spirit, his intrepidity and tenderness" may be "displayed in wider scenes"—whereupon "tears stopped her tongue," and the chaise carries her half fainting from the door. Seven chapters are then omitted. In Chapter XV, itself a fragment of only fifty words, Charles's father, the upright "Welch Parson," dies, leaving his family in penury. Did Charles go to London? Was the lost Charlotte also saved from the fury of the storm? Did the two young people meet and fall in love? These and other questions are raised and intentionally left unanswered by this fragmentary romance, in which the most striking signs of Sterne's influence are its moments of excessive sensibility and its highly self-conscious method of narration, which frequently calls attention to itself, and contemplates its own involutions. The love story also possesses Mackenzian features.

"The Woman of Feeling" follows a similar method, and again the tears of Mackenzie are mingled with those of Sterne, a very popular blend among magazine writers. In general, the Man of Feeling had fewer mourners than Yorick, but it was still an imposing retinue. This magazine piece tells the story of a young girl, left penniless by her father's untimely death, and forced into service after her period of schooling. A number of potential lovers enter and traverse the scene, perhaps to return later. Their real importance is obscure, since we are offered only Chapters II to V of her sentimental history, which breaks off in a flood of tears at the moment when her seduction by a handsome officer seems imminent.

> Mistaken tenderness! [declares the author] which has deprived the world of a story pregnant with nature and sentiment. Should they [her too-scrupulous auditors] not have known, that the heart is relieved by disclosing its griefs? and that sorrow, like a divided stream, is lessened every time it is told?[68]

Both "The Woman of Feeling" and "The Welch Parson," like most other magazine pieces in the same manner, are completely devoid of humor, and the tongue-in-cheek, half-ironical touches that made Sterne's novels so fascinating to cultivated readers.

The "Sentimental Journey" of the LADY'S

In addition to these and a great many other magazine stories of medium length written under the influence of Sterne or his disciples, the magazines produced a considerable number of full-length serial works that sought to emulate *Tristram Shandy* and *A Sentimental Journey* in their entirety. The first long magazine imitation of Sterne (this time the manner curiously blended with Smollett's) was "The Disasters of Tantarobobus" in the *Universal Museum* of 1762. The second, and most ambitious of all, was "A Sentimental Journey, by a Lady," which ran with only a few interruptions in the *Lady's Magazine* for over six years, and achieved the doubtful distinction of being the longest original work of magazine fiction, in number of words, ever published in an eighteenth-century miscellany. "A Sentimental Journey" is more than twice as long as "Harriet Vernon," the longest magazine novel in letter form; three times the length of "Sir Launcelot Greaves" (which ran to 86,000 words); and over six times the length of Sterne's original of which it was ostensibly a copy. Despite changes in taste, the reader today finds it possible to imagine how the "Memoirs of a Young Lady," "The Monks and the Robbers," and even "The Welch Parson" might have interested their eighteenth-century audience, but difficult to understand how any pleasure could be derived from "A Sentimental Journey, by a Lady," the most tedious, the most affected, and (in its entirety) the most unreadable of all contemporary works of magazine fiction—except perhaps for other works in the same class. In its own day, however, it passed for a striking novelty, and aroused the obvious envy of other magazine editors.

Commencing its run in August, 1770, about two years after the publication of Sterne's *Sentimental Journey*, this work was projected as the principal serial feature of the new *Lady's Magazine*, prominently mentioned in the initial "Address to the Fair Sex," and given the leading position in each month's offerings from the first issue until 1777, an honor that Smollett accorded "Sir Launcelot" on only a few occasions. Its basic structure is that of a tour or "progress" through the kingdom, presented impressionistically, rather than "historically." After a motto drawn from Watts, on the tendency of travel to "*enlarge* the mind," the story opens abruptly with "A Night Scene" in a stage-coach, denoted by a burst of asterisks, a favorite sign with magazine writers that the muse of Sterne had descended. Then follows a vapid exchange between the author and another, *un*feeling, lady passenger, succeeded in turn by other sketches in the alleged manner of Sterne's *Sentimental Journey*—scenes and portraits, odd events illustrative of "humanity," whimsical digressions, interpolated stories, and snatches of conversation, one succeeding the other in a desultory fashion, but broken up in the orthodox manner with little sub-headings intended to formalize the identity of each paragraph as a significant moment of consciousness.

The numerous ambiguities in Sterne's original, and the hints that suggest a larger purpose for his journey, look both forward and backward in time, glance at *Tristram Shandy*, and provide at least the shadow of an intrigue, were all lost on the author of "A Sentimental Journey," whose only visible motive (as the editor said) was to "enrich" the contents of the *Lady's Magazine* by providing each month five or six pages of modish eccentricities. The carriage is overturned on the Maidenhead road, eliciting a lifeless display of humors; the traveller dines at an inn, takes a seat in the post chaise for Oxford, and later falls into a dream from which she is awakened by a highwayman. In this manner the story progresses by leisurely stages to Henley, Dorchester, and Oxford (where the author lingered for eleven installments); Bath, Bristol, the southwestern counties, London, Canterbury, Dover, and (by a sudden leap) Dublin and the midlands.

> The historical traveller, if I may call him so, is confined to his *rout* [she wrote at one point]... he must take places as he successively approaches

THE

Lady's Magazine;

For AUGUST, 1770.

A SENTIMENTAL JOURNEY.

By a Lady.

"Nothing tends ſo much to *enlarge* "the mind as TRAVELLING, that "is, making a viſit to other "towns, cities, or countries, be- "ſides thoſe in which we were "born and educated."

WATTS's *Improvement*, &c.

The STAGE COACH;

A

NIGHT SCENE,

* * * * *
* * * * *
* * * * *
* * * * *
* * * * *
* * * * &c. &c.

——THIS was all we ſaw, or heard for one quarter of an hour.—A ſuprizing thing when two women, a Frenchman, &c. &c. were in company!

"Oh la! Lord bleſs me! ſays the lady, we are all as dead as a herring!—We ſhall be overturned, and then what will become of us!—The coach indeed was very much aſide.

Pray Ma'am, ſays I, let us not be ſo anxious about ourſelves.—The poor people on the outſide are in a ſituation more dangerous.

People on the *outſide!* replies the lady with an air of diſdain. What have we to do with them? if a thouſand of ſuch creatures were knocked on the head at once, proviſions would be cheaper, and thoſe of their claſs, that remain, might live ſo much the better.

The reflection ſhocked me. — I was in no good humour before.— The inhumane temper ſhe diſcovered made me conſiderably worſe.— On our entrance into the coach, I had received a perſonal affront from this very lady. As I was going to enter the coach, ſhe rudely puſhed me by, ſeized the ſtep, and ſeated herſelf before I knew where I was, or what ſhe was about. The confuſion her rudeneſs occaſioned to me, gave the opportunity to the gentlemen to get before

The Leading Article of the *Lady's Magazine* from 1770–1777
(Here Pictured in the First Issue).

> to them, and dares not deviate from the straight way... The sentimental traveller is not confined to such narrow limits; he ranges over a whole district in the twinkling of an eye... I think that sentimental travelling may in some respect be compared to dreaming, the objects pass alternately before your eyes, and the intermediate spaces become insensible...[69]

As the years went by, however, and her meager fund of humors and sentiments became depleted, the traveller tended to leave the dream world of her sensibility, which alone justified her method, and become much more "historical," focusing more sharply upon the "objects" before her eyes—local oddities, representative scenes and personages, picture galleries, and guidebook information of various kinds—with the result that at least one of her readers complained, and it became necessary to reassure her audience that the "writer of the Sentimental" was "the same who began the work, who planned the *Lady's Magazine*, and who has continued the Journey without intermission."

> Her intention was not [she went on to say] to imitate *Sterne*, but to embellish a description of Great Britain with *sentimental reflections*; and the descriptions will be found to be as accurate as any that have been published; in one respect more valuable... as the modern improvements made in places through which the traveller has passed have been noticed, and are not to be found in any other publication.[70]

What readers of the *Lady's Magazine* thought of this odd defense of "A Sentimental Journey" on the score of objectivity is not recorded, possibly because it enjoyed the special favor of the editor, who seems to have been its author. But the story was allowed to drag its long slow length along for three more years, at the end of which time (it was later acknowledged) the serial was quietly "*dropped* on account of the desire of *many* Correspondents."[71]

But though "A Sentimental Journey" passed unregretted by readers of the *Lady's Magazine*, it made a deep impression on contemporary editors, who paid it the homage of frequent imitation. Partly as a result of its prominent position in this leading magazine, other miscellanies during the next quarter of a century, felt impelled to give place to serialized imitations of *Tristram Shandy* and *A Sentimental Journey*, or essay-series in the Shandean manner. In March, 1773, when the new *Sentimental Magazine* was launched by Kearsley as a rival publication of the *Lady's*, the proprietors could think of nothing better than to promise as the first of the publication's new serial features, "A Sentimental Journey through Life." This work was likewise elevated to the leading position in the monthly roster, and for nine months competed feebly for the favor of the same audience.

There was one difference, however. Kearsley's "Journey" was an imitation of *Tristram Shandy* rather then *A Sentimental Journey*. Unfortunately, for this purpose, "Chastity of Sentiment" was the avowed first principle of the new periodical, and the author was impelled to avoid even a hint of coarseness or vulgarity. Proceeding crayfish fashion, in the manner readers had now come to expect of Sterne's disciples, the story begins with "Part IV" of the novel, in which the Author sits in an "Elbow Chair" and contemplates the York River, ruminating on the events of his life which brought him to this pass. "Parts I" and "II," which then follow, describe with sluggish facetiousness the difficult pregnancy of the author's mother, his father's dispute with the doctors, the altercations among his mother's attendants at his birth, the disagreements over his methods of nursing, his baptism, and so on. Punctuated by numerous digressions and interpolations, the lying-in and its comic consequences occupy eight months of the nine, whereupon in a few sentences the author slides over his boyhood, his education at the university, and his subsequent adventures in London and Paris. At this point the narrative was abruptly terminated with a note explaining that the author, being accustomed to read abed at night, had fallen asleep, and been accidentally consumed in a holocaust that destroyed all his manuscripts. One would like to think that this precipitant close to "A Sentimental Journey through Life" was accomplished by public demand. But the continued popularity of nearly identical pieces in other magazines suggests some other reason.

Other magazine serials of novel length, similarly inspired by *Tristram Shandy* or *A Sentimental Journey* (or by one another) are "A Trip to Margate, by Ansegise Clement, Gentleman" (*London Magazine*, 1781–1782), "A New Sentimental Journey through England, Written by a Lady" (*New Lady's*, 1786–1788), "The Life and Amusements of Isaac Bickerstaffe, Junior" (*General*, 1787–1792), "The Sylph, or the History of Sophia Merton" (*Weekly Entertainer*, 1798–1800), "Benevolent Rambles, or the History of Sentonius" (*Lady's Monthly Museum* 1804), and "The Adventures of a Bad Shilling, in the Kingdom of Ireland" (*Ireland's Mirror*, 1805–1806). There is no more striking sign of Sterne's hold on the popular fancy than the fact that so many London and provincial magazines should give such marked attention to full-length works in his alleged manner. Moreover, in the *New Lady's Magazine*, the *General*, and the *Weekly Entertainer*, these serials were regarded, during their various periods of survival, as the leading articles of the magazines. "Isaac Bickerstaffe" was maintained, without interruption, during the whole run of Bellamy's *General Magazine* (1787–1792), and was left unfinished at the end. The "*New* Sentimental Journey" of the *New Lady's* was ostentatiously offered as the principal buttress of a periodical containing

> More in Quantity, and a much greater Variety of New, Original, and select Pieces (in Prose and Verse) on [e]very curious, useful, and entertaining subject... than are to be found in any other Work of the Kind whatever.

But Hogg's "Journey" was in fact so little new that it might count for a plagiarism, its author obviously writing with the old "Sentimental Journey" open in front of her. She began her story with a similar night-scene in a stage on the same road, and after an identical overturn and transfer to a post chaise, pursued the same route to Henley, Dorchester, and Oxford—affecting throughout the same lifeless humors and stale sentiments, the same species of banal reverie, the same wearisome digressions and interpolations, and the same appalling cuteness of manner that distinguish the whole tribe of Shandean imitations.

In addition to this imposing list of magazine novels, there were numerous essay-series that also came deeply under the influence of Sterne, and two of them, "The Sceptic" and "Manners of the French" in the *Biographical and Imperial* and the *Belle Assemblée*, are sufficiently narrative in character to be included in the Catalogue. Sterne made a deep impression on essay-writers as well as story-tellers, who found that his subjects, methods, manner, and animating ideas were easily assimilated in the essay tradition, at the same time that they lent a modish touch to the essayists' comments on manners and society. Like the author of *The Vicar of Wakefield*, Sterne himself had written partly under the influence of Spectatorial tradition, and in the end he gave it back its own, and more of the same.

Other Influences on Magazine Writers: French Fiction

Addison and Steele, Richardson, and Sterne, and their numerous followers, therefore, were the leading literary forces operating on magazine writers in the eighteenth century. But two others may be mentioned in passing—the French novelists of sensibility and the Gothic romancers. The pervasive influence of the first is more to be suspected than proved, since it blended so deceptively with the native school of sensibility. But the abundance of French fiction in British miscellanies during the whole of the eighteenth century (much of it translated by amateurs) indicates that magazine writers were highly aware of the growing corpus of French fiction, and presumably were influenced by it in their own scribblings. Something further is said about foreign fiction in translation in Appendix III. What found favor in British miscellanies was chiefly the milder forms of French sentimentalism. Editors were notoriously cautious. Readers were traditionally outspoken in expressing their views, and an alert minority of self-appointed censors stood by, ready to voice objections to all signs of excessive sensibility, especially when offered in conjunction with improprieties or displays of libertinage. Furthermore, most miscellany readers were incurably optimistic, and had little stomach for the gloomier aspects of the *roman noir.*

The principal French authors of novels and long short stories that won the approval of magazine readers were Marmontel (by a large majority), Mme. de Genlis, the Chevalier de Florian, and Baculard D'Arnaud—the last-named only in his less somber moods. There were numerous reprintings of *Julie*, *Fanny* and *Le Sire de Créqui* in translation, but none of *Makin* or *Liebman*, and only ephemeral appearances of *Varbeck.*[72] The unacknowledged translation of Arnaud's *Daminvile* in the *Lady's Magazine* of 1779–1780, under the title of "Military Distress," probably impressed readers as a conventional story of suffering lovers, intensified in a number of striking ways, but not greatly out of line with what they were already accustomed to. Its principal departures from the native tradition in magazine fiction were the surprising prolongation of the hero's agonies, the far-flung range of the narrative action (which involves shipwreck on the high seas and enslavement in Africa), the story's highly charged scenes of ecstasy and grief, the feeling of conspiratorial evil generated by the malign forces of the book, and the extraordinary emphasis upon human callousness and barbarity, in contrast to isolated examples of virtue and benevolence. A number of the same features were found in Mme. de Genlis's "Histoire de la Duchesse de C——" and Mme. de Tencin's "Comminge"—both widely circulated in magazine translations. In general, the effect of such works on native periodical writers was to increase the emphasis upon love (if this was possible), intensify the climate of sensibility in their works, and to encourage them to employ continental backgrounds of chateaux, convents, and dungeons.

The anonymous author of the "Memoirs of a Young Lady," cited earlier among the epistolary novels of the magazines, had obviously read French fiction, probably Marivaux's *Vie de Marianne* and the translation of *Daminvile*, just mentioned, which appeared a few years earlier in the same magazine. Beaumont's father, the implacable Lord Devereux, is an English version of Arnaud's Monsorin, supported by the power of patriarchal authority, but not by the power of the throne. But in other respects the novel resembles *Evelina*, whose author, incidentally, had likewise fed on French fiction. Most writers of miscellany stories, being presented with the choice between simple, yet affecting incidents, "rational sentiments, just reflections, and an elegant narrative," and what the *Critical* reviewer called "that hurricane of distress and those romantic situations which bedizen the works of French novelists and their imitators,"[73] elected to produce the former, but it is not always easy to differentiate between the two strains, which (as Foster has shown) were already deeply entwined in the English school of sensibility. We can only say that in the magazines one tended to draw support from the other, but that English models were followed more frequently than French.

Falling in with the fashion for foreign fiction, some writers disguised their own writings as stories "From the French" (just as others passed their French translations off as originals), and of these it may be remarked that they are very little different in manner or substance from the usual magazine story, except for their tendency to employ continental backgrounds.

Gothic Fiction

In contrast with the followers of Arnaud, Florian, and Mme. de Genlis, the Gothicists are easy to recognize, and very numerous. The shorter pieces in this mode are found nearly everywhere, though the longer tended to be confined to those periodicals that published quantities of prose fiction, and had the courage of their readers' predilections-magazines like the *Lady's*, the *New Lady's*, the *General*, the *Monthly Mirror*, the *Lady's Monthly Museum*, and the *Theatrical Inquisitor*. The registers of new fiction indicate that about a third of all fiction published in volume form between 1796 and 1806 was frankly "Gothic" in character, or at least included important scenes of sentimental terror. The patrons of circulating libraries for many years had an insatiable appetite for these fashionable condiments. But only in periodicals with a large feminine following were Gothic novels and novelettes given a status commensurate with their general popularity. As in the case of French sentimentalism, the proprietors of miscellanies were obviously subjected to pressures to which booksellers and the proprietors of circulating libraries were not, since the purchasers of magazines naturally acquired everything in them and were accustomed to expressing their approval or disapproval in letters to the editor. Furthermore, it was the ill fortune of Gothic romance in the late eighteenth century to draw a good deal of the hostile lightning in conservative opinion, which was determined to strike at *some* fiction *some*where.

The Gothic fiction of the magazines has already received close attention elsewhere, and may therefore be dealt with summarily.[74] In general, it may be said that the numerous shorter pieces in this mode were of two kinds —the Gothic *tale* and the Gothic *fragment*. The principal prototype of the first was the eighteenth-century apologue combined with *The Castle of Otranto* and *The Old English Baron*, and other English classics in the Gothic mode; the second was modelled on the Shandean fragment, plus Mrs. Barbauld's "Sir Bertrand," first published in *Miscellaneous Pieces in Prose* (1773), and Nathan Drake's "Sir Gawen" (1790), both of which were widely reprinted and endlessly imitated in British miscellanies for more than twenty years. In the Gothic fragments, which were frequently dreams, and derive in part (via "Sir Bertrand") from the terrors of the damned in "The Inchanted Palace" of the *Visions of Sir Heister Ryley* (1710–1711), the supernatural was freely admitted. The only limit on their marvels was their authors' powers of imagination, usually very feeble. Elsewhere, however, among the magazine Gothicists, the *surnaturel expliqué* was the rule. Eighteenth-century readers were greeted by very few real ghosts or goblins in the columns of the *Lady's*, the *General*, and the *Lady's Monthly Museum*, although they suffered from a good many false alarms. This caution was, again, a result of editorial timidity, but also a sign of Mrs. Radcliffe's influence. Sustained works of sentimental terror began to appear in the women's magazines only after her brilliant successes in 1790–1791. The moral bias of her novels, their abiding emphasis on propriety, their modish interest in the benign as well as the frightening aspects of nature, and their view of love as a gentle tremor of the heart with few more serious consequences than a dreamy melancholy, made them highly congenial to magazine writers of a whole generation. Though occupied with outlaws, bandits, and unscrupulous noblemen in a foreign clime, *A Sicilian Romance*, *The Romance of the Forest*, and *Udolpho* are squarely in the genteel tradition in prose fiction.

At the same time, Radcliffean romance, with its long-drawn suspense, its slow unfolding of a central mystery and labored "explanations," its sustained episodes of terror, and its cumulative atmosphere, suffered even more than other types of fiction from the rule of *multum in parvo*. In the end, as we have seen, the author of "The Monks and the Robbers" found it beyond his powers to complete his novel on episodic principles, and most other magazine Gothicists gave up the attempt. The best of the magazine novels in the Gothic mode, and one of the few full-length stories ever to graduate from miscellany to volume publication, was the Rev. George Moore's "Grasville Abbey," which made not the slightest effort to accommodate itself to the requirements of installment publication. Moore obviously wrote his romance for the general trade, and then for some reason transferred it to the columns of a popular miscellany. About three-fourths the length of *The Romance of the Forest*, of which it is in part an imitation, it is a very striking example of a work of fiction designed to be read in its entirety in a few sittings, but agonizingly protracted in the *Lady's Magazine* for a period of four and a half years.

The writers of Gothic novelettes, on the other hand, were more successful in meeting the problems of serialization imaginatively. In the *Lady's Monthly Museum*, in particular, they learned how to achieve Radcliffean effects to scale, and, within the compass of two to six installments, how to project a story in which the division into parts was not only accepted, but effectively exploited. But in this magazine Gothic romance unexpectedly encountered the shrill opposition of governesses and boarding-school mistresses, who denounced these "frantic productions" as designed to "enflame the passions" of their charges and "tincture both the fancy and the heart with extravagance and romance"—with the result that, after the first volume, the amount of Gothic fiction in the *Museum* was sharply curtailed.

Many other literary fashions are reflected in the novels and novelettes of the miscellanies. All the breezes of the popular fancy sweep across the broad stream of magazine fiction between 1740 and 1815, setting up ripples and eddies in the shallow current; and since many of the stories were themselves written by readers, they provide an intimate revelation of their real tastes and interests. On an almost month-by-month basis, in the London and provincial periodicals, it is possible to follow the fluctuating fascination of the magazine audience not only with epistolary novels and sentimental journeys, but with pseudo-travel literature of all kinds, "tête-à-têtes" and "secret histories," Moorish and Arabian tales, folk literature, "historical" fiction and stories of primitive life, Ossianism, German, Swiss, and American subjects, and other vagaries of the popular fancy—sometimes blended and combined in curious ways. The original writers of the magazines were in no real sense experimental. On the contrary, as a class they were extremely conventional. They followed fashions rather than led them. But they were often capricious and amateurishly uninhibited, and capable of affecting more than one manner at the same time—the Ossianic and the Shandean, for example, or the "eastern" and the "Gothic" modes.

The Essential Character of Miscellany Fiction

There is nothing in the over-all picture from which the eighteenth-century apologist can take heart. With a few conspicuous exceptions, already noted, the original miscellany fiction published between 1740 and 1815 was trashy, affected, and egregiously sentimental. Judged as literary art, it was devoid of imagination and wretchedly written. It made few demands upon its readers, and its range of allusiveness extremely restricted. Its basic substance was the cliché. Considered in terms of its real subjects and themes, it was almost exclusively concerned with the problems of courtship and social advancement in the upper middle-class—with fulfillment of self through love, with finding a lost father, or winning family and fortune by marriage to a person of superior social connections. Its favorite formula was suffering goodness in a universe providentially weighted in favor of the same. Occasionally a pair of deserving lovers was sacrificed in order to obtain striking theatrical effects.

In "The Temple of Sensibility," written by a reader of the *Lady's Monthly Museum* in 1800, Charles Westerville, the son of a rich merchant, and Louisa Mansfield, a country clergyman's daughter, are two lovers of exquisite sensibility. They exchange their tremulous vows in a sylvan temple, built by Charles to celebrate their first place of meeting. The unfeeling Mr. Westerville, however, disapproves of this unequal match, and sends his son on a long sea voyage. A great storm blows up. Mourning over her lover's absence, Louisa walks along the seashore, and stumbles on the body of a shipwrecked sailor, whose "clay-cold" breast contains "*her own portrait.*" It is the hapless Charles!

Usually, however, as in "Nancy Pelham" and the "Memoirs of a Young Lady", the deserving lovers ride out the storms of parental disapproval, intriguing enemies, and adverse circumstances, and reach a haven of spiritual and material blessings to which even the most sentimental reader could take no exception. Their final union is one long promise of fulfillment, unqualified by irony, or unalloyed by any possibility of failure or disenchantment, or even by uncertainty. The approved values of this dubious literature are the joys of love and mutual affection ("sincere esteem," not the passion that wrecks and destroys), the consolations of friendship, the genteel pleasures of country life, and the delights of benevolence and domestic felicity, fortified, if possible, by £10,000 a year and a baronetcy. Its corresponding dangers and evils are seduction or loss of reputation, betrayal in love, treacherous friendship, implacable parenthood, poverty, snobbishness, libertine principles, and prodigality of all kinds, especially gambling and loose living.

The writers themselves of miscellany fiction emphasized its truth to real life and its moral efficacy. But beyond its intense preoccupation with happy and unhappy love, the domestic virtues and vices, and social failure and success, it would seem to have had little relevance to the lives of the persons who wrote it or of those who read it, viewed in the larger framework of history. The same pre-occupation with genteel subjects and domestic themes, of course, was shared by the majority of English novels during the same period. But in the magazines we find no saving minority concerned even remotely with the problems of social justice, the rights of man, Deism and Methodism, enfranchisement, enclosure, India, the American War, or the French Revolution—except for the sufferings of beautiful and virtuous émigrées. During the critical years between 1789 and 1815, most miscellanies faithfully summarized the news each month in double columns, fine print, but it never wakened the story-writers from their long dream of love.

With Smollett's and Goldsmith's retirement from the miscellanies in 1762–1763, the satirical and anti-sentimental modes of magazine fiction were allowed to lapse, and with them any tendency to examine critically English society at large, or even to reflect the upper middle-class world with partial fidelity. In spite of the hundreds of stories by school-boys and girls in eighteenth-century miscellanies, not one, apparently, was written about daily life in an academy or college, the cruelties of headmasters, or the adventures or misadventures of boarding-school misses. On the other hand, they favored readers with a great many accounts of love at first sight in an elevated social sphere, courtship in great country houses, the pleasures of the London season, and life in fashionable watering places or in Paris; and a considerable literature of Gothic romance dominated by tyrannical marquises and marchionesses, robber barons, wicked monks, and scheming abbesses. The scenes in London shops and rooming houses that made *Evelina* such a delight to contemporary readers, were all passed over in miscellany novels and novelettes. The world of this fiction is the daydream world of idle persons of extremely limited experience but greatly enlarged social aspirations who had fed their minds on the trivialities of the magazines and the circulating libraries—or the surrogate world of hacks and sub-professionals who had viewed at best the fringes of fashionable society, but were prepared to give readers what they wanted. One has only to recall the subjects of Ned Ward's *London Spy* and *Weekly Comedy*, the adventures of Pacolet in the *Tatler*, Sir Roger de Coverley, Defoe's narrative letters to Mr. Mist and Mr. App, Mrs. Haywood's unvarnished case histories in the *Female Spectator*, Johnson's "pictures of life," Goldsmith's newspaper and magazine pieces, and Smollett's "Sir Launcelot Greaves" to be struck by the degree to which later writers of periodical fiction had withdrawn from the world of familiar life into a make-believe realm of fashion and elegance, or of flamboyant melodrama.

The original magazine fiction of the eighteenth century is not mass literature, since it was still read by only a minority of English society (with a potential audience of perhaps 200,000 in 1800), but, in a very real sense, it displays mass literature in the making, since much of it was written to create as well as to satisfy a set of specialized predilections on the part of the largest possible circle of readers in its day. Beginning in 1759–1760, when the circulations of the common miscellanies entered their period of most rapid expansion, a kind of descending spiral was set in motion, wherein magazine proprietors won larger and still-larger audiences by an increasing sacrifice of their inherited ideals. The professed aim of the miscellanies after 1731 was "Knowledge and Pleasure" combined, that is, knowledge as a form of pleasure; and most of them continued for the rest of the century to affect a great air of self-improvement—since readers were eager to be improved. To be cultivated and informed was a necessary first step in order to qualify for the polite world. In their annual prefaces and addresses to the public, editors called conspicuous attention to the many edifying features of their compilations, which were further supported by pretentious title pages and emblematic frontispieces. But except in a few historical miscellanies, repositories, annuals, and reviews, they never made good on these boats. Most miscellanies are an undiscriminated jumble of elegant trifles, moral essays, foreign and domestic news, charades, prose fiction, occasional poems, "enigmas," anecdotes, and articles designed to satisfy a very fickle and flimsy curiosity.

Hogg's *New Lady's Magazine* of 1786, like Bellamy's *General* of a year later, is Goldsmith's "Infernal Magazine" thrice compounded. In the first number readers were invited to enter the pantheon via a pretentious series of prefatory archways—beginning with a copper-plate engraving displaying Minerva as "the Genius of This Work," flanked by Truth and History, presenting a copy of Hogg's new magazine to the Ladies of England. This was followed by a crowded title-page itemizing *forty* areas of "Knowledge and Pleasure" in which the *New Lady's* intended to keep abreast; a grandiose dedication to the Princess Royal; and a royal patent that managed to suggest not merely the protection but the auspices of the throne. All these typographical flourishes, these spacious promises, and this thrashing around by the editor were sheer flummery, since the magazine was actually a routine collection of fashionable fribbles, moral vacuities, flagrant imitations, and unacknowledged borrowings from other magazines, including old copies of the *Lady's*, which the new magazine proposed to supplant. Hogg's methods were more egregious than most other booksellers', but not different in kind. All of them in some sort misled the public by insisting on the informative character of their compilations, and by pretending to bring readers in close touch with the world of fashion and polite learning.

THE
NEW LADY'S MAGAZINE;
Or, POLITE *and* ENTERTAINING
COMPANION FOR THE FAIR SEX:

Entirely Devoted to their Uſe and Amuſement.

A WORK far Superior to every other PUBLICATION of the KIND hitherto PUBLISHED, or now PUBLISHING.

CONTAINING

More in Quantity, and a much greater Variety of New, Original, and ſelect Pieces (in Proſe and Verſe) on very curious, uſeful and entertaining ſubject—together with a greater and more elegant Variety of Copper-plates, than are to be found in any other Work of the Kind whatever.—And including, among an infinite Variety of other uſeful and intereſting Particulars, Eſſays, Letters, Diſſertations, Treatiſes, and curious Productions, relating to

Hiſtory,	Happineſs,	Sentiments,	Affluence,	Virtue,
Geography,	Manners,	Accompliſhments,	Voyages,	The Stage,
Muſic,	Literature,	Honour,	Travels,	Dreſs.
Amuſement,	Biography,	Improvement,	Medicine,	Education,
Politeneſs,	Criticiſm,	Inſtruction,	Prudence,	Conduct,
Cookery,	Tranſlations,	Entertainment,	Faſhion,	The Married State,
Confectionary,	Taſte,	Gardening,	Philoſophy,	Proſperity,
Friendſhip,	Wit,	Œconomy,	Morality,	Poetry, &c. &c.

And many other Miſcellaneous Subjects of Knowledge and Pleaſure, which will render this New Lady's Magazine a moſt agreeable Companion (far preferable to any other Work of the Kind) to Female Readers, of every Age, Rank, and Condition in Life.

TOGETHER WITH

A faithful Regiſter and Journal of the whole Tranſactions of the Times, Foreign and Domeſtic; Births, Marriages, Deaths, Promotions, Preferments, &c. and a Critical and Impartial Review of ſuch new Books and Publications as are offered to the Ladies either for their Improvement or Entertainment.

The Whole Publiſhed under the immediate Inſpection of

THE REV. MR. CHARLES STANHOPE,

Of QUEEN'S-SQUARE, GREAT ORMOND-STREET.

BY THE KING'S ROYAL LICENCE AND PROTECTION,

AND

INSCRIBED TO THE PRINCESS ROYAL OF ENGLAND.

VOL. I.

EMBELLISHED with the greateſt Variety of elegant, ſuperb, and numerous Copper-Plates, Portraits, Patterns, Songs ſet to Muſic, and other EMBELLISHMENTS which will be worth of themſelves alone above four TIMES the Price of the whole Work.

LONDON:

Printed, by Royal Authority, for ALEX. HOGG, at the KING'S ARMS, No. 16, Paternoſter-Row, and ſold by all Bookſellers, Stationers, and Newſcarriers, in Town and Country.

[*To be Publiſhed Monthly*, Price only 6d.]

An Encyclopedic Title-Page (1786)

The truth is that, in spite of their endless complaints about plagiarists and their public outrage at the practices of their competitors, most magazine publishers learned to live very comfortably under the prevailing copyright system. They were quite content to feed upon one another and upon the general trade, letting writers of talent and reputation find employment elsewhere, and engaging hacks and semi-professionals to supply them with the necessary novelties. With a shrewd sense of their audience's vanities and naive aspirations, they carefully cultivated its writing members, cajoling them into working for them gratis, praising their efforts effusively, and (what is worse) printing them as models of elegant composition. On the fringes of the rapidly expanding circle of semi-literate readers, new writers in turn were led to take up their pens in the same sterile enterprise. By thus catering to readers' desires to realize themselves as novelists, poets, and essayists, miscallany editors no doubt satisfied a deep urge on the part of the writing audience, but they cannot be exculpated from the charge of venally exploiting it in the mercantile interest. The profits were enormous, of course, as the great number of miscellanies in the field after 1770 demonstrates. Starting in 1764, George Robinson, in a relatively short period, amassed a fortune of £ 200,000, much of it from his phenomenal business as a wholesale dealer, but part also from his profits from the *Town and Country* and the *Lady's* magazines, which must have amounted to at least £ 5000 a year.[75]

We have sometimes been invited by the critics of mass culture to view the eighteenth century with special approval, as an age with a homogeneous reading public, when popular and cultivated taste were happily united, and when the common reader was blissfully content to take his standards from above, free from the pernicious effects of commercialism that mar the popular literature of our own age. This picture is lent some support by the piratical practices of the miscellanies, the publishers of which (as we have seen) tended to abridge and excerpt the approved novels of the day, following the dictates of the larger book-sellers and the monthly reviewers. But it is very seriously qualified by the "original" fiction of the same magazines, in which editors took increasing pride. This fiction reveals anything but a homogeneous literary culture, dominated by the best poets, essayists, novelists, and critics. Rather it exhibits in abundance those very qualities of daydream, poverty of feeling, and separation from life as known to its readers that are usually laid at the door of the modern novelist.[76]

During a very brief period in the early eighteenth century, if we may judge from their phenomenal circulation, the *Tatler* and *Spectator* seemed to effect a union of popular and cultivated taste, but the public involved was only a tiny fraction of the whole population. And already in the *Gentleman's Journal* of 1692–1694, and the *Records of Love* of 1710 (if not in the *Tatler* and *Spectator* themselves), the literature of sensibility had found an easy access into periodical publications, poisoning the air with its oversimplifications and fantasy-spinning about love. The earliest magazine criticism of the novel we have noted, that in the *Athenian Mercury* of 1692, expressed a feeling of alarm at the spread of this very disease. By the 1730's the vapors had infected other popular miscellanies, though they were still largely concentrated in the women's magazines. Twenty to thirty years later, during the very zenith of Richardson's, Fielding's, and Smollett's reputations, they had become the dominant mode of most popular fiction in the magazines as well as outside, against the tide of which the monthly reviewers and the essay-critics could make little headway. Almost any volume of the *Monthly* or *Critical* from their earliest years will show that vulgar romances, scandalous histories, and trashy pseudo-biographies outnumbered the acceptable novels by two or three to one—and later the ratio became even more unfavorable. This literature was different in many respects, naturally, from modern best-sellers, but not superior in literary quality. In some respects it was worse.

The cleavage between popular and cultivated taste was serious, therefore, even in the middle years of the eighteenth century, and what we seem to witness in the succeeding 150 years is not the disintegration of a homogeneous literary culture, but the gradual extension, on its lower levels, of an amorphous one, among a large reading public which previously had no literary taste at all. We may seriously doubt whether the new readers of fiction in the *Lady's*, the *Town and Country*, the *New Lady's*, the *General*, and the *Belle Assemblée* were lured from a sober concern with the major eighteenth-century novelists, or with serious literature chosen by their betters. More likely, like Isabella Thorp in *Northanger Abbey*, they were coddled on circulating library fiction, or on magazine stories like "A Series of Letters," "The Temple of Sensibility," "Nancy Pelham," "Memoirs of a Young Lady," "The Monks and the Robbers," and "The Treacherous Husband." The record of the magazines, in any case, indicates that the expansion and decline of popular taste in prose fiction were not successive, but simultaneous phenomena. In the miscellanies of the eighteenth century there is only feeble evidence for a prelapsarian age in literary culture. The fall of the common reader (if fall there was) was successfully engineered in Paternoster Row during the very process of his creation.

APPENDIX I

The Fiction of the Religious Magazines

The stories of the religious miscellanies constitute a more sharply defined corpus of fiction than those of other specialized magazines, yet confirm a number of the general observations that have been made about periodical fiction in the last years of the eighteenth century. As a class of publication, the religious magazines are themselves somewhat removed from other miscellanies, and the quantity of fiction that they contain is small. Editors naturally displayed a good deal of prejudice against most forms of popular entertainment, of which novels, like the theater, were reckoned among the most godless. On the famous "Spiritual Barometer" published by the *Evangelical Magazine* in 1800, the "Love of Novels, &c." was ranked with "Scepticism," total neglect of private prayer, and the prizing of "Deistical company" at 40° below zero, just above drunkenness and adultery. As late as 1806 the same magazine was even attacking allegory as a devilish device for "perverting the word of God, and whipping it into froth." And when the *Christian Observer* in 1809 at last found a novel which it could tolerate, it would not allow it to be called a novel.[1]

Nevertheless, the urge to introduce narrative ingredients into the religious magazines, the *Evangelical* and the *Christian Observer* included, was almost irresistible. This was especially true of the evangelical miscellanies, whose hold was chiefly on working-class readers, to whom questions of doctrine and abstract morality were less interesting than graphic pictures of piety and goodness. Despite bitter doctrinal differences among themselves, all the evangelical magazines were inclined to follow a similar plan, consisting usually of pious tracts, sermons, and exhortations of the faithful; religious poetry; exemplary lives and deaths; and accounts of strange and providential happenings. It is in the last two categories that fiction tended to intrude.

The *Arminian Magazine* is the most interesting of the religious miscellanies, since it was founded by Wesley, and received his close personal attention from 1778 until his death in 1791. Wesley was a man of far greater sophistication and intellectual grasp than most other editors of eighteenth-century miscellanies, religious or otherwise, and he put a good deal of himself into the magazine. He announced in the first volume that the *Arminian* would publish verse (which was traditional)—adding, however: "But we faithfully promise not to insert any Doggerel: nothing which shall shock either the understanding or the taste of the serious reader."[2] In conformity with this policy he revived in the *Arminian* a good deal of seventeenth and early eighteenth-century verse, not all of it religious in character, and pursued a much more liberal policy in other respects than did his competitors, or even his successors in the same magazine. He reprinted, for instance, a long extract from Giovanni della Casa called "The Refined Courtier,"[3] and included other works of secular interest. He published also a good many anecdotes, apologues, oriental tales, dreams, visions, and allegories from earlier authors (including Addison and Dr. Johnson), intended to amuse and edify his readers, not all of whom, he recognized, embraced Arminianism. Some of these narratives were even serialized, as, for example, "The Account of Ambrose Gwinett" (originally published in the *Gentleman's*, but widely reprinted in other miscellanies), "Superstition and Religion" (a dream allegory), "The Sufferings of Thecla" (an early saint's life), and Addison's "Vision of Mirza." The longest piece of serial fiction that Wesley published was "God's Revenge Against Murder and Adultery," taken from John Reynold's *Triumphs of God's Revenge* (1621). Though greatly abridged, this sensational chronicle of betrayal, lust, assassination, intrigue, and providential punishment, ran regularly from May, 1787, to December of the following year, curiously interlaced with the sermons, pious testimonials, and last words of dying Christians that made up the principal part of the magazine.

Wesley's annual prefaces in the *Arminian*, compared with his contemporaries', were distinguished by an admixture of good sense and humility. They admitted criticisms of the magazine, most of which were directed against its lack of variety. Some of the stories and verses published in the *Arminian* were obviously designed to meet this objection. To this end he also invited twenty-four of his ministers to write the stories of their own lives, to be published from time to time in the magazine. Some of these pious autobiographies read like novels themselves, although all are allegedly true. The most surprising, "An Account of Mr. Silas Told (Written by Himself)," ran for eighteen months, contemporaneously with "God's Revenge Against Murder and Adultery."[4] Born in 1711, Told shipped as an apprentice seaman in 1724, bound for a term of eleven years. He endured many hardships and suffered many barbarities in the West Indies and Africa and on the high seas. But none of the native savagery he witnessed, or his sufferings from hurricane, pestilence, privation, shipwreck, and piracy, could compare with the inhumanity, greed, and wanton cruelty of some of his own English captains in the slave trade. Viewed as a Methodist tract, the "Account of Silas Told" is a persuasive argument for Wesleyan ideals of personal conduct; viewed as popular entertainment, it is a picaresque story of adventure on the Spanish Main which would have delighted readers of both Defoe and Smollett.

The *Arminian* printed no fictitious narratives in excess of 5000 words except "God's Revenge Against Murder and Adultery," but some of its later contemporaries did, and altogether eleven religious miscellanies contributed, between 1797 and 1815, twenty-five stories to the Catalogue of magazine novels and novelettes, practically all of them "originals." In general this fiction was of two kinds: *first*, highly moral or religious tales, allegories, dream visions, adventure stories, "histories," and "cases" ("The Honest Farmer, a Tale," "The Temple of Faith," "The Palace and the Castle, an Allegory," "Letter[s] of a Country Squire to the Editor," "The Farmer's Sabbath," "The History of an Old Pocket Bible, Supposed to be Written by Itself," and so on)—in other words, traditional kinds of magazine fiction (mostly essay-type), adapted to the uses of religious instruction or moral uplift; and *second,* more indigenous types of narrative based upon subjects and forms peculiar to the religious miscellanies. This second kind, because it anticipates Dickens and other nineteenth-century novelists, has greater interest in the history of fiction.

A basic ingredient of most evangelical magazines was homiletic history and biography—that is, striking instances of piety and goodness, accounts of "exemplary lives" and "happy deaths," and miraculous "experiences," designed to show Christians how to live and die, and to demonstrate the operation of divine grace in human affairs. The autobiographies of Silas Told and other disciples of Wesley were intended to serve this kind of testimonial function in the *Arminian,* but there was a long tradition for such pieces in the religious miscellanies, even before Wesley's ministers took up their pens. In the early magazines these homiletic histories were usually short and highly factual in character. Many of them were written by readers, and a primary emphasis was upon their authenticity. With time, however, such pieces became highly stereotyped, and the emphasis was shifted towards authentic *effects,* and away from names, dates, and other documentary details. In addition, even when dealing with real persons and events, writers discovered the advantages of the sustained narrative episode. Death-bed scenes that were prolonged for months were common. The last moments of little children were particularly admired, and thousands of eighteenth-century and early nineteenth-century readers who never read *Clarissa,* or probably any novel at all, must have wept over the passing of these juvenile saints, distinguished always by their never-murmuring sweetness and goodness, their universal forgiveness, and their transcendent faith in the scriptures. By a long process of trial and error writers learned to give these lingering departures the proper magnitude by including touching farewells to home and friends, glimpses of heaven beyond the grave, bedside prayers punctuated by the sobs of the bereaved, and sometimes the complete conversion of sinful spectators.

"The Life and Death of a Sunday Scholar," from the *Cottage Magazine,* a story emanating from the parsonage at "H———," is a typical 6000-word pseudo-biography in this mode, presenting "the case of a young lad, belonging to our Sunday School," whose exemplary life demonstrated "the final triumph of faith in a most glorious death"— and, incidentally, the many pious benefits to be derived from sabbath schools.[5] The literal truth of this story, which was six months in the telling, would be less suspect, were it not anticipated in so many particulars by the lives and deaths of other juvenile saints, and accompanied by numerous other fables in the same magazine about people with names like "Abraham Faithful," "Nathaniel Upright," and "Thomas Goodman." "The Young Cottager" in the

Christian Guardian, later collected with a few other stories by the Reverend Legh Richmond in a volume entitled *Annals of the Poor*,[6] is another sustained piece of necrological literature (18,750 words), in which the little girl's death leads the narrator to an enhanced awareness of the "inward and inbred corruption" of himself and the rest of the world, and the divine harmony of the universe. "The Village Apprentice" in the *Watchman*, on the other hand, is a story of the happiness and moral regeneration wrought by a country parson who liberated "a poor parish apprentice from the brutality of her master." All three of these "cases" may have had some basis in fact, but they have obviously been greatly embroidered in the telling; and like the "Secret Histories of the Court" and the amorous "Tête-à-Têtes" in the townish magazines of an earlier period, also about real people, it seems proper to classify them as fiction.

Jane S———, the heroine of "The Young Cottager" is "a young bud of grace" who will "blossom in paradise," but other pieces in the religious magazines describe the horrible deaths of blasphemers, drunkards, and infidels, and give accounts of apparitions, striking conversions, and miraculous deliverances. The effect of such pieces in the "mad Methodist Magazines" upon the occupants of the parsonage at Haworth has long been known, and their influence upon young Marian Evans is also suspected. Coleridge himself had written in 1797, in a well-known letter to Thomas Poole, "I never yet read a Methodist's 'Experience' in the Gospel Magazine without receiving instruction & amusement."[7] It is possible that Dickens also came under their influence. The intense dislike that he later displayed for professional pietism and sabbath-day prohibitions does not preclude this possibility. Even if Dickens was not acquainted with the marginal fiction and highly charged biographies and pseudo-biographies of the evangelical magazines, many of his readers were. He therefore inherited a large audience of humble background and unsophisticated tastes, long prepared by pious compilations like the *Cottage Magazine*, the *Christian Guardian*, the *Herald*, the *Watchman* and the *Evangelical Magazine* to be moved and edified by the sufferings of Oliver Twist and David Copperfield, and the striking deaths of Little Nell, Paul Dombey, Steerforth, and Bill Sikes.

APPENDIX II

Magazines Specializing in Prose Fiction

Only about nine periodicals specializing in prose fiction were published in the three-quarters of a century from 1740–1815. They were not, therefore, a conspicuous feature of the period. In fact, they were much less numerous than the serials devoted exclusively to poetry, music, history and biography, politics, the theater, and religion. Moreover, all nine of the fiction magazines appeared between 1780 and 1810. Thus they belong not to the generation of Richardson, Fielding, and Smollett, but to a much-later day when the number of novel-readers had greatly increased, and when there was a sufficient audience to support periodicals devoted entirely to prose fiction.

The surviving magazines of this class are of two kinds: (1) collections of classics in reprint; and (2) redactions of Gothic romances and sentimental adventure stories for readers with a taste for marvels, terrors, and hectic melodrama. The first group, which includes the *Novelist's Magazine* (1780–1789), the *New Novelist's* (1786–1787), the *Gleaner* (1805–1806), *Harvest Home* (1807–1808), the *New Gleaner* (1809–1810), and the *New Magazine of Choice Pieces* (1810), was the more conservative, tending to reflect the approved taste for prose fiction as expressed in the reviews and elsewhere. The readers of these magazines were eager to improve themselves by reading the best fiction and acquiring libraries of the same, for a very small outlay of money each week. The second group, which includes the *Marvellous Magazine* (1802–1804), the *Tell-Tale* (1803–1805), and at least one other magazine,[1] belongs to the years from 1802–1805 when Gothic fiction was at the flood-tide of its popular favor. These periodicals were so little concerned with received opinion and the approved monuments of the past that they usually disguised the authorship of even classics in this genre. Neither group, normally, published new fiction—that is, original stories or new translations of foreign works. Both were largely content to exploit the corpus of existing fiction under prevailing copyright conditions. The *new*-fiction magazines belong to a still-later generation, when there was a much-larger audience for the novel, one less interested in reprints of standard works and vulgar redactions, and more attracted by the facile productions of a new breed of journalistic writer.

The earliest and most famous of the eighteenth-century periodicals specializing in prose fiction is the *Novelist's Magazine,* a collection of classics of English and foreign fiction, published in weekly numbers over the course of nine years, and amounting in the end to twenty-three volumes. The *Novelist's* enjoyed one of the most phenomenal sales of any eighteenth-century magazine. According to Rees, in its period of greatest public favor 12,000 copies of each number were sold weekly.[2] It may be described as the first all-fiction magazine, however, only if we place a very broad interpretation upon the term *magazine*, and disregard the various precedents provided by (1) old comic journals like *News, from the Land of Chivalry*, the *London Spy*, and the *Weekly Entertainment* of 1700, which employed narrative or sub-narrative forms almost exclusively; (2) Ozell's *Monthly Amusement* of 1709; and (3) the numerous serial books published from the earliest years of the century, particularly novels and collections of stories. The first of these three classes of works, the comic journals, may be disregarded, since their purpose and methods were so completely different from those of the *Novelist's Magazine*, but the last two require closer attention.

The *Monthly Amusement*, a short-lived periodical published between April and September, 1709, and found advertised in early numbers of the *Tatler*, represents a pioneer effort to establish a kind of semi-fiction magazine upon a radical new principle. Its design, as unfolded in the "Advertisement by the Proprietors" in the first number, was

> to publish every Month a Novel or a Play, and sometimes both together, selected from the best *Spanish, French*, and *Italian* Writers. All the Novels of CERVANTES and the best Plays of MOLIÈRE, are already done, and will head the Van in this intended Collection.

In conformity with this program, "Number I" contained "The Little Gypsie, a Novel," translated from Cervantes's *La Gitenilla*, and "Number II," an English version of Molière's *Misanthrope*. The succeeding four numbers offered *Le Malade imaginaire*, two additional "novels" of Cervantes ("The Jealous Estremaduran" and "The Deceitful Marriage"), and a "Pleasant and Delightful" collection of shorter "histories," entitled "Love's Academy."

The essential difference between the *Monthly Amusement* (1709) and the *Records of Love* (1710), which gave equal emphasis to prose fiction, is that the latter was a literary miscellany, like the *Gentleman's Journal*, attempting to provide a mélange of poems, sketches, and little stories, new as well as old, within the prescribed limits of a certain number of pages every month. The *Monthly Amusement*, on the other hand, was a kind of serial anthology. It worked with a more flexible quota of pages (the first number was 117 pages; the third was 66), but was committed from the outset to an exclusive program of novels and plays. Furthermore these were to be drawn only from "the best *Spanish, French*, and *Italian* Writers." Neither periodical survived for more than a few numbers—suggesting that the public for both was much more engrossed with the *Tatler* and its imitators; but ultimately the more flexible principle of the *Records of Love* was to prevail. As far as is known, no further efforts were made for three-quarters of a century to publish a magazine along the lines laid down by Ozell.

Though differing fundamentally in its plan from the miscellanies, however, the *Monthly Amusement* was a genuine periodical publication, appearing in regular installments, numbered and dated, and preserving in volume form the identity of its monthly parts;[3] Harrison's *Novelist's Magazine* of 1780, on the other hand, was really a collection of novels issued in sheets, without any effort to preserve the identity of the separate numbers. Therefore, it has a much closer affinity with the serial books of the eighteenth century, particularly the narrative works. In Wiles's list of nearly 400 serial books published between 1678 and 1749, roughly ten per cent may be classified as fiction. Most of the 35 or 40 narrative works are single titles, like *Pamela, Telemachus,* and *Robinson Crusoe,* but others are collections of stories, as, for example, *Polite Tales for Young Gentlemen and Ladies* (1744–1745) and the *Modern Story-Teller, or General Entertainer* (1748–1749), or novels in series, like *Religious Novels* (1729) and the *Weekly Novelist* (1735–1736). The first-named, the *Polite Tales,* appeared in ten weekly "numbers" of four sheets each between November, 1744, and the following January, selling for 6d a bundle—about the same quantity and price as an issue of the *Gentleman's Magazine,* in which it is found advertised. The tales, drawn "from The Most Celebrated Authors," were all short, apparently. According to Wiles, however, at least two novels in reprint, Mrs. Manley's *New Atalantis* and La Calprenède's *Cleopatra,* were issued in the *Weekly Novelist,* an intended "Select Collection of the Best Novels," which ran to at least 36 parts.[4] Presumably there were other works similarly published in the thirty years between 1750 and 1780.

The only real differences between the *Novelist's Magazine* and earlier serial collections like these were (1) the magnitude of Harrison's enterprise, which included a much longer series of more imposing works of fiction; (2) the fact that his novels (though not his weekly numbers) were separately and chronologically dated, and gathered into successive volumes, each with a separate title page, like periodicals; and, most important, (3) the fact that Harrison called his collection a *magazine* and thus associated it with the miscellanies rather than with the serial books. But these points of difference should not be labored, and it is very difficult to make a precise distinction between the *Novelist's* and the *New Novelist's Magazine,* and other serial anthologies like Harrison's *British Classics* (of the essay-serial), Cooke's *British Novelists,* and Hogg's *New Weekly Novelist* of a slightly later period. All five were closely associated with the comprehensive movement towards cheap books in the eighteenth century, in which the miscellanies were also involved. But none of the five was published under conditions permitting that interplay between editor and audience which characterizes genuine periodical publications. There were no "correspondents" for the *Novelist's* or *New Novelist's Magazine.* Nevertheless, in deference to tradition, Harrison's and other publications of the same class have been included among the periodicals (where Graham canonized them in 1930)[5] and their contents have been gathered into the Catalogue, although it must be recognized that *Tom Jones* and *Clarissa* published in fascicules at weekly intervals are hardly to be viewed as serial novels, and that it is only by sufferance that they may be regarded as magazine fiction at all.

Except that it was devoted exclusively to fiction, which would repel many purchasers, the *Novelist's Magazine* was really an extremely conservative collection. The care and expense which Harrison lavished upon the engravings show that it was obviously designed to attract more than the circulating library trade or the audience of the *Lady's Magazine.* There is nothing modish or mawkish about the *Novelist's Magazine.* Owing to copyright restrictions, which he scrupulously observed, and from which, of course, he immeasurably benefited, most of the native English novels Harrison included were at least fourteen years old, and many of them were considerably older. The magazine appeared among a crowded new generation of fiction-writers in the 1780's, but its "novelists" do not include Fanny Burney, Clara Reeve, Sophia Lee, Mrs. Brooke, Mackenzie, Henry Brooke, Charlotte Smith, Dr. Moore, or even Walpole. There is Goethe's *Werther* near the end of the series—a surprising contemporary touch; but most of the foreign fiction, like the English, is heavily weighted in favor of old stand-bys and accepted masterpieces. At first view, therefore, the *Novelist's Magazine* seems quite removed from the eddying stream of the new English novel. On closer scrutiny, however, it reveals a considerable degree of contemporaneity, and by its omissions as well as its admissions reflects the general contours of late eighteenth-century taste. It does not include, as Graham carelessly stated, "all the famous novels of the century."

Harrison began his collection with a relatively recent and very popular work in the oriental mode, Hawkesworth's *Almoran and Hamet,* and then followed in rapid succession (since the arrangement in the bound volumes was perfectly chronological), *Joseph Andrews, Amelia,* Langhorne's *Solyman and Almena,* and *The Vicar of Wakefield,* alternating older and newer, lighter and more serious, with a shrewd eye to the fickle public palate. Before it completed its eight-years' run, however, the *Novelist's* had published all the novels of Richardson, Fielding, Smollett, and Sterne; *Rasselas,* Mrs. Lennox's *Female Quixote, Pompey the Little, The Memoirs of Miss Sidney Bidulph* and *Nourjahad, David Simple,* and a number of lesser, once-admired, but now largely forgotten mid-century works like Dr. Dodd's *The Sisters* and Kelly's *Memoirs of a Magdalen*—works designed "to recommend virtue" and "decry vice" or otherwise "support the interest of morality."[6]

The magazine obviously could not ignore French fiction without disappointing many purchasers, but selection must have presented a problem, since French novels, though highly approved in some circles, were strongly disapproved in others, because of their sentimental excesses and their alleged licentiousness. The principal writers whom Harrison recognized were those likely to be least offensive to the greatest number of conservative readers—Voltaire, Le Sage, and Gueullette (with two titles each); Fénelon, Marmontel, the Chevalier de Mouhy, Mme. de Grafigny, and Treyssac de Vergy (with one). He included also *Marianne,* but no other Marivaux, no Prévost, Crébillon, Diderot, or Rousseau—in spite of the great esteem in which the latter, in particular, was held in both the reviews and the miscellanies. Among the numerous older works of English and foreign fiction which Harrison could safely admit, he chose the *Arabian Nights, Tales of the Genii, Gulliver's*

Travels, and *Robinson Crusoe.* But there was no other Defoe, and (some conspicuous absences) no Aphra Behn, Mrs. Manley, or Ned Ward, all three of whom had fascinated earlier generations. Mrs. Haywood is represented by three selections, but they are all from her later, reformed period. The *Novelist's Magazine* published no secret histories, no collections of *novelle,* no pastoral romances, no picaresque fiction before Le Sage and Smollett. Except for *Don Quixote,* as a matter of fact, it included no fiction written prior to 1700—no Boccaccio, no Scarron, no *novelle* of Cervantes, no *Arcadia,* no romances of Scudéry, D'Urfé, or La Calprenède. The editor of the *Novelist's* still considered *The Female Quixote* to be of interest to his readers, but not the fiction that Mrs. Lennox had felt it necessary to attack. In short, compared with the panoply of names and titles spread before readers of the *Literary Panorama* twenty-five years later,[7] the roster of the *Novelist's* seems austere and somewhat oppressively "classical." But it more or less accurately reflects the structure of late eighteenth-century taste as represented by the serious reviews and other journals of literary opinion, including the more liberal of the essay-critics.

In the *New Novelist's Magazine* of 1786–1787, published also in weekly numbers, Harrison made an effort to supplement the offerings of the *Novelist's Magazine* with a serial anthology of shorter pieces of various kinds—fragments, tales, little histories, and novelettes, many of them drawn from magazine literature. The shortest novel in the *Novelist's* had been *Solyman and Almena* (22,500 words); whereas the longest in the *New Novelist's* was the "History of the Count de Comminge" (20,000), in Mrs. Lennox's translation. The new magazine offered only three stories of novel-length, as against twenty-nine in the 5000 to 12,000-word bracket. A few of the pieces included may be originals or new translations, but most of them are familiar repertory pieces like Mackenzie's "Father Nicholas," Mrs. Haywood's "Lady's Revenge," Mrs. Lennox's "Tale of Geneura," Miss Aikin's "Sir Bertrand," Johnson's "Vision of Theodore," and other classics derived from essay-serials, volumes of literary essays, and collections of "miscellanies." Three are by Harrison himself, two of them reprinted from the *British Magazine* of 1782–1783, which was published by the same house.

The record shows that the *New Novelist's* was a favorite with editors of provincial miscellanies, who depended upon it to fill their monthly or fortnightly quotas of prose fiction, and a great many of its selections reappear in later serial anthologies: the *Gleaner* (1805–1806), *Harvest Home* (1807–1808), *New Gleaner* (1809–1810), and *New Magazine of Choice Pieces* (1810), supplemented with more recent translations from the French and German, extracts from new magazines and collections of stories, and detached episodes from novels of the previous twenty years.

Closely associated in method with serial anthologies like these and other collections of old favorites, yet very different in intention, are the serial chapbooks, which specialized in sensational fiction, retailed in monthly parcels—usually one novel or tale at a time—but later collected in volumes. The *Marvellous Magazine and Compendium of Prodigies* (1802–1804), the *Tell-Tale, or Universal Museum* (1803–1805), and *Radcliffe's New Novelist's*

Pocket Magazine (1802) all belong to this class of periodical, which made a regular practice of butchering the classics of Gothic romance, compressing them to a fraction of their original length, intensifying (if possible) their melodrama, and subjecting them to a general rechristening. The *Marvellous Magazine*, for example, published in monthly numbers a series of disguised redactions of this kind, tailored precisely to seventy-two pages (or in a few cases to exactly thirty-six). Mrs. Radcliffe's *Italian*, the first of about thirty such "prodigies," was thus reduced to one-fifth its normal size, outfitted with a substitute cast of characters, and offered as "The Midnight Assassin, or Confession of the Monk Rinaldo." Obviously the readers of this blood-curdling tale, from which, of course, all the author's artful graces had evaporated, were less interested in the fact of her authorship than in a new set of counters and a fresh parade of marvels and prodigies. Most of Mrs. Radcliffe is found in the first twelve numbers of the *Marvellous Magazine,* transformed far beyond any requirements of the copyright situation. *The Mysteries of Udolpho,* now 30,000 words instead of 275,000, emerged as "The Veiled Picture, or the Mysteries of Gorgono, the Appenine Castle of Signor Androssi." Lewis's *Monk,* similarly transmogrified, found a new identity as "Father Innocent, Abbot of the Capuchins, or the Crimes of Cloisters."

In this manner the *Marvellous Magazine* published a long series of "Gothick," "romantic," and "pathetic" tales between May, 1802, and April, 1804, with only two acknowledgments. During 1803–1805 the *Tell-Tale* offered more than eighty "interesting Adventures, Voyages, Histories, Lives, Tales, and Romances" of a similar provenience, of which fifty-one were of novel or novelette length, numbered, but undated except by years. A few bore authors' names, like "Marmontel," "Mme. de Genlis," and "the late T. Bellamy" (whose "British Barons," already hectically compressed, suffered still-further excisions, and was re-titled "The Barons of Old"). Ten were attributed to Sarah Wilkinson—indicating that she was probably the curator of the "Universal Museum" as well as its busy redactor. The literary quality of both the *Marvellous Magazine* and the *Tell-Tale* was inferior, judged even by magazine standards. Their contents were obviously designed for an audience somewhat less discriminating than that of the serial anthologies. Many of their readers, one suspects, were schoolboys and girls. The titles we have mentioned are really those of chapbook romances, intended to be sold singly as well as in collected form. A great many, therefore, are found listed also in Andrew Block's *English Novel.*[8]

The serial chapbooks, on the other hand, were more up-to-date than the serial anthologies. *The Italian* had been only five years before the public when "The Midnight Assassin" appeared. These periodicals also contained German romances, very much the fashion after 1794–1795. Being very limited in range however, they tell us less about the general taste than the *Novelist's Magazine,* except to demonstrate how far, by 1802–1803, prose fiction was now embraced by readers in the lower levels of the reading public. The degree of literacy demanded by the *London Spy* of 1698–1700 and the *Marvellous Magazine* of 1802–1804 was roughly the same, but the intervening one hundred years had seen a revolution in popular taste as a result of which the common reader now frankly accepted prose fiction as a medium of popular entertainment, without expecting it to describe the world in which he himself lived, or without requiring the support of famous authors' names. "Rinaldo" in "The Midnight Assassin" was only Mrs. Radcliffe's Schedoni, thinly disguised, but in the history of British journalism he was really a creature of the new age, an age in which a large popular audience could now interest itself in sensational fiction divested of its genteel trappings.

APPENDIX III

Foreign Fiction in Translation

Among the accepted boundaries of literary geography that need to be adjusted in order to accommodate large tracts of magazine fiction hitherto unknown or only dimly apprehended are those of stories in translation. The amount of French, German, and other foreign fiction in eighteenth-century British periodicals is imposing, and it is not entirely drawn from writers of the first eminence. Magazine readers were naturally influenced by the approved taste of the age, but they were also instinctively attracted to second and third-rate fiction. Therefore, although a good many foreign classics were reprinted in the *Novelist's Magazine* and elsewhere—works like Galland's *Arabian Nights,* Fénelon's *Telemachus,* and Boccaccio's *Decameron*—the statistics run heavily in favor of writers of lesser stature. All together the Catalogue lists works by fifty-one known French authors, fourteen German, five Italian, two Spanish, two Danish, and one Russian writer[1]—in addition to which we find many stories of undisclosed authorship that are simply labeled "From the French" or "A German Story," or otherwise indicate a foreign provenience.

The first long German story to be published in a British magazine appeared in 1776; the third, in 1786. The great Teutonic vogue, however, chiefly for Lafontaine and Kotzebue, came after 1800, and was largely a nineteenth-century phenomenon.[2] The interest in French fiction, on the other hand, was sustained during the whole period from 1740–1815, and reflects, albeit dimly, the larger movements of French taste over three quarters of a century. Important new works of French fiction like *Candide* and *La Nouvelle Héloise* were often noticed in the *Monthly* and *Critical* even before they were translated into English. Most reviews, abstract journals, and historical miscellanies kept their readers informed on important literary events across the channel, and the popular miscellanies exploited some of the same interest by publishing quantities of French apologues, fairy stories, oriental tales, and full-length novels and romances. With a few exceptions, all of the best-known figures in French fiction from Fénelon to Chateaubriand achieve at least one entry in the Catalogue, and some many more than one. Among eminent authors Voltaire is the leader with nine entries; then Lesage with seven; Rousseau, Montesquieu, and St. Pierre with three each; Fénelon with two; and Crébillon *fils*, Marivaux, Diderot, Duclos, and Chateaubriand with one, although several of these stories were printed more than once.

In general, however, very little interest was expressed in what we think of today as major fiction. Marivaux's *Marianne* appeared once, in the *Novelist's Magazine,* where it enjoyed an enormous circulation, but forty to fifty years after the book's first publication in both French and English. Although Marivaux's name was occasionally invoked in discussions of *Pamela* and *Clarissa,* magazine readers were not directly exposed to any of his fiction, not even long excerpts, until 1784, by which time *Marianne* was ready to be regarded as a classic.

On the other hand, the novels of Rousseau, who belongs to a later literary generation, were received with striking signs of contemporary interest. The *Monthly Review* and the *Critical* gave signal attention to *La Nouvelle Héloise* and *Émile* in 1761–1763, and short extracts and epitomes of these novels are frequently encountered in the miscellanies. But the only works of Rousseau to figure in the Catalogue are "Queen Fantasque," "The Levite of Ephraim," and "Emilius and Sophia"—all brief, and all printed only once.[3] We may say, therefore, that Rousseau's influence as a fiction-writer, to the degree that it was transmitted through the magazines, was spread not by means of the novels themselves, long extracts, or abridgments, but through critical commentary, short excerpts, and reviews, or popular intermediaries like Mme. de Genlis, whose pedagogical novel, *Adèle et Théodore* was translated and widely circulated in both the *Universal* and the *Lady's Magazine.*

Among the masters of eighteenth-century fiction, the most conspicuous absence in the Catalogue is that of the Abbé Prévost, who received no attention from magazine translators or redactors. The *Novelist's Magazine,* which published seventeen full-length works of French fiction between 1780 and 1789, most of them eighteenth-century classics, for some reason passed over Prévost completely—a surprising omission in view of the importance attached to his works by twentieth-century historians of the novel. Another sign of neglect is the fact that Prévost was seldom mentioned in the anecdotes, little biographies, and memoirs of contemporary novelists which are so familiar a feature of the eighteenth-century miscellanies, and which provide a rough index to popular tastes and interests. By discriminating readers, like Clara Reeve, and members of the Burney circle, Prévost was esteemed as an important novelist. But the record of the miscellanies indicates that the *Le Doyen de Killerine, Mémoires d'un Homme de Qualité,* and *Cleveland* did not figure in the consciousness of the average magazine reader, although he was otherwise occupied with sentimental fiction. Possibly translators and editors with whom the decision rested felt that the miscellany audience would be repelled by Prévost's hurricanes of distress and his agonizing pictures of passion as a destructive force. They may also have felt that the novels were too long and too compact with incident to make good risks as serial fiction. No doubt, too, his works seemed a little old-fashioned by 1759–1760, when the great run on French fiction began in the miscellanies, although in the same period this condition did not inhibit the translators of Fénelon, Le Sage, Mme. de Tencin, and other authors of the same or an earlier literary generation.

The lack of general interest in Prévost, though surprising, is not extraordinary, since sharp discrepancies between polite and popular taste were a normal feature of the eighteenth-century miscellanies. Readers of the *Lady's*, the *Town and Country*, and the *General Magazine* were sometimes willing to be dictated to by their betters, but usually they indulged their own preferences, which tended to subvert the hierarchy of merit promulgated by the reviews and other organs of approved opinion. The record of the Catalogue shows that major French fiction received only perfunctory homage from the popular miscellanies, compared with the attention squandered on writers of lesser stature. About half of the fifty-one French authors mentioned in it are minor fabulists, *conteurs*, and romancers like Mlle. L'Héritier, Mme. D'Ormoy, Bricaire de la Dixmerie, Barthelmy Imbert, Ducray-Duminil, Saint-Lambert, and Mme. de Saint-Venant, writers of interest today only to literary antiquarians.

Viewed in terms of numbers of entries, the principal French authors encountered in magazine translation, in order of frequency, are Marmontel, Mme. de Genlis, the Chevalier de Florian, Bricaire de la Dixmerie, Baculard D'Arnaud, Mme. de Gomez, and Voltaire, and of these Marmontel was the overwhelming favorite. Voltaire is a striking exception to the sentimental rule, his satirical romances being considerably removed in manner and intention from run-of-the-mill magazine fiction in England. The marked attention given to *Candide* upon its first appearance, which included two English translations within a matter of weeks, a long two-part review in the *Critical*, and abridgments of the novel in Lloyd's *Evening Post* and in Kinnersley's *Grand Magazine of Magazines* are signs of an international reputation that tended to overrule the usual predilections of the miscellany audience. But the thinness of Voltaire's magazine record (except, of course, for shorter pieces) is exposed if we look beyond the number of his entries in the Catalogue, and take into account the total number of his *citations*—that is, if we measure the general interest in his works not merely by the titles first printed in nine periodicals, but also by the frequency with which they were *reprinted* in others. Voltaire's fiction has a very low repetition count. Of the nine entries, only one is a double citation.[4] His novels and novelettes make a grand total of only ten magazine appearances over a span of forty-six years, most of them in collections of classics like the *Novelist's* or *New Novelist's Magazine*, or in periodicals like the *Gentleman's* or Smollett's *British*, which were pitched to readers of a superior degree of literary sophistication.

In contrast, Arnaud, with only nine entries in the Catalogue (actually eight) achieves a grand total of twenty-three citations, more than twice as many as Voltaire. Equivalent totals for Marmontel are forty-two entries (eighty-six citations); Mme. de Genlis, thirty entries (thirty-eight citations); the Chevalier de Florian, eighteen entries (thirty-four citations); Bricaire de la Dixmerie, eleven entries (nineteen citations). A single story of Florian, "Claudine," was printed ten times in the magazines; another, "Célestine," nine, in four different translations. Records like these, of course, were achieved only with the support of periodicals like the *Lady's*, the *General*, and the *Bon Ton Magazine*, motivated primarily by the desire to please the greatest number of potential readers in their day. The phenomenal run on "Claudine," which occurred within the space of only five months in 1792, is partly accounted for by the appearance in September of *New Tales from the French of Florian*, published by Egerton, on which collection magazine proprietors made routine drafts. But it was anticipated in August by an original translation of the same story in the *European*, whose editor had discovered Florian's *Nouvelles nouvelles* on his own. The *European's* version was quickly transferred to the columns of five other miscellanies, including the *Lady's*, the *Scots*, the *Hibernian*, and the *Bon Ton*, where it could be read concurrently with the piracies from the trade edition in other magazines.

In selecting French fiction for magazine circulation, editors were obviously motivated by several different principles, which sometimes operated singly, sometimes in conjunction with one another. One was the principle of reputation, which helps to explain the high incidence of both Voltaire and Arnaud. Readers were eager to be exposed to the works of continental authors whose names were celebrated in fashionable circles, either as masters of the art of fiction, or writers in the pink of fashion.[5] A separate but related principle to reputation was accessibility—the availability of both French and English texts. Only a handful of miscellanies like the *European* were willing or able to provide new translations of foreign fiction. Most of them depended upon other magazines, or upon trade editions of works as they came before the public. Editors, in other words, usually made their choice of stories not from the whole range of French fiction spread out in panoply, but from someone else's preliminary screening, usually that of the London booksellers, which was itself fairly rule of thumb. Even when they published new translations, unless these works were directly commissioned, magazine editors were dependent upon the taste and interests of their writers, who were sometimes professionals, but often amateurs, working from odd copies of lesser fiction not always easy to come by. When Clara Reeve suddenly abandoned her translation of Lamarche-Courmont's *Lettres d'Aza* in 1778, it took the editor of the *Lady's* more than six months to obtain the French original, and some of the other foreign fiction published in the same magazine is still unidentified.

A third principle operating in editors' minds, in selecting translations for magazine publication, was that of novelty—the obvious fascination of readers with stories that showed slight but startling deviations from the expected in subject matter or manner. As an ingredient of prose fiction, of course, novelty was a very complex and ephemeral quality, extremely difficult to isolate. It depended upon a thousand particulars, now vanished, which were once an unmistakable part of the literary climate. Furthermore, it frequently appeared in combination with the most egregious clichés. But there is no question that some of the interest shown by the miscellany audience in Marmontel, Arnaud, Florian, and Mme. de Genlis, and to a certain extent in Voltaire also, was prompted by their unusual subjects, or by their novel approaches to the familiar themes and hackneyed situations of eighteenth-century fiction.

Still another principle of choice was brevity. Under the rule of *multum in parvo* only a few editors were willing to embark upon works of one hundred or two hundred thousand words. Therefore, except in the *Novelist's Magazine*, the *petits conteurs* and novelette-writers enjoyed a considerable advantage over the authors of longer works of fiction, some of which, in serial form, would have required years to bring to completion. Mme. de Genlis's *Adèle et Théodore*, one exception to the rule of brevity, ran for four and a half years in the *Universal*, even though abridged in the process, and a competing translation in the *Lady's* was abandoned after four years, perhaps because the novel was already available in circulating libraries. Both magazines published quantities of foreign fiction in translation, but the bulk of it was of medium length or shorter. Of the thirty titles of Mme. de Genlis listed in the Catalogue, twenty-four are novelettes, and three others are less than 18,000 words.

The most important principle at work in the minds of proprietors of magazines, however, and an obverse corollary of that of novelty, was the rule of conformity—the affinity of the subjects, themes, and dominant attitudes of French or German fiction with those of already-current popular magazine literature. Translators and editors sometimes gave way to caprice or heeded the exhortations of reviewers and essay-critics, but they usually inclined towards fiction that their experience told them would be attractive to a large and miscellaneous audience of readers, uninterested in fine strokes of irony and satire, complicated states of mind, or literary and philosophical subtleties. Here the minor sentimental and didactic writers enjoyed their greatest advantage, for there was in the magazines from the middle years of the century a strong current running in favor of edifying stories of happy and unhappy love, suffering goodness, and triumphant virtue projected in terms of high life, or domestic life at the genteel level.

The principle of conformity is seen operating in conjunction with other principles in the case of Arnaud, where editors and translators passed over the more morbid of the *Épreuves du sentiment*, like "Makin" and "Liebman," showing a tacit preference for the author's less extravagant flights of sensibility. The composite image of Arnaud presented by the English magazine translations is a recognizable version of the original, toned down to satisfy conventional expectations. Besides novelty and conformity, Arnaud had the additional advantage of brevity. All but one of his magazine translations could easily be encompassed in the normal span of two to four installments. He was also for a period extremely fashionable, as the record shows.

The first Arnaud to appear in a British magazine was "Fanny, or the Happy Repentance," offered in the *Universal* for July, 1766. This translation was taken without acknowledgment from the trade edition just published by Becket under the same title. Arnaud was coolly received in critical quarters. Becket's edition was derided in both reviews for its numerous absurdities, and the *Monthly* went out of its way a few years later to warn readers against "Adelson et Salvini" as "a monstrous, unnatural romance," even before it had been translated into English.[6] Although "Fanny" may have been interesting to advanced readers of the *Universal* in 1766, Arnaud's entrance into the popular miscellanies was obviously premature, for the story was not reprinted in another periodical until 1780. Eight years later, however, in 1774, prompted perhaps by Murdoch's new collection of translations, called *Tears of Sensibility*, one of which was reprinted in the *London Magazine* (under Arnaud's name, but without Murdoch's), the *Universal* published its own translation of "Salisbury," one of the *Nouvelles historiques*. This time the French writer seems to have caught on, and a mild rash of Arnaud broke out in the London miscellanies, fed by the *Universal,* that lasted for about ten years. The magazine translations of Arnaud, like those of Voltaire, almost invariably carried the author's name, a sign of the rule of reputation. But "Daminvile," the longest of the magazine translations, which ran in the *Lady's* as "Military Distress" for thirteen installments, was offered without any sign of its origin, showing that by 1779–1780 *darnauderie* could sustain its own weight in a popular magazine.[7]

The interest in Arnaud was succeeded in 1791–1792 by the briefer, but more intense vogue for the Chevalier de Florian. In France Florian's novels and short stories had for some years enjoyed a considerable popularity, and the *Six Nouvelles* of 1784 had already been mined by two English trade editions. But both of these, for some reason, had been generally ignored by the miscellanies. Then, prompted perhaps by the serialization of two full-length romances, "Numa Pompilius" and "Gonzalvo de Cordova," in the *Town and Country* and the *Lady's,* partly perhaps by new French and English collections of his tales, editors of English periodicals suddenly discovered Florian. Eighteen magazine appearances are recorded within the space of twenty months. This number would be still larger, if it did not exclude shorter pieces like "Selico" and "Zulbar," which were equally popular.[8]

The coming of Florian to the periodicals was long prepared for by Gessner, whose tiny idylls had flooded the women's magazines for nearly twenty years, but it was also anticipated by the current interest in Gothic romance. Exotic backgrounds and astonishing adventures, some of them terrifying, were major ingredients of Florian's fiction. Although the themes and dominant ideas of all of his productions were very much the same, each called for a striking new *mise-en-scène*. The setting of "Claudine," where the author interrupted his story to hymn the praises of Gessner, was Savoy; that of "Valérie" was Italy. In "Camiré" it was the jungles of Paraguay; in "Célestine," Grenada and the Sierra Nevada. Florian's tales usually involve a pair of young lovers, separated by parental rapacity or the usages of a supposedly civilized society, but finally united under the most romantic circumstances. In "Valérie," the heroine, tricked into marrying a man she detests, lies dead (or seemingly so) in a tomb beneath a Florentine church. Her lover forces his way to her bier at midnight and restores her to life by the passionate intensity of his grief. In "Camiré" the hero, a noble American savage, rescues the niece of the governor of the colony from a jungle serpent; buys her hand with a Chilean goldmine; and flees with her to his own people, where they may live in perfect innocence and liberty. In "Célestine" the lovers, again the victims of civilized greed, are separated during an attempted elopement, and wander for years in search of one another. At length, disguising herself as a shepherd, the heroine becomes the revered leader of a pastoral community by the sea, where she is discovered by her lover when he is fleeing from Algerian pirates. Leaving the village only long enough to claim Célestine's inheritance, the happy pair returns to make a virtuous life among the peasants.

Florian's elegant make-believe is devoid of Marmontel's ironical overtones, or Arnaud's philosophical questionings. He found his principal home, therefore, not in the *Universal* (which had led the vogue for Arnaud, but ignored Florian completely), or in the *European* (except for "Claudine"), but in very popular magazines with large numbers of feminine subscribers, like the *Lady's,* the *General,* and the *Sentimental and Masonic Magazine* of Dublin. The phenomenal interest in Florian faded out after several years, but was successfully revived in the period from 1805–1808, when it competed with the new taste for Mme. de Genlis, whose didactic romances and edifying tales of high life flooded the miscellanies of the early nineteenth century.

The magazine vogues of Arnaud, Florian, and Mme. de Genlis are on the whole successive phenomena, depending in part upon special circumstances that conspired to bring each writer in turn to popular attention. The rage for Marmontel, however, commenced ten years earlier than the first of these, and survived the eighteenth century. It seemed to transcend transient conditions of the literary climate, and govern the taste of a whole age. It was supported by all kinds of magazines, including the *Gentleman's,* and even won the grudging approval of the monthly reviewers. It is altogether the single most extraordinary phenomenon in the realm of magazine fiction in translation, although the *Contes moraux* have received only slight attention from modern historians of the novel.

Marmontel was a writer of humble origin who rose rapidly to eminence in court circles, owing partly to his literary talents, partly to his ingratiating personal qualities. He received a solid education at several provincial schools, where it was expected that he would enter the priesthood. Instead, with the encouragement of Voltaire, who had read his verses, he came to Paris with the hope of becoming a poet. At Voltaire's prompting, Marmontel wrote several tragedies, two of which were highly successful. Then, coming under the powerful patronage of Mme. de Pompadour, he served for several years as Secretary to the Public Buildings at Versailles. Finally, in 1756, he obtained a position under Boissy on the *Mercure de France,* the official literary journal, and a highly lucrative publishing monopoly. Later he succeeded Boissy as editor. Seeking to revive interest in the *Mercure,* he wrote for it a series of short stories and novelettes, beginning in 1756 with "Le Moi." This story won an immediate success, and was quickly followed by others in a similar vein. During his first three years with the *Mercure* Marmontel published a total of twelve tales in the magazine.

In 1761 he lost his connection with the journal by unintentionally offending the Duc d'Aumont, but in the same year he collected his stories in two volumes of *Contes moraux*, adding several new pieces. The *Contes* enjoyed a prodigious sale, and earned their author a European reputation. Later he wrote literary articles for the *Encyclopédie,* a number of popular plays and operas, and two successful novels, *Bélisaire* (1767) and *Les Incas* (1778). In 1791 he collected two new volumes of short stories, *La Veillée* and *Les Déjeuners du village*. After the revolution he served briefly in the Assembly of the Electors of the Third Estate, but then he retired from public life, wrote a celebrated volume of memoirs (published posthumously), and died in a cottage in Normandy on the last day of the year 1799.

As a story-teller Marmontel possessed numerous qualities designed to appeal to readers of very different sensibilities. His forte was the finely-lined portrait, the adroitly-managed scene, the piquant situation, built up and resolved in a climate of elegance and fine feeling. The *Contes moraux* are generally disregarded today. To modern readers they seem shallow and contrived, and unrelated to the real concerns of common life. Among readers of his own day, however, they passed as fascinating studies of human nature, possessing a high degree of contemporaneity. The scene of Marmontel's first story is ancient Athens, but the theme is the essentially egotistical character of love between the sexes. The principal interest in "Soliman II," one of the most popular of the tales, is the manner in which a despotic monarch and a great amoureux yearns for some check upon his irrational impulses. His antagonist is a saucy young European in his harem, whom he finally takes to wife in spite of the laws of sultans. Both antique and oriental subjects, of course, were extremely trite. Marmontel's special competence lay in his ability to lend freshness and pungency to the time-worn counters of the eighteenth-century short story.

The "Shepherdess of the Alps," according to Marmontel's own account, was a daydream inspired by the sight of a thatched cottage on a country estate near Paris. The shepherdess herself was a portrait of Mme. Gaucher, the mistress of Lord Albermarle, the English ambassador at Versailles, who had entranced the young novelist with her beauty and ingenuousness. But the theme of this story, which is developed with some irony, is the heroine's fidelity to her lover in a relationship outside the law. As in the other *Contes moraux*, although prompted by personal factors, Marmontel's fancy was guided by elusive conditions in the literary and social climate that made his stories extremely interesting to several generations of readers on both sides of the Channel.

The prodigious popularity of the *Contes moraux*, of which there is much contemporary evidence, is confirmed by the numerous French editions of the work, listed in the catalogue of the Bibliothèque Nationale: four in the first year alone (1761), and at least ten others between 1763 and 1780. By this time their vogue seems to have subsided in France, although Marmontel continued to attract many imitators (two of them being Arnaud and Mme. de Genlis), and the two volumes of *Nouveaux contes moraux* went through five French editions between 1791 and 1818.

In England the response to the *Contes moraux* was slightly delayed, but it was of even longer duration, if we take into account the record of the magazines. The first English Marmontel in volume form was *Select Moral Tales,* translated by Miss Roberts and published in 1763. This little volume, which included only four of the tales, went unnoticed by both the *Monthly* and the *Critical.* Two competing translations of the whole collection, however, quickly followed—*Moral Tales, by Marmontel,* by an anonymous translator, published by Becket and De Hondt, and the *Moral Tales of M. Marmontel,* translated by Denis and Lloyd, and published by Kearsley. These two versions, each dated 1764, but really published in November, 1763, were favorably reviewed together in the *Monthly* and the *Critical* for January, 1764. In both cases, however, reviewers felt that the anonymous translation was superior, for which reason, no doubt, it was more frequently reprinted, and enjoyed the favor of magazine pirates. It went through a second edition in 1766, at which time a third volume of more recent tales was appended, and later became the basis for at least five further English editions between 1768 and 1800.[9] In addition, Mrs. Pilkington published in 1799 a new collection of selected translations.

The record of English interest in Marmontel is even more striking when the magazine versions are brought into the picture. In fact, four of the *Contes moraux* made their first appearance in English dress in the *St. James's Magazine,* which was then edited by Robert Lloyd. Beginning in June, 1763, Lloyd published in the *St. James's* a series of four "Moral Tales, from Mr. Marmontel," which became the nucleus of the Denis and Lloyd two-volume collection, published in November. Between July and October, 1763, there were four reprintings in other miscellanies from the *St. James's* series, and during the succeeding eighteen months we discover ten additional piracies from the Becket and De Hondt *Moral Tales.* Later there were many others from the supplementary Volume III. Between 1763 and 1766, a total of fifteen out of a possible twenty-one Marmontal stories found their way into periodicals, most of them more than once.

The intense popularity of Marmontel diminished slightly after 1766, but it never fully lapsed until the nineteenth century. "The Shepherdess of the Alps," one of the most popular of the stories, was printed a total of nine times in the magazines, eight of them after 1777; "Friendship Put to the Test" also appeared nine times, five after 1781. Readers and editors were not satisfied to reprint the existing versions, but offered translations of their own. "Soliman II" and "L'Amitié à l'épreuve" each circulated in three different versions, four of the six being magazine originals. In 1781 the *Lady's* embarked upon a series of new translations of the *Contes moraux,* made by young ladies, presumably readers of the magazine. The project was intended to embrace the whole collection of twenty-three stories, but for some reason was abandoned after five were printed and a sixth was noted as received. Perhaps the editor felt that the stories were already too familiar. Rapidly becoming the leading purveyor of magazine fiction in the early 1780's, the *Lady's* tended increasingly to emphasize originals, or translations of unfamiliar foreign fiction.

The record of the *Nouveaux contes moraux* (1792) in the magazines, however, demonstrates that Marmontel had lost little of his hold upon the popular audience. Eight different stories from the new collection quickly appeared in English miscellanies, most of them taken from the trade edition, published by Bew, but many of them in fresh translations. Between 1792 and 1810 these same eight stories went through twenty-four printings, representing fourteen different versions.

The popularity of Marmontel with English readers was the result of a variety of factors, not all of which are easy to specify. To an extraordinary degree the *Moral Tales* fulfilled all the editorial expectations that we have cited. That is, Marmontel enjoyed a tremendous international reputation, and was greatly admired in elite circles. Most of his fiction was of the proper length for magazine publication, and readily available in several English editions. His stories possessed a great deal of novelty, at the same time that they offended few of the prejudices of popular or polite readers and struck many familiar notes. Each story was a somewhat special concoction, displaying striking differences in subject and theme, but nearly all turn upon some question of love, or some problem of courtship and marriage. Marmontel often took his subjects from leisured society, approached from some unusual direction. Though superficially unlike others of the *Contes moraux*, "The Shepherdess of the Alps," therefore, may be considered as representative of all.

In this popular story the Marquis and Marchioness of Fonrose, returning to Italy, are benighted in a remote valley in Savoy, and are astonished to encounter a beautiful and unhappy shepherdess. She lives with two aged rustics, from whom the marchioness is unable to learn more than that she appeared mysteriously in the valley four years previously, and is obviously of genteel origin. The Marquis and Marchioness return to Turin marveling over their romantic adventure, the account of which makes a deep impression upon their young son, Fonrose, who determines to penetrate the mystery. Disguising himself as a peasant, he seeks the acquaintance of Adelaide, who in time confides to him her mournful story. She comes from a family of wealth and distinction, which broke all ties with her when she accepted as a lover the young Count d'Orselan, whose parents refused to accede to his marriage. The Count was commanding officer of a French regiment, unexpectedly ordered into battle at a moment when he was absent without leave—an absence occasioned by his passion for Adelaide. Believing himself disgraced, the Count took his own life in the valley which the guilt-ridden shepherdess now haunts, and in which she keeps an eternal vigil near his grave.

The young Fonrose falls hopelessly in love with the Shepherdess of the Alps, and sickens under the influence of his secret passion, which, under the circumstances, he is unable to confide, and which she does not suspect. Her pity for him, however, causes her to forget some of her own grief, and when in time he reveals to her the source of his own affliction, she sends for his parents. The Marquis and Marchioness now add their entreaties to their son's, and Adelaide at length consents to subjugate her own desires and restore Fonrose to life by giving him her hand, not in love, she says, but in "esteem" and "friendship."

There are some delicate ironies in this happy-unhappy love story, chiefly resulting from Adelaide's inconsistent behavior. When she agrees to marry Fonrose (the decision has been left to him!), Marmontel asks: "Did she yield only to pity, to gratitude? I would fain believe it, in order to admire her the more." But he has prepared for a quite different impression by dwelling, since the lovers' first meeting, on the attraction Adelaide feels for the handsome young shepherd. After consenting to marry him, she goes to take leave of her first lover's grave, and must be forced from the spot "not without some sort of violence." She insists on a monument to his memory, and periodically revisits his tomb. In closing, Marmontel writes:

> Time, the assiduities of Fonrose, the fruits of her second marriage, have since opened her soul to the impression of a new affection: and she is cited as an example of a woman remarkable and admirable even in her infidelity.[10]

Urbanities like these unquestionably helped to sustain Marmontel's reputation in elite circles, though they were probably lost on most readers of popular miscellanies, for whom the most striking features of "The Shepherdess of the Alps" would be its scenes of romantic passion in an alpine setting, its idealized pictures of rustic life, and its elements of mystery and surprise, those precise features, in fact, that later fed the fertile imagination of the author of *The Romance of the Forest* and *The Mysteries of Udolpho*.

But there were other ingredients of "The Shepherdess of the Alps" which it shared with other Marmontel stories of very different theme and background, and which also help to account for the author's perennial popularity as a magazine author: namely, its essential optimism (most of the *Contes moraux* have happy endings), its simple ideals of benevolence and philanthropy, its quasi-egalitarian ideas, and its appeal to "nature" on several scores. Marmontel was always an indulgent spokesman for the philosophy of the tender heart, urging directly and by implication the primacy of the life of the feelings, and the fulfillment of self through love. Nearly every story in the collection presents a problem that is solved by an appeal to the sentimental philosophy. That this tendency in Marmontel was of much greater interest to the popular audience than his delicate touches of humor and satire is indicated by a series of affected imitations appearing in the *St. James's Magazine* in 1774, called "The English Marmontel, or the School of Sentiment," in which the guiding themes were declared to be "Humanity, Beneficence, Justice, Virtue, Honour." All of the characters in "The Shepherdess of the Alps," without exception, are motivated by these ideals of personal conduct.

In addition to these popular ingredients, there was in Marmontel a pronounced interest in psychology, in states of feeling, in manners, and in moral sentiments, which for a great many years had been fed by Richardson and other novelists in the English school of sensibility. Marmontel's stories are much less didactic then Richardson's, but they usually involve some moral choice or conflict of duties, or present for our approval some signal act of self-abnegation, generosity, or forgiveness. Like Richardson, also, Marmontel was not above giving piquancy to his narratives by dwelling on scenes of physical passion or adding sensuous touches. This tendency brought a few demurrers from his English critics. Reviewers questioned the appropriateness of the appellation "Moral Tales" (a mistranslation of *Contes moraux*), and expressed some doubt whether the stories should be placed in youthful hands, though they contained "very agreeable pictures" of modern manners, and some "good strokes of humour and satire."[11] Less liberal than the monthly reviewers, the essay-critic in No. 14 of *Essays, by a Society of Gentlemen, at Exeter* (1796), discovered "a very bad tendency" in all the tales:

> Not a single story, perhaps, is spotless—not one is untainted by some indelicate allusion such as a young lady, possessing the genuine modesty of her sex, could read without a blush.

We may seriously doubt, however, whether Marmontel's improprieties were an impediment to his acceptance by the miscellany audience, especially since the stories laid many scruples to rest with their general air of moral concern.

Marmontel's high reputation with English readers continued until at least 1820, as shown by the number of new editions of his works. Leigh Hunt gave marked attention to the *Moral Tales* in 1806–1807 by including eleven of them in his *Classic Tales*. They account, in fact, for more than half of his French selections. But by this period Marmontel's magazine vogue was on the wane, and other foreign authors in translation had begun to catch the popular fancy. Of the total number of magazine citations for Marmontel between 1763 and 1815, which comes to eighty-six, only eight are dated later than 1800, and these appear in collections of old favorites like the *New Gleaner* and the *Entertaining Magazine*. But beginning in 1802–1803, the most popular imitator of Marmontel, Mme. de Genlis, entered the very zenith of her magazine reputation, and with stories like "Pamrose, ou Le Palais et la chaumière" and "La Princesse des Ursins" in the *Nouvelle bibliothèque des romans* offered an equivalent combination of passion, propriety, and elegant sentiments adapted to the altered climate of the Napoleonic era.

NOTES

INTRODUCTION

1. See Majorie Plant, *The English Book Trade* (London, 1939), pp. 273ff.

2. The remark was made in the "Introduction" to the *Works of Tobias Smollett,* edited by Saintsbury in 1895, and reprinted in *Prefaces and Essays by the Late George Saintsbury* (London: Macmillan, 1933), p. 69.

CHAPTER I

1. George M. Smith, "Our Birth and Parentage," *Cornhill Magazine,* n.s.X (January, 1901), 6.

2. Anthony Trollope, *An Autobiography,* Chap. 8.

3. *The Works of the Learned,* ed. J. de la Crose, "To the Reader," I (1691), [ii].

4. *Compleat Library, or News for the Ingenious... by a London Divine* [*i.e.,* Richard Wolley, for John Dunton], I (May, 1692), 25.

In the *History of the Works of the Learned* (1699), modelled on La Crose's earlier serial, the editor assured his readers that "we shall be so far from giving an Account of Books that are Trifling, or contrary to good Manners, that we shall not so much as mention their Titles." ("The Preface," I, [iii].)

5. *Memoirs of Literature, Second Edition, Revised and Corrected,* London, I (1722), [ix-xiv].

6. *Literary Magazine, or the History of the Works of the Learned... by a Society of Gentlemen,* II (1736), 155. For earlier attacks on fiction in the same journal, see Vol. I, 144, 231, 232.

There had also been a brief notice of an English translation (Hamburg printed) of *The Adventures of Telemachus* in La Roche's *Literary Journal* (III, 1731, pp. 266–269). It was partly through news and casual reviews of French fiction that notices of English novels began eventually to find their way into literary periodicals in England.

7. *History of the Works of the Learned, Containing Impartial Accounts and Accurate Abstracts of the Most Valuable Books Published in Great-Britain and Foreign Parts,* 1740 (2), pp. 433–439.

8. "Advertisement," *The Supplement to the First Volume of the Athenian Gazette,* London (1691), [p. iv].

9. Vol. III, No. 19 (October 3, 1961). Quest. [1].

10. "The Preface to the Third Volume" (1691), [p. iii].

11. *The Life and Errors of John Dunton,* I (London, 1818), 193.

Among the "politer sort" he mentions the Marquis of Halifax, Sir William Temple, Sir Thomas Pope Blount, Sir William Hedges (who sent "several complete sets into the Indies, to his Friends"), and Sir Peter Pett. (*Ibid.,* pp. 193–194.)

12. The title of the "Little Review", beginning June 6, 1705, was: "The Little Review; or,

an Inquisition of Scandal; Consisting in Answers of Questions and Doubts, Remarks, Observation and Reflection."

The first number contains an inquiry regarding the reading of sermons; the second, a grammatical inquiry, a letter about the methods of Parliamentary voting, a complaint about the mackerel monopoly of the Fishmongers Company, and a protest about the conditions which create old maids "in the Parish of St. S—p—res" (pp. 6–8).

Like the *Athenian*, the "Little Review" also offered many "cases" for consideration.

13. Ian Watt, *The Rise of the Novel* (Berkeley and Los Angeles, 1957), pp. 31–34.

14. *Gentleman's Journal*, I (March, 1792), 3. For a judicious study of Motteux's publication, see Dorothy Foster, "The Earliest Precursor of Our Present-Day Monthly Miscellanies," *PMLA*, XXII (March, 1917), 22–58.

15. "The Treacherous Guardian," II (April, 1693), 116. The story is introduced thus: "The following Novel will not only shew us, that the power of Love adds to the natural quickness of the beautiful Sexes Wit, but also give an Example of Constancy and Virtue." (P. 115.)

16. *Ibid.*, II (June, 1793), 181.

17. "Now, for a Novel. I am sometimes much put to it, to discover Adventures worth relating: Take that which follows for a Fable if you please; however, I am credibly inform'd, that most of the Particulars are true." (*Ibid.*, II, June, 1693, 181.) Earlier, Motteux had described his novel "The Widow by Chance" as a "Piece of News" (II, January, 1693, p. 7), and defended his stories as being "not only true but moral" (II, February, 1693, p. 38).

18. "To the Right Honourable William Earl of Devonshire," *Gentleman's Journal*, I (1692), [iv].

19. For example, see "A Description of the Kingdom of Poetry," I (January, 1692), 16–20; "By Apollo, a Proclamation," I (February, 1692), 8–10; "A Discourse Concerning the Ancients and the Moderns," *ibid.*, 18–22, and I (March, 1692), 19–23—pieces found in the first three issues alone.

20. *Athenian Mercury*, IX (December 17, 1692), No. 2, Quest. 2.

Some other literary questions: "Which is the best *Poem* that ever was made?" (II, No. 3, July 11, 1691, Quest. 3); "Whether *Sappho* or Mrs. *Behn* were the better Poetess?" (V, No. 13, January 12, 1691/1692, Quest. 8); "What's your Opinion of Reading or Seeing *Plays*, whether *Comedy* or *Tragedy*?" (VI, No. 17, March 22, 1692, Quest. 1).

21. As far as I know, Graham Pollard was the first writer to call attention to this curious example of early magazine fiction. See "Serial Fiction," *New Paths in Book Collecting*, ed. John Carter (1934). p. 254.

22. See *A Ramble Round the World, or the Travels of Kainophilos*, 1689; Dunton's *Night Walker, or Evening Rambles in Search after Lewd Women*, 1696–1697; also, the "Six Nights Rambles" of a young gentleman in the *Athenian Mercury*, III, iv, No. 2. According to Graham (*English Literary Periodicals*, p. 53), the *Secret Mercury, or the Adventure of Seven Days* (1702) contained "rambles" for the seven days of the week. A later example, in the same mode, is "The Rake's Progress, or the Humours of Drury-Lane, a Poem, in Eight Cantos, in Hudibrastick Verse, Being the Ramble of a Modern Oxonian," *Weekly Amusement*, Nos. 40–41 (August 9–16, 1735).

23. Ward begins his second number with this statement, which may of course be exag-

gerated, but it is supported by the numerous reprintings of the *Spy* during the succeeding thirty or forty years.

Walter Graham, in the *Cambridge Bibliography* (II, 1941, p. 565), classifies the *London Spy* among the "semi-literate satires" of the period. Ward's work is coarse; it implies a very low order of sensibility, if that is what Graham means, but it is not reading for the barely literate. A partial breakdown of what Ward himself may have thought of as his audience is suggested by the *Weekly Comedy* of 1699 (probably written by Ward). The journal is entirely given over to dialogue and the cast of characters includes a merchant, a news-writer, a lawyer, a poet, a projector, and other representatives of occupations where more than marginal literacy would be expected.

24. In the *Wandering Spy, or the Way of the World*, the Spy sets out to test the truth of the adage "That all the World is a Cheat." On his way to London he meets an old hag who gives him a magic ring that will make him invisible to all (cf. Gyges's enchanted ring in *Tatler* Nos. 138, 243), and "a perspective Glass" that will enable him to penetrate through all walls and into the minds of men (cf. the powers of Mr. Bickerstaff's Guardian Angel). The results of his quest are unfolded in a series of "fables" or allegorical visions descried from the top of the "Monument" in London.

25. A slight exception to this statement is the *Monthly Miscellany*, which contains one "Novel," a sentimental love story of 1800 words, "translated from a Miscellaneous Collection in the French" (I, August 1707, pp. 317–319). The *Post Angel* was about to embark on a program of prose fiction when it ceased publication. The June, 1702, issue announced that the magazine would thenceforth appear in new dress, "continu'd by a *Society of Ingenious Gentlemen, Clergymen*, and others," and that it would include "*Poems, Letters, Novels*, &c." The new plan was already partly in operation, since the same issue contained a "diverting" (i.e., ribald) piece entitled "The Last Nights Adventure, in a Letter of Gallantry to B. H. Esq." But the new *Post Angel* was stillborn.

26. Ozell's *Monthly Amusement* was printed in six monthly numbers between April and September, 1709, and is found advertised in early numbers of the *Tatler*. Its design was "to publish every Month a Novel or a Play, and sometimes both together, selected from the best *Spanish, French,* and *Italian* writers." In accordance with this plan, the magazine offered Cervantes and Molière in alternate numbers for the first five, and in the sixth a set of "Pleasant and Delightful Novels" entitled "Love's Academy." It is less a genuine miscellany, however, than a serial collection of novels and plays, and it is therefore reserved for comment in Appendix II, with other periodicals of the same class. The *Amusement* was obviously intended for polite readers, who needed no introduction to Cervantes and Molière.

27. "The Introduction and Design of the Book," *Gentleman's Journal*, I (January, 1692), 1; the October, 1693, issue carried the title "The Lady's Journal" inside (p. 323), though not on the title-page, and an address "To the Fair Sex," signed P. Motteux.

Motteux's references to his feminine readers were frequent—usually in connection with the fiction of the magazine.

28. In all that relates to the *Ladies' Diary* and *Delights for the Ingenious*, I am indebted to the admirable survey of these two publications in Bertha Monica Stearns, "Early English Periodicals for Ladies," *PMLA*, XLVIII (March, 1933), 38–60.

29. The account of Cleanthes, the "Unfortunate Courtier," was begun (evidently) in the 1705 volume, which I have been unable to see; and was continued in 1706, 1708, 1709, and 1710. The story, which was offered as a warning to women regarding the wiles of gallantry, is surprisingly ribald for a miscellany which pretended to observe all the proprieties.

The amount of fiction in the *Ladies' Diary* was extraordinary for its day. Fourteen other almanacs for the year 1708 were examined. Only two contained stories (Partridge's *Merlinus Liberatus* and *Poor Robin*), and these were mere anecdotes.

30. *Ladies' Diary*, 1706, "The Womens Almanack," pp. [14–15].

31. *Ibid.*, 1711, "The Charming-Fair," p. [ii]; "Advertisement," p. [19].

32. *The Records of Love, or Weekly Amusements for the Fair*, I, No. 1 (January 7, 1710), p. 15.

33. Q. D. Leavis, *Fiction and the Reading Public* (London, 1932), pp. 126 ff.

34. "The Generous Heiress, a True Story," Nos. 6–7 (February 11–18, 1710); "The Wandering Dancing Master," Nos. 10–12 (March 11–25, 1710).

35. *Records of Love*, I, No. 1 (January 7, 1710), p. 15.

36. *Tatler*, Nos. 1, 4 [a portrait of "Clarissa"], 5, 22, 35, 58, 85—running between April 12 and October 25, 1709.

The edition of the *Tatler* used throughout is that edited by George A. Aitken, 4 vols. (1898–1899); the quotations from the *Spectator* are from the eight-volume Aitken edition (1898).

37. "Cynthio" is alleged to be Edward Lord Viscount Hinchinbroke, who did not actually die until 1722. Presumably the identity of the portrait would be known by hearsay.

38. *Tatler*, Nos. 13, 15, 26, 44, 48, 138, 243.

39. A two-act farce based on the "Vision of the Golden Rump" (which appeared in *Common Sense* on March 19 and 26, 1737), submitted to Giffard, the proprietor of the theater in Lincoln's Inn Fields, was used by Walpole as a pretext to dictate the Licensing Act of June, 1737. (See F. Homes Dudden, *Henry Fielding, His Life, Works, and Times*, I, Oxford, 1952, pp. 206–210.)

40. *The Visions of Sir Heister Ryley, with Other Entertainments*, Nos. 1–80 (1710–1711). The author's "main Design," according to the Preface, was "to instill into the Mind of the Reader sound Principles of Morality, under the Vail of a pleasing Vision, an apposite Allegory, or a lively Emblem." "The Inchanted Palace" is found in Nos. 12, 18, 24, and 43 (September 15–November 27, 1710). It totals 5250 words.

41. Martha Pike Conant, *The Oriental Tale in England in the Eighteenth Century* (New York, 1908).

42. There are three stories *formally* continued in the *Tatler* ("The History of Orlando the Fair," Nos. 50–51; "The Vision of the Goddess of Justice," Nos. 100, 102; "The Vision of the Three Roads of Human Life," Nos. 120, 123); and two in the *Spectator* ("The Endeavour of Mankind to Get Rid of Their Burdens," Nos. 558–559; "The Story of Hilpa," Nos. 584–585). "The Vision of the Three Roads" was intended to extend into a third number, but was never completed.

In addition to these, of course, there are a number of casual narrative sequences like the "Progress of Cynthio" and the story of "John Trott."

43. *Spectator*, Nos. 296 (February 8, 1712), 308 (February 22), 314 (February 29). There are also two later references to John Trott, in Nos. 316 and 376. The total length of the series, however, including Mr. Spectator's comments, is only about eight hundred words.

44. See pp. 52–54, below.

45. The *Free-Thinker* was dedicated "To the Ladies of Great Britain." The *Plain Dealer* gave them special attention from his first number:

> The LADIES, when they hear, That my Design is PLAIN DEALING, will consider me perhaps, as an Old-fashion'd Fellow, who can have nothing to do with Them; yet I know they will be frequently kind enough to furnish me with Business, and I shall handle them, as often as they allow me Opportunity. (I, 1730, p. 6.)

46. *The Free-Thinker: or, Essays on Ignorance, Superstition, Bigotry, Enthusiasm, Craft, &c... in Three Volumes*, the Second Edition, 1733, Vol. I, 224. This edition is employed for all quotations used in the text.

See Nicholas Joost, "The Authorship of the *Free-Thinker*," *Studies in the Early English Periodical*, ed. Richmond P. Bond (Chapel Hill, 1957), 105–134.

47. *Free-Thinker*, No. 92 (II, 172).

48. See Nicholas Joost, "The *Fables* of Fénelon and Philips' *Free-Thinker*," *Studies in Philology*, XLVII (January, 1950), 51–61.

The continued stories of this serial are "The History of Astolfo" (Nos. 88, 94, 101); Fénelon's "Tale of Florio" (Nos. 109–110), "History of Alibez" (Nos. 128–129), "Adventures of Aristonous" (Nos. 177–180), and "Adventures of Melesichthon" (Nos. 191–192); "Psychostaticks" (Nos. 149, 157–158); and the "Story of Miranda" (see Note 49).

49. The "Story of Miranda" occupies parts of Nos. 95, 103, 108, 123, 136, 140, 190, appearing at irregular intervals between February 16, 1718, and January 15, 1719. According to Joost ("The Authorship of the *Free-Thinker*," *op. cit.*, p. 133), James Heywood wrote most of the letters, and Philips provided the commentary.

50. The quotations in the text are from Nos. 1, 13, and 117 of the first collected edition (2 vols., London, 1730).

51. The new journal came out on Saturdays, but there was a Wednesday "Supplement," presumably also of six pages. This supplement, like the Saturday publication, was designed to "be agreeable to all Lovers of News in general. And to Tradesmen, Merchants, and other Gentlemen in particular, who are Delighted with the Works of Learning and Ingenuity." (See Stanley Morison, *The English Newspaper*, Cambridge, 1932, p. 91.)

52. *Mist's Weekly Journal*, April 26, 1718 (quoted in William Lee, *Daniel Defoe: His Life, and Recently Discovered Writings*, London, 1869, Volume II, 36–37). Similarly Defoe wrote in *Applebee's* on June 10, 1721:

> Having thus enter'd a Protest, in your Behalf, against all unbecoming Reflections [*i.e.*, "upon our Governor and Government"], let me tell you, in the next Place, that the Field is large enough without it. The Publick Credit, the Commerce, the State of our Morals, the Decrease of Virtue, the Increase of Crime, the Assaults made by mad Men upon Religion, the Growth of Atheism, the ill Habits, the ill Manners, and the ill Customs of the Age, afford you room enough to shew all the Wit, the Humour, the Rage, and the Satyr, that you can be Master of, or at least that you ought to exert in this Introductory Part of your Work. (*Lee*, II, 387–388.)

For convenience I have assumed that all the writings collected in *Lee*, Volumes II and III, are actually Defoe's, although many of them may be by other writers in *Mist's* and *Applebee's*. Lee ascribes to Defoe over five hundred separate items, published in seven different newspapers and journals between May, 1716, and January, 1729. But Lee never defines his criteria.

53. James Sutherland, *Defoe* (London, 1937), p. 228.

54. *Mist's*, March 19, 1720. Reprinted in *Lee*, II, 212–213.

55. (1) *Mist's*, March 29, May 21, October 8, 1720; (2) *Mist's*, May 7, May 28, June 4, 1720; (3) *Applebee's*, June 13–20, 1724; (4) *Applebee's*, October 31, November 14, 1724; January 30, 1725; (5) *Applebee's*, November 21–28, 1724; (6) *Applebee's*, April 3–10 1725.

The above are reprinted in *Lee* as follows: (1) II, 214–215, 234–236, 288; (2) II, 227–229, 236–240; (3) III, 272–277; (4) III, 323–325, 330–332, 359–361; (5) III, 333–335, 336–338; (6) III, 371–376.

56. *Mist's*, February 21, February 28, March 7, March 14, March 21, April 4, 1719 (reprinted in *Lee*, II, 104 ff.).

57. "Imitate then such of your Predecessors as have found the Method of pleasing the Publick, by presenting them with a delicious Variety of Entertainments fit for all Palates, and remain no longer upon one Topick than whilst the same may prove agreeable; let the Ladies share in the Entertainment you give us, and believe, that by engaging them in your Favour, you make too Powerful a Party to be oppos'd by your Contemporaries..." (Applebee's *Original Weekly Journal*, October 12, 1728.)

58. During the ten-year period from 1728–1737, R. M. Wiles (see Note 60) lists four works of serial fiction from the *Universal Spectator*:

1. [Story of Eudocius and Selinda], Nos. 46–47 (August 23–30, 1729). 2 parts.
2. [Olgny and Hariot], Nos. 354–356 (July 19–August 3, 1735). 3 parts.
3. [Autobiography of a Lincolnshire Farmer's Daughter], Nos. 366–368 (October 11–25, 1735). 3 parts.
4. [A Novel from Bandello], Nos. 373–375 (November 29–December 13, 1735). 3 parts.

But there were several others—one being the "Private Memoirs of the God of Love, &c.," Nos. 459, 462, (July 23, August 13, 1737); another being the imitation of "Miranda," which may be summarized as follows:

In No. 95 (August 1, 1730) Mr. Stonecastle receives a letter from a young lady named Annabella who asks him to take her under his protection, and assist her in the choice of a husband. She is twenty-one, "tall, straight, healthy," and "handsome"; and she has a fortune of £ 5000. She is willing "to receive *Proposals* from all *Batchelors* above Twenty-five, and all *Widowers* under Forty, provided they are without children." Candidates must have "a competent Share of *Good-Nature*, *Sense* and *Virtue*, as well as *Fortune*."

In No. 101 (September 12, 1730), Mr. Stonecastle reports on the eager response to Annabella's offer. Applicants have overwhelmed him with flattery, and tendered him numerous bribes. None, however, have interested themselves in Annabella's person; all have occupied themselves solely with her fortune—a sign of the "*Corruption, Avarice,* and *Depravity* of the Age."

In No. 112 (November 28, 1730) he is forced indignantly to quash a rumour that he intends to marry Annabella himself, and this leads to a little sermon on ill-sorted matches. He intends, on the contrary, that the prize shall go to Honestus, an excellent young tradesman, of good parts, fine temper, and high principles. This proposal Annabella blushingly accepts, and therefore no further offers will be entertained.

The whole series totals about 3700 words.

59. "A Letter to a *Lady*, concerning Books of *Piety* and *Romances*," *Universal Spectator*, No. 91 (August 1, 1730).

60. *The British-Mercury, Printed for the Company of the Sun-Fire-Office, in Threadneedle-Street, behind the Royal Exchange, London*. The three serial stories are: "A Voyage into Another World," Nos. 381–387 (October 22–December 3, 1712); "A Letter from Madrid," Nos. 391–395 (December 31, 1712–January 28, 1713); "The Rover," Nos. 471–482 (July 14–September 29, 1714).

I have been unable myself to examine the first of these three stories. The citation is from Roy McKean Wiles, *Prose Fiction in English Periodical Publications before 1750* (Unpublished dissertation, Harvard, 1935). I am deeply indebted in this part of my study to Wiles's "Bibliographical Register" of 421 "pieces of prose fiction [both short and long] which were printed as such in English periodical publications before 1750." His list is far from complete (partly the result, perhaps, of too narrow a definition of prose fiction). For example, it ignores all the fiction published in the *Gentleman's Magazine*, the *London*, and other historical miscellanies published between 1731–1749. But it is particularly thorough in covering many of the hard-to-find journals and newspapers of the period, and it has been an immeasurable advantage to be able to follow him through this very difficult and unfrequented terrain.

61. The problem is discussed in H. C. Hutchins, *ROBINSON CRUSOE and Its Printing, 1710–1731* (New York, 1925), pp. 161–163; also in Wiles, *Serial Publication in England*, pp. 28–29. Particularly suggestive is Heathcote's statement in 1724 that his printing of *A General History of the Pyrates* in serial form in the *Original London Post* was "with the Consent and Approbation of the Proprietor" (Wiles, p. 29). According to Moore, Defoe was probably the author (see Note 66).

62. Walter Graham, *English Literary Periodicals* (New York, 1930), p. 378.

63. R. M. Wiles, *Serial Publication in England before 1750* (Cambridge, 1957). Wiles's dissertation has been cited in Note 60.

64. A total of 44 serial stories (or 36 different titles) from 1719–1739 inclusive. These figures include only pieces of four or more installments (roughly 5000 words upwards).

65. Mist's *Weekly Journal*, May 23, 1724. The writer in the journal returns to the subject again on June 6 and August 29, 1724. The *History* is advertised on May 16 and June 6.

66. Mist's name seems not to have appeared on the early editions, but Parker's *London News* on September 9, 1724, identified Mist as the "Proprietor" of the work (see Wiles, *Serial Publication, op. cit.*, p. 29).

Moore is confident that Defoe was author of the *Pyrates*. See "The Canon of Defoe's Writings," *Library*, Ser. V, Vol. XI (September, 1956), 155–169.

67. See Wiles, *Serial Publication*, pp. 29–30.

68. Wiles finds a total of about twelve serial novels published in six newspapers in the period from 1740–1750. All but one are confined to the years from 1740–1743. Four of the six are believed to be farthing papers, furtively avoiding the stamp tax, and existing today in only very fragmentary runs: *All-Alive and Merry* (two different titles), the *London Evening Adver-*

tiser, and *Robinson Crusoe's London Daily Evening Post.* (See Wiles, *Serial Publication*, pp. 43–54.)

69. Ian Watt's penetrating analysis of the social and economic factors that limited the diffusion of the novel in the later eighteenth century (*Rise of the Novel*, pp. 41ff.) throws light on this period (see also J. M. S. Tompkins, *Popular Novel in England, 1770–1800*, pp. 10–12). The cost of novels was prohibitive, and remained so for most of the century. *Tom Jones* "cost more than a labourer's average weekly wage" (Watt, p. 42). Under prevailing copyright conditions, of course, the serialization of novels in newspapers offered an easy way round this obstacle. But a taste for fiction among newspaper readers had to be created before it could be satisfied, and historical conditions conspired to delay this advance for nearly a century.

70. The *Craftsman* was conducted by an imaginary editor named "Caleb D'Anvers, of Gray's-Inn, Esq.," a "Gentleman of an ancient Family, and no inconsiderable Estate in the North of England" (No. 1). He entertained letters from numerous correspondents, both real and imaginary, interspersed with satirical sketches, stories, and essays, some written "From [his] own Chambers." He also made numerous references to the *Tatler* and *Spectator*. But these resemblances are only superficial. In all important respects the *Craftsman* was a non-literary journal, as its feeble complement of prose fiction demonstrates.

71. A few examples of the short fiction of the *Craftsman* are: "The First Vision of Camilick" (No. 16), "The Kingdom of Timbutam" (No. 92), "The Case of Jack Teazle the West-Country Clothier" (No. 157). The only long serial story is "The History of the Norfolk Steward [*i.e.*, Robert Walpole]," which is divided into three parts, and totals 5000 words (No. 61, September 2, 1727; and "Appendix," Vol. III, 1731, pp. 304–310, 311–317).

Concerning this political satire, David Harrison Stevens wrote:

> The *Hyp-Doctor*, always hostile to Pope, charged him (No. 48, November 9, 1731) with writing against Walpole, as follows: "We are told that Mr. P[op]e wrote the Poem call'd *The Dawley Farm* and the *Norfolk Steward*, in *Fog* and *Craftsman*; if so, he is very ungrateful to some of his Subscribers and Benefactors." (*Party Politics and English Journalism 1702–1742*, Chicago, 1916, p. 126 n.)

72. The *Lady's Curiosity* is assigned to 1752 by the Bodleian Library's *Catalogue of Periodicals* on the basis of the title-page (the separate numbers being undated), but the Hamilton College copy in the U.S.A. is dated 1738, the year in which the work was advertised in the *Craftsman* (see Wiles, p. 314). The 1752 copy in the Bodleian is undoubtedly a re-issue.

73. *The Lady's Magazine, or the Compleat Library, Containing a Very Curious Collection of Histories, Travels, Novels, Poems, Songs, Letters, &c.*, I (1738–1739), [i].

74. *The Weekly Amusement, or the Universal Magazine*, Nos. 1 (November 9, 1734)–61 (January 4, 1736). The "Advertisement" was run on the second page of the first four numbers. There was a Dublin periodical also called the *Weekly Amusement* (1735), of which only a few pages survive, but which seems to have been either a close imitation or a piracy of the London publication.

75. *The Oxford Magazine, or Family Companion* (1736), known only through Professor Sutherland's notes, was destroyed in World War II. It contained installments of Aphra Behn's *Oroonoko* (see Wiles, p. 69).

76. "Introduction," *The Universal Spy, or the London Weekly Magazine*, No. 1.

77. Wiles lists a periodical (no longer extant) entitled *Walker's Half-Penny London Spy* (1736), which offered parts of the *London Spy* and other works of Ward in installment form (p. 69); another, called the *Reading Mercury, or the London Spy* (1736), reprinting the *London Spy* in serial form on the front page (pp. 63, 305); and a thrice-weekly journal entitled the *London Spy Revived* (1737), which offered the *London Spy* in a regular supplementary sheet (pp. 63, 310).

78. Wiles includes the *Pleasant, and Surprizing Adventures of Mr. Robert Drury*, however, among his list of serial books for 1741 (p. 327). Serial books, of course, were not periodicals.

CHAPTER II

1. Catalogue Nos. 184, 328, 1101.

2. The *Cambridge Bibliography* lists about one-hundred titles of genuine essay-serials between 1740 and 1800. Melvin R. Watson, in *Magazine Serials and the Essay Tradition, 1746–1820*, pp. 16–17, estimates 120 from 1750–1810.

3. For purposes of clarity it will be necessary hereafter to make a distinction in terminology between (1) the *essay-serial* (or *single-essay periodical*), a genuine serial publication, appearing usually at weekly or twice-weekly intervals, and (2) the *essay-series*, a mere sequence of essays, published in a miscellany, weekly journal, or newspaper, or as a collection in volume form. For examples of essay-series in volume form, see Note 6.

4. The essayists, of course, frankly accepted the doctrine of imitation. In the "Introduction" to the fourth edition of the *Looker-On* (1797), William Roberts wrote:

> As there is no room for originality in this species of composition, disadvantaged as in many respects are the efforts of imitation, yet it is all that we can aspire to; and grace and dignity in the execution of a secondary part must content our ambition. The delicacy of Addison's morality, the vivacity of his comments, and above all the spirit of his plan, are the just objects of judicious imitation; and he will most egregiously have failed, who aims only at forcing into his work a few of the principal ingredients of the Spectator, without having sounded the secret of those happy combinations of language, and that easy controul of imagery and illustration, which finish and adorn the admonitions, the raillery, and the reasonings of that master-production. (*British Essayists*, XLI, 1817, [4].)

5. Hugh Kelly, in "The Babler," published in *Owen's Weekly Chronicle* in 1763–1765, expressed some of the essayist's feelings of frustration at the narrow compass of the traditional essay, when he wrote in the last number that

> before he [the essayist] can well begin, the scanty limits of his Paper renders it necessary to conclude; and his whole Essay must be contained in a quantity of words, which is scarcely sufficient to serve it for an introduction. (*The Babler*, London, II, 1767, p. 274; see also the "Preface" to Vol. I.)

"The Babler," as it happens, was a newspaper series, but though this fact made the writer's problem more acute, it did not alter its essential character.

6. For example: *The Dreamer* [by Dr. William King], London, 1764; *The Medley, Consisting of Thirty-One Essays, on Various Subjects,* Newcastle, 1766; *Essays, Moral and Literary* [by the Rev. Vicesimus Knox], London, 1777; *Literary Amusements, Evening Entertainer, by a Female Hand,* Dublin, 1782; *Variety, a Collection of Essays, Written in the Year 1787* [by H. Repton], London, 1788; *The Reflector, a Selection of Essays on Various Subjects of Common Life,* London, 1788; *Winter Evenings* [by the Rev. Vicesimus Knox], London, 1788; *Farrago, Containing Essays, Moral, Philosophical, Political, and Historical,* London, 1792; *Essays, by a Society of Gentlemen, at Exeter,* Exeter, 1796; *The Peeper, a Collection of Essays, Moral, Biographical, and Literary* [by John Watkins], London, 1796; *The Philanthrope* ["after the manner of a Periodical Paper"], London, 1797; Nathan Drake, *Literary Hours,* London, 1798; *The Portfolio, Containing Essays, Letters, and Narratives,* London, 1814—to name some of the better known.

Not all of these, of course, adopted Spectatorial methods *in toto.* The *Medley, Variety,* and the *Reflector,* for example, are hardly distinguishable from genuine essay-serials, but others, like *Essays, by a Society of Gentlemen,* Knox's *Essays,* and Drake's *Literary Hours* are simply collections of moral and literary essays. Most of the above titles, however, contain essay-type fiction.

7. Catalogue, Nos. 945, 1050.

Cumberland's "Remarkable History of Nicolas Pedrosa," first published in the *Observer,* Nos. 142–144, was one of the most popular of all magazine pieces, judged by the number of its reprintings (thirteen appearances between 1790 and 1815).

8. The "Voyages" have recently been reprinted (1958) by the Augustan Reprint Society (No. 67), and edited with a judicious introduction by S. J. Sackett. Sackett does not take account, however, of the long journalistic tradition for satirical voyages, which goes back to the seventeenth century. Fantastic journeys, like that in Chapter IV of "Don Rugero" (1681), were a familiar ingredient of the comic journals in the seventeenth century. Later examples are "A Voyage into Another World" in the *British Mercury* (1712); "Travels through the Globes of the Sun and Moon," in the *Universal Mercury* (1724); and the spurious continuation of *Gulliver's Travels* in *Applebee's* (1728). Moreover, short satirical journeys, especially in the form of dreams, were fairly common in the polemical serials.

A magazine piece in the same tradition with the travels of "Vinegar" and "Drake" is "Topsy-Turvy Island" in Books XVI and XIX of the *Female Spectator* (1745). Like Fielding's series, Mrs. Haywood's satirical description of the absurdities of English life avoids a narrative structure. Also presented as a series of extracts, it allegedly derives from "an old book of voyages."

9. "Drake's Travels" appeared in six numbers of the *Universal Spectator,* published between July 26 and November 8, 1740. The subject of the series, however, had already been broached in the May 31 and June 7 numbers with several excerpts from Bishop Hall's *Mundus alter et idem,* translated by "the late ingenious Dr. [William] King of the Commons."

Chapters 1 and 2 of the "Travels," which occupy Nos. 616, 617, and 621 of the *Universal Spectator,* sketch the "Private History" of the narrator, and explain the reasons which led him to explore the Southern World—namely, his interest in the customs, manners, and government of mankind. Chapters 3 to 9 (compressed into two numbers) describe his discoveries in the country of Pamper-Belly and the two provinces of Eat-Allia and Drink-Allia. Beginning with the third chapter Drake more or less abandons the narrative method, resolving never to "speak of [himself] or then but when it is absolutely necessary." But subsequent events represent a progress in his understanding of mankind, and in the last "extract" (*U. S.* No. 631) he arrives at the capital in time to witness the election of the new duke of Pamper-Belly, with whose proclamation the series suddenly terminates. Most of Drake's discoveries are derived from Bishop Hall's original, but he is given more identity as a character than is the narrator of the *Mund us alter et idem.*

Drake's series in the *Universal Spectator,* which is moral rather than political satire, commenced several months after the one in the *Champion,* and may therefore have been prompted by Fielding's. On the other hand, it begins directly with "An Account of the Author, and His Motives to Travel" (July 26, 1740), which was published five days before Job's belated "Introduction to His Travels" in the *Champion.* There may, consequently, have been some reciprocal influence. Job's "Introduction" of July 31, incidentally, is thought by Sackett not to be by Fielding (cf. Augustan Reprints, No. 67, *op. cit.,* pp. i–ii).

10. The earliest piece of magazine fiction listed in the Catalogue is "Drake's Travels" (see Note 9). In addition to this satirical voyage, the *Universal Spectator* published in 1743–1744 three new translations of novelette length from Mlle. L'Héritier.

11. None of the weekly journals was perfectly static in method or policy. At the beginning of its run the *Champion* affected more Spectatorial features than it did later. From 1741 it became increasingly occupied with political matters, and the dream visions, oriental tales, narrative episodes, and "cases," fairly common before, tended to give way to argumentative and expository essays.

It is probably owing to the increasing polemical character of the periodical that satirical novels like the two *Anti-Pamelas* and *Shamela* were more persistently advertised in the paper than sentimental ones. In No. 401 (June 10, 1742), the leading essay, allegedly written by a correspondent, began:

> Novels having, of late, been recommended from the Pulpit [an allusion to *Pamela*], I hope you will not think your Paper disgraced by a little piece of that kind . . .

What follows is a short story of a coquette in high life, "reduced, by her own abominable Vices, to Infamy and Contempt"—an essay more in the mode of the *Universal Spectator* than in that of the *Champion.* Such pieces were more appropriate to the early *Champion.*

12. Hill's column—judging from the selection of 152 of its pieces made at the end of the run (*Inspector,* 2 vols., London, 1753)—offered occasional fiction in the manner of the essay-serial, but not much. Furthermore, the more literary essays were probably the ones considered worth collecting. There are a few references to Smollett and Fielding (e.g., Nos. 24, 27, 49, 128), including the famous beginning of the Battle of *Amelia,* but no critical essays on prose fiction or on specific novels, like those found about the same time in the *Rambler,* the *Adventurer,* the *World,* and, of course, the *Monthly Review.*

13. For example, the collected essays of "The Visitor," first published in the *Ledger* in 1760–1761, offer out of a total of eighty-five numbers three stories in two parts; another, an "Indian Tale," in three; and another in four. The latter is an intermittent letter-series from "Selima Seeker" detailing her adventures in the world. Even this slight degree of emphasis on serial fiction was unusual for a newspaper series.

14. No. 129 (from the *Calcutta Chronicle*) and No. 516 (from the *Morning Chronicle*)—both collected in the *Spirit of the Public Journals*.

15. Melvin R. Watson, *Magazine Serials and the Essay Tradition, 1746–1820*, Louisiana State University Studies, Humanities Series, No. VI (Baton Rouge, 1956).

16. "The Observer," *Town and Country Magazine*, 1773–1790 (Watson's No. 44, p. 115); "The Matron," *Lady's Magazine*, 1774–1791 (Watson's No. 53, pp. 116–117).

17. Watson, *Magazine Serials*, p. 28.

18. *Ibid.*, pp. 23–24.

19. See George C. Brauer, Jr., "Recommendations of the 'Spectator' for Students during the Eighteenth Century," *Notes and Queries*, CC (May, 1955), 207–208. In the story, "Amanda," published in the *Edinburgh Museum*, I (April, 1763), p. 156, it was said of the heroine:

> From the *Spectator* she inbibed a manner of thinking elevated and just, and a conversation sensible and elegant; her mind was fraught with the most rigid punctilios of honour, and, from never harbouring an improper sentiment herself, she entertained a high opinion of the integrity of everybody else.

In "The Vision of Female Excellence" (Catalogue No. 1323), the "Goddess" who appears to the writer cautions her against the dangers of reading "Novel and Romances," but approves the English essayists in the following terms: "Be conversant likewise with the *Spectator, Tatler, Guardian, Idler, Rambler, Adventurer, Mirror,* and other publications of a similar kind; you will find them a perpetual fund of rational entertainment and instruction." (*Aberdeen* (1), III, 1790, p. 341.) In the *Edinburgh Museum,* however, Amanda's elevated thinking was her undoing.

20. Some essay-series published no fiction at all, owing to the growing tendency in the magazines to specialize in various ways; but others for the same reason concentrated on narrative materials. Series like "The English Marmontel" in the *St. James's Magazine* and "The Collector" in the *New Lady's Magazine* are really collections of short stories in serial form. Occasionally, as in Mrs. Trimmer's "Moral Tales" in the *Family Magazine*, and "The Story-Teller" in the *Wit's*, attempts were made to integrate these series in some manner. But genuine experimentalism was alien to the spirit of the essay-series, their writers being too timid, and lacking in imagination and literary experience. The more sustained efforts in prose fiction, like "The Night-Walker" and "The Traveller" in the *Wit's*, are usually routine magazine novelettes, divided into chapters numbered like essays, garnished with mottoes, and so on. Actually, the writers in genuine essay-serials, traditional as they were in most respects, displayed more ingenuity and elasticity in adapting the novel to the special requirements of the essay form.

21. For example, "Essays after the Manner of Goldsmith" (*European*); "The Reasoner" and "Domestic Lessons for the Use of the Younger Part of the Female Readers of the *Lady's Magazine*" (*Lady's Magazine*); "The Old Woman" and "Village Tattle" (*Lady's Monthly Museum*).

22. See Chap. I, pp. 57–58.

23. *Female Spectator, by Mrs. Eliza Haywood*, The Seventh Edition (London, 1771), II, 102. All the quotations in the text are taken from this edition, but the citations in the Catalogue are from the original edition.

24. *Ibid.*, III, 105.

25. *Ibid.*, I, 5–6.

26. *Ibid.*, IV, 208–209.

27. Clara Reeve, *The Progress of Romance*, Reproduced from the Colchester Edition of 1785 (New York: Facsimile Text Society, 1930), I, 120–121.

28. See Note 19, Chapter I. The continuing association of "Rambler" with raffishness until after Johnson's time is indicated by the appearance of the notorious *Rambler's Magazine* (1783–1790). See also "Particulars of a Night's Ramble," *London Magazine,* XLIII (March, 1774), 110–112.

29. Quotations from the *Rambler* are from the *Works of Samuel Johnson, LL.D., in Nine Volumes* (Oxford and London, 1825), Vols. II–III.

30. See the chapter on "Pleasure" in J. H. Hagstrum, *Samuel Johnson's Literary Criticism* (Minneapolis, 1952), pp. 76–96.

31. *Jacobite's Journal*, No. 5

32. *Covent Garden Journal*, No. 24 (March 24, 1752).

33. *Adventurer*, No. 1 (November 7, 1752), p. 6. Quotations from the *Adventurer,* used in the text, are all from the original edition.

34. "Biographical Preface," *British Essayists,* XXIII (1817), iii.

35. *The Life of Samuel Johnson, LL.D., by Sir John Hawkins, Knt.* (Dublin, 1787), p. 275.

36. *Boswell's Life of Johnson*, ed. G. B. Hill, rev. L. F. Powell (Oxford, 1934), I, 253.

37. A later contemporary wrote of Hawkesworth:

> It was an age of novels, as of periodical essays, in which he wrote. Hawkesworth was evidently a diligent reader of the best novels. All those incidents in human life, which were the most susceptible of being introduced with advantage in a fictitious narrative, were familiar to his mind. ("Memoirs of the Life of Dr. John Hawkesworth," *Universal,* CXI, October, 1802, p. 235.)

38. The distinction is Hawkesworth's. It is made in *Adventurer* No. 4, in speaking of the difference between the novel and the eastern tale.

39. Martha Pike Conant, *The Oriental Tale in England in the Eighteenth Century* (New York, 1908), p. 95f.

40. Hawkins, *Life of Samuel Johnson*, p. 275.

The qualities that the eighteenth century admired in Hawkesworth are set forth in the *Universal's* "Memoir" of 1802. His "beautiful tales," the writer declares, "for beauty of design, for natural diversity and propriety of incidents, for the force and clearness with which they suggest the moral truths, which they were severally intended to convey, greatly excel whatever has been given to the world of the same sort, in any other periodical publication." (*Universal Magazine*, CXI, 235.)

41. "Acknowledgements to Our Correspondents," *Universal*, LXIX (September, 1781), 160.

42. "Notes to Correspondents," *Lady's Monthly Museum*, n.s. XIV (May, 1813), 300.

43. "The Story of Zulima" in three numbers of the *Prater* (1756). In Nos. 13 and 15 Mr. Babble visits the house of his friend Miss Aimwell, and tells the story of Zulima to the assembled company. In No. 16 the various reactions of the listeners are described. The three papers total 5900 words.

44. The short chapters, of approximately essay length, framed in a useful moral; the episodic manner in which the story is conducted; the character of the narrator, as a kindly and witty observer of the human scene; the emphasis upon humors and sentiments; and the numerous urbanities, new to the English novel, but very familiar in Spectatorial tradition.

If Goldsmith's first attempt at a novel is viewed as an effort to approach the form via the separate but associated tradition of the essay-serial, in which he was already an accomplished craftsman, a good deal of the scrappiness of the second volume is accounted for.

For the influence of the *Spectator* on the popular novel of a later period, see J. M. S. Tompkins, *Popular Novel in England, 1770–1800*, p. 343.

45. "Historical and Biographical Preface to the *World*," *British Essayists*, XXVI, x.

The quotations from the *World* used in the text are taken from Chalmers's edition.

46. Moore was author of *Fables for the Female Sex* (three editions by 1749), two comedies (*The Foundling*, 1744, and *Gil Blas*, 1751), and a successful domestic tragedy, *The Gamester* (1753).

47. The quotations are from the *Mirror*, No. 1. All the quotations from the *Mirror* and *Lounger* are taken from Chalmers's *British Essayists* (1817), Vols. XXXIV–XXXVII.

48. "La Roche," *Mirror* Nos. 42–44; "Louisa Veroni," *Mirror* Nos. 108–109; "Father Nicholas," *Lounger* Nos. 82–84.

49. "Henry Mackenzie," *The Lives of the Novelists*, Everyman Library Edition (1910), p. 301.

50. A striking illustration of the encroachment of the novel on the essay-serial is provided by the *Adviser* (1803). This collection of 141 essays, published in four successive volumes, includes a series of thirty-one papers called "The Narrative," beginning in the fourth number and resumed at intervals. The story, like that of "Eugenio," is allegedly based upon "a manuscript left [to the Author], as a legacy, by a much-loved and lamented friend, alas cut off at an early period" (I, 3). As "The Narrative" unfolds, however, it sheds some of its alleged autobiographical character and becomes instead the vehicle for a good deal of expository material, obviously the opinions of the Adviser himself. By the fourth volume the *personae* of the two so completely converge that there is even a reference in this pretended bundle of old papers to the periodical in which it is being published. "The Narrative," even though uncompleted, extends to 60,000 words, and is the longest single serial story in the history of the essay-serial.

51. "A Postscript, Which Should Have Been a Preface," *Waverley* (Chapter 43).

52. *Trifler, a Periodical Paper, Published at Edinburgh, by Richard Maw-Worm, Esq.*, No. 17 (April 10, 1796).

Trifler No. 19 (April 24, 1796), on the other hand, published a "Vindication of Novels" by a correspondent called "Candidus," who declared that though novel-reading is carried to excess in some quarters, it is capable of conveying "the sublimest truths" and inculcating "the most useful maxims" in young people—if properly administered by parents.

53. *Lounger*, No. 20 (June 18, 1785), "On Novel Writing."

In addition to this celebrated essay, Mackenzie wrote two other critiques on a germane subject, Nos. 27–28 (August 6–13, 1785), "An Examination of the Moral Effects of Tragedy."

54. *Sylph* (London; Deptford), No. 5 (October 6, 1795).

Sylph No. 19 (December 5, 1795), also an attack on contemporary fiction, contains a mock petition from the "Proprietors of circulating libraries," followed by a "Humble Petition of the Lady and Gentleman Novel-Makers."

55. *Peeper, a Collection of Essays, Moral, Biographical, and Literary* (London, 1796), No. 15, "On the Prostitution of Literature and the Arts to the Purposes of Vice."

56. *Busy Body* (London), No. 15 (February 3, 1787).

Busy Body No. 22 (February 20, 1787), also, contains a derisive essay on "How to write an elegant Novel."

57. *Miniature, a Periodical Paper, by Solomon Grildig, of the College of Eton* (Windsor), No. 10 (June 25, 1804), "Letter from *Miserlos* on Novels." A more bitter attack is found in *Miniature* No. 2 (April 30, 1804), "Remarks on Novels and Romances—Receipt for a Modern Romance."

Similarly, the *Ghost* (Edinburgh), in an essay "On Novels" (No. 34, August 24, 1796), declared: "I deem it highly probable that even the best Novels are pernicious to youth."

58. *Lounger*, No. 60 (March 25, 1786), "Scheme of a literary Projector, for a new Sort of Periodical Publication," attributed in the *British Essayists* to Dr. Henry.

59. *Looker-On*, No. 84 (December 28, 1793), "Eulogy on Female Literature."

60. *Olla Podrida* (Oxford and London), No. 34 (November 3, 1787). In this mock discourse serial "Tales" are defined as "those narrations of blended fiction and sentiment, which, too inconsiderable from their size to swell into circulatory duo-decimos, assume the general humble denomination of *Tales*, and are distinguished by the epithets *tender, pathetic, sentimental, founded on fact*, &c. &c." (p. 339). The quotations are from the second edition of 1788.

Olla Podrida contains two important critiques on the novel: No. 15 (June 23, 1787), an attack on the vulgarity and absurdity of sentimental fiction; and No. 16 (June 30, 1787), a defence of mixed characters. The first was presumably written by Thomas Monro, the principal author of the series; the second by Henry Headley of Norwich, editor of *Select Beauties of Ancient English Poetry*.

61. *Loiterer* (Oxford), No. 9 (March 28, 1789).

62. *Observer* (Chalmers' *British Essayists*, 1807 ed., XXXVIII, XXXIX, XL).

63. *Variety, a Collection of Essays, Written in the Year 1787* (London, 1788), Nos. 25–26 (pp. 213–232). The larger part of the collection was written by Humphry Repton, but Miss Seward contributed the two essays on *Clarissa*, as the following passage from her letters indicates:

> I feel great satisfaction in the approbation you express of my strictures in defense of Richardson, against the injustice of Mr Cumberland. They are honoured in the situation you have assigned them in this your ingenious book… (Letter XIII, to H. Repton, Esq., on the Publication of his Essays entitled *Variety*, Lichfield, March 30, 1788, *Letters of Anna Seward*, Edinburgh, 1811, Vol. II, p. 80.)

64. Frederick T. Blanchard, *Fielding the Novelist, a Study in Historical Criticism* (New Haven, 1926).

65. *Speculator* No. 4 (April 6, 1790) is a discussion of the pleasure derived from objects of terror—illustrated by a poem in No. 7 (April 17), and by the celebrated fragment of "Sir Gawen" in Nos. 10–12.

66. *Flapper* (Dublin), No. 24 (April 23, 1796).

Flapper No. 5 (February 16, 1796) attacks novel-reading in general as enervating to the mind, and recommends biography, history, and poetry.

67. *Adviser, by Abraham Briarcliff* (Edinburgh), No. 5 (March 11, 1797).

The aesthetic of Richardson is further supported in *Adviser* No. 14 (May 13, 1797), where it is recommended that novelists "confine themselves to the study of characters worthy of imitation." The writer is of the opinion "that it is better to have impressed upon our minds, the idea of a *Grandison*, than of a *Count Fathom*."

An adverse judgment on Fielding and Smollett, curiously, was later rendered in Hogg's *Spy* for precisely opposite reasons. Hogg objected to Fielding and Smollett because of their romantic idealization of the human situation. In the "Scot's Tutor" (*Spy*, No. 38, May 18, 1811) he wrote:

> With the works of Smollet and of Fielding, I became, about this time acquainted. These writings contained pictures of life, and manners which pleased me, by their novelty and the brilliancy of their colours, but they tended, at the same time, to generate hopes of ultimate success in worldly concerns, which experience does not realize. A man may be born a Tom Jones or a Roderick Random, but may struggle with misfortunes, and he may indulge his passions, without reaping any other fruit at last than poverty, shame, and remorse.

68. *Microcosm, a Periodical Work, by Gregory Griffin, of the College of Eton*, The Second Edition (Windsor), No. 26, "On Novel-Writing" (May 14, 1787).

No. 30 of this serial, "On Mr. Newbery's Little Books" (June 11, 1787), is an ironic eulogy of Newbery's books for children, but also an oblique attack on modern fiction

69. *Moral and Literary Essays*, No. 14, "On Novel Reading." The quotations in the text are from the edition of Knox's essays published in *British Essayists*, ed. James Ferguson (1819), Vols. XLI–XLIII.

70. *Olla Podrida*, No. 16 (June 30, 1787). See Note 60.

71. "On Novels—Plain Sense—Camilla—Romances," *Literary Leisure*, No. 56 (November 20, 1800).

No. 49 (October 2, 1800), written on the subject of "Readers," contains an ironic tribute to "the many Novels which have, of late years, rescued that line of composition from its state of degradation," thus impugning a good deal of modern fiction, without mentioning any exceptions.

CHAPTER III

1. The most celebrated of the protests against the piratical practices of newspapers and magazines was uttered in connection with Johnson's "Idler." In No. 42 of the *Universal Chronicle*, in which Johnson's series had been appearing for about two months, the following notice was published:

> The Proprietors of this Paper having found that their Essays, entitled *The Idler*, are inserted in the News-Papers and Magazines with so little Regard to Justice or Decency, that this CHRONICLE, in which they first appear, is not always mentioned, think it necessary to declare to the Publishers of those Collections, that however patiently they have hitherto endured these Injuries, made yet more injurious by Contempt, they have determined to endure them no longer. They have already seen Essays, for which a very large Price is paid, transferred,

> with the most shameless Rapacity, into the Weekly or Monthly Compilations, and their Right, at least for the present, alienated from them, before they could themselves be said to enjoy it. (January 13/20, 1759, p. 17.)

As a consequence they threatened to make retribution by seizing copies of the offending publications, reprinting them *in toto*, selling them "at an humble price," and using the profits "for the Support of Penitent Prostitutes."

2. "History" in the eighteenth century was frequently used in this enlarged sense to include not only the study of the past, but organized knowledge of every kind (natural history, geography, politics, commerce, and so on) that could increase our understanding of man or the world he inhabits. (See Louis L. Martz, *The Later Career of Tobias Smollett*, New Haven, 1942, pp. 1–5.)

3. The 1746 "Preface" boasted that the circulation was then 3000 copies. Johnson's and Hawkins's assertions that the magazine attained a sale of ten or fifteen thousand are believed to be exaggerated. Cf. C. Lennart Carlson, *The First Magazine, a History of the GENTLEMAN'S MAGAZINE* (Brown University Studies, 1938), pp. 62, 63n. In my treatment of the *Gentleman's* for the period from 1731–1754, I am greatly indebted to this excellent monograph. Carlson, however, gives little attention to fiction, since it was such a minor feature of the magazine.

4. Cave was so egocentric that he regarded all miscellanies as his competitors, even when they were very different in purpose. In the 1750 "Preface," for example, he denounced the following "reptile" imitators: *Polite and General Entertainer; Kapelion, or Poetical Ordinary; Magazine of Magazines; Grand Magazine; Living World; Traveller's Magazine; Prisoner's Magazine; Theological Magazine; Quaker's Magazine; Religious Magazine; Royal Magazine; British Magazine; Ladies Magazine; Old Woman's.*

5. "A Story Strange as True," *Gentleman's*, VII (1737), 230–31, 278–80, 342–43, 425–26, 491–93; VIII (1738), 18–19, 115–118. The story was later reprinted in the *Wonderful Magazine* (1765), the *Edinburgh Weekly Magazine* (1780), the *Berwick Museum* (1786–1787), and the *Wonderful Magazine* (1793).

6. See Carlson, *The First Magazine*, pp. 110ff.

7. "The Apotheosis of Milton, a Vision," *Gentleman's*, VIII (1738), 232–234, 469, 521–522; IX (1739), 20–21, 73–75. Beginning in May 1738, the vision was continued in the September, October, January, and February numbers. The work was attributed to Johnson by Hawkins in 1787, but the attribution was denied by Boswell, who declared that William Guthrie was the author (*Life of Johnson*, ed. G. B. Hill, Oxford, 1934, I, 140).

8. See Carlson, *The First Magazine*, pp. 140ff. On a table in the assembly room are placed two large folio volumes containing the prose works of Milton—*i.e.*, Birch's edition (IX, 20).

9. For example, readers of the *Gentleman's* in March 1738 had been offered "The Temple of Detraction" from *Old Common Sense*, and in April a selection from the *Reveur* an essay-serial given over entirely to dreams and visions.

10. Besides reappearing in the *Scots* and the *Gentleman's and London* in 1751, "Asem and Salned" (*Gentleman's* XXI, 552–555, 604–606) was reprinted in the *Magazine of Magazines* (Limerick, 1751) and the *Ladies Magazine* (1752).

"Rosetta and Chamont" (*Gentleman's*, XXV, 401–406, 441–445) was reprinted in the

Gentleman's and London (Dublin, 1755), the *Magazine of Magazines* (Limerick, 1755), the *Newcastle General* (1755), the *Weekly Miscellany* (Sherborne, 1776), the *Scots Town and Country* (Edinburgh, 1778), the *Lady's* (1781–1782), and the *Hibernian* (Dublin, 1781).

11. The first title of the magazine, under which it was advertised in 1731, was the *Gentleman's Magazine, or Trader's Monthly Intelligencer*, indicating its initial orientation towards the mercantile classes. (Cf. Carlson, *The First Magazine*, p. 30.)

12. See Appendix III, pp. 376ff.

13. *Universal*, n.s. I (April, 1804), 359.

14. *Gentleman's*, XX (December, 1750), 575.

15. In his very useful study *Fielding the Novelist* (pp. 35ff), Frederick T. Blanchard seems to make a glacier out of what is only a light frost in the *Gentleman's*. He tends to describe all qualified references to *Tom Jones*, however minor, as "slaps," "slurs," and "slights," and all favorable or neutral ones as "stowaway compliments" that somehow escaped the hostile editors' vigilance, or as signs that they "could not afford to crush out every reference to [the book]." For a period of its history when Cave's magazine took almost no notice of novels, it is surely an exaggeration to write (as Blanchard does): "For a full year [1749–1750] the *Gentleman's Magazine* had kept out of its columns any actual review of Fielding's novel" (p. 43).

16. See Alan Dugald McKillop, *Samuel Richardson, Printer and Novelist* (Chapel Hill, 1936), p. 252. The "Short Character of *Clarissa*," containing the letter from Sir Charles Easy was published in the magazine in December, 1748 (XVIII, 548–550); the "Essay" with "OBJECTIONS ANSWERED" the following June and July (XIX, 245–246, 345–349).

17. See McKillop, *Samuel Richardson*, p. 218. The puff of *Sir Charles* in November, 1753, also included a short extract from the novel (*Gentleman's*, XXIII, 511–513).

18. ["The Story of *Yorick*, from *Tristram Shandy*,"] *Gentleman's*, XXX (January, 1760), 35–37; "The Story of *Le Fever*, from the Sixth Volume of *Tristram Shandy*," XXXII (January, 1762), 28–32. The notice of Volume IX of the novel (February, 1767, pp. 75–76) displays some prejudice, but still less than that usually shown by the monthly reviewers and essay-critics. The novel is indecent, but "does no mischief," since it "tends as little to inflame the passions as *Culpepper's Family Physician*." This is a distinction that few eighteenth-century critics of Sterne were willing to make.

19. *Universal*, XXXVI (April, 1765), 202. The *Critical's* excoriation of *Otranto* had been published in January, 1765.

20. *London*, XXXVIII (April, 1769), 180f. "The Benevolent Society" ran until October, 1771.

21. The accounts of the trial itself in the *Gentleman's* and the *London* are about the same length. But the *Gentleman's* published only one of the letters read at the trial, that of Miss Vernon to her sister (Lady Grosvenor), which the magazine offered as testimony of "the effects of Virtue, when directed by natural good Sense" (*Gentleman's*, XL, 1770, pp. 318–319); whereas the *London* printed thirteen of the secret letters that passed between the Duke of Cumberland and Lady Grosvenor, the contents of which were highly sensational (*London*, XXXIX, 1770, pp. 347–356).

22. "To the Publick," *London*, XL (October, 1771), 477–478.

The 1770 "Advertisement" of the *Town and Country* had boasted that it already enjoyed "a sale, far beyond the limits of any cotemporary Magazine" (p. 1), and that its "History of

Têtes-à-Têtes" was being "received with universal applause." The frontispiece of the same volume displayed Minerva "crowning the Genius of the *Town and Country Magazine* with a wreath of laurel," and in the foreground "the Genii of Intrigue displaying a Tête-à-Tête."

The attitude of the *Universal* towards this species of magazine fare is suggested by the remark made to a correspondent who had submitted to the magazine the scandalous account of an assignation:

> The tête à tête by U.Z. is inadmissable. There are other periodical publications to the plan of which it is perfectly well suited. The *Universal Magazine* is a repository of morality and useful knowledge, not a vehicle of abuse and obscene compositions. ("To our Correspondents," LI, August, 1772, p. 103.)

23. *London*, XL, 477.

The third and fourth members of the series were the "Memoirs of Squire Morgan and His Spouse," December, 1771, pp. 581–583; and "Memoirs of the Churchbuilding Peer, and His Dolcina, or of Lord D——r and Miss B——y," February, 1772, pp. 47–49.

The "Anecdotes of the Maid of Bath," offered in September, 1772, pp. 406–408, may be a remnant of this now-abandoned series, since it is in the same manner. But it is not so designated.

24. "The School of Love" began in January, 1773 (p. 16), and ran through the year. The series on "Court Beauties" began in January, 1774 (p. 3), and appeared irregularly until December, 1775.

25. "*The Generous Husband*," *London*, XL (October, 1771), 509.

In November, 1771 (p. 570) the editor of the "Impartial Review" stigmatized an alleged collection of "Love Letters which passed between his R——l H———s the Duke of C—— and the Hon. Mrs. H——n" as "A contemptible catchpenny calculated only for the perusal of ignorance or credulity."

See also the attack on *The Precipitate Choice* in April, 1772 (p. 189), for "indelicacy of sentiment" and false *ton*, "of which the author seems to know nothing but what is to be gathered from the scandal and ribaldry of news-papers."

26. "Advertisement," *London*, XLI (December, 1772), 608.

27. "*Ermina: or the Fair Recluse*," *ibid.*, XLI (October, 1772), 491.

28. "*The Memoirs of Miss Williams*," *ibid.*, XLI (August, 1772), 386. The novel is described as "near 600 pages of lying adventures."

29. *Compendious Library, or Literary Journal*, February, 1752, p. 175.

30. See Joseph B. Heidler, *The History, from 1700 to 1800, of English Criticism of Prose Fiction* (Urbana, 1928); and W. F. Gallaway, Jr., "The Conservative Attitude toward Fiction, 1770–1800," *PMLA*, LV (December, 1940), 1041–1059. Both the monthly reviewers and the essay-critics were conservative, but it is possible to discriminate fairly sharply between kinds and degrees of conservatism. The reviewers were better informed on the theory of fiction than is sometimes supposed, and more receptive to new ideas.

I am indebted to J. M. S. Tompkins (*Popular Novel in England,* pp. 14–19, 330–332) for some of my remarks on the reviewers, though her area of interest is naturally more restricted than mine.

31. Some cases from the *Critical* in which criteria are stated or strongly implied:

> The story is simple, uniform and interesting; the stile equal, easy, and well kept up, sinking no where below the level of genteel life, a compliment which cannot be paid to one of the most celebrated novel-writers we have [Fielding? Smollett?]. The characters are natural and properly supported... The whole is interspersed with some short and spirited reflections aptly introduced, and here and there are some light sketches of humour very entertaining. ("*Henrietta*," V, February, 1758, p. 130.)

> With regard to the execution of this piece, it deserves our highest approbation. The sentiments are unaffectedly elegant, and its tendency unexceptionably moral. The situations of the parties are interesting and well described, and the characters in general are admirably sustained. ("*The History of the Marquis de Roselle*," XIX, May, 1765, p. 351.)

> In estimating the merits of *Vancenza*, it is not necessary, with all the formality of an Aristarchus, to lay down rules for the conduct of an epopeia of the familiar kind. It is enough that the plot be artfully involved and naturally unravelled, while each part co-operates to produce the event. In reality, nothing extraneous should be introduced, and each trifling episode should be remotely connected with the catastrophe. This, however, is a rule which must occasionally be dispensed with. ("*Vancenza; or, the Dangers of Credulity*," n.s. IV, March, 1792, p. 268.)

32. "*The History of Miss Sally Sable*," *Critical*, V (January, 1758), 31; "*The Mother, or the Happy Distress*," *ibid.*, VII (May, 1759), 409.

33. "*The Adventures of Peregrine Pickle*," *Monthly Rev.*, IV (March, 1751), 355–364.

34. "*The History of Pompey the Little*," *Monthly Rev.*, IV (February–April, 1751), 316–317, 329–337, 457–465.

35. "*Amelia*, by Henry Fielding," *Monthly Rev.*, V (December, 1751), 510–515.

In this essay, Cleland defended Fielding's "low" subjects in the same terms he had used for *Peregrine Pickle*, saying "it would even be an absurd affectation to omit them, in compliance to a false delicacy," although he admitted that Fielding perhaps dwelt overmuch on such subjects.

36. "*Memoirs of a Coxcomb*," *Monthly Rev.*, V (October, 1751), 385–387.

37. *The History of the English Novel*, V (1929), 21.

38. *Critical*, XI (March, 1761), 186.

39. "*Emily, or the History of a Natural Daughter*," *Monthly Rev.*, XIV (April, 1756), 289.

40. "*The Adventures of Jack Smart*," *ibid.*, 361.

There are many signs in the reviews of appreciation and understanding of the difficulties of the novelist's art. The following are two citations from the *Critical* two decades later:

> The writers of novels, more than authors of any other class, appear to be chiefly governed, in the contrivance of incidents, by fashion and prevailing example; though there be no species of composition in which greater variety is required, and where it may likewise be more plentifully supplied by a fertile imagination... Let it be acknowledged... that to furnish a novel in which judgment and imagination are happily blended together; where the characters are also natural, strongly conceived and well supported, and the incidents entertaining, requires a degree of genius which will ever entitle an author to the warm approbation of impartial criticism. ("*The Benevolent Man; or the History of Mr. Belville*," XL, October, 1775, p. 264.)

The review of *Juliet Grenville* in the *Critical* began:

No species of literature affords more useful instruction than that which leads to the knowledge of human characters through the intricate mazes of the heart... Utility, however, though the principal, is not the sole consequence derived from writings of this sort. For if they be the work of a masterly hand, of a hand that is guided by a regular and lively fancy combined with just reflexion, and accomplished in the art of elegant composition, they present us with the most agreeable entertainment that the mind can receive. (XXXVI, December, 1773, pp. 443–444.)

41. The complete review of *The Memoirs of a Gentleman* reads:

As pitiful, miserable a romance as we remember to have read; with false English in the first page. (*Critical*, XXXVI, December, 1773, p. 477.)

That of *The History of Philario and Clementina:*

Which is too stupid, and vulgar, for particular criticism. (*Monthly*, LVII, July, 1777, p. 75.)

That of *The False Friends:*

Flimsy sentiments, dressed up in stiff formal language. (*Monthly*, LXXIII, December, 1785, p. 466.)

That of *The Dangers of Coquetry* begins:

The moral to be drawn from this work is so good, that we are blind to the dulness, the insipidity, and improbability of the narrative. (*Critical*, LXX, September, 1790, p. 339.)

This is followed by a single sentence from the book stating its moral.

42. "*The Adventures of Miss Beverly,*" *Critical*, XXVI (September, 1768), 209.

43. "*The Fool of Quality,*" *ibid.*, XXII (September, 1766), 204.

44. "Two Novels," *ibid.*, XXVIII (August, 1769), 132.

45. "*The History of Tom Fool,*" *Monthly Rev.*, XXIII (August, 1760), 163.

46. *Critical*, XXI (April, 1766), 281; XXIV (December, 1767), 430; XXV (April, 1768), 284. Despite his air of disapproval, the reviewer allotted these three novels seven, six, and nine-and-a-half pages respectively.

47. "*The History and Adventures of an Atom,*" *Monthly Rev.*, XL (June, 1769), 441–455.

48. *Critical*, n.s. XI (August, 1794), 361–372.

The reviewer's reply to the "remonstrance" of a reader is found in "Correspondence", n.s., XII (November, 1794), 359–360, in the course of which he says:

It could not be our intention to speak slightingly of a work which all admire, and which we have no hesitation in pronouncing 'The most interesting novel in the English language.' If such indeed had been our view, the very specimen which we selected would have completely refuted our decision.

But he adds: "It does not at all destroy the merit of Udolpho to say that it is *not perfect.*"

The review of the *Mysteries of Udolpho* was attributed to Coleridge by Garland Greever (*A Wiltshire Parson and His Friends*, London, 1926, 165 ff.) and is reprinted in T. M. Raysor, *Coleridge's Miscellaneous Criticism* (London, 1936, pp. 355–370), but it has been conclusively shown by Charles I. Patterson that the young poet had no hand in it ("The Authenticity of Coleridge's Reviews of Gothic Romances," *JEGP*, L, 1951, pp. 517–521).

49. "*Memoirs of Miss Sidney Bidulph*," *Critical*, XI (March, 1761), 186–198; "*Belisarius*," ibid., XXIII (March, 1767), 168–179; "*The Spiritual Quixote*," XXXV (April, 1773), 275–286.

50. "*Almoran and Hamet*," *Monthly Rev.*, XXIV (June, 1761), 415–435; "*A Sentimental Journey*," *ibid.*, XXXVIII (March–April, 1768) 174–185, 309–319; "*The Fool of Quality*," *ibid.*, XXXV (August–November, 1766), 145–146, 286–297, 346–356.

51. "*Eloisa*," *Monthly Rev.*, XXIV (April, 1761), 227–235; XXV (September–October, 1761), 192–214, 241–260.

The *Critical* gave much more attention to Rousseau's *Emilius and Sophia* between October, 1762, and January, 1763—a four-part review totalling 25,000 words. But the emphasis was almost entirely upon Rousseau's educational theories.

52. "*The Life of John Buncle, Esq.*," *Critical*, II (October, 1756), 219–227; "Vol. II," XXI (June, 1766), 470.

53. "*The Life of John Buncle, Esq.*," *Monthly Rev.*, XV (November–December, 1756), 497–512, 585–604; XXXV (July–August, 1766), 33–43, 100–123.

54. "*The Life and Opinions of Tristram Shandy, Gentleman*," *Monthly Rev.*, XXI (App., 1759), 561–571; "Vols. III, IV," *ibid.*, XXIV (February, 1761), 101–116; "Vols. V, VI," *ibid.*, XXVI (January, 1762), 31–41; "Vols. VII, VIII," *ibid.*, XXXII (February, 1765), 120–139; "Vol. IX," XXXVI (February, 1767), 93–102.

These reviews, however, were written by four different critics—Kenrick, Ruffhead, Langhorne, and Griffiths, according to B. C. Nangle (*The Monthly Review: First Series, Indexes*).

The same volumes were reviewed in the *Critical*, IX (January, 1760), 73–74; XI (April, 1761), 314–317; XIII (January, 1762), 66–69; XIX (January, 1765), 65–66; XXIII (February, 1767), 135–138.

CHAPTER IV

1. Using as a scale the "Chronological Index" of R. S. Crane and F. B. Kaye, *A Census of British Newspapers and Periodicals, 1620–1800* (Chapel Hill, 1927). Crane and Kaye's list for 1740 may not be fully exhaustive, but it makes no important omissions, and the general distribution of news-sheets and magazines is certainly accurate.

2. "To the Publick," *Ladies*, I (November 18, 1749), p. [1]. The same address was printed in subsequent issues.

3. "This *Magazine* will be published once a Fortnight; so that, at the End of the Year, the Customers will have Twenty-six Numbers; which, together with a *Supplement*, will make one handsome compleat Volume, and cost them no more than Four Shillings and Sixpence for the whole Year: It will fully answer the End of any Weekly Journal, as it contains the earliest Intelligence both Foreign and Domestick, and will be found at the Year's End to be much cheaper, being no more than One Penny *per* Week." ("To the Publick," *Ladies*, I, March 24/April 7, 1750, p. 161.)

4. "Mr. *Goodwill* having received Letters from many of his female Correspondents, desiring he will insert in his *Magazine* such Novels as may, at the same time, divert and instruct—He

resolved immediately to comply with this Request; and as he knows of nothing more engaging than the *Royal Slave,* of the celebrated Mrs. *Behn,* from which Mr. *Southern* took his Play of that Name, he hopes it will be agreeable to his Readers. When that is finished he will give constantly a Novel from some of the best Writers of that Class." (Prefatory note to the "History of the Royal Slave," *Ladies,* IV, April, 14/28, 1753, p. 115.)

5. See W. C. Sydney, *England and the English in the Eighteenth Century* (New York, 1892), II, 137. In comparison, the total sale of *Waverley* (1814), a sensationally popular success, amounted to 11,000 copies in the fifteen years from 1814 to 1829.

6. The full title of the first was the *Covent Garden Magazine, or the Amorous Repository*; that of the second was the *Rambler's Magazine, or the Annals of Gallantry, Glee, Pleasure, and the Bon Ton.*

7. "Advertisement," *Sentimental,* I (1773), 3.

8. See Nos. 932 and 1370 in the Catalogue.

9. "Perplexities of a Man of Letters, from the German" (1807). The *New Annual Register,* its only serious competitor from 1780, printed no long fiction.

The "repositories" and "registers" of the later eighteenth century were typically weekly, fortnightly, monthly, or annual compilations, displaying a serious interest in domestic and foreign affairs, politics, and new works of learning. Although they were not all impartial, they usually aspired to some measure of completeness.

10. See J. R. MacGillivray, "An Early Poem and Letter by Wordsworth," *RES,* January, 1954, pp. 62–66; and Robert Mayo, "Two Early Coleridge Poems," *Bodleian Library Record,* V (October, 1956), 311–318.

11. See "To the Reader," *Arminian,* VII (1784). The 1807 "Preface" of the *Evangelical* (Vol. XV) claimed a circulation "far exceeding that of any periodical publication, not religious." The following year, in the same place, it declared that it had "20,000 readers," but did not specify how many to each copy.

12. *Evangelical,* "Preface" to Volume I (1793).

13. As described by Austin Dobson, *Samuel Richardson* ("English Men of Letters," New York, 1902), p. 31. The alleged popularity of Fielding and Smollett among "poor country people in general" is described in *Memoirs of the First Forty-five Years of the Life of James Lackington... Written by Himself* (London, 1803, p. 250; first ed., 1791). Dobson's story is only hearsay. Lackington's views are probably colored by nostalgia, as well as by his characteristic expansiveness.

14. "A View of the Commencement and Progress of Romance," printed in *The Works of Tobias Smollett, M.D.* (London, 1797), I, xcii. Moore's complaint reads as follows:

> There were, for a considerable time, so many novels written of this description, with so few exceptions, that the very words Romance or Novel conveyed the idea of a frivolous or pernicious book. Even this, however, did not diminish the number, though it made many people at pains to declare, that for their part they never read novels—a declaration sometimes made by persons of both sexes, who never read anything else.

15. The claims are sometimes invalid. "The Beggar's Tale," for example, which was printed first in the *Caledonian Magazine, or Aberdeen Repository,* for 1790, in a communication

signed "Philanthropos," reappeared verbatim in the *Monthly Visitor* eleven years later (1801) over the same signature, labelled as written "For the *Monthly Visitor.*" Such spurious labels are not uncommon. Sometimes, of course, editors were themselves deceived.

16. *Town and Country*, XIII (April, 1781), 282. The continuation of the story was suspended from February to July because (the editor explained) the author "has been for some Time very much indisposed."

17. "Great part of the *Champion of Virtue* is received, and will be inserted as soon as we have cleared up a few of our arrears." (*European*, LXVII, April, 1815, p. 377.) "The first part of *The Champion of Virtue*, a Gothic Story, will certainly appear in the July Magazine..." (*Ibid.*, May, 1815, p. 473.) "The *Champion of Virtue* will be commenced in our next." (*Ibid.*, June, 1815, p. 563.) "For 'Champion of Virtue,' *vide* 'Old English Baron,' *verbatim*!!!." (LXVIII, July, 1815, p. 89.)

18. *London*, "Acknowledgements to Correspondents," XLVIII (September, 1779), 432.

19. The *Universal Magazine*, in February, 1786, publicly complained that the *New London Magazine* had reprinted "The Lord of Crequi" as well as "several other Articles" from "Old Numbers of our Magazine," and that such plagiarisms often amounted to half its contents—all "imposed on the Public for *New* and *Original* Matter." ("To our Correspondents," LXXVIII, 104.)

20. (1) "Hypocrisy Out-done": *Universal Spectator*, No. 329 (January 25, 1735); *Gentleman's*, V (January, 1735), 38–39; (2) "The Treacherous Guardian": *Ladies*, I (1749–50), 307, 323–324; *Lady's*, XXII (August, 1791), 397–400.

Another surprising example of longevity in a repertory piece is "The History of Amanda, Written in the Year 1712, by John Hughes, Esq.," found printed the *Lady's*, VIII (Supplement, 1777), 694–696. This piece was taken from *Spectator* No. 375 (May 10, 1712). Later it reappeared as "Amanda and the Country Squire" in the *Britannic*, II, No. 22 (1794), 229–231, and the *Hibernian*, 1795 (January), pp. 67–69, without any mention of the *Spectator* or the *Lady's Magazine* (the *Britannic*'s probable source). In both the *Hibernian* and the *Britannic* the story was included in the series "Memoirs of Love and Gallantry."

21. Stories in the *Magazine of Magazines*, the *Gentleman's and London*, the *Newcastle General*, and the *Scots*, for example, were frequently carried in issues bearing the same date as the London originals. (See "Asem and Salned," "Rosetta and Chamont," "The Happy Consequences Which Result from Good Nature.") Evidently these publications awaited the arrival of the London magazines before going to press. The same kind of "simultaneous" publication also occurred in London—for example, see "The History of Philander and Clarinda."

In 1777 the Editor of the *Selector* announced:

> We shall be obliged to defer the publication of our *Selector* for the future till Thursday Morning; because the Original Pieces in it are copied immediately into the papers, and sent into the world before the *Selector* can be properly circulated. We have no objections to this mark of approbation from our Fellow Publishers. We only wish the Editors of Magazines and News Papers would do us the justice of acknowledging their obligations to us. (No. 4.)

22. *Lady's*, XXXV (1804), 87.

23. In October 1785, the *Town and Country Weekly Magazine* (Dublin) began the serializa-

tion of *Anna, or Memoirs of a Welch Heiress,* by Agnes Maria Bennett, recently published in London. The story was pursued without any abridgment through the 17th chapter of Volume I, at which point the magazine appears to have expired. But this form of piracy was unusual, and as far as is known was not repeated elsewhere in the Irish periodical press, though the novel was an extremely popular one, and there was no copyright impediment.

24. This cautionary statement was incorporated in the title, beginning in Volume II.

25. *New Lady's*, IX (1794), "Notes to Correspondents," 298, 346.

26. "On Saturday next will be published Number I. (the succeeding Numbers to be issued Weekly in the most Regular and Punctual Manner) of HOGG'S NEW NOVELIST'S MAGAZINE; OR GENTLEMAN'S AND LADY'S ENTERTAINING LIBRARY." (*New Lady's Magazine*, IX, January, 1794, p. 2.) The first novel in this new collection of serial books was *Pamela*. The "serialization" of Richardson's novel in the *New Lady's* began the following July. Hogg obviously used the sheets for *Pamela* to pad the contents of his ailing magazine.

27. *London*, XVIII (February, 1749), 51–55.

28. *Gentleman's*, XXXI (January, 1761), 34–35; *ibid.*, XXXII (February, 1762), 71–76; *London*, XXXI (May, 1762), 273–275.

29. *Scots*, XXIV (January, 1762), 29–33. This review, which was signed "C.," is identical with that appearing the following month in the *Critical Review* (XXIV, February, 1762), of which the *Scots* must have obtained an advance copy.

30. "Story of Almoran and Hamet, an Oriental Tale," *Gentleman's*, XXXI (June, 1761), 273–276 ("From the *Public Ledger*."); "Account of Almoran and Hamet, an Eastern Tale," *London*, XXX (June, 1761), 303–306; "Almoran and Hamet, an Oriental Tale," *Scots*, XXIII (July, August, 1761), 359–365, 411–415; "Story of Almoran and Hamet, an Oriental Tale," *Universal*, XXVIII (Supplement, 1761), 370–373.

The summary in the *Scots*, which was signed "M.," was reprinted from the *Monthly Review*, XXIV (June, 1761), 415–435.

31. See the brief discussion of the *Marvellous Magazine* and the *Tell-Tale* in Appendix II.

32. The abridgment of *Candide* (Part I) in *Lloyd's Evening Post and British Chronicle* has not been available for examination, but is known through the reprinting in the *Edinburgh Chronicle* for May 17/19 to May 31/June 2, 1759, which is described as "extracted from *Lloyd's Chronicle*." Presumably it appeared in *Lloyd's* earlier in the same month.

Kinnersley's abridgment of *Candide* is identical with that of the *Edinburgh Chronicle* except for his prefatory remarks. We may assume, therefore, that his version was also taken from *Lloyd's*. In the absence of the original, however, the introductory comments have been attributed to Kinnersley.

The abridged translation of *Candide* published in *Lloyd's*, the *Edinburgh Chronicle*, and the *Grand Magazine*, of course, was not a piracy, since it did not encroach upon an English copyright. The first bookseller's translation of *Candide* (Part I) was evidently that published by Scott and Gritton, which is found excerpted in the *London Chronicle* for May 24/26, 1759. Still another translation, published by Nourse, was noticed in the *Monthly Review* for July, 1759.

33. See *Coninger on the Law of Copyright*, ed. F. E. Skone James, 6th edition (London, 1927), p. 135. For a briefer treatment of the case see Augustine Birrell, *Seven Lectures on the Law and History of Copyright in Books* (London, 1899), p. 158, and A. S. Collins, *Authorship in the Days*

of Johnson (London, 1927), pp. 56, 59. Collins gives the impression, however, that Dodsley was successful in his suit, and thus reverses the consequences of this legal action.

34. Twelve years after *Dodsley v. Kinnersley*, in 1773, the question of abridgments again arose, in connection with *Stackhouse's History of the Holy Bible*, first published in 1737, of which a London bookseller claimed perpetual copyright by common-law right. In a suit against three Scottish booksellers, John Hinton sought to restrain them from publishing *Stackhouse* on the grounds that it infringed upon the author's rights, though the original author was unknown (Stackhouse having been himself a redactor). Ten of the judges in the Court of Session offered opinions in the case, of which only one supported Hinton. One of the counsel for the defense was James Boswell, who published in 1774 an account of the proceedings (*The Decision of the Court of Session, upon the Question of Literary Property, etc.*, Edinburgh, 1774).

In exposing the inconsistencies of the booksellers' claims, Lord Hailes, one of the judges who rendered opinions, made reference to contemporary magazine publishing. He said, in part:

> This common-law right [to literary property] is strangely interpreted by the London booksellers.
>
> The Bishop of Gloucester, in his admirable Charge to his Clergy, has bestowed on the London booksellers the appellation of *The Sages of St. Paul's Church-yard* [i.e., Paternoster Row].
>
> The doctrine of these *sages* is commodious: they *limit* or *enlarge* this common-law right as best suits their own conveniency.
>
> They *limit* it, 1. when, maintaining that an author has a right to the *whole* of his work, they take the liberty of borrowing whatever *part* of the work may be a proper ingredient for their monthly hashes of literature, their *Universal Magazines of knowledge and pleasure.*
>
> If a work chance to be short, they retail it in a news-paper under the appellation of a *criticism*, or an *extract.*
>
> 2. Again they *limit* this common-law right by exciting their dependents to make abridgements of valuable works. [They *limit* it further in compiling dictionaries of arts and sciences, he went on to say; and they *enlarge* it by including in it property whose authorship is unknown or forgotten, and by claiming "the name of *original author* for any *tasteless compiler.*"] (Boswell, *The Decision*, pp. 6–7.)

35. *Universal*, LXI (July, 1777), 28; LXXII (March, 1783), 118.

36. See Chapter V, pp. 336–341.

37. The *London Chronicle*, during the more-than-two years of its existence previous to April, 1759, noticed about 280 books, of which only two were frankly fiction (Fordyce's *Temple of Virtue* and Mme. Riccoboni's *History of the Marquis of Cressy*). Obviously novels counted for little in the editor's plans, although he had published between December 13, 1757, and January 12, 1758, a 9500-word series of entertaining extracts from *The Voyages and Adventures of Capt. John Holmesby to the Southern Ocean* (London, 1757). The long excerpts from *The Countess of Dellwyn* and *Rasselas* in the spring of 1759, therefore, mark a new departure for the *London Chronicle*, and suggest a turning point in the fortunes of the English novel. Johnson's *Rasselas* in 1759 received more attention in the miscellanies than any previous work of prose

fiction, French or English, for at least twenty years. It is a pivotal novel in the history of magazine fiction.

38. Published by Robinsons: (1) White, *The Adventures of John of Gaunt*, 1790; (2) *The Negro, Equalled by Few Europeans*, 1790; (3) Chavis and Cazotte, *Arabian Tales*, 1792; (4) Le Sage, *Vanillo Gonzales*, 1797; (5) *The Spaniard, or the Pride of Birth*, 1807; (6) Wilmot, *Scenes in Feudal Times*, 1809; (7) Catherine Cuthbertson, *The Forest of Montalbano*, 1810. The *Lady's* twice offered extracts from the *Arabian Tales*.

39. See *The Progress of Romance* (Facsimile Text Society), II (1785), 47:

> *Hort.* Is it not equally injurious to Authors, to publish extracts of books in Magazines and other periodical publications?
> *Euph.* Certainly.—And unless I am mistaken, the method I propose would put an end to these pilfering practices, for they deserve to be called so.

The first long extract from a new work of fiction published in *Monthly Extracts* (September, 1791) was "Memoirs of the House of Marny" (11,700 words), taken from Clara Reeve's *School for Widows*, just published.

40. *Monthly Rev.*, n.s. II (June, 1790), 161–165.

41. *Universal*, LXXXV (Supplement, 1789), 365. In the original, Mrs. Montgomery's story occupies pp. 128–185 of Volume I (1789).

42. Listed in the *Monthly Review* in 1789–1790: (1) *The Narrative Companion and Entertaining Moralist, Being a Selection of Histories, Novels, Tales, &c.* (August, 1789); (2) *Evening Amusements for the Ladies* (December, 1789); (3) *Tales, Entertaining and Sympathetic, Inscribed to the Heart* (March, 1790); (4) *Norman Tales, from the French of M. Le Grand* (July, 1790); (5) *Louisa Forrester, or Characters Drawn from Real Life* (September, 1790); (6) Montesquieu, *Fugitive Pieces* (September, 1790).

These six, however, received only very brief notice. A possible seventh short-story collection is *Family Sketches* (April, 1790).

Given *major* attention in the *Critical Review* during 1791–1793 were: (1) *Fugitive Pieces, by M. de Montesquieu* (May, 1791); (2) Musaeus, *Popular Tales from the German* (September, 1791); (3) Marmontel, *The Tales of an Evening* (May, 1792); (4) *Tales of a Parrot, Done into English, from a Persian Manuscript* (November, 1792); (5) Chavis and Cazotte, *Arabian Tales* (November, 1792); (6) *New Tales, from the French of Florian* (December, 1792); (7) Anna Maria Porter, *Artless Tales* (September, 1793).

All except the last were translations.

43. In the Catalogue, see "Historie d'Emilie" (1777–1780), "Histoire de Monsieur Le Grand" (1781–1782), and "La Dame Genereuse" (1782–1783).

This genteel activity began in the second number of the magazine (September, 1770), with "Générosité d'un égyptien," of which a translation was requested. It was shrewdly calculated to win favor in boarding schools, where the magazine was taken in.

44. The change in English taste which brought native collections to the fore is strikingly reflected in Block's *English Novel* (pp. 354–357), where he lists 213 titles emphasizing the word "Tales" published between 1740 and 1850. Of these 213, less than ten appeared previous to 1800.

45. "Sir Bertrand" was largely responsible for the rash of Gothic fragments in British

miscellanies after 1773. It was reprinted at least a dozen times, and was endlessly imitated in both prose and verse.

46. The fullest account of Helen Maria Williams, with an accurate bibliography of her writings on France, is found in M. Ray Adams, "Helen Maria Williams and the French Revolution," *Wordsworth and Coleridge, Studies in Honor of George McLean Harper* (Princeton, 1939), pp. 87–117. Adams seems to accept as fact, however, all the "biographical" details of the *Letters Written from France*, making insufficient allowance for artistic license. If Miss Williams's correspondent in this volume is fictitious, including his alleged reactions to her letters, why may not some of the personal data also be re-arranged for effect—the date of her arrival in Paris, for example? A clue to Miss Williams's intentions is provided by the closing comment she made upon the "Memoirs" of her friend's husband: "Such is the history of Mons. du F——. Has it not the air of romance?" (*Letters Written in France*, 5th ed., pp. 192–193.)

47. The story, allegedly transmitted to Miss Williams by a French cleric, is included in "Letter XIX" of her collection, following accounts of "Suwarrow's escape across the mountains of Glarus" and "the French Army in Palestine" (*Sketches of the State of Manners and Opinions in the French Republic towards the Close of the Eighteenth Century*, London, 1801, Vol. I, 238–298). Her text is described as "a transcript of the copy which I have received from the Abbé, who assures me that he knew some of the parties and that little is due to the embellishment of the narrator" (p. 247).

48. See M. Ray Adams, *op. cit.*, p. 110; also the article on Miss Williams in the *DNB*.

49. "The Evil Effects of Reading Novels and Romances," *University*, I (February, 1795), 108; "Remarks on the Dangerous Tendency of Novels," *New Lady's*, V (April, 1790), 204–205; "Character and Effects of Modern Novels," *London*, XLII (May, 1773), 247.

50. "On Novel-Writing and Reading," *Lady's*, XI (July, 1780), 375–376; "Cursory Thoughts on the Modern Novel," *ibid.*, Supplement (1780), p. 693.

51. For example, the author of a letter signed "Una" in the *Lady's Magazine* (XXVI, August, 1795, pp. 369–370) attacked the story called "Julia, or the Clandestine Marriage" published in the previous May issue (pp. 232–236) as "a jumble of inconsistency and nonsense" whose real tendency was to reverse the perfunctory moral attached at the close.

52. *Monthly Preceptor*, I (1800), No. 2, pp. 121–129.

53. *Strabane*, II (December, 1800), 577.

54. *Lady's Monthly Museum*, I (1798), 388–393, 420, 467–473.

55. "Character of a Sentimental Lady," *Edinburgh Weekly*, XLIX (September 21, 1780), 343–344.

56. "The Novelist, a Fragment," *Monthly Mirror*, XIII (June, 1802), 389–391; "On the Utility of Periodical Publications," *ibid.*, XVIII (September, 1804), 161–163.

On the other hand, the heroine of "The Benevolent Fair" in the *Town and Country* (XV, October, 1783, pp. 545–547) benefited from her reading, which included *Tom Jones, Roderick Random, Peregrine Pickle, Sir Charles Grandison, Pamela,* and a few other novels "of established reputation," though she despised "the trash of the town" and "was no regular subscriber to circulating libraries." As a consequence of this judicious eclecticism, she gained a very genteel lover, "the heir to a large fortune," and the two are now pronounced "the happiest couple in all Bedfordshire."

57. *European*, XIX (March, 1791), 197.

58. "Hints on Reading," *Lady's*, XX (February, April, 1789), 79–81, 177–178.

59. "Critical Observations on the Novel of *Tom Jones*, in a Series of Letters from an Uncle to His Niece," *Lady's*, Vol. XXXIV (February–October, 1803). The fifteen letters make nine installments. The *Town and Country's* "Short View" of Fielding appeared in the June, 1777, issue of the magazine.

60. *Lady's*, XXVIII (1797), 353; XXXVI (1805), 264.

61. "The long story sent us by a *Subscriber*, not having any moral tendency, is inadmissable." (*Strabane*, I, April, 1799, p. 196.)

62. (1) *Edinburgh* (1), VI (April, June, 1762), 186–188, 277–279; (2) *Westminster*, III (May, 1775), 258–260; (3) *Edinburgh Weekly*, LVIII (October 9, 1783), 33–36; (4) *ibid.*, November 13, 1783, pp. 193–195; (5) *Universal*, LXXVI (February, 1785), 81–86; (6) *Weekly Entertainer*, IX (April 30, 1797), 420–421; (7) *European*, XV (February, 1789), 99–101; (8) *ibid.*, January, 1789, pp. 22–24.

63. *Lady's Monthly Museum*, n.s. III (December, 1807), 451–452; n.s. V (November, 1808), 217–218; n.s. IX (July, 1810), 2–4; n.s. XII (May, 1812), 341–343; n.s. XIV (June, 1813), 313–315. "The Literary Spy" appeared in the same magazine in six numbers between January and July, 1808.

"On Novels and Romances, with a Cursory Review of the Literary Ladies of Great-Britain," *Belle Assemblée*, I (November, 1806), 531–533.

64. "A View of French Literature for the Present Century" appeared in nine parts in the *European* between February, 1782, and December, 1783. It consisted of fingernail biographies of leading contemporary writers in France. Of the first twenty-five authors surveyed in the two 1782 volumes, nine were novelists, though this proportion fell off sharply in the two later numbers.

"On the Literature, Wit, and Taste of Some European Nations" was published in the May and June, 1784, issues of the *European*. This two-part essay gave its entire attention to historical works and prose fiction.

"The Lady's Librarian" appeared in fifteen issues of the *New Lady's* between August, 1787, and January, 1789.

65. "Cursory and General Hints on the Choice of Books," No. 174, *Essays, Moral and Literary*; "On Novel Reading," No. 14, *ibid.*

66. No. 15, "The Lady's Librarian, *New Lady's*, IV (January, 1789), 31.

67. "Remarks upon Novels, and Particularly of *Clarissa Harlow*, by Mr. Cumberland," *New Lady's*, IV (January, 1789), 12–15; "Remarks on the Dangerous Tendency of Novels," *New Lady's*, V (April, 1790), 204–205.

In December, 1793, while it had at least half a dozen serial stories running, the *New Lady's* published still another essay "On the Dangerous Influence of Novels" (VIII, 512–517). These contradictory postures were so common that they must be considered as a conscious effort by editors to disarm criticism by seeming to accede to it.

CHAPTER V

1. The quotation is from *The Adventures of Sir Launcelot Greaves* (Oxford: Shakespeare Head Press, 1926), p. [ix]. But the same idea has been frequently expressed, as, for example: (1) "It [*Sir Launcelot Greaves*] was published as a serial, and may well have been the first piece of fiction written in English to that end. Two of Defoe's—*Robinson Crusoe* (First Part) and *Captain Singleton*—had been so published, but both had existed for some time in book form." W. S. Henley, "Introduction," *The Works of Tobias Smollett*, I (New York, 1899), xl; (2) "... two years later he [Smollett] was concerned with the *British Magazine*, in which appeared in serial form (a method of publication popular in the nineteenth century, but at that time an innovation) the novel *The Adventures of Launcelot Greaves*." L. Rice-Oxley, Editor, *The Expedition of Humphry Clinker*, World's Classics (Oxford, 1922), p. vii; (3) "It was for this magazine [the *British*] that Smollett wrote *Sir Launcelot Greaves*, apparently the first novel to make its bow to the public in serial form. Defoe's *Captain Singleton* and the first and second parts of *Robinson Crusoe* had previously been published serially, but only after existing for some months in book form." Arnold Whitridge, *Tobias Smollett, a Study of His Miscellaneous Works*, Published by the Author, 1925, p. 52; (4) "It is worth noting that in the history of periodicals this [*Sir Launcelot Greaves*] is the first instance of a work of fiction being serialized." Lewis Melville, *The Life and Letters of Tobias Smollett* (London, 1926), p. 183; (5) "With the exception of such disjointed things as *The Coverley Papers*, *Launcelot Greaves* was the first novel to appear serially in English." E. A. Baker, *The History of the English Novel*, IV (1930), 222.

Saintsbury's more cautious statement on the subject has already been quoted (cf. Chapter I, Note 2).

2. "The History of the Fair Maria" in Goldsmith's *Lady's Magazine* of 1759–1760 similarly broke with precedent. This original story of 11,300 words began in October, 1759, and ran until September, 1760. But it seemed a much less striking novelty than Smollett's because its installments were of normal length for magazine serials, and its manner was quite conventional. Only two, of less than 1500 words each, had been published by the time that Chapter 1 of *Sir Launcelot* appeared. Furthermore, the author of "Fair Maria" was never identified.

3. "Tobias Smollett," *The Lives of the Novelists*, Everyman's Library (London, 1928), p. 92.

4. Lewis M. Knapp, *Tobias Smollett, Doctor of Men and Manners* (Princeton, 1949), p. 229.

5. Louis L. Martz, *The Later Career of Tobias Smollett*, Yale Studies in English, No. 97 (New Haven, 1942) pp. 176–180. Martz believes that Smollett also wrote "The History of Canada," which began its run in the first number of the *British Magazine* (January, 1760), and was interrupted at the time Smollett's health broke in the spring of 1763.

6. The advertisement for the February number, printed in the *London Chronicle* for January 29/31, 1760, p. 106, reads as follows:

> By the KING's Authority. / Dr. SMOLLETT having represented to his MAJESTY, that he has been at great Labour and Expence in writing Original Pieces himself, and engaging other Gentlemen to write Original Pieces, to be published in the *British Magazine; or Monthly Repository for Gentlemen and Ladies*; his Majesty was pleased to signify his Approbation of the said Work, by granting his Royal Licence to the said Dr. SMOLLETT. / *And To-morrow will be*

published, Price 6d. / No. II. embellished with three Copper-plates, of *THE BRITISH MAGAZINE*; or Monthly Repository for Gentlemen and Ladies. By T. SMOLLETT, M.D. and others.

For some reason the advertisements for the first number in the same newspaper did not carry Smollett's name, although they did describe in general terms the contents of the new magazine, and promised (among other things) "Tales, Allegories, and Essays, Humorous, Oriental and Moral" (see the *London Chronicle*, December 18/20, December 20/22, December 22/25, 1759).

The *British* broke with precedent in other respects, besides openly publishing the editor's name. The first issue, appearing on January 1, 1760, was called the "January" number, although according to normal practice it should have been dated "December, 1759." The *British*, therefore, enjoyed an advantage in being (so to speak) always a month ahead of its competitors. But this was a disadvantage also, since readers who sought summaries of February news in the February number would find that the magazine was already a month old. After four months, therefore, the *British* retreated from its advanced position, by publishing an undated number. The May issue contained *May* news, and was published at the beginning of June.

7. *Works of Oliver Goldsmith*, ed. Peter Cunningham, "Library Edition" (New York and London, 1900), VI, 91. The essay appeared in the *Public Ledger* for February 16, 1760.

8. James Beattie, "An Essay on Laughter, and Ludicrous Composition," *Essays* (Edinburgh, 1776). Beattie wrote:

> Sir Launcelot Greaves is of Don Quixote's kindred, but a different character. Smollett's design was, not to expose him to ridicule; but rather to recommend him to our pity and admiration. He has therefore given him youth, strength, and beauty, as well as courage, and dignity of mind, has mounted him on a generous steed, and arrayed him in an elegant suit of armour. Yet, that the history might have a comic air, he has been careful to contrast and connect Sir Launcelot with a squire and other associates of very dissimilar tempers and circumstances. (Pp. 350–351.)

9. The quotation is from Chapter 2 of the novel (Shakespeare Head Press edition, p. 16). The succeeding quotations are from Chapter 2 of the same edition.

In his subtle and persuasive treatment of Smollett in *The Early Masters of English Fiction* (University of Kansas Press, 1956), A. D. McKillop wrote of *Sir Launcelot Greaves* as follows: "Though the book is not well organized, it has some fine sketches of humorous characters and some remarkable genre pieces . . ." (P. 169.) McKillop speaks of *Sir Launcelot Greaves* as a two-volume novel, of course. As a magazine serial, it was admirably organized. Smollett's *tableaux* are perfectly suited for a long story published in monthly parts, and far in advance of their time.

10. Viewed in this light, *Sir Launcelot Greaves* may be considered as part of the medieval revival. The attitude towards chivalry is ambivalent. Its customs are travestied, but its enthusiastic idealism is used to expose the venality of eighteenth-century officialdom. Smollett's point of view was strikingly expressed by Helen Maria Williams many years later, though in a very different connection:

> For my part, while I contemplate these things [*i.e.*, the new spirit in France], I sometime think that the age of chivalry, instead of being passed for ever, is just returned, not indeed in its erroneous notions of loyalty, honour, and gallantry, which are as little "à l'ordre du jour" as its dwarfs, giants, and imprisoned damsels; but in its noble contempt of sordid cares, its

spirit of unsullied generosity, and its heroic zeal for the happiness of others. (*Letters from France*, Vol. II, 1792, p. 5.)

11. "Preface," *Royal Female Magazine*, II (1760), ii.

In the background of "The Fortune-Hunter" is a pair of true lovers, Eusebius and Amanda, who remain faithful despite efforts to divide them; in the foreground, the principal interest is in the farcical misadventures of the titular character, who seeks to win Amanda for himself, but becomes the victim of his own intrigues.

12. Thirteen years later, in 1773, "The Fortune-Hunter" was reprinted in the *Caledonian Weekly Magazine*; twenty-six years after its run in the *Universal Museum*, the "Disasters" was revived in abridged form in the *New London Magazine* of 1788. These are the only recorded reprintings of either story.

13. The advertisement for the first number of the *Lady's Museum*, printed in the *London Chronicle* for February 28/March 1, 1760, p. 212, reads as follows:

> By the KING's Authority, / *This Day was published*, / Price 1 s. embellished with Copper-plates, / (To be published the first of every Month with the Magazines) Number I. of / THE LADY'S MUSEUM. Consisting of a Variety of Original Pieces in Prose and Verse, for the Information and Amusement of the Ladies. / By the Author of the *Female Quixote, Henrietta*, &c.

Earlier advertisements in the *Chronicle* actually carried Mrs. Lennox's name (see the February 19–21 issue, p. 178, for example).

14. See the letter from "Perdita" in No. 4 (p. 244). The reminder was made regarding the authorship of "The Trifler," but naturally it extended to the other contents of the magazine.

15. Miriam Rossiter Small, *Charlotte Ramsay Lennox*, Yale Studies in English, No. 85 (New Haven, 1935), p. 30.

16. The announcement of No. 2 of the *Bee* in the *Public Advertiser*, October 14, 1759 (reproduced in the *Works of Oliver Goldsmith, op. cit.*, V, 6). Compare with Goldsmith's equivalent statement in the "Translator's Preface" to Marteilhe's *Memoirs* (1757):

> If there be any who can be pleased with a Narrative inspired by Truth; and, perhaps, executed with Modesty; if we cannot deserve the Approbation of such Readers, we shall contentedly acquiesce in their Censure. (*Memoirs of a Protestant*, ed. Austin Dobson, 1895, p. 6.)

17. See Goldsmith's remark on the editorship of the *Lady's*, quoted on p. 294.

18. *Works*, VIII, 73–74.

19. "The Indigent Philosopher," No. 3 (January 29–February 1, 1762), *New Essays by Oliver Goldsmith*, ed. R. S. Crane (Chicago, 1927), pp. 111–112.

20. "Essay IX," *Works*, V, 192 and n. This essay was originally No. 4 of "The Indigent Philosopher."

21. See *The Citizen of the World*, Letters LIII and LXXIII (the same charges were repeated in the letter to the Rev. Henry Goldsmith, *Works*, VIII, 247); and the review of *Jemima and Louisa* in the *Critical Review* for August, 1759 (*Works* VIII, 51–55).

22. "Essay XIX," *Works*, V, 236.

23. And since this is true of four which Professor Crane admits without question to the canon ("A Reverie at the Boar's-Head-Tavern," "The Distresses of a Common Soldier," "The

History of Carolan, the Last Irish Bard," "The Adventures of a Strolling Player"), it may also be true of the fifth, "The History of Miss Stanton"—the story containing the germ of *The Vicar of Wakefield*. The puerilities of this piece are usually excused as being the result of Goldsmith's writing under pressure, but the story may with equal justice be regarded as a sly joke upon magazine readers, a kind of mock-sentimental romance wittily undercutting some of their most cherished clichés.

24. *Memoirs of the Life, and Writings of Percivale Stockdale* (1809). Stockdale wrote:

> During a part of the year 1771, I compiled the universal magazine for Mr. Hinton, a bookseller in pater-noster-row. For this business I had seven guineas a month; which at that time, was a sum of great importance to my circumstances. But my paymaster was so sordid, and suspicious a creature; it was so difficult to please him; he was such a pretender to judgment, in matters of which he was totally ignorant; and he was so doubtful, that he had not labour enough for his money, that, in a few months, I was obliged to quit my attention to him, and his magazine. (II, 74.)

25. *Monthly Mirror*, III (1797), vi; *Lady's Monthly Museum*, n.s. IV (1808), iii; *Beau Monde, or Literary and Fashionable Magazine,* I (1806–1807), 358; *New Universal Magazine,* title page July, 1787, *et seq.*

In its 1773 "Preface" the *London* professed to enjoy the "Correspondence of some of the most distinguished Characters in the Republic of Letters." Again in 1781, they assured their readers that they had "sollicited and obtained the assistance of gentlemen of the first reputation in the republic of letters, whose joint labours will enliven and improve, by giving fresh spirit and vigour to their Miscellany." ("Advertisement," L, December, 1781, p. 560.) Boswell at this time was writing for them an anonymous series of essays called "The Hypochondriack," but this is the only known original in the *London* by an author of reputation.

26. The condition of the Yeames family was called to the attention of the readers of the *Lady's Magazine* in the editor's column of July, 1814 (XLV, 298).

27. Miss D. P. Campbell's case was laid before readers of the *Lady's Monthly Museum* in 1815 (s.3.II, 120). She was the author of a serial novel, "Agnes Addison, a Simple Tale" in 1814, and many poems and shorter pieces in the same magazine.

28. The only examples of magazine novels known to have graduated from the miscellanies into volume publication are: (1) Smollett's "Sir Launcelot Greaves" (*British*, 1760–1761), 1762. (2) Mrs. Lennox's "Harriot and Sophia" (*Lady's Museum*, 1760–1761); later published as *Sophia*, 1762. (3) George Moore's "Grasville Abbey" (*Lady's*, 1793–1797), 1797. (4) A. Percy's "The Monks and the Robbers" (*Lady's*, 1794–1805), 1808. (5) "Memoirs of Dick, the Little Pony" (Young Gentleman's and Lady's, 1799–1800), 1800. (6) A. Kendall's "Derwent Priory" (*Lady's*, 1796–1797), 1798. (7) Rev. Legh Richmond's "The Young Cottager," *et al.* (*Christian Guardian*, 1809–1814), later collected in *Annals of the Poor*, 1814. (8) John Jones's "Hawthorn Cottage" (*European*, 1812–1814), 1815.

A slightly larger number of magazine novelettes, like Goldsmith's "Reverie at the Boar's-Head-Tavern," found their way into later collections of essays and stories. For examples, see various pieces in the Catalogue attributed to Holcroft, Potter, Ryan, Moser, Murdoch, Keate, Bellamy, and Denis and Lloyd. But publishers were wary, for the simple reason that anything published in a miscellany was in the public domain unless protected by a royal license.

29. See the memoir entitled "The Late Mr. Thomas Bellamy," published in the *Monthly Mirror*, X (September, 1800), 132–134.

Bellamy was also the author of *The Benevolent Planters*, a short dramatic piece performed at the Theatre Royal, Haymarket, and printed in 1789; three novels, including a posthumous work called *The Beggar Boy* (published in 1801); and a collection of "Miscellanies" (1794), garnered from the then-defunct *General Magazine*.

30. "Preface," *Monthly Mirror*, I (December, 1795), x.

31. Anne Blower may be a relative of Elizabeth Blower, author of at least four novels between 1780–1788; or possibly the same person—although Bellamy would hardly be receiving extensive contributions from a well-known novelist without puffing her work.

32. Editors flattered their correspondents shamelessly. Concerning four of his principal contributors, the editor of the *Biographical and Imperial Magazine* wrote:

> The want of variety, of elegant originality, and of an ingenious and candid system of criticism... can no longer be urged against this publication; nor... while a WALSH and a BALMANNO, a REID, and a COURTNEY WENTWORTH continue, among others, to enrich the miscellaneous pages with the voluntary communications of original genius... can it be doubted, that the amusing and the polite literature which adorn the *Imperial Magazine*... will as far eclipse every rival publication..." ("Preface to the Third Volume," III, 1790, iv–v.)

The editor of the *Biographical and Imperial* in 1790 was John Thelwall. Three months later, when one of the above poets, W. Hamilton Reid, fell upon evil days, the editor lent him the following sympathy:

> W. Hamilton Reid's beautiful poems are received. We lament with him the fate of neglected genius, and wish him, from the benevolence of feeling patrons, a speedy relief from the misfortune which has fallen upon him. ("Correspondence," III, 138.)

The praise that editors heaped upon correspondents was intended to be read by both authors and readers. The December, 1779, editor's column of the *Lady's Magazine* acknowledged the receipt of a new novel in the following terms:

> We are greatly obliged to a new correspondent for *The Fortunate Sequel, or the Adventures of Ella Worthy, a Novel, in a Series of Letters, by a Lady*: and as they display an uncommon knowledge of the human heart, are wrote with spirit and elegance, and are fraught with sentiments that are necessary for the conduct of the sex in general, they shall begin our collection for January next, and be continued every succeeding month without interruption. (X [618].)

The same praise was repeated in equivalent terms in the 1779 Supplement, which announced other "admired Pieces" and "ingenious Originals" to be offered in the forthcoming volume. (X, [674].)

33. "Correspondence," *General*, V (January, 1791), ii.

34. *Lady's Monthly Museum*, n.s. XI (1811), 352; *Weekly Mirror* (Edinburgh), No. 2 (September 29, 1780), 32, and No. 18 (January 19, 1781), 288.

In the provincial presses editor and printer were often one. The Editor of the *Museum* (Cork) wrote of himself in 1796:

As EDITOR, he has to compose, or transcribe each number — as PRINTER, he has to work at Press, and Case, without the help of Journeyman, or Apprentice, — and without having served one hour to the business. (No. 6, May 18, 1796.)

35. For example, in the *Lady's Magazine* there were nine pieces of novelette length signed "R." published between the 1771 and the 1773 Supplements ("The Distressed Pair," "Cleomir and Dalia," "Melinda, or the Folly of Ambition," "The Dissemblers," "The Danger of Trying Experiments," "Sophia, or the Advantages of Adversity," "Melusina," "Cleora," and "The Travels of Heraclitus and Democritus"). Obviously, we are here presented with the work of a staff-writer, or a series of commissioned pieces by a single hand.

In the *Belle Assemblée* of 1807–1808 there was a similar series of pieces signed "E.R."

36. "To Correspondents," *Monthly*, III (March, 1797), 250.

37. For example, there were two translations of LeSage in the *Lady's* of 1775–1776 presented as the work of "Elfrida"; but the second was also initialed "D——." Later the same initial was appended to the continuation of the translation of the "Lettres d'Aza" in 1779–1780. There were many such double signatures in the *Lady's*: "The Extraordinary Wife, from Marmontel, a New Translation, by Louisa D'Argent" (signed "E."); "Lauretta, a New Translation from the French of Marmontelle, by Harriot Delany" (signed "J——"); "The Sylph Husband, a Moral Tale, a New Translation from Marmontel, by Miss Georgiana H———t, a Young Lady between Sixteen and Seventeen" (signed "R———"). It is difficult to resolve these ambiguities, except to note that Spectatorial tradition authorized the use of a public name, often signed to an introductory letter, in conjunction with a quite different initial, added at the end of the paper. The above translations of Marmontel may have been corrected by a staff-member.

38. *Monthly Visitor*, VI (January, 1799), 108.

39. *Lady's*, I (August, 1770), [3]. In the 1773 Supplement the magazine published a letter from "The Author of the Sentimental, &c.," in which he identified himself as the same writer "who planned the *Lady's Magazine*, and who has continued the Journey without intermission."

Accepting this as a true statement, we infer that the compiler of the *Lady's* was indeed a "Lady," though he sometimes referred to himself as *he* in his correspondence column. There was a venerable tradition for placing female periodicals in female hands (e.g., Mrs. Haywood, Mrs. Lennox, Matilda Wentworth, and others). On the other hand, Goldsmith's *Lady's* (1759–1761) probably only pretended to be conducted by a matron ("Mrs. Stanhope"), and fictions like this were common.

In the absence of any precise knowledge on this score, the more neutral pronoun *he* has been used to designate the compiler and editor of Robinson's *Lady's Magazine*.

40. See *European*, LII (July, 1807), LVI (November, 1809), 322.

The gratuitous contributions to the *Lady's Monthly Museum* were so numerous in March, 1802, that rejected articles were not returned to the sender, but thrown into the waste-basket (p. 216).

41. (1) *Lady's*, VIII (April, 1777), [170]; (2) *Lady's*, X (October, 1779), [506]; (3) *Town and Country*, XVIII (October, 1786), [506]; (4) *New Lady's*, V (June, 1790), [282]; (5) *Monthly Mirror*, XI (June, 1801), [362]; (6) *Lady's Monthly Museum*, XV (December, 1805), 427; (7) *Monthly Mirror*, n.s. III (March, 1808), [210]; (8) *Lady's*, XLII (August, 1811), [346]; (9) *Belle Assemblée*, n.s. XIV (November, 1816), 167.

42. The song, "Shall I all the truth discover," was published in Volume IV of the *Lady's Magazine* (October, 1773), facing page 544. The novelist's reply, signed "C. Reeve," and dated November 5, 1773, from Colcester, is found in the November issue (p. 568). Her offer to write for the magazine is phrased as follows:

> If my testimony will be of any service to you, I give it in favour of your Magazine, as the most *unexceptionable* of any publication of that kind. I should sometimes be tempted to become your correspondent, if I did not perceive that you have already but too many, and to increase the number would be only increasing your trouble in selecting, choosing, and rejecting them: the subject of this will, I hope, be its excuse.

Miss Reeve's real intentions in thus volunteering are uncertain. It seems unlikely that the recent translator of Barclay's *Argenis*, a woman already of some literary reputation, who later complained bitterly about the "pilfering practices" of "Magazines and other periodical publications," was offering her services *gratis* to the prosperous *Lady's Magazine*—although it is thus that the editor would seem to have regarded her offer, in replying as follows:

> We should be obliged to this lady for the honour of her correspondence, for however numerous our friends are, we shall endeavour to make room for her fav[o]urs. (*Lady's*, IV, 568.)

He returned the same invitation, less formally, several months later, writing in his correspondence column: "We depend upon *Miss Clara Reeve* for a completion of her promise..." (*Lady's*, V, January, 1774, [p. 2]).

Possibly Miss Reeve was hinting at a responsible connection with the magazine, and was repeating her offer in 1778, when she submitted copy to the editor.

43. *Lady's*, IX (April, 1778), 192.

44. *Ibid.*, IX (June, 1778), [282].

45. *Ibid.*, X (August, 1779), [394].

This episode in the history of the *Lady's Magazine* is curiously anticipated by the magazine's difficulties with Mme. Fauques de Vaucluse four years earlier. See "The Transmigrations of Hermes" in the Catalogue (No. 1255).

46. *Ibid.*, VII (August, 1776), [394].

47. The magazine had published a hair remedy in an earlier volume, which correspondents were eager to have reprinted, but the editor was unable to oblige, writing:

> we must assure our correspondents, that we have not yet been able to lay our hands upon it; yet we imagine it may be found in Vol. VI. but have it not by us at present... (XII, November, 1781, [562].)

48. *Lady's*, XII (August, 1781), [394]; XIII (May, 1782), 257.

49. "Alcander and Lucinda, a Moral Tale, *Lady's*, VIII (June–November, 1777); XV (January, 1784). The 650-word conclusion to this 2900-word tale, over six years delayed, was offered with a desire to "make retribution," and set an example for others who might be led similarly to "atone for the past." (XV, 41.)

The conclusion to "Artemisia, or the Happy Conclusion, a Moral Tale" (*Lady's*, VIII, January, February, 1777; XII, November, Supplement, 1781; XIII, February, 1782) was supplied by "A Constant Reader," after a lapse of over four years—whereupon the editor commented:

> The reason why this story was suspended, was because the editor suspected the originality; and now finds himself not mistaken! (XII, 577.)

50. "The Continuation offered by A. Percy will be willingly received if she will please to transmit it." (*Lady's*, XXIX, January, 1798, p. [2].) The story was resumed three months later. The editor began to call for a conclusion in July, 1801 (XXXII, [338]); and repeated his request in February, 1804 (XXXV, [58]). But the story ran until May, 1805.

51. Two other phenomenally long runs, both in the *Lady's Magazine*, were: "A Sentimental Journey, by a Lady" (August, 1770–April, 1777); and "The Elville Family Secrets, a Novel" (January, 1804–August, 1810).

Mention should also be made here of "The Matron," an essay-series that appeared regularly in the *Lady's Magazine* for over seventeen years (1774–1791). It has been described by Melvin R. Watson (*Magazine Serials and the Essay Tradition, op. cit.*, pp. 59–60, 117; and *Periodical Post Boy*, No. 14, November, 1953, pp. 2–5).

This series, extraordinary for the length of its run, was also remarkable for the amount of narrative material it contained, based upon the family life and domestic relationships of "Mrs. Grey," the fictitious editor. Over the course of the years a kind of cumulative family history was unfolded involving Mrs. Grey's children, grandchildren, and niece. "The Matron" has not been included in the Catalogue, however, since, though the picture of family life is consistently maintained, there was very little effort in the monthly columns to achieve narrative continuity. The model for the Greys, Watson believes, was the Lizard family of the *Guardian*.

52. *Universal Spectator*, No. 329 (January 25, 1735).

53. *Boswell's Life of Johnson*, ed. G. B. Hill, rev. L. F. Powell, III (1934), 19 (and note).

54. (1) *Edinburgh Weekly*, XL (May 20, 1778), 178; (2) *Weekly Magazine and Literary Review*, I (January 2, 1779).

55. Richmond P. Bond, *New Letters to the TATLER and SPECTATOR* (Austin, 1959).

56. *European*, I (1782), "Introduction," pp. [iii]–iv; *ibid.*, LVI (November, 1809), [322].

The Spectatorial base for a good deal of magazine correspondence is also suggested by the following notice, published in the "Correspondence" column of the *General Magazine* (November, 1787):

> The patrons of the *General Magazine* are respectfully informed, that a well-wisher proposes in No. 8, to introduce a paper to be occasionally continued upon the plan of the Mirror, Lounger, &c. &c. under the title of *The Friend*. To enable him to furnish a pleasing variety, he has desired us to solicit the assistance of ingenious and classical correspondents. (p. 282.)

57. *Serial letters*: Nos. 456, 568, 685, 1292. *Simple letter-series*: Nos. 941, 970, 1128. *Intermittent series*: Nos. 756, 757, 762, 763. *Dynamic series*: Nos. 758, 1130.

58. Frank G. Black, *The Epistolary Novel in the Late Eighteenth Century, a Descriptive and Bibliographical Study* (Eugene, 1940), p. 16.

59. *Lady's*, X (August, 1779), 432; X (December, 1779), 641.

60. "Our worthy correspondent Curiosus, can only receive all the information the publisher is able to give respecting the history of Nancy Pelham; it was written by an American lady, but he never knew either her name or rank in life. It will be continued in our next, and will soon be concluded." (*London*, "Acknowledgements to Correspondents," XLVIII, June, 1779, p. 288.)

61. The time-lapse of the first 31 letters of *Pamela* (Part I) is indefinite. The reader's impression is that several months elapse. But the period of the heroine's "bondage and misery" and of her subsequent "happiness" is precise: 78 days from beginning to end. This part of the narrative action comprises more than four-fifths of the novel, quantitatively speaking.

The first letter of *Clarissa* is dated January 10; the last, December 18, of the same year.

62. *London*, XLVIII (October, 1779), 448.

63. The Catalogue indicates that "Anna, a Fragment," was reprinted in the magazines at least six times between 1797 and 1815. The unlisted "Gentoo Story" from the same volume, being shorter, was even more popular.

Brandon, of course, was not a leader in the vogue, since his *Fragments* did not appear until 1797. But the frequency with which his collection was pilfered even at this late period shows how keen the appetite for Shandean imitations still was.

64. *Edinburgh Weekly*, XLV (July 21, 1779), 85.

65. *European*, LXI (March, 1812), 195.

66. *Edinburgh Weekly*, XLVI (December 22, 1779), 292–294; *European*, II (November, 1782), 325–328 [No. 6 of "The Man of the Town"]; *Town and Country Weekly*, II (January 21, 1786), 49–54; *Asylum*, III (February 23, 1796), 296–298; *Lady's Monthly Museum*, XI (October, 1803), 236–242; *Ireland's Mirror*, II (September, 1805), 485; *Monthly Mirror*, XX (July, 1805), 22–24; *Dublin Magazine, or Monthly Memorialist*, I (November, 1812), 18–19. Many of these were widely reprinted, and the above citations may not represent the earliest magazine appearances.

A now-famous "fragment" in verse is Coleridge's "Foster Mother's Tale" in the *Lyrical Ballads* of 1798. Versified fragments were nearly as common as prose pieces by the time the *Ballads* were published.

67. *Gentleman's*, XXXVII (January, 1767), 75–76; *Oxford*, VII (August, 1771), 67–69.

In an essay "On the Imitations of Sterne" (*Westminster*, XIII, November, 1785, pp. 585–587), the pseudonymous author attacked the flood of insipid and affected pieces in the supposed manner of Sterne in periodical publications of the previous ten years. "I remember," he wrote, "to have told in one magazine ten [such] titles in two pages." Sterne's true "simplicity and nature" had misled the inexperienced. They were to be achieved only by "consummate learning," "originality of sentiment," and the "most delicate sympathy."

68. *Town and Country*, VII (January, 1775), 16.

69. *Lady's*, IV (January, 1773), 3.

70. *Ibid.*, IV (Supplement, 1773), 676–680.

71. *Ibid.*, XIII (October, 1782), 506.

72. "Julia, or the Penitent Daughter" appeared in the magazines five times; "Fanny, or the Happy Repentance," four; "The Lord of Crequi," five. (See Catalogue Nos. 733, 399. 811.) "Warbeck" was begun in the *Oxford Magazine* in 1776, but was left uncompleted. Two later appearences, in the *Sentimental* and the *Monthly Miscellany*, in 1777, were also fragmentary.

73. "*The History of Eliza*," *Critical*, XXII (December, 1766), p. 434.

74. See Robert D. Mayo, "Gothic Romance in the Magazines," *PMLA*, LXV (September, 1950), 762–789; and "The Gothic Short Story of the Magazines," *Modern Language Review* XXXVII (1942), 448–454.

75. Both magazines sold for a shilling a copy (containing about 50 pages apiece). Allowing for a monthly circulation of 10,000 for each, a conservative estimate, since both are said to have attained fifteen to sixteen thousand, the gross income from both would amount to £ 1000 a month, or £ 12,000 a year. It is doubtful that compiling, printing, and distributing the two cost much more than half this amount—considering the casual manner in which they were conducted. The *Town and Country* was published from 1769–1796; the *Lady's*, established in 1770, survived well into the 19th century. George Robinson died a very wealthy man in 1801.

76. See Q. D. Leavis, *Fiction and the Reading Public* (London, 1932), pp. 126 *et seq.*

APPENDIX I

1. See "On the Abuse of Allegory in Preaching," *Evangelical*, XIV (1806), 489–491. In reviewing *Coëleb's in Search of a Wife* the critic in the *Christian Observer* began: "It may be very true that novels are mischievous; but we cannot allow this work to be called a novel." (VIII, February, 1809, p. 109.)

The "Spiritual Barometer" (*Evangelical*, VIII, December, 1800, p. 526) is reproduced in Maurice J. Quinlan, *Victorian Prelude* (Columbia University Press, 1941), p. 115.

2. "To the Reader," *Arminian*, I (1778), vi.

3. There were at least six English translations of the *Galateo* of Giovanni della Casa made between 1675 and 1774. Wesley's abridgment is from the version by "N.W." called *The Refin'd Courtier*, first published in 1663.

4. "God's Revenge" appeared in twenty installments between May, 1787, and December, 1788; the "Account of Mr. Silas Told" was published in 18 parts between February, 1787, and August, 1788.

5. *Cottage Magazine*, III (1814), 201. The story is told in the form of three letters to the editor of the magazine. The last is inscribed "E.T.M.P., H———, Parsonage, Nov. 1814." (IV, 1815, p. 29.)

6. The homiletic fiction of the *Annals of the Poor*, first published in the *Christian Guardian*, was later reprinted in the form of tracts, and enjoyed an enormous 19th-century circulation. By 1844, according to William Jones, the Religious Tract Society had distributed a total of 1,354,616 copies of Richmond's "Young Cottager," "Dairyman's Daughter," and "Negro Servant" (see *The Jubilee Memorial of the Religious Tract Society*, London, 1850, p. 150). It is these pieces, or others like them, that Thackeray is ridiculing with Lady Southdown's tracts in *Vanity Fair*.

7. See G. E. Harrison, *Methodist Good Companions* (1935), p. 113. Coleridge's letter to Poole is No. 174 of the *Collected Letters*, ed. E. L. Griggs, Volume I (1956).

Toplady's *Gospel Magazine* expired in 1784, and therefore Coleridge may have been thinking of his boyhood reading. The *Gospel Magazine* was not Methodist, however, but Calvinistic, although Coleridge may merely have meant by "Gospel Magazine" any evangelical periodical, of which there were a great many in existence by 1797.

On the other hand, if Coleridge was speaking of the new *Gospel Magazine and Theological Review,* founded in 1796, he would be referring to pieces like the following: "Remarkable Passages in the Life of Mr. Vavasor Powel, Minister of the Gospel in Wales, Written by Himself" (I, May, June, 1796); "An Abridgement of the Singular Experience and Great Sufferings of Mrs. Agnes Beaumont, Afterwards Mrs. Story" (I, August, 1796); "Conversion of Mr. John Biggs, of Rothwell. Northamptonshire, in the Year 1689" (II, May, 1797).

The value of "experiences" like these as a method of gaining and holding reader interest was recognized by all evangelical magazines. As the *Evangelical* declared in its initial volume: "Biography, Memoirs, Diaries, Authentic Anecdotes, Striking Providences, and the Expressions of Dying Christians, arrest the mind of the reader, and make a deep impression." (I, 1793, p. 4.)

APPENDIX II

1. Graham Pollard cites a third such magazine, *Radcliffe's New Novelist's Pocket Magazine* (1802), but this serial is unavailable in any of the public collections. See *New Paths in Book Collecting*, ed. John Carter (London: Constable, 1934), p. 257.

2. See *Reminiscences of Literary London from 1779 to 1853*. By Dr. Thomas Rees, with Extensive Additions by John Britton, F.S.A. (New York: Harper, 1896), p. 23.

3. The "Advertisement" of the *Monthly Amusement* reminded readers of this fact, saying that should the periodical fall short of its intention "Buyers... will suffer no Disappointment; because every Piece will be an entire work of it self."

4. R. M. Wiles, "Short-Title Catalogue of Books Published in Fascicules before 1750," *Serial Publication in England before 1750*, p. 341 (*Polite Tales*); p. 355 (*Modern Story-Teller*); p. 279 (*Religious Novels*); pp. 300, 304 (*Weekly Novelist*).

5. Walter Graham, *English Literary Periodicals* (New York, 1930), pp. 182, 185.

6. "The Sisters," *Novelist's*, V, iii; "Memoirs of a Magdalen," *ibid.*, VII, iii.

7. "Morality of the English Novel and Romance," published in the *Literary Panorama* between 1811–1814, is an anthology of extracts or "Selections," designed to show the range and perspicuity of the novelists as moral teachers, under such headings as "Slavery," "Charity," "Happy Family," "Duelling," and "Unsullied Conscience." The series, which was conducted by a well-known popular novelist, S. J. Pratt, included over a hundred extracts, drawn not only from classical authors like Fielding, Richardson, Mackenzie, Fanny Burney, and Goldsmith, but from newer works of fiction like *Thaddeus of Warsaw, Hermsprong, St. Botolph's Priory,* Mrs. Parson's *Girl of the Mountains, The Milesian Chief,* and Mrs. Opie's *Father and Daughter.*

8. For example, *The Cavern of Horrors, or Miseries of Miranda*, 1802, and *De La Mark and Constantia, or Ancient Heroism, a Gothick Tale*, 1803 (both from the *Marvellous Magazine*, where they bear the same dates); *Banditti of Monte Baldo, or the Lass of the Lake*, 1805, and *Edwin, or the Wandering Fugitive*, 1805 (from the *Tell-Tale*). About half the contents of both magazines are found listed in *Block*, bearing the same publishers' names.

APPENDIX III

1. *French writers* named or identified in Catalogue entries are Baculard D'Arnaud, Godart de Beauchamps, Beaurieu, Mlle. Bernard, Bitaubé, Bonneville, Boufflers, Bricaire de la Dixmerie, Chateaubriand, Chavis and Cazotte, Crébillon *fils*, Diderot, Dubois-Fontanelle, Duclos, Ducray-Duminil, Fénelon, Mme. Fauques de Vaucluse, Florian, Galland, Mme. de Genlis, Mme. de Gomez, Mme. de Grafigny, Gueullette, La Calprenède, Imbert, Lamarche-Courmont, La Motte, Legrand d'Aussy, Le Sage, Mlle. L'Héritier, Louvet de Couvray, Marivaux, Marmontel, Mercier, Montesquieu, Mme. Montolieu, the Chevalier de Mouhy, Mme. D'Ormoy, Pétis de la Croix, Mme. Riccoboni, Mme. Roland, Rousseau, Saint-Lambert, Saint-Pierre, Mme. de Saint-Venant, Savary, Mme. de Tencin, the Count de Tressan, Treyssac de Vergy [who wrote in English], Voisenon, Voltaire.

German: Boettiger, Gellert, Gessner, Goethe, Kahlert, Kotzebue, Lafontaine, Marie Sophie von La Roche, Meissner, Musaeus, Rabener, Schiller, Vogel, Wieland.

Italian: Ariosto, Boccaccio, Croce, Da Porto, Tasso.

Spanish: Cervantes, Fernandez de Avellaneda.

Danish: Anderson, Suhm.

Russian: Karamzin.

2. Of the forty-three German titles of known authorship listed in the Catalogue, nineteen belong to the twenty-five-year period from 1776–1800, twenty-four to the decade and a half between 1801 and 1815. These figures do not take into account the supplementary reprintings of these titles in other magazines, which are heavily weighted in favor of the nineteenth century on a four-to-one ratio.

The earliest long works of German fiction in British periodicals, in order of appearance are: (1) "The Adventures of Sophia Sternheim," by Marie Sophie von La Roche, published in the *Universal Magazine* for 1776. (2) "The Remarkable History of the Countess of G——, a Swedish Lady," by C. F. Gellert, in the *Weekly Miscellany* (Sherborne) for 1778. (3) An original translation of Gessner's *Der erste Schiffer,* printed in the *Yorkshire Magazine* for 1786.

The first, and probably the second, of these items was extracted without acknowledgment from a recently published trade edition. The third was taken from a French intermediary. Much of the German fiction published in British magazines before 1815 was probably translated from French sources, which were more accessible to English writers, and offered a less formidable language barrier.

The above analysis, of course, takes into account only German fiction in excess of 5000 words. The tiny prose idylls of Gessner enjoyed a considerable magazine vogue in the *Lady's* and elsewhere somewhat earlier than 1776. Outside Gessner, the most frequently encountered German writers in British periodicals are Lafontaine and Kotzebue, whose magazine runs began in 1800 and 1807 respectively.

3. All three also appeared after 1782—i.e., posthumously.

There were a few long extracts from the novels in the miscellanies, but they were all discursive passages, not narrative. See "Abstract of the Savoyard Curate's Profession of Faith, from Rousseau" (*Gentleman's*, XXXIV, 1764, pp. 13–16, 79–82); and "Rousseau's *Emilia*, a

New Translation by "J. E——y" (*Lady's*, IX, 1778, pp. 507–508, 590–592; X, 1779, pp. 117–118; XI, 1780, pp. 146–148, 183–184). The latter was an extract from the novel totalling 6300 words.

The *Monthly Review's* serialized review of *La Nouvelle Héloïse*, already mentioned in Chapter III (p. 207), totalled 30,000 words, and consisted of a full summary of the story with intercalated excerpts.

4. "The Black and the White," taken from Smollett's translation of the *Works* and printed in the *British* in 1765; reprinted in the *Oxford* four years later.

This story was also translated in the *Gentleman's* in 1765, where it figures under the title "A Story from the French of Voltaire." But being a different translation, this version has been cited in a separate entry.

5. The English magazine versions of Mme. de Gomez, on the other hand, illustrate the non-operation of the reputation principle. Not a single one of the ten stories found in British miscellanies between 1782 and 1807 (mostly in provincial repositories and collections of old favorites) bore her name or any other sign of their origin.

6. *Monthly*, XLVI (Appendix, 1772), 696. The reviews of "Fanny, or the Happy Repentance" are found in the *Monthly*, XXXV (August, 1766), 97–100; and the *Critical*, XXII (July, 1766), 90.

7. The editor was certainly aware of the deception, since the story in the *Lady's* was embellished with a copper-plate engraving copied from one in Volume V (1778) of the *Oeuvres de M. D'Arnaud.*

8. There were at least five appearences of "Selico, nouvelle africaine" (see the *Bee*, 1792; *Universal Magazine and Review*, 1792; *Sentimental and Masonic*, 1792; *Lady's*, 1792; *Weekly Entertainer*, 1793); and four of "Zulbar, nouvelle indienne" (see *Universal*, 1792; *Universal Magazine and Review*, 1792; *Sentimental and Masonic*, 1792; *Weekly Entertainer*, 1793). "Selico" is found in three different translations.

9. In this analysis of Marmontel's reputation, the edition of the "Moral Tales" published in the *Novelist's Magazine* (1781) has been regarded as a trade edition rather than a magazine printing, since it is usually so considered. Counted as magazine fiction, of course, it would have increased the already-large incidence of Marmontel.

10. The quotations are taken from the Becket and De Hondt translation, the only full-length version of the story to be printed in the magazines.

11. Thus spoke the *Critical* reviewer (XVII, January, 1764, pp. 43–44). The critic in the *Monthly* (XXX, January, 1764, pp. 59–61) took approximately the same line. Clara Reeve, in the *Progress of Romance* (1785), found Marmontel "a charming writer," but noted that the *Moral Tales* "have some things in them that are offensive to *good Morals*." (Facsimile Text Society ed., II, 35.)

A GLOSSARY

ABRIDGMENT: A condensed version of a work of fiction, not greatly reduced in scale. Most abridgments followed more or less the author's own wording, and therefore attempted to afford the same pleasures as the original. An example is Kinnersley's abridgment of Johnson's *Rasselas,* which became a *cause célèbre* in the copyright struggle (see pp. 239–243). See also EPITOME, REDACTION, and "REVIEW."

COMMON MISCELLANY: A generic term used to denote all miscellanies of a non-"historical" character, including not only periodicals designed to amuse and inform a more popular audience of readers than that of the *Gentleman's Magazine,* but serials of a more specialized character. See also HISTORICAL MISCELLANY, REVIEW-MISCELLANY, GENERAL MAGAZINE, PROVINCIAL REPOSITORY, and SPECIALIZED MAGAZINE.

CUMULATIVE EPISODE: A type of *episodic narrative* (q.v.), indigenous to the essay-serial, in which a story, continued at intervals and always complete at the end of any given episode, eventually came to a climax or reached a conclusion which was the consummation of all that preceded. Examples are the "Progress of Cynthio" in the *Tatler,* the "Story of Miranda" in the *Free-Thinker* and the "Story of Colonel Caustic" in the *Lounger* (see pp. 34–35, 46–47, 133–135).

DETACHED EPISODE: A long extract from a novel, either an inset story or a discrete part, offered as a self-contained work of fiction. Examples are "The Adventures of Imlac" from *The History of Rasselas,* "The Story of Old Edwards" from *The Man of Feeling,* and "The Affecting History of Caroline Montgomery" from *Ethelinde* (see pp. 243–253). Related forms of magazine fiction are the "*review,*" the *epitome,* the *abridgment,* and the *redaction* (qq.v.).

DREAM NARRATIVE or DREAM VISION: A species of essay-type fiction in which the author allegedly falls asleep and dreams, or has a vision that unfolds some moral, philosophical, or political truth (see pp. 38–39). Frequently combined with allegory, the dream narrative became one of the most familiar forms of magazine fiction in the eighteenth century. Some early examples are "The Vision of Mirza" in the *Spectator,* "The Inchanted Palace" in the *Visions of Sir Heister Ryley,* and "The Vision of the Golden Rump" in *Common Sense.*

DYNAMIC LETTER-SERIES: A type of epistolary narrative in which the story is presented from more than one point of view, or through the agency of two or more correspondents (see pp. 53–54). Examples are the story of "John Trott" in the *Spectator,* Johnson's "History of Hymenaeus's Courtship," and Mackenzie's "History of the Homespuns." See also SIMPLE LETTER-SERIES and INTERMITTENT LETTER-SERIES.

EPISODIC NARRATIVE: A type of serial story the separate parts of which were more or less self-contained (see p. 42). Examples are Mr. Bickerstaff's various adventures with his guardian angel Pacolet in the *Tatler,* and "Drake's Travels" in the *Universal Spectator.* More loosely organized than the *serial tale* (q.v.), the *episodic narrative* was usually continued intermittently, the story being considered complete at the end of any given installment. Some episodic narratives, however, ran their course to an end which was the consummation of all that preceded, and we call this sub-species the *cumulative episode* (q.v.).

EPITOME: A highly condensed summary of a work of fiction, intended chiefly to acquaint readers with the fable of the book (see pp. 236–239). See also ABRIDGMENT, REDACTION, and "REVIEW."

ESSAY-MISCELLANY: A type of hybrid periodical combining features of both the *essay-serial* and the *miscellany* (qq.v.), and offering a medley of new and reprinted pieces on which the personal stamp of the editor was very marked. Examples are Goldsmith's *Bee* and Mrs. Lennox's *Lady's Museum.*

ESSAY-SERIAL (or SINGLE-ESSAY PERIODICAL): A type of periodical publication, usually published at weekly or twice-weekly intervals, in which attention tended to be focussed on a single essay or story in each issue (see Chapter II, pp. 71 ff). There were two main classes of *essay-serial*—the "literary" and the "polemical." The first, in the direct line of the *Tatler* and *Spectator,* included much more prose fiction than the second variety, which was largely devoted to partisan controversy. See also ESSAY-SERIES and ESSAY-MISCELLANY.

ESSAY-SERIES: A series of essays conducted in the manner of the *essay-serial* (q.v.), but published in a weekly journal, miscellany, or newspaper, or printed in volume-form (see pp. 75–84). Some well-known examples are Johnson's "Idler" (published in Payne's *Universal Chronicle*), Goldsmith's "Chinese Letters" (*Public Ledger*), Boswell's "Hypochondriack" (*London Magazine*), and Cumberland's *Observer,* which was first published as a collection of essays. See ESSAY-SERIAL.

GENERAL MAGAZINE: A type of miscellany that attempted to combine various "historical" ingredients with others of a more popular character. Examples are the *Universal Magazine* (after 1764) and the *Newcastle General Magazine* (see pp. 182–183, 215–216). See also COMMON MISCELLANY and HISTORICAL MISCELLANY.

HISTORICAL MISCELLANY: A type of miscellany that attempted to record contemporary "history," by summarizing the news, and keeping readers informed on parliamentary affairs, new advances in science and learning, and contemporary opinion on a broad front. The most successful and the longest-lived of the historical miscellanies was Cave's *Gentleman's Magazine* (see Chapter III). In their encyclopedic purpose the historical miscellanies are closely associated with the *reviews* (q.v.). See also COMMON MISCELLANY, GENERAL MAGAZINE, and REVIEW-MISCELLANY.

INTERMITTENT LETTER-SERIES: A story told in the form of letters from a single correspondent, who chronicled events more or less as they occurred. In this type of story, as opposed to the *simple letter-series* (q.v.), readers received periodic reports on a developing narrative action (see pp. 52–53). Examples are Defoe's story of "Tom Manywife" (p. 52), and Johnson's stories of "Euphelia" and "Eumathes" (p. 104). See also LETTER-SERIES, DYNAMIC LETTER-SERIES, and SIMPLE LETTER-SERIES.

LETTER-SERIES: Any of several types of magazine stories told in the form of two or more letters, as opposed to the *serial letter,* in which a single letter was divided for installment publication. See SIMPLE LETTER-SERIES, INTERMITTENT LETTER-SERIES, DYNAMIC LETTER-SERIES, and SERIAL TALE.

MAGAZINE: Any of a wide variety of periodical publications, exclusive of newspapers and technical serials that made no effort to entertain. The term *magazine* was given wide currency in the eighteenth century by the popularity of Cave's *Gentleman's Magazine* and therefore tended to be pre-empted by the *miscellany* (q.v.), but in these pages it is applied also to weekly journals, essay-serials, essay-miscellanies, and specialized serials (except newspapers) that show some desire to amuse as well as inform their readers.

MISCELLANY: A serial collection of writings on several subjects or in several manners, designed to amuse and inform a somewhat general audience of readers. In the eighteenth-century the term was also applied to any collection of writings on various subjects and in various manners (see Arthur E. Case, *A Bibliography of English Poetical Miscellanies, 1521–1750,* Oxford, 1935), but in these pages it is used exclusively to denote periodical publications like the *Gentleman's Journal,* the *Gentleman's Magazine,* the *European Magazine,* and the *Lady's,* which offered a flexible combination of poems, stories, essays, letters, and informational articles, some original, some collected from outside sources, or translated from foreign literature. Because of the dominant position of the *Gentleman's Magazine* among eighteenth-century serial publications, the term *magazine* was frequently synonymous with *miscellany.* See MAGAZINE, COMMON MISCELLANY, HISTORICAL MISCELLANY, ESSAY-MISCELLANY, PROVINCIAL REPOSITORY, REVIEW-MISCELLANY, and SPECIALIZED MAGAZINE.

MOCK-HEROIC and MOCK-SENTIMENTAL TALE: A type of magazine story, indigenous to the essay-serial, intended to ridicule conventional ideas of love, heroism, and gallantry, or parodying fiction giving expression to these views. Examples are "The History of Orlando the Fair" in the *Tatler,* "The Story of Hilpa" in the *Spectator,* and "Anningait and Ajut" in the *Rambler.*

NEWS-SHEET (or NEWSPAPER): Any periodical primarily concerned with disseminating intelligence; in these pages opposed to the term *magazine* (q.v.).

NOVEL: Here used to apply to any magazine story in excess of 12,000 words (see p. 6). During most of the eighteenth century the term *novel* was synonymous with the term *history* and was used to denote a work of fiction of any length, usually contemporary in setting. By the end of the century, however, it began to be more frequently employed to designate longer works of fiction. See NOVELETTE.

NOVELETTE: Here used to denote any magazine story of 5000 to 12,000 words (see pp. 5–6). The term *novelette* was very infrequently employed in the eighteenth century. The earliest magazine use noted was in 1774 (see Catalogue No. 1113), when it was applied to a translation from the Spanish. See also NOVEL.

PICTURE OF LIFE (or LIVING PICTURE): A term used by Dr. Johnson to describe the narrative portraits of the *Rambler.* The *picture of life,* as presented by Johnson, was a history of some representative character, or the account of some person's unhappy experience in life, offered as an illustration of a moral or social evil, and intended to excite satirical laughter or abhorrence. Examples are Johnson's "History of Zosima" and "Hymenaeus's Courtship" (see pp. 101–105).

PROVINCIAL REPOSITORY: A magazine primarily of regional interest, designed to attract a fairly general audience of readers in some area outside the principal urban centers of England, Scotland, and Ireland. Examples are the *Berwick Museum,* the *Cumberland Magazine,* and the *Weekly Entertainer* (Sherborne). Such magazines typically combined "historical" features copied from the London magazines, with articles of regional interest, repertory pieces, and a certain amount of original material, some of it of local origin (see pp. 217–218).

REDACTION: A condensed version of a work of fiction, usually avoiding the phraseology of the original, and frequently changing also the title and all of the proper names. The *Tell-Tale* and *Marvellous Magazine* specialized in redactions of famous works of Gothic fiction (see Appendix II).

REVIEW: A type of periodical almost exclusively devoted to notices of new books and pamphlets. The principal eighteenth-century reviews were the *Monthly* and the *Critical* (see pp. 190–208), but there were many others. The review also combined with the miscellany to produce hybrids like the *European* and Phillips's *Monthly Magazine.* See REVIEW-MISCELLANY.

"REVIEW": A form of surrogate magazine fiction, very popular in the miscellanies, consisting of a summary of a new work of fiction, "specimens," and a few critical comments (see pp. 235–236). The "*review*" is distinguished from the *epitome* (q.v.) in being prefaced with a bibliographical citation giving the title of the work, its publisher, price, etc.

REVIEW-MISCELLANY: A type of miscellany giving a regular part of its attention to notices of new books; for example, the *British Magazine and Review,* the *European Magazine and London Review,* and Phillips's *Monthly Magazine* (see pp. 215–217). See also REVIEW and MISCELLANY.

SATIRICAL ADVENTURE STORY: A familiar species of essay-type fiction designed to ridicule human vices and follies from an odd or somewhat impersonal point of view, usually through the imagined experience of some inanimate, or non-human, being (see p. 38). Early examples are "The Adventures of a Shilling" in the *Tatler,* and "The Letter from a Monkey" in the *Spectator.*

SERIAL ANTHOLOGY: A collection of classics or old favorites of English and foreign fiction, issued in fascicules, normally unnumbered and undated, but later collected into volumes bearing volume numbers and dates, like periodicals. Examples are the *Novelist's Magazine* and the *New Novelist's Magazine* (see Appendix II). The *serial anthology* is associated with the *serial chapbook* (q.v.).

SERIAL CHAPBOOK: A serial collection of stories, usually of a very popular or sensational character, published at regular intervals, and sometimes separately numbered and dated. The single issues of the serial chapbooks usually contained one or sometimes two stories, tailored to a prescribed number of pages, and were sold separately and also in bound volumes, like magazines. Examples are the *Tell-Tale* and the *Marvellous Magazine,* which specialized in redactions of Gothic fiction (see Appendix II). See also SERIAL ANTHOLOGY and REDACTION.

SERIAL LETTER: A story told in the form of a single letter, somewhat mechanically divided for installment publication. This type of story was given wide currency by the popularity of Hawkesworth's *Adventurer* (see p. 107). The method of the *serial letter* is closely associated with that of the *serial tale* (q.v.), and sharply differentiated from that of the *letter series* and the *episodic narrative* (qq.v.).

SERIAL TALE: A type of magazine story, usually short, somewhat mechanically divided for installment publication. Examples are the "History of Orlando the Fair" in the *Tatler,* "The History of Melissa" in the *Adventurer,* and "The Story of La Roche" in the *Mirror.* The method of the *serial tale* is allied with that of the *serial letter* (q.v.), and contrasted with that of the *episodic narrative* and *letter series* (qq.v.), in which each installment is more or less a self-contained unit.

SIMPLE LETTER-SERIES: A story told by means of two or more letters addressed to the same correspondent, and giving a consecutive view of events in retrospect. Examples are Defoe's "Village Love" and Johnson's "Story of Eubulus" (see pp. 52–53, 103–104). In the *simple letter-series,* as in the *serial letter* (qq.v.), the divisions between the parts are somewhat perfunctory; in the *intermittent* and *dynamic letter-series* (qq.v.), on the other hand, these divisions tend to be genuinely functional.

SINGLE-ESSAY PERIODICAL. See ESSAY-SERIAL.

SPECIALIZED MAGAZINE: A type of miscellany addressed to a single class of readers, or to persons with some special area of interest like agriculture, religion, art, commerce, or the theatre; for example, the *Juvenile Magazine, Recreations in Agriculture, Bellamy's Picturesque Magazine,* the *Tradesman, or Commercial Magazine,* and the *Theatrical Review* (see pp. 218–220).

SUPPORTING NARRATIVE: A method of unifying a series of periodical essays by enclosing them in a narrative framework or creating the impression of a background intrigue. Examples are the *Plain Dealer* and Goldsmith's "Chinese Letters" (see pp. 47, 123–124).

WEEKLY JOURNAL: A type of periodical designed to evade the tax on newspapers imposed in 1712 (see pp. 48ff). The *weekly journal* combined features of the *news-sheet,* the *essay-serial,* and the *miscellany* (qq.v.). They were usually six-page (later four-page) periodicals, printed in double columns, with leading articles or introductory letters, followed by summaries of the news, obituary articles, prices of stocks, and other miscellaneous features. Important examples of the weekly journal are *Mist's, Applebee's,* the *Universal Spectator,* and Fielding's *Champion.*

A CATALOGUE OF MAGAZINE NOVELS AND NOVELETTES
1740–1815

Introduction

The historians and bibliographers of the English novel have almost entirely disregarded periodical literature, though miscellanies and essay-serials were two very widely frequented avenues of publication, and contain quantities of narrative material. In the three volumes which he devotes to the eighteenth century, for example, E. A. Baker has almost nothing to say about magazine fiction, although he occasionally dwells upon narrative poetry and the drama. Andrew Block's *English Novel* lists some nine thousand works published between 1740 and 1850, but completely ignores periodical literature, which could have supplied him with many hundreds of additional titles. His catalogue reveals so little about its sources of information, its methods, and its criteria that it is impossible to say whether his silence on this score represents an oversight or a conscious limitation of his area of operation. When the need to review some thousands of English periodicals (some of them in series of over a hundred volumes) is added to his other burdens, the bibliographer, like the historian, is disposed to throw up his hands and look the other way. The field of magazine literature is so vast, and its outlying areas so barren and inaccessible, that he is likely to feel that the only feasible approach to the magazines is to ignore them. There is not even a full, accurate, and up-to-date bibliography of English literary periodicals with which he can begin.

Similarly, most specialized studies of eighteenth-century fiction, like Miss Conant's *Oriental Tale in England in the Eighteenth Century*, F. G. Black's *Epistolary Novel in the Late Eighteenth Century*, and Montague Summers's *Gothic Bibliography* (to name only three) take little or no account of periodical literature, although magazines like the *Lady's*, the *New Lady's*, the *Universal*, the *London*, the *Belle Assemblée*, and the *Edinburgh* contain quantities of oriental tales, epistolary novels, and Gothic fiction in a variety of modes, lying within easy reach in British and American libraries. The same reticence prevails among other students of eighteenth-century fiction. Except for mention of Sir Roger de Coverley, the oriental tales of the *Rambler* and *Adventurer*, Smollett's *Sir Launcelot Greaves*, and Goldsmith's *Citizen of the World*, most literary historians have been content to let periodical literature before *Blackwood's* go by the board. From the point of view of literary merit, this neglect is no doubt deserved. But in those studies occupied with trends and influences, the growth and decline of novelists' reputations, and the development of various literary genres, and in all works on eighteenth-century fiction which describe literary fashions or show their relation to the history of taste, it is a serious omission to disregard so large and so widely circulated a corpus of prose fiction.

The following catalogue, although not a bibliography in the fullest technical sense, is intended to provide easier access to one part of this forgotten literature—namely, all narrative works in excess of 5000 words, published in British magazines between 1740 and 1815. By *magazines* is meant serial publications, exclusive of newspapers. Within this range the Catalogue aspires to completeness, although this is necessarily only an approximation. Some eighteenth-century periodicals are today known only by title. Others survive only in a mutilated condition. A few, formerly available, were destroyed in the war. No doubt some magazines in small libraries have been overlooked, and a few stories escaped the net in other ways. But the Catalogue may safely claim to cover all the major and most of the minor periodicals published in London, Newcastle, Edinburgh, Glasgow, and Dublin, and the great majority of still-extant provincial publications over a seventy-five year period (actually seventy-six). A grand total of over nine hundred different periodicals were examined in whole or in part in preparing this list, and, of these, 238 were found to contain what have been designated as "novels" and "novelettes." A Register of the magazines offering long fiction is appended to the Catalogue, together with a key to the short titles employed throughout.

The problem of what does or does not constitute magazine fiction is often perplexing. The Aristotelian distinction between "real" and "feigned" history is easy to state, but difficult to apply in practice, since a great many factual narratives sought to achieve effects traditionally associated with imaginative writing, and a great deal of eighteenth-century fiction was motivated by a desire to pass itself off as real history. The claim that stories, obviously invented, are "true," "genuine," or "founded on fact" is one of the most common labels of magazine fiction. The age was eminently biographical as well as historical. Magazines were filled with anecdotes of the great and the near-great, odd and curious lives, and memoirs of statesmen, peers, poets, and actors. Writers of magazine stories were inevitably led to trade upon this predilection, especially since they could not fail to be aware of how extensive was the prejudice against prose fiction. As "novelists" they enjoyed only dubious literary standing; as "historians" they were admired and approved.

The relations between *real* and *feigned* history in the eighteenth century were devious, and they are still largely unexplored. But in general, voyages and travels, history, and biography in which the dominant aim appears to have been to present an accurate account of events that actually occurred have been excluded from the Catalogue as non-fiction, and those in which the genius of fiction seems to preside, albeit feebly, have been included, even though such stories may involve real people and historical subjects. Thus we have excluded works like Sully's "History of the Dutchess of Beaufort" (translated by Mrs.

Lennox), the "Sufferings of Christiana, Princess of Zell," and the "History of Bampfylde Moore Carew, King of the Beggars," to name several items at random, even though all three were obviously composed with an eye to imaginative effects; and we have classified as fiction the scandalous "tête-à-têtes" of the *Town and Country*, the "secret histories" of the *Court, City and Country Magazine*, the lives of secular saints in the evangelical magazines, and some of the memoirs of footpads, sporting men, and celebrated stage beauties found in the *Sporting Magazine*, the *Rambler's*, and the *Ladies*, even though these accounts indubitably contain at least a substratum of truth. Such a separation is obviously forced, however, and probably a certain amount of marginal fiction has been ruled out which another classifier, operating on the same principles, would have included, and *vice versa*.

Equally perplexing has been the distinction between narrative and other literary genres—particularly the essay form, which, owing to the sovereign influence of Addison and Steele, and the didactic motive that informed almost all magazine fiction, is highly ambiguous. The difference between a long story with a labored moral, and a didactic essay with a prolonged illustrative narrative, is a question of emphasis which it is not always easy to answer. Magazine authors often seem to write as if purposely attempting to blur the distinction between narrative and non-narrative writing. Some essay-series are found divided into "Chapters," like novels; and some magazine novels affect Spectatorial titles, numbered parts, and other paraphernalia of the essay tradition. A great many essay-serials and essay-series, of course, contain serial narratives, and these, when long enough, have been gathered into the Catalogue. Some magazine series, in fact, are little more than collections of short stories and novelettes. Others, more conservative, are projected in terms of assumptive characters, whose histories are casually unfolded, or whose adventures or domestic experiences are made the subject of weekly or monthly lucubrations. The mere presence of narrative episodes, or even of a background story, has not been considered sufficient to warrant including the whole series in the Catalogue, unless it becomes the principal engine, as in "The Sceptic" or "The Night Walker." Sustained episodes that achieve a degree of autonomy, on the other hand, like the stories of "Colonel Caustic" in the *Lounger* and "Eugenio" in the *Looker-On* have been admitted. But the decision has occasionally been difficult to make, as in the case of the *Busy Body* of 1759, which begins promisingly with the life and adventures of the assumptive character, but from which, after a few numbers, the story quickly evaporates. The *Busy Body* has not been admitted, whereas "Drake's Travels" in the *Universal Spectator* has been classified as fiction, since the "story," however vaguely conceived, has been maintained throughout.

A similar problem of differentiation exists also in the case of magazine voyages and tours, sentimental journeys, diaries and journals, "letters," and "epistolary exchanges"—works which are sometimes narrative, sometimes descriptive, sometimes discursive, and sometimes all three. Here again the presence of a narrative line, however attenuated, has been required. For this reason Fielding's "Voyages of Mr. Job Vinegar," though similar in other respects to "Drake's Travels," has been excluded. For this reason, also, collections of short stories have not been listed unless they possess a frame story or guiding theme, or show some equivalent effort to integrate the series, like the "Moral Tales" of Mrs. Trimmer's *Family Magazine*—or "The Novelist" of the *Lady's*, where several stories are enclosed one inside the other. The latter work was left uncompleted by its author, but unfinished narratives—if they achieved sufficient length—have been given bibliographical recognition, since they are fairly numerous, and sometimes even though fragmentary, very long. The uncompleted "Narrative" of the *Adviser* (1803) is 60,000 words in length. Furthermore, we find it difficult to determine from the contents of some magazine stories whether they are actually finished or not. Occasionally editors were themselves deceived.

Long epitomes of novels have been included (but not of plays and operas); also abridgments, detached episodes, and fragments, when they are self-contained narrative units; and book reviews published in miscellanies, when they exceed 5000 words, and when the several excerpts (if there is more than one) are articulated in some manner, or enclosed in a synopsis or partial summary of the story. Here, as elsewhere, in the Catalogue, a kind of rule of thumb has prevailed. But reviews of novels in the *Monthly*, the *Critical*, the *British Critic*, and other strictly book-review periodicals have been ruled out, since they would have added unnecessarily to the length of the Catalogue. Reviews in these journals are relatively easy to find (such periodicals being typically well indexed), and are already accessible to readers. To exclude them and include others is an inconsistency, no doubt, but one that has some basis in reason. Most of the review-epitomes included in the Catalogue were published in miscellanies, outside book-review departments, where they mixed indiscriminately with more formal types of magazine fiction, and thus competed for the general reader's eye.

An alphabetical arrangement, by title, has been adopted in the Catalogue, as the simplest and most generally useful of several possible methods. However suitable for works in volume form, a chronological scheme is impractical for magazine fiction, owing to the confused situation created by serialization and by successive reprintings of the same story, sometimes at intervals of twenty or thirty years. For students who are interested in specific years, or in cross sections of the public taste, however, a Chronological Index has been provided, indicating by number which stories were published during any given year, and whether they are first or later printings, and new stories or continuations. The lists of stories in the Register of Periodicals are also arranged chronologically, so that readers may follow successive changes in taste within the same periodical.

The disadvantages of a strictly alphabetical arrangement have also been partly overcome by the Index of Catalogue References by title and by authors' names. In the Catalogue, the observed appearances of any given story are always given under the title of the first, the others following in chronological order, or (when they bear the same date) in order of importance, the larger periodicals being mentioned first. But when the same story appeared under different titles, all the important variants are listed in the Index. Thus all ten of the reprintings of the story of "Albert and Matilda" from *Variety* discussed in Chapter IV will be found entered under "The Friar's Tale," which was the title employed by the *General Magazine* upon the story's first magazine appearance. But cross references will also be found under "Albert and Matilda" and "The Friar and His Dog," the other names under which the story circulated in the *Britannic* and the *Edinburgh*.

Identical or nearly identical texts are always brought together in the Catalogue, but different translations or strikingly different versions of the same story have been listed separately, even when they bear the same title, as, for example, "Abbas and Sohry," which exists in two quite different renderings of Dixmerie's original. The same procedure has been followed in dealing with epitomes, abridgments, detached episodes, and reviews. Each entry, however, though separate, will always lead to the others. Thus Johnson's *History of Rasselas* will be found entered under that title for its full-length version, reprinted in the *Novelist's Magazine* (No. 633), and for its various condensations (Nos. 634–636); and elsewhere for the extracted "Adventures of Imlac" (No. 48) and the disguised redaction called "A Young Prince's Search after Happiness" (No. 1365), since they really represent different versions of the novel. All six, however, are mentioned in each of the entries, and are brought together in the Index under both "HISTORY OF RASSELAS" and "JOHNSON, Samuel."

In the Catalogue, therefore, all works of whatever origin are submerged in the alphabetical scheme, but their authorship when known is always mentioned in the entry, and also recorded under the writer's name in the Index, which therefore provides a short-title list of all the works by any given author in the Catalogue. In other words, the five long stories that Mackenzie wrote for the *Mirror* and *Lounger*, plus three long pieces extracted from *The Man of the World* and *The Man of Feeling*, are all listed in the Index under "MACKENZIE, Henry." Unless it is specifically stated or implied in any given entry, however, that the authorship was identified, it may be assumed that it was not. Mackenzie was a very popular writer, whose name was considered an ornament, but the authorship or origin of many magazine extracts was completely suppressed. At least seven different novels of Mme. de Gomez reappeared in the magazines in nine different versions, in which her name was never mentioned once, nor that of her principal translator, Mrs. Haywood.

A serious effort has been made to identify important works of fiction and to bring together identical pieces, or stories by the same author, but no attempt has been made to trace the origins of every run-of-the-mill oriental tale and sentimental history, or to establish the priorities of all magazine texts as against versions published outside. This is a problem that users of the Catalogue may face on their own as the need arises. Roughly half of the entries in the Catalogue constitute "new" fiction in some sense—that is, originals, adaptations, or new translations. But appearances are deceptive, and it is very difficult to expose all the manipulations of plagiaristic editors, who were accustomed to omit authors' names and other signs of origin, change the titles of stories, condense and expunge, and shamelessly address to themselves authors' introductions already twenty or thirty years old. As a general rule, most stories found published in *essay-serials* and *essay-series* are "new" fiction, as is a good deal of the anonymous and pseudonymous fiction of the London magazines. But the fact that a title stands at the head of an entry is no guarantee of originality, especially if the vehicle is a miscellany. Unless it was affirmed that the story was written *for* the magazine (and sometimes even if it was), very likely it was taken without acknowledgment from some already-published novel, essay-serial, book of travel, collection of short stories, or volume of literary sketches; or translated from the French, German, Italian, or Spanish. Editors liked to give even their borrowed pieces an air of novelty—as when the *Universal* published in 1774 "The Travels of Himilco," described as "by the Author of *Chrysal*," without giving the slightest indication that it was lifted verbatim from Johnstone's new novel, *Arsaces.* To all appearances, though the proprietors never said so, it was written for the *Universal.*

Editors were often reluctant to acknowledge their debts to others. They were also casual about assigning titles to their fiction, thus greatly adding to the cataloguer's other problems. Sometimes they gave the story no title at all; sometimes they used more than one for the same piece, as in "A Story Strange as True" in the *Gentleman's*, which figures under three different titles in a single run of only five parts. In listing stories like this one, the title of the *first* installment has been adopted as standard, although striking departures in later installments have always been noted. Parts 1 and 2 of the story of Harry Careless in the *Rambler's Magazine*, for example, bore no title at all, appearing simply as two autobiographical letters addressed to the editor of an essay-series called "The Rambler." In Part 3 the story was suddenly elevated to the rank of formal serial fiction, receiving the title "Further Adventures of Harry Careless," and, later, Part 4 was called "Harry Careless' Amour with Lady D———." In this case the title adopted for the story was "The Adventures of Harry Careless" (based on Part 3), and it has been placed in square brackets to call attention to its unauthorized status. In other instances, where the story, as printed, bears to title at all, one has been supplied from the table of contents of the magazine, the index to the collected volume, the page-heading, or the author's prefatory letter. A few names have simply had to be invented. But the source for titles enclosed in square brackets has always been noted.

With these exceptions, the titles given in the Catalogue are always complete and verbally accurate, and the original orthography has been preserved. But no effort has been made to reproduce the original punctuation and typography, which were often complicated and unsystematic. A single title in the *European* or the *Lady's* was frequently projected as a kind of title-page in miniature, with a generous outlay of space, utilizing half a dozen fonts—all of which have here perforce been reduced to one or two. Similarly, all lineation in the originals has been disregarded; capitalization has been regularized throughout; titles of books, when mentioned, have been italicized for clarity; parentheses have been substituted for square brackets (which are here reserved for editorial interpolations), and commas and periods for the ornamental combinations of colons, semi-colons, and dashes with which printers and editors liked to garnish their headings. This standardization has been accomplished at the expense of some quaintness, no doubt, but with considerable gain in terms of simplicity and legibility. It must be remembered that most miscellanies, typographically considered, were slapdash productions, executed in haste and, often, under divided control. Editors and printers were careless and forgetful, and did not worry very much about consistency. Pages were frequently misnumbered, and parts of stories mislaid. Sometimes their order was reversed. Different sections of the magazine were evidently set up at different times, probably by different compositors, who no doubt were allowed a good deal of authority over the text, since they worked directly from a variety of authors' MSS. Except for adhering to the original wording and spelling (even when incorrect), and preserving in the punctuation some of the shades of emphasis suggested by the original, it has seemed sensible not to perpetuate the state of partial disorder reflected in the titles of magazine stories.

No page numbers have been included in the entries, except when magazines are undated, or when continued stories are not identified as serial fiction or are otherwise difficult to locate. The practical advantages of this economy in dealing with novels of ten, twenty, or thirty installments are obvious. The disadvantages are mostly imaginary, since the page numbers of essay-serials in their original issue are usually not cumulative anyway; and the annual and semi-annual volumes of miscellanies are almost invariably well indexed. Even when they are not, it is fairly easy to locate fiction in monthly, fortnightly, or weekly numbers when its presence is expected, especially since in continued stories editors usually began each installment by citing the last page-number of the previous one. It has been deemed sufficient, therefore, even with very long runs, to give the dates of the first and last parts, together with the total number of installments, signaling only when there have been long interruptions in the narrative.

The word *part*, as employed in the Catalogue, means simply "installment," not a formal division within the story itself. The *part* is the basic unit of magazine fiction, and usually reflects a decision made by the editor of the magazine, rather than the author. A story labelled "1 part (5000)" is a narrative of approximately 5000 words, published in a single installment; and "5 parts (12,000)" indicates a story of novel-length in five weekly or monthly installments, without regard to chapters or other formal divisions in the narrative, of which there may be fewer or more. Many magazine stories, of course, were divided by their authors into "chapters," "essays," "letters," and even "books" and "volumes," but except in essay-serials and essay-series, these formal separations have no necessary correlation with those made by the editor (or the printer). Even in original eighteenth-century miscellany fiction, author and editor rarely worked in perfect step. As a consequence, single "chapters" of a story were sometimes subdivided by the editor into several installments; and, conversely, one installment might contain many chapters—or, in the case of the *Novelist's Magazine*, a whole novel. The weekly numbers of the *Novelist's* were issued in sheets, which, when bound together, show no sign of their original division. They are therefore considered in the Catalogue as combining into a single *part*, except *Clarissa* and *Sir Charles Grandison*, which proved so long that the editor was forced to allocate two whole volumes to each. The same distinction, however arbitrary, has been maintained for other "magazines" published in fascicules. In the Catalogue, in other words, the *part* has been construed as the smallest visible unit preserved in the collected columns of the periodical.

The "parts" of even typical magazine stories are so irregular in length, and the "page" itself is so uncertain a quantity, varying from a few hundred words in tiny magazines to a thousand or fifteen hundred in others, that it seemed advisable to provide some more accurate and convenient scale of magnitude for magazine fiction. For this reason, an estimated length in numbers of words has been given in the first citation of every entry (and in later citations, if the number changes appreciably). These numbers, which are mere approximations, accurate in most cases within only ten per cent, obviously have little value or interest for most readers. Nevertheless, some standard means of distinguishing length is necessary in a Catalogue where stories within the same narrative convention and with similar titles are sometimes twenty times the length of others, and where undivided stories may be much longer than serial novelettes of ten or a dozen parts.

When stories were left unfinished, as frequently happened, the number of parts and the estimated length apply only to the fragments, except when otherwise stated. Unfinished stories in the Catalogue are of two kinds: first, those that were broken off as the result of some failure on the part of the author, some change of plan by the editor, or perhaps the extinction of the magazine (all such stories, which never had an ending, are described as "Uncompleted"); second, pieces of which some part is missing because the magazine is inaccessible, or survives only in a broken run. Such stories are marked "*Inc.*,"—that is, the *citations* are "incomplete," rather than the works themselves. But since we are sometimes in doubt whether a magazine actually survived longer than the existing files indicate, or whether a story was actually completed in a missing number, there is a corresponding area of uncertainty between *un*completed works and *in*complete citations.

A question mark inserted after a date (as: July?, 1792; or merely 1792?) indicates that the month or year is inferential, the number of the magazine in which the story was published being undated. A question mark preceding a date, on the other hand (as: ?July, 1792; or simply ?1792), means that earlier or later parts of the story are believed to have existed, but that one or sometimes both of its terminal dates are in doubt.

Users of the Catalogue are reminded that, contrary to modern practice, almost all miscellanies were post-dated, the magazine being viewed as an epitome of the period whose date it bears. For example, the December issue always summarized the December news, and was usually published during the first week of January. Similarly, magazines dated "December 1/15" invariably appeared after the second of the two dates. "Supplements" were usually undated, but typically those of monthlies appeared about ten days after the last issue of any given volume, that is, July 15 or January 15, and were accompanied by an index to the volume, a title page, and an "Address" to readers of the magazine, although the latter was sometimes issued at the beginning of the year.

Annual or semi-annual volumes are always given in roman numerals in Catalogue entries, if the volumes bear any number at all. But the serial numbers of separate issues are given in arabic, even when the originals are in roman.

The term *entry*, as employed in these pages, applies to all the items gathered under any given number without respect to letters; the term *citation* applies to the separate bibliographical descriptions, each of which signals a separate magazine appearance. Thus "Abadir and Zatima," the first "entry" in the Catalogue, is made up of three "citations" (Nos. 1, 1a, and 1b) plus two sets of "notes," containing supplementary information.

Initial articles, definite and indefinite, in titles are always included in the citations, if found in the original, but they have been ignored in the alphabetical scheme. A few other introductory words and phrases like "From," "Selection from," "An Account of," and "Interesting Extract from" have likewise been disregarded in alphabetizing the entries.

All dates, attributions, and other information enclosed in square brackets are interpolated by the present editor, and will not be found in the original, unless otherwise stated.

The following abbreviations have occasionally been employed in the notes:

Block — Andrew Block, *The English Novel*, 1740–1850 (Grafton, 1939)

DNB — *Dictionary of National Biography*

McBurney — W. H. McBurney, *A Check List of English Prose Fiction, 1700–1739* (Harvard University Press, 1960).

Nangle — B. C. Nangle, *The Monthly Review* (*First Series, Indexes of Contributors and Articles* (Oxford, 1934); *Second Series* (Oxford, 1955).

1. [ABADIR AND ZATIMA.] *Juvenal,* Nos. 5–6 (March 18/April 1–April 1/15, 1805). 2 parts (9500). Signed "O.R."

The title is from the address to "Correspondents" (No. 4, p. 16).

a. The Story of Abadir and Zatima. Being a Continuation of the Arabian Mornings, by Ferdinand Fullerton Weston, Esq. *Monthly Literary Recreations,* II (May, 1807)–III (August, 1807). 4 parts (5200). Uncompleted.

In this reprinting the story was offered as a supplementary tale to the series "Arabian Mornings" (No. 112), presumably also by Weston, since the beginning of "Abadir and Zatima" was used to introduce the whole series. The story was described as "From the *Juvenal.*"

b. The Story of Abadir and Zatima. *Cyclopaedian,* I (December, 1807)–II (February, 1808). 3 parts. Uncompleted.

2. ABBAS AND SOHRY, a Persian Tale. [By Bricaire de la Dixmerie.] *Lady's,* I (January, 1771). 1 part (6300).

An unacknowledged translation of "Abbas et Sohry, nouvelle persanne"

(*Contes philosophiques et moraux, par M. de la Dixmerie,* 1765). For a different translation of the same story, see No. 3.

a. Abbas and Sohry, a Persian Tale. *Harvest Home,* I (1807), 236–246. 1 part.

3. ABBAS AND SOHRY, a Persian Tale. *Edinburgh*(2), IX (February, 1789). 1 part (5500).

Another translation of Bricaire de la Dixmerie, "Abbas et Sohry" (see No. 2).

4. The ABBEY OF CLUNEDALE, a Tale, by Dr. Drake. *Universal,* CVIII (February, 1801). 1 part (5100).

From Nathan Drake's *Literary Hours, or Sketches Critical and Narrative* (1798; 2nd edition, "Corrected and Enlarged," 1800).

a. The Abbey of Clunedale, a Tale, by Dr. Drake. *Hibernian,* 1801 (March–April). 2 parts.

b. The Abbey of Clunedale. *Britannic,* IX, No. 124 (1802). 1 part.

Part of the series "Memoirs of Love and Gallantry."

c. The Abbey of Clunedale, a Tale. *Edinburgh*(2), n.s. XX (November–December, 1802). 2 parts.

5. ABDALLAH AND ALMIRA, or the Constant Couple. *Lady's,* VII (July, 1776)–VIII (February, 1777). 5 parts (5000). Signed "Aurelia B——d"; later "Aurelia Burf——d."

6. ABDULSELAM AND CHELNISSA, a Turkish Novel. *New Lady's,* IV (April–May, 1789). 2 parts (6800).

7. ACTIVE EXERTION AND MENTAL EXERCISE INDISPENSABLE TO HAPPINESS. By the Nursery Reformer. *Belle Assemblée,* n.s. VIII (November, 1813)–n.s. IX (June, 1814). 4 parts (7500). Uncompleted.

8. ADELA, an Helvetic Story. *Universal,* CXI (1802). 1 part (5000).

a. Adela, an Helvetic Story. *Weekly Entertainer,* XLI (January 31–February 14, 1803). 3 parts.

9. ADELA AND THEODORE, or Letters on Education. [By Mme. de Genlis.] *Universal,* LXX (June, 1782)–LXXIX (December, 1786). 27 parts (103,000).

This work was offered (LXX, 285) as the "Translation of an excellent little Work just published at *Paris,* intitled *Adela & Théodore, ou Lettres sur l'Education.*" A final note (LXXIX, 305) declared that "Having thus conducted our readers through such parts of these letters, as may be supposed to be most interesting to an English reader, it is now proper to bring them to a conclusion"—whereupon the rest of the story was summarized in about 750 words.

For a different translation of *Adèle et Théodore* (1782), running concurrently in the *Lady's,* see No. 12.

Part 13 of "Adela and Theodore" (September, 1784) contains "The History of Saint-André"; and Parts 18–20 (July–September, 1785) "The History of the Dutchess of C———. Written by Herself." Both were later reprinted separately (see Nos. 68 and 888). Parts 5–11 contain "The History of Seraphina the Beautiful Nun," elsewhere offered as "The History of Cecilia" (No. 566)

10. ADELAIDE, an Original East Indian Story. *Sentimental and Masonic*, IV (March, 1794)–VI (June, 1795). 16 parts (37,000).

"For the *Sentimental and Masonic Magazine*."

11. ADELAIDE, or Filial Affection. By Miss Anne Blower. *General*, III (March–May 1789). 3 parts (8000).

"For the *General Magazine*."

a. Adelaide and the Two Brothers. *Britannic,* VI, Nos. 75–76 (1798). 2 parts.

Part of the series entitled "Memoirs of Love and Gallantry."

12. ADELAIDE AND THEODORE, or Letters on Education. Containing All the Principles Relating to Three Different Plans of Education for Princes, Young Ladies, and Young Gentlemen. *Lady's*, XVI (May, 1785)–XX (April, 1789). 49 parts (126,000). Uncompleted.

An unacknowledged translation of Mme. de Genlis's *Adèle et Théodore, ou Lettres sur l'éducation* (1782), about three-fifths the length of the original. For another translation of the same novel, running concurrently in the *Universal*, see "Adela and Theodore" (No. 9).

Parts 26–28 (June–August, 1787) contain the "History of Saint Andre." For another translation of the same, see No. 68. Parts 40–46 (July–Supplement, 1788) contain the "History of the Duchess of C——, Written by Herself," of which the *Lady's* had already printed another translation, called "Female Fortitude" (No. 421). For another version of the same inset story, see No. 888.

13. ADELAIDE OF FLORIDA. *Belle Assemblée*, n.s. VII (March, 1813)–n.s. VIII (September, 1813). 5 parts (11,600).

"Novel II" of a series entitled "Spanish Novels."

14. The ADOPTED CHILD, a Novel. By Two Sisters. *Lady's,* XLIII (November, 1812)–XLVI (January, 1815). 30 parts (63,000).

15. The ADOPTED CHILD, or the Castle of St. Villereagh. By Sarah Wilkinson. "Tale 77," *Tell-Tale,* VI (1805). 1 part (13,400).

16. ADVENTURE OF A YOUNG WOMAN WHO WAS CONFINED IN A HOLLOW OAK. A Tale. *Edinburgh*(2), XVI (October, 1792). 1 part (5000).

17. The ADVENTURE OF THE INN, a Short History. *Town and Country*, X (April, June, 1778). 2 Parts (7700).

a. The Adventure of the Inn, a Short History. *Gentleman's and London,* 1778 (May, July). 2 parts.

18. ADVENTURES AND AMOURS OF A BAR-MAID, a Series of Facts. *Bon Ton,* III (January, 1794)–IV (April, 1794). 3 parts (6250).

19. The ADVENTURES AND TRAVELS, IN VARIOUS PARTS OF THE GLOBE, OF HENRY VOGEL, Translated from the German. *Universal,* n.s. XII (July, 1809)–n.s. XIV (October, 1810). 8 parts (18,000). Uncompleted. The introductory letter is signed "W."

    From *Heinrich Vogel's Beschreibung seiner dreyssigjährigen... Seereisen, nebst der Geschichte seines Lebens* (Leipsig, 1797).

20. The ADVENTURES OF A BAD SHILLING, in the Kingdom of Ireland. *Ireland's Mirror,* II (June, 1805)–III (April, 1806). 11 parts (20,000).

    "For *Ireland's Mirror.*"

21. The ADVENTURES OF A CAT. *Westminster,* II (August–September, 1774). 2 parts (5750). Signed "Mopsey./Adelphi, Sept."

    "For the *Westminster Magazine.*"

22. The ADVENTURES OF A DANCING MASTER. *Rambler's,* I (February–May, 1783). 4 parts (8200).

23. Selection from the *ADVENTURES OF A DRAMATIST ON A JOURNEY TO THE LONDON MANAGERS. Belle Assemblée,* n.s. VI (Supplement, 1812). 1 part (6000).

    From Benjamin Frere, *Adventures of a Dramatist* (1813 [actually 1812]).

24. ADVENTURES OF A GOLD RING. *Rambler's,* I (March–July, 1783). 5 parts (6600).

25. ADVENTURES OF A LADY'S LAP-DOG, in Which Will Be Included the History of Several Characters, Accurately Drawn from Real Life. *Lady's Monthly Museum,* VIII (March, 1802)–IX (December, 1802). 9 parts (20,600).

26. ADVENTURES OF A MIRROR. *Lady's,* XXII (January, February, May, 1791). 3 parts (6750). Uncompleted.

27. [The ADVENTURES OF A NORTH BRITAIN.] *Rambler's,* II (August, 1784)–III (October, 1785). 13 parts (20,700).

    The title is not used until Part 2. It is later corrected to read "Adventures of a North Briton." The story is addressed "To the Editor of the *Rambler's Magazine,*" and Part 13 is signed "A North Briton."

28. ADVENTURES OF A PEN. *European,* L (July–October, 1806). 3 parts (9400). Signed "Dionysius."

    a. Adventures of a Pen. *Hibernian,* 1806 (August–November). 3 parts. Signed "Dionysius."

29. ADVENTURES OF A QUIRE OF PAPER. *London,* XLVIII (August–October, 1779). 3 parts (7800). Signed "RUSTICUS."

"For the *London Magazine.*"

a. Adventures of a Quire of Paper. *Edinburgh Weekly,* XLVI (October 20–November 17, 1779). 3 parts. Signed "RUSTICUS."

b. Adventures of a Quire of Paper. *Gentleman's and London,* 1779 (October–December). 3 parts.

30. ADVENTURES OF A RAKE. Written by Himself. *Covent Garden,* II (March–June, 1773). 4 parts (7500 words).

The introductory letter and Part 4 are both signed "A reformed Rake." At the end of this story (II, 230) the Editor of the *Covent Garden* wrote: "We request the correspondence of this gentleman upon any other occasion."

a. The Adventures of a Rake. Written by Himself. *Rambler's,* IV (November, 1786)–V (February, 1787). 5 parts.

The introductory letter and the last part are also signed "A reformed Rake."

31. The ADVENTURES OF A SHILLING. *New Lady's,* III (August, 1788)–IV (November, 1789). 16 parts (20,000). Signed "J. D——T."

In July, 1788 (III, 338), the Editor wrote: "The Adventures of a Shilling, communicated by *Josephus,* will have an early insertion."

32. ADVENTURES OF A SOPHA. *Rambler's,* IV (Supplement, 1786)–VIII (June, 1790). 45 parts (69,000). *Inc.*

A continuation of this story was promised in the final extant copy of the *Rambler's Magazine.* This story is not a version of *Le Sopha* by Crébillon *fils,* although possibly inspired by its notoriety (see No. 870).

33. ADVENTURES OF A STAGE COACH. *Rambler's,* VI (July–December, 1788); VII (April, 1789). 7 parts (5800).

34. The ADVENTURES OF A THREE-SHILLING BANK TOKEN. *Town Talk,* V (November 1, 1813). 1 part (6700).

35. The ADVENTURES OF ALPHONSO AND MARINA, an Interesting Spanish Tale. *Universal,* LXXX (June–Supplement, 1787). 2 parts (5500).

a. The Adventures of Alphonso and Marina, an Interesting Spanish Tale. *Hibernian,* 1787 (September–October). 2 parts.

36. ADVENTURES OF AN ALGERIAN CAPTIVE. By Dr. Updike Underhill, an American Physician, Who Had Been Taken Prisoner by the Algerians, on Board an American Vessel, and Remained in a State of Slavery Upwards of Six Years. *Entertaining* (1), I, No. 7 (July, 1802). 1 part (7100).

An extract from Chapters 61–78 of Underhill's [i.e., Royall Tyler's] *Algerian*

Captive (1802). For a full-length reprinting of the same novel in the *Lady's*, see No. 83.

37. The ADVENTURES OF BERTHOLDE, Extracted from the French. With His Effigy Curiously Engraved. *London,* XXII (June, 1753). 1 part (5000).

From the *Histoire de Bertholde* (La Haye, 1752), a French translation of the Italian poem of Giulio Cesare Croce (d.1620), entitled *Astuzie sottilissime di Bertholdo,* and described in the *Nouv. Biog. Gén.* as a "récit des aventures grotesque d'un paysan à la fois rusé et stupide."

a. The Adventures of Bertholde, Extracted from the French. *Gentleman's and London,* 1753 (June). 1 part.

b. The Adventures of Bertholde, Extracted from the French. *Ladies,* IV, No. 15 (July 21, 1753). 1 part.

A still later appearance of this piece, in abridged form, is found "The Singular Life and Adventures of Bertholde," *New Wonderful Museum,* V, No. 58 (1807).

38. The ADVENTURES OF CHARLES VILLERS, an Unfortunate Court Dependant, a Novel, in Two Volumes. *Universal,* XXXIX (November–Supplement, 1766). 3 parts (17,100).

An abridgment of *The Adventures of Charles Villars* (1766). The editor of the *Universal* wrote: "We have here only extracted what relates to the principal Story, omitting the incidental Parts, which are little interesting." (XXXIX, 239.)

a. The Adventures of Charles Villers, an Unfortunate Court Dependent, as Related by Himself. *Weekly Misc.* (Sherborne), XII (August 9, 1779)–XIII (October 18, 1779). 4 parts.

b. The Adventures of Charles Villers, an Unfortunate Court Dependent, as Related by Himself. *Moral and Entertaining,* V (August–November, 1779). 4 parts.

c. The Adventures of Charles Villars, an Unfortunate Court Dependent, as Related by Himself. *Hibernian,* 1779 (September)–1780 (February). 7 parts.

39. The ADVENTURES OF COLIN M'LOON, or Newspaper Editors. *Scourge,* VIII (October, November, 1814); IX (January, 1815). 3 parts (7000).

The story is told in three letters, each signed "M'Loon." The title of the third reads "The Life and Adventures of Colin M'Loon."

40. The ADVENTURES OF CUPID THE LITTLE. *Lady's,* V (January–April, 1774). 4 parts (8500).

The story contains two acts of a play entitled "The Romantic Lady, a Comedy." Both the story and the play were left uncompleted. There were complaints from readers on this score as late as November, 1778.

41. The ADVENTURES OF DAVID SIMPLE. Containing an Account of His Travels through the Cities of London and Westminster, in the Search of a Real Friend. By Miss [Sarah] Fielding. *Novelist's,* IX (1782). 1 part (118,000).

First published in 1744. The reprinting in the *Novelist's* includes four engravings, dated August 10–31, 1782.

42. ADVENTURES OF DOLIGNY. (From the French of M. Florian.) *Lady's Monthly Museum,* XVI (May–June, 1806). 2 parts (5600). Signed "E.F."

The attribution to Florian is doubtful. The story is not found in the collected works of 1802 or 1804. A note in the *Museum* (p. 402) explained that the original story had been abridged.

43. [ADVENTURES OF EMMA, a Moral Tale.] *Ranger,* II, Nos. 23–26 (May 31–June 21, 1794). 4 parts (13,000). Signed "O."

Written by the authors of the *Ranger,* the Hon. M. Hawke and Sir Robert Vincent. The title is from the table of contents of the collected edition.

a. The Adventures of Emma, a Moral Tale. (From the *Ranger.*) *Lady's,* XXVI (Supplement, 1795)–XXVII (March, 1796). 4 parts.

b. Albert and Emma, an Interesting History. *Universal,* XCVIII (March, April, June, 1796). 3 parts.

The editor wrote: "With particular Pleasure... we present our Readers with the following History, from a Series of Periodical Papers, the joint Production of the Hon. *M. Hawke* and Sir *Robert Vincent,* Bart. now first collected into 2 Vol. 12 mo." (p. 176).

c. Albert and Emma, an Interesting History. *Edinburgh*(2), n.s. VII (April, May, 1796); n.s. VIII (July, 1796). 3 parts.

d. Albert and Emma, an Interesting History. *Hibernian,* 1796 (April, May, July). 3 parts.

e. Albert and Emma, an Interesting History. (From a Series of Periodical Papers, the Joint Production of the Hon. M. Hawke and Sir Robert Vincent, Bart. now first collected into a 2 Vol. 12 mo.) *Weekly Entertainer,* XXVII (May 9, 1796)–XXVIII (July 25, 1796). 9 parts.

f. Albert and Emma. *Scots,* LVIII (November–Appendix, 1796). 3 parts.

"From a series of periodical papers by the Hon. M. Hawke and Sir Robert Vincent."

g. Albert and Emma, a Tale. *Lady's,* XXXI (December–Supplement, 1800). 2 parts.

See No. 43a above, in the same magazine.

h. Clairville and Emma. *Britannic,* VIII, Nos. 111–113 (1801). 3 parts (12,500).

Part of the general series "Memoirs of Love and Gallantry." There are a few abridgments, and some slight changes in phrasing.

i. Albert and Emma. (The Honourable M. Hawke, and Sir Robert Vincent, Bart.) *New Magazine of Choice Pieces,* I, Nos. 12–13 (1810). pp. 325–353.

44. The ADVENTURES OF FERDINAND COUNT FATHOM. By Dr. [Tobias] Smollett. In Two Volumes. *Novelist's,* VII (1782). 1 part (162,000).

First published in 1753. The reprinting in the *Novelist's* included four engravings, dated February 9–March 2, 1782.

45. The ADVENTURES OF GIL BLAS OF SANTILLANE. Translated from the French of Monsieur Le Sage. By Dr. [Tobias] Smollet[t]. In Four Volumes. *Novelist's*, IV (1781). 1 part (300,000).

First published in 1750. The reprinting in the *Novelist's* includes ten engravings, dated December 23, 1780–February 24, 1781. For a short extract from *Gil Blas*, see No. 1294.

46. [Adventures of Harry Careless.] *Rambler's*, II (May, 1784); III (March–June, 1785). 4 parts (6600).

Nos. 17, 28, 29, 31 of an essay-series called "The Rambler". The title is taken from No. 29 (called "Further Adventures of Harry Careless").

47. The ADVENTURES OF HENRY METLAND. *New Gleaner*, II (1809), 299–319. 1 part (12,150).

48. The ADVENTURES OF IMLAC, the Poet. From *The History of Rasselas, Prince of Abyssinia*, by the Author of the *Rambler*. *Edinburgh*(1), III (May–June, 1759). 2 parts (5100).

An extract from Chapters 8–12 of Johnson's *Rasselas* (1759). For several magazine versions of the novel, see Nos. 633–636, and 1365.

49. ADVENTURES OF KITTY PRY. *Rambler's*, I (September, 1783)–III (November, 1785). 29 parts (55,000). The introductory letter is signed "Kitty Pry."

50. ADVENTURES OF LORD M——. *Rambler's*, IV (July–November, 1786); V (March–May, 1787). 7 parts (8000).

"From a manuscript, which was found in an old garret."

51. The ADVENTURES OF MADAM FLIRT, Written by Herself. *Rambler's*, V (June–December, 1787). 7 parts (9400).

52. The ADVENTURES OF MAHOMET, the Wandering Sultan; or a Sketch of Men, Manners and Opinions in the Seventeenth Century. Written in 1796. By Joseph Moser, Esq. *European*, LIV (August, 1808)–LIX (May, 1811). 33 parts (135,000).

53. The ADVENTURES OF MISS SOPHIA STERNHEIM. From the German of Mr. Weiland [i.e., C. M. Wieland]. *Universal*, LIX (November–Supplement, 1776). 3 parts (8100). Signed "B."

Adapted, without acknowledgment, from Joseph Collyer, *The History of Lady Sophia Sternheim, Attempted from the German of Mr. Wieland* (1776), a translation of Marie Sophie von La Roche, *Geschichte des Fräuleins von Sternheim* (1771). The work was erroneously attributed to Wieland because of his sponsorship of it. The original translation runs to about 45,000 words.

a. The Adventures of Miss Sophia Sternheim, etc. [Same title as above.] *Hibernian*, 1776 (December)–1777 (February). 4 parts.

b. The Adventures of Miss Sophia Sternheim, etc. [Same title.] *Gentleman's and London*, 1776 (December); 1777 (January, March).

54. The ADVENTURES OR MR. GEORGE EDWARDS, a Creole. By Sir John Hill. *Novelist's*, XXIII (1788). 1 part (47,000).

First published in 1751. The reprinting in the *Novelist's* includes two engravings, dated May 1 and June 2, 1788.

55. The ADVENTURES OF MRS. BILSON, Selected from *The History of the Countess of Dellwyn. Newcastle*, XIII (April–May, 1759). 2 parts (7500).

From Sarah Fielding, *The History of the Countess of Dellwyn* (1759). This episode was extracted and published first in the *London Chronicle* (April 7/10–10/12, 1759), whence it was probably taken by the *Newcastle General Magazine*.

56. The ADVENTURES OF MOSES McFUN, Written by Himself. *Rambler's*, V (Supplement, 1787)–VII (January, 1789). 13 parts (12,250). Uncompleted.

57. The ADVENTURES OF OMAR. [By Everard Ryan.] *Edinburgh Mag. and Rev.*, I (January, March, April, 1774). 3 parts (5400).

This story, written first "For the *Edinburgh Magazine*," was later collected in Ryan's *Reliques of Genius* (1777) under the title "The Progress of Ambition."

a. The Adventures of Omar, a Tale. *Edinburgh*(2), XI (June, 1790). 1 part.

b. The Adventures of Omar. *Weekly Misc.*(Glasgow), n.s. III, Nos. 61–64 (September 4–September 25, 1793). 4 parts.

c. The Progress of Ambition, a Tale. *New Gleaner*, II (1810), 100–109.

Attributed to "Ryan."

58. The ADVENTURES OF PEREGRINE PICKLE. In Which Are Included Memoirs of a Lady of Quality. In Four Volumes. By Dr. [Tobias] Smollett. *Novelist's*, VI (1781). 1 part (335,000).

First published in 1751. The reprinting in the *Novelist's* includes eleven engravings, dated August 4–October 21, 1781. For a short epitome of Smollett's novel, see No. 59.

59. The ADVENTURES OF PEREGRINE PICKLE, in Which Are Included the Memoirs of a Woman of Quality. *Royal*(1), II (January/February/March, 1751). 1 part (5900).

Called an "extract," but really a summary of Smollett's novel, which appeared in the same year. For a later full-length reprinting of the same novel, in the *Novelist's*, see No. 58.

60. The ADVENTURES OF RODERICK RANDOM. In Two Volumes. By Dr. [Tobias] Smollet[t]. *Novelist's*, II (1780). 1 part (200,000).

First published in 1748. The title-page in the *Novelist's* is dated 1781, but the work preceded No. 1367 (dated 1780), and the six plates are all dated 1780 (June 3–July 8).

61. The ADVENTURES OF SIGNOR GAUDENTIO DI LUCCA. Being the Substance of His Examination before the Fathers of the Inquisition, at Bologna, in Italy. Giving an Account of an Unknown Country in the Midst of the Desarts of Africa. Copied from the Original Manuscript in St. Marks Library, at Venice. With Critical Notes by the Learned Signor Rhedi, Translated from the Italian. [By Simon Berington.] *Novelist's*, XXI (1786). 1 part (74,000).

Originally published in London in 1737. The reprinting in the *Novelist's* includes three engravings, dated March 25–April 8, 1786.

62. ADVENTURES OF SINDBAD THE SAILOR. "Tale 5," *Tell-Tale*, I (August, 1803). 1 part (13,200).

The seven voyages from the standard translation of Galland's *Arabian Nights*. For a complete reprinting of Galland, see No. 113.

63. The ADVENTURES OF TELEMACHUS, the Son of Ulysses. Translated from the French of Messire Francois Salignac de la Mothe-Fenelon, Archbishop of Cambray. By John Hawkesworth, LL.D. *Novelist's*, XVII (1784). 1 part (153,000).

This translation was first published in 1768. The reprinting in the *Novelist's* includes six engravings, dated December 11, 1784–January 15, 1785. For another English version of Fénelon's *Télémaque*, see No. 147.

64. The ADVENTURES OF THE BARON DE LOVZINSKI. Extracted from *The Life of the Chevalier de Faublas* [by Jean Baptiste Louvet de Couvray]. *Lady's* XXV (October, 1794)–XXVI (April, 1795). 8 parts (27,000).

From *The Life and Adventures of the Chevalier de Faublas* (1793), a translation in part of "Une Année de la Vie," *Les Aventures du chevalier de Faublas* (1787–1789).

a. The Adventures of the Baron de Lovzinski. *Hibernian*, 1794 (November)–1795 (June). 8 parts.

65. The ADVENTURES OF WM. ANNESLEY. By [Henry] Mackenzie. *Harvest Home*, I (1807), 355–365. 1 part (6000).

From *The Man of the World* (1773), Chapters 18–20.

66. The AFFECTING HISTORY OF CAROLINE MONTGOMERY. From *Ethelinde, or the Recluse of the Lake*, a New and Beautiful Novel, by Mrs. Charlotte Smith. *Universal*, LXXXV (December–Supplement, 1789). 2 parts (9700).

Extracted from Volume I of *Ethelinde* (1789), pp. 128–185.

a. The Affecting History of Caroline Montgomery. From *Ethelinde, or the Recluse of the Lake*, a Beautiful Novel, by Mrs. Charlotte Smith. *New London*, VI (January–March, 1790). 3 parts.

b. The Affecting History of Caroline Montgomery, etc. [Same title as *Universal*.] *Hibernian*, 1790 (January–March). 3 parts.

c. The Affecting History of Caroline Montgomery. *Caledonian*(2), IV (January–March, 1790). 2 parts.

A note (p. 36) attributes the story to "a new beautiful novel" by Mrs. Smith.

d. The Affecting History of Caroline Montgomery, etc. [Same title as *Universal.*] *Weekly Entertainer*, XV (February 22–March 22, 1790). 5 parts.

e. The Affecting History of Caroline Montgomery. From *Ethelinde, or the Recluse of the Lake*, by Mrs. Charlotte Smith. *European*, XVII (May–June, 1790). 2 parts.

f. The History of Caroline Montgomery. From *Ethelinde, or the Recluse of the Lake*, by Mrs. Charlotte Smith. *Scots*, LII (May–June, 1790). 2 parts.

g. The History of Caroline Montgomery. By Mrs. Charlotte Smith. *Edinburgh*(2), XIV (December, 1791). 1 part (8400).

67. The AFFECTING HISTORY OF MISS AMELIA NEVIL. (From *A Philosophical Essay on Old Maids.*) *Universal*, LXXVIII (March–April, 1786). 2 parts (5250).

Extracted from Part I, Chapter 5, "On the Envy and Ill-Nature of old Maids," in Hayley's *Philosophical, Historical, and Moral Essay on Old Maids* (1785). For other extracts from the same work see Nos. 245 and 700.

a. The Affecting History of Miss Amelia Nevil. (From *A Philosophical Essay on Old Maids.*) *Hibernian*, 1786 (April–May). 2 parts.

b. Malevolence Defeated, or the History of Mrs. Winifred Wormwood. By Mr. Hayley. *New Novelist's*, I (1786), 140–146.

c. Malevolence Defeated, or the History of Mrs. Winifred Wormwood. *Weekly Entertainer*, IX (January 15–22, 1787). 2 parts.

d. The Envy and Ill-Nature of Old Maids. (Taken from an *Essay on Old Maids.*) *Caledonian*(2), I (March–April, 1788). 2 parts (6700).

A longer extract from the same chapter.

e. [The Story of Mrs. Wormwood.] *Town and Country*, XXI (June, September, October, 1789). 3 parts (5250).

The title is taken from Parts 2 and 3.

f. Amelia Neville, or the Disappointment of Envy, and the Reward of Benevolence. A True Story. By Mr. Hayley. *Harvest Home*, II (1808), 342–350. 1 part (5250).

68. AFFECTING HISTORY OF ST. ANDRE. (By the Countess de Genlis.) *Weekly Misc.* (Glasgow), IV, Nos. 95–99 (April 13–May 11, 1791). 5 parts (7000).

From the "Histoire de Saint-André" in Mme. de Genlis, *Adèle et Théodore* (1782). This is not a new translation, however, but a reprinting of the inset "History of Saint-André" in the *Universal's* "Adela and Theodore" (No. 9).

For another translation of the same story, see No. 12.

a. History of Saint Andre. From *Adela and Theodore. Gleaner*, II (1806), 131–142.

The same translation as the above.

69. [AFFECTING STORY OF A MENDICANT.] *Intruder*, Nos. 15–21 (June 25–August 6, 1802). 7 parts (11,000).

The title is from the table of contents.

70. AGNES ADDISON, a Simple Tale. By Ora. *Lady's Monthly Museum*, n.s. XVI (May, 1814)–n.s. XVII (December, 1814). 8 parts (16,600).

"Ora" was later identified as Miss D. P. Campbell (s.3.II, 120).

71. AGRARIUS DENTERVILLE, or the Victim of Discontent, a Tale. *Monthly Mirror*, IV (October, 1797)–VI (November, 1798). 8 parts (18,400). Signed "G./Gloster."

72. ALAN, or the Folly of Idle Curiosity, a Tale. *Edinburgh*(2), n.s. XV (May–June, 1800). 2 parts (6500).

73. ALBANI, or the Murderer of His Child. Containing the Different Views of His Character, as a Libertine in Palermo, an Officer in the Spanish Service, a Planter in the Island of Cuba, and an Independent Gentleman, on his Return to Italy. *Marvellous*, II (March 1, 1803). 1 part (30,000).

74. ALBERT. [By Thomas Bellamy.] *General*, V (August, 1791)–VI (April, 1792). 6 parts (6600).

Bellamy's name was lent to the story only in Part 5. This piece was later collected in the author's *Miscellanies in Prose and Verse* (1794).

75. ALBERT, or the Village Curate. *Aberdeen*(2), I (December, 1796)–II (June, 1797). 5 parts (7600). Signed "B.C."

"For the *Aberdeen Magazine.*"

76. ALBERTINA. An Anecdote Extracted from the Secret History of the Court of ———. *Town and Country*, XVIII (October, 1786)–XIX (January, 1787). 4 parts (7500).

Note (XIX, 28): "This Anecdote was originally written in German by Mr. Wall. It has been translated into French by Mr. [Nicolas] de Bonneville, and published in a collection intitled, *Choix de petits romans, imités de l'allemand* [1786], sold by the publisher of this Magazine. The anecdote, as here given, differs in some respects, both from the original and from the French translation. An attempt has been made to adapt it to the taste of the English reader."

For other translations of Bonneville's "Albertine," see Nos. 77–78, and 815.

a. Albertina, an Anecdote Extracted from the Secret History of the Court of ———. *Hibernian*, 1786 (December)–1787 (February). 4 parts.

77. ALBERTINA. From the Secret History of the Count of ———. *Edinburgh*(2), IV (December, 1786). 1 part (6800).

Attributed in a note to Nicolas de Bonneville's *Choix de petits romans, imités de l'allemand* (1786). For other translations of the same story, see Nos. 76, 78, and 815.

78. ALBERTINA, a Tale, from the German. *Universal*, LXXXV (July–August, 1789). 2 parts (5400).

An unacknowledged translation of "Albertine" by Nicolas de Bonneville (see Nos. 76–77 above). Bonneville's story provided the basis for Mme. de Montolieu's *Caroline de Lichtfield* (1786), and the editor of the *Universal* replied as follows to a reader who complained of a plagiarism: "*Eliza* is mistaken in her assertion that the story of *Albertina* in our Magazine for July and August is an Extract from *Caroline of Lichtfield*; on the contrary, the Author of that work has founded his Novel, without acknowledging the Circumstance, on the German original of *Albertina*, extending it by a number of Incidents, like the Variations in a favourite Tune." (LXXXV, 279.) For a later plagiarism of the translation in the *Universal*, see No. 815.

a. Albertina, a Tale, from the German. *Weekly Entertainer*, XIV (September 28–October 5, 1789). 2 parts.

79. ALBERTUS, or the Ingrate. *Lady's Monthly Museum*, n.s. II (May, 1807). 1 part (5000).

80. The ALBUM, or Ministeral Amusements. *European*, XII (December, 1787)–XIII (January, April, 1788). 3 parts (6000).

Parts 2 and 3 in both this magazine and the following are titled "The Streatham Album, or Ministerial Amusements."

a. The Album, or Ministerial Amusements. *Hibernian*, 1788 (January, February, May, 1788). 3 parts.

81. ALCIONE, a Tale. *Edinburgh*(2), n.s. I (May–June, 1793). 2 parts (6600).

82. ALEXIS, or the Cottage in the Woods. An Original Novel, from the French [of F. G. Ducray-Duminil]. *Lady's*, XXII (March, 1791)–XXIV (July, 1793). 31 parts 101,000).

From *Alexis, ou la Maisonnette dans les bois* (1789).

a. Alexis, or the Cottage in the Woods. An Original Novel, from the French. *Hibernian*, 1791 (April)–1793 (September). 30 parts.

83. The ALGERIAN CAPTIVE, or the Life and Adventures of Doctor Updike Underhill, Six Years a Prisoner among the Algerines. [By Royall Tyler.] *Lady's*, XXXV (January–Supplement, 1804). 13 parts (54,500).

An editorial note explains that this work was published "somewhat more than a year ago. but nearly the whole of the impression was consumed in the dreadful fire" which destroyed the warehouses of "Mr. Hamilton," and therefore "The Proprietors now present it to the readers of the *Lady's Magazine*." (XXXV, 37.) For an earlier extract from the same work (1802), see No. 36.

84. ALL FOR THE BEST, a Dream. *Belle Assemblée*, IV (February, 1808). 1 part (6200) Signed "E.R."

a. All for the Best, a Tale. *Hibernian*, 1808 (March–April). 2 parts. Signed "E.R."

85. [ALL OR NOTHING, a Moral Tale.] [By Marmontel.] *Weekly Amusement*, II (January 12–February 2, 1765). 4 parts (6000).

A translation of Marmontel's "Tout ou rien" (*Contes moraux*, 1761); extracted From the *Moral Tales* (Becket and De Hondt, 1764). The title is taken from Parts 2–4. For a slightly different version of the same translation, see "Moral Tales" (No. 917).

86. ALLADIN THE PERSIAN, an Eastern Tale. *Bee*, XVIII (November 20, 1793–January 1, 1794). 7 parts (13,000). Signed "T.J."

"For the *Bee*."

87. ALMORAN AND HAMET. An Oriental Tale. In Two Volumes. By Dr. [John] Hawkesworth. *Novelist's*, I (1780). 1 part (38,000).

First published in 1761. The reprinting in the Novelist's included two plates, dated November 1, 1779, and May 6, 1780. For an epitome of *Almoran and Hamet*, see No. 88.

88. ALMORAN AND HAMET, an Oriental Tale. Dedicated to the King. By J[ohn]. Hawkesworth, L.L.D. *Scots*, XXIII (July–August, 1761). 2 parts (8600). Signed "M" [*Monthly Review*?].

This long epitome of *Almoran and Hamet* (1761), enclosed in a few critical comments, is taken verbatim from the *Monthly Review*, XXIV (June, 1761), 415–435. According to Nangle, the review was written by Owen Ruffhead. For a full-length version of the same novel, see No. 87.

89. ALPHONSINE D'ARGENNES, or the Victim of Ambition. *Belle Assemblée*, V (October–December, 1808). 3 parts (18,000). Signed "E.R."

a. Alphonsine d'Argennes, or the Victim of Ambition. *Hibernian*, 1809 (January–May). 5 parts. Signed "E.R."

90. ALPHONSO, or the Natural Son. From the French of Madame de Genlis. *Beau Monde*(2), I (July, 1809)–II (April, 1810). 9 parts (70,000).

A translation of *Alphonse, ou le Fils naturel* (Paris, 1809).

a. Alphonso, or the Natural Son. From the French of Madame de Genlis. (Never Before Translated.) *Monthly Panorama*, I (February, 1810). Discontinued after only one part.

91. ALPHONSO AND ALMIRA, or the Noble Forester. A Sardinian Tale. By a Lady. *Lady's* XXXVIII (April–July, 1807). 4 parts (10,600).

92. AMANDA, a Tale, Founded on Fact. *Lady's Monthly Museum*, III (July–September, 1799). 3 parts (5700).

93. Les AMANTS SANS AMOUR. Par Mad. de Genlis. *Ambigu*, VII, No. 59 (November 20, 1804). 1 part (9800).

First published in the *Mercure de France* (No. 153, June 2, 1804). For an English translation of the same story, see No. 710.

94. AMAZAN, an Eastern Tale. *Monthly Literary Recreations,* I (July–November, 1806). 5 parts (9000). Signed "I."

95. The AMBITIOUS MOTHER, an Interesting Story. (From *The Rambles of Fancy,* Just Published.) *Rambler's,* IV (December, 1786)–V (January, 1787). 3 parts (5300). Uncompleted.

From Lucy Peacock, *The Rambles of Fancy* (1786).

96. AMELIA. By Henry Fielding, Esq. *Novelist's,* I (1780). 1 part (220,000).

For an early magazine epitome of this novel (1751), see No. 97. The reprinting in the *Novelist's* included seven engravings, dated March 18, 1780–April 23, 1780.

97. An Account of a Novel Lately Published, Intitled *AMELIA,* by Henry Fielding, Esq., to Which Are Added Some General Remarks. *London,* XX (December–Appendix, 1751). 2 parts (7400).

A summary of the fable, volume by volume, followed by a few critical comments. For a full-length reprinting of the same work see No. 96.

An Account of a Novel Lately Published, Intitled *Amelia,* etc. [Same title as above.] *Ladies,* III (January 25/February 8–March 21/April 4, 1752). 5 parts.

98. AMELIA, a Novel. From the French of Madam D'Ormoy. *Caledonian Mag. and Rev.,* I (May 1, 1783)–III (April 2, 1784). 13 parts (28,000).

An introductory note declared that this was "a genuine Translation, and indeed the first that has ever made its appearance in the English language, being done by a Gentleman of abilities, who has made the French language a principal study." (I, 148.) At the end of the serial the translator was thanked for "his friendly attention," and it was stated that "a beautiful Edition of this interesting Novel corrected, is printing apart and will be speedily published." (III, 73.)

The original is Mme. C. C. D'Ormoy, *Les Malheurs de la jeune Émélie* (1777).

99. AMELIA'S LETTERS. *Repository of Arts, etc.,* I (March, 1809)–V (March, 1811). 22 parts (56,000).

Each letter occupies a single installment.

100. AMESTAN ET MÉLÉDIN, ou l'Expérience a l'épreuve. Conte oriental. *Ambigu,* XIX (November 30, 1807). 1 part (7000).

101. AMIABLE ERRORS, or How to Make a Husband Miserable. *Lady's Monthly Museum,* n.s. XVI (February–April, 1814). 3 parts (6100). Signed "E.T."

102. The AMIABLE WIFE AND ARTFUL MISTRESS. (An Extract from *Santo Sebastiano,* a Novel, by the Author of *The Romance of the Pyrenees.*) *Lady's,* XXXVIII (July–August, 1807). 2 parts (6700).

From Catherine Cuthbertson's *Santo Sebastiano, or the Young Protector* (Minerva Press, 1806). Other, shorter extracts from the same novel, totalling 9000 words, were published in the *Lady's* in April, November, and December, 1807.

103. The AMOURS OF CECIL, Lord Burleigh. *Rambler's*, II (February–April, 1784). 3 parts (6200).

"For the *Rambler's Magazine.*"

104. AMOURS OF THE EARL OF ESSEX AND THE COUNTESS OF RUTLAND, Supposed to Be Written by Herself, and Addressed to a Lady. *Rambler's*, IV (July–November, 1786). 5 parts (6400).

Nos. 13–17 of the series "The Amorous Novelist."

105. The AMOURS OF WIT AND OECONOMY. From an Original MSS. [sic] *Beauties of All the Magazines*, I (May–September, 1762). 5 parts (8000). Uncompleted.

Part 5 is entitled "Continuation of the Amours of Wit and Oeconomy; with the History of Mercury at a Horse-Race Meeting." (I, 337.)

106. [AMURATH, an Eastern Story.] [By John Hawkesworth.] *Adventurer*, Nos. 20–22 (January 13–January 20, 1753). 3 parts (6700).

The title is from the Table of Contents of the first collected edition which reads: "Imperceptible deviation to vice. Moral use of punishment. Remonstrances of conscience universal. AMURATH, an eastern Story."

a. [Amurath, Sultan of the East, an Eastern Story.] *Weekly Amusement*, I (December 15–29, 1764). 3 parts.

The title is from Parts 2 and 3.

b. Amurath, an Oriental Tale. *Universal Museum*, n.s. VIII (March–May, 1772). 3 parts.

c. The Impulse of Conscience Ought Always to Be Attended to. *Weekly Misc.* (Sherborne), II, Nos. 31–32 (May 2–9, 1774). 2 parts.

d. The Impulse of Conscience Ought Always to Be Attended to. *Weekly Misc.* (London), III, Nos. 86–87 (1774). 2 parts.

e. The Story of Amurath. *Edinburgh Repository*(2), I (1793). 2 parts.

The story is attributed to the *Adventurer* (p. 468).

f. Amurath, an Eastern Story. *Ipswich*, I (October–November, 1799). 2 parts.

107. ANDROMACHE DELAINE, a Tale. By Catherine Bremen Yeames. *Lady's*, XL (April–May, 1809). 2 parts (5000).

108. ANGELICA DE LORIS. *Belle Assemblée*, n.s. VII (June, 1813)–n.s. VIII (August, 1813). 3 parts (9900).

Third of a series of "Spanish Novels."

109. ANNA, a Fragment. (From *Fragments, in the Manner of Sterne*, Lately Published.) *Lady's*, XXVIII (October–December, 1797). 3 parts (5000).

From the collection by Isaac Brandon, published in 1797, Vol. II, 97–129.

a. Anna, a Fragment. (From *Fragments, in the Manner of Sterne.*) *Universal,* CII (January, 1798). 1 part.

b. Anna, a Fragment. From *Fragments, in the Manner of Sterne. Scots,* LX (March–April, 1798). 2 parts.

c. Anna, a Fragment. *Harvest Home,* I (1807), 57–65. 1 part.

d. Anna, a Fragment. In the Manner of Sterne. *Entertaining*(2), I (September–November, 1813). 3 parts.

e. Anna, a Fragment. In the Manner of Sterne. *Sunderland Literary Misc.,* I, Nos. 2–5 (February–May, 1815). 4 parts.

110. ANNA, or Memoirs of a Welch Heiress. [By Agnes Maria Bennett.] *Town and Country Weekly,* I, No. 29 (October 29, 1785)–II, No. 3 (January 21, 1786). 12 parts (27,500). Uncompleted.

An unacknowledged reprinting of the first 17 chapters of A. M. Bennett's novel of the same name (1785).

111. ANNETTE, a Fairy Tale. By Master George Louis Lenox. *British Mag. and Rev.,* III (October, December, 1783). 2 parts (5600).

"Master *Lenox* has begged us to apologize for delaying the Conclusion of his *Fairy Tale,* which he promises to compleat in the first Week of his ensuing Holidays." ("Answers to Correspondents," November, 1783, p. [326].)

a. Annette, a Fairy Tale. By Master George Louis Lenox. *Hibernian,* 1783 (December); 1784 (June). 2 parts.

b. Annette, a Fairy Tale. By Master George Louis Lenox, Aged Only Twelve Years. *Edinburgh Weekly,* LVIII (December 18, 1783)–LIX (January 1, 1784). 2 parts. Uncompleted.

"The *Fairy Tale,* by Master Louis Lenox, which was begun some numbers ago... is not yet finished by the young author; though by a note in the *British Magazine* for November (from which publication we extracted it), he had promised to conclude it as [sic] about the last holidays." (To Our Correspondents," March 4, 1784, p. 296.) The Editor had evidently overlooked Part 2 in the December issue of the *British.*

c. Annette, a Fairy Tale. By Master George Louis Lenox. *New Novelist's,* I (1786), 187–194. 1 part.

Embellished with an engraving dated November 1, 1786.

d. Annette, a Fairy Tale. By Master George Louis Lenox. *Gleaner,* I (1805), 320–329.

112. The ARABIAN MORNINGS. *Monthly Literary Recreations,* II (March, 1807)–III (November, 1807). 6 parts (16,000). Uncompleted. Signed "A."

Running parallel with this series from May–August, 1807, was "The Story of Abadir and Zatima" by Ferdinand Fullerton Weston, reprinted from the

Juvenal (see No. 1). Since part of "Abadir and Zatima" was used to introduce "The Arabian Mornings," Weston was presumably the author of both.

a. The Arabian Mornings, after the Manner of the *Arabian Nights Entertainments. Cyclopaedian*, I (April, 1807)–II (July, 1808). 7 parts. Uncompleted.

113. ARABIAN NIGHTS ENTERTAINMENTS. Consisting of One Thousand and One Stories, Told by the Sultaness of the Indies, to Divert the Sultan from the Execution of a Cruel Vow. Translated from the French of M. Galland. In Four Volumes. *Novelist's*, XVIII (1785). 1 part (500,000).

The original English version of Galland's *Les Mille et une nuits* (in 6 vols.) was published in 1712. The 4-volume edition, reprinted by the *Novelist's*, was published by Longman in 1778. In the *Novelist's* the text has been embellished with sixteen engravings, dated March 19–July 2, 1785. For a short extract from the same translation, see No. 62.

114. An ARABIAN TALE. *Repository of Arts, etc.*, XIV (July–October, 1815). 4 parts (9100).

Nos. 52–55 of the series "The Modern Spectator."

115. ARDEN OF FEVERSHAM. "Tale 29," *Tell-Tale*, II (1804). 1 part (6300).

116. ARMORICA, an Epic Poem [in prose]. By J. H[uddleston]. Wynne. *Imperial*, III (May–November, 1762). 5 parts (5200).

Described by the author in an introductory letter as "a poem in prose," authorized by the examples of *Telemachus* and *Fingal*. (III, 249.)

117. The ARMOUR OF TIMANDER, or the Contest between the Eye and the Tongue. A Tale. *Edinburgh*(2), n.s. II (July, 1793). 1 part (5000).

118. ARSACES AND ISMENA, an Oriental History. Now First Translated from the Posthumous Works of the Celebrated Montesquieu. *Universal*, LXXIV (May–June, 1784). 2 parts (14,500). Signed "L."

From Montesquieu's *Arsace et Isménie, histoire orientale* (1783). For another translation of the same work, see No. 119.

a. Arsaces and Ismena, an Oriental History. *Caledonian Mag. and Rev.*, III June 14–August 27, 1784). 4 parts. Signed "L."

b. Arsaces and Ismena, an Oriental History, etc. [Same title as *Universal*.] *Hibernian*, 1784 (June–September). 4 parts.

119. ARSACES AND ISMENIA, an Oriental Story, by M. de Montesquieu. *Edinburgh*(2), I (March–April, 1785). 2 parts (13,850).

"The following Story, published lately in France, is universally acknowledged to be a production of Montesquieu. We hope the translation will be acceptable to many of our Readers." (I, 250.) For a slightly earlier translation of *Arsace et Isménie* (1783), see No. 118.

120. The ARTFUL LOVER, or the Amours of Miss L'F——r and Mr. D——. *Court and City*, I (October, 1770). 1 part (5000).

121. ARTFUL VILLAINY BROUGHT TO LIGHT. A Chinese History. *Weekly Amusement*, III, (March 22–April 12, 1766). 4 parts (8000).
   a. Artful Villainy Brought to Light. A Chinese History. *Weekly Misc.* (London), I, Nos. 36–38 (1772–1773). 3 parts.
   b. The Sufferings of Ouang, or Artful Villainy Discovered. A Chinese Story. *New Novelist's*, II (1787), 161–171. 1 part.
   c. The Sufferings of Ouang, or Artful Villainy Discovered. A Chinese Story. *Weekly Entertainer*, XI (February 11–March 3, 1788). 4 parts.
   d. Artful Villainy Brought to Light. A Chinese Tale. *Edinburgh*(2), XIV (September, 1791). 1 part.
   e. The Sufferings of Ouang, or Artful Villainy Discovered. A Chinese Story. *Gleaner*, I (1805), 273–285.

122. ASEM AND SALNED, an Eastern Tale. [By La Motte.] *Gentleman's*, XXI (December–Supplement, 1751). 2 parts (5000).

   An unacknowledged translation of "Salned et Garaldi, nouvelle orientale, par feu M. de la Motte," in the *Mercure de France* (October, 1751), pp. 45–65. For another translation of the same story, see No. 393.

   a. Asem and Salned. An Eastern Tale. *Magazine of Magazines*, II (December–Supplement, 1751). 2 parts.
   b. Asem and Salned. An Eastern Tale. *Gentleman and London's*, 1751 (December–Appendix, 1751). 2 parts.
   c. Asem and Salned. An Eastern Tale. *Scots*, XIII (Appendix, 1751). 1 part.
   d. Asem and Salned. An Eastern Tale. *Ladies*, III (January 25/February 8–February 22/March 7, 1752). 3 parts.

123. ASPASIA AND AGIS, or the Innocent Impostor. [By Charles Dibdin] *Bystander*, Nos. 2–20 (1789–1790). 10 parts (16,500). Published in alternate numbers of the magazine. Signed "★★★★."

   Part of the series called "The Novelist." Dibdin was author and editor of the *Bystander*.

124. ASSAD AND ALANE, or the Noblest Man. A Tale. (From the German of Augustus Lafontaine.) *Lady's*, XXXII (March, May, June, 1801). 3 parts (6400).

   A translation of "Der edelste Mann" (see *Kleine Romane und moralische Erzählungen*, 3rd ed., Vol. III, 1804).

125. ATALA. From the French of Mr. de Chateaubriand. *Harvest Home*, II (1808), 136–159. 1 part (13,800).

   There was an English edition of *Atala* (1801) published by G. and J. Robinson in 1802, on which this version was probably based.

126. The ATONEMENTS OF SENSIBILITY, a Novel. *Universal*, LXXXVIII (May–June, 1791). 2 parts (7800).

a. The Atonements of Sensibility, a Novel. *Universal Mag. and Rev.*, V (June, 1791)–VI (July, 1791). 2 parts.

b. The Atonements of Sensibility, a Novel. *Weekly Entertainer*, XVIII (September 19–October 3, 1791). 3 parts.

127. The ATTACHED INDIAN. *Lady's Monthly Museum*, n.s. II (February, 1807). 1 part (5200).

a. The Attached Indian. *Hibernian*, 1807 (February–March). 2 parts.

128. AUCASSIN AND NICOLETTE, a Tale. From the *Tales of the Minstrels, Translated from the French of M. Le Grand. Lady's*, XXVII (October–November, 1796). 2 parts (5000).

A translation of "Aucassin et Nicolette" by Legrand d'Aussy. The collection called *Tales of the Minstrels* (1796) had appeared earlier under the titles of *Tales of the XIIth and XIIIth Centuries* (1786) and *Norman Tales* (1789). The identical translation is found in both.

129. The AUCTION, a Dream. (From the *Calcutta Chronicle*.) *Spirit of the Public Journals for 1803*, VII (1804). 174–191. 1 part (6000).

130. AUGUSTA AND EMILY, a Tale. (By Miss C. B. Yeames.) *Lady's*, XXXIV (April–July, 1803). 4 parts (7000).

131. The AUTHOR'S PORTFOLIO, No. 9. *Lady's*, XLVI (November, 1815)–XLVII (February, April, June, 1816). 4 parts (7600).

The ninth item in a general series bearing the same title.

132. BABOUC, or the World as It Goes. Translated from the French of M. de Voltaire, by Mr. [Joseph] Collyer. *New Novelist's*, I (1786), 47–55. 1 part (6200).

A translation of "Babouc, ou le Monde comme il va" (1749). Collyer's translation was first published in *Select Pieces of M. de Voltaire, Translated from the French, by Joseph Collyer* (1754).

133. The BAD MOTHER, a Moral Tale. By the Author of "The Shepherdess of the Alps" [i.e., Marmontel]. *Weekly Amusement*, I (February 18–March 10, 1764). 4 parts (5000).

A translation of Marmontel's "La Mauvaise Mère" (*Contes moraux*, 1761); extracted from the *Moral Tales* (Becket and De Hondt, 1764). For another reprinting of the same tale, see No. 917.

a. The Bad Mother, a Moral Tale. *Caledonian Weekly*, I (?–June 30, 1773–?). 1 part. *Inc.*

Part 2 of the version in the *Weekly Amusement.*

b. The Bad Mother. A Moral Tale. By M. Marmontel. *Bristol and Bath*, II, No. 13 (1783). 1 part.

134. The BANDEAU OF LOVE, or the Blindness of Dulilot. (By Madame Roland. From Her *Works.*) *Universal,* CVIII (May–June, 1801). 2 parts (5900).

A translation of "Le Bandeau de l'amour, ou L'Aveuglement de Dulitot" (1774), extracted from *The Works (Never Before Published) of Jeanne-Marie Phlipon Roland* London, 1800), pp. 63–82.

a. The Bandeau of Love, or the Blindness of Dulilot. A Tale, by Madame Roland. *Edinburgh*(2), n.s. XVIII (July–August, 1801). 2 parts.

b. The Bandeau of Love, or the Blindness of Dulilot. (By Madame Roland.) *Hibernian,* 1801 (August–September). 2 parts.

c. Dulilot and Nervalle. *Britannic,* X, Nos. 131–132 (1802). 2 parts (5400).

A slightly abridged version of the above. Part of the series "Memoirs of Love and Gallantry."

135. The BANDITTI OF MONTE BALDO, or the Lass of the Lake. "Tale 60," *Tell-Tale,* V (1805). 1 part (12,500).

136. The BANDITTI OF THE FOREST, or the Mysterious Dagger. *Lady's Monthly Museum,* n.s. XI (July, 1811) – n.s. XII (February, 1812). 8 parts (15,750). Signed "C."

137. The BANKS OF THE DART, a Tale. *Lady's Monthly Museum,* n.s. IX (August 1810) – n.s. X (February, 1811). 6 parts (10,400).

138. The BANQUET OF THE GODS. *Edinburgh Weekly,* VIII (April 12–May 3, 1770). 4 parts (12,500).

"The intent of the following Piece is to expose the heathen Mythology, which the Author ridicules in an uncommon strain of Pleasantry and Humour." (VIII, 33.)

139. The BARON'S WEDDING, a Romance. By E. T. *Lady's Monthly Museum,* n.s. VI (March–June, 1809). 4 parts (7900).

140. The BARONS OF OLD. By the Late T. Bellamy. "Tale 11," *Tell-Tale,* I (1803). 1 part (7900).

A redaction of "The British Barons" (No. 168), by Thomas Bellamy, first published in the *General Magazine.*

141. BASEM, or the Blacksmith. An Oriental Apologue. By William Beloe, F.S.A., Translator of Herodotus, &c., &c. *Freemason's,* IV (April, 1795)–V (July, 1795). 4 parts (17,000).

a. Basem, or the Blacksmith, etc. [Same title as above.] *Hibernian,* 1795 (June–October), 1796 (April). 6 parts.

b. Basem, or the Blacksmith of Bagdat. *Britannic,* V, Nos. 59–63 (1797). 5 parts.

142. BASIL, or the Happy Family. A Moral Tale. *Hibernian,* 1811 (October). 1 part (5000).

143. BATHMENDI, a Persian Tale. [By M. de Florian.] *Edinburgh*(2), XIII (January, 1791). 1 part (5000).

A translation of "Bathmendi, nouvelle persane" (*Les Six Nouvelles de M. de Florian,* Paris, 1784). For other translations of the same story, see Nos. 144 and 164.

144. BATHMENDI, or the Search after Happiness. A Tale. By M. de Florian. *Lady's,* XXVIII (January–February, 1797). 2 parts (5500).

A translation of "Bathmendi, nouvelle persane" (1784), extracted without acknowledgment from *Tales, Romances, Apologues, Anecdotes, and Novels* (1786). For other translations of the same story see Nos. 143 and 164.

a. Bathmendi, or the Search after Happiness. By M. de Florian. *Harvest Home,* I (1807), 65–74.

145. The BEACON, or the Execution Improved! Being an Humble Attempt to Check the First Approaches to Vice. Founded on a Circumstance Which Really Happened, and Addressed to the Publishers of the *Cheap Magazine. Cheap,* I (January, 1813). 1 part (8200).

A note at the end recommends to the author, "Observant Pedestrian," greater brevity in the future, while thanking him for his contribution, and expressing the wish for further contributions from the same pen (I, 31).

146. The BEAU MONDE, or a History of the New World. *Belle Assemblée,* I (February–April, 1806). 3 parts (5700). Uncompleted.

147. The BEAUTIES OF *TELEMACHUS. Universal,* LX (January, 1777)–LXVI (February, 1780). 18 parts (46,000). Uncompleted.

A redaction of Fénelon's *Télémaque,* with translations of "some of the finest Passages" (LX,3); appearing sporadically over a three-year period, and covering the first twelve of the twenty-four books. During the course of this series, the editor of the *Universal* declared that his English text was adapted from the translations of "Dr. *Hawkesworth,* Dr. *Smollet,* and other eminent Writers" (LXI, July, 1777, p. 1). For a full-length reprinting of the Hawkesworth translation, see No. 63.

148. The BEAUTIFUL AFRICAN, or Love and Slavery. "Tale 63," *Tell-Tale,* V (1805). 1 part (13,500).

There are striking verbal similarities between this piece and No. 432, but the stories are very different.

149. The BEGGAR BOY, or History and Adventures of James Altamont. "Tale 75," *Tell-Tale,* VI (1805). 1 part (13,400).

A disguised redaction of James Annesley's *Memoirs of an Unfortunate Young Nobleman* (1743). For a short extract from the same book, see No. 876.

150. The BEGGAR'S TALE. *Caledonian* (2), V (December, 1790). 1 part (10,200). Signed "PHILANTHROPOS."

Addressed "To the Editor of the *Caledonian Magazine,*" by an "ingenious Correspondent."

a. The Beggar's Tale. *Monthly Visitor,* XIV (October–December, 1801). 3 parts. Signed "PHILANTHROPOS."

"For the *Monthly Visitor.*"

151. BELISARIUS. By M. Marmontel. *Scots,* XXXIX (April, 1767). 1 part (5300). Signed "M" [i.e., *Monthly Review?*].

A review of the first English translation of Marmontel's *Bélisaire* (1767), containing a long summary of the story with extracts. The last 3500 words of this review is identical with the review of the same novel in the *Monthly Review* for April, 1767 (pp. 290–298), assigned by Nangle to William Rose. Since the two reviews were published simultaneously, it seems likely that Rose sent his review to both periodicals. The *Scots* published it in full; Griffiths omitted the first 1700 words. A similar example of double publication, again involving the *Monthly* and the *Scots,* is found in No. 88 above.

152. BENEDICT, a True History. [By Mrs. Mary Pilkington.] *Lady's,* XL (November, 1809) – XLI (May, 1810); XLII (November, 1811) – XLIII (March, 1812).

The story was suspended between May, 1810, and November, 1811, owing to "the serious indisposition of the Author." (XLI, 242.) The story had been announced as forthcoming from her pen (XL, [434], 459), but did not carry her name when it appeared.

153. BENEVOLENCE AND GRATITUDE, a Novel. *Sentimental,* III (October–December, 1775). 3 parts (9000).

a. Benevolence and Gratitude, a Novel. *Caledonian Mag. and Rev.,* II (November 14–28, 1783).

154. BENEVOLENCE REWARDED, a Tale. *Lady's,* XXVI (August–October, 1795). 3 parts (5500).

155. BENEVOLENCE REWARDED, or the History of Miss Harriet Worthy. A Moral Tale. *Lady's,* XV (June, 1784)–XVI (February, 1785). 9 parts (14,900).

156. The BENEVOLENT ORPHAN, or the History of James Logan. Shewing That Opportunities of Doing Good Are Not Confined to the Rich. *Scotch Cheap Rep.,* No. 9 (1808). 1 part (5800). Signed "F."

157. BENEVOLENT RAMBLES, or the History of Sentonius. *Lady's Monthly Museum,* XII (February–June, 1804). 4 parts (15,300).

The story was missing from the April number, and the editor expressed the wish that the author would pursue her story "without intermission, till concluded." (XII, 283.)

158. The BLACK AND THE WHITE. A Tale from Voltaire. *British* (2), VI (June–July, 1765). 2 parts (5000).

A translation of "Le Blanc et le noir" (1764), extracted from Vol. XIX of Smollett's edition of the *Works of Mr. de Voltaire* (1761–65). For an earlier translation of the same piece, see No. 1178.

a. The Black and the White. Translated from Voltaire. *Oxford,* II (February, 1769). 1 part (4800).

A slight abridgment of the above.

159. BLANCHE AND CARLOS, or the Constant Lovers. Including the Adventures of Valville and Adelaide, a Mexican Tale. *Marvellous,* III (October 1, 1803). 1 part (30,000).

160. BLIOMBERIS. [By M. de Florian.] *Belle Assemblée,* II (February–April, 1807). 3 parts (11,600). Signed "E.R."

An unacknowledged translation of Florian's "Bliombéris, nouvelle française" (*Six Nouvelles,* 1784).

161. The BOND OF BLOOD. Original Romance. *Theatrical Inquisitor,* VI (March, 1815) – VII (August, 1815). 6 parts (9250). Signed "G.S." in black letter. Uncompleted.

162. The BOND-STREET LOUNGER. *Belle Assemblée,* VI (April, 1809). 1 part (5000).

163. The BOOK OF THE CHRONICLES OF THE THREE SISTERS. From the *Popular Tales of the Germans* [by Johann Carl August Musaeus]. *Lady's,* XXII (October-Supplement, 1791). 4 parts (15,000).

A translation of Musaeus, "Die Bücher der Chronika der drey Schwestern" (*Volksmährchen der Deutschen,* 1782–1786), made by William Beckford and published in *Popular Tales of the Germans* (1791). Parts 2–4 in the *Lady's* are entitled "Books of the Chronicles," etc. For other excerpts from Beckford's collection, see Nos. 522 and 1063.

164. BOTHMENDI. Translated from the French of M. Florian, by a Lady. *Belfast Monthly,* XIII (December, 1814). 1 part (5000).

"For the *Belfast Monthly Magazine.*"

A translation of "Bathmendi, nouvelle persane" (*Les Six Nouvelles de M. de Florian,* 1784). For other translations of the same story, see Nos. 143–144.

165. The BRAZIER. [By Mme. de Genlis.] "Tale 73," *Tell-Tale,* VI (1805). 1 part (5200).

An unacknowledged translation of "Le Chaudronnier, ou la Reconnaissance réciproque" (*Les Veillées du château,* 1784). The translation is Thomas Holcroft's ("The Brazier, or Reciprocal Gratitude," *Tales of the Castle,* Vol. I, 1785). For other translations from *Les Veillées,* see Nos. 291, 347, and 406.

a. The Brazier, or Reciprocal Gratitude. From the French of Madame [de] Genlis. *Gleaner,* II (1806), 15–23.

166. The BRAZIER'S DAUGHTER, or History of Ethelred and Ethelgive. "Tale 46," *Tell-Tale,* IV (1804). 1 part (13,300).

An abridged version of Mme. de Gomez, "Histoire d'Etelred, roi d'Angleterre" ("Quinzième journée," *Les Journées amusantes,* 1722–1731). The original translation, from which this abridgment was made, is Mrs. Haywood's, published under the title "The History of Ethelred, King of England," in *La Belle Assemblée* (1724–1726). For a full-length reprinting of Mrs. Haywood's translation of the same story, see No. 574; and for still another abridged translation of the "Histoire d'Etelred," No. 341.

167. A BRIEF ACCOUNT OF WHAT BEFEL SOME GENTLEMEN, Who Were Ship-Wrecked on the Coast of Summatra, in the East-Indies. *Female Spectator,* Book XVIII (1745), pp. 337–363. 1 part (5800).

The story is followed by several pages of commentary.

168. The BRITISH BARONS. By Thomas Bellany. *General,* VI (February–December, 1792). 9 parts (9500).

This piece was collected in Bellamy's *Miscellanies in Prose and Verse* (1794). For a later redaction of the story, see No. 140.

a. The British Barons. *Universal Mag. and Rev.,* VII (March, 1792)–IX (January, 1793). 8 parts.

169. BRITISH OAK, or a Solider's Benevolence. "Tale 19," *Tell-Tale,* II (1804). 1 part (10,000).

170. BROMLEY MELMOT, a Novel. *Lady's Monthly Museum,* II (February–June, 1799). 5 parts (28,000).

171. The BROTHERS, a Moral Tale. *Lady's,* XLII (September, 1811)–XLV (February, 1814). 30 parts (58,000).

172. BURBACH, a Spanish Anecdote. *Repository of Arts, etc.,* VII (January–February, 1812). 2 parts (7100).

173. The CABINET, or Fatal Curiosity. "Tale 2," *Tell-Tale,* I (1803). 1 part (5200).

A reprinting of "Fatal Curiosity, an Arabian Tale," published in *Literary Amusements, or Evening Entertainer, by a Female Hand* (1782).

174. The CACIQUE OF ONTARIO, an Indian Tale. *Gleaner,* I (1805), 165–175. 1 part (6000).

A complete reprinting of the novel of the same title, reviewed in the *Critical,* LXII (1786), 392–393.

175. CAMIRA, an American Tale. [By M. de Florian.] *Monthly Extracts,* IV (September, 1792). 1 part (8100).

A translation of Florian's "Camiré" (1792), extracted, in the course of review, from *New Tales from the French of M. Florian* (1792). For another translation of the same story, see No. 176.

176. CAMIRE, an American Tale. [By M. de Florian.] *Belle Assemblée,* III (July–August, 1807). 2 parts (8800). Signed "E.R."

An unacknowledged translation of Florian's "Camiré, nouvelle américaine" (*Nouvelles nouvelles,* 1792). For an earlier translation, see No. 175.

a. Camire, an American Tale. *Hibernian,* 1807 (October); 1808 (January). 2 parts. Signed "E.R."

177. CANDIDE, or the Optimist. *Grand Magazine*(1), II (May, 1759)–III (July, 1759). 3 parts (15,800).

A translation and condensation of Part I of Voltaire's *Candide ou l'Optimisme* (1759). The above version is probably based upon that published serially in *Lloyd's Evening Post and British Chronicle* a few weeks earlier. (See Chapter IV, pp. 239–240.)

178. The CAPRICE OF FORTUNE, a True Story. *Matrimonial,* I (January–March, 1775). 1 part (7300).

The title of Parts 2 and 3 is "The Caprice of Fortune, or Charlotte and Maria, a True Story."

179. The CAPTAIN'S DAUGHTER, or a Journal of Vicissitudes. *Lady's Monthly Museum,* n.s. IX (August, 1810) – n.s. XI (August, 1811). 10 parts (38,600).

180. The CAPUCHIN, a True Story. *Weekly Misc.* (Glasgow), n.s. I, Nos. 11–16 (September 12–October 17, 1792). 6 parts (7900).

181. CAROLINE, or the Blessings of Adversity. *Lady's,* XLVI (April, 1815)–XLVII (October, 1816). 19 parts (46,500).

182. CAROLINE COURTNEY. [By Thomas Bellamy.] *Monthly Mirror,* I (December, 1795–April, 1796). 4 parts (5300). Signed "T. BELLAMY."

a. Caroline Courtney. By the late Mr. T. Bellamy. *Gleaner,* II (1806), 23–32. 1 part.

183. CAROLINE OF ABBYVILLE, an Instructive Tale. *Parlour Window,* Nos. 1–8 (1795–1796). 8 parts (18,000). Uncompleted.

The novel was obviously not written for *Parlour Window,* which is an essay-serial. The first installment breaks off in the middle of a sentence. In October, 1793, Part 1 of a story bearing practically the same title ("Caroline of Abbyville, an Original Tale") had been printed in the *Sentimental and Masonic Magazine* (Dublin), but had been left unfinished. It seems to be an earlier draft of the story in the *Parlour Window*. In the Bodleian copy of *Parlour Window,* the periodical is attributed to "Mrs. Eustace and her sister."

184. The CASE OF MR. JOHN BULL, Clothier, of Wooton-Under-Edge, in the County of Gloucester, as Drawn up by Dr. Galen. *Monitor,* No. 35 (April 3); No. 39 (May 1, 1756). 2 parts (6500). Signed "D."

Part 2 is called "The Second Part of the History of Mr. John Bull." Both parts were offered in the form of letters signed "PUBLICOLA," although they were also initialed.

185. The CASKET, a Moral Tale. By Marmontel. *Edinburgh*(2), n.s. II (August–September, 1793). 2 parts (7750).

 A translation of "La Cassette, conte moral," first published in the *Mercure* (1792). For another translation of the same story, see No. 670. Both are different from the translation ("The Casket") published in *New Moral Tales*, Vol. IV (1794).

186. The CASTLE DE WARRENNE, a Romance. *Lady's Monthly Museum*, V (July–December, 1800). 6 parts (31,000).

187. The CASTLE OF GLENCROICH, a Romance of the 12th Century. *Glasgow*, III (January–June, 1812). 5 parts (10,700).

 "For the *Glasgow Magazine*." Part 5 is signed: "NUBILIA. / Glasgow, June 30, 1812."

188. The CASTLE OF KOLMERAS, a Romance. Supposed to Be Written by the Hero. (Translated from the French of Madame de Genlis.) *Entertaining*(1), No. IX (September, 1802). 1 part (9600).

 A translation of "Le Château de Kolméras," first published in the *Nouvelle bibliothèque des romans*, année 4, tom. 9 (1802).

189. The CASTLE OF LANGARRAN, a Welch Story. From the MSS. of the Late James Petit Andrews, Esq., F.S.A. *Monthly Mirror*, VII (April, 1799)–XI (May, 1801). 22 parts (29,600).

 The receipt of the story was gratefully acknowledged in the Editor's column for April, 1799 (p. 194).

 a. The Castle of Langarran, a Welch Story. In a Series of Letters. *Hibernian*, 1799 (August)–1801 (June). 20 parts.

190. The CASTLE OF MONTALBERT, or the Fatal Prediction. "Tale 44," *Tell-Tale*, III (1804). 1 part (11,250).

191. The CASTLE OF SAVINA, or the Irishman in Italy. A Tale. *Weekly Selector*, I, Nos. 16–23 (May 19–July 7, 1812). 8 parts (16,500).

192. CASTLE OF THE PYRENEES. "Tale 6," *Tell-Tale*, I (1803). 1 part (13,400).

 A disguised redaction of "The Interesting History of the Count de Bellegarde" (see No. 706), from Charlotte Smith's *Celestina*.

193. The CASTLE ON THE CLIFT, a Romance. By Juvenis. *Lady's*, XXIX (November, 1798); XXX (January, March, 1799). 3 parts (9300). Uncompleted.

194. On the CAUSES AND EFFECTS OF EARLY MARRIAGES. *Belle Assemblée*, I (June, October, 1806). 2 parts (6100). Signed "H.T."

195. The CAVE OF ST. SIDWELL, a Romance. *Lady's Monthly Museum*, n.s. II (January, 1807)–n.s. III (August, 1807). 6 parts (11,000). Signed "E.F."

196. The CAVERN OF HORRORS, or Miseries of Miranda. A Neapolitan Tale *Marvellous,* I (December 1, 1802). 1 part (30,000).

197. CECILIA, or Memoirs of an Heiress. [By Madame D'Arblay.] *Universal,* LXXII (March–June, 1783). 4 parts (23,000).

A long summary of the novel (1782), with extensive extracts.

a. Cecilia, or Memoirs of an Heiress. *Hibernian,* 1783 (April–September); 1784 (January). 7 parts.

198. CELESTINA. [By M. de Florian.] "Tale 68," *Tell-Tale,* V (1805). 1 part (5100).

An unacknowledged translation of "Célestine, nouvelle espagnole" (1784), taken from *The Works of M. le Chevalier de Florian... Translated from the Last Paris Edition, by Mr. Robinson* (1786). For other translations of the same story, see Nos. 199, 244, and 824.

199. CELESTINA, A SPANISH TALE. [By M. de Florian.] *Belle Assemblée,* II (June, 1807). 1 part (5800). Signed "E.R."

An unacknowledged translation of "Célestine, nouvelle espagnole" (*Six Nouvelles de M. de Florian,* 1784). For other translations, see Nos. 198, 244, and 824.

200. CELESTINA, or Innocence. *Belle Assemblée,* n.s. IX (May, 1814)–n.s. X (July 1814). 1 part (6300).

201. The CHAMPION OF VIRTUE, a Gothic Story. [By Clara Reeve.] *Berwick Museum,* I (January, 1785) – II (June, 1786). 18 parts (46,500).

A long abridgment of Clara Reeve's novel of the same name, first published in 1777.

202. The CHANCES, or Adventure of a Night. A Tale. *New London,* IV (January, 1788). 1 part (5000).

203. The CHAPEL OF ST. BENEDICT. A Romance of the Fifteenth Century. *Belle Assemblée,* n.s. VIII (September, 1813)–n.s. X (July, 1814). 11 parts (25,000).

204. The CHARACTER OF A MAN OF GALLANTRY. *Hibernian,* 1776 (July). 1 part (7500).

The story is introduced by a letter signed "Hilario. / Henry-street, June 29th, 1776." and addressed "To the Editor of the *Hibernian Magazine,*" affirming the truth of the story and emphasizing its moral efficacy (p. 455).

205. CHARACTER OF PIERRE DE LA MOTTE. With the Adventure Which Placed Adeline under His Protection, and His Retreat to the Ruined Abbey of St. Clair, in the Forest of Fontanville. [By Ann Radcliffe.] *Monthly Extracts,* III (August, 1792). 1 part (7800).

A long extract from the *Romance of the Forest* (1791), Chaps. 1–2. For a further extract from the same novel, see No. 889.

206. CHARLES EDMUNDS, or the Freethinker. A Novel. By R[ippin]. Porter. *Lady's Monthly Museum,* n.s. XIV (April, 1813)–n.s. XV (September, 1813). 6 parts (10,800).

"Should we approve the Tale mentioned by R. P. we will insert it with pleasure: we beg leave to observe, that although the professors of Deism be unfortunately numerous, we believe that Atheism is nearly exploded." ("Notes to Correspondents," January, 1813, p. 60.) The receipt of the ms. was acknowledged the following month, and the editor asked leave "to compress it" (p. 120).

207. CHARLES MARTEL, an Anecdote. *Lady's,* III (September, 1772). 1 part (7900).

a. Charles Martell, an Anecdote. *Weekly Misc.*(Sherborne), XV (February 5–19, 1781). 3 parts.

b. Charles Martel. *New Gleaner,* I (1809), 348–360.

The story is labeled "Anon."

208. The CHARMS AND REWARD OF VIRTUE IN DISTRESS. An Interesting Story in Private Life, Shewing the Effects of Education. *Universal,* XXIV (April, 1759). 1 part (6100).

a. The Charms and Reward of Virtue in Distress, etc. [Same title as above.] *Magazine of Magazines,* XVII (April, 1759). 1 part.

b. The Triumph of Virtue, a True History. *British*(2), IV (October–November, 1763). 2 parts.

c. The Triumph of Virtue, a True History. *Beauties of All the Magazines,* II (December, 1763). 1 part. Uncompleted.

d. The History of a Widow and Her Family. *Weekly Entertainer,* XVI (December 20, 1790)–XVII (January 3, 1791). 3 parts.

e. Agathius and Eliza. *Britannic,* II, No. 24 (1794). 1 part.

An abridged version of the above. Part of the series "Memoirs of Love and Gallantry."

209. The CHATEAU OF ROUSSILLON. *Belle Assemblée,* n.s. III (March, 1811) – n.s. V (February, 1812). 8 parts (25,750).

a. The Chateau of Roussillon. *Hibernian,* 1811 (April–November). 6 parts. Uncompleted.

210. The CHILD OF HUMILITY. By Thomas Bellamy. *General,* V (February–December, 1791); VI (May–August?, 1792). 10 parts (13,000). Uncompleted.

This piece was later reprinted in completed form in Bellamy's *Miscellanies in Prose and Verse* 1794), I, 56–110.

a. The Child of Humility. By Thomas Bellamy. *Hibernian,* 1791 (March–December); 1792 (June). 7 parts. Uncompleted.

Abandoned by the *Hibernian* after Part 6 of the original.

211. The CHILD OF SORROW. A Sentimental Novel. *Royal*(3), I (January–November, 1788). 10 parts (10,000).

212. The CHILD OF SUSPICION, a Romantic Tale. *Lady's Monthly Museum,* n.s. XI (July, 1811)–n.s. XII (January, 1812). 5 parts (13,000).

213. The CHILD OF THE BATTLE. By H. Finn. *Lady's Monthly Museum,* n.s. XV (November, 1813)–n.s. XVI (June, 1814). 8 parts (15,600). Uncompleted.

The first part of this novel was received in August, 1813, (p. 120), at which time the editor requested to see the whole (in order "that we may form our own judgment as to its moral and extent"). He must have seen only part, however, since the printing was broken off in June, 1814, by the "indisposition" of the author. In November he was ready to resume publication, but decided (n.s. XVII, 300) that the novel, having "excited such general interest, and obtained an increased demand for the 15th and 16th volumes of this work," would be "republished, and the Narrative completed, in the *improved series* of the *Lady's Monthly Museum,*" beginning in January, 1815—and thus:

a. The Child of the Bəttle. By H. Finn. *Lady's Monthly Museum,* 3. s. I (January, 1815)–3. s. V (February, 1817). 22 parts (43,750).

214. The CHIMNEY-SWEEPER, or the School for Levity. A Novel. *Lady's Monthly Museum,* VIII (January–June, 1802). 6 parts (15,200).

215. CHINESE TALES, or the Wonderful Adventures of the Mandarin Fum-Hoam. Related by Himself, to Divert the Sultana, upon the Celebration of Her Nuptials. Written in French by M. Gueulette. Translated by the Rev. Mr. [Thomas] Stackhouse. *Novelist's,* V (1781). 1 part (80,000).

From Thomas Simon Gueullette, *Les Contes chinois, ou les Aventures merveilleuses du mandarin Fum-Hoam* (1723), first translated into English in 1725. Stackhouse's, however, is a new translation, first published in the *Novelist's.* It is embellished with three engravings, dated June 16–30, 1781.

216. A CHRISTMAS TALE. By Joseph Moser, Esq. *European,* XXXII (November–December, 1797). 2 parts (6300).

a. A Christmas Tale. By Joseph Moser, Esq. *Edinburgh*(2), n.s. X (December, 1797)–n.s. XI (January, 1798). 2 parts.

b. A Christmas Tale. By Joseph Moser, Esq. *Scots,* LX (January–February, 1798) 2 parts.

217. CHRISTOPHER CURIOUS. *Rambler's,* VI (February; Supplement, 1788)–VIII (June, 1790). 21 parts (33,000).

There was a ten-month's interruption in this story after Part 1. When resumed, the story was called "The Adventures of Christopher Curious.

218. CH——S F——X IS ENTERTAINED BY JULIUS CAESAR. *Westminster,* XI (July, 1783): 1 part (5750).

Offered as "An Extract from the New Novel Called *The Man in the Moon*, Chap. IX."—written by William Thomson, and published in 1783. "For the *Westminster Magazine*."

219. CHURKUMGURKUM, or the Gift of Tongues. *Bon Ton,* IV (August–December, 1794). 2 parts (8500).

220. The CIRCASSIAN SLAVE. *Belle Assemblée,* n.s. I (January–February, 1810). 2 parts (7000).

a. The Circassian Slave, a Tale of Facts. *Hibernian,* 1810 (February–March). 2 parts. Uncompleted.

221. CLARISSA, or the History of a Young Lady. Comprehending the Most Important Concerns of Private Life. And Particularly Shewing the Distresses That May Attend the Misconduct Both of Parents and Children, in Relation to Marriage. By Mr. Samuel Richardson. In Eight Volumes. *Novelist's,* XIV–XV (1784). 2 parts (975,000).

First published in 1747–1748. The reprinting in the *Novelist's* is embellished with thirty-four engravings, dated December 20, 1783–August 7, 1784.

222. CLAUDINA, a Savoyard Tale. [By M. de Florian.] *Monthly Extracts,* IV (September, 1792). 1 part (7500).

A translation of "Claudine, nouvelle savoyarde" (*Nouvelles nouvelles,* 1792), extracted from *New Tales, from the French of M. Florian* (1792). For another translation of the same story, see No. 223.

a. Claudina, a Savoyard Tale. *Edinburgh*(2), XVI (September, 1792). 1 part.

Printed without any indication of source.

b. [Claudina, a Savoyard Tale.] *General,* VI (1792), 228–244. 1 part.

Extracted from the *New Tales,* cited above, and printed in the "Impartial Review."

c. *New Tales, from the French of M. Florian. Universal Mag. and Rev.,* VIII (December, 1792). 1 part.

No title was given to the story, which was printed in the course of review.

223. CLAUDINE, a Swiss Tale. From the French of M. de Florian. *European,* XXII (August–September, 1792). 2 parts (6300).

An original translation of "Claudine, nouvelle savoyarde" (*Nouvelles nouvelles, par M. de Florian,* Paris, 1792). For another version of the same story, see No. 222.

a. Claudine, a Charming Swiss Tale. From the French of the Celebrated M. de Florian. *Bon Ton,* II (August–September, 1792). 2 parts.

b. Claudine, a Swiss Tale. (From the French of M. de Florian.) *Scots,* LIV (September–October, 1792). 2 parts.

c. Claudine, a Swiss Tale. From the French of M. de Florian. *Sentimental and Masonic,* I (September–October, 1792). 2 parts.

d. Claudine, a Swiss Tale. (From the French of M. de Florian.) *Lady's,* XXIII (October–November, 1792). 2 parts.

e. Claudine, a Swiss Tale. (From the French of M. de Florian.) *Hibernian,* 1792 (October–November). 2 parts.

224. CLEOMAR AND DALIA. A Novel, from the French [of Bricaire de la Dixmerie]. *Selector*(1), Nos. 2–3 (1776). 2 parts (6750).

A translation of "Cléomir et Dalia, nouvelle gauloise" (*Contes philosophiques et moraux, par M. de la Dixmerie,* 1765). For another translation of the same story, see No. 225.

225. CLEOMIR AND DALIA. From the Celtic. *Lady's,* III (January, 1772). 1 part (7500). Signed "R."

An earlier magazine translation of Bricaire de la Dixmerie, "Cléomir et Dalia, nouvelle gauloise" (see No. 224).

a. Cleomir and Dalia. From the Celtic. *New Gleaner,* I (1809), 121–139.

Attributed to the "*Lady's Mag.*"

226. CLEORA, or the Assassination. *Lady's,* IV (December–Supplement, 1773). 2 parts (5000). Signed "R."

227. CLIFFORD AND LOUISA, or the Evils of the Vice of Gaming. A True Story. From Mrs. Crespigny's *Letters. Weekly Entertainer,* XLV (November 11–25, 1805). 3 parts (5400).

From Lady Mary Champion de Crespigny, *Letters of Advice from a Mother to Her Son* (1803).

228. CLITANDER AND CLEORA, a Tale. *European,* XL (October, 1801). 1 part (5000). Signed "Dionysius."

a. The Folly of Idle Inquisitiveness, a Tale. *Edinburgh*(2), n.s. XVIII (December, 1801). 1 part (4750).

A disguised version of the same story, slightly abridged. The names of the principal characters are changed.

229. A COLLECTION OF GENUINE LETTERS, Written by a Lady in a Convent at Douay, in Flanders, to Her Friends in England. *Covent Garden,* I (July, 1772)–II (December, 1773). 13 parts (18,000).

230. COLVILLE, a West Indian Tale. *Freemason's,* X (April–May, 1798). 2 parts (6100).

231. The COMMUNICATIVE POCKETS. By Augustus von Kotzebue. *Repository*

232. The COMPETITORS, a Moral Tale. By Mr. Bacon. *Pocket,* III (September–October, 1795). 2 parts (8500).

Possibly by James Bacon, of Lincoln's Inn, author in 1795 of at least one novel and a play; or Robert Bacon, the author of *Miscellaneous Pieces in Verse and Prose* (1790). The same "Mr. Bacon" was author of a number of signed pieces in the *Pocket Magazine,* and may have been its editor.

233. CONCEALMENT, a Tale. *Lady's Monthly Museum,* XV (November–December, 1805). 2 parts (6800).

234. The CONFESSION OF JULIEN DE JOINVILLE. A Moral Tale. *European,* LVII (June, 1810). 1 part (6800).

a. The Confession of Julien de Joinville. A Moral Tale. *Weekly Entertainer,* L (July 16–23, 1810). 1 part.

235. CONFESSIONS OF A METHODIST. *Satirist,* IV (January 1–June 1, 1809); VI (January 1–March 1, 1810). 6 parts (15.000). Signed "MISOPHENAX."

The purpose of the series was "to expose the hypocrisy and shocking blasphemy of the Methodists." (IV, 562).

236. CONFESSIONS OF A POLITICIAN. *Satirist,* VI (May 1, 1810)–VII (July 1, 1810). 3 parts (5200). Uncompleted.

237. The CONFLICT BETWEEN REASON AND LOVE. A True Story. *Universal Museum,* n.s. II (September, 1766)–n.s. III (January, 1767). 5 parts (11,200).

A notice to the reader in December, 1766, declared that to avoid tedium "we have this month taken the liberty to abridge [the letters] into a narrative" (n.s. II, 636).

238. CONJUGAL INFIDELITY, or Authentic Memoirs of Lydia Lovemore. In a Series of Letters to Eliza. *Rambler's,* VII (Supplement, 1789)–VIII (April, 1790). 5 parts (11,700).

239. The CONJURER, a Tale. *Asylum,* II, Nos. 28–52 (March 25?–August 26, 1795). 22 parts (35,000).

A condensation of Lawrence Flammenberg [i.e., K. F. Kahlert], *The Necromancer, or the Tale of the Black Forest* (Minerva Press, 1794), translated by Peter Teuthold from *Der Geisterbanner* (1792). (See Montague Summers, *A Gothic Bibliography,* p. 335.) "The Conjurer" is about half the length of the Teuthold translation, on which it is based.

Der Geisterbanner and *The Necromancer* were extremely interesting to magazine writers and editors, who published at least three other versions in the magazines (see Nos. 240, 944, and 949).

a. The Conjurer, a Tale. *Gleaner,* II (1806). 5 parts.

240. The CONJUROR, a Romance. *Hibernian,* 1810 (May–June). 2 parts (5200). Uncompleted.

A disguised redaction of Lawrence Flammenberg [i.e., K. F. Kahlert], *The Necromancer, or the Tale of the Black Forest* (London: Minerva Press, 1794), but abandoned after only a few thousand words. For other versions of the same novel, or of *Der Geisterbanner,* on which it was based, see Nos. 239, 944, and 949.

241. The CONNOISSEUR. From Marmontel's *Tales. Universal,* XXXIII (Supplement, 1763). 1 part (5400).

A translation of "Le Connoisseur" (*Contes moraux,* 1761), extracted from the *Moral Tales* (Becket and De Hondt, 1764; actually 1763). For another magazine printing of the same story, see "Moral Tales" (No. 917).

a. The Connoisseur. *Weekly Misc.*(Sherborne), X (September 14, 1778). 1 part.

b. The Connoisseur. *Moral and Entertaining,* III (September, 1778). 1 part.

242. The CONQUESTS OF THE HEART, a Novel, by a Young Lady. *London,* n.s. IV (February, 1785). 1 part (5000).

A review of the novel of the same name (1785)—containing two long extracts connected by a thread of narrative.

243. CONRADINE, or Innocence Triumphant. *Belle Assemblée,* VI (January–February 1809). 2 parts (9100).

244. The CONSTANT LOVERS, or the Adventures of Pedro and Celestin[a]. A Tale. By the Chevalier de Florian. *Edinburgh*(2), XIII (May, 1791). 1 part (5400).

A translation of "Célestine, nouvelle espagnole" (1784), taken from "The Constant Lovers, or the Adventures of Pedro and Celestina, by the Chevalier de Florian," published in *Tales, Romances, Apologues, Anecdotes, and Novels* (1786). For other translations of the same story, see Nos. 198–199, and 824.

a. The Constant Lovers, etc. [Same title as above.] *Lady's,* XXII (September, 1791). 1 part.

b. The Constant Lovers, etc. [Same title.] *Hibernian,* 1791 (October). 1 part.

c. The Constant Lovers, etc. [Same title.] *Aberdeen*(1), IV (October, 1791). 1 part.

d. The Constant Lovers, or the Adventures of Pedro and Celestina. By the Chevalier de Florian. *New Gleaner,* I (1809), 110–120. 1 part.

245. CONSTANTIA, an Affecting History. (From *A Philosophical Essay on Old Maids,* 3 Vols.) *Universal,* LXXVIII (January–February, 1786). 2 parts (6000).

A reprinting of Part II, Chapter 2, "On the Patience of Old Maids," in Hayley's *Philosophical, Historical, and Moral Essay on Old Maids* (London, 1785). For other extracts from the same work, see Nos. 67 and 700.

a. Constantia, or Unexampled Magnanimity. By Mr. Hayley. *New Novelist's,* I (1787), 395–401. 1 part (5100).

A slightly shorter version of the above.

b. Constantia, or Unexampled Magnanimity. By Mr. Hayley. *Caledonian*(1), I June 15–29, 1787). 2 parts (5100).

c. On the Patience of Old Maids. (From an *Essay on Old Maids.*) *Caledonian*(2), I (July–August, 1788). 2 parts (6000).

d. Constantia, or Unexampled Magnanimity. A Tale. *Edinburgh*(2), n.s. IV (October, 1794). 1 part (5100).

e. The Unfortunate Constantia, or a Picture of Unexampled Magnanimity. By William Hayley, Esq. *Entertaining*(1), I, No. 9 (September, 1802). 1 part (5100).

246. [The CONTENTED CURATE.] [By Charles Dibdin.] *Bystander*, Nos. 10 (August 15, 1789)–26 (February 6, 1790). 8 parts (11,000).

Addressed "To the *By-Stander.*" The story has no title, but most of the letters are signed "The Contented Curate." Dibdin was author of the *Bystander.*

a. [The Contented Curate. By Mr. Charles Dibdin.] *General,* V (November, 1791)–VI ([June,] 1792). 7 parts.

"From that store-house of wit and pleasantry, *Dibdin's Bystander.*" The title is from Part 2 and after.

247. The CONTENTED SHEPHERD. *Lady's Monthly Museum,* n.s. I (December, 1806)–n.s. II (January, 1807). 2 parts (5300).

248. A CONTINUATION OF THE HISTORY AND ADVENTURES OF THE RENOWNED DON QUIXOTE DE LA MANCHA. Written Originally in Spanish, by the Licentiate Alonzo Fernandez de Avellaneda. Translated into English [from the French version of Le Sage] by William Augustus Yardley, Esq. In Two Volumes. *Novelist's,* XVI (1784). 1 part (183,000).

First published in 1784. The reprinting in the *Novelist's* includes six engravings, dated August 21–September 25, 1784.

249. The CONTRAST. *Lady's,* XXI (April, 1790)–XXII (January, 1791). 11 parts (14,200).

250. The CONVERSATIONS OF A YOUNG MESOPOTAMIAN and an English Merchant at Ispahan, in Persia, with the Occurrences of Their Travels from Thence to Bassora. *Weekly Amusement,* II (April 27–May 18, 1765). 4 parts (5000).

The story figures under several titles. The page-headings read "The History of Abbas the Hermit."

251. CORRESPONDENCE BETWEEN TWO FRIENDS. *Monthly Literary Recreations,* I (September, 1806)–III(November, 1807). 14 parts (16,200). Signed "V." Uncompleted.

A series 20 (actually 19) numbered letters, published one or two at a time. The early letters are dated 1806, and some of the later ones take account of a dispute occurring elsewhere in the magazine regarding the writings of Smollett.

252. The COTTAGE OF GLENMORE, a Story. *New Lady's,* VI (October, 1791)–VIII, (March, 1793). 5 parts (7000).

The story appeared irregularly, and was interrupted for eleven months in 1792.

253. The COTTAGE OF THE PYRENNEES. *Belle Assemblée,* n.s. VI (November–December, 1812). 2 parts (7500).

One of a series of "Spanish Novels."

254. A COTTAGE TALE. *Edinburgh*(2), n.s. XVI (July–August, 1800). 2 parts (6800). "For the *Edinburgh Magazine.*"

255. The COTTAGER'S DAUGHTER. "Tale 12," *Tell-Tale,* I (1803). 1 part (11,500).

256. The COTTAGER'S WIFE. *Christian Observer,* XII (March–May, 1813). 3 parts (9300). Signed "EVANDER."

"For the *Christian Observer.*"

257. [COUNT H——G AND SIGNORA CAMPIONI.] *Literary Reg.,* II, Nos. 45–46 (1770). 2 parts (5100).

A scandalous chronicle involving real persons, including "W–rt–y M–g–ue." For still another story about Count H——g, see No. 877.

The title of the above is from the Index to Vol. II.

258. COUNT SCHWEITZER, or the Mysterious Adventure. A Tale. *Lady's,* XXXIII (January–August, 1802). 7 parts (10,000). Uncompleted.

259. The COUNTRY LAIRD. A Tale by John Miller [i.e., James Hogg]. *Spy,* Nos. 24–26 (February 9–23, 1811). 3 parts (10,400).

Later revised and reprinted as "The Woolgatherer" in *The Brownie of Bodsbeck, and Other Tales, by James Hogg* (1818).

260. The COURT OF JUNO. A Vision. *Belfast Monthly,* III (October, 1809)–IV (February, 1810). 4 parts (24,900). Signed "NEMORENSIS."

"For the *Belfast Monthly Magazine.*"

261. CRAFT AND CRUELTY PREVAILING OVER JUSTICE. A Story Founded upon Fact. *Lady's Monthly Museum,* XV (September–December, 1805). 4 parts (15,000).

262. CREDULITY AND SUPERSTITION EXEMPLIFIED, or the Story of the Bleeding Finger. *Hibernian,* 1784 (February). 1 part (5300). Uncompleted.

263. The CREOLE. By Miss [Lucy] Peacock. *New Novelist's,* II (1787), 16–27. 1 part (8000).

From *The Rambles of Fancy* (1786).

a. The Creole. By Miss Peacock. *Caledonian*(1), I (September 21–Appendix, 1787). 3 parts.

264. CRIME AND PUNISHMENT. *Belle Assemblée,* IV (June, 1808)–V (July, 1808). 2 parts (8100).

265. The CRIMINAL. By Mr. [James] Harrison. *New Novelist's,* I (1786), 3–10. 1 part (5300).

Embellished with an engraving dated May 1, 1786.

a. The Criminal. By Mr. Harrison. *Caledonian*(1), I (February 23–March, 23, 1787). 3 parts.

b. The Criminal. Respectfully Inscribed to the Bench and the Bar. By Mr. Harrison. *Entertaining*(1), No. 8 (August, 1802). 1 part.

c. The Criminal. By Mr. Harrison. *Gleaner,* I (1805), 175–183. 1 part.

266. The CRIMINAL. From "Lost Honour," by Schiller. *German Museum,* III (October–December, 1800). 3 parts (8300).

A translation of Schiller's "Der Verbrecher aus verlorener Ehre" (*Thalia,* Vol. II, 1786). For other translations of the same story, see Nos. 267 and 1254.

a. The Criminal. *Belle Assemblée,* III (August–September, 1807). 2 parts.

b. The Landlord of the Sun. A True Story. *Hibernian*(2), II (October–December, 1810). 3 parts (7200).

A slight abridgment of the above, but with mottoes added. There is no acknowledgment of the source in either 266a or 266b.

267. The CRIMINAL. From "Lost Honour," By Schiller. *Universal,* n.s. XII (September, 1809) – n.s. XIII (January, 1810). 4 parts (7700). Signed "R.H."

A third translation of Schiller's "Der Verbrecher aus verlorener Ehre" (*Thalia,* Vol. II, 1786). For two earlier translations of the same story, see Nos. 266 and 1254.

268. The CRUEL BROTHER. In a Series of Letters. *Lady's,* VII (February, 1776)–VIII (March, 1777). 15 parts (20,000).

269. The CRUEL FATHER. *Lady's Monthly Museum,* XI (November, 1803); XII (January, 1804). 2 parts (6900).

270. The CRUELTY OF DESERTING NATURAL CHILDREN, and the Danger of Slight Breaches of Duty: Exemplified in the History of a Natural Daughter, as Related by Herself. *Weekly Amusement,* III (October 25–November 8, 1766). 3 parts (6100).

271. The CRUSADER, a Legend. From the Novel of *Scenes in Feudal Times,* by R. H. Wilmot, Lately Published. *Lady's,* XLI (September, 1810). 1 part (5000).

Wilmot's novel was published in 1809. In the December number and Supplement (1810), the *Lady's* published a shorter extract (4500 words) from the same novel, entitled "The Tournament."

272. The CULTIVATION OF PHILOSOPHY, or Virtuous Sensibility Necessary to Consistency of Character and Conduct. An Essay, Illustrated by an Affecting

Story Founded on Fact. *Universal,* XC (April–May, 1792). 2 parts (5100). Signed "C.W."

273. The CURATE AND HIS DAUGHTER, a Tale. *Bon Ton,* I (September, 1791) – II (March, 1792). 5 parts (10,000).
 a. The Curate and His Daughter. *Hibernian,* 1791 (October–November). 2 parts. Uncompleted.

274. CURIOUS ACCOUNT OF A DUMB PHILOSOPHER. Communicated by a Gentleman on a Tour in Germany. *Freemason's,* X (June, 1798) – XI (December, 1798). 7 parts (16,800). Signed "M." Uncompleted.

 The magazine expired with the December number.

275. CUTHBURGA, an Anglo Saxon Tale. *Monthly Misc.*(Dublin), I (April–July, 1796). 4 parts (9000). Uncompleted.

276. CYTHERIDA, a Tale. *Oxford,* X (July–September, 1773). 3 parts (5800).
 a. Cytherida, a Tale. *Literary Reg.,* V, Nos. 33, 37, 38, 42 (1773). 4 parts.

277. The DAIRYMAN'S DAUGHTER. [By the Rev. Legh Richmond.] *Christian Guardian,* II (February, 1810)–III (March, 1811). 5 parts (14,400). Signed "SIMPLEX."

 Part of the series called "The Poor Man's Friend." There is a later "Account of the Father of the 'Dairyman's Daughter'" in the same magazine (V, October, 1813), followed by "Recollections Concerning the Dairyman's Daughter" (VII, March, September, 1815). The latter is also signed "SIMPLEX."

 This story "considerably enlarged" was later gathered in a collection by Richmond entitled *Annals of the Poor* (1814). See No. 1361.

278. DALIDOR AND MULCE. A Moral Tale. (From the French of Madame de Genlis.) *Lady's,* XXXVI (October–November, 1805). 2 parts (7500).

 A translation of "Les Rencontres" in Vol. IV (1805) of Mme. de Genlis, *Nouveaux contes moraux et nouvelles historiques.* For a magazine reprinting of the French original, see No. 279.

279. DALIDOR ET MULCÉ. Par Mad. de Genlis. *Ambigu,* VII, No. 60 (November 30, 1804). 1 part (6400).

 This story was collected in the *Nouveaux contes moraux et nouvelles historiques,* Vol. IV (1805), under the title "Les Rencontres." For an English translation, see the preceding entry.

280. La DAME GENEREUSE. *Lady's,* XIII (March–October, 1782); XIV (May, July, 1783). 8 parts (7600). Signed "J—— H——."

 This story is in French, and readers were invited to submit translations (see No. 281).

281. La DAME GENEREUSE. Translated from the French. *Lady's,* XIV (February, May, 1783). 2 parts (6800).

Part 1, which is signed "J—— H——r," was offered as a translation of Parts 6–8 of the previous entry, and was probably written by the same person, who expressed a hope that someone else would translate "the former part." (P. 73.)

Part 2, offered in May, is a translation of Parts 1–5 of the previous entry, and is entitled "Translation of the Generous Lady." This version is signed "H./ Reading," who may again be the same writer.

a. The Generous Lady. Translated from the French. *Hibernian*, 1783 (June–July) 2 parts.

This reprinted, without acknowledgment, the above translation, but placed the parts in the proper order.

282. [The DANGER OF CHANGING OCCUPATIONS: Verified in the Life of a Berwickshire Farmer.] [By James Hogg.] *Spy*, Nos. 3–4 (September 15–22, 1810). 2 parts (9000).

The title is from the table of contents of the collected edition. This story was later revised and reprinted as "The Renowned Adventures of Basil Lee" in Hogg's *Winter Evening Tales* (1820).

283. The DANGER OF IMITATION. *Lady's*, XVIII (June–November, 1787). 6 parts (5500).

Part of a series entitled "Domestic Lessons for the Use of the Younger Part of the Female Readers of the *Lady's Magazine*."

284. The DANGER OF THE PASSIONS. An Allegorical Tale. [By John Murdoch.] *Universal Museum*, n.s. V (November–December, 1769). 2 parts (7800).

Later collected in Murdoch's *Pictures of the Heart, Sentimentally Delineated*, (1783).

285. The DANGER OF TOO GREAT SINCERITY IN MEN, and Too Great an Attachment to Money in the Fair Sex. *Weekly Mirror*, Nos. 2–3 (September 29–October 6, 1780). 2 parts (6300). Signed "T."

286. The DANGER OF TOO MUCH KNOWLEDGE without Solidity of Judgement. *Weekly Mirror*, Nos. 13–14 (December 15–22, 1780). 2 parts (5800).

a. The Danger of Too Much Knowledge without Solidity of Judgement. *Glasgow Mag. and Rev.*, I (October–November, 1783). 2 parts.

"For the *Glasgow Magazine and Review*."

287. The DANGER OF TRYING EXPERIMENTS. *Lady's*, III (October, 1772). 1 part (6800). Signed "R."

288. The DANGEROUS EFFECTS OF A WRONG EDUCATION, or the Fatal Contest. A Genuine Narrative of an Authentic Story. *Westminster*, II (July–August, 1774). 2 parts (6800). Signed "Z."

"For the *Westminster Magazine*."

289. The DANGERS OF DELAY. By John Gifford, Esq. [i.e., John Richards Green.] *New Novelist's,* II (1787), 325–337. 1 part (9600).

Embellished with an engraving dated April 1, 1788. But Volume II of the *New Novelist's* bears the date 1787.

a. The Dangers of Delay. By John Gifford, Esq. *Weekly Entertainer,* XI (May 26–June 23, 1788). 5 parts.

b. The Dangers of Delay, by John Gifford, Esq. *Gleaner,* II (1806), 213–228. 1 part.

290. The DANGERS OF DISSIPATION. *Lady's,* XIII (December, 1782)–XVI (January, 1785). 29 parts (30,000).

291. DAPHNIS AND PANDROSE, a Moral Tale. [By Mme. de Genlis.] *New Lady's,* VII (June–October, 1792). 4 parts (7250).

An unacknowledged translation of "Daphnis et Pandrose, ou les Oréades," included in *Les Veillées du château* (Paris, 1784). For other translations from the same work, see Nos. 165, 347, and 406.

292. DE COURVILLE CASTLE, a Romance. By a Young Lady. *Lady's,* XXVI (February, 1795) – XXVIII (April, 1797). 14 parts (18,100). Signed "E.F."

This may be the same story as that published much later under the title *The Gothic Story of De Courville Castle, or the Illegitimate Son* (1825?), cited in Block.

293. DE LA MARK AND CONSTANTIA, or Ancient Heroism. A Gothick Tale. *Marvellous,* IV (November 1, 1803). 1 part (29,000).

294. DE VALCOUR AND BERTHA, or the Prediction Fulfilled. A Romance. *Lady's Monthly Museum,* X (January–June, 1803). 6 parts (10,000).

295. DEBORAH, or the History of an Old Maid, Written by Herself. *Lady's,* XII (Supplement, 1781) – XIII (December, 1782). 13 parts (13,800).

296. The DEBTORS, a Narrative Found of Facts. By Maria. *Lady's,* XLIII (August–October, 1812). 3 parts (7100).

297. Selections from Boccaccio's *DECAMERON. Belle Assemblée,* n.s. VI (September, 1812) – (December, 1812). 4 parts (18,500). Uncompleted.

Only 13 "novels" are included in this selection, plus "Boccaccio's Introduction"; the series is interrupted after the 2nd novel of the 5th day. The text is that of the Charles Bagley translation (2nd edition, 1804).

298. The DELIGHTS OF BENEVOLENCE. By a Lady. *General,* V (February–November, 1791). 10 parts (21,000).

The receipt of the novel, a gratuitous contribution from "a Lady who forbids us to mention her name," was acknowledged in January, 1791 (p. ii). It is an imitation of Sterne.

a. The Delights of Benevolence. *Universal Mag. and Rev.,* V (March, 1791) – VI (December, 1791). 9 parts.

299. The DELUSIONS OF THE HEART. By Anna Maria Porter. *Lady's,* XXVI (November–Supplement, 1795). 3 parts (6300).

a. The Delusions of the Heart, a Tale. By Anna Maria Porter. *Scots,* LVIII (January–February, 1796). 2 parts.

300. The DENOUEMENT. A Scene from the "Clergyman's Tale." From the 3d Volume of *Canterbury Tales,* by Miss Harriet and Sophia Lee. *Universal,* CV (July, 1799). 1 part (5000).

From the new volume of *Canterbury Tales,* published in 1799. For another extract, from Vol. IV, see No. 1099.

a. The Denouement, etc. [Same title as above.] *Weekly Entertainer,* XXXIV (August 19–September 2, 1799). 3 parts.

b. The Denouement, a Tale. From the 3d Volume of *Canterbury Tales,* by Miss Harriet and Sophia Lee. *Scots,* LXI (August, 1799). 1 part.

c. The Denouement, etc. [Same title as No. 300b.] *Edinburgh*(2), n.s. XIV (August, 1799). 1 part.

d. The Denouement, a Scene from the *Canterbury Tales. Hibernian,* 1799 (August–September). 1 part.

301. DEO AND BETTINA, a Venetian Story. Introduced by Reflections on Plebeian Heroism, and Some Account of the Forms, Customs, and Usages of a Regatta. From the Countess of Rosenberg's *Moral and Sentimental Essays,* Lately Published. *European,* VIII (September–November, 1785). 3 parts (12,000).

From *Moral and Sentimental Essays, by J. W., C——t——ss of R——s——g* [i.e., Justin Wynne, Countess of Rosenberg] (1785).

a. Deo and Bettina, a Venetian Story, etc. [Same title as above.] *Gentleman's and London,* 1785 (October)–1786 (January). 4 parts.

302. The DEPENDENT, a Tale. By Mr. Bacon. *Pocket,* IV (April–June, 1796). 3 parts (12,500).

Possibly by James or Robert Bacon (see No. 232).

303. La DERNIÈRE VISION DE BUONAPARTÉ, telle qu'il l'a racontée à son confident Duroc. *Ambigu,* XL, Nos. 354 (January 30); 356 (February 20, 1813). 2 parts (5100).

Offered as Nos. 49–50 of the series "Le Logographe, ou le Moniteur secret."

304. DERWENT PRIORY, a Novel. In a Series of Letters. [By A. Kendall.] *Lady's* XXVII (January, 1796)–XXVIII (September, 1797). 22 parts (60,000).

The receipt of the MS. was acknowledged in December, 1795 (p. 538). After the completion of its run in the *Lady's,* the novel was reprinted as *Derwent Priory, or Memoirs of an Orphan. In a Series of Letters. First Published Periodically;*

now Republished with Additions. By the Author of THE CASTLE ON THE ROCK. London: Symonds, 1798. 2 vols. There was also a Dublin edition dated 1799.

a. Derwent Priory, a Novel. In a Series of Letters. *Hibernian,* 1796 (April)–1797 (November); 1801 (November–December). 22 parts.

The four-years interruption of this reprinting was never explained.

b. Derwent Priory, a Novel. In a Series of Letters. *Aberdeen*(2), I (June, 1796)–III (March, 1798). 22 parts.

305. The DESERTED VILLA, a Tale. *North British,* I, No. 9 (February 20, 1783)–II, No. 6 (October 24, 1783). 5 parts (5400).

"To the Editor of the *Caledonian Miscellany.*"

306. The DEVIL UPON TWO STICKS. Translated from the *Diable boiteux* of Monsieur Le Sage. To Which are Prefixed, Asmodeus's Crutches, a Critical Letter upon the Work, and Dialogues between Two Chimneys of Madrid. In Two Volumes. *Novelist's,* II (1780). 1 part (107,000).

This translation of *Le Diable boiteux* was first published in 1741. The reprinting in the *Novelist's* includes four engravings, dated July 22–August 12, 1780. For two magazine extracts from Le Sage's novel, see Nos. 461 and 645.

307. The DIAMOND RING, or Successful Artifices of Three London Wives. *Bon Ton,* IV (August, 1794)–V (June, 1795). 11 parts (20,500).

308. Extracts from *DINARBAS, A TALE, Being a Continuation of RASSELAS, PRINCE OF ABISSINIA. Gentleman's and London,* 1790 (August–September). 2 parts (5100).

A series of connected passages from the novel by Ellis Cornelia Knight (1790).

309. The DISASTERS OF TANTARABOBUS, Surnamed the Unfortunate, a Tale. Faithfully Transcribed from a Genuine Manuscript of the Learned Bumbulkius, Preserved in the Quidnunckian Library, and Now First Translated from the Original Low Dutch. *Universal Museum,* I (January–August, 1762). 8 parts (15,250).

a. The Disasters of Tantarabobus, etc. [Same title as above.] *New London,* I (July–December, 1788). 6 parts (5400). Uncompleted.

An unfinished and greatly condensed version of the above.

310. The DISBANDED FENCIBLE, a Tale. *Historical, Biographical, etc.,* II (August–September, 1800). 2 parts (5000). Signed "R."

a. The Disbanded Fencible, a Tale. *Hibernian,* 1800 (September–October). 2 parts.

b. The Disbanded Fencible, a Tale. *Literary and Masonic,* I (March, 1802). 1 part.

311. The DISSEMBLERS. By a Lady. *Lady's,* III (August, 1772). 1 part (7000). Signed "R."

312. DISSIPATION, or the Pernicious Effects of Bad Example. A Narrative Founded upon Fact. *Female Preceptor,* III, Nos. 3–4 (September–October, 1814). 2 parts (6200).

313. The DISTRESSED FUGITIVE. *Royal*(3), I (May–August, 1788). 4 parts (5000).

314. The DISTRESSED PAIR, or the History of Mrs. and Mrs. Morton. *Lady's,* II (Supplement, 1771). 1 part (6600). Signed "R."

315. DISTRESSFUL SITUATION OF GERALDINE. *Monthly Extracts,* III (August, 1792). 1 part (10,000).

Published as part of a review of Charlotte Smith, *Desmond, a Novel* (1792).

316. The DIVORCE, a Tale. Related by a Mother to her Daughter. *Belle Assemblée,* n.s. X (July–October, 1814). 4 parts (12,900).

317. The DOG OF MELAI. (Translated from Meissner.) *German Museum,* I (January–February, 1800). 2 parts (6200). Signed "M.G."

A translation of A. G. Meissner, "Der Hund des Melai" (*Erzählungen und Dialogen,* Vol. I, 1788). For other translations of the same story, see Nos. 856–857.

a. The Dog of Melai. *Belle Assemblée,* III (December, 1807). 1 part. Signed "M.G."

b. The Dog of Melai. (From the German of Meissner.) *General Chronicle,* VI (November–December, 1812). 2 parts.

318. DOMESTIC MISERY, or the Victim of Seduction. A Pathetic Tale, Addressed to the Unprincipled Libertine. *Marvellous,* II (February 1, 1803). 1 part (14,400).

319. DON ALGONAH, or the Sorceress of Montillo. A Romantic Tale. *Marvellous,* I (June 1, 1802). 1 part (29,600).

320. DON ALVARO, a Spanish Tale. *Belle Assemblée,* V (July, 1808). 1 part (5200). Signed "M.I.O."

a. Don Alvaro, a Spanish Tale. *Monthly Pantheon,* I (October, 1808). 1 part.

321. [DON QUIXOTE JUNIOR.] *Scots Town and Country,* I (July 21, 1778)–II (May 25, 1779). 13 parts (28,700).

The title is taken from the signatures, and from the index. The author published a sequel under the same title a year later (see the following entry).

322. [DON QUIXOTE JUNIOR.] *Edinburgh Eighth-Day,* I (September 1, 1779)–II (February 19, 1780). 5 parts (8300). Uncompleted?

"I am the great DON QUIXOTE jun. whose adventures made such a conspicuous figure in the *Scots Town and Country Magazine* [see No. 321], and whose succeeding adventures are always more extraordinary if possible than the past." (I, 12.) The title is from the table of contents of Vol. I.

323. DORILAS AND SAPPHIRA. *Lady's,* VIII (May–October, 1777); IX (March, 1778). 4 parts (6200).

324. DOUBLE CUCKOLDOM. From *The Art of Cuckoldom,* a New Work, Just Published, Price 2s.6d. With a Capital Engraving. *Bon Ton,* IV (May–August, 1794). 4 parts (6500).

Published "By Permission of the Translator." (IV, 136.)

325. The DOUBLE MISTAKE. A Tale, from the French. *Gentleman's,* XXXVI (September–November, 1766). 3 parts (8600).

326. DOVEDALE HALL, a Novel. By Mr. W[illiam]. Holloway. *Lady's Pocket,* IV Nos. 21–22 (October–November, 1796). 2 parts (7500). Uncompleted.

327. [DRAKE'S TRAVELS.] *Universal Spectator,* Nos. 616, 617, 621, 624, 625, 631 (July 16–November 8, 1740). 6 parts (10,000).

A free adaptation of Bishop Hall's *Mundus alter et idem* (1605), Book I, Chaps. I–XI. The title is taken from No. 621 ("The Second Chapter of Drake's Travels, continued.").

328. DREAM OF ZACHARY TORPEDO, ESQ. *Devil,* I, Nos. 2–7 (October 9–November 11, 1786). 6 parts (10,100).

For another dream of "Zachary Torpedo," see No. 1101.

329. A DREAM UPON THE OCCUPATIONS OF DEPARTED SOULS. Extracted from the *Satires* of [Gottlieb Wilhelm] Rabener. *German Museum,* I (March–June, 1800). 3 parts (9200).

A translation of "Ein Traum von den Beschäftigungen der abgeschiedenen Seelen" (*Neuen Beyträgen zum Vergnügen des Verstandes und Witzes,* 1744). The title of Parts 2 and 3 in the *Museum* reads "A Dream on the Occupation of the Departed Souls."

a. A Dream on the Occupations of Departed Souls. *Belle Assemblée,* III (August–October, 1807). 3 parts.

b. Occupation of Departed Souls. From the *Satires* of Rabener. *Entertaining*(2), III (October–December, 1815). 3 parts (6400).

An abridged version of the same translation.

330. The DRUID, a Tale. From the *Tales of Imagination. Glasgow Misc.,* II (1801), 290–318.

For another extract from the same collection, published in 1800, see No. 521.

331. A DRUID'S TALE, Written by Himself. *Edinburgh*(2), VII (June, 1788)–VIII (July, 1788). 2 parts (7700).

a. A Druid's Tale, Written by Himself. *Hibernian,* 1788 (October-November). 2 parts (6750).

An abridged version of the above.

332. The DUELLIST. *Belle Assemblée,* n.s. VIII (October–December, 1813). 3 parts (7600).

"Novel IV" of a series of "Spanish Novels."

333. The DUKE OF MILAN. By Master George Louis Lennox. *New Novelist's,* I (1787), 351–369. 1 part (13,800).

a. The Duke of Milan. By Master George Louis Lenox. *Weekly Entertainer,* IX (April 23–May 28, 1787). 6 parts.

334. The DUMB LOVER, a True Story. From the French of Madame M——. *Belle Assemblée,* n.s. X (November, 1814)–n.s. XI (February, 1815). 4 parts (8600).

Included under "Original Communications."

335. The DUPE OF LOVE AND FRIENDSHIP, or the Unfortunate Irishman. A Moral Tale, Founded on a Fact Which Happened at Leverpool [sic]. *Westminster,* I (July, 1773). 1 part (7700). Signed "F."

a. The Dupe of Love and Friendship, or the Unfortunate Irishman. A Moral Tale. Founded on a Fact Which Happened at Liverpool. *Hibernian,* 1773 (August). 1 part. Signed "F."

b. The Dupe of Love and Friendship, etc. [Same title as *Hibernian.*] *Perth,* V (September 24–October 1, 1773). 2 parts. Signed "F."

c. The Unfortunate Irishman. A Moral Tale, Founded on a Fact Which Happened in Liverpool. *Town and Country Weekly,* I, Nos. 35–38 (December 10–31, 1785). 4 parts.

d. The Unfortunate Irishman. Founded on a Fact Which Happened at Liverpool. *New Gleaner,* II (1810), 306–318.

Attributed to "Griffith." [Mrs. Elizabeth Griffith?]

336. The DUTCH PATRIOTS OF THE SIXTEENTH CENTURY. (A Free Translation, or Paraphrase, from the French of Mons. Bitaubé, Member of the National Institute.) *Lady's,* XLII (March, 1811)–XLVI (August, 1815). 47 parts (95,000).

From Paul Jérémie Bitaubé, *Les Bataves* (Paris, 1797). A prefatory note explains that "a very limited edition" of this history ("for it is not romance, but real history, only embellished with poetic ornament") was published by Robinsons under a different title several years before, but was destroyed, and is here revived "at the request of several respectable subscribers." The original English edition referred to was *The Batavians, or Virtue and Valour Crowned by Perseverance, from the French of C. Bitaubé* (London: Robinsons, 1799)–reviewed in the *Monthly Review* for October, 1800 (p. 208).

337. EARLY HISTORY OF THE HEROINE. [From the *Memoirs of a Scots Heiress.*] *Monthly Extracts,* I (October, 1791). 1 part (8300).

From the novel published in 1791—reprinted in the course of review. For another extract from the same review see No. 1358.

338. An EASTERN NOVEL. The Following Example Shews That the Practice of Virtue Renders a Family Illustrious. *Freemason's,* I (June–August, 1793). 3 parts (6600).

339. The EASTERN TURRET, or Orphan of Navona. "Tale 56," *Tell-Tale,* IV (1804). 1 part (9900).

340. ECCENTRICITIES OF A MODERN PHILOSOPHER. *Flowers of Literature for 1806,* V (1807), 275–297. 1 part (5000).

Attributed to "*Flim Flams,* 2nd Edition" [i.e., Isaac Disraeli, *Flim-Flams! or the Life and Errors of My Uncle and the Amours of My Aunt,* 1805].

341. EDMUND AND ALGITHA. *Britannic Mag. and Chronological Rep.,* n.s. I (May–October, 1807). 6 parts (14,500).

A translation and adaptation of Mme. de Gomez, "Histoire d'Etelred, roi d'Angleterre" ("Quinzième journée," *Les Journées amusantes,* 1722–1731). For other versions of the same story, see Nos. 166 and 574.

342. EDWARD AND PAULINA. *Lady's Monthly Museum,* n.s. XVI (April, 1814)–n.s. XVII (August, 1814). 5 parts (9600).

The title of Parts 2 and 3 is "Edward and Paulina, a German Tale."

343. EDWARD III AND THE COUNTESS OF SALISBURY. An Historical Novel [by Arnaud], Never Before Published. *Universal,* LV (November–December, 1774). 2 parts (5000).

A translation of Baculard D'Arnaud, "Salisbury" (*Oeuvres,* VI, 1774), acknowledged in the prefatory paragraph in the *Universal,* which also copied the engraving from the French edition. Written "For the *Universal Magazine.*" The editor of the magazine has added some historical information.

Curiously, Arnaud's original may have been prompted by an earlier piece also printed in the *Universal.* In a note appended to the 1774 edition of "Salisbury" Arnaud wrote: "Le fonds de cette Nouvelle ne m'appartient pas; il est emprunté d'une espèce d'anecdote insérée dans un journal intitulé le *magazin Anglais.*" This piece to which Arnaud refers was probably "The Triumph of Virtue" first printed in the *Universal,* dealing with the relations of Edward III and the Countess of Salisbury (see No. 1278).

344. EDWIN, or the Wandering Fugitive. "Tale 80," *Tell-Tale,* VI (1805). 1 part (13,400).

345. The EFFECTS OF SELFISH PRINCIPLES. *Belle Assemblée,* V (July–September, 1808). 3 parts (11,800).

346. The EFFECTS OF SENSIBILITY, a True Story. *Edinburgh*(2), n.s. III (March–April, 1794). 2 parts (12,000).

347. EGLANTINE, or Indolence Reformed. From the *Tales of the Castle.* [By Mme. de Genlis.] *New Gleaner,* II (1810), 182–198. 1 part (9200).

A translation of "Églantine, ou l'Indolente corrigée" in Volume I of Mme. de Genlis, *Les Veillées du château* (1784)—hence "Tales of the Castle." This is a quite different translation, however, from that in Holcroft's *Tales of the Castle* (1785), even though it bears the same title. For other translations of stories in *Les Veillées,* see Nos. 165, 291, and 406.

348. The ELDER BROTHER AND THE YOUNGER BROTHER. *New Novelist's,* I (1787), 316–323. 1 part (6000).

Embellished with an engraving dated March 1, 1787.

a. The Elder Brother and the Younger Brother. *Harvest Home,* II (1808), 248–258.

349. The ELDER SISTER AND THE YOUNGER SISTER. Written during the American War. *New Novelist's,* I (1787), 406–415. 1 part (7000).

Embellished with an engraving dated May 1, 1787.

a. The Elder Sister, etc. [Same title as above.] *Caledonian*(1), I (July 13–August 10, 1787). 3 parts.

350. ELEAZAR AND NAPHTALI. From the French of M. Florian. By J. J. *European,* LXVI (September–December, 1814). 4 parts (18,750).

A prose translation of Florian's *Éliézer et Nephtali* (Paris, an X) [1802–1803]. For another translation of the same, see "Eliezer and Nephtaly."

351. ELIEZER AND NEPHTALY, a Free Translation from the French of Florian. *Monthly Literary Recreations,* I (July–October, 1806). 4 parts (12,300). Signed "Y."

A prose translation of Florian's *Éliézer et Nephtali* (Paris, an X) [1802–1803]. For another translation of the same story, see No. 350.

352. ELIZA, or the Hermit's Cell. A Novel. By Miss Eliza Yeames. *Lady's,* XXXVI (April–August, 1805). 5 parts (19,250).

353. ELIZA, or the Northern Heiress. *New Lady's,* VIII (May–November, 1793). 6 parts (12,000).

354. ELIZA GORDON, or the Fair Run-a-Way. A Sentimental Story from Real Life. *Rambler's,* II (September–November, 1784). 1 part (5000).

355. ELIZA LASCELLS, a Tale. *Universal,* CXIII (September–November, 1803). 3 parts (15,500).

a. Eliza Lascells, a Tale. *Weekly Entertainer,* XLIII (January 2–February 27, 1804). 9 parts.

356. ELLEN, or the Parsonage. A Tale. In a Series of Letters. *Lady's Monthly Museum,* n.s. X (June, 1811)–n.s. XIII (November, 1812). 14 parts (23,500). Signed "W.R."

357. The ELOPEMENT, or the Amours of Lady J—— and Mr. O——. *Court and City,* I (January–March, 1770). 3 parts (8300).

358. The ELVILLE FAMILY SECRETS, a Novel. By the Author of "Emily de Veronne." *Lady's,* XXXV (January–November, 1804); XXXVII (March, April, May, July, September, November, 1806); XXXVIII (January, May, August, 1807); XXXIX (January, March, June, August, 1808); XL (February, July, 1809); XLI (March, August, 1810). 23 parts (62,200).

The Editor of the *Lady's* had a great deal of difficulty in securing continuations of this novel, which was interrupted for fifteen months in 1804–1806.

"Emily Veronne" was published five years earlier in the same magazine (see No. 364).

359. The EMBARRASSMENTS OF LOVE, a Dramatic Novel. [By John Murdoch.] *Westminster*, I (October, 1773). 1 part (7000).

"For the *Westminster Magazine*." Later revised and reprinted in Murdoch's *Pictures of the Heart, Sentimentally Delineated* (1783), from which Nos. 359a and 359b were derived.

a. The Embarrassments of Love. By Mr. Murdoch. *New Novelist's*, I (1786), 122–132. 1 part (7700).

b. Embarrassments of Love. By Mr. Murdoch. *Caledonian*(1), I (December 15, 1786–February 9, 1787). 4 parts.

360. The EMIGRANTS. *Belle Assemblée*, n.s. V (April–May, 1812). 2 parts (5000). Signed "Eliza."

361. EMILIUS AND SOPHIA, or the Recluse. *Universal*, n.s. XIV (August–November, 1810). 4 parts (9750). Uncompleted. Signed "T."

Attributed to "the works of Rousseau" (p. 117). This translation, slightly abridged, covers only about half of the posthumous novel *Émile et Sophie, ou les Solitaires* (1780).

362. Mr. Kett's New Novel, *EMILY*. *Belle Assemblée*, VII (October–November, 1809). 2 parts (11,800).

An extract from the Rev. Henry Kett, *Emily, a Moral Tale* (1809), offered in the course of a review.

363. EMILY ATKINS. By Mr. [Henry] Mackenzie. *Gleaner*, II (1806), 88–98. 1 part (6100).

Adapted from Chapters 26–29 of *The Man of Feeling* (1771).

364. EMILY VERONNE, or the Perfidious Friend. A Novel. *Lady's*, XXX (January, 1799)–XXXII (October, 1801); XXXIII (February, 1802). 23 parts (80,000).

By the author of "The Elville Family Secrets" [see No. 358]. The novel was continued irregularly after March, 1800.

365. EMMA, or the Artist. *Universal*, CXII (April, June, 1803). 2 parts (5100).

366. EMPIRE OF NOTHING, a Vision. [By William Roberts.] *Looker-On*, Nos. 16 (May 1); 20 (May 15, 1792). 2 parts (9450).

367. The ENCHANTED LOVERS, a Fairy Tale. *Westminster*, I (December, 1773). 1 part (6000).

"For the *Westminster Magazine*."

368. The ENGLISH HERMIT; or Unparalleled Sufferings and Surprizing Adventures of Mr. Philip Quarll, Who Was Lately Discovered on an Uninhabited Island in the South-Sea, Where He Had Lived above Fifty Years, without any Human Assistance. [By Edward Dorrington (*pseud.*?).] *Novelist's,* XXI (1786). 1 part (81,000).

First published in 1727. The "Preface" is signed "P.L." [i.e., Peter Longueville], who declares that the work is by Dorrington. It has been attributed to Alexander Bicknell. The reprinting in the *Novelist's* includes two engravings, dated May 6 and May 13, 1786.

369. L'ÉPOUSE IMPERTINENTE PAR AIR. Nouvelle, par Madame de Genlis. *Ambigu,* VI, No. 50 (August 20, 1804). 1 part (8000).

First published in the *Mercure de France* (No. 125, November 19, 1803).

370. ERNESTINA, or the Fair German. "Tale 47," *Tell-Tale,* IV (1804). 1 part (13,500).

An unacknowledged translation of Mme. Riccoboni's *Histoire d'Ernestine* (1765). For an early magazine version of the same story see No. 573.

371. The ERROR OF A GOOD FATHER. A Tale, by M. Marmontel. *Universal,* XC (April–May, 1792). 2 parts (11,000).

A translation of "L'Erreur d'un bon père" (first printed in the *Mercure,* 1791), extracted without acknowledgment from *Tales, Translated from the French of M. Marmontel* (1792).

a. The Error of a Good Father, *Monthly Extracts,* III (May, 1792). 1 part.

Extracted from the same volume of translations, as part of a review.

b. The Error of a Good Father. A Tale, by M. Marmontel. *Universal Mag. and Rev.,* VII (June, 1792)–VIII (October, 1792). 4 parts.

c. The Error of a Good Father. A Tale, by M. Marmontel. *Weekly Entertainer,* XX (July 2–30, 1792). 5 parts.

372. ESSAYS ON TRANSMIGRATION. *Royal*(3), I (January–June, 1788). 7 parts (5100). Uncompleted?

There were two February numbers of the *Royal Magazine.*

373. EULALIA, or the Force of Prejudice. *Lady's,* II (September, 1771). 1 part (5600).

374. EUPHEMIA. In Two Volumes. By Mrs. Charlotte Lennox. *Universal Mag. and Rev.,* IV (November, 1790)–V (March, 1791). 3 parts (9500).

A summary of *Euphemia* (1790) with extracts from the "Dublin printed" edition.

375. EVANDER AND CARAMANTA, a Love Romance. *New Lady's,* III (December–Supplement, 1788). 2 parts (8000).

a. Evander and Caramanta, a Love Romance. *Hibernian,* 1789 (January–February). 2 parts.

376. "EVERYTHING DEPENDS ON THE MANNER." A Tale, from the Spanish. *Belfast Monthly,* I (October–November, 1808). 2 parts (9300).

"For the *Belfast Monthly Magazine.*"

377. The EXCELLENT WIFE. From *Edward: Various Views of Human Nature, Taken from Life and Manners, Chiefly in England,* by Dr. [John] Moore. *Universal,* XCIX (October, 1796). 1 part (5000).

From the same novel, recently published (1796), the *Universal* also offered "Excellent Lessons against Youthful Cunning" (December, 1796) and "Lessons of Humanity, a Conversation" (February, 1797). The three extracts from *Edward* total 11,500 words.

a. The Excellent Wife, etc. [Same title as above.] *Weekly Entertainer,* XXVIII (November 14–December 5, 1796). 1 part.

The *Entertainer* also published the first of the supplementary extracts.

b. The Excellent Wife. *Scots,* LIX (January, 1797). 1 part.

Attributed to Dr. Moore's novel.

c. The Excellent Wife. By Dr. Moore. *Aberdeen*(2), II (April–May, 1797). 2 parts.

378. The EXCURSION, by Mrs. Brooke, Author of *Lady Julia Mandeville* and *Emily Montagu*[*e*]. *Universal,* LXI (July–October, 1777). 4 parts (15,500).

An abridgment of Frances Brooke's novel of the same name (1777).

a. The Excursion, by Mrs. Brooke, etc. [Same title as above.] *Hibernian,* 1777 (August–November). 4 parts (13,700).

A slightly abridged version of the above.

379. The EXILE. By Miss Anna Maria Porter. *Lady's Pocket,* IV, Nos. 18–19 (July–August, 1796). 2 parts (5800).

380. The EXPEDITION OF HUMPHRY CLINKER. By Dr. Smollett. In Three Volumes. *Novelist's,* XIX (1785). 1 part (146,000).

Originally published in 1771. The reprinting in the *Novelist's* includes four engravings, dated July 9–July 30, 1785.

381. EXPERIENCE, a Tale. *Edinburgh Weekly,* XIV (November 28–December 5, 1771). 2 parts (5000).

382. EXTRAORDINARY CONVERSION OF AN ACTRESS. Found among the Papers of the Celebrated French Writer [Charles Pinot] Duclos. *Belle Assemblée,* n.s. II (October, 1810). 1 part (5000).

A translation of "La Conversion de Mademoiselle Gautier, imprimée sur le manuscrit autographe" (*Oeuvres complètes de Duclos,* X, 1806, pp. 285ff.).

383. EXTRAORDINARY PROPHECY! The Visions of Aaron, the Son of Adriel,

Which He Saw Concerning the Rise and Fall of the Sister Nations. *Monthly Pantheon,* III (June, 1809). 1 part (5400).

384. The EXTRAORDINARY WIFE. From Marmontel. A New Translation. By Louisa D'Argent. *Lady's,* XI (March–May, 1780). 3 parts (9100). Signed "E."

A translation of "La Femme comme il y en a peu" (*Contes moraux.* Vol. III, 1765). For other translations of the same story, see Nos. 475, 917, and 1348.

385. The FAIR ADULTERESS, or the Treacherous Brother. A Novel. *Universal,* XXXVII (December–Supplement, 1765). 2 parts (11,100).

A slight abridgment of the novel published under the same title in 1743.

386. The FAIR APOSTATE, a True History. *St. James's*(2), I (April–November, 1774). 8 parts (11,750).

"For the *St. James's Magazine.*"

387. The FAIR FUGITIVE, or the Elopement of Miss E—— with Captain ****. *Court and City,* I (July, 1770). 1 part (6000).

388. The FAIR HIBERNIAN, a Turkish Tale. *Edinburgh*(2), n.s. V (February–March, 1795). 1 part (9000).

a. The Fair Hibernian. *Britannic,* V, Nos. 70–71 (1798). 2 parts.

Part of the series entitled "Memoirs of Love and Gallantry."

389. The FAIR PENITENT, an Historical Romance. (From the French of Madame de Genlis.) *Lady's,* XXXVII (January–November, 1806). 6 parts (12,100).

A translation of "La Jeune Pénitente" (*Mercure de France,* No. 129, December 17 1803). For a magazine printing of the French original, see No. 723.

390. The FAIR PHILOSOPHER, a Moral Tale. *New Musical,* I (September, 1774–January, 1775). 5 parts (6200).

391. The FAIR SAVAGE, or History of Cleodon and Felidia. [By Mme. de Gomez.] "Tale 32," *Tell-Tale,* III (1804). 1 part (12,900).

An unacknowledged adaptation of the "History of Cleodon" in Mrs. Haywood's *Belle Assemblée* (1724–1726), translated in turn from Mme. de Gomez "Histoire de Cleodon" ("Septième journée," *Les Journées amusantes,* 1722–1731). For other extracts from the same English translation, see BELLE ASSEMBLÉE (Index).

392. The FAITHFUL PAIR. *Belle Assemblée,* n.s. IV (January–May, 1814). 5 parts (12,200).

"Novel V" of a series of "Spanish Novels."

393. The FALSE APPEARANCES, or Innocence Vindicated. A Persian Tale. [By La Motte.] *Every Man's,* I (March–April, 1772). 2 parts (5000).

A translation of "Salned et Garaldi, nouvelle orientale, par feu M. de la Motte," in the *Mercure de France* (October, 1751), pp. 45–65. Concerning this translation, the Editor of the *Every Man's* wrote: "The editor of this moral tale, assures his readers, that it has never appeared before in an English dress; and that the ground work of the story is founded on facts, though it is decorated with the ornaments of romance." (I, 438.)

For an earlier translation, which was widely reprinted, see "Asem and Salned" (No. 122).

394. FALSE APPEARANCES, or the History of the Viscountess de Vassy. *Lady's,* XXVIII (December, 1797)–XXIX (April, 1798). 6 parts (14,000).

395. The FALSE KEY, a Tale. *Edinburgh*(2), n.s. X (July–September, 1797). 3 parts (8800).

396. FAMILY ANECDOTES. By a Disappointed Lover. *Lady's Monthly Museum,* n.s. VII (September, 1809)–n.s. IX (July, 1810). 9 parts (25,600). Uncompleted.

Addressed "to the Editor of the *Lady's Museum.*"

397. FAMILY ANECDOTES. (Founded on Facts.) By Sophia T——. *Lady's,* XXXVII (April, 1806)–XXXVIII (March, 1807). 11 parts (34,250).

By Sophia Troughton, the author of "Sketches from Nature" (No. 1159).

398. The FAMOUS AND RENOWNED HISTORY of the Life and Glorious Actions of the Mighty Hercules of Greece. *Penny Medley,* No. 11 (1746). 1 part (5900).

399. FANNY, or the Happy Repentance. From the French of M. D'Arnaud. *Universal,* XXXIX (July, 1766). 1 part (7500).

A translation of Baculard D'Arnaud, *Fanni, ou l'Heureux repentir, histoire angloise* (1764). This is the first observed appearance of Arnaud in an English magazine. The text is a slight abridgment (unacknowledged) of the English version recently published in a trade edition by Becket under the same title.

a. Fanny, etc. [Same title as above.] *Weekly Misc.*(Sherborne), XV (December 25, 1780–January 1, 1781). 2 parts.

b. The Happy Repentance, or Memoirs of Lord Whatley. *Bouquet,* II, Nos. 7–9 (January–March, 1796). 3 parts (6500).

A further abridgment of the above text.

c. Fanny, or the Happy Repentance. From the French of M. D'Arnaud. *Gleaner,* I (1805), 190–201. 1 part.

The same version as that printed in the *Bouquet.*

400. The FARMER'S DAUGHTER, an Interesting Story. *Universal,* CXIII (July–August, 1803). 2 parts (6900). Signed "ANONYMOUS."

Addressed "To the Editor of the *Universal Magazine.*"

a. The Farmer's Daughter, a Tale. *Edinburgh*(2), n.s. XXII (August–September, 1803). 2 parts.

401. The FARMER'S DAUGHTER OF ESSEX. A Novel, by James Penn, Vicar of Clavering cum Langley, in the County of Essex, and Lecturer of St. Ann and Agnes, Aldersgate. *Universal,* XL (June, 1767). 1 part (5000).

a. The Farmer's Daughter of Essex. *New London,* IV (November, 1788). 1 part.

402. The FARMER'S SABBATH. *Scotch Cheap Repository,* Nos. 6–7 (1808). 2 parts (9400).

403. The FATAL DISCOVERY. No Novel. *Westminster,* I (November, 1773). 1 part (6200).

"For the *Westminster Magazine.*"

a. The Fatal Discovery. *Hibernian,* 1773 (December). 1 part.

404. [The FATAL EFFECTS OF FALSE APOLOGIES AND PRETENCES: a Story.] [By John Hawkesworth.] *Adventurer,* Nos. 54–56 (May 12–May 19, 1753). 3 parts (5200).

The title is from the table of contents of the first collected edition.

a. [The Fatal Effects of False Apologies and Pretences: The History of Charlotte and Maria.] *Weekly Amusement,* III (May 17–June 14, 1766). 3 parts.

The title appears only on Parts 2 and 3.

b. That Truth Should Always Be Adhered to, Exemplified. *Weekly Misc.* (Sherborne), I (October 11–18, 1773). 1 part.

c. That Truth Should Always Be Adhered to, Exemplified. *Weekly Misc.* (London), II, Nos. 58–59 (1773). 1 part.

405. [The FATAL EFFECTS OF FASHIONABLE LEVITIES: The Story of Flavilla.] [By John Hawkesworth.] *Adventurer,* Nos. 123–125 (January 8–15, 1754). 3 parts (6400).

The title is from the table of contents of the first collected edition.

a. Fatal Effect of Fashionable Levities, Exemplified in the Story of Flavilla. *Weekly Amusement,* II (May 18–June 1, 1765). 3 parts.

b. The Necessity of Abstaining from the Appearance of Evil. *Weekly Misc.* (Sherborne), II (May 16–23, 1774). 2 parts.

c. The Necessity of Abstaining from the Appearance of Evil. *Weekly Misc.* (London), Nos. 88–89 (1774). 2 parts.

d. The Story of Flavilla. By Dr. Hawkesworth. *Harvest Home,* I (1807), 150–159. 1 part.

406. The FATAL EFFECTS OF INDULGING THE PASSIONS: Exemplified in the

History of M. de la Paliniere. By Madame [de] Genlis. *European,* VI (December, 1784) – VII (February, 1785). 3 parts (14,500).

A translation of "Histoire de M. de la Palinière" (*Les Veillées du château,* 1784). The translation is presumably Thomas Holcroft's since it is identical with that of "The History of M. de la Paliniere" (*Tales of the Castle,* Vol. I, 1785), published the following year. In the *European,* it is described as written "For the *European Magazine,*" and ornamented with an engraving (facing p. 93, Vol. VII) showing "M. de la Paliniere at Julia's Tomb." For other translations from *Les Veillées,* see Nos. 165, 291, and 347.

a. The Fatal Effects of Indulging the Passions, etc. [Same title as above.] *Hibernian,* 1785 (January–May). 5 parts.

b. The Slave of Sensuality, or Fatal Effects of Indulging the Passions. A Moral Story. From the French of Madame Genlis. *New Novelist's,* II (1787), 224–244. 1 part.

407. FATAL EFFECTS OF JEALOUSY, a Spanish Novel. *Universal,* XLI (November–December, 1767). 2 parts (12,000).

408. The FATAL EFFECTS OF REVENGE. From the French. *Court Miscellany,* IV (July–September, 1768). 3 parts (7100).

409. FATAL EFFECTS OF SEDUCTION. A Tale, by A. K. *Monthly Visitor,* XIII (May–August, 1801). 4 parts (5400).

"For the *Monthly Visitor.*" By A. Kendall (?).

410. FATAL INCONSTANCY. *Britannic,* XII, Nos. 167–168 (1805). 2 parts (6100).

Part of the series entitled "Memoirs of Love and Gallantry."

411. The FATAL MISTAKE, or the History of Mr. Elliot. Written by Himself. (From *Female Stability,* a Novel. See Our Review.) *London,* L (July–August, 1781). 2 parts (5000).

From the novel by Charlotte Palmer, published in 1780. The review mentioned in the title is found on p. 338 of the July number of the magazine.

a. The Fatal Mistake, or the History of Mr. Elliot. Written by Himself. (From *Female Stability,* a New Novel.) *Edinburgh Weekly,* LIII (September 27–October 4, 1781). 2 parts.

The *Edinburgh* also reprinted the review from the *London* (p. 159).

412. The FATE OF ANGELLA, or the Spectre of the Ruins. A Romance. (Written Expressly for This Work.) *Compiler,* II, Nos. 8–14 (1808). 7 parts (10,000).

413. The FATHER AND DAUGHTER, a Tale of Saffron-Hill. *Scourge,* VI (August, October, 1813). 2 parts (7100).

The introductory letter, which is signed "Sam Shamble," dedicates this "affecting narrative" to Mrs. Opie [author of *The Father and Daughter,* 1801].

414. FATHER INNOCENT, Abbot of the Capuchins; or the Crimes of Cloisters *Marvellous,* II (April 1, 1803). 1 part (30,000).

A disguised redaction and condensation of Lewis's *The Monk.*

415. FATHER PAUL, or the Castle of Conradsburg. A Story of the Years 1296 and 1796. *German Museum,* III (May–June, 1801). 2 parts (6000).

416. Le FAUX PRINCE DE MODENE, anecdote du dix-huitième siècle. *Ambigu,* VII, No. 56 (October 20, 1804). 1 part (9000).

417. The FAVOURITE. *Lady's,* XIX (May–November, 1788). 7 parts (7200).

The "Fifth Lesson" in a series entitled "Domestic Lessons for the Use of the Younger Part of the Female Readers of the *Lady's Magazine.*"

418. FELISA. (Said to Be a True Story of Former Times.) *European,* XLV (May–June, 1804). 2 parts (5250). Signed "DIONYSIUS."

419. FEMALE CORRESPONDENCE. Miss Maria Vernon to Lady Walbrook. *Lady's,* XII (January, 1781)–XIII (March, 1782). 14 parts (13,700).

Each part represents a single letter in the series.

420. FEMALE CORRESPONDENCE, on the Moral, Social, and Relative Duties, Interspersed with Observations on Various Subjects. *Court, City and Country*(2), I (January–April, 1788). 4 parts (7500). Uncompleted.

421. FEMALE FORTITUDE, or the History of the Duchess of C——, Written by Herself. [By Mme. de Genlis.] *Lady's,* XVII (January–July, 1786). 7 parts (16,000).

Translated from the "Histoire de la duchesse de C***, écrite par elle-même," in Mme. de Genlis's *Adèle et Théodore* (1782). For other translations of the same story see Nos. 9, 12, and 888.

"Adela and Theodore" was being serialized in the *Lady's* (1785–1789), when "Female Fortitude" began its seven-month's run, but the interpolated history of the novel was still several years in the future. Since "Female Fortitude" is an unacknowledged translation of Mme. de Genlis's story, the editor of the *Lady's* was probably unaware of the duplication.

422. [FEMALE FORTITUDE REWARDED.] *Hibernian,* 1776 (December–Appendix). 2 parts (7100). Signed "ACASTO."

The title is from Part 2.

423. FEMALE GRATITUDE, or the History of Eliza Bentley. *Universal,* LXXXIII (August–September, 1788). 2 parts (5400). Signed "SERAPHINA."

a. Female Gratitude, etc. [Same title as above.] *Beauties of Magazines, etc.,* II (November, 1788). 1 part.

b. Female Gratitude, etc. [Same title.] *Caledonian*(2), I (December, 1788)–II (January, 1789). 2 parts.

c. Female Gratitude, etc. [Same title.] *Alston,* I, Nos. 8–9 (November–December, 1799). 2 parts. Signed "SERAPHINA."

424. The FEMALE QUIXOTE, or the Adventures of Arabella. By Mrs. Lenox. In Two Volumes. *Novelist's,* XII (1783). 1 part (158,000).

First published in 1752. The reprinting in the *Novelist's* included four engravings dated May 17–June 7, 1783.

425. The FEMALE TOURISTS. In a Series of Letters, from a French Lady, during a Summer's Tour in England. *Lady's Monthly Museum,* 3.s.I (January, 1815)–3.s.III (January, 1816). 10 parts (13,300).

426. [FEMALE VIRTUE AND GREATNESS DISPLAYED in Principle and Refined Improvements.] *London,* XLVI (January, 1777)–XLVIII (October, 1779). 27 parts (87,000). Signed "ARPASIA."

The story figures under several titles, most of them variants of the above, which was employed in Part 2. It was also labeled (from Part 16) "The History of Nancy Pelham." Addressed "To the Editor of the *London Magazine.*"

The story was written by a "correspondent" of the *London,* concerning whom the Editor wrote: "Our worthy correspondent Curiosus, can only receive all the information the publisher is able to give respecting the history of Nancy Pelham; it was written by an American lady, but he never knew either her name or rank in life." ("Acknowledgements to Correspondents," June, 1779, p. 288.)

There was some question whether the novel would be published by Baldwin separately, after its conclusion in the *London,* but evidently the proprietors decided against it. (See XLVII, 192.)

a. Female Virtue and Greatness Displayed. A New Novel. *Hibernian,* 1777 (February)–1779 (November). 31 parts. Signed "ARPASIA."

427. The FEMALE VOLUNTEER. A Pathetic History. *London,* XLIX (December–Appendix, 1780). 2 parts (10,400).

"For the *London Magazine.*"

a. The Female Volunteer. A Pathetic History. *Hibernian,* 1780 (Appendix)–1781 (January). 2 parts.

b. The Female Volunteer. A Pathetic History. *Cumberland,* IV (January–April, 1781). 4 parts.

c. The Female Volunteer. A Pathetic History. *Weekly Misc.*(Sherborne), XV (March 12–April 2, 1781). 4 parts.

428. La FEMME DE LETTRES. *Ambigu,* XXVII, No. 236 (October 20, 1809). 1 part (10,500).

429. FERDINAND AND ISABEL, or Love at First Sight. A Tale, By Mr. Bacon. *Pocket,* V (September, 1796). 1 part (5200).

Possibly by James or Robert Bacon (see No.232).

430. FERNANDO OF CASTILE, or the Husband of Two Wives. *Marvellous,* IV (March 1, 1804). 1 part (8400).

431. FICTITIOUS MEMOIRS. A Fragment. *Universal,* CII (April, June, 1798). 2 parts (5000).

Addressed "To the Editor of the *Universal Magazine*" by "A Correspondent" who says it is the work of a deceased friend, who "evidently had Fielding in his eye" (p. 102). The work contains only two "chapters."

432. FIDELIA AND ERNESTUS, the Unfortunate Lovers. *London,* XLIII (February, March, June, 1774). 3 parts (5400).

"For the *London Magazine.*" There are verbal similanties to No. 148.

433. The FIERY CROSS, or Affecting Story of Tom Bragwell, Brought Home to the Consciences of Those It May Concern. *Cheap,* II (September–December, 1814). 3 parts (24,000). Signed "O.P."

434. FILIAL AFFECTION, or Fraternal Hatred. The Names Fictitious, But the Story Founded upon Fact. *Lady's Monthly Museum,* I July–September, 1798). 3 parts (6500).

435. The FIRST NAVIGATOR, by [Salomon] Gessner. In Two Cantos. Translated from the French, by George Moore, Author of *Grasville Abbey. Lady's,* XXXII (February–June, 1801). 5 parts (8800).

A translation of *Der erste Schiffer* (1762), of which there were already several French translations. For an earlier magazine translation of the same poem, see "A Tale from the French." "Grasville Abbey," published first in the *Lady's* (1793–1797) [No. 478], had been re-issued as a 3-volume novel (1797).

a. The First Navigator, by Gessner, etc. [Same title as above.] *Hibernian,* 1801 (September–December). 4 parts.

436. FITZALBERT AND OLIVIA. *Lady's Monthly Museum,* n.s. VIII (May–June, 1810), 2 parts (6100).

437. FITZMAURICE, an Hibernian Tale. *Lady's Monthly Museum,* n.s. VIII (March. 1810)–n.s. IX (July, 1810). 5 parts (9600). Uncompleted.

438. FITZWALTER, or the Sophistry of the Passions. *Beau Monde*(1), I (April, 1807)–II (September, 1807). 6 parts (10,500). Signed "M.C."

439. The FLEET PRISON; or a Cure for Extravagance, and a Convincing Proof of the Fallacy of Fashionable Friendship. [By Mrs. Mary Pilkington?] *Lady's,* XLI (February, April, 1810); XLIII (April–June, 1812). 5 parts (15,400).

The two-year's interruption in the story was ascribed to "the unfortunate illness of the ingenious Authoress" (XLIII, 147; also XLI, [242]), who seems to be Mrs. Pilkington (see XL, 441).

440. The FLOWERS, or the Artists. (From the French of Madame de Genlis.) *General Chronicle,* I (March, 1811)–II (Supplement, 1811). 7 parts (14,500).

Extracted (and translated) from *La Botanique historique et littéraire... suivie d'une nouvelle intitulée: Les Fleurs, ou les Artistes, par Madame de Genlis* (1810).

441. [The FOLLY OF ASPIRING TO EXPENSIVE AMUSEMENTS.] *Town and Country*, I (February, 1769). 1 part (5400).

Addressed "To the Printer of the *Town and Country Magazine*." The title is taken from the heading of p. 81.

a. Folly of Aspiring to Expensive Amusements, and the Fatal Consequences of a Love of Dissipation. *Strabane*, II (May, 1800). 1 part.

442. [FOLLY OF EXTRAVAGANCE. The Story of Misargyrus.] [By Dr. Samuel Johnson.] *Adventurer*, Nos. 34 (March, 3 1753), 41, 53, 62 (June 9, 1753). 4 parts (7000). Signed "T."

The title is from the table of contents of the collected edition.

443. The FORCE OF DESPAIR, a Most Affecting Novel. Founded on Facts, Authenticated by Two Sentences of the Parliaments of Dijon and Thoulouse, in France. (Never before Published.) *Hibernian*, 1772 (December) – 1773 (January). 2 parts (11,150). Signed "J. S. Dodd."

Part 1 of this story appeared in both versions of the *Hibernian* (see the Note under *Hibernian* in the "Register of Periodicals"). But Part 2 was printed only in Marchbank and Seguin (January, 1773, pp. 691–698). It is surprising to find the more piratical of the two periodicals publishing the more complete version of the story. This possibly represents a maneuver on the part of Marchbank and Sequin, intended to present evidence of priority.

444. The FORCE OF PATERNAL LOVE, a Dramatic Tale, Founded on Fact. *Universal Museum*, n.s. VII (February–March, 1771). 2 parts (5000).

445. The FOREST OF ALSTONE. An Original Tale, Founded on Fact. By E. Caroline Litchfield. *Lady's*, XXIII (April–September, 1792). 4 parts (5800). Uncompleted.

The editor made numerous unsuccessful appeals for a continuation of this story.

446. The FORTUNATE COUNTRY MAID, or Memoirs of the Marchioness of L—— V——. Translated from the French of the Chevalier de Mouhy. In Two Volumes. *Novelist's*, VII (1782). 1 part (226,000).

A translation of Charles de Fieux, *La Paysanne parvenue, ou les Mémoires de Mme. la Marquise de L. V., par M. le chevalier de M.* (1735–1736). The text is that of the first English translation of 1740. The reprinting in the *Novelist's* is embellished with six engravings, dated December 2, 1781–January 5, 1782.

447. The FORTUNATE FOUNDLING. *Lady's*, XIV (June, August, 1783); XV (May–August, 1784); XVI (May–August, 1785). 10 parts (7000). Signed "NOCTIS-AMATOR."

448. The FORTUNATE SEQUEL, or the Adventures of Ella Worthy. A Novel, in a

Series of Letters. By a Lady. *Lady's,* XI (January, 1780) – XIII (July, 1782) 32 parts (48,000).

a. The Fortunate Sequel, etc. [Same title as above.] *Cumberland,* III (February, 1780) – IV (December, 1781). 31 parts (34,600). Uncompleted.

Reprints only through Part 23 of the above.

449. The FORTUNE-HUNTER. A Modern Tale. *Royal Female,* II (July–December, 1760). 6 parts (16,750).

a. The Fortune Hunter. *Caledonian Weekly* (?–June 30, 1773–?). 1 part. *Inc.*

Only the second half of Part 1 appears in this broken run.

450. The FOUNDLING OF THE LAKE, or the Mysterious Wanderer. An Original Romance. *Hibernian,* 1810 (September–December). 4 parts (9300).

451. The FOUNTAINS, a Tale. [By Dr. Johnson.] From Essays Lately Published by Mrs. Williams. *Universal Museum,* n.s. II (April–May, 1766). 2 parts (5000).

Extracted from *Miscellanies in Prose and Verse* (1766), by Anna Williams.

a. The Fountains, a Tale. *British*(2), VII (May–June, 1766). 2 parts.

b. The Fountains, a Fairy Tale. *European,* XII (July, 1787). 1 part.

A letter signed "C.D.," and addressed to the "Philological Society," declares that the story is by Dr. Johnson, although not included in "the late edition of that Author's Works," that is, Hawkins's edition (1787). A version of the same letter is found also in Nos. 451c, e, f.

c. [The Fountains, a Fairy Tale.] *Northern Gazette,* I, Nos. 22–24 (August 30–September 13, 1787). 3 parts.

The title is taken from Parts 2 and 3.

d. The Fountains, a Fairy Tale. By Dr. Johnson. *Edinburgh*(2), VI (September, 1787). 1 part.

e. The Fountains, a Fairy Tale. *Hibernian,* 1787 (October). 1 part.

f. The Fountains, a Fairy Tale. *English Lyceum,* III, No. 7 (January, 1788). 1 part.

g. The Fountains, a Fairy Tale. *Weekly Misc.*(Glasgow), V (October 26–November 23, 1791). 5 parts.

452. FOUR MORAL REPRESENTATIONS IN ONE, or Amusements at a Royal Wedding. *New Town and Country,* I (June–August, 1787). 3 parts (8700).

a. Four Moral Representations in One, etc. [Same title as above.] *New Lady's,* VI (March, 1791). 1 part (5600).

An abridged version of the above.

453. FRANK PRINRAKE, an Original Novel. By T. Dutton, Esq. *Bon Ton,* III (July, 1793)–IV (August, 1794). 13 parts (29,000).

a. Frank Prinrake, an Original Novel. *Hibernian,* 1793 (September–December). 4 parts (11,800). Uncompleted.

Reprints only 10 of the original 23 chapters.

454. FREDERICA, a Novel, in a Series of Letters. By Simonides Pure. *New Lady's,* VII (January, 1792)–IX (January, April, 1794). 12 parts (10,000). Uncompleted.

Continued irregularly from the beginning.

455. FREDERICK OSMOND, a Tale. *Edinburgh*(2), n.s. XIX (January–February, 1802). 2 parts (7800). Signed "Juvenis./Cupar, 20th Jan. 1802."

"For the *Edinburgh Magazine.*"

a. Frederick and Emily. *Britannic,* XII, No. 169 (1805). 1 part (5250).

An abridged version of the above, under the general heading of "Memoirs of Love and Gallantry."

456. FREDRICA: A Romance. *Lady's Monthly Museum,* VII (July–December, 1801). 6 parts (15,000).

The story makes a single letter, signed "Fredrica."

457. The FRENCH FAMILY, a Tale. By Miss Eliza Yeames. *Lady's,* XXXIX (December, Supplement, 1808). 2 parts (6400).

458. The FRENCH PRIZE, an Adventure at Margate, with Some Observations on the Pleasures of Friendship. Written by a Gentleman. *Weekly Misc.*(Sherborne), XVIII (May 6–13, 1782). 2 parts (5000).

459. The FRIAR'S TALE. *General,* II (July-August, 1788). 2 parts (5000).

Offered as an extract from *Variety, a Collection of Essays, Written in the Year 1787* – a volume of essays by Humphry Repton (1788).

a. The Friar's Tale. *Hibernian,* 1788 (August–September). 2 parts.

b. The Friar's Tale. *Aberdeen*(1), I, No. 26 (December 31, 1788)–II, No. 27 (January 14, 1789). 2 parts.

c. The Friar's Tale. *Weekly Misc.* (Glasgow), IV, Nos. 88–90 (February 23–March 9, 1791). 3 parts.

d. The Friar's Tale. (From a Collection of Essays, Entitled *Variety.*) *Lady's,* XXIII (June, July, September, 1792). 3 parts.

e. The Friar's Tale, etc. [Same title as 459d.] *Universal Mag. and Rev.,* VIII (July August, October, 1792). 3 parts.

f. The Friar's Tale. *Sentimental and Masonic,* I (July, August, October, 1792). 3 parts.

g. The Friar and His Dog, a Tale. *Edinburgh*(2), XVI (July–August, 1792). 2 parts.

h. Albert and Matilda. *Britannic,* VI, Nos. 85–86 (1799). 2 parts.

Offered as part of a series entitled "Memoirs of Love and Gallantry."

i. The Friar's Tale. From *Variety, a Collection of Essays. Gleaner,* II (1806). 1 part.

460. FRIBURGH-CASTLE, or the Wife of Two Husbands. *Marvellous,* IV (March 1, 1804). 1 part (5800).

461. The FRIENDS, from the French of Le Sage. Translated, Altered, and Enlarged. By a Lady. *Lady's,* V (November, 1774)–VI (March, 1775). 5 parts (20,000). Signed "R——."

A translation of Chapter XIII ("La force de l'amitié, histoire") and Chapter XV ("Suite et conclusion de l'histoire de la force de l'amitié") of Le Sage, *Le Diable boiteux* (1707). For other magazine versions of this novel, see "The Devil upon Two Sticks," and "History of the Amours of the Count de Belflor and Leonora of Cespedes."

Part 3 of "The Friends" is entitled "The Force of Friendship"; Part 4, "The Friend, a History."

a. The Friends. By a Lady. *New Lady's,* V (November, 1790)–VI (May, 1791). 8 parts.

462. FRIENDSHIP PUT TO THE TEST. A Moral Tale. [By Marmontel.] *Universal Museum,* n.s. III (November–December, 1767). 2 parts (6200).

A translation and abridgment of "L'Amitié à l'épreuve" (*Contes moraux,* Vol. III, 1765), based upon the version in *Moral Tales,* Vol. III (1766). For other translations of the same story, see Nos. 463, 917, and 1267.

463. FRIENDSHIP PUT TO THE TEST. From the French of Marmontel. Translated by a Young Lady. *Lady's,* XII (March–July, 1781). 5 parts (13,750). Signed "R."

A new translation of "L'Amitié à l'épreuve" (*Contes moraux,* Vol. III, 1765). For earlier translations of the same story, see Nos. 462, 917, and 1267.

a. Friendship Put to the Test, etc. [Same title as above.] *Hibernian,* 1781 (April–October). 5 parts.

b. Friendship Put to the Test. [By] Marmontel. *Harvest Home,* II (1808), 114–136. 1 part.

464. The FROLIC, a Story Founded on Fact. *Rambler's,* V (October, 1787)–VI (February, 1788). 6 parts (8500).

"For the *Rambler's Magazine.*"

465. The FUGITIVE. By Simonides Pure. *New Lady's,* VII (October–Supplement, 1792). 4 parts (5500).

466. The GENEROUS GUARDIAN. (From *The Mysterious Protector,* a Novel, Lately Published, Dedicated by Permission to Lady Crespigny.) *Lady's,* XXXVI (December, 1805). 1 part (5000).

The novel was published anonymously in 1805.

467. The GENEROUS LOVER. *Freeholder's,* III (October–December, 1770). 3 parts (6400).

468. The GIPSEY. *Rambler's,* I (May–September, 1783). 5 parts (6200).

"For the *Rambler's Magazine.*" The introductory letter is signed "An Egyptian"; Part 5 is signed "your constant reader, and occasional correspondent, S. J——s."

469. GOD'S REVENGE AGAINST MURDER AND ADULTERY. *Arminian,* X (May, 1787) – XI (December, 1788). 20 parts (18,000).

A greatly abridged version of John Reynolds, *The Triumphs of God's Revenge against the Crying and Execrable Sin of Murther* (1621); made by "J.W." (i.e., John Wesley).

470. The GOLDEN MIRROR, or the Kings of Scheschian. From the Original Scheschianese. (Translated from the German of M. Wieland.) *Lady's,* XXIX (January, 1798) – XXX (October, 1799). 20 parts (35,600). Uncompleted.

A translation of C. M. Wieland. Der *goldne Spiegel, oder die Könige von Scheschian, eine wahre Geschichte, aus dem Scheschianischen übersetzt* (1772), Part 1, Chaps. 1–8, amounting to about one-third of the original. For other translations from the same work, see Nos. 471 and 473.

a. The Golden Mirror, etc. [Same title as above.] *Hibernian,* 1798 (April) – 1799 (June). 13 parts (28,000). Uncompleted.

This reprinting breaks off after Part 16 in the *Lady's.*

471. The GOLDEN MIRROR, or the Kings of Sheshian: a True History [by C. M. Wieland], Translated from the Sheshianese. *Belle Assemblée,* I (June, 1806) – II (June, 1807). 9 parts (26,000). Uncompleted.

A translation of *Der goldne Spiegel* (see the previous entry), Part I, Chaps. 1–5, amounting to about one-fourth of the original. For still another translation from the same work, see No. 473.

472. GONZALO DE CORDOVA, or Granada Recovered. An Heroic Romance. (Translated from the French of M. de Florian, Author of *Numa Pompilius, Tales,* &c.) *Lady's,* XXIII (May, 1792) – XXVI (June, 1795). 27 parts (70,000).

A translation of *Gonzalve de Cordoue, ou Grenade reconquise, par M. de Florian* (Paris, 1791). The introductory letter is signed "Eliz. M——./May 2, 1792.)"

473. The GOOD KING, a Moral Tale. Translated from the German of Wieland. *Edinburgh*(2), XIV (November, 1791). 1 part (5700).

Taken from Part II, Chaps. 5–10, of C. M. Wieland, *Der goldne Spiegel* (1772) [see Nos. 470–471 above].

474. The GOOD MOTHER, a Moral Tale. [By Marmontel.] *Weekly Amusement,* I (March 17–April 14, 1764). 5 parts (6900).

A translation of "La Bonne Mère" (*Contes moraux,* 1761), taken without acknowledgment from the *Moral Tales* (Becket and De Hondt, 1764) [see No. 917].

a. The Good Mother, a Moral Tale. *Caledonian Weekly,* I (?July 21–?July 28, 1773). 2 parts. *Inc.*

These fragments comprise Parts 2 and 3 of the above.

b. The Good Mother. A Moral Tale. *Weekly Misc.*(Sherborne), X (September 28, 1778) – XI (October 5, 1778). 2 parts.

c. The Good Mother. A Moral Tale. *Moral and Entertaining,* III (October, 1778). 1 part.

475. The GOOD WIFE, a Moral Tale. [By Marmontel.] *Court Miscellany,* I (November–December, 1765). 2 parts (8300).

An abridged translation of "La Femme comme il y en a peu" (*Contes moraux,* Vol. III, 1765). For other translations of the same story, see Nos. 384, 917, and 1348.

476. [GOTHIC STORY OF THE CASTLE OF OTRANTO.] *Universal,* XXXVI (April–May, 1765). 2 parts (11,250).

An abridgment of Walpole's *Castle of Otranto* (1764), amounting to slightly more than a third of the original. The magazine title is taken from the headnote, which reads: "We have inserted the following *Gothic* Story of the Castle of *Otranto,* in Hopes that such of our Readers, as delight in Romance and Novel, will find Matter of agreeable Entertainment in it." (XXXVI, 202.)

a. The Wonderful Gothic Story of the Castle of Otranto. *Wonderful*(2), IV, No. 40 (1793–1794). 1 part.

477. The GOVERNESS. A Narrative Written for the Amusement and Instruction of Those Young Ladies Who Have Been Genteelly Educated, But Who Have Little or No Fortunes. *Lady's,* IX (August, 1778) – XI (December, 1780). 31 parts (42,200).

478. GRASVILLE ABBEY, a Romance. By G[eorge]. M[oore]. *Lady's,* XXIV (March, 1793) – XXVIII (March, August, 1797). 47 parts (113,000).

The author was addressed in February, 1793, when "further specimens" of his novel were requested (XXIV, [58]). A note at the end of the Part 47 reads: "At the request of several of our readers, this much-admired romance is now reprinted in volumes, for G. G. and J. Robinson, Paternoster-row." (XXVIII, 356.) It was reviewed in the *Monthly Review* for April, 1798.

a. Grasville Abbey, a Romance. By G. M. *Sentimental and Masonic,* II (April, 1793)–VI (?June, 1795). 21 parts. *Inc.*

This reprinting was evidently interrupted by the extinction of the magazine.

479. The GRATEFUL NEGRO. [By Maria Edgeworth.] *Monthly Epitome,* n.s. III (April, 1804). 1 part (6900).

The story was extracted from Miss Edgeworth's *Popular Tales* (1804), and offered as "a fair specimen of the whole," which was under review.

480. Of the GREAT DANGER OF TOO MUCH BEAUTY. The Story of Lesbia and Sylvius. *Weekly Mag. and Literary Rev.*, Nos. 15–16 (July 22–29, 1758). 2 parts (5300).

481. The GREEN PETTICOAT, a German Anecdote, Translated from the French of Madame de Genlis. *Entertaining*(1), I (December, 1802). 1 part (5600).

A translation of "Le Jupon vert, anecdote," first published in the *Nouvelle bibliothèque des romans*, année 3, tom. 10 (1801).

a. The Green Petticoat, a German Anecdote from the French of Madame de Genlis. *New Gleaner*, II (1810), 73–82.

482. GROUNDLESS HATRED, a Real History. *Lady's*, I (February, 1771). 1 part (5500).

a. Groundless Hatred Changed into Love, a Real History. *Weekly Misc.*(Sherborne), IV (May 8–15, 1775). 2 parts.

b. Groundless Hatred Changed into Love, a Real History. *Weekly Misc.* (London), IV, Nos. 140–141 (1775). 2 parts.

c. Groundless Hatred, a Real History. *New Lady's*, IV (August–September, 1789). 2 parts. Signed "R. J. O——R./Lambeth."

The editor of the *New Lady's* acknowledged the receipt of this plagiarized story in May, 1789 (p. [226]).

483. The GUARDIAN, or Conjugal Infidelity. *Rambler's*, I (Supplement, 1783) – II (April, 1784). Signed "S. J——S." 5 parts (5000).

"For the *Rambler's Magazine*."

484. GYRON THE COURTEOUS, a Tale of the Times of King Arthur. *Edinburgh*(2), XII (July–August, 1790). 2 parts (7500).

"Translated from the German of [C. M.] Wieland." This story is a prose redaction of Wieland's blank-verse poem "Geron, der Adeliche, eine Erzählung aus König Artus Zeit" (1777).

485. HANNIBAL FERACUTI, Prince of Sabionetta. *Belle Assemblée*, n.s. V (May–June, 1812). 2 parts (5250).

486. HAPPILY. A Moral Tale. [By Marmontel.] *St. James's*(1), II (June, 1763). 1 part (5900). Signed "D." [i.e. Charles Denis].

The first English translation of "Heureusement" (*Contes moraux*, 1761), made by Charles Denis. This version was later collected in the *Moral Tales of M. Marmontel, Translated from the French by C. Denis and R. Lloyd* (1764). In the *St. James's* the story appears under the general heading "Moral Tales, from Mr. Marmontel." See "Moral Tales" (No. 917).

a. Happily. A Moral Tale. *Beauties of All the Magazines*, II (July, 1763). 1 part. Signed "D."

"From the *Saint James's Magazine.*"

b. Happily. A Moral Tale from the French. *New Lady's,* VIII (Supplement, 1793) – IX (February, 1794). 3 parts.

c. Happily. A Moral Tale from the French. *Hibernian,* 1794 (March–April). 1 part.

487. HAPPINESS IS NOT TO BE PROCURED BY RICHES OR LUXURY. *Weekly Misc.*(Sherborne), I (November 15–22, 1773). 2 parts (5600).

An expanded version of Dr. Johnson's "History of Seged, Emperor of Ethiopia," in *Rambler* Nos. 204–205.

a. Happiness Is Not to Be Procured by Riches or Luxury. *Weekly Misc.* (London), II, Nos. 63–64 (1773). 2 parts.

488. HAPPY ARE THOSE WHOM THE MISFORTUNES OF OTHERS MAKE WISE. *Weekly Misc.* (London), II, No. 40 (1773). 1 part (5200).

489. [The HAPPY CONSEQUENCES WHICH RESULT FROM GOOD-NATURE.] *Universal,* XIII (September, 1753). 1 part (5600).

A disguised redaction of the "History of Dorimon and Alithea," published in Mrs. Haywood's *Female Spectator* in 1744 (see No. 571). The names of the principal characters are borrowed from the story of "Amasina and Palamon," published in Book V of the *Female Spectator.*

The title is taken from the introductory letter addressed "To the Proprietors of the *Universal Magazine,*" and signed "Your constant Reader and Well-wisher, R. C."

a. [The Happy Consequences Which Result from Good-Nature.] *Magazine of Magazines,* VI (September, 1753). Signed "R.C."

The title is taken from the introductory letter, addressed to the "Proprietors of the *Magazine of Magazines.*"

b. The School for Wives. A Domestic History. *Lady's,* X (December–Supplement, 1779). 1 part (5100).

An abridged version of the above.

c. The Happy Consequences Resulting from Good-Nature. *Bristol and Bath,* I, Nos. 5–7 (1782). 3 parts.

490. The HAPPY DIVORCE. A Moral Tale. [By Marmontel.] *Weekly Amusement,* I (July 14–September 8, 1764). 9 parts (11,700).

A translation of "L'Heureux Divorce" (*Contes moraux,* 1761), extracted without acknowledgment from the *Moral Tales* (Becket and De Hondt, 1764). See No. 917.

491. The HAPPY FAMILY. A Tale, in a Series of Letters. *Oxford,* XI (September, 1774) – XII (January, 1775). 5 parts (5100).

492. The HAPPY PAIR, or the Affecting and Instructive History of Mr. and Mrs. Palmer. *Hibernian,* 1798 (March). 1 part (6200). Signed "J. ALEXANDER."

493. HARRIET, OR THE NOVICE. A Cautionary Tale, Founded upon Facts. *Lady's Monthly Museum,* n.s. XV (July, 1813) – n.s. XVI (June, 1814). 12 parts (17,200). Signed "C."

In his "Notes to Correspondents" (June, 1813), the editor wrote: "Harriet, a Tale, shall appear; but we hope it will prove a Nouvellette." (P. 375.) In May, 1814, he complained publicly that "Mr. C's last Tale" was proving "too gloomy and melancholy." (P. 300.)

494. HARRIET VERNON, or Characters from Real Life. A Novel, in a Series of Letters. By a Lady. *Lady's,* XXXVIII (January, 1807) – LX (March, 1809). 29 parts (113,000).

In a note addressed to his "Correspondents" in November, 1808, the editor asked for the address of the "ingenious authoress" of this novel (p. [474]).

495. HARRIOT, a Moral Tale. *Universal Museum,* n.s. I (October, 1765) – n.s. II (January, 1766). 1 part (12,500).

496. HAWTHORN COTTAGE, a Tale. By J[ohn]. J[ones]. *European,* LXII (October, 1812) – LXV (June, 1814). 21 parts (75,000).

Readers were informed at the end of the serial (p. 491) that in consequence of its very favourable reception, "an edition is in preparation for the press, carefully revised and corrected, and will be published in the course of the ensuing autumn" [i.e., *Hawthorn Cottage, or the Two Cupids, a Tale* (London: Asperne, 1815), 2 vols.].

a. Hawthorn Cottage, a Tale. By J. J. *Dublin*(2), I, Nos. 2–11 (December, 1812–September, 1813). 8 parts (31,500). Uncompleted.

Carried only through Part 9 of the original.

497. The HEIR OF STRATHMORE, a Novel in Miniature. *Glasgow,* II (May–November, 1811). 7 parts (12,100). Signed "Nubilia./Glasgow, Nov. 18. 1811."

"For the *Glasgow Magazine.*"

498. The HEIR OF THE HOUSE OF OLDFIELD, a Moral Tale. By Mr. [James?] Harrison. *Pocket,* I (September, 1794). 1 part (6000).

499. The HEIRESS OF DEVON, a Tale. By a Lady. *Sentimental and Masonic,* II (May, 1793) – III (August, 1793). 4 parts (15,500).

"For the *Sentimental and Masonic Magazine.*" The receipt of the novel was acknowledged in the May, 1793, number (p. 394).

500. HENRIETTA. By Mrs. [Charlotte] Lennox. In Two Volumes. *Novelist's,* XXIII (1787). 1 part (118,000).

First published in 1758. The reprinting in the *Novelist's* includes four engraving, dated August 1 – November 1, 1787.

501. HENRIETTA, COUNTESS OSENVOR. A Sentimental Novel. In a Series of Letters to Lady Susannah Fitzroy. By Mr. Treyssac de Vergy, Counsellor in the Parliament of Paris. In Two Volumes. *Novelist's,* XVII (1785). 1 part (47,000).

This novel was published first in English, in 1770. The reprinting in the *Novelist's* includes two engravings, dated January 22 and 29, 1785.

502. HENRY AND ELIZA, a Sentimental Tale. *European,* I (May, 1782) – IV (July, 1783). 7 parts (10,300). Uncompleted. Signed "CLIO."

The receipt of this story, written by a reader, was acknowledged in April, 1782 (p. 238). Its publication was attended by many delays, occasioned, first, by the "indisposition" of the author (II, 398), second, by "a *Matrimonial Expedition*" (III, 242). Finally, after seven short installments, extending over fifteen months, the story was left unfinished.

503. HENRY AND HENRIETTA. *New Novelist's,* II (1787), 36–43. 1 part (5800).

504. HENRY COMPTON, a Tale. *Edinburgh*(2), n.s. XVIII (September–October, 1801). 2 parts (7300).

505. The HERMIT. *European,* LX (July–December, 1811). 6 parts (11,200).

The title of Parts 2–6 is "The Hermit of the Vale, or the Man of Sorrows." The receipt of the tale was acknowledged in March, 1811 (p. 162).

506. The HERMIT, an Oriental Tale. By M. Hays. *Universal,* LXXVIII (April–May, 1786. 2 parts (6000).

Probably Mrs. Mary Hays, the author from 1796 of several novels and various juvenile works.

a. The Hermit, an Oriental Tale. By M. Hays. *Hibernian,* 1786 (May). 1 part (2800). Uncompleted.

A reprinting of Part 1 only of the above.

b. The Hermit, an Oriental Tale. *Edinburgh*(2), n.s. II (December, 1793). 1 part.

507. The HERMIT OF SNOWDEN, or Memoirs of Albert and Lavinia. Written by Himself, and Found after His Death near the Place of His Retirement. *Weekly Entertainer,* XVII (May 2, 1791) - XVIII (July 18, 1791). 11 parts (25,000).

A reprinting of Elizabeth Ryves, *The Hermit of Snowden* (1789), but slightly abridged.

508. The HERMIT OF THE CAVERN, a Spanish Story. By Thomas Bellamy. *General,* III (March–May, 1789). 3 parts (5700).

This piece was later collected in Bellamy's *Miscellanies in Prose and Verse* (1794).

a. The Hermit of the Cavern, a Spanish Story. *Universal Mag. and Rev.,* I (April–June, 1789). 3 parts (5700).

b. Felix and Elvira. *Britannic,* VI, Nos. 78–79 (1798). 2 parts.

Part of the series "Memoirs of Love and Gallantry."

509. The HERMIT OF THE GROVE. "Tale 33," *Tell-Tale,* III (1804), 1 part (13,250).

510. The HERMITS OF MURCIA. By Marmontel. *New Gleaner,* II (1810), pp. 321–354. 1 part (19,200).

A translation of "Les Solitaires de Murcie, conte moral" (*Mercure,* 1791). For another translation of the same story, see No. 1045.

511. [The HERO DISTINGUISHED FROM THE MODERN MAN OF HONOUR: Account of Eugenio by Benevolus.] [By John Hawkesworth.] *Adventurer,* Nos. 64–66, 70 (June 16–July 7, 1753). 4 parts (7000).

The title is taken from the table of contents of the first collected edition.

a. [The Story of Eugenio and Amelia.] *Scots,* XVI (May, 1754). 1 part (5200).

Nos. 64–66 of the *Adventurer,* printed successively in the same issue. The title is from the index of Volume XVI.

b. [The Hero Distinguished from the Modern Man of Honour.] *Weekly Amusement,* III (July 19–August 2, 1766). 3 parts (5200 words).

All four papers of the *Adventurer,* slightly abridged. The title is taken from Part 2.

c. Eugenio. From the *Adventurer. New Gleaner,* II (1810), 201–210. 1 part.

The version of the *Weekly Amusement,* with further abridgments. Attributed to Hawkesworth.

512. HEROICK VIRTUE, or Love and Duty Reconciled. A Moral Tale, from the French. *London,* L (April–May, 1781). 2 parts (8300).

"For the *London Magazine.*"

a. Heroic Virtue, or Love and Duty Reconciled. A Moral Tale, from the French. *Weekly Misc.*(Sherborne), XVI (August 20–September 3, 1781). 3 parts.

513. The HEROISM OF LOVE AND FRIENDSHIP. *Lady's Monthly Museum,* n.s. XVII (August–December, 1814). 5 parts (10,750).

514. HERVORAR SAGA, or the History of Hervora, Her Ancestors and Posterity. Translated from an Ancient Manuscript. *Monthly Literary Recreations,* II (January, 1807) – III (July, 1807). 7 parts (15,750). Signed "I."

A redaction of the Icelandic *Hervarar Saga,* probably based upon current Latin or German translations. (For a bibliography of early texts and translations of this saga, see *Islandica,* V, 22–26.)

515. L'HEUREUX ACCIDENT. Conte, par M. [Stanislas Jean] de Boufflers. *Ambigu,* XXI, No. 183 (April 30, 1808). 1 part (15,750).

Reprinted from the *Mercure de France* XXX (December 12–19, 1807), where it appeared under the same title, and was signed "M. de Boufflers."

516. The HIEREU-MANIA. *Spirit of the Public Journals for 1811,* XV (1812).

Four letters signed "PRAISE-GOD BARE-BONES" and addressed "To the Editor of the *Morning Chronicle,*" who wrote: "We have received the following letter; whether it be genuine, or a hoax, we leave our readers to determine." The letters are dated Oct. 11, Oct. 18, Nov. 12, Nov. 23, [1811].

517. HIGHLAND CHARACTERS, or the Communicative Tourist. *Lady's Monthly Museum,* n.s. V (November, 1808) – n.s. VIII (May, 1810). 12 parts (36,400).

518. The HIGHLAND HERMITAGE, or the History of the Laird of Calderwood and His Family. In a Series of Letters. *Lady's,* XLII (August, 1811) – XLVI (January, 1815). 43 parts (92,000).

519. HIGHLAND HEROISM, or the Castles of Glencoe and Balloch. *Marvellous,* II (February 1, 1803). 1 part (14,400).

A disguised redaction of Mrs. Radcliffe's *Castles of Athlin and Dunbayne, a Highland Story* (1789).

520. A HIGHLAND STORY. *North British Mag. and Rev.,* II (October, December, 1804). 2 parts (7750).

The editor in November, 1804, was forced to beg for the remainder of the story (p. 258).

a. A Highland Story. *Female Preceptor,* I, Nos. 8–9 (May–June, 1813). 2 parts.

521. The HIGHLANDERS. From *Tales of the Imagination. Glasgow Misc.,* II (1800). 171–201. 1 part (10,000).

For another extract from *Tales of Imagination* (1800), see No. 330.

522. The HIRSCHBERG TAILOR, a Tale [by Johann Carl August Musaeus]. *Edinburgh* (2), XIV (July, 1791). 1 part (5400).

A translation from the "Legenden von Rübezahl" (*Volksmährchen der Deutschen,* 1782–1787), extracted from William Beckford's *Popular Tales of the Germans* ("Legends concerning Number-Nip," Vol. II, 1791, 46–79). For other extracts from *Popular Tales,* see Nos. 163 and 1063.

a. The Taylor of Hirschberg, a Tale. *Weekly Misc.* (Glasgow), V (August 17–31, 1791). 3 parts.

523. HISTOIRE D'EMILIE. *Lady's,* VIII (February, 1777) – XI (November, 1780). 25 parts (11,300). Signed "GERTRUDE."

A serial novelette in French, written by a reader of the magazine in minute installments and with numerous interruptions.

524. HISTOIRE DE LA RUINE DE LA VILLE DE MEXICO, tirée des *Incas* de M. Marmontel. *Magazin à la mode,* I (October–November, 1777). 2 parts (10,000).

An extract from Marmontel, *Les Incas, ou la Destruction de l'empire du Pérou* (1777), following a long epitome of the novel in the September number (pp. 423–444). For an abridgment in English of *Les Incas,* see No. 653.

525. HISTOIRE DE MONSIEUR LE GRAND, écrite par lui-même. (The History of Monsieur Le Grand, Written by Himself.) *Lady's,* XII (October, 1781) – XIII (June, 1782). 9 parts (5600). Signed "J——s G——t, Cavendish Square."

A short serial novelette in French, written by a reader. Though the story was ostensibly completed in June, the editor of the *Lady's* is found querying the author in the following January about "a chasm in his manuscript, which we would wish to receive before we proceed in our continuation." (XIV, [ii].)

An English translation was begun in the 1781 Supplement, but abandoned; and a list of "ERRATA to the History of Monsieur Le Grand" was printed in August, 1782 (pp. 416–417).

526. HISTORICAL ANECDOTE OF ALEXIS PETROWITZ. *Belle Assemblée,* V (August–September, 1808). 2 parts (9600). Signed "E.R."

527. The HISTORY AND ADVENTURES OF A BEDSTEAD. *Rambler's,* II (December, 1784) – V (April, 1787). 28 parts (42,500). Uncompleted.

528. The HISTORY AND ADVENTURES OF AN ATOM. By Dr. Smollett. In Two Volumes. *Novelist's,* XXI (1786). 1 part (61,000).

First published in 1769. The attribution to Smollett has been questioned, but is accepted in the *Cambridge Bibliography.* In the *Novelist's,* the reprinting includes two engravings, dated April 15 and 22, 1786.

529. The HISTORY AND ADVENTURES OF THE RENOWNED DON QUIXOTE. Translated from the Spanish of Miguel de Cervantes Saavedra. To Which is Prefixed Some Account of the Author's Life. By Dr. [Tobias] Smollett. In Four Volumes. *Novelist's,* VIII (1782). 1 part (430,000).

Smollett's translation was first published in 1755. The reprinting in the *Novelist's* included sixteen engravings, dated March 23–June 22, 1782.

530. [HISTORY OF A COUNTRY CURATE.] [By T. F. Middleton.] *Country Spectator,* Nos. 16, 21, 28 (January 22, February 26, April 16, 1793). 3 parts (5000).

Three letters signed "*Mutabilis./Lincolnshire,*" and initialed "S."; but written by the Author of the *Spectator.* The title is from the table of contents.

531. HISTORY OF A GAMBLER. From the New Novel of *The Metropolis. Sporting,* XXXVIII (July–August, 1811). 2 parts (5000).

From *The Metropolis, a Novel* (1811?; 8th ed., 1819).

532. The HISTORY OF A GOOD WARM WATCH-COAT, with Which the Present Possessor Is Not Content to Cover His Own Shoulders, Unless He Can Cut out of It a Petticoat for His Wife, and a Pair of Breeches for His Son. [By Laurence Sterne.] *Westminster,* III (July, 1775). 1 part (5250).

The piece is identified as a "production of the celebrated author of *Tristram Shandy*" – i.e., *A Political Romance, Addressed to* ——— ———, *Esq., of York* (1759; reprinted as *History of a Watch Coat,* 1775).

a. The History of a Good Warm Watch-Coat, etc. [Same title as above.] *Hibernian,* 1775 (August), 1 part.

b. The History of a Good Warm Watch-Coat, etc. [Same title as above.] *Monthly Misc.,* III (August, 1775). 1 part.

c. History of a Good Warm Watchcoat. In a Letter to a Friend. By the Rev. Mr. Sterne. *New Novelist's,* I (1786), 73–80. 1 part.

533. The HISTORY OF A HAIR-DRESSER. Found Wrapped up in a Paper with His Curling-Irons. Written by Himself. *Covent Garden,* I (November, 1772) – II (April, 1773). 6 parts (12,700).

534. The HISTORY OF A MAN OF THE MODE, or a Sketch of Real Life under Fictitious Names. *Belle Assemblée,* I (June, 1806). 1 part (5900). Signed "RH—."

535. The HISTORY OF A MILLINER'S GIRL. *Covent Garden,* I (July–November, 1772). 5 parts (14,850).

536. The HISTORY OF A PHILOSOPHICAL VAGABOND, Pursuing Novelty, But Losing Content. From *The Vicar of Wakefield,* a Tale, Just Published. *Universal Museum,* n.s. II (March, May, 1766). 2 parts (5000).

Taken from Volume II, Chapter 1, of Goldsmith's novel (1766) [see No. 1306].

a. The History of a Philosophical Vagabond, Pursuing Novelty, But Losing Content. *British*(2), VII (April–May, 1766). 2 parts.

The story is preceded by a two-page summary of the novel from which it is taken.

b. The History of a Philosophical Vagabond, etc. [Same title as *British.*] *Royal*(2), XIV (April–May, 1766). 2 parts.

Identical with the piece in the *British.*

537. The HISTORY OF A REPROBATE, Related by Himself, from the Third Volume of *The Fool of Quality* [by Henry Brooke], Just Published. *Universal Museum,* n.s. IV (May–July, 1768). 3 parts (16,000).

Extracted from Chapter 16 of the new volume published in 1768 (pp. 113–217). For another extract, from Volumes I–II of the same novel, see No. 655.

a. The History of an Englishman's Slavery in Algiers, from the Third Volume of Brooke's *Fool of Quality,* Just Published. *Court Misc.,* IV (May–June, 1768). 2 parts (7000).

A shorter extract from the above work (III, 180–214).

b. The History of a Reprobate. *Harvest Home,* II (1808). 1 part (14,300).

The longer version of the *Universal Museum,* slightly abridged.

538. HISTORY OF A TETE SEULE, or Memoirs, Amours, Anecdotes, and Adventures of Dick Sprightly. *Town and Country,* IV (October, 1772). 1 part (9000).

539. HISTORY OF ALBERTO AND ANGELICA. *Belle Assemblée,* n.s. III (February–March, 1811). 2 parts (8300).

Part of the series "Historic Romances, or Wonders in Real Life."

a. History of Alberto and Angelica. *Hibernian,* 1811 (March–May). 3 parts.

540. The HISTORY OF ALPHONSUS OF CASTILE. Translated by a Lady. *Town and Country,* XXI (January–June, 1789). 6 parts (11,800).

541. The HISTORY OF ALSALEH, an Eastern Courtier. [By John Murdoch.] (From *Pictures of the Heart, Sentimentally Delineated,* in 2 Vols. 12 mo.) *Universal,* LXXIII (October–November, 1783). 2 parts (5700).

Part 1 is preceded by a brief review that attributes the work to Murdoch. Part 2 is entitled "The Adventures of a Friend to Truth," the title it bears in the original collection (1783).

a. The History of Alsaleh, etc. [Same title as above.] *Hibernian,* 1783 (November–December). 1 part.

542. [HISTORY OF AMANDA.] *Lady's,* IV (August–October, 1773). 3 parts (5250).

Nos. 5–7 of the series called "The Reasoner." The story was given no further title.

543. The HISTORY OF AMELIA. *Lady's,* XV (January–April, 1784). 4 parts (7000).

Introduced by a letter signed "A constant Reader." Part 2 of this story was inadvertently printed before Part 1.

a. The History of Amelia. *New Lady's,* VI (June–August, 1791). 2 parts.

In reprinting this story, the editor arranged Parts 1 and 2 in the proper order.

544. The HISTORY OF AMELIA, from Facts. *Jester's,* I (August–November, 1766). 4 parts (6500). Signed "E.H."

545. The HISTORY OF AMELIA STANFORD, Written by Herself. *Lady's,* XXVIII (June–September; Supplement, 1797). 4 parts (8700).

546. [The HISTORY OF AMYNTOR AND EUDOSIA, or Polite Friendship.] *Royal Female,* II (August–October, 1760). 3 parts (6400).

The story occupies Nos. 6, 7, and 8 of a series called "The Meddler." The title is from the index of Volume II.

547. HISTORY OF AN EMIGRANT FAMILY. (From *A Tour in Swisserland* by Helen Maria Williams.) *Universal,* CII (April, 1798). 1 part (5500).

Extracted from *A Tour of Switzerland* (1798), Vol. I, Chap. 19.

a. History of an Emigrant Family. From *A Tour in Swisserland. Scots,* LX (May, 1798). 1 part.

b. History of an Emigrant Family, etc. [Same title as *Universal.*] *Edinburgh*(2), n.s. XI (May, 1798). 1 part.

c. History of an Emigrant. (From *A Tour in Swisserland* by Helen Maria Williams.) *Weekly Entertainer,* XXXI (May 28, June 4, June 18, 1798). 3 parts.

d. The History of Madame and Monsieur C——. A Real and an Affecting Tale, Produced by the French Revolution during the Tyranny of Robespierre. Related by Miss Williams. *Freemason's,* XI (July–August, 1798). 2 parts.

e. The History of an Emigrant Family. (From *A Tour in Switzerland,* by Helen Maria Williams.) *Lady's,* XXIX (December–Supplement, 1798). 2 parts (7350).

A slightly longer extract, reprinting the whole chapter.

548. The HISTORY OF AN HEIRESS, Written by Herself. *Lady's,* III (December, 1772) – V (August, 1774). 23 parts (56,000).

549. The HISTORY OF AN HUMBLE FRIEND, Written by Herself. *Lady's,* V (September, 1774) – VII (Supplement, 1776). 21 parts (41,000).

550. The HISTORY OF AN INTENDED DIVINE. *Belfast Monthly,* XI (November, 1813) – XII (May, 1814). 4 parts (8000). Uncompleted.

"To the Proprietors of the *Belfast Magazine.*"

551. [The HISTORY OF AN IRISH FAMILY.] *Cheap,* II (January–November, 1814). 8 parts (32,000). Signed "Th.N.R."

The title of each part differs, but all carry the above label. That of Part 1 is "Difference in Human Characters the Result of Education: Exemplified in the History of an Irish Family." That of Part 2 is "Times Are Altered! Being a Continuation of the History of an Irish Family," etc.

552. The HISTORY OF AN OLD POCKET BIBLE, Supposed to Be Written by Itself. *Cottage,* I (March, 1812) – II (December, 1812). 6 parts (11,200). Signed "X."

553. The HISTORY OF AN ORPHAN. In a Series of Letters between Miss Brudenell and Miss Campbell. *New Lady's,* II (January–November, 1787). 11 parts (22,000).

The receipt of this story, communicated by "Mary Eliza," was acknowledged in the December, 1786, number (p. [562]).

554. The HISTORY OF AN UNFORTUNATE ROYAL CAPTIVE. *Weekly Entertainer,* XXV (March 23– June 29, 1795). 14 parts (21,600).

An unacknowledged abridgment of Ann Yearsley, *The Royal Captive, a Fragment of Secret History* (1795), about one-sixth the length of the original.

555. HISTORY OF ANASTIA DORIA, a Genoese Lady, Written by Herself. *Universal,* XLV (November–December, 1769). 2 parts (10,000).

556. The HISTORY OF APHERIDON. *Lady's,* V (December, 1774) – VI (August, 1775). 8 parts (6900). Signed "MEZORAIM/Aberdeen, 1775."

557. The HISTORY OF APPRIUS, King of Merryland. Extracted from the Chronicles of the World. A Modern Apologue. *Bon Ton,* IV (October, 1794) – V (June, 1795). 8 parts (11,000).

A translation of Godart de Beauchamps, *Histoire du prince Apprius* [i.e., Priapus] (1728); reprinted from *The History of King Apprius, &c., Extracted from the Chronicle of the World, from Its Creation* (1728) [McBurney, No. 236].

558. [The HISTORY OF ARIANA.] *Universal,* XIII (October–November, 1753). 2 parts (8600). Signed "R.C."

A disguised redaction of Mrs. Haywood, "The Triumph of Fortitude and Patience over Barbarity and Deceit," in the *Female Spectator* (see No. 1276). The origin of the story is unnamed, and all the proper names have been changed. The title is taken from Part 2.

a. [The History of Ariana.] *Magazine of Magazines,* VI (October–November, 1753). 2 parts. Signed "R.C."

559. The HISTORY OF AUGUSTA PEMBROKE AND MISS WOODLEY. In a Series of Letters. *Lady's,* XII (May, 1781) – XIV (March, 1783). 18 parts (24,400).

560. The HISTORY OF AURELIA. *Lady's,* V (September, 1774) – VI (May, 1775). 6 parts (5700).

561. The HISTORY OF BELISA, ORSAMES, AND JULIA. [By Mme. de Gomez.] *Weekly Entertainer,* VIII (September 24–November 6, 1786). 7 parts (13,100).

An unacknowledged translation of Mme. de Gomez, "Histoire de Belise, d'Orsame, et de Julie" ("Première journée," *Les Journées amusantes,* 1722–1731), adapted from the translation published under the same title in Mrs. Haywood, *La Belle Assemblée* (1724–1726). For other magazine extracts from the same collection, see BELLE ASSEMBLÉE (Index).

562. The HISTORY OF BIANCA CAPELLO. [By Charlotte Lennox.] *Lady's Museum,* I, Nos. 5–7 (1760). 3 parts (6700).

The story is introduced with a letter from the alleged translator, "Offaria Cellini," but it is believed to be the work of Charlotte Lennox (see M. R. Small, *Charlotte Ramsay Lennox,* p. 225).

a. Bianca Capello, an Historical Novel, Translated from the Italian by Lady Pomfret. *New Novelist's,* I (1786), 16–24.

The attribution is to Henrietta Louisa Fermor, Countess of Pomfret (d. 1761), but the text is identical with the above.

563. The HISTORY OF BLANCHE, or the Enchanting Effects of Eloquence and Soft Language. [By Mlle. Marie-Jeanne L'Héritier.] *Universal Spectator,* No. 832 (September 15) – No. 835 (October 6, 1744). 4 parts (8750).

A translation of "Les Enchantemens de l'éloquence," *Oeuvres meslées* (1696).

564. The HISTORY OF CAPTAIN HERBERT AND MISS AUGUSTA NUGENT, in a Series of Letters. *Lady's,* VII (April, August, 1776) – VIII (January, 1777); X (January, February, August, 1779) – XI (January, 1780). 16 parts (10,300). Uncompleted.

The story was abandoned by its first author after Part 8, and resumed by another two years later—only to be broken off a second time.

565. The HISTORY OF CAPTAIN WINTERFIELD. *British Mag. and Rev.,* II (March–April, 1783). 2 parts (7000). Signed "H——."

Probably written by James Harrison, the publisher of the *British Magazine* (see No. 565d).

a. The History of Captain Winterfield. *Gentleman's and London,* 1783 (May–June). 2 parts.

b. The History of Captain Winterfield. *Edinburgh Weekly,* LVII (July 17–31, 1783). 3 parts.

c. The History of Captain Winterfield. *Bristol and Bath,* II, No. 16 (1783). 1 part.

d. Affecting History of Captain Winterfield. *New London,* I (July–August 1785). 2 parts.

In the editor's remarks, attributed to "Mr. Harrison of Pater-noster Row" (p. 58).

e. Affecting History of Captain Winterfield. *Gentleman's and London,* 1785 (August–October). 3 parts.

The second appearance of the story in the same magazine (see No. 565a).

f. The History of Captain Winterfield. *Newcastle,* I (December, 1785). 1 part.

g. History of Captain Winterfield. By Mr. Harrison. *New Novelist's,* II (1787), 3–12.

Embellished with an engraving dated January 1, 1787.

h. The History of Captain Winterfield. *Weekly Misc.*(Glasgow), n.s. I, No. 19 (November 7) – No. 22 (November 28, 1792). 4 parts.

i. History of Captain Winterfield. *Entertaining*(1), I, No. 12 (December, 1802). 1 part.

j. History of Captain Winterfield. By Mr. Harrison. *Weekly Entertainer,* XLI (March 28–April 18, 1803). 4 parts.

k. The History of Captain Winterfield. By Mr. Harrison. *New Gleaner,* I (1809), 46–57.

566. The HISTORY OF CECILIA, or the Beautiful Nun, by Madame [de] Genlis. "Tale 37," *Tell-Tale,* III (1804). 1 part (13,000).

A translation (and adaptation) of the story of "Cécile," told in Mme. de Genlis, *Adèle et Théodore* (1782), Vol. I, Letters XXII–LIV. A translation of the same story, but entitled "The History of Seraphina, the Beautiful Nun," was included in the abridged version of the novel published in the *Universal* (see No. 9 above). The translation in the *Universal,* in fact, seems to be the original of the version in the *Tell-Tale.*

a. The History of Cecilia, the Beautiful Nun, by Madame [de] Genlis. In a Series of Letters from the Baroness d'Almane to the Viscountess de Limours. *Gleaner,* II (1806), 162–182.

567. [The HISTORY OF CHARLES KEMPTON AND MISS SELBY.] *Town and Country,* XI (August–September, 1779). 2 parts (6500).

The title is taken from Part 2.

a. [The History of Charles Kempton and Miss Selby.] *Cumberland,* II (September–November, 1779). 2 parts.

568. HISTORY OF CLARA DAVENPORT, in a Letter to a Friend. *New Lady's,* IV (February, May, June, 1789); V (February, March, 1790). 5 parts (10,500). Signed "MARY ELIZA, Edward-Street, Cavendish-Square."

Addressed "To the Editor of the *New Lady's Magazine.*"

569. The HISTORY OF COUNT DE SALMONY, and of Isabella de Mayrand. [By Mme. de Gomez.] *Weekly Entertainer,* VII (April 24–June 19, 1786). 9 parts (17,900).

An unacknowledged translation of the "Histoire du comte de Salmony, et de Isabelle de Mayrand," found in the "Quatorzième journée" of Mme. de Gomez, *Les Journées amusantes* (1722–1731). The original translation, from which the above is taken, is Mrs. Haywood's, first published in *La Belle Assemblée* (1724–1726). For other extracts from the same collection, see BELLE ASSEMBLÉE (Index).

570. HISTORY OF DON ZAMBOGA AND SERAPHINA, Written by Himself. *Belle Assemblée,* n.s. III (March–May, 1811). 3 parts (13,000). Uncompleted.

Offered under the general heading of "Historic Romances."

a. History of Don Zamboga and Seraphina, Written by Himself. *Hibernian,* 1811 (May–July). 3 parts.

571. [HISTORY OF DORIMON AND ALITHEA.] [By Eliza Haywood.] *Female Spectator,* Book VI (1744), 356–383. 1 part (6500).

The story is told in the course of a much-longer paper. For a disguised redaction of this story, see "The Happy Consequences Which Result from Good Nature" (No. 489).

a. Prudence and Virtue Rewarded, or the History of Dorimon and Alithea. Written by a Lady. *Weekly Misc.*(Sherborne), XVII (December 3–10, 1781). 2 parts.

572. The HISTORY OF EDWARD AND MARIA. *London,* XLIII (September, 1774) – XLIV (Appendix, 1775). 11 parts (18,000).

a. The History of Edward and Maria. *Dumfries Weekly,* IX (?March 14, 1775) – XII (February 13, 1776). 9 parts. *Inc.*

573. The HISTORY OF ERNESTINE, Translated from the French of Madam Riccoboni. *Universal,* XXXVII (September–October, 1765). 2 parts (11,000).

The first English translation of Mme. Riccoboni's *Histoire d'Ernestine* (1765). For a later version of the same story, see No. 370.

a. The History of Ernestine. *Weekly Amusement,* IV (December 12–26, 1767). 3 parts.

b. The History of Ernestine. *Weekly Misc.*(Glasgow), n.s. II, Nos. 31–37 (February 6–March 20, 1793). 7 parts.

574. The HISTORY OF ETHELRED, King of England. [By Mme. de Gomez.] *Weekly Entertainer,* V (April 4) – VI (July 4, 1785). 13 parts (22,000).

An unacknowledged translation of the "Histoire d'Etelred, roi d'Angleterre," found in the "Quinzième journée" of Mme. de Gomez, *Les Journées amusantes* (1722–1731). The translation is Mrs. Haywood's, published under the same title in *La Belle Assemblée* (1724–1726). For a shortened version of the same translation, see No. 166, and for another translation, No. 341. For other extracts and adaptations from the same collection, see Belle Assemblée (Index).

575. The HISTORY OF EXCHANGE ALLEY. *Beauties of All the Magazines,* I (December, 1762) – II (May, 1763). 5 parts (12,800).

576. HISTORY OF FRANCIS COUNT MONTGOMERY, and the Sieur d'Anglade. Translated from the French. *Court Misc.,* II (September–October, 1766). 2 parts (6450).

577. The HISTORY OF FREDERICK AND AMELIA, in a Series of Letters. By Mr. Mavor. *Fashionable,* I (June–December, 1786). 7 parts (7100).

The author was probably the Rev. William Fordyce Mavor.

578. The HISTORY OF GEORGE BARNWELL. Carefully Abridged from Mr. Surr's Celebrated Novel. By Sarah Wilkinson. "Tale 54," *Tell-Tale,* IV (1804). 1 part (13,400).

A condensation of Thomas Skinner Surr, *George Barnwell, a Novel* (1798).

579. The HISTORY OF GOSTANZA AND MARTUCCIO, a Florentine Tale. *Belle Assemblée,* I (October–November, 1806). 2 parts (10,000).

580. [The HISTORY OF HYMENAEUS'S COURTSHIP.] [By Dr. Samuel Johnson.] *Rambler,* Nos. 113 (April 16), 115, 119, 167 (October 22, 1751). 4 parts (6750).

The title is from the table of contents of the collected edition.

581. The HISTORY OF ISAAC JENKINS, His Wife, and Children. Extracted from a Pamphlet Written by Dr. Beddoes of Bristol, under That Title, Which Has Lately Been Published. *Weekly Entertainer,* XXIII (June 2–30, 1794). 5 parts (9500).

From Thomas Beddoes, *The History of Isaac Jenkins, and of the Sickness of Sarah His Wife, and Their Three Children* (1792).

582. The HISTORY OF JAMES LE BRUN. (From *The Romances of Real Life,* by Charlotte Smith.) *Political,* XIV (January–February, 1788). 2 parts (7500).

From *The Romance of Real Life* (1787).

a. The History of James Le Brun. (From *The Romances of Real Life.*) *Hibernian,* 1788 (February, May). 2 parts (6000).

Part of the story has been omitted, probably accidentally.

583. The HISTORY OF JEMMY AND JENNY JESSAMY. By Mrs. [Eliza] Haywood. In Three Volumes. *Novelist's,* XVII (1785). 1 part (160,000).

First published in 1753. The reprinting in the *Novelist's* includes six engravings, dated February 5–March 12, 1785.

584. The HISTORY OF JOHN OF CALAIS. [By Mme. de Gomez.] *Weekly Misc.* (Sherborne), XIX (December 9–December 23, 1782). 3 parts (9000).

An unacknowledged translation of the "Histoire de Jean de Calais," found in the "Quatrième journée" of Mme. de Gomez, *Les Journées amusantes* (1722–1731). The translation is Mrs. Haywood's, first published under the same title in *La Belle Assemblée* (1724–1726). For other extracts from the same collection, see BELLE ASSEMBLÉE (Index).

a. The History of John of Calais. "Tale 3," *Tell-Tale,* I (September, 1803). 1 part.

585. The HISTORY OF JOHN WINCHCOMB, Otherwise Jack of Newbury. "Tale 76," *Tell-Tale,* VI (1805).

Probably a version of *The History of Jack of Newbury, Called the Clothier of England,* (1750?).

586. The HISTORY OF JONATHAN WILD THE GREAT. By Henry Fielding, Esq. *Novelist's,* IX (1782). 1 part (72,000).

First published in 1743 (rev. ed., 1754). The reprinting in the *Novelist's* included two engravings, dated October 12 and October 19, 1782.

587. HISTORY OF JOSEPH PIGNATA. From the German of [August von] Kotzebue. *Theatrical Inquisitor,* V (September, 1814) – VI (February, 1815). 6 parts (14,000). Signed "FLOSCULUS."

A translation of "Die Flucht" (*Die jüngsten Kinder meine Laune, von A. v. Kotzebue,* Vol. V, 1796). The editor of the *Theatrical Inquisitor* wrote: "Some important liberties have been taken with the original, both to shorten the story, and render it more suited to the English reader." (V, 151.)

588. HISTORY OF KEMSARAI AND MEIMOUNA, or the Three Talismans. An Oriental Tale. *Lady's,* XXXI (November–December, 1800). 2 parts (5100).

589. The HISTORY OF KITTY WELLS, a True Story. *European,* I (January–March, 1782). 3 parts (6600). Signed "P."

a. The History of Kitty Wells, a True Story. *Hibernian,* 1782 (April–May). 2 parts.
b. History of Kitty Wells. *New Novelist's,* II (1787), 79–87. 1 part.
c. The History of Kitty Wells. *Harvest Home,* II (1808), 355–365. 1 part.

590. The HISTORY OF LADY BRADLEY, Written by Herself, and Addressed by Mrs. Falkland, to the Lady to Whom She Communicated the Memoirs of Her Own Life, Published under the Title of "Memoirs of a Young Lady of Family" in the First, Second, and Third Volumes of This Magazine. *Lady's,* VII (Supplement, 1776) – IX (August, 1778). 22 parts (23,500).

See No. 873 below, of which the present story was a continuation.

591. The HISTORY OF LADY JULIA MANDEVILLE. *London,* XXXII (July–August, 1763). 2 parts (7400).

An epitome of Frances Brooke's novel of the same name (1763), offered as a notice of the work.

a. The History of Lady J. Mandeville. *Beauties of All the Magazines,* II (August, 1763). 1 part. Uncompleted.

"From the *London Magazine.*" Reprints only Part 1 of the above.

592. HISTORY OF LADY P———. *Belle Assemblée,* n.s. XII (October, 1815) – n.s. XIII (February, 1816). 5 parts (9800).

Extracted from Mrs. Grant, of Leggan, *Popular Models and Impressive Warnings, for the Sons and Daughters of Industry* (1815), according to the editor (p. 168).

593. The HISTORY OF LADY SHELLY. *Beauties of All the Magazines,* I (December, 1762) – II (March, 1763). 4 parts (6000).

The story is told in the form of a letter, signed "Constance./Harrum Lodge, Oct. 22, 1762." It is labelled "From the *Ladies Magazine*" [i.e., Cooke's *Lady's Magazine* of 1762?].

594. The HISTORY OF LAMBERG. *German Misc.,* 1796, pp. 229–268. 1 part (8400). Uncompleted.

Translated by Alexander Thomson, from the German of A. G. Meissner. The original has not been identified.

595. [The HISTORY OF LAURA.] *Lady's Monthly Museum,* VII (September–November, 1801). 3 parts (4900).

Nos. 38–40 of the series called "The Old Woman." The story bears no title in the original.

596. The HISTORY OF LAURETTA. A Moral Tale. [By Marmontel.] *Court Misc.*, I (July–October, 1765). 4 parts (10,350).

The earliest English translation of "Laurette" (*Contes moraux*, Vol. III, 1765). For other translations of the same story, see Nos. 747, 748, and 917.

597. HISTORY OF LEONORA CLELAND, or the Jealous Mother. *Town and Country*, XV (November, 1783) – XVI (April, 1784). 7 parts (14,500).

a. History of Leonora Cleland, or the Jealous Mother. *Hibernian*, 1783 (December) – 1784 (May). 7 parts.

598. The HISTORY OF LEOPOLD DE CIRCÉ, or the Effects of Atheism. Translated from the French of M. de St. Venant. *Universal*, CXIII (August, October, 1803). 2 parts (7500).

From *Leopold de Circé, ou les Effets de l'athéisme, par Mme. de Saint-Venant* (1803).

599. HISTORY OF LORD WARTON. *Berwick Museum*, III (April–December, 1787). 8 parts (14,700).

600. The HISTORY OF LOUISA. *Westminster*, I (June, 1773). 1 part (7600).

"For the *Westminster Magazine*."

a. The History of Louisa. *Town and Country Weekly*, I (? – July 30, 1785). 1 part. *Inc.* This fragment contains only the end of the story.

601. The HISTORY OF LOUISA LEESON, or the Triumph of Virtue, and Punishment of Vice, Exemplified. *New Lady's*, IV (March–June, 1789). 4 parts (10,500). Signed "Charlotta."

602. The HISTORY OF MANTHORN, the Enthusiast. *Town and Country*, X (March, 1778) – XI (March, 1779). 7 parts (17,750). Uncompleted.

Attributed to Thomas Holcroft in a later biographical article (*European*, I, 1782, p. 49).

a. The History of Manthorn, the Enthusiast. *Gentleman's and London*, 1778 (April) – 1779 (April). 7 parts. Uncompleted.

b. The History of Manthorn. *Cumberland*, I (?1778) – II (April, 1779). 7 parts? *Inc.*

Vol. II (February, April, 1779) of the *Cumberland* offers Chaps. 6 and 7 of this uncompleted story. Vol. I was not examined.

603. The HISTORY OF MARCELLA. *Royal*(1), I (October/December, 1750). 1 part (6100).

a. Disinterested Love, or the Triumph of Constancy. *Scots*, XII (Appendix, 1750). 1 part.

Attributed to a "French Magazine."

b. The History of Marcella. *Weekly Mag. and Literary Rev.*, I, Nos. 6–7 (May 20–27, 1758). 2 parts.

c. The History of Marcella. *Court, City and Country*(1), III (April–June, 1765). 3 parts (5300).

A slightly abridged version of the foregoing.

d. The History of Marcella. *General,* I (October–December, 1787). 3 parts.

e. St. Albert and Marcella. Written by Marcella. *Britannic,* IV, Nos. 52–53 (1796–1797). 2 parts.

Part of the series of "Memoirs of Love and Gallantry."

604. [HISTORY OF MARIA.] *Town and Country,* XV (May–June, 1783). 2 parts (8800).

The title is from the index to Volume XV.

605. HISTORY OF MATILDA, in Letters to a Friend. *New Lady's,* V (December, 1790) – VI (December, 1791). 7 parts (12,000).

606. The HISTORY OF MELISSA. [By John Hawkesworth.] *Adventurer,* Nos. 7–8 (November 28–December 2, 1752). 2 parts (5250).

In the table of contents of the first collected edition, the story is called "Distress encouraged to hope: the history of MELISSA."

a. The History of Melissa. *Scots,* XIV (November–December, 1752). 2 parts.

b. [Distress Encouraged to Hope: The History of Melissa.] *Weekly Amusement,* III (May 10–May 31, 1766). 4 parts.

The title is from Parts 2–4.

c. Hope Ordained by Providence for Man's Consolation, Exemplified in the Story of Melissa. *Weekly Misc.*(Sherborne), I (October 4–11, 1773). 2 parts.

d. The History of Melissa. From the *Adventurer* of Dr. Hawkesworth. *General,* II (January–March, 1788). 3 parts.

e. The History of Melissa. By Dr. Hawkesworth. *New Gleaner,* I (1809), 142–150. 1 part.

607. The HISTORY OF MIRRIL, A Grecian Tale, Translated from the *Triomphe de l'amitié. Oxford,* I (December–Supplement, 1768). 2 parts (8250).

Taken from Mme. Fauques de Vaucluse, *Le Triomphe de l'amitié, ouvrage traduit du grec par Mlle. de* * * (1751).

608. The HISTORY OF MISS BETSY THOUGHTLESS. By Mrs. [Eliza] Haywood. In Four Volumes. *Novelist's,* XIII (1783). 1 part (236,000).

First published in 1751. The reprinting in the *Novelist's* includes eight engravings, dated September 13–October 31, 1783.

609. The HISTORY OF MISS CLEVELAND. *Town and Country,* XII (September–October, 1780). 2 parts (6100). Signed "THEODOSIA."

a. The History of Miss Cleveland. *Hibernian,* 1780 (November). 1 part. Uncompleted. Reprints Part 1 of the above only.

610. The HISTORY OF MISS INDIANA DANBY. *Universal Museum,* n.s. I (June, 1765). 1 part (5100).

611. HISTORY OF MISS JENNY, Written and Sent by Her to the Countess of Roscommon, Lady to the English Ambassador at the Court of Denmark. Translated from the French of Madame Riccoboni. *Universal,* XXXV (September–December, 1764). 4 parts (28,500).

Translated from *Histoire de Miss Jenny, écrite et énvoyee par elle à Milady Comtesse de Roscomond, par Mme. Riccoboni* (1764).

612. The HISTORY OF MISS SIDNEY. *New Lady's,* II (May–June, 1787). 2 parts (6700).

Addressed "To the Editor of the *New Lady's Magazine*" in a letter signed "Mary Eliza / Primrose-Street."

a. The History of Miss Sidney. *Hibernian,* 1787 (June–July). 2 parts. Signed "Mary Eliza."

b. The History of Miss Sidney. *Berwick Museum,* III (June–July, 1787). 2 parts.

Addressed "To the Editor of the *Berwick Museum*" in an identical letter signed "Mary Eliza."

613. HISTORY OF MR. AND MRS. RESTLESS. *Lady's,* XX (December, 1789) – XXI (March, 1790). 3 parts (5600).

614. The HISTORY OF MR. ELDRIDGE. (From *Charlotte, a Tale of Truth.*) *Glasgow Misc.,* II (1800), 130–145. 1 part (5000).

From the novel by Susanna Rowson, published by the Minerva Press (1791).

615. HISTORY OF MR. FRAZER. From *Helen of Glenross. Universal,* CX (January–February, 1802). 2 parts (12,000).

From the novel by H. Martin, published in 1802.

616. The HISTORY OF MR. SAWYER DICKINS, a Wealthy Banker. (From a New and Interesting Novel, Entitled *A Winter in London.*) *Weekly Entertainer,* XLVI (November 10–24, 1806). 3 parts (5500).

From *A Winter in London, or Sketches of Fashion, a Novel* (1806), by Thomas Skinner Surr.

617. The HISTORY OF MRS. MORDAUNT, an Original Tale. *Sentimental and Masonic,* III (September–December, 1793). 4 parts (10,000).

"For the *Sentimental and Masonic Magazine.*"

618. The HISTORY OF MONSIEUR D'AMILCAR. A Tale of Other Times. *Belle Assemblée,* n.s. VIII (November, 1813) – n.s. IX (January, 1814). 3 parts (8300).

619. HISTORY OF MONSIEUR DU F———. (From Miss H. W. Williams's *Letters Written in France, in the Summer [of] 1790.*) *European,* XVIII (December, 1790) – XIX (January, 1791). 2 parts (10,500).

The "Memoirs of Mons. and Madame Du F———," taken from Letters XVI–XXII of Helen Maria Williams's *Letters Written in France* (1790).

a. The Affecting History of Monsieur and Madame Du F———. *Universal,* LXXXVIII (January–February, 1791). 2 parts.

Attributed to the *Letters Written in France.*

b. History of Monsieur Du F———. (From Miss H. M. Williams's *Letters Written in France, in the Summer 1790.*) *Universal Magazine and Review,* V (January–February, 1791). 2 parts.

c. History of Monsieur Du F———, etc. [Same title as *European.*] *Gentleman's and London,* 1791 (January–March). 3 parts.

d. The Affecting History of Monsieur and Madame Du F———. (From *Letters Written in France in the Summer of 1790,* by Miss Helen Maria Williams, Who Had a Personal Knowledge of the Unfortunate Sufferers.) *Weekly Entertainer,* XVII (March 28–April 25, 1791). 5 parts.

e. The Affecting History of Monsieur and Madame Du F———. *Aberdeen*(1), IV (March–April, 1791). 2 parts.

Attributed in a note to the *Letters* of Miss Williams, "whose Writings are so much esteemed by the Public" (p. 172).

f. [History of Monsieur Du F———.] *Historical,* III, Nos. 29–30 (March–April, 1791). 2 parts.

Reprinted as part of a review of the *Letters.*

g. Family Pride and Parental Cruelty, Exemplified in the Interesting "History of Mons. and Madame Du F———." (From *Letters Written in France, in the Summer of 1790,* by Miss Helen Maria Williams.) *Lady's,* XXIII (January–March, 1792). 3 parts.

620. The HISTORY OF NOURJAHAD. By Mrs. [Frances] Sheridan. *Novelist's,* XXIII (1788). 1 part (26,000).

First published in 1767. The reprinting in the *Novelist's* includes an engraving dated December 1, 1787, though the title-page reads "1788". For a magazine epitome of the same novel, see No. 621.

621. The HISTORY OF NOURJAHAD. *Universal,* XLI (August, 1767). 1 part (5750).

An unacknowledged condensation of Frances Sheridan's novel of the same name (1767). For a full-length reprinting see No. 620.

622. The HISTORY OF OMRAH, the Son of Abulfaid. An Oriental Tale. *British,* I (January–March, 1760). 3 parts (8900).

Attributed to Smollett in *The Orientalist,* a collection of eastern tales (Dublin 1764), probably because it was the leading article in the first number of Smollett's *British Magazine.*

a. The History of Omrah, etc. [Same title as above.] *Edinburgh Museum,* I (July–August, 1763). 2 parts.

b. Omrah, Son of Abulfaid, an Oriental Tale. *Ipswich,* I (May–June, 1799). 2 parts.

623. The HISTORY OF OPHELIA. By Miss [Sarah] Fielding. In Two Volumes. *Novelist's,* XIX (1785). 1 part (105,000).

First published in 1760. The reprinting in the *Novelist's* includes three engravings, dated August 20–September 3, 1785.

624. The HISTORY OF OPTIMA, Supposed to Be Related by Herself. By Mr. Williams. *New Novelist's,* I (1786), 210–220. 1 part (7800).

Probably by John Williams (Anthony Pasquin).

625. The HISTORY OF PARMENIO, Written by Himself. *Lady's,* XVIII (May–October, 1787). 6 parts (12,250).

626. The HISTORY OF PAUL AND VIRGINIA, Translated from the French of Bernardin St. Pierre, by Miss Helen Maria Williams. *Weekly Entertainer,* XXIX (February 27–May 29, 1797). 13 parts (23,500).

An abridgment of Miss Williams's translation of *Paul et Virginie* (1787). The magazine version amounts to about two-thirds the length of the Williams translation, which was first published in 1795.

627. The HISTORY OF PEROUROU, or the Bellows-Mender, Written by Himself. (From Miss [Helen Maria] Williams' *Sketches of the State of Manners and Opinions of the French Republic.*) *Universal,* CVIII (January–February, 1801). 2 parts (9250).

From the author's two-volume collection of *Sketches* published in 1801.

a. The History of Perourou, or the Bellows-Mender, Written by Himself. (From Miss Williams's *Sketches of the State of Manners and Opinions in the French Republic.*) *Lady's,* XXXII (January–March, 1801). 3 parts.

b. Story of Perourou, or the Bellows-Mender. *Edinburgh*(2), n.s. XVII (February-April, 1801). 3 parts.

Attributed in a note to the *Sketches.*

c. The History of Perourou, etc. [Same title as *Universal.*] *Scots,* LXIII (March–April, 1801). 2 parts.

d. The History of Perourou, etc. [Same title as No. 627a]. *Hibernian,* 1801 (May–August). 4 parts.

e. Perourou, the Bellows-Mender. *Britannic,* IX, Nos. 117–119 (1801). 3 parts.

Part of the series "Memoirs of Love and Gallantry."

f. The History of Perourou, or the Bellows-Mender, Written by Himself. *Glasgow Misc.*, II (1801), 229–256.

g. The History of Perourou, or the Bellows-Mender. Supposed to Be Related by Himself. By Miss Helen Maria Williams. *Entertaining*(1), I, No. 4 (April, 1802). 1 part.

h. The History of Perourou, etc. [Same title as No. 627g.] *Weekly Entertainer*, XXXIX (May 17–June 21, 1802). 5 parts.

i. The History of Perourou, or the Bellows-Mender. By Miss Helen Maria Williams. *Gleaner*, I (1805), 222–236. 1 part.

628. [HISTORY OF PHILANDER AND CLARINDA.] *British*(2), VIII (June–July, 1767). 2 parts (6000). Signed "J. BURTON/Baker's Buildings, Bishopsgate."

Addressed "To the Authors of the *British Magazine*." The title is from Part 2.

a. The History of Philander and Clarinda. *Royal*(2), XVI (June, 1767) – XVII (July, 1767). 2 parts. Signed "J. BURTON, Bishopsgate."

Addressed "To the Author of the *Royal Magazine*." The simultaneous appearance of this story in two London miscellanies suggests that the author may have submitted it to both at the same time.

629. [The HISTORY OF PHILIP DELLWYN.] *Literary Leisure*, I, No. 5 (October 24) – No. 7 (November 17, 1799). 3 parts (7500).

The title is from the table of contents of the collected edition.

a. Affecting History of Philip Dellwyn, Taken Chiefly from His Own Manuscript. By Solomon Saunter, Esq. *Entertaining*(1), I, No. 10 (October, 1802). 1 part.

630. The HISTORY OF POLYDORE AND EMILIA. *Weekly Misc.*(Sherborne), XI (January 11, 1779). 1 part (6250).

Taken, without acknowledgment, from "Letter XXXI" of George, Lord Lyttelton, *Letters from a Persian in England to His Friend at Ispahan* (1735).

a. The History of Polydore and Emilia. *Moral and Entertaining*, IV (January, 1779). 1 part.

631. The HISTORY OF POMPEY THE LITTLE, or the Life and Adventures of a Lap-Dog. By Mr. [Francis] Coventry. *Novelist's*, XIX (1785). 1 part (53,000).

First published in 1751. The reprinting in the *Novelist's* includes two engravings, dated August 7 and 15, 1785.

632. The HISTORY OF PRINCE NOUROUN SALNAIM AND THE PRINCESS AXIANIA. An Oriental Tale. *Grand*(2), III (January–August, 1760). 6 parts (25,000). Uncompleted.

633. The HISTORY OF RASSELAS, Prince of Abissinia. A Tale, in Two Volumes, by Dr. Johnson. *Novelist's*, XXIII (1787). 1 part (38,000).

A reprinting of Johnson's *Rasselas* (1759), embellished with two engravings dated June 1 and July 1, 1787. For extracts and abridgments of the same work, see Nos. 48, 634–636, and 1365.

634. The HISTORY OF RASSELAS, Prince of Abissinia. *Grand Magazine*(1), II (April–May, 1759). 2 parts (9300).

The earliest of several abridgments of Johnson's novel (1759). It is this piracy, by Kinnersley, that led Dodsley to seek an injunction (see Chapter IV, pp. 240–241). For other versions of the novel see Nos. 48, 633, 635–636, and 1365.

635. [The HISTORY OF RASSELAS, Prince of Abissinia.] *London*, XXVIII (May–June, 1759). 2 parts (9600).

An epitome of Johnson's novel (1759), preceded by a note praising the work for its moral tendency, its "agreeable and enchanting Manner," and its "sententious Stile." The title is from Part 2.

For other versions of the same novel see Nos. 48, 633–634, 636, and 1365.

636. An Account of *The HISTORY OF RASSELAS, Prince of Abissinia. Universal*, XXIV (May, 1759) – XXV (September, 1759). 4 parts (12,000). Uncompleted.

A series of discrete fragments from Johnson's novel (1759), separately titled, but making a kind of continuous narrative. For other versions of the same work, see Nos. 48, 633–635, and 1365.

637. The HISTORY OF ROBERT, Surnamed the Brave, Created a Knight by Raimond, Count of St. Gilles, Rovergue, Provence, and Count of Toulouse after the Death of William the Fourth, His Brother. *Lady's*, XXXII (January–December, 1801). 12 parts (34,000).

The translator of the work, "Eliza M****," declares that it is a posthumous work of the Count de Tressan" (i.e., *Histoire de Robert, Surnommé le Brave, ouvrage posthume de L. E. de Lavergne*, 1800).

a. The History of Robert, Surnamed the Brave, etc. [Same title as above.] *Hibernian*, 1802 (January–December). 12 parts.

638. The HISTORY OF ROSETTA. Translated from the French of D'Arnaud. *London*, XLII (January–February, 1773). 2 parts (6600).

"Rosetta, or the Fair Penitent Rewarded," extracted, without acknowledgment, from John Murdoch, *The Tears of Sensibility, Translated from the French of Mons. D'Arnaud* (1773). The original of Murdoch's piece is *Clary, ou le Retour à la vertue recompensé* (1767).

a. The History of Rosetta. Translated from the French of D'Arnaud. *Hibernian*, 1773 (February–March). 2 parts (5800).

An abridged version of the above. This story was published in Pott's edition of the *Hibernian*, but not in the pirated edition (see the Note under *Hibernian* in the "Register of Periodicals").

639. The HISTORY OF SALLY RESTLESS. *Lady's,* XX (June–December, 1789). 7 parts (7000).

Part of the series "Domestic Lessons for the Use of the Younger Part of the Female Readers of the *Lady's Magazine.*"

640. The HISTORY OF SIR CHARLES GRANDISON. In a Series of Letters. By Mr. Samuel Richardson. In Seven Volumes. *Novelist's,* X (1783) – XI (1783). 2 parts (780,000).

First published in 1753–1754. The reprinting in the *Novelist's* included twenty-eight engravings, dated November 2, 1782 – May 12, 1783.

641. The HISTORY OF SIR LAUNCELOT EDGEVILE. *Court Misc.* III (November, 1767) – IV (May, 1768). 5 parts (10,200).

642. The HISTORY OF SOLIMAN AND ELMIRA. Translated from the French [of Marmontel], and Illustrated with a Beautiful Copper-Plate. *Court Misc.,* IV (July–August, 1768). 2 parts (5800).

A translation of "Soliman II," from the *Contes moraux* (1761). This English version was extracted, without acknowledgment, from *Moral Tales* (Becket and De Hondt, 1764) [see No. 917]. For other translations of the same story, see Nos. 1162–1163.

a. The History of Soliman II. By M. Marmontel. *Bristol and Bath,* II, No. 9 (1783). 1 part.

643. The HISTORY OF SOPHIA EVERAD. *New Lady's,* VII (September, 1792) – VIII (August, 1793). 5 parts (8900). Signed "W./Islington."

644. The HISTORY OF THE ADVENTURES OF JOSEPH ANDREWS, and of His Friend Mr. Abraham Adams. Written in Imitation of the Manner of Cervantes, Author of *Don Quixote.* By Henry Fielding, Esq. In Two Volumes. *Novelist's,* I (1780). 1 part (134,000).

First published in 1742. The reprinting in the *Novelist's* included four engravings, dated December 1, 1779–March 1, 1780.

645. HISTORY OF THE AMOURS OF THE COUNT OF BELFLOR AND LEONORA OF CESPEDES. From the French of Mons. Le Sage. *Lady's,* VI (May–October, 1775); VII (January, 1776). 7 parts (13,000). Signed "ELFRIDA."

A translation of Chapter IV ("Histoire des amours du comte de Belflor et de Léonor de Cespèdes") and Chapter V ("Suite et conclusion des amours du comte de Belflor") of Le Sage, *Le Diable boiteux* (1707). For a complete translation of *Le Diable boiteux,* see No. 306; and for another extract, No. 461. The translation in the *Lady's* was broken off by "Elfrida," and the editor was forced to find another writer to "deliver [readers] from the pangs of suspence." (VII, 34.) The last part is signed "D——."

646. The HISTORY OF THE COUNT DE COMMINGE, Written by Himself. *Lady's Museum,* I, Nos. 2–8 (1760). 9 parts (20,000).

Translated for the *Museum* by Mrs. Lennox, from Mme. de Tencin, *Mémoires du comte de Comminge* (1735). The above story was republished by Mrs. Lennox, with a few changes, as the *History of the Marquis de Lussan and Isabella* in 1764. For another version of *Comminge,* see No. 887.

a. The History of the Count de Comminge, Written by Himself. *Town and Country,* XIII (January–Supplement, 1781). 9 parts.

This printing of Mrs. Lennox's translation was interrupted between February and July, 1781, because the author was "very much indisposed." (XIII, 282). Though Mrs. Lennox was still alive in 1781, it is evident that the alleged "author" in the *Town and Country* was a mere plagiarist.

b. The History of the Count de Comminge, Written by Himself. *Hibernian,* 1781 (February) – 1782 (January). 9 parts.

c. The History of the Count de Comminge, Supposed to be Written by Himself. Translated from the French, by Mrs. Lennox. *New Novelist's,* II (1787), 275–301.

d. History of the Count de Comminge, Written by Himself. Translated from the French, by Mrs. Lennox. *New Gleaner,* I (1809), 255–287.

647. The HISTORY OF THE COUNT DE FERNAIS. *Dundee Repository,* I (November 15–29, 1793). 2 parts (5600).

648. HISTORY OF THE DECAYED ENGLISH MERCHANT AND HIS DAUGHTER. From Pratt's *Gleanings. Lady's,* XXVII (January–May, 1796). 3 parts (5000).

From S. J. Pratt, *Gleanings through Wales, Holland and Westphalia, etc.* (1795).

a. The Decayed English Merchant and His Daughter. From Pratt's *Gleanings. Scots,* LVIII (March–June, 1796). 3 parts.

649. HISTORY OF THE FAIR ARDELIA. *Court Misc.,* VII (June–August, 1771). 3 parts (5600).

a. History of the Fair Ardelia. *Universal Museum,* n.s. VII (June–August, 1771). 3 parts.

650. The HISTORY OF THE FAIR MARIA. A Novel Founded on Truth. *Lady's*(2), I (October, 1759) – II (September, 1760). 6 parts (11,300).

651. HISTORY OF THE FAMILY OF D——y, Related by Mr. Hughes, in His *Tour through the Western Provinces of France. Monthly Visitor,* n.s. VIII (July–August, 1804). 2 parts (5000).

From the Rev. W. Hughes, *A Tour through Several of the Midland and Western Departments of France, in the Months of June, July, August, and September, 1802* (1803).

a. History of the Family of D——y, etc. [Same title as above.] *Weekly Entertainer,* XLIV (October 8–22, 1804). 3 parts.

652. [HISTORY OF THE HOMESPUNS.] [By Henry Mackenzie.] *Mirror,* Nos. 12 (March 6), 25, 53 (July 27, 1779). 3 parts (5600).

The story, which bears no title in the original, was continued in the *Lounger,* Nos. 17 (May 28, 1785) and 98 (December 16, 1786), making a total of 5 parts (9400). The two letters from John Homespun in the *Lounger* interlock also with the chronicle of the Mushroom family in *Lounger* Nos. 36, 52, and 62 (see No. 938 below).

a. [History of the Homespuns.] *Weekly Misc.*(Sherborne), XII (April 19, June 21, August 30, 1779). 3 parts.

A reprinting of the *Mirror,* Nos. 12, 25, 53. No title was employed, except the general title of "*The Mirror.*"

b. [History of the Homespuns.] *Moral and Entertaining,* IV (May, 1779) – V (September, 1779). 3 parts.

A reprinting of *Mirror* Nos. 12, 25, and 53 only, under the title "The Mirror, a New Periodical Paper, Just Published at Edinburgh."

653. The HISTORY OF THE INCAS, or the Destruction of the Empire of Peru. Translated from the French of the Celebrated Mr. Marmontel. *Universal,* LXI (November, 1777) – LXII (February, 1778). 3 parts (9500).

A highly condensed abridgment of Volume I of *The Incas, or the Destruction of the Empire of Peru, by M. Marmontel* (1777), translated in turn from *Les Incas, ou la Destruction de l'empire du Pérou* (1777). For an extract in French from the same novel, see No. 524. In the *Universal* only the French source was acknowledged.

a. The History of the Incas, etc. [Same title as above.] *Westminster,* VI (March–May, 1778). 3 parts.

"For the *Westminster Magazine.*"

654. [HISTORY OF THE LIFE OF DUNCAN CAMPBELL, His Difficulties, Escapes, Re-encounter with a Ghost, and Other Adventures.] [By James Hogg.] *Spy,* Nos. 49 (August 3), 51 (August 17, 1811). 2 parts (8300).

The title is from the table of contents of the collected edition. This story was later reprinted as "Duncan Campbell" in Hogg's *Winter Evening Tales* (1820).

655. The HISTORY OF THE MAN OF LETTERS. *Strabane,* II (January–December, 1800). 11 parts (41,000).

Attributed to "Brook" – i.e., Henry Brooke, *The Fool of Quality* (Vols. I–II, 1766), from Chaps. 7 and 8 of which the story is largely extracted. For other extracts from the same novel, see No. 537.

a. The Man of Letters. By Mr. Brooke. *Harvest Home,* II (1808), 192–235. 1 part (26,000).

An abbreviated version of the above.

b. The Man of Letters. *Entertaining*(2), III (February–May, 1815). 4 parts (5000).

A greatly abbreviated version of the same story.

656. The HISTORY OF THE OLDCASTLE FAMILY, an Original Novel, Written Exclusively for This Work. *Belle Assemblée,* VII (September, 1809) – n.s. II (December, 1810). 16 parts (73,000).

657. The HISTORY OF THE PRINCESS RAKIMA AND THE SULTAN AMURAT IV. [By Mme. de Gomez.] *Weekly Entertainer,* VI (December 26, 1785) – VII (February 27, 1786). 10 parts (15,000).

An unacknowledged translation of the "Histoire de Rakima, et du Sultan Amurat," found in the "Treizième journée" of Mme. de Gomez, *Les Journées amusantes* (1722–1731). The English translation is Mrs. Haywood's ("The History of Rakima," *La Belle Assemblée,* 1724–1726). For other extracts from the same collection, see BELLE ASSEMBLÉE (Index).

658. The HISTORY OF THE ROYAL SLAVE. [By Aphra Behn.] *Ladies,* IV (April 14–November 10, 1753). 15 parts (30,500).

A complete reprinting of Mrs. Behn's novel, offered by the *Ladies* as the first of a projected series of classics in the novel form.

659. The HISTORY OF THE SECOND USHER, a Comic Tale. From *The Adventures of John of Gaunt,* an Entertaining Novel [by James White] Just Published. *Lady's,* XXI (May, 1790). 1 part (8000).

Adapted from "Visits" XIII–XVI of the novel, published in 1790. For other extracts from the same work, see No. 660 (not the same story, though it bears the same title) and No. 1010. In April, 1790, the *Lady's* had published another extract from White's novel, entitled "History of the First Usher" (4500 words).

a. The History of an Usher, a Comic Tale. From *The Adventures of John of Gaunt,* an Entertaining Novel Just Published. *Weekly Entertainer,* XV (June 21–28, 1790). 2 parts.

b. History of the Second Usher, etc. [Same title as *Lady's Magazine.*] *Hibernian,* 1790 (July–August). 2 parts.

660. The HISTORY OF THE SECOND USHER, a Comic Tale. From *The Adventures of John of Gaunt, Duke of Lancaster,* by James White, Esq., Author of *Earl Strongbow,* etc. *Weekly Entertainer,* XVI (July 12–August 23, 1790). 7 parts (11,750).

Taken from "Visits" XII, XVII, XX–XXI of White's novel. For other extracts, see No. 659 (not the same story) and No. 1010.

661. The HISTORY OF TOM JONES, a Foundling. In Four Volumes. By Henry Fielding, Esq. *Novelist's,* III (1780). 1 part (360,000).

First published in 1749. The reprinting in the *Novelist's* includes twelve engravings, dated September 30–December 18, 1780.

662. The HISTORY OF WENTWORTH AIRCASTLE. By Mr. Scawen. *New Novelist's,* I (1786), 34–45. 1 part (8500).

The author is otherwise unidentified (see No. 662a). Embellished with an engraving dated June 1, 1786.

a. Vicissitudes of Wentworth Aircastle. By Mr. Schoen. *Entertaining*(1), I (June, 1802). 1 part.

Possibly George L. Schoen, author of a poem published in 1793.

b. The History of Wentworth Aircastle. By Mr. Scawen. *Gleaner,* I (1805), 366–380.

663. The HISTORY OF YOUSSUF-BEY AND OF GUL-BEYAZ, a Turkish Story. *Weekly Amusement,* III (August 16–October 25, 1766). 10 parts (9250).

664. The HOBGOBLIN AT THE SPA. Translated from the German. *New Novelist's,* I (1787), 328–336. 1 part (6000).

665. The HONEST BRETON. [By Marmontel.] *Monthly Extracts,* II (April, 1792). 1 part (13,750).

A translation of "Le Franc Breton" (*Mercure,* 1790), extracted, in the course of review, from *Tales of an Evening, Followed by the Honest Breton, Translated from the French of M. Marmontel* (1792). For another translation of the same story, see No. 666.

a. Montalde, or the Honest Breton. By M. Marmontel. "Tale 55," *Tell-Tale,* IV (1804). 1 part.

666. The HONEST BRETON. [By Marmontel.] *Weekly Entertainer,* XLVIII (May 16–July 11, 1808). 8 parts (14,500).

A translation of "Le Franc Breton" (*Mercure,* 1790). For another translation of the same story, see No. 665.

a. The Honest Breton. *New Gleaner,* II (1810), 257–279.

667. The HONEST FARMER, a Tale. *Scotch Cheap Repository,* Nos. 1–2 (1808). 2 parts (9600). Signed "A."

668. The HONOUR OF CHIVALRY, or the Renowned and Famous History of Don Bellianis of Greece. *Penny Medley,* No. 8 (1746). 1 part (5200).

669. The HORRORS OF A MONASTERY, a Tale. *Edinburgh*(2), n.s. VI (August–September, 1795). 2 parts (6900). Signed "J.G."

670. HORTENSIA, or the Wisdom of Explanation. A New Moral Tale, by M. de Marmontel. *Universal,* XCIV (April–May, 1794). 2 parts (7900).

A translation of "La Cassette, conte moral," first published in the *Mercure* (1792). For another translation of the same story, see No. 185.

a. Hortensia, etc. [Same title as above.] *Hibernian*, 1794 (May–June). 2 parts.

b. Hortensia, a Moral Tale. *Scots*, LVI (June–July, 1794). 2 parts.

c. Hortensia, etc. [Same title as *Universal*.] *Weekly Entertainer*, XXXIII (June 10, 1799) – XXXIV (July 1, 1799). 4 parts.

671. The HOUSE ON THE CLIFF, a Novel. *Lady's Monthly Museum*, n.s. IX (October, 1810) – n.s. X (June, 1811). 8 parts (20,000).

672. The HOUSEHOLDER, a Conversation, by Torquato Tasso. *Universal*, CV (September–October, 1799). 2 parts (7800).

An abridged translation of *Il Padre de famiglia* (1583).

673. The HOVEL ON THE HEATH, a Moral Tale, by Mr. Harrison. *Pocket*, IV (February, 1796) – V (October, 1796). 7 parts (13,000). Uncompleted.

Probably by James Harrison.

a. The Hovel on the Heath, a Moral Tale. *Hibernian*, 1796 (November) – 1797 (February). 4 parts. Uncompleted.

674. HULKEM. (By Lafontaine.) *German Museum*, I (May–June, 1800). 2 parts (7500).

The German original (by Augustus Lafontaine) has not been identified. The same story later appeared in a French translation as "Hulkem and Hassan" (*Nouveaux contes moraux d'Auguste Lafontaine, traduits de l'allemand*, 1802).

a. Hulkem, a Tale. *Belle Assemblée*, VI (March–April, 1809). 2 parts.

b. Hulkem, a Tale. *Hibernian*, 1809 (April–May). 2 parts (5500).

A slight abridgment of the same translation.

675. HUMAN LIFE, an Allegory. *Universal Museum*, n.s. VI (September–November, 1770). 3 parts (5300).

676. HUMAN VICISSITUDES. *Lady's Monthly Museum*, II (March–May, 1799). 3 parts (5100).

677. HUMAN VICISSITUDES, or the History of the Hon. Mrs. M———. *Universal*, CXI (November, 1802). 1 part (5000).

A quite different story from No. 676.

678. The HUMILIATION OF PRIDE AND AMBITION. *Belle Assemblée*, n.s. XI (May, 1815) – n.s. XII (July, 1815). 3 parts (6200).

"Novel VI" of a series of "Spanish Novels."

679. The HUMOROUS LIEUTENANT AND THE FAIR MAID OF GREECE, a Tale. *New Universal*(2), I (August–September, 1787). 2 parts (5100).

680. The HUSBAND TURNED SYLPH. A Tale. Translated from the Third Volume of Marmontel's *Tales,* Lately Published. *British*(2), VI (November–December, 1765). 2 parts (5000).

The first English translation of "Le Mari sylphe" (*Contes moraux,* Vol. III, 1765). For other translations see No. 917 ("Moral Tales") and No. 1224.

681. HYMENAEA IN SEARCH OF A HUSBAND. *Belle Assemblée,* VI (March, 1809) – n.s. VI (November, 1812). 43 parts (116,000). Uncompleted.

682. The HYPOCRITES, a Novel. *Sentimental,* I (August, 1773) – II (April, 1774). 10 parts (17,000).

a. The Hypocrites, a Novel. *Dumfries Weekly,* III (September 21, 1773) – V (May 10, 1774). 9 parts.

683. IDDA OF TOKENBURG, or the Force of Jealousy. A Tale, Translated from the German of Augustus Lafontaine. *Lady's,* XXXII (January–August, 1801). 8 parts (18,000).

A translation of "Idda von Tokenburg, oder die Stärke der Eifersucht" (see *Kleine Romane und moralische Erzählungen von August Lafontaine,* III, 3rd ed., 1804).

a. Idda of Tokenburg, etc. [Same title as above.] *Hibernian,* 1802 (February–October). 8 parts.

684. ILDEFONZO AND ALBERONI, or Tales of Horrors. *Marvellous,* III (August 1, 1803). 1 part (30,000).

685. The ILLUSIONS OF LOVE, a Sentimental Tale, in a Letter Addressed to a Young Lady of Family, from a Female Friend. *Lady's,* XVII (April, 1786) – XVIII (February, 1787). 11 parts (23,000).

686. The ILLUSTRIOUS LOVERS, or Secret History of Malcolm and Matilda, a Scottish Story. *Rambler's,* III (December, 1785) – IV (February, 1786). 4 parts (7100).

The four parts comprise Nos. 6–8 of the series "The Amorous Novelist."

687. IMPERIAL CLEMENCY, a Moral Tale. *British Mag. and Rev.,* III (October, 1783). 2 parts (5000). Signed "F———."

Possibly by James Fisher (see No. 687d below), the author of a number of poems and essays published between 1790 and 1810.

a. Imperial Clemency, a Moral Tale. *Gentleman's and London,* 1783 (November–December). 2 parts.

b. Imperial Clemency, a Moral Tale. *Weekly Entertainer,* II (December 8–15, 1783). 2 parts.

c. Imperial Clemency, a Moral Tale. *Edinburgh Weekly,* LIX (January 29–February 5, 1784). 2 parts.

d. Imperial Clemency. By Mr. Fisher. *New Novelist's,* I (1787), 387–393. 1 part

e. Imperial Clemency, a Moral Tale. *Edinburgh*(2), X (December, 1789). 1 part.

f. Imperial Clemency, a Moral Tale. *Dundee Rep.,* I (July 12–26, 1793). 2 parts.

g. Imperial Clemency, a Moral Tale. *Edinburgh*(2), n.s. IV (September, 1794). 1 part.

A second appearance of this story in the *Edinburgh* (see No. 687e).

h. Imperial Clemency. By Mr. Fisher. *Harvest Home,* II (1808), pp. 240–248. 1 part.

688. The IMPRESSED SEAMAN, a Moral Tale. [By Thomas Bellamy.] *General,* II (July–October, 1788). 4 parts (7000).

The piece was unclaimed by Bellamy in the *General,* but was later collected in his *Miscellanies in Prose and Verse* (1794) as "Henry Randolph, or the British Seaman."

a. The Impressed Seaman, a Moral Tale. *New Gleaner,* I (1809), 202–215.

Attributed to the *General Magazine.*

689. The INDIAN COTTAGE. By [Bernardin de] St. Pierre. *Harvest Home,* I (1807), 29–50. 1 part (13,000).

From *La Chaumière indienne, par Jacqúes-Bernardin-Henri de Saint-Pierre* (1791). For another version of the same story, see No. 690.

690. The INDIAN COTTAGE, a Tale. [By Bernardin de Saint-Pierre.] Translated from the French for the *Bee. Bee,* XVII (September 4–October 2, 1793). 5 parts (8750).

A translation, considerably condensed, of Saint-Pierre, *La Chaumière indienne* (1791). For another translation of the same story, see No. 689.

691. The INDIANS. [By William Richardson.] *County,* II (March–August, 1788). 4 parts (6000). Signed "The Mental Chymist/Feb. 1788."

Labeled "For the *County Magazine,*" but actually a plagiarism (see No. 691a).

a. The Indians. *General,* IV (January–February, 1790). 2 parts.

The story is identified as a "selection" from the "elegant pen of Professor [William] Richardson," author of *The Tragedy of the Indians* [1790]. "The Indians, a Tale," was first published in Richardson's *Poems, Chiefly Rural* (Glasgow, 1774), which went into its fourth edition in 1781. A shorter version than No. 690 is found printed in the *Dumfries Weekly Magazine,* X (August 15, 1775), pp. 289–296 (4500 words).

b. The Indians, a Tale. By Professor Richardson. *Hibernian,* 1790 (January–April). 3 parts.

c. The Indians, a Tale. From *The Tragedy of the Indians. Universal Mag. and Rev.,* III (March, 1790). 1 part.

d. The Indians. *Britannic,* V, Nos. 68–69 (1798). 1 part.

Included in the series "Memoirs of Love and Gallantry."

692. The INDIGENT, INDUSTRIOUS CHILD. *Juvenile,* I (May, 1788) – II (October, 1789). 5 parts (9250). Signed "M.P."

693. The INDISCREET LOVER. *Britannic,* XI, No. 159 (1804). 1 part (5000).

Part of the series "Memoirs of Love and Gallantry." [See Addenda, p. 647.]

694. The INDISCRETIONS OF YOUTH, or Entrance into Life, a Novel, in a Series of Letters. *Fashionable,* I (June–December, 1786). 7 parts (13,750).

a. The Indiscretions of Youth, etc. [Same title as above.] *Berwick Museum,* III (March, 1787). 1 part. Uncompleted.

A reprinting of Part 1 of the above only.

695. INDUSIATA, or the Adventures of a Silk Petticoat. *Westminster,* I (June–December, 1773). 7 parts (10,000). Signed "N."

"For the *Westminster Magazine.*"

696. The INEXORABLE RESOLUTION, a Tale. *Universal,* LXXXII (June–Supplement, 1788). 2 parts (8000).

a. The Inexorable Resolution, a Tale. *Beauties of Magazines, etc.,* I (June, 1788) – II (August, 1788). 2 parts.

697. The INEXPERIENCED TRAVELLER, or Characteristic Traits. *Lady's Monthly Museum,* XIII (August–December 1804). 5 parts (25,000).

698. The INFIDEL PARSON, a Moral Story Founded on Truth. *London,* XL (November, 1771) – XLI (January, 1772). 3 parts (7800).

699. [The INFLUENCE OF INFIDELITY UPON MORAL CONDUCT: Story of Opsinous.] [By John Hawkesworth.] *Adventurer,* Nos. 12–14 (December 16–23, 1752). 3 parts (6300).

The title is from the table of contents of the collected edition.

a. The History of Opsinous. *Scots,* XIV (Appendix, 1752). 1 part.

Attributed to the *Adventurer.*

b. The History of Opsinous. *Harvest Home,* I (1807), 269–278.

700. On the INGENUITY OF OLD MAIDS. (Taken from the Same [i.e., Hayley's *Essay on Old Maids*].) Containing the Story of Dr. Coral and His Daughter. *Caledonian*(2), I (April–May, 1788). 2 parts (5000).

From Part II, Chapter 1, of William Hayley's *Philosophical, Historical, and Moral Essay on Old Maids* (1785). For other extracts from the same work, see Nos. 67 and 245. A shorter version of the "Story of Dr. Coral and His Daughter" was frequently reprinted in the magazines.

701. INNOCENCE PRESERVED: Being the Adventures of Miss Arabella R———y. A Narrative Founded on Some Late Extraordinary Matters of Fact. *Ladies,* II (November 3/17, 1750 – December 29/January 12, 1751). 5 parts (12,000).

A reprinting, in its entirety, of *The Temple Rakes, or Innocence Preserved, Being the Adventures of Miss Arabella R———y,* etc. (1735?) [McBurney, No. 298].

a. Innocence Preserved, etc. [Same title as above.] *Beauties of All the Magazines,* II (January, March, 1763). 2 parts (5500). Uncompleted.

This piece is labeled "From the *Ladies Magazine,*" but it reprints only about one-half of the original.

702. INNOCENCE PROTECTED, a Sentimental Story, by Mr. [James?] Harrison. *Entertaining*(1), I (March, 1802). 1 part (9100).

703. The INTELLIGENT TRAVELLER, or Human Nature Displayed. *Lady's Monthly Museum,* n.s. III (July, 1807) – n.s. VI (February, 1809). 16 parts (55,000).

In August, 1807, the editor requested "considerable alterations" in the MS. (p. 96). The story was interrupted between May and August, 1808, owing to "the indisposition of the Author" (n.s. IV, 320).

704. [INTERESTING ADVENTURES of a Spanish Lady, a Story Founded on Fact.] *Newry,* I (May/June, 1815) – II (March/April, 1816). 6 parts (20,000). Signed "S."

"For the *Newry Register.*" The title is taken from Parts 2–6.

705. INTERESTING ADVENTURES OF AN ENGLISH MERCHANT, Who Was Banished for Life to Siberia. Never Before Published. *Oxford,* I (September-October, 1768). 2 parts (5300).

706. The INTERESTING HISTORY OF THE COUNT DE BELLEGARDE. (From *Celestina, a Novel,* by Mrs. Charlotte Smith.) *Universal,* LXXXIX (September-December, 1791). 4 parts (20,000).

The extract is from Volume IV, Chaps. 7–11, of *Celestina* (1791). In the *Universal* it is prefaced with the label, "Sublime and Picturesque Scenery in the Pyrenean Mountains." For a disguised redaction of the same story, see No. 192.

a. History of the Count de Bellegarde. *Monthly Extracts,* II (January, 1792). 1 part (15,000).

The same extract as the above, but beginning at a later point.

b. The Interesting History of the Count de Bellegarde, with a Description of the Sublime and Picturesque Scenery in the Pyrenean Mountains. (From *Celestina, a Novel,* by Mrs. Charlotte Smith.) *Weekly Entertainer,* XIX (February 27–April 23, 1792). 9 parts.

Identical with the extract in the *Universal.*

707. INTERESTING HISTORY OF THE MONMOUTH FAMILY. *Lady's,* XI (August–November, 1780). 4 parts (8700).

708. [INTERESTING STORY OF MRS. S———.] *Literary Reg.,* III (1771), Nos. 5 and 9. 2 parts (7900).

The title is from Part 2 ("The Sequel of the Interesting Story of Mrs. S———").

709. INTERESTING STORY OF REBECCA, Founded on Facts. *Dublin Museum,* I (January–December, 1807). 12 parts (35,000).

710. The INTRIGUE, or the Lovers Who Were Persuaded to Be in Love. A Tale, from the French [of Mme. de Genlis]. *Lady's,* XXXVI (January–April, 1805). 4 parts (9800).

An unacknowledged translation of "Les Amants sans amour" (*Mercure de France,* 1804). For an earlier appearance of the same story, in the original French,. see No. 93.

711. The INVISIBLE SPY. By Explorabilis [sic]. [By Eliza Haywood.] In Two Volumes. *Novelist's,* XXIII (1788). 1 part (170,000).

First published in 1754 (dated 1755), as *The Invisible Spy, by Exploralibus.* For an early extract from the same novel, see No. 1180. The reprinting in the *Novelist's* includes five engravings, dated July 1 to October 1, 1788.

712. IONIA. The New Nosegay for the Year 1749, or Memoirs of the Late Ridotto. *British*(1), IV (March, 1749). 1 part (5000).

713. From ISABELLA TO ALBERT. *Bee,* XI (September 26, 1792) – XII (November 28, 1792). 4 parts (9400).

The introductory letter, signed "ALBERT," declares that the letters are "the artless effusions of a favourite sister... scarcely sixteen when she wrote them... The names only are disguised, and the places and dates suppressed." (XI, 131.) Addressed "To the Editor of the *Bee.*"

714. ISMAEL, a Moorish Tale. *Edinburgh*(2), n.s. I (January, 1793). 1 part (5400).

715. IVAN CZAROWITZ, or the Rose without Prickles That Stings Not, a Tale. Written by Her Imperial Majesty. Translated from the Russian for the *Bee. Bee,* XVII (September 11–25, 1793). 3 parts (5000).

716. JACQUELINE, or Memoirs of an Exile. *Hibernian,* 1811 (August–October). 3 parts (11,000).

717. Some Account of JANE S———, THE YOUNG COTTAGER. [By the Rev. Legh Richmond.] *Christian Herald,* I (April 18–September 19, 1814). 6 parts (12,750). Signed "SIMPLEX."

An introductory note explains that the story has been extracted from "a Magazine very little known in this country" [i.e., the *Christian Guardian*], and that "it is understood to come from the same pen which wrote 'The Dairyman's Daughter,'" (p. 142). The version in the *Christian Herald,* however, has been abridged about a third. The original, called "The Young Cottager," and "The Dairyman's Daughter" were reprinted in a collection by Richmond called *Annals of the Poor* (1814). See Nos. 277 and 1361.

718. JE VIENS. A French Tale. *Lady's Monthly Museum,* n.s. II (April, 1807). 1 part (5000). Signed "W.I.M."

a. Je Viens. A French Tale. *Hibernian,* 1807 (April–May). 2 parts. Signed "W.I.M."

719. The JEALOUS HUSBAND, a True Story. *Universal,* XLVI (March, 1770). 1 part (5200).

a. The Jealous Husband, a True Story. *Weekly Misc.*(Sherborne), X (July 27, 1778). 1 part.

b. The Jealous Husband. *Salmon's Mercury.* I, Nos. 25 (May 7?), 26, 29–31, 36 (July 23, 1779). 6 parts. Signed "I.H./Bristol/April 12th."

Addressed "To the Printer of the *Weekly Mercury.*"

720. JEALOUSY, a Novel. *Lady's,* XLI (December, 1810) – XLII (September, 1811). 10 parts (16,500).

721. JEALOUSY, a Sentimental History, Founded upon Facts. *Lady's,* IV (July–August, 1773). 2 parts (5800).

722. JEALOUSY, a Tale, from the French. *Lady's Monthly Museum,* n.s. X (February–May, 1811). 4 parts (10,750).

723. La JEUNE PÉNITENTE, NOUVELLE. [By Mme. de Genlis.] *Ambigu,* VII, No. 58 (November 10, 1804). 1 part (12,500). Signed "D. [i.e., Ducrest] GENLIS."

First published in the *Mercure de France* (No. 129, December 17, 1803). For a later English translation of the story see No. 389.

724. JOHANNA AND UBALDUS, a Tale of the Fourteenth Century. *Bon Ton,* V (May–December, 1795). 8 parts (7300).

725. JOHN DE LANCASTER AND AMELIA JONES, a Tale. (From *John de Lancaster,* a Novel, Just Published, by Richard Cumberland, Esq.) *Weekly Entertainer,* XLIX (July 31–October 30, 1809). 12 parts (21,000).

Largely taken from Vol. III of the novel, published in 1809.

726. The JOURNEY. *Lady's Monthly Museum,* n.s. X (March–April, 1811). 2 parts (5000). Signed "W.R."

727. A JOURNEY FROM THIS WORLD TO THE NEXT. By Henry Fielding, Esq. *Novelist's,* XII (1783). 1 part (49,000).

First published in Volume II of *Miscellanies* (1743). The reprinting in the *Novelist's* includes three engravings, dated June 14–28, 1783.

728. The JOURNEY TO LONDON, a Tale. *Edinburgh*(2), n.s. VI (October, 1795). 1 part (5600).

729. A JOURNEY TO THE MOON. *Monthly Visitor,* IV (May–June, 1798). 2 parts (5500). Signed "FERDINAND ST. JULIAN."

a. A Journey to the Moon. *Aberdeen*(2), III (July–September, 1798). 3 parts. Signed "FERDINAND ST. JULIAN."

730. JOURNIES OF JULIUS. *Youth's,* III (January–December, 1808). 12 parts (16,000).

731. JULIA. Karamsin's *Russian Tale. German Museum,* II (September, 1800). 1 part (5900).

A first translation into English of a tale by Nikolai Mikhailovich Karamzin. An abridged version of this translation, called "Julia, a Russian Tale" (4200 words) was published in the *Universal Magazine* for October, 1800, and was reprinted in a number of contemporary periodicals, including the *Hibernian Magazine.*

a. Julia, a Russian Tale. *Belle Assemblée,* VI (February, 1809). 1 part (5900).

b. Julia, a Russian Tale. *Monthly Pantheon,* II (May, 1809). 1 part (5900).

732. JULIA, or Adventures of a Curate's Daughter. *Westminster,* I (January–March, 1773). 3 parts (14,000).

"For the *Westminster Magazine.*"

a. Julia, or Adventures of a Curate's Daughter. *Hibernian,* 1773 (March–May). 3 parts.

This story is found only in the piratical issues of the *Hibernian,* published by Marchbank and Seguin (see the Note under *Hibernian* in the "Register of Periodicals").

b. Julia, or Adventures of a Curate's Daughter. *Town and Country Weekly,* I (?May 14–?June 4, 1785). 3 parts. *Inc.*

c. The History of Julia, or the Adventures of a Curate's Daughter. *Weekly Entertainer,* VI (August 22–September 26, 1785). 6 parts (11,250).

An abridged version of the above.

d. Julia of Elmwood. *New Gleaner,* I (1809). 1 part.

Attributed to the *Westminster Magazine.*

733. JULIA, or the Penitent Daughter, an Affecting History. [By Baculard D'Arnaud.] *Universal,* LXX (February–March, 1782). 2 parts (9400). Signed "L."

In an introductory note (p. 60), this story is attributed to "the truly excellent M. Arnaud," the "author of *Trials of Sentiment.*" It is a translation of "Julie, anecdote historique" (*Épreuves du sentiment,* 1772).

a. Julia, etc. [Same title as above.] *Hibernian,* 1782 (March–May). 3 parts.

b. Julia, etc. [Same title.] *Weekly Entertainer,* I (June 9–30, 1783). 4 parts.

c. Julia, or the Penitent Daughter. A Tale, from the French of M. Arnaud. *Lady's,* XXIV (1793). 3 parts.

d. Julia, etc. [Same title as *Universal.*] *New Gleaner,* I (1809), 153–168. 1 part.

734. JULIA AND PALMIRA, a Tale. By Miss Eliza Yeames. *Lady's,* XLVI (September, 1815) – XLVII (January, 1816). 6 parts (11,000).

735. JULIANA, or the Maid of the Inn, a Tale. *New Lady's,* IV (January–February, 1789). 2 parts (5750).

736. KAIS AND LEILA. *Britannic,* VII, Nos. 92–97 (1799–1800). 6 parts (16,250).

An unacknowledged abridgment of Isaac Disraeli, "Mejnoun and Leila, the Arabian Petrarch and Laura" (1797) [see *Romances, by I. D'Israeli,* 1799, pp. 1–203]; included in the series "Memoirs of Love and Gallantry."

737. The KING AND THE COUNT. *Universal,* n.s. XV (May, 1811) – n.s. XVI (July, November, 1811). 4 parts (15,000). Uncompleted. Signed "MOMUS."

738. The KNIGHT OF ST. JOHN OF JERUSALEM, an Historical Legend. *Lady's Monthly Museum,* I (September–December, 1798). 4 parts (9200). Signed "A.K. [i.e., A. Kendall?], Isleworth."

739. The KNIGHT OF THE BROOM FLOWER, or the Horrors of the Priory. "Tale 52," *Tell-Tale,* IV (1804) 1 part (8200).

740. KOENIGSMARK THE ROBBER, or the Terror of Bohemia. In Which Is Introduced "Stella, or the Maniac of the Wood, a Pathetick Tale." By H. J. Sarrett. *Marvellous,* III (June 1, 1803). 1 part (33,000).

741. The LADY'S REVENGE. [By Eliza Haywood.] *Female Spectator,* Book XIV (1745), 103–119 [actually 127]. 1 part (5700). Signed "ELISMONDA/Kensington, April 16, 1745."

Offered as a letter from a reader, on which the Female Spectator herself made some remarks (pp. 119–126).

a. The Lady's Revenge. *Newcastle General,* II (September–October, 1748). 2 parts.

"From the *Female Spectator.*"

b. The Lady's Revenge. *British* (Edinburgh), II (November, 1748). 1 part.

"From the *Female Spectator.*"

c. The Lady's Revenge. Written by a Lady. *Weekly Entertainer,* IV (July 19–26, 1784). 2 parts.

d. The Lady's Revenge. By Mrs. Haywood. *New Novelist's,* I (1786), 57–64. 1 part.

e. The Lady's Revenge. *Weekly Misc.*(Glasgow), VI, Nos. 142–144 (March 7–22, 1792). 3 parts.

f. The Lady's Revenge. By Mrs. Haywood. *Gleaner,* I (1805), 102–111. 1 part.

742. The LAPSE OF THE HEART. A Real History. *Sentimental,* II (December, 1774) – III (February, 1775). 3 parts (8750).

743. LAUNCELOT LASTHOPE, the Bachelor. *Belle Assemblée,* n.s. III (February, May, 1811). 2 parts (5000).

744. LAURA ALDOBRANDINI. *Repository of Arts, etc.,* XIV (October–November, 1815). 2 parts (5000).

745. LAURA LABARRE, Countess of Strathmore, a Fragment. Taken from the Novel of *The Idiot Heiress. Compiler,* II, Nos. 8–13 (1808). 6 parts (8000).

The Idiot Heiress was published by the Minerva Press in 1805.

746. LAURENTINA, or the Modern Circe, a Tale. *Belle Assemblée,* n.s. IX (February–April, 1814). 3 parts (6500).

747. LAURETTA. A Moral Tale. [By Marmontel.] *Weekly Amusement,* III (January 11–March 1, 1766). 8 parts (12,000).

A translation of "Laurette" (*Contes moraux,* Vol. III, 1765), extracted from *Moral Tales,* Vol. III (1766) [see No. 917]. For other translations of the same story, see Nos. 596 and 748.

a. Lauretta. A Moral Tale. *Thespian,* II (November, 1793) – III (April, 1794). 7 parts.

748. LAURETTA. A New Translation from the French of Marmontelle. By Harriot Delany, a Young Lady of Nineteen. *Lady's,* XI (August–November, 1780). 4 parts (12,600). Signed "J———."

A translation of Marmontel's "Laurette" (*Contes moraux,* Vol. III, 1765). For other translations of the same story see Nos. 596, 747, and 917.

749. LAZY LAWRENCE, a Tale. *Edinburgh*(2), n.s. IX (January–February, 1797). 2 parts (9900).

750. LERMOS AND ROSA, or the Fortunate Gipsey. An Interesting Adventure, Which Really Happened in Spain, about Forty Years Ago. *Marvellous,* IV (December 1, 1803). 1 part (29,000).

751. A LESSON FOR ADVERSITY. By Marmontel. *New Gleaner,* II (1810), pp. 89–99. 1 part (6500).

Translated from "La Leçon du malheur, conte moral" (*Mercure,* 1791). For other translations of the same tale, see Nos. 752–753.

752. A LESSON FROM ADVERSITY. A Tale, Translated from the French of Marmontel, by a Friend. *Bee,* XIII (January 30–February 13, 1793). 3 parts (6300).

Translated from "La Leçon du malheur, conte moral" (*Mercure,* 1791). "For the *Bee.*" For other translations of the same tale, see Nos. 751 and 753.

753. The LESSON OF MISFORTUNE, a Moral Tale. [By Marmontel.] *Universal,* XC (March, 1792). 1 part (6600).

A translation of "La Leçon du malheur, conte moral" (*Mercure,* 1791), extracted from "a second Volume of new Tales, by the celebrated M. Marmontel" (i.e., *Tales, Translated from the French of M. Marmontel,* 1792). For other translations of the same story, see Nos. 751–752.

a. The Lesson of Misfortune. From Marmontel. *Gentleman's and London,* 1792 (March–May). 3 parts.

b. The Lesson of Misfortune, a Moral Tale. From the French of the Celebrated M. Marmontel. *Weekly Entertainer,* XIX (May 21–June 4, 1792). 3 parts.

c. The Lesson of Misfortune. *Monthly Extracts,* III (May, 1792). 1 part.

Extracted as part of a review of the *Tales.*

d. The Lesson of Misfortune, a Moral Tale. *Universal Mag. and Rev.,* VII (May–June, 1792). 2 parts.

e. The Lesson of Misfortune. *General,* VI (1792). 1 part.

Published in the magazine's "Impartial Review of British Literature," pp. 4–18, as part of the notice of the *Tales.*

754. LETTER FROM A PERUVIAN PRINCESS TO HER LOVER Giving an Account of Her Being Taken out of the Temple of the Sun by the Spaniards. [By Mme. de Grafigny.] *Weekly Amusement,* II (July 6, 1765) – III (September 20, 1766). 36 parts (34,000).

The *Catalogue* of the British Museum lists three early translations of the *Lettres d'une Péruvienne* (1747), of which this is a reprinting of the first: *Letters Written by a Peruvian Princess, Translated from the French* (1748). The *Weekly Amusement,* however, prints only 37 letters of the 45 included in the translation of 1748. For a later magazine translation of the *Lettres,* see No. 764.

755. LETTER FROM A YOUNG GENTLEMAN IN LONDON. *Adviser,* II (1803), Nos. 50–53. 1 part (5600).

756. LETTER FROM AN ENGLISH GENTLEMAN in France to His Brother in England. *Lady's,* XIX (March–November, 1788). 9 parts (20,400).

Actually a series of three letters, the last dated from Paris, February 10, 1773.

757. LETTER OF A COUNTRY SQUIRE TO THE EDITOR. *Christian Observer,* I (December, 1802); III (February, 1804); V (March, 1806); VI (September, 1807). 4 parts (8000). Signed "S.T."

Actually a letter-series, continued at intervals of 14 to 25 months. Addressed "To the Editor of the *Christian Observer.*"

758. [LETTERS BETWEEN HORATIO AND MISS W———.] *Weekly Mag. and Literary Rev.,* I, Nos. 3–9 (April 29–June 10, 1758). 6 parts (5000).

The editor pretended that this correspondence was genuine, but the letters were dated contemporaneously with their publication, and ended with an intention to marry. The title is from the table of contents of Volume I.

759. LETTERS BETWEEN PEOPLE OF FASHION. *Lady's,* XVI (December, 1785) – XVII (April, 1786). 6 parts (12,000). Uncompleted.

760. LETTERS BETWEEN THEODOSIUS AND CONSTANTIA. By Dr. [John] Langhorne. In Two Volumes. *Novelist's,* VII (1782). 1 part (45,000).

First published as the *Letters That Passed between Theodosius and Constantia* (1763). The reprinting in the *Novelist's* includes two engravings, dated January 26 and February 2, 1782.

761. LETTERS FROM FELICIA TO CHARLOTTE. Containing a Series of the Most Interesting Events, Interspersed with Moral Reflections, Chiefly Tending to Prove That the Seeds of Virtue Are Implanted in the Mind of Every Reasonable Being. By Mr. [actually Mary] Collyer. In Two Volumes. *Novelist's,* XXIII (1788). 1 part (130,000).

First published as *Felicia to Charlotte: Being Letters from a Young Lady in the Country to Her Friend in Town* (1744; Volume II, 1749). The reprinting in the *Novelist's* includes four engravings, dated January 1–April 1, 1788.

762. LETTERS FROM MISS AMELIA DEAN TO MISS LOUISA DANBY. *Lady's,* IV (May, 1773) – VI (January, 1775). 14 parts (21,250).

The series was offered to the editor in a letter signed "Alexis" (IV, [234]), but later attributed to "W.B." (VII, 429).

763. LETTER[S] FROM MISS BEAUCHAMP TO MISS GRANBY. *Lady's,* VII (April–December, 1776). 8 parts (12,400). Uncompleted.

The editor of the *Lady's* signaled that his present supply was "exhausted" in January, 1777, but no further installment was forthcoming. There were complaints from readers as late as November and December, 1778. The title was changed to read "Letters" in Parts 2–8.

764. LETTERS OF A PERUVIAN PRINCESS, with the Sequel. Translated from the French of Madame de Grafigny, by Francis Ashmore, Esq. In Two Volumes. *Novelist's,* IX (1782). 1 part (43,000).

This is the third English version of *Lettres d'une Péruvienne* (1747) listed in the *Catalogue* of the British Museum (see "Letter from a Peruvian Princess" above). The translator's "Apology" in the *Novelist's* is dated Sept. 28, 1782. This version also includes, as a "Sequel," a translation of Lamarche-Courmont's "Letters of Aza" (see No. 1122), and is embellished with two engravings, dated October 5 and October 25, 1782.

765. LETTERS OF AN UNKNOWN. *Champion,* Nos. 69–72 (April 30–May 21, 1814). 4 parts (5000). Signed "MERCURATOR."

Parts 2–4 are entitled "Letters of an Unknown Spanish Gentleman."

766. LETTERS OF AZA. [By Lamarche-Courmont.] Translated by the Author of *The Old English Baron* [*i.e.,* Clara Reeve]. *Lady's,* IX (June–July, 1778); X (July, 1779) – XI (February, 1780). 11 parts (17,000).

A translation of *Lettres d'Aza ou d'un Péruvien* (1749). For another translation, in the *Novelist's Magazine,* see No. 1122.

Only the first two letters of the version in the *Lady's* were done by Clara Reeve, who suddenly withdrew from the project without any explanation. After making numerous fruitless appeals to Miss Reeve to resume her work, the editor found another translator. Parts 3–11 are therefore entitled "Letters of Aza, But Not by the Author of *The Old English Baron.*" These parts are signed "D———." (See Chapter V, pp. 312–317, above.)

767. The LETTERS OF DE CLAIRVILLE. *Cabinet,* n.s. I (April, 1809) – n.s. II (August, 1809). 4 parts (6400).

a. The Letters of De Clairville. *Monthly Pantheon,* III (June–August, 1809). 3 parts. Uncompleted.

Reprints Parts 1–3 of the above only.

768. LETTERS OF THE MARCHIONESS DE M———. Wrote by the Celebrated Mr. Crebillon. *Weekly Mag. and Literary Rev.,* I (June 3–July 22, 1758). 6 parts (13,500). Uncompleted.

Reprinted without acknowledgment, from *Letters from the Marchioness de M***, to the Count de R***, Translated from the Original French, by Mr.* [*Samuel*] *Humphreys,* first published in 1735, and re-issued in 1758 [McBurney, No. 304]. Humphreys's translation was made from Crébillon's *Lettres de la marquise de M*** au comte de R**** (1732). The version in the *Weekly Magazine* printed only the first fifteen of the seventy letters in the Humphreys edition.

769. LETTERS WHICH PASSED BETWEEN CHARLES WALLER, Chaplain to Oliver Cromwell, and Frances, One of the Protector's Favourite Daughters. *Lady's,* XXVII (March–June, 1796). 3 parts (7000).

770. LETTRE DE MADAME N. À MADAME L. À VIENNE. *Ambigu,* XXXII, No. 283 (February 10, 1811). 1 part (5000).

A "secret history" of the court life under Napoleon. Offered as No. 3 of the series called "Le Logographe, ou le Moniteur secret."

771. The LEVITE OF EPHRAIM, Translated from the Posthumous Works of Rousseau. *Westminster,* X (September–October, 1782). 2 parts (7400).

A translation of "Le Lévite d'Éphraïm" (*Oeuvres posthumes de Jean-Jaques Rousseau,* I, Geneva, 1781). "For the *Westminster Magazine.*"

772. LEWIS TYRRELL, or the Depraved Count. Including the Pathetick Adventures and Tragical End of Ella Clifford and Oscar Henry Hampden, or the Victims of Treachery. An English Tale of the Fourteenth Century. *Marvellous,* IV (February 1, 1804). 1 part (29,000).

773. The LIAR. *Lady's,* XVIII (November, 1787) – XIX (May, 1788). 7 parts (7800).

Described as the "Fourth Lesson" of the series "Domestic Lessons for the Use of the Younger Part of the Female Readers of the *Lady's Magazine.*"

774. The LIFE AND ADVENTURES OF AMBROSE GWINETT, Formerly Well Known to the Public as the Lame Beggar Man, Who, in the Year 1734, and for a Long Time After, Swept the Way between the Meuse-Gate and Spring-Garden, Charing-Cross. Said to Be Taken Almost Literally from His Own Mouth. *Gentleman's,* XXXVIII (Supplement, 1768) – XXXIX (January, 1769). 2 parts (7300).

Attributed (XXXIX, 14) to the "*Gent. Journ.*" [1768]. Abridgments of the above story were frequently published in miscellanies for the rest of the century.

775. The LIFE AND ADVENTURES OF JOE THOMPSON. A Narrative Founded on Fact. By Mr. [Edward] Kimber. In Two Volumes. *Novelist's,* XII (1783). 1 part (163,000).

First published in 1750. The reprinting in the *Novelist's* includes four engravings, dated July 5–August 1, 1783.

776. The LIFE AND ADVENTURES OF PETER WILKINS, a Cornish Man. Taken from His Own Mouth, in His Passage to England, from off Cape Horn in America, in the Ship *Hector.* By R. S., a Passenger in the *Hector.* In Two Volumes. *Novelist's,* XII (1783). 1 part (138,000).

By Robert Paltock; first published in 1751. The reprinting in the *Novelist's* includes six engravings, dated August 2–September 6, 1783.

777. The LIFE AND ADVENTURES OF ROBINSON CRUSOE. In Two Volumes. By Daniel Defoe. *Novelist's,* IV (1781). 1 part (225,000).

Includes both the *Adventures* (1719) and the *Farther Adventures* (1719). The reprinting in the *Novelist's* is embellished with seven engravings, dated March 3–April 14, 1781.

778. An Account of the LIFE AND ADVENTURES OF SIR HUMPKIN BUZ, and His Journey to the City of Nubibub. Written by Himself. *Scots,* LXXVI (November, 1814) – LXXVII (January, 1815). 3 parts (5500). Uncompleted.

779. The LIFE AND ADVENTURES OF SIR LAUNCELOT GREAVES. [By Tobias Smollett.] *British*(2), I (January, 1760) – II (December, 1761). 25 parts (85,000).

a. The Adventures of Sir Launcelot Greaves. By Dr. Smollett. In Two Volumes. *Novelist's,* IX (1782). 1 part.

First collected in volume form in 1762. The reprinting in the *Novelist's* is embellished with a set of four engravings, dated September 7–28, 1782.

780. The LIFE AND AMUSEMENTS OF ISAAC BICKERSTAFFE, Junior. An Original Work, with Observations Historical, Critical, Illustrative, &c. &c. *General,* I (July, 1787) – VI (February, 1792). 38 parts (51,000). Uncompleted.

a. The Life and Amusements of Isaac Bickerstaffe, Junior, etc. [Same title as above.]

Gentleman's and London, 1787 (September) – 1790 (November). 30 parts. Uncompleted.

Reprints only Parts 1–30 of the original.

781. The LIFE AND DEATH OF A SUNDAY SCHOLAR. *Cottage,* III (June, 1814) – IV (January, 1815). 3 parts (6000). Signed "E.T.M.P./H———, Parsonage, Nov. 1814."

782. The LIFE AND MEMOIRS OF DENNIS O'CARROL M'GUFFIN M'FRAME, Written by Himself. *Rambler's,* VI (June–September, 1788). 4 parts (7100).

783. The LIFE AND OPINIONS OF TIMOTHEUS RANDY, Stay-Maker. *Covent Garden,* II (April–June, 1773). 3 parts (5000).

784. The LIFE AND OPINIONS OF TRISTRAM SHANDY, Gentleman. By the Rev. Mr. [Laurence] Sterne. *Novelist's,* V (1781). 1 part (210,000).

First published 1759–1767. The reprinting in the *Novelist's* includes eight engravings, dated April 21–June 9, 1781.

785. LIFE AND SINGULAR ADVENTURES, SUFFERINGS, AND CAPTIVITY, OF ROBERT DRURY, Including His Fifteen Years Confinement in the Island of Madagascar. Taken from His Own Journal, Published by Himself. [By Daniel Defoe?] *New Wonderful Museum,* VI, Nos. 67–68 (1808). 2 parts (7000).

An epitome *of Madagascar, or Robert Drury's Journal, during Fifteen Years Captivity on That Island* (1729). Drury's original, which is sometimes attributed to Defoe, runs to about 108,000 words.

786. The LIFE OF A BEE. *Children's,* I (December, 1799) – III (April, 1800). 5 parts (8800).

787. LIFE OF A LOUNGER. *Belle Assemblée,* VII (July–October, 1809). 4 parts (5500). Uncompleted.

a. Life of a Lounger. *Hibernian,* 1809 (August–October). 3 parts. Uncompleted. Reprints Parts 1–3 of the above only.

788. LIFE OF A MODERN MAN OF FASHION. *Bon Ton,* II (March–April, 1792). 2 parts (6900).

789. [LIFE OF A PROFLIGATE STUDENT.] [By James Hogg.] *Spy,* Nos. 6, 8, 9, 11 (October 6–27, 1810). 4 parts (17,000).

The title is from the table of contents of the collected edition.

790. The LIFE OF A WOMAN OF THE TOWN. *Beauties of All the Magazines,* I (December, 1762) – III (April, 1764). 10 parts (28,000).

791. [The LIFE OF AN OLD DEBAUCHEE.] [By John Hawkesworth.] *Adventurer,* Nos. 86 (September 1, 1753); 134–136 (February 16–23, 1754). 4 parts (9000).

The title is from the table of contents of the collected edition.

792. The LIFE OF DANIEL DANCER, Esquire. *New Gleaner,* I (1809), 216–226. 1 part (6000).

793. The LIFE OF DICK EN—L——D, Alias Captain En—g——d, of Turf Memory. *Bon Ton,* II (October, 1792–February, 1793). 5 parts (6250).

Taken from *The Life of Dick En—l——d* [i.e., Richard England] (1792).

794. The LIFE OF JOHN GILPIN. *Town and Country Weekly,* I (?July 27–September 10, 1785). 6 parts (7500). *Inc.*

Probably *The Life of J. G. ... to Which Is Added, by Way of Appendix, the ... History of His Journey to Edmonton* [in verse, by W. Cowper] (Dublin, 1785).

a. The Life and Adventures of John Gilpin. Tale "62," *Tell-Tale,* V (1805). 1 part (11,000).

A version of the same original as the above fragment.

795. The LIFE OF JUMPING JOE, a Notorious Surrey Footpad, Lately Executed for a Crime of Which He Declared Himself Innocent. *Bon Ton,* II (October, 1792) – IV (September, 1794). 18 parts (24,000).

796. The LIFE OF MISS B———, Written by Herself. *Lady's,* VIII (March, 1777) – IX (February, 1778). 7 parts (8900).

The story was interrupted in August, 1777, because the continuation was lost in transit (VIII, [562]); and resumed in December when the manuscript was recovered "by an uncommon and unforeseen event" (VIII, 649) – whereupon the author once more took up her pen.

797. LIFE OF MISS WENTWORTH, Written by Herself. *Britannic,* VIII, Nos. 103–106 (1800). 4 parts (13,500).

Part of the series "Memoirs of Love and Gallantry."

798. LIFE OF MRS. GOOCH. *Bon Ton,* II (May, 1792) – III (October, 1793). 16 parts (20,000).

An abridged version of *The Life of Mrs. Gooch, Written by Herself* (1792). The original extends to about 50,000 words.

799. A Short Account of the LIFE OF PATTY SAUNDERS, Lately Published. *Ladies,* III (February 22/March 7–March 21/April 4, 1752). 3 parts (5000).

Probably taken from *The Life of Patty Saunders, Written by Herself,* noticed in *Monthly Review,* VI (January, 1752), 77.

800. [The LIFE OF QUEEN MARIAMNE.] *New Universal*(1), XIV (?July–October, 1758). 3 parts (7600). *Inc.*

The title is one of several used in Vol. XIV (Vol. XIII is not available for comparison). "The Life of Queen Mariamne" was followed in November by "Anecdotes of Herod after the Death of Mariamne, His Queen" (2 parts, *inc.*). The story in both seems to be a version of that told in La Calprenède, *Cléopâtre,* Book I (1647).

801. LIFE OF THOMAS SAINVITZ, Written by Himself. Translated from the Latin. *Cyclopaedian,* I (September, 1807) – II (February, 1808). 6 parts (11,000).

Nos. 6–11 of the series "Narrative Sketches of Men and Manners."

802. LISSETTE OF SAVOY, or the Fair Maid of the Mountains. By Sarah Wilkinson. "Tale 39," *Tell-Tale,* III (1804). 1 part (9200).

803. The LITERARY ADVENTURES OF PETER POSITIVE OF GOTHAM, in Nottinghamshire. *Universal,* n.s. XII (October, 1809) – n.s. XIII (January, 1810). 3 parts (6300). Uncompleted.

"Addressed to the Editor of the *Universal Magazine.*"

804. The LITTLE ACTRESS. *Lady's,* XIX (November, 1788) – XX (May, 1789). 8 parts (8000).

The "Sixth Lesson" of "Domestic Lessons for the Use of the Younger Part of the Female Readers of the *Lady's Magazine.*"

805. The LITTLE EPICURE. *Lady's,* XX (December, 1789) – XXI (March, 1790). 4 parts (5300).

Part of the series "Domestic Lessons for the Use of the Younger Part of the Female Readers of the *Lady's Magazine.*"

806. The LITTLE HAY-MAKERS, or the Metamorphose. *Juvenile,* I (May, 1788) – II (July, 1788). 3 parts (5000).

807. The LITTLE HERMITAGE. *Juvenile Library,* I, Nos. 4 (March, 1800), 7, 12, 14, 16, 17 (June, 1801). 6 parts (12,000).

808. The LONG FAREWELL. *Lady's,* X (December, 1779) – XI (January, 1780). 3 parts (5750). Signed "J."

809. The LONG PACK, a Tale. By the Ettrick Shepherd [i.e., James Hogg]. *Weekly Entertainer,* XLIX (November 6–November 20, 1809). 3 parts (5000).

The earliest appearance of this story listed in Batho (*Ettrick Shepherd,* p. 196) is 1817. The tale was later collected in *Winter Evening Tales* (1820).

810. LORD GOWEN, or the Forester's Daughter. By Sarah Wilkinson. "Tale 10," *Tell-Tale,* I (1803). 1 part (5300).

811. The LORD OF CREQUI, a New Historical Novel. From the French of the celebrated M. D'Arnaud. *Universal,* LXXI (October, November, 1782); LXXII (January, 1783). 3 parts (16,000). Signed "L."

A translation of "Le Sire de Créqui" (*Oeuvres de M. D'Arnaud,* VI, 1774).

a. The Lord of Crequi, etc. [Same title as above.] *Caledonian Mag. and Rev.,* I (April 4–May 16, 1783). 4 parts. Signed "L."

b. The Lord of Crequi, etc. [Same title.] *New London,* II (January–April, 1786). 4 parts.

c. The Lord of Crequi, etc. [Same title.] *Gentleman's and London,* 1786 (March–May). 3 parts (11,300). Uncompleted.

d. The Lord of Crequi, etc. [Same title.] *Berwick Museum,* II (June, 1786) – III (January, 1787). 8 parts.

812. The LOST DAUGHTER RECOVERED, A Story Founded on Fact. *European,* I (June, 1782) – III (January, 1783). 4 parts (7400).

813. The LOST SON, an Affecting History. From *Euphemia,* a Novel... by Mrs. Charlotte Lennox, Author of *The Female Quixote,* etc. *Universal,* LXXXVII (October–Supplement, 1790). 3 parts (11,200).

From the novel published in 1790.

a. The Lost Son, an Affecting History, etc. [Same title as above.] *Weekly Entertainer,* XVII (February 7–March 14, 1791). 6 parts.

814. LOUISA, A POETICAL NOVEL, by Miss Seward. *Universal,* LXXIV (May, 1784). 1 part (5100).

A prose summary, with numerous extracts, of Anna Seward, *Louisa, a Poetical Novel, in Four Epistles* (1784).

815. LOUISA, A PRUSSIAN TALE. *Gleaner,* I (1805), 87–97. 1 part (5600).

An unacknowledged plagiarism of Nicolas de Bonneville, "Albertine" (*Choix de petits romans, imités de l'allemand,* 1786); adapted from the translation published in the *Universal* in 1789 (cf. No. 78). For other translations of the same story, see Nos. 76–77.

816. LOUISA, A TALE OF TRUTH. *Belle Assemblée,* n.s. II (October, 1810). 1 part (6500).

817. LOUISA, OR THE FOUNDLING. *Universal,* CXII (January–April, 1803). 3 parts (13,000).

818. LOVE AND LITERATURE. From the French of Madame de Genlis. *Belle Assemblée,* n.s. III (January, 1811). 1 part (5200). Signed "M."

A translation of "La Nouvelle poétique, ou les deux Amans rivaux de gloire" (*Nouveaux contes moraux et nouvelles historiques,* Vol. II, 1802).

819. LOVE AND SUICIDE. *Belle Assemblée,* V (October, 1808). 1 part (5500).

820. LOVE AND VENGEANCE. *Belle Assemblée,* V (November–December, 1808). 1 part (8900).

821. The LOVE CAMPAIGNS OF BARON D———N. *Freeholder's,* III (October, 1770). 1 part (6400).

822. LOVE IN A VILLAGE, or the Charms of Simplicity. *Westminster,* I (August, 1773). 1 part (5000).

"For the *Westminster Magazine.*"

823. LOVE MATCHES, or the History of Paladel and Patty. *Bon Ton,* V (November, 1795–February, 1796). 4 parts (6000).

For a different version of the same story, see No. 1030.

824. The LOVERS, a Spanish Romance. (Translated from the French of M. Florian.) *Lady's Monthly Museum,* XVI (March, 1806). 1 part (5000). Signed "E.F."

A translation of "Célestine, nouvelle espagnole" (*Six Nouvelles de M. de Florian,* Paris, 1784). For other versions of the same story, see Nos. 198–199, and 244.

a. The Lovers, etc. [Same title as above.] *Weekly Entertainer,* XLVI (May 26–June 2, 1806). 2 parts. Signed "E.F."

825. The LOVES OF ANAS-ELOUJOUD AND OUARDI, a Tale. Translated from the Arabic by Mons. Savary, the Celebrated Author of *Letters on Egypt,* and *On Greece;* and Now First Translated into English for This Miscellany. *Attic Misc.,* I (February–May, 1790). 4 parts (13,250). Signed "G."

Translated from Claude Savary, *Les Amours d'Anas-Eloujoud et de Ouardi* (Bagdad and Paris, 1789). The *Letters on Egypt* and *Letters on Greece* were published in London in 1787 and 1788.

826. The LOVES OF OTHNIEL AND ACHSAH, Translated from the Chaldee. *Universal Museum,* n.s. V (April–May, 1769). 2 parts (5200).

Extracted, without acknowledgment, from the two-volume novel of the same title, published in the same year.

827. The LOVES OF ZOELLO AND AGRIPPINA, an Italian Novel. *New Novelist's,* I (1786), 157–165. 1 part (5700).

828. LUCINDA, an Amorous History. In a Series of Letters to Clarinda. *Rambler's,* VII (June–December, 1789). 6 parts (15,500).

829. The LUCKY IMPUDENCE, a Novel Founded on Facts. *Hibernian,* 1773 (February–March). 1 part (6250).

This story is found only in the piratical issues of the *Hibernian,* published by Marchbank and Seguin (see the Note under *Hibernian* in the "Register of Periodicals").

830. LUCY AND EMMA, a Tale. *Belfast Monthly,* V (September–October, 1810). 2 parts (9100). Signed "R."

"For the *Belfast Monthly Magazine.*"

831. LYDIA, or Filial Piety, a Novel. [By John Shebbeare.] *Novelist's,* XXII (1786). 1 part (204,000).

First published in 1755. The reprinting in the *Novelist's* includes six engravings, dated May 20–July 1, 1786.

832. MAC—— BLUNDER. *Lady's Monthly Museum,* n.s. I (July–October, 1806). 4 parts (5400).

Attributed (p. 36) to "[George] Pinckard's *Notes on the West Indies,*" published in 1806.

a. Mac Blunder. (Pinckard's *Notes on the West Indies,* Lately Published.) *New Magazine of Choice Pieces,* I, Nos. 1–2 (1810).

833. The MAID OF LOCHLIN, or Mysteries of the North. By Sarah Wilkinson. "Tale 48," *Tell-Tale,* IV (1804). 1 part (10,200).

834. The MAID OF ST. MARINO, an Historical Legend. *Lady's Monthly Museum,* I (July–November, 1798). 5 parts (8100). Signed "M."

835. The MAID OF SWITZERLAND. By Miss Anne Blower. *General,* III (January–February, 1789). 2 parts (5500).

The receipt of the story was acknowledged in November, 1788 (II, 562).

a. The Maid of Switzerland. By Miss Anne Blower, *Universal Mag. and Rev.,* I (February–March, 1789). 2 parts.

b. The Maid of Switzerland. By Miss Anne Blower. *Gentleman's and London,* 1789 (February–March). 2 parts.

c. The Maid of Switzerland. *Britannic,* V, No. 65–66 (1797). 1 part.

Part of the series "Memoirs of Love and Gallantry."

d. The Maid of Switzerland. *Hibernian,* 1797 (December) – 1798 (January). 2 parts.

836. [The MAN IN THE MOON.] *Pic Nic,* I, No. 4 (January 29, 1803) – II, No. 13 (April 2, 1803). 7 parts (6500). Uncompleted.

A series of seven "Letters" with the above signature. The story was left unfinished when *Pic Nic* ceased publication; in a later periodical (*Cabinet,* 1803) there are several new letters bearing the same signature (May 21, June 4, June 18, 1803), but they are not a continuation.

837. The MAN OF INTEGRITY, a Novel. *Lady's Monthly Museum,* IX (July–December, 1802). 6 parts (19,250). Signed "E.F."

838. The MAN OF PRINCIPLE, a Character. *Universal,* LXXXV (November–December, 1789). 2 parts (6700).

A long extract from Dr. John Moore, *Zeluco* (1789), and the last of a series of more of less discrete fragments presented in the *Universal* between June and December, 1789, and offered as a review of the book. For other magazine versions of the same novel, see Nos. 1370–1371.

a. The Man of Principle, a Character. From *Zeluco. Caledonian*(2), IV (January–February, 1790). 2 parts.

839. MANNERS OF THE FRENCH. *Belle Assemblée,* n.s. IX (June, 1814) – n.s. XIV (October, 1816). 27 parts (43,000). Uncompleted.

A series of Sternean sketches, various signed "A Free Speaker," "Guillaume the Free Speaker," "M. Guillaume," and "Guillaume le Franc Parleur."

840. MARCELLUS, or the Old Cobbler of the Cottage. From the French of Madame [Isabelle] de Montolieu. *General Chronicle,* III (September–October, 1811). 2 parts (5300).

A translation of "Le Vieux savetier de la cabane et les huit louis" (*Mercure de France,* Vol. XLII, June 16, 1810).

841. MARIA MONTFORD, or the Consequences of Indiscretion. *Weekly Entertainer,* LI (September 16–23, 1811). 2 parts (5000).

842. MARLTON ABBEY, or the Mystic Tomb of St. Angelo, a Romance. By M. Chapman. "Tale 64," *Tell-Tale,* V (1805).

843. MARMOISAN, or the Innocent Deceit, a Novel. [By Mlle. Marie-Jeanne L'Héritier.] *Universal Spectator,* Nos. 806 (March 17), 808, 809, 811 (April 21, 1744). 4 parts (10,000).

A translation of "L'Innocente tromperie" (*Oeuvres meslées,* 1696), offered as "another Piece" by the author of *Finette* (No. 1331).

a. Marmoisan, or the Innocent Deceit, a Novel. *Scots,* VI (August–September, 1744). 2 parts (9250).

Attributed to the *Universal Spectator.*

In March, 1775, the *Lady's Magazine* began reprinting the same translation, which was offered as an original story by a correspondent of the magazine, but terminated it, without explanation, after printing only about a third of the story. Probably the editor discovered the deception.

844. The MARRIAGE PROMISE. By Sarah Wilkinson. "Tale 7," *Tell-Tale,* I (1803). 1 part (12,000).

845. The MARRIAGES OF THE SAMNITES. An Ancient Anecdote. [By Marmontel.] *St. James's*(1), II (August, 1763). 1 part (6100).

The Denis and Lloyd translation of "Les Mariages samnites, anecdote ancienne" (*Contes moraux,* 1761), later collected in their *Moral Tales* of 1764 (see No. 917). In the *St. James's* the story was offered as part of a series entitled "Moral Tales, from Mr. Marmontel."

846. The MARRIED DEMONESS. *Belfast Monthly,* IV (June, 1810) – V (September, 1810). 3 parts (10,850).

"For the *Belfast Monthly Magazine.*"

847. The MASQUERADE. [By Augustus von Kotzebue.] *Flowers of Literature for 1807,* VI (1808), 17–36. 1 part (5200).

A translation of "Das Grab auf dem Hügel" (*Kleine Romane, Erzählungen, Anecdoten und Miscellen von August von Kotzebue,* Vol. II, 1807). Attributed in the table of contents of the *Flowers of Literature* to "*Kotzebue's Novelettes,*" but actually taken from *The Pastor's Daughter with Other Romances* (2nd ed., Vol. II, 1807).

a. The Masquerade. (Kotzebue.) *New Magazine of Choice Pieces,* I (1810), 181–192.

848. The MASQUERADE. (An Extract from the Novel Intitled *The Forest of Montalbano,* Lately Published.) *Lady's,* XLI (October–December, 1810). 3 parts (12,200).

From Catherine Cuthbertson, *The Forest of Montalbano, a Novel, by the Author of SANTO SEBASTIANO, &c.* (1810).

849. MASSOUD, a Tale, from the French. *Edinburgh*(2), V (February, 1787). 1 part (6000).

a. Massoud, a Tale, from the French. *Gentleman's and London,* 1787 (May–June). 2 parts.

850. MATERNAL ADVICE, and the Good Effect of a Virtuous Education: Exemplified in a Series of Letters, Alternately Passing between an Attached Parent and Her Son and Daughter, Who, by a Singular Turn in the Wheel of Fortune, Had Unexpectedly Come into the Possession of Riches and Rank. *Lady's Monthly Museum,* n.s. IV (June, 1808); n.s. V (November, 1808) – n.s. VII (October, 1809). 11 parts (28,000).

The title from Part 2 reads "Epistolary Correspondence."

851. MATILDA, a Moral Tale. *Fashionable,* I (November–December, 1786). 2 parts (6400).

852. MATILDA, or the Adventures of an Orphan, an Interesting Tale. *Marvellous,* IV (March 1, 1804). 1 part (14,000).

853. MATILDA FORRESTER, or the Exemplary Daughter. (A Tale, Alas!, Too True.) *Lady's Monthly Museum,* n.s. XIII (November, 1812) – XIV (May, 1813). 7 parts (9500). Signed "John."

"For the *Lady's Monthly Museum.*"

854. MAURICE. *Lady's,* XVIII (October–December, 1787). 3 parts (6400).

The three parts constitute No. 15 of the series "The Children's Friend."

855. MAXIMILIAN AND SELINA, or the Mysterious Abbot, a Flemish Tale. *Marvellous,* IV (January 2, 1804). 1 part (29,000).

856. MELAI, a Constantinopolitan Tale. [By Meissner.] *Bee,* III (May 11–18, 1791). 2 parts (7700).

A translation of A. G. Meissner, "Der Hund des Melai" (*Erzählungen und Dialogen,* Vol. I, 1788). For other translations of the same tale, see Nos. 317 and 857.

857. MELAI'S DOG. [By Meissner.] *Lady's,* XLVI (January–March, 1815). 3 parts (6500). Signed "ARMIUM AMATOR."

A translation of A. G. Meissner, "Der Hund des Melai" (see No. 856). For a third translation of the same story, see No. 317.

858. The MELANCHOLY MAN, a Dramatic Tale, in Three Parts. *Westminster,* VI (January–March, 1778). 3 parts (5200).

"For the *Westminster Magazine.*"

a. The Melancholy Man, a Dramatic Tale, in Three Parts. *Hibernian,* 1778 (February–April). 3 parts.

859. MELINDA, or the Folly of Ambition. *Lady's,* III (February, 1772). 1 part (5250). Signed "R—."

a. Melinda, or the Folly of Ambition. *Weekly Misc.*(Sherborne), III (December 26, 1774–January 2, 1775). 2 parts.

A slightly abbreviated version of the above.

b. Melinda, or the Folly of Ambition. *Weekly Misc.*(London), III, Nos. 121–122 (1774–1775). 1 part.

c. Melinda, or the Folly of Ambition. Translated from the French. *New Novelist's,* II (1787), 60–67. 1 part.

860. MELUSINA, a Tale, Addressed to the Younger Part of the Fair Sex. *Lady's,* IV (November, 1773). 1 part (5000). Signed "R—."

861. MELVIN FAMILY, a Novel, in a Series of Letters. By Maria. *New Lady's,* VIII (January–December, 1793). 7 parts (6300).

862. MEMOIR I. *Compiler,* II (1808), 121–127, 147–155, 195–206. 3 parts (6250).

The story was offered as part of the series "Scenes of Life," written "For the *Compiler.*" A fourth number (pp. 241–242) was devoted to "reflections" on the story.

863. MEMOIRS OF A CAPTAIN. *London,* XLII (May–June, 1773). 2 parts (8100).

a. Memoirs of a Captain. *Hibernian,* 1773 (June–July). 2 parts. Uncompleted.

This story is found in both versions of the *Hibernian* (see the Note under *Hibernian* in the "Register of Periodicals").

b. Memoirs of a Captain. *Dumfries Weekly,* II (June 29–July 20, 1773). 4 parts.

864. MEMOIRS OF A MAGDALEN, or the History of Louisa Mildmay. By Hugh Kelly, Esq. In Two Volumes. *Novelist's,* VII (1782). 1 part (61,000).

First published in 1767. The reprinting in the *Novelist's* included two engravings, dated January 12–19, 1782.

865. MEMOIRS OF A MAID OF HONOUR, Written by Herself. *Covent Garden,* II (April–September, 1773). 6 parts (16,300).

866. MEMOIRS OF A MISSIONARY. *Satirist,* VI (June 1, 1810); VII (August 1, 1810); VIII (April 1, 1811). 3 parts (5000). Signed "AN OLD FRIEND."

867. MEMOIRS OF A WIDOW, Written by Herself. *Lady's,* XI (December, 1780) – XII (Supplement, 1781). 13 parts (12,250).

868. MEMOIRS OF A WIG. *Scourge,* VII (June, 1814); VIII (July, 1814). 2 parts (6500).

Presented in two letters signed "PERUKE, JUN."

869. MEMOIRS OF A WIT. *Westminster,* II (August–September, 1774). 2 parts (5000). Signed "DICK RAMBLE."

Addressed "To the Editor of the *Westminster Magazine.*"

870. MEMOIRS OF A WOMAN OF PLEASURE. *Covent Garden,* II (May, 1773) – III (?March, 1774). 11 parts (15,000). *Inc.*

The heroine of this chronicle is called "Fanny Hill," but it bears only a very slight resemblance to Cleland's novel of the same name.

871. MEMOIRS OF A YOUNG LADY. Communicated by Our Old and Valuable Correspondent C.B.I.A. *Bon Ton,* IV (November, 1794) – V (April, 1795). 5 parts (13,750).

872. MEMOIRS OF A YOUNG LADY, in a Series of Letters. *Lady's,* XIV (April, 1783) – XVII (November, 1786). 46 parts (96,000).

873. MEMOIRS OF A YOUNG LADY OF FAMILY, Written by Herself, and Addressed to a Female Friend. *Lady's,* II (April, 1771) – III (December, 1772). 22 parts (67,000).

For a sequel to this story, see "The History of Lady Bradley," published in the same magazine in 1776–1778 (No. 590).

874. MEMOIRS OF AN ENGLISH SERAGLIO, by a Lady Who Has Been One of the Sultanas. *Rambler's,* III (December, 1785) – IV (June, 1786). 5 parts (6650). Uncompleted.

875. MEMOIRS OF AN INDIVIDUAL, Written by Himself. *Attic,* I, No. 8 (May, 1790) – II, No. 21 (June, 1791). 9 parts (9000). Uncompleted.

876. From the MEMOIRS OF AN UNFORTUNATE YOUNG NOBLEMAN, Return'd from a Thirteen Years Slavery in America, Where He Had Been Sent by the Wicked Contrivances of His Cruel Uncle. *Gentleman's,* XIII (February–June, 1743). 4 parts (5300). Uncompleted.

An epitome, with a long extract, of James Annesley's work of the same title, published in 1743, and listed in the *Gentleman's* "Register of Books" for February (p. 112). A continuation was promised at the end of the fourth part, but not forthcoming. For a disguised redaction of the same work, see No. 149. Leslie Stephen called Annesley's *Memoirs* "a doubtful narrative of his life in America" (*DNB*, II, 6).

877. MEMOIRS OF COUNT H———G AND MRS. M———ER. *Town and Country,* II (October, 1770). 1 part (5800).

Part of the series "Histories of the Tête à Tête Annexed." For another scandalous history involving "Count H———g," see No. 257.

878. MEMOIRS OF DICK, the Little Pony, Supposed to be Written by Himself. *Young Gentleman's and Lady's,* I (1799) – II (1800). 12 parts (19,000).

At the end of Part 11 the editor wrote (II, 350): "At the request of several of our subscribers, the favourite *Memoirs of Little Dick* are now printing in a small volume, with additions and corrections, and will be ready on Saturday, the 14th of December: an elegant frontispiece, taken from an interesting scene, will embellish the work." *The Memoirs of Dick, the Little Pony,* published by Walker and dated 1800, was noticed in both the *Critical* and the *Monthly.*

879. MEMOIRS OF EMERALD STAR OF THE GREEN ISLES. *Scourge,* V (February, April, June, 1813). 3 parts (8500).

Part of the series "Fashionable Biography."

880. MEMOIRS OF MISS SIDNEY BIDULPH. Extracted from Her Own Journal. By Mrs. [Frances] Sheridan. In Five Volumes. *Novelist's,* XXII (1786). 1 part (300,000).

First published in 1761 (Vols. I–III) and 1767 (Vols. IV–V). The reprinting in the *Novelist's* includes ten engravings, dated August 1, 1786–May 1, 1787.

881. MEMOIRS OF MONTALBERT, by Margaret B. *Lady's,* XLI (Supplement, 1810) – XLII (April, 1811). 4 parts (7700).

882. MEMOIRS OF MRS. HERBERT, by Miss Anne Blower. *General,* IV (February–October, 1790). 8 parts (14,000).

a. Memoirs of Mrs. Herbert. *Hibernian,* 1790 (March–November). 8 parts.

b. Memoirs of Mrs. Herbert. *Universal Mag. and Rev.,* III (March, 1790) – IV (November, 1790). 8 parts.

883. MEMOIRS OF MRS. J—S—N, by a Lady. *Rambler's,* I (September, 1783) – III (September, 1785). 20 parts (17,750).

With Part 2 the title becomes "History of Emma J———n"; with Part 13 "The History of Emma J——nson." Part 2 is signed "EMMA./Windsor, September 2."

884. [The MEMOIRS OF MRS. WILLIAMS.] *Universal,* XLVI (May, June, Supplement, 1770). 3 parts (16,000).

Extracted from *Letters between an English Lady and Her Friend at Paris, in Which Are Contained the Memoirs of Mrs. Williams; by a Lady* (1770). The title is from Parts 2 and 3. The heading of Part 1 reads as follows: "The Following Memoirs of Mrs. Williams, Being of a Very Interesting Nature, Will, We Hope, Be Acceptable to Many of Our Readers."

a. The Authentic and Entertaining Memoirs of Mrs. Williams. *Weekly Misc.* (Sherborne), XVIII (August 26–September 30, 1782). 6 parts.

885. MEMOIRS OF NED VERSATILE. *Meteor,* I (November–December, 1813). 2 parts (5500).

Offered in two letters signed "NICHOLAS VERSATILE."

886. MEMOIRS OF SOPHIA. *New Novelist's,* II (1787), 183–195. 1 part (9000).

Embellished with an engraving dated December 1, 1787.

887. MEMOIRS OF THE COUNT D'COMMINGE, and Adelaid, of Laussan. Translated from the French of Monsieur D'Arnaud [actually Mme. de Tencin]. *Universal,* LVI (February–March, 1775). 2 parts (5600).

An abridgment of *Memoirs of the Count of Comminge* (1774), "For the *Universal Magazine.*" The attribution to Arnaud is erroneous. In 1764 Arnaud published a celebrated tragedy based upon Mme. de Tencin's *Mémoires du comte de Comminge* (1726) in a volume entitled *Les Amans malheureux, ou le Comte de Comminge, drame en 3 actes et en vers, précédé d'un discours préliminaire et suivi des Mémoires du comte de Comminge* (1764). In the accompanying "discours" Arnaud attributed the subject of his piece to Mme. de Tencin, but in reprinting the *Mémoires* in full, as an appendix to his tragedy, he did not again mention her name. This led to a confusion of authorship in the English translation.

In 1774 Kearsley published in London an English translation of the *Mémoires,* based upon Arnaud's edition, omitting the "discours" and the "drame", and attributing the novel to him (*Memoirs of the Count of Comminge, from the French of Monsieur D'Arnaud,* 1774). The error was compounded in the *Universal,* which condensed the Kearsley translation (without acknowledgment), adopting much of its phraseology, but shifting from a first to a third-person narrative. In Part 2 the title was corrected to read "Count de Comminge." For a full-length magazine translation of Mme. de Tencin, see No. 646.

a. Memoirs of the Count de Comminge, and Adelaid of Laussan, a Novel. Translated from the French of Monsieur D'Arnaud. *Edinburgh Mag. and Rev.,* V (February, 1776). 1 part.

888. MEMOIRS OF THE DUTCHESS OF C———. *New Magazine of Choice Pieces,* II, No. 17 (1810). 1 part (17,500).

Attributed to "Adelade and Theodore" (p. 40) – that is, the "Histoire de la duchesse de C****" in Mme. de Genlis, *Adèle et Théodore* (1782). This translation is not new, however, but taken from "The History of the Dutchess of C———, Written by Herself," contained in the *Universal's* "Adela and Theodore" (No. 9).

For other translations of the same story, see Nos. 12 and 421.

889. MEMOIRS OF THE FAMILY OF LA LUC. *Monthly Extracts,* III (August, 1792). 1 part (5500).

Offered as an extract from Ann Radcliffe, *The Romance of the Forest* (1791), recently published; taken from Chap. 15 of the novel. For another extract from the same novel, see No. 215.

890. MEMOIRS OF THE HOUSE OF MARNY. *Monthly Extracts,* I (September, 1791). 1 part (11,700).

Identified as from *The School for Widows, a Novel, by Clara Reeve, Author of the OLD ENGLISH BARON, &c.* (1791).

a. Memoirs of the House of Marny. Extracted from *The School for Widows,* a Novel Lately Published. *Hibernian,* 1791 (November). 1 part.

891. The MENDICANT, a Narrative Founded upon Facts, by Mrs. [Mary] Pilkington. *Female Preceptor,* II, Nos. 1–2 (July–August, 1813). 2 parts (7000).

892. The MERCHANT'S DAUGHTER, a Novel. *Lady's Monthly Museum,* n.s. VII (August, 1809)–n.s. IX (September, 1810). 12 parts (26,700). Signed "E.T."

a. The Merchant's Daughter, a Novel. *Hibernian,* 1809 (August–October). 3 parts (8100). Uncompleted.

Reprints Parts 1–3 of the above only.

893. The MIDNIGHT ASSASSIN, or Confessions of the Monk Rinaldi; Containing a Complete History of His Diabolical Machinations and Unparalleled Ferocity, Together with a Circumstantial Account of That Scourge of Mankind the Inquisition, with the Manner of Bringing to Trial Those Unfortunate Beings Who Are at Its Disposal. *Marvellous,* I (May 1, 1802). 1 part (30,000).

A disguised redaction of Mrs. Radcliffe's *Italian* (1797), greatly condensed.

894. MILITARY DISTRESS, or Daminville, an Anecdote. [By Arnaud.] *Lady's,* X (February, 1779)–XI (April, 1780). 13 parts (30,000). Signed "E———."

An unacknowledged translation of Baculard D'Arnaud, "Daminvile, anecdote" (*Oeuvres de M. D'Arnaud,* V, 1778). The illustration used to embellish this translation in the *Lady's* was copied from the same volume of Arnaud.

895. MILITARY PROCESSION, a Vision. *Edinburgh Weekly,* XLI (July 22–August 12, 1778). 3 parts (5000). Signed "ZENO."

"For the *Weekly Magazine.*"

896. The MILL, a Tale. *Universal,* XC (January, 1792). The Good Vicar, a Sequel to "The Mill, a Tale," by M. Marmontel. *Ibid.*(February, 1792). 2 parts (5400).

A translation of two connected stories in "La Veillée" (*Mercure,* 1792); extracted from *Tales of an Evening* (1792), to which work the editor of the *Universal* drew attention in his prefatory note. Many miscellanies published "The Mill" (2200 words), without the sequel.

a. The Mill, a Tale. *Gentleman's and London,* 1792 (February). The Good Vicar, etc. [Same title as above.] *Ibid.,* (March). 2 parts.

Reprints the entire notice of the *Universal.*

b. The Mill, a Tale. From the French of the celebrated Marmontel. *Weekly Entertainer,* XIX (February 13, 1792). The Good Vicar, etc. [Same title.] *Ibid.,* XX (December 24, 1792). 2 parts.

897. MIRTH AND MOONSHINE. *Belle Assemblée,* n.s. VI (November, 1812)–n.s. VIII (September, 1813). 9 parts (21,000).

898. The MISANTHROPE. *Perth,* I (July 3–10, 1772). 2 parts (6100). Uncompleted. Signed "HEARTILY."

899. [The MISCHIEFS OF SUPERSTITION AND INFIDELITY: The History of Fidelia.] *Adventurer,* No. 77 (July 21)–No. 79 (August 7, 1753). 3 parts (9000). Signed "Y."

Written for the *Adventurer* by Hester Mulso (later Mrs. Chapone). The title is from the table of contents of the collected edition.

a. The Happiness Arising from Revealed Religion, Exemplified by the History of a Lady, Related by Herself. *Weekly Misc.*(Sherborne), I, Nos. 14–15 (January 3–10, 1774). 2 parts.

b. The Happiness Arising from Revealed Religion, etc. [Same title as No. 899a.] *Weekly Miscellany* (London), II, Nos. 70–71 (1774). 2 parts.

c. Fidelia, a Tale; or the Insufficiency of Morality, without Religion, for Attaining Real Happiness. *Edinburgh Repository*(2), I (1793), 47–70.

The story was attributed to the *Adventurer.*

900. The MISER CONVINCED OF HIS ERROR. *Sentimental,* I (March–July, 1773). 2 parts (9250).

901. The MISERIES OF IMPROPER EDUCATION, or the History of the Family of the Leverets, Taken from Real Life. *Lady's,* XX (February–May, 1789). 3 parts (7700).

a. The Miseries of Improper Education, or the History of the Family of the Leverets. *Hibernian,* 1789 (March–June). 3 parts.

902. [The MISFORTUNES OF ALIENA.] [By Eliza Haywood.] *Female Spectator,* Book XIV (1745), 65–101. 1 part (6400). Signed "CLARIBELLA/Red-Lyon-Square, March 29, 1745."

The story was addressed as a letter "To the Authors of the *Female Spectator,*" and was followed by a long passage of commentary. The title is drawn from the index to Vol. III.

a. [The Misfortunes and Character of the Once-Admired Aliena.] *Ladies,* I (December 16/30, 1749–January 27/February 10, 1750). 4 parts. Signed "MATILDA."

This version is a literal reprinting of Mrs. Haywood's, but it is addressed "To Jasper Goodwill, Esq.," the editor of the *Ladies*. In Part 4 Jasper Goodwill added his own "Reflections on the Unfortunate Case of Aliena," also extracted without acknowledgment from Book XIV of the *Female Spectator*. In the *Ladies* the title is found on Parts 2–4 only.

b. [The Misfortunes of Aliena.] *Beauties of All the Magazines,* I (November–December, 1762). 2 parts (5300).

A condensed version of the same story. Part 1 bears no title except "From the *Lady's Magazine*" – that is, the *Ladies* of 1749–1750 (No. 902b)? or Cooke's *Lady's* of 1762 (cf. No. 593).

c. The Fatal Effects of Excessive Love, or the History of the Unfortunate Aliena, Written by a Lady. *Weekly Entertainer,* III (June 7–14, 1784). 2 parts.

A slightly different condensed version.

903. The MISFORTUNES OF LUCINDA. *Lady's,* V (January–May, 1774). 5 parts (7350).

Prefaced by a letter signed "J. C——n."

904. MISNAR, THE PERSIAN, or the Temple of Hymen, by Marina. *Lady's,* XLVI (March–May, 1815). 3 parts (5750).

905. MISS CHARLOTTE JARVIS TO MISS ELIZA SWANSFORD. *Lady's,* IV (January–December, 1773). 10 parts (22,000).

After Part 2 "Swansford" is spelled "Swanford"; and in Part 9 the title becomes "Miss Charlotte Camply to Miss Eliza Swanford."

906. MISS SALLY BROOKS, or the Seduced Female. *New Lady's,* V (March, 1790)–VIII (July, 1793). 15 parts (45,000). Uncompleted.

a. Miss Sally Brooks, or the Seduced Female. *Hibernian,* 1790 (April, June, August). 3 parts (10,000). Uncompleted.

Reprints Parts 1–3 of the above only.

907. La MODE. Par le chevalier [Stanislas Jean] de Boufflers. *Ambigu,* XXXIII, No. 206 (December 20, 1808). 1 part (7100).

Reprinted from the *Mercure de France,* XXX (October 10–24, 1807), where it appeared under the same title, and was signed "M. de Boufflers."

908. MODERN LIFE DELINEATED, or the History of Gertrude and Emma Lloyd. *Lady's,* XLIII (September, 1812)–XLV (July, 1814). 20 parts (47,500).

In commencing the publication of this story, the editor of the *Lady's* wrote: "The fair Author of this novel is requested to favor us with her address." (XLIII, 395.)

909. MODERN SEDUCTION, a Tale Too True. *Lady's,* XLI (August–September, 1810). 2 parts (7850). Signed "Y.C.R./London, July 9, 1810."

910. MODERN TIMES, or the Adventures of Gabriel Outcast. *Ulster Rep.*, I, Nos. 6–26 (1785). 21 parts (53,000).

911. The MONASTERY. *Asylum*, I (July 30–September 3, 1794). 6 parts (7700).

912. MONASTIC RUINS, or the Invisible Monitor. By Sarah Wilkinson. "Tale 72," *Tell-Tale*, VI (1805). 1 part (6100).

913. The MONKS AND THE ROBBERS, a Tale. *Lady's*, XXV (August 1794–November, 1794); XXIX (April, 1798)–XXXVI (May, 1805). 53 parts (86,500).

The story, written by a reader, was abandoned after only three parts, and resumed by a volunteer, "A. Percy," in 1798, who pursued it for seven more years. After 1801, however, its appearance was very irregular. The novel was reprinted in 1808 as a two-volume novel, *The Monks and the Robbers, a Tale of the Fifteenth Century*.

a. The Monks and the Robbers, a Tale. *Hibernian*, 1794 (October–December); 1798 (May)–1805 (June). 50 parts.

914. MONTRAVERS AND LAVINIA, or One Winter in London. A Tale, by L. M., Author of Several Approved Works of Fancy. *Lady's Monthly Museum*, n.s. IX (October–November, 1810). 2 parts (9500).

915. The MOOR'S REVENGE. *Repository of Arts, etc.*, XIII (February–March, 1815). 2 parts (5200).

916. MOORAD, or Filial Piety, a Tale. *Lady's*, XXXIX (February–July, 1808). 6 parts (15,250).

917. MORAL TALES, by M. Marmontel. Translated from the French, by C. Dennis and R. Lloyd. In Three Volumes. *Novelist's*, VI (1781). 1 part (177,000).

First published in 1763–1765 (but dated 1764 and 1766), this full translation of the *Contes moraux* (1761–1765) contains the following: Vol. I – "Original Preface," "Alcibiades, or Self," "Soliman II," "The Scruple, or Love Dissatisfied with Itself," "The Four Phials, or the Adventures of Alcidonis of Megara," "Lausus and Lydia (*)," "By Good Luck," "The Two Unfortunate Ladies," "All or Nothing," "The Pretended Philosopher"; Vol. II – "The Bad Mother," "The Good Mother," "The Shepherdess of the Alps," "The Happy Divorce," "Annete and Lubin, a True Story (*)," "The Samnite Marriages, an Ancient Anecdote," "The Good Husband," "The Connoisseur," "The School of Fathers"; Vol. III, "The Sylph-Husband," "Lauretta," "A Wife of Ten Thousand!," "Friendship Put to the Test," "The Misanthrope Corrected." [NOTE: Items marked with an asterisk (*) are of less than novelette-length.]

The attribution of the above translation to Charles Denis and Robert Lloyd, however, is erroneous. Actually there were two translations of Marmontel published in 1764 [November, 1763]:

1. *Moral Tales, by Marmontel* [by an anonymous translator] (Becket and De Hondt).

2. *The Moral Tales of M. Marmontel,* Translated from the French by C. Denis and R. Lloyd (Kearsley).

The latter both the *Monthly* and *Critical* reviewers found inferior to the anonymous translation. In 1766 Becket published a supplementary third volume of *Moral Tales,* of which the translator was again unnamed. It is these three volumes of anonymous translations that form the real basis for the corrected and improved text in the *Novelist's Magazine.*

Both the *Moral Tales* of Becket and De Hondt, and the Denis and Lloyd translations, however, were pirated by the miscellanies, and these and other competing translations of the *Contes moraux* circulated in the magazines for the rest of the 18th century. See MORAL TALES, DENIS AND LLOYD, and MARMONTEL (Index). The reprinting in the *Novelist's* was embellished with six engravings, dated October 13–November 25, 1781.

918. MORAL TALES. [By Sarah Trimmer.] Amusement and Instruction for Leisure Hours in the Week Days. *Family,* I (January, 1788)–III (June, 1789). 18 parts (75,000).

An interlocking series of 25 tales, of varying lengths. Those in excess of 5000 words are Nos. XX ("The Rural Economists"), XXII ("The Good Nurse"), and XXIV ("The Gamester"), published in January, March, and May, 1789.

919. The MOST AGREEABLE WOMAN IN THE WORLD! *Weekly Entertainer,* XXXVI (September 22; October 27, 1800). 2 parts (6000).

Offered in two letters addressed "To the Editor," and signed "PAUL PLIANT."

920. The MOST PARTICULAR FORTUNES AND MISFORTUNES of the Famous Moll Flanders, Extracted from Her Own Life. *Wonderful*(2), IV, No. 42 (1793–1794). 1 part (9500).

An unacknowledged epitome of Defoe's *Moll Flanders* (1721).

921. The MOTHER AND NURSE'S FRIEND. By the Authoress of "Intellectual Education." *Belle Assemblée,* n.s. VII (January, 1813)–n.s. VIII (December, 1813). 11 parts (20,500). Uncompleted.

922. The MOTHER-IN-LAW, a New Work, Written by Herself, and Addressed to the Editor of the *Lady's Magazine. Lady's,* XVI (January, 1785)–XVII (Supplement, 1786). 26 parts (27,000).

923. The MOUNTAIN COTTAGER, or the Deserted Bride. By Sarah Wilkinson. "Tale 81," *Tell-Tale* (1805). 1 part (9600).

924. The MUTUAL ASTONISHMENT, AN ORIENTAL NOVEL, Translated from the French [of Bricaire de la Dixmerie]. *Universal,* XL (January, 1767). 1 part (5000).

A translation of "L'Étonnement réciproque, nouvelle orientale" (*Contes philosophiques et moraux, par M. de la Dixmerie,* 1765). For other translations of the same story, see Nos. 925 and 927. A still different, but much shorter version was published in the *Selector,* No. 3 (1776).

a. The Mutual Astonishment, etc. [Same title as above.] *New Town and Country,* II (June–July, 1788). 2 parts.

925. MUTUAL ASTONISHMENT, AN ORIENTAL TALE. *Lady's,* I (June, 1771). 1 part (5000).

A translation of Bricaire de la Dixmerie, "L'Étonnement réciproque, nouvelle orientale" (see No. 924). For a third translation of the same story, see No. 927.

a. Mutual Astonishment, an Oriental Tale. *Bath and Bristol,* I, Nos. 10–12 (1782). 3 parts.

b. Mutual Astonishment, an Oriental Tale. *New Lady's,* III (February–March, 1788). 2 parts.

926. MUTUAL LOVE, an Eastern Tale. *Court Miscellany,* V (April–May, 1769). 2 parts (5600).

927. The MUTUAL SURPRIZE, an Oriental Tale. *Lady's,* XXVI (March, May, 1795). 2 parts (5500).

A translation of Bricaire de la Dixmerie, "L'Étonnement réciproque, nouvelle orientale" (see Nos. 924 and 925, the latter also published in the *Lady's*).

928. MY COUSIN KATE, by a Whimsical Bachelor. *Lady's Monthly Museum,* n.s. XVII (October–December, 1814). 3 parts (5600). Signed "E.T."

929. MY LUMBER ROOM. *Enquirer,* I (1811), 12–17, 114–123, 183–192, 246–256; II (1812), 36–45, 179–183. 6 parts (17,000). Signed "C.D.E."

930. MYRON, an Arabian Tale, by Joseph Moser, Esq. *European,* LI (January–April, 1807). 4 parts (12,300).

931. MYRTLE-WOOD, a Tale. By Clarissa. *General,* III (June–July, 1789). 2 parts (9250).

"For the *General Magazine.*" The editor acknowledged the receipt of Part 1 in April (III, 142) and Part 2 in May (III, 190).

a. Myrtle-Wood, a Tale. *Universal Mag. and Rev.,* II (July–October, 1789). 3 parts.

932. The MYSTERIES OF UDOLPHO, a Romance, Interspersed with Some Pieces of Poetry. By Ann Radcliffe, Author of *The Romance of the Forest,* &c. *European,* XXV (June, 1794). 1 part (6000).

A summary of the story, with excerpts, tendered as a review of the novel, which had just appeared.

a. Account of the *Mysteries of Udolpho,* a Tale, by Mrs. Radcliffe. *Hibernian,* 1794 (July–August). 2 parts.

Identical with the above, but omitting the critical comments at the close.

933. The MYSTERIOUS BRIDE, or the Statue-Spectre. *Marvellous,* IV (April 2, 1804). 1 part (12,000).

934. The MYSTERIOUS RECLUSE. *Belle Assemblée,* IV (February–June, 1808). 5 parts (22,800).

a. The Mysterious Recluse. *Hibernian,* 1808 (May–October). 6 parts. Uncompleted.

Interrupted after Part 4 of the *Belle Assemblée.*

935. NADIR, a Tale of Former Times. *Belle Assemblée,* n.s. X (September–November, 1814). 3 parts (10,400).

936. NANCY, or the Village Beauty. *London,* XLII (October–Appendix, 1773). 4 parts (6600).

"For the *London Magazine.*"

937. [The NARRATIVE.] *Adviser,* I, No. 4 (1803)–IV, No. 121 (1803). 31 parts (60,000). Uncompleted.

Allegedly based on "a manuscript left [the author], as a legacy, by a much loved and lamented friend." The title is from the headings of the various "Essays" ("The Narrative Begun," "Narrative Continued," etc.).

938. [NARRATIVE OF A COUNTRY FAMILY Raised to Sudden Affluence by the Arrival of a Son from India.] [By Henry Mackenzie.] *Lounger,* Nos. 36 (October 8, 1785), 56, 62 (April 8, 1786). 3 parts (5800).

The story, told in three letters from "Marjory Mushroom," is connected also with the "History of the Homespuns" in *Lounger* Nos. 17 and 98 (see No. 652 above). The title is taken from the table of contents of the collected edition.

939. NARRATIVE OF DON PEDRO DE MENTIROSO. (From the same [i.e., from James Murphy, *A General View of the State of Portugal,* 1798].) *Universal,* CII (February, 1798). 1 part (5300).

a. Interesting Story of Don Pedro de Mentiroso. From *A General View of the State of Portugal,* by James Murphy. *Edinburgh*(2), n.s. XI (March, 1798). 1 part.

b. Narrative of Don Pedro de Mentiroso. (From *The Four Ages, etc.,* by Mr. William Jackson, of Exeter.) *Weekly Entertainer,* XXXI (March 19–April 2, 1798). 3 parts.

Erroneously attributed to Jackson's *Four Ages* (1798).

c. Don Pedro de Mentiroso. *Britannic,* VI, No. 73 (1798). 1 part.

Part of the series "Memoirs of Love and Gallantry."

940. [NARRATIVE OF ELIZA.] *Female Preceptor,* II, Nos. 2–3 (August–September, 1813). 2 parts (5000). Signed "ELIZA."

The title is from Part 2. Addressed "To the Editor of the *Female Preceptor.*"

941. [NARRATIVE OF JULIA.] [By William Mudford.] *Universal,* n.s. VIII (November, 1807; n.s. IX (February, 1808); n.s. X (July, 1808). 3 parts (10,000).

The story is included in Nos. 5, 7, and 9 of the series called "The Contemplatist," written by Mudford for the *Universal.* The title of the story is taken from the collected edition of 1811.

No. 5 is signed "JULIA / London, H——y-street, Nov. 4, 1807"; No. 7 bears the same signature, but is dated Dec. 11, 1807. No. 10 is signed "Maria S——y" and dated July 7, 1808.

942. NARRATIVE OF MRS. DHOLSON, a Widow Lady, as Related by Herself to the Writer. *Edinburgh*(2), n.s. IX (April–May, 1797). 2 parts (5800). Signed "J.F."

943. NATURE AND ART. By Mrs. Inchbald. *Moral and Political,* I (June–September, 1796). 3 parts (5900).

A review with a long epitome of Mrs. Inchbald's novel of the same title (1796).

944. The NECROMANCER. Comprising a Series of Wonderful Events, Founded on Fact. Translated from a New German Work, Purposely for This Magazine, by T. Dutton, Esq. *Conjuror's,* II (June, 1793)–III (November, 1793). 6 parts (26,000).

A translation and condensation of Lawrence Flammenberg [i.e., K. F. Kahlert], *Der Geisterbanner, eine Wundergeschichte aus mündlichen und schriftlichen Traditionen gesammelt* (1792). (See Montague Summers, *A Gothic Bibliography,* p. 335.) This magazine version of the novel appeared a year before the more celebrated Minerva Press translation, *The Necromancer, or the Tale of the Black Forest* (1794). For other magazine versions of the novel, see Nos. 239–240, and 949.

945. NED DROWSY, a Story, by Mr. [Richard] Cumberland. *Edinburgh*(2), VII (April–May, 1788); XII (October, 1790). 3 parts (18,000).

Attributed to the "*Observer,* Vol. IV"–i.e., to the supplementary volume of Cumberland's essay-series, published in 1788, containing the story of "Ned Drowsy" in Nos. 118–122. Cumberland completed his story in Nos. 127–128 of Volume V (1790)—whence Part 3 of the above was extracted.

a. Ned Drowsy, a Story, by Mr. Cumberland. *Caledonian*(2), I (June–October, 1788). 4 parts (12,400). Uncompleted.

Includes Parts 1 and 2 of the above only (i.e., *Observer* Nos. 118–122).

b. History of Ned Drowsy. From *The Observer,* by Mr. Cumberland. *Hibernian,* 1791 (October–November). 2 parts (7100). Uncompleted.

Reprints *Observer* Nos. 118–120 only.

c. The History of Ned Drowsy. Related by Mr. Cumberland. *Harvest Home,* I (1807), 210–236. 1 part.

Includes the whole series.

946. The NEGRO, Equalled by Few Europeans. An Extract from a Beautiful Novel of That Name Just Published in Three Volumes by Messrs. Robinsons. Containing the False Imprisonment of Itanoko (the Negro), His Examination before the Judges, and Other Matters. *Lady's,* XXI (June–September, 1790). 4 parts (10,000).

A translation of *Le Nègre, comme il y a peu de blancs* (noticed in the *Mercure de France,* September 26, 1789, pp. 87–90). The English translation was published by Robinsons in 1790.

a. The Negro. An Extract from a Novel of That Name Just Published. Containing the False Imprisonment of Itanoko (the Negroe), His Examination before the Judges, and Other Matters. *Hibernian,* 1790 (August–November). 4 parts.

947. The NEGRO SERVANT. [By the Rev. Legh Richmond.] *Christian Guardian,* I (May, August, 1809); II (January, 1810). 3 parts (7400). Signed "SIMPLEX."

Nos. 4–5 of the series "The Poor Man's Friend." This story was later gathered in a collection by Richmond entitled *Annals of the Poor* (1814). See No. 1361.

948. The NET-MAKER OF BAGDAD, or the Fool and His Cousin. *Weekly Selector,* I, Nos. 7–14 (March 17–May 5, 1812). 8 parts (14,500).

949. A NEW GERMAN STORY. *Hibernian,* 1793 (July–October); 1794 (December)–1796 (May). 26 parts (76,000).

A translation of Lawrence Flammenberg [*i.e.,* K. F. Kahlert], *Der Geisterbanner, eine Wundergeschichte aus mündlichen und schriftlichen Traditionen gesammelt* (1792). (See Montague Summers, *Gothic Bibliography,* p. 335.) The early parts of this magazine version of the novel appeared a year before the Minerva Press translation, *The Necromancer, or the Tale of the Black Forest* (1794), mentioned in *Northanger Abbey;* and ran almost contemporaneously with a different translation in the *Conjuror's Magazine* (see No. 944). For other magazine versions of *Der Geisterbanner* and *The Necromancer,* see Nos. 239–240.

a. A New German Story. *Minerva,* I (August–December, 1793). 4 parts (8700). Uncompleted.

Reprints Part 1, and most of Part 2, of the above.

950. The NEW PYGMALION. *European,* III (April–May, 1783). 2 parts (5500).

a. The New Pygmalion. *Caledonian Mag. and Rev.,* I (May 16, July 11, 1783). 2 parts.

951. A NEW SENTIMENTAL JOURNEY THROUGH ENGLAND, Written by a Lady. *New Lady's,* I (February, 1786)–III (May, 1788). 33 parts (76,000).

952. The NEW YEAR'S GIFT, a Tale. *Monthly Visitor,* VI (January–April, 1799). 4 parts (13,000). Signed "E.B./Sidbury, Devon."

953. The NEW YEAR'S GIFT, a Tale, By Joseph Moser, Esq. Written January 1, 1805. *European,* XLVII (January, 1805). 1 part (5000).

a. The New Year's Gift, etc. [Same title as *European.*] *Hibernian,* 1805 (February–March). 2 parts.

954. The NIGHT-WALKER. *Wit's,* I (July, 1784)–II (March, 1785). 8 parts (11,400). Signed "H——."

955. The NOBLE GENTLEMAN, a Tale. *New Universal*(2), I (October–November, 1787). 2 parts (5350).

956. Le NOURISSON, Translated from the French by Wm. Sh-w. *New Lady's,* II (October, 1787)–III (April, 1788). 6 parts (15,000). Signed "WM. SHAW./Argyll-Street."

In Parts 3–6 the title is spelled "Le Nourrisson."

a. Le NOURISSON. Translated from the French. *Gentleman's and London,* 1788 (May–August). 4 parts (11,700). Signed "WM. SHAW."

An abridged version of the above. The title of Parts 3 and 4 is spelled "Le Nourrisson."

957. NOURMAHALL, or the Queen of the Indies, a Turkish Tale. From *Turkish Tales,* in Two Volumes, by J. Moser. *Universal,* XCV (November–December, 1794). 2 parts (5800).

From the collection by Joseph Moser, published in 1794.

a. Nourmahall, or the Queen of the Indies, a Turkish Tale. *Hibernian,* 1794 (December)–1795 (January).

958. A NOVEL, from the Italian. *Lady's,* XXVII (December, 1796)–XXVIII (January, 1797). 3 parts (9400).

959. The NOVELIST. *Weekly Entertainer,* III (January 5–June 28, 1784). 17 parts (28,250). Uncompleted.

An epistolary novel, written by a reader (see III, 7).

960. The NOVELLIST, Consisting of Histories, Narratives, Moral Allegories, &c. *Lady's,* XV (February, 1784)–XVII (May, 1786). 20 parts (16,000). Uncompleted.

An articulated collection, addressed "To Mrs. D——— of Ackworth-Park, Yorkshire" in an introductory letter signed "W—d—s—n." Abandoned by its reader-writer without explanation after twenty parts.

961. Les NUITS D'ASSUÉRUS. *Ambigu,* XXXVI, No. 321 (February 29, 1812), No. 323 (March 20); XXXVII, No. 325 (April 10, 1812). 3 parts (7000).

A political satire, consisting of a series of "conversations" between Napoleon, the historiographer Réal, and Josephine.

962. Account of NUMA POMPILIUS, Second King of Rome. Translated from the French of M. de Florian, by a Lady. *Town and Country,* XXIII (April, 1791)–XXIII (October, 1793). 24 parts (65,000).

A translation of *Numa Pompilius, second roi de Rome, par M. de Florian* (Paris, 1786). There were at least three earlier English translations of this work.

963. The NUN. *European,* XXV (May–June, 1794). 2 parts (7800).

Addressed "To the Editor of the *European Magazine*" in a letter signed "S.P./ March 31, 1794," and purporting to have been told the writer by a friend while they were traveling through Normandy. Enclosed in the story is another, entitled the "Memoirs of Angelique" (4700), sometimes reprinted by itself (see *Bon Ton,* IV, July–August, 1794).

a. The Nun. *Hibernian,* 1794 (June–July). 2 parts.

The introductory letter was addressed "To the Editor of the *Hibernian Magazine.*"

b. The Nun, or Memoirs of Angelique, a Tale. *Edinburgh*(2), n.s. III (June, 1794)–n.s. IV (July, 1794). 2 parts (6400).

An abbreviated version of the above.

c. Angelica, a Tale. *Scots,* LVI (September–October, 1794). 2 parts (7400).

A slightly condensed version of Nos. 963 and 963a.

964. The NURSERY REFORMER. *Belle Assemblée,* n.s. VI (November, 1812)–n.s. VII (May, 1813). 7 parts (11,600).

965. The NUT-SHELL, a Tale, [translated] from Meissner's *Sketches,* Vol. III [by Alexander Thomson]. *German Misc.,* 1796, pp. 135–178. 1 part (7900).

A translation of A. G. Meissner, "Die Haselnussschale" (*Skizzen,* Dritter Theil, Carlsruhe, 1792).

966. NYTRAM, Prince of Paramania, an Oriental Tale. *British Mag. and Rev.,* I (September–December, 1782). 4 parts (7400). Signed "H——."

Probably by James Harrison (see No. 966a). Harrison was publisher of both magazines.

a. Nytram, Prince of Paramania, an Oriental Tale, by Mr. Harrison. *New Novelist's,* I (1786), 228–238. 1 part.

Embellished with an engraving dated December 1, 1786.

b. Nytram, etc. [Same title as *New Novelist's.*] *Entertaining*(1), I No. 10 (October, 1802). 1 part.

c. Nytram, etc. [Same title.] *New Gleaner,* II (1810). 154–166.

967. OAKWOOD HOUSE, an Original Novel. *Belle Assemblée,* n.s. III (January, 1811)–n.s. VIII (September, 1813). 33 parts (77,000).

The title is later changed to "Oakwood House, an Original Descriptive Novel."

968. ODELIA, a Philosophical Romance. Translated from a French MS. *Ireland's Mirror,* I (June, 1804)–II (June, 1805). 11 parts (24,000).

969. The OFFICIOUS FRIEND, a Tale. From *The Man of Nature,* a Work Lately Translated from the French. *Universal,* LII (January–February, 1773). 2 parts (5800).

Extracted from James Burne, *The Man of Nature* (1773), a translation of G. Guillard de Beaurieu, *L'Élève de la nature* (1766).

970. [The OLD BACHELOR.] *Lady's Monthly Museum,* n.s. I (July, August, December, 1806). 3 parts (7200).

Presented in two letters, addressed "To the Editor of the *Lady's Museum,*" explaining the writer's reasons for his celibacy. The story elicited several replies from readers (n.s. II, 11–13). The title is from Parts 2 and 3.

971. The OLD MAN'S TALE, a Traveller's Adventure in Switzerland. *Pocket,* III (November, 1795). 1 part (5000). Signed "W.G.H."

972. OLYMPIA, or the Acquisitions of Experience. Translated from the French by a Lady. *Lady's,* VII (December, 1776)–VIII (June, 1777). 7 parts (14,500). Signed "I——."

973. OMAR AND FATIMA, or the Apothecary of Ispahan. A Persian Tale by Joseph Moser, Esq. *European,* XLVI (July–December, 1804). 6 parts (20,000).

974. OMILIUS TO SAPPHIRA. *Female Preceptor,* I, No. 8 (May, 1813)–II, No. 3 (September, 1813). 5 parts (5000).

This exchange of letters, which is partly in verse, is prefaced by a letter "To the Editor of the *Female Preceptor,*" signed "Aspasia / March 25, 1813."

975. OPTIMISM, a Dream, by M. [Louis Sébastien] Mercier, *European,* XI (January–February, 1787). 2 parts (5400).

A translation of "L'Optimisme" (*Songes philosophiques,* Vol. I, 1768).

a. Optimism, a Dream, by M. Mercier. *Hibernian,* 1787 (February–March). 2 parts.

b. Optimism, a Dream. *Weekly Misc.* (Glasgow), IV, Nos. 92–94 (March 23–April 6, 1791). 3 parts.

976. The ORACLE, an Oriental Tale. *Universal,* XL (February, 1767). 1 part (6200).

An unacknowledged translation of Bricaire de la Dixmerie, "L'Oracle journalier" (*Contes philosophiques et moraux,* 1765).

a. The Oracle, an Oriental Tale. *New Town and Country,* II (January–February, 1788). 2 parts.

b. The Oracle, an Oriental Tale. *Weekly Misc.*(Glasgow), n.s. II (January 9–February 6, 1793). 5 parts.

977. ORASMIN, or the Folly of Despondency, an Oriental Fable. *Universal,* XC (March–April, 1792). 2 parts (8500).

a. Orasmin, or the Folly of Despondency, an Oriental Fable. *Universal Mag. and Rev.,* VII (April–May, 1792). 2 parts.

978. ORIGINAL LETTERS. *General,* I (July, 1787)–II (December, 1788). 18 parts (21,000). Signed "G.M."

The prefatory letter, signed "G.M." and dated July 9, 1787, declares that the letters are "genuine," though the names are fictitious. A final letter, also to the editor, is dated November 12, 1788. The series is labeled "For the *General Magazine*."

979. ORIGINAL LETTERS. Miss Clifford to Miss Granby. *Lady's,* IX (December, 1778)–X (May, 1779). 6 parts (5000). Uncompleted.

The editor of the *Lady's* acknowledged a further "pacquet of *Letters from Miss Clifford,* &c" in September, 1779, but postponed printing them "as they seem to want some little polishing" (X, [450]). But the series was never resumed.
After Part 3 the title reads "A Series of Letters, by a Young Lady."

980. ORIGINAL LETTERS FROM THE WIFE OF A BRITISH OFFICER IN PORTUGAL to Her Friend in London. *Belle Assemblée,* n.s. VI (September, 1812)–n.s. VII (March, 1813); n.s. VIII (July, October, 1813). 8 parts (10,500). Uncompleted

"Letter I" is dated September 18, 1812; "Letter IX" (the last), June 20, 1813.

981. ORIGINAL LETTERS WRITTEN FROM SPAIN, Containing the History of Don Alonzo, or the Noble Hermit. *Universal,* LXXXVIII (January–May, 1791). 5 parts (14,000).

An introductory letter addressed "To the Editor of the *Universal Magazine,*" and signed "A.B.," declares that the letters were written several years before "by an English Gentleman, on a Tour through Spain and Italy, to a Friend in London," although the real names are concealed (p. 27).

a. Original Letters Written from Spain, etc. [Same title as above.] *Hibernian,* 1791 (February–June). 5 parts.

b. The Spanish Lovers. Extracted from the Private Correspondence of an English Gentleman on His Travels through Spain, a Short Time Previous to That Country Being Invaded by Buonaparte. *New Magazine of Choice Pieces,* I (1810), 51–73. 1 part (10,500).

Reprints only the "History of Don Alonzo," adapted from Parts 2–5 of the above.

982. ORLANDO, or the Knight of the Moon, by Sarah Wilkinson. "Tale 15," *Tell-Tale,* II (1804). 1 part (5300).

983. ORLANDO FURIOSO. *Universal,* LXIX (July, 1781)–LXXVIII (Supplement, 1786). 26 parts (68,000).

A prose translation of Ariosto carried through Book XIV of the original. A note at the end of the fragment (LXXVIII, 360) explained that this translation had been offered as "a Specimen of Italian Literature, which, till very recently, has been little known in our Language," but now that the Hoole translation (*Orlando Furioso, Translated into English Verse... by John Hoole,* 1783) had been published, the *Universal* had decided to discontinue its translation.

984. OSBORNE FITZROY, a Caledonian Romance. *Lady's Monthly Museum,* XII (February, 1804)–XIII (December, 1804). 9 parts (24,800).

985. OSMAN, an Eastern Tale. *Lady's,* XXXIII (March–April, 1802). 2 parts (5200).

Evidently a translation from the French. In July and August, 1773, the *Lady's* had published a shorter version of the same tale: "Osman, or Modern Gratitude, Translated by a Lady" (4600 words).

986. The OXONIAN'S SENTIMENTAL TRIP TO LONDON. *British Mag. and Rev.,* I (July, 1782)–II (January, 1783). 1 part (8000).

987. [The PALACE AND THE CASTLE, an Allegory.] *Christian Mirror,* Nos. 17–18 (1805). 2 parts (5100). Signed "I."

The title is from the table of contents.

988. PAMELA, or Virtue Rewarded. In a Series of Familiar Letters from a Beautiful Young Damsel to Her Parents. Published in Order to Cultivate the Principles of Virtue and Religion in the Minds of the Youth of Both Sexes... By Mr. Samuel Richardson. In Four Volumes. *Novelist's,* XX (1785). 1 part (475,000).

A reprinting of both parts of the original (1740; 1741), which is here embellished with sixteen engravings, dated October 8, 1785–January 21, 1786.

a. Pamela, or Virtue Rewarded. *New Lady's,* IX (July, 1794)–X (November, 1795). 1 part.

Parts I and II of Richardson's novel, issued as a serial book and distributed as a regular supplement of the *New Lady's Magazine* for 18 months. Hogg's *New Novelist's Magazine* (of which the first offering was *Pamela*) had been announced in January, 1794, and the bookseller evidently disposed of the unsold sheets in the above manner. Hogg described *Pamela* in the *New Lady's* as "the most valuable and entertaining Novel ever written" (IX, 298), and later declared that its reprinting in the magazine was meeting with "universal applause" (X, 34). But the magazine ceased publication the same year.

989. PAMROSE, or the Palace and the Cot. [By Mme. de Genlis.] *Entertaining*(1), I (November, 1802). 1 part (12,000).

A translation of "Pamrose, ou le Palais et la chaumière," first published in the *Nouvelle bibliothèque des romans,* année 3, tom. 9 (1801). For a slightly earlier translation of the same story, see No. 990.

a. Pamrose, or the Palace and the Cot, Translated from the French of Madame de Genlis. *Weekly Entertainer,* XL (December 13, 1802)–XLI (January 17, 1803). 6 parts.

990. PAMROSE, or the Palace and the Cottage, a Novel, by Madame de Genlis. *Lady's,* XXXIII (August–October, 1802). 3 parts (10,750).

A translation of "Pamrose, ou le Palais et la chaumière" (1801). For another translation of the same story, see No. 989.

991. PANTHEON ANECDOTES. *London,* LI (April–December, 1782). 7 parts (13,500).
"For the *London Magazine.*"

992. PARENTAL RESENTMENT EXEMPLIFIED, or a Biographical Sketch. *Belle Assemblée,* I (May, 1806). 1 part (5000).

993. PARENTAL TYRANNY, or the History of Louisa and Narcissa. *Universal,* LXXIII (July, 1783). 1 part (5000).
For a later version or translation of the same story see No. 1212.
a. Parental Tyranny, or the History of Louisa and Narcissa. *Hibernian,* 1783 (September). 1 part.

994. The PASSIONS, an Allegorical Tale. *St. James's*(2), II (January, 1775). 1 part (5500). Uncompleted.
No. 4 of the series "The English Marmontel, or the School of Sentiment."

995. PAULIN, or the Happy Effects of Virtue. *Lady's Monthly Museum,* XIV (January–June, 1805). 6 parts (19,500).

996. The PEASANT BOY, or the Events of De Courcy Castle. "Tale 67," *Tell-Tale,* V (1805). 1 part (8200).

997. A PEEP AT MY NEIGHBORS, or Asmodeus in the Country. *Lady's,* XLV (June, 1814)–XLVI (July, 1815). 6 parts (9500). Signed "T****."

998. The PERFIDIOUS DECEIVER, a True History. *Caledonian Mag. and Rev.,* I (March 7–21, 1783). 2 parts (5000).

999. PERIANDER OF CORINTH, or Revenge, a Tale. Translated from the German of Augustus Lafontaine. *Lady's,* XXXII (September–November, 1801). 3 parts (7500).
A translation of "Die Rache" (see *Kleine Romane und moralische Erzählungen von August Lafontaine,* 3rd ed., Vol. VI, 1804).

1000. PERPLEXITIES OF A MAN OF LETTERS. From the German. *Annual Reg., 1805,* XLVII (1807), 932–946. 1 part (7400).
For another translation of the same story, see No. 1001.

1001. The PERPLEXITIES OF A MAN OF LETTERS. From the German. In Letters from Goodwin to His Friend. *Sporting,* XXXII (August, October, 1808); XXXIII (January, 1809). 3 parts (7000).
For another translation of the same story, see No. 1000.

1002. PERUVIAN TALES, Related in One Thousand and One Hours, by One of the Select Virgins of Cusco, to the Ynca of Peru, to Dissuade Him from a Resolution He Had Taken to Destroy Himself by Poison. Translated from the Original French by Samuel Humphreys, Esq. In Three Volumes. *Novelist's,* XXI (1786). 1 part (200,000).

An old translation of Thomas Simon Gueullette, *Les Milles et une heure, contes péruviens* (1733). Humphrey's preface is dated May 1, 1734. The reprinting in the *Novelist's* includes seven engravings, dated February 4–March 18, 1786.

1003. PERVONTE, or the Wishes, a Fairy Tale. Translated from the German [of C. M. Wieland]. *New Novelist's*, II (1787), 27–36. 1 part (6400).

A prose translation of the poem "Pervonte, oder die Wünsche," Parts 1 and 2 (1779).

a. Pervonte, etc. [Same title as above.] *Gleaner,* I (1805), 124–134.

1004. PHANTASMAGORIA, or the Developement of Magical Deception. *Marvellous,* III (July 1, 1803). 1 part (30,000).

1005. PHILADELPHIA, a Novel, in a Series of Letters, Written by J. L. H. *New Lady's,* III (September, 1788)–IV (Supplement, 1789). 9 parts (8700).

The introductory letter, signed "S. Pure," declares that this is "the production of a young gentleman of only 12 years of age" (III, 458).

1006. PHILARIO AND CLARINDA. From *Philario and Clarinda, a Warning to Youth against Scepticism, Infidelity, and Vice,* by the Rev. John Thorowgood. *Universal,* CXI (November, 1802). 1 part (5000).

From the novel published in 1802.

1007. [The PIGEON.] [By Augustus von Kotzebue.] *Universal,* n.s. VII (June, 1807). 1 part (5000).

A translation of "Die Taube, eine Erzählung" (*Die jünsten Kinder meiner Laune, von A. v. Kotzebue,* Vol. III, 1795). Included as part of a review of "Kotzebue's *Novellettes*" (i.e., *Novelettes,* 3 vols., London, 1807). For another extract from the same English collection, see No. 1057.

a. [The Pigeon.] *Hibernian,* 1807 (September). 1 part.

Attributed to "*Novellettes.*" The title is included in the introductory remarks.

b. The Pigeon, by Kotzebue. *Weekly Entertainer,* XLVII (October 26–November 9, 1807). 3 parts.

1008. The PILGRIM, A TALE. From *Vancenza,* a Novel, in 2 Vol. by Mrs. M. Robinson. *Universal,* XC (February–March, 1792). 2 parts (5500).

Extracted from Mary Robinson, *Vancenza, or the Dangers of Credulity* (1792), Vol. II, Chaps. 2–6. Part 2 contains "The Pilgrim's Story."

a. Vancenza, or the Dangers of Credulity, by Mrs. M. Robinson. *Monthly Extracts,* II (February, 1792), 176–185. 1 part.

A double extract called "The Pilgrim" and "The Pilgrim's Story." In addition to the above, the magazine printed the "Description of the Castle of Vancenza" (pp. 167–176), "Preparations for the Nuptials of Elvira and Prince Almanza" (pp. 185–192), and "Death of Elvira" (pp. 192–193). The excerpts from *Vancenza* published in the *Monthly Extracts* total about 12,000 words.

b. The Pilgrim, a Tale. A Novel, by Mrs. Robinson. *Universal Mag. and Rev.,* VII (March–April, 1792). 2 parts.

c. The Pilgrim, etc. [Same title as *Universal.*] *Weekly Entertainer,* XX (November 26–December 3, 1792). 2 parts.

1009. The PILGRIM, A TALE FROM HISTORY. *Hibernian,* 1796 (October)–1797 (December). 13 parts (40,000). Uncompleted.

An Ossianic tale, introduced by a letter addressed "To the Editor" and dated "August 20th, 1796," dwelling on the story's "historical" character.

a. The Pilgrim, a Tale from History. *Literary and Masonic,* I (November–December, 1802). 2 parts (6200). Uncompleted.

Reprints only through the middle of Part 3 of the above.

1010. A PILGRIM'S NARRATION OF HIS OWN HISTORY. From *The Adventures of John of Gaunt* [by James White]. *Weekly Entertainer,* XVI (October 11–25, 1790). 3 parts (5600).

Adapted from "Visits" XVII–XX of White's novel (1790). For other extracts, see Nos. 659–660. On September 6–13, 1790, the *Weekly Entertainer* had also published "The History of Raymond Bushy Beard," (4500 words), making a total of four extracts (about 30,000 words) from the same novel within the year.

1011. The PLEASANT AND DELIGHTFUL HISTORY OF MONTELION, the Most Valiant and Renowned Knight of the Oracle. *Penny Medley,* No. 9 (1746). 1 part (5600).

1012. PLEASURE, a Vision. *Universal Museum,* n.s. VI (January–February, 1770). 2 parts (5100).

1013. The PLEASURES OF BENEVOLENCE, or the History of Lady Mortimer. *Lady's,* XLII (December, 1811)–XLIII (August, 1812). 9 parts (19,500).

The story was declared to be "from the pen of a lady, whose entertaining and instructive productions we *know* to have heretofore been highly approved by our fair readers." (XLII, 490.)

1014. PLINDARMON'S SONG. *General,* IV (August, 1790)–V (September, 1791). 9 parts (8600). Uncompleted?

An Ossianic narrative. The receipt of the story from "our greatly esteemed Correspondent, *Recluse,*" was acknowledged in August (IV, 340). The first installment of the story, signed "R.", is dated June, 1790.

1015. POOR JACK THE HUNTSMAN, a Pathetic Tale. *Sporting,* XXXI (July, 1808)–XXXII (January, 1809); XXXIII (June, 1809). 5 parts (12,000). Signed "M."

Nos. 7–11 of the series "The Philosophical Sportsman."

1016. POOR LISE. *German Museum,* III (January–February, 1801). 2 parts (6300). Signed "M.G."

a. Lise and Login. *Britannic,* IX, Nos. 120–121 (1801). 2 parts (5250).

A slight abridgment of the above. Part of the series "Memoirs of Love and Gallantry."

1017. The PORTRAIT, or Incidents in My Own Life. *Lady's,* XXXVII (June–August, 1806). 3 parts (6200).

a. The Portrait, or Incidents in My Own Life. *Dublin Museum,* I (February–May, 1807). 3 parts.

1018. [The POWER OF CORRUPT SOCIETY AND FALSE SHAME over the Natural Feelings of Virtue. Story of Father Nicholas.] [By Henry Mackenzie.] *Lounger,* Nos. 82–84 (August 26–September 9, 1786). 3 parts (5200). Signed "Z."

The title is from the table of contents of the collected edition.

a. The Affecting History of Father Nicholas. From the *Lounger,* a Series of Periodical Papers in Three Vols. *Universal,* LXXX (June–Supplement, 1787). 2 parts.

b. The Affecting History of Father Nicholas. *Gentleman's and London,* 1787 (August–September). 2 parts.

c. Story of Father Nicholas. By Mr. Mackenzie. *Weekly Entertainer,* X (September 17–October 1, 1787). 3 parts.

d. The Power of Corrupt Society and False Shame over the Natural Feelings of Virtue: Exemplified in the Story of Father Nicholas. From the *Lounger,* Lately Published. *European,* XII (December, 1787). 1 part.

e. Story of Father Nicholas. By Mr. Mackenzie. *New Novelist's,* II (1787), 105–112.

f. The Story of Father Nicholas. By Mr. Mackenzie. *Caledonian*(2), I (January–February, 1788). 2 parts.

g. History of Father Nicholas. *Weekly Misc.*(Glasgow), II, Nos. 27–30 (December 23, 1789–January 13, 1790). 4 parts.

h. The Story of Father Nicholas. *Town and Country,* XXV (April–May, 1793). 2 parts.

i. The Story of Father Nicholas. *Minerva,* I, No. 4 (September, 1793). 1 part. Uncompleted.

Offers Part 1 of the preceding only.

j. Father Nicholas. *Gleaner,* II (1806). 115–123.

Attributed to the *Lounger.*

1019. The POWER OF DESTINY, or Story of the Journey of Giafar to Damascus, Comprehending the Adventures of Chebib and His Family. *Monthly Extracts,* IV (October, 1792). 1 part (32,000).

Attributed to *Arabian Tales, or a Continuation of the Arabian Nights Entertainments* (1792), translated by Robert Heron from Chavis and Cazotte, *Suite des Mille et une nuits* (1788–1789). For other extracts from the same translation, see ARABIAN TALES (Index).

1020. The POWER OF FAITH. *Belle Assemblée,* n.s. I (May–June, 1810). 2 parts (6900).

1021. The PRATER, by Charlotte King. *New Lady's,* IX (May, 1794)–X (Supplement, 1795). 17 parts (13,500). Uncompleted.

1022. The PRETENDED MARTIN GUERRE. Extracted from the *Causes Celebres.* By Miss C. Smith. *Edinburgh*(2), VI (August, 1787). 1 part (5100).

A note (p. 116) explains that the story is taken from Charlotte Smith, *The Romance of Real Life* [1787].

a. The Pretended Martin Guerre. Extracted from the *Causes Celebres.* By Miss C. Smith. *Caledonian*(1), I (September 21–October 5, 1787). 2 parts.

b. The Pretended Martin Guerre. An Authentic History. *Weekly Misc.*(Glasgow), III, Nos. 74–76 (November 17–December 1, 1790). 3 parts.

1023. The PRETENDED PHILOSOPHER. A Humorous Character, from Marmontel's *Moral Tales. Universal Museum,* II (November, 1763)–III (January, 1764). 3 parts (6300).

An extract from "The Pretended Philosopher" (*Moral Tales,* Becket and De Hondt, 1764), translated from Marmontel's "Le Philosophe soi-disant" (*Contes moraux,* 1761). For other extracts from the same collection, see No. 917. For some reason the *Universal Museum* omitted the first 1200 words of the translation.

a. [The Pretended Philosopher. A Moral Tale.] *Weekly Amusement,* II (March 23–April 13, 1765). 4 parts (7500).

A complete reprinting of the above translation, taken from the *Moral Tales.* The title is from Parts 2–5.

1024. The PRETTY VILLAGER, a Tale. *Universal,* LXXXVIII (April, 1791). 1 part (5600).

a. The Pretty Villager, a Tale. *Aberdeen*(1), IV (May, 1791). 1 part.

b. The Pretty Villager, a Tale. *Weekly Entertainer,* XX (October 1–15, 1792). 3 parts.

c. The Pretty Villager, a Tale. *Harvest Home,* II (1808), 1–12.

1025. The PRINCE OF BRITTANY, a New Historical Novel, by the Author of "The Lord of Crequi." *Universal,* LXXVI (March–June, 1785). 4 parts (19,500). Signed "L."

A translation of Baculard D'Arnaud, "Le Prince de Bretagne" (*Oeuvres de M. D'Arnaud,* VII, 1777). The *Universal* had published "The Lord of Crequi" in 1782–1783 [see No. 811].

a. The Prince of Brittany, a New Historical Novel. *Hibernian,* 1785 (April–September). 6 parts.

b. The Prince of Brittany, a New Historical Novel. *Weekly Entertainer,* IX (June 11, 1787)–X (July 30, 1787). 8 parts. Signed "L."

1026. The PRINCE OF CARIZIME, and the Princess of Georgia, an Arabian Tale. *Belle Assemblée,* IV (May, 1808)–V (July, 1808). 3 parts (12,500). Signed "M.R."

A translation of the "Histoire du prince de Carizme et de la princesse de Géorgie" (Petis de la Croix, *Contes turcs,* 1707).

a. The Prince of Carizime, etc. [Same title as above.] *Cyclopaedian,* II (October, 1808)–III (January, 1809). 3 parts (6400). Uncompleted.

Reprints only about half of the above.

1027. The PRINCESS DES URSINS, an Historical Novel, by Madame de Genlis. Translated from the French. *Lady's,* XXXIII (July–August, 1802). 2 parts (6600).

A translation of "La Princesse des Ursins, nouvelle historique" (*Nouvelle bibliothèque des romans,* année 4, tom. 10 [1802]). For another translation of the same story, see No. 1028.

1028. The PRINCESS DES URSINS, an Historical Spanish Novel, Translated from the French of Madame de Genlis. *Entertaining*(1), No. 10 (October, 1802). 1 part (6900).

A translation of "La Princesse des Ursins, nouvelle historique" (1802). See No. 1027.

1029. The PROGRESS OF LOVE, a Novel. *Sentimental,* III (March–July, 1775). 5 parts (12,000).

a. The Progress of Love, a Novel. *Hibernian,* 1775 (April–August). 4 parts.

1030. The PROGRESS OF PASSION, or Love-Matches and Money-Matches Illustrated. The True Story of Paladel and Patty. *Westminster,* V (March–June, 1777). 4 parts (5400). Signed "C.M."

"For the *Westminster Magazine.*" For a different version of the same story, see No. 823.

1031. The PROTECTING SPIRIT. [By Augustus von Kotzebue.] *Flowers of Literature, for 1807,* VI (1808), 95–123. 1 part (7600).

Attributed in the table of contents to "Kotzebue's *Romances*" (i.e., "Der Schutzgeist," *Kleine Romane, Erzählungen, Anecdoten und Miscellen von August von Kotzebue,* Vol. II, 1807). Actually the translation is an abridged version of "The Protecting Spirit," published in *The Pastor's Daughter with Other Romances* (2nd. ed., Vol. II, 1807).

a. The Protecting Spirit. *New Magazines of Choice Pieces,* I, No. 9 (1810), 233–250. 1 part.

Attributed to Kotzebue.

1032. The PROVERB REVERSED, or Dishonesty the Worst Policy. Being a Letter from Mr. David Longhead, the Dishonest Farmer, Containing the History of His Life. *Scotch Cheap Rep.*, No. 8 (1808). 1 part (5100). Signed "A."

Addressed "To the Editors of the *Scotch Cheap Repository*." Dated "Isle of Man, 1st Nov. 1808."

1033. The PROWESS AND DEATH OF CAPTAIN TRANCHEMONT, and His Brave Companions. A Tale, from the *Continuation of the Arabian Nights Entertainments. Edinburgh*(2), n.s. III (January–February, 1794). 2 parts (11,750).

An extract from the Edinburgh translation of Chavis and Cazotte, *Suite des Mille et une nuits* (1788–1789), called *Arabian Tales, Being a Continuation of the Arabian Nights Entertainments* (II, 1792, pp. 366–417). For another translation of the same story, see No. 1207. A number of other extracts were made from the same collection. See Arabian Tales (Index).

1034. The PUBLIC BREAKFAST, a Scene from Camilla, a Novel, by Mrs. D'Arblay (late Miss Burney). *Universal*, XCIX (August, 1796). 1 part (6000).

From the novel published in 1796. A shorter extract (3350), called "The Sermon," was published in the *Universal* for September, pp. 201–205.

a. The Public Breakfast, etc. [Same title as above.] *Weekly Entertainer*, XXVIII (September 19–October 10, 1796). 4 parts.

1035. PURGATORY, a Vision. *Ayrshire*, I (August, 1815–July, 1816). 12 parts (18,000). Uncompleted. Signed "Plato, May 20, 1815."

"For the *Ayrshire Magazine*."

1036. The PURSUITS OF LITERATURE, or Memoirs of Horace Laurelless and His Patrons. *Meteor*, I (November, 1813–February, 1814). 4 parts (10,000).

1037. The PYRENEAN HERMITS. *Lady's*, I (March–April, 1771). 2 parts (9100).

A translation of Bricaire de la Dixmerie, "Les Solitaires des Pyrénées, nouvelle espagnole et françoise" (*Contes philosophiques et moraux*, 1765). For other translations of the same story, see Nos. 1038–1039.

Part 1 of this story had already appeared in the *Lady's* when the magazine divided (see the Note under *Lady's* in the "Register of Periodicals"). Wheble's rival magazine continued the story in its April issue (I, 409–414), but in a different translation from the one listed above.

1038. The PYRENEAN HERMITS, A TALE. By M. Dixmerie. *Edinburgh*(2), VIII (December, 1788). 1 part (7900).

A translation of "Les Solitaires des Pyrénées" (see Nos. 1037 and 1039).

a. The Pyrenean Hermits, etc. [Same title as above.] *Hibernian*, 1789 (February–April). 3 parts.

1039. The PYRENEAN HERMITS, OR THE DOUBLE DISCOVERY. Translated from the French [of Bricaire de la Dixmerie]. *New Lady's,* I (February–March, 1786). 2 parts (6100).

A translation of "Les Solitaires des Pyrénées" (see Nos. 1037–1038).

1040. QUEEN FANTASQUE, a Tale, from the French of J. J. Rousseau. Translated for This Work. *Attic Misc.,* I (November–December, 1789). 2 parts (6600).

A translation of *La Reine fantasque, conte, par Jean-Jacques Rousseau* (1762) [1772?].

1041. RAYMOND CASTLE, a Legendary Tale, by Mr. Bacon. *Cabinet Mag.,* I (April–May, 1797). 2 parts (5000).

Possibly by James or Robert Bacon (see No. 232).

1042. The RECESS, a Tale of Past Times, Originally Written by Miss [Sophia] Lee. Third Edition. *Marvellous,* I (July 1, 1802). 1 part (30,000).

An abridgment of the *Recess, or a Tale of Other Times* (1785), about one fifth the length of the original. The third edition of the full-length novel was published in 1787.

1043. [The RECLUSE.] [By James Anderson?] *Recreations,* I (April–June, 1799); III (August, 1800). 4 parts (16,250).

Included in the series "Lucubrations of Timothy Hairbrain." The title of the story is from Part 2. Anderson was editor of the *Recreations.*

1044. The RECLUSE. *Monthly Museum,* I (February–April, 1814). 3 parts (5000).

1045. The RECLUSES OF MURCIA. A New Tale by Marmontel. *Carlton House,* I (January–April, 1792). 4 parts (7200).

A translation, greatly abridged, of "Les Solitaires de Murcie, conte moral" (*Mercure,* 1791). For another translation of the same tale, see No. 510.

1046. The RECLUSES OF SNOWDEN, a Tale. *Lady's Monthly Museum,* n.s. IV (February–April, 1808). 3 parts (8000).

1047. The RECRUITING PARTY, a Tale. *Lady's Monthly Museum,* n.s. XII (March–April, 1812). 2 parts (5600).

1048. The REFUSAL. [By Jane West.] *Belle Assemblée,* n.s. I (April, 1810). 1 part (9000).

A summary of Mrs. West's recent novel of the same title (1810), with copious extracts.

a. The Refusal. *Hibernian,* 1811 (March–April). 2 parts.

Identified, as above.

1049. REGINALD DU BRAY, an Historic Tale. *Berwick Museum,* I (November, 1785)–II (October, 1786). 12 parts (27,300).

An unacknowledged reprinting of *Reginald Du Bray, an Historick Tale, by a Late Lord* (1779), republished by the Minerva Press in 1786 (actually 1785?).

1050. The REMARKABLE HISTORY OF NICOLAS PEDROSA, and His Escape from the Inquisition in Madrid. From *The Observer,* Vol. V, by Richard Cumberland, Esq. *Universal,* LXXXVII (August–October, 1790). 3 parts (7000).

Nos. 142–144 of Cumberland's *Observer,* Volume V, published in 1790.

a. The Remarkable History of Nicolas Pedrosa, etc. [Same title as above.] *Hibernian,* 1790 (September–November). 3 parts.

b. The Remarkable History of Nicolas Pedrosa, etc. [Same title as above.] *Universal Mag. and Rev.,* IV (September–November, 1790). 3 parts.

c. The Remarkable History of Nicolas Pedrosa, etc. [Same title as above.] *Weekly Entertainer,* XVI (November 29–December 13, 1790). 3 parts.

d. The History of Nicolas Pedrosa, and His Escape from the Inquisition in Madrid. *Edinburgh*(2), XII (November, 1790). 1 part.

Attributed, in a note, to Volume V of the *Observer.*

e. The History of Nicholas Pedrosa. From Mr. Cumberland's *Observer. Town and Country,* XXIII (January–February, 1791). 2 parts.

f. History of Nicolas Pedrosa, a Tale, by Mr. Cumberland. *Attic Misc.,* II (February–March, 1791). 2 parts.

g. History of Nicholas Pedrosa, with an Account of His Escape from the Inquisition. *Weekly Misc.*(Glasgow), n.s. I (July 4–August 1, 1792). 5 parts.

h. History of Nicolas Pedrosa. *Culler,* I (October 28–November 27, 1795). 5 parts.

i. Nicolas Pedrosa. By Mr. Cumberland. *Gleaner,* I (1805), 355–366.

j. Nicolas Pedrosa. By Richard Cumberland, Esq. *Weekly Entertainer,* XLVI (October 13–November 3, 1806). 4 parts.

k. Nicolas Pedrosa (Cumberland). *New Magazine of Choice Pieces,* II, No. 20 (1810), 78–93.

l. The History of Nicolas Pedrosa. *Sunderland Literary Misc.,* I (September–December, 1815). 4 parts.

1051. The REMARKABLE HISTORY OF THE COUNTESS OF G——, a Swedish Lady. *Weekly Misc.*(Sherborne), IX (January 5, 1778)–X (June 29, 1778). 14 parts (47,000).

A translation of C. F. Gellert, *Leben der schwedischen Gräfinn von G**** (1746). There were two earlier appearances of this novel in English, *The Life of the Countes of G———. Translated from the German, by a Lady* (1747; reprinted 1776), and *The Life of the Sweedish Countess of G***, Translated from the German by the Rev. Mr. N**** (1776). Although different from both, the version in the *Weekly Miscellany* was probably based on the second.

a. The Remarkable History of the Countess of G——, a Swedish Lady. *Moral and Entertaining,* II (January, 1778)–III (July, 1778). 7 parts.

1052. The REPRESENTATIONS OF LIFE. Contained in Works of Fiction. Not to Be Considered as Having Any Existence in Nature. *Belle Assemblée,* II (January–April, 1807). 4 parts (12,000).

1053. RESCHID AND ALMENA, an Oriental Tale. *Pocket,* IV (March, 1796). 1 part (5000). Signed "J. Jackson."

1054. The RESTORED SON AND DAUGHTER. *Asylum,* III, Nos. 53–59 (October 14–November 25, 1795). 7 parts (9700).

Addressed "To the Editor" in a letter signed "R.C.", and dated Glasgow, Oct. 1, 1795."

1055. The RESUSCITATED MARINER, or the Incidents of Myrtle Grove. By Mrs. [Mary] Pilkington. *Lady's,* XL (October, December, 1809). 2 parts (6400).

The receipt of this story was announced in September 1809 (p. [384]).

1056. RETRIBUTION, a Tale, Founded on Facts. By Thomas Bellamy. *Monthly Mirror,* II (October–December, 1796). 3 parts (6900).

a. Retribution, a Tale, Founded on Facts. By Thomas Bellamy. *Hibernian,* 1798 (February–March).

b. Retribution. By T. Bellamy. *Harvest Home,* I (1807), 97–109.

1057. The REVENGE. [By Augustus von Kotzebue.] *Universal,* n.s. VII (May, 1807). 1 part (6000).

A translation of "Die Rache" (*Kleine Romane, Erzählungen, Anecdoten und Miscellen,* Vol. II, 1807). In the *Universal* the story was offered as a "sample" of the newly translated "*Novellettes*" (i.e., *Novelettes,* 3 vols., London, 1807). For another extract from the same English collection, see No. 1007.

a. The Revenge. *Hibernian,* 1807 (July–August). 2 parts.

Offered under the general title of "Substance of Kotzebue's *Novellettes,* Lately Published."

b. The Revenge. From Kotzebue's *Novellettes. Weekly Entertainer,* XLVII (August 24–September 7, 1807). 3 parts.

1058. The REVENGE, A MORAL TALE, by the Celebrated Diderot, Member of the French Academy. *Belle Assemblée,* n.s. I (February, 1810). 1 part (7900).

A translation of "Exemple singulier de la vengeance d'une femme, conte moral, ouvrage posthume de Diderot" (1793), deriving ultimately from a German version of Diderot's *Jacques le Fataliste* (written 1773, but not published until 1796).

a. The Revenge, etc. [Same title as above.] *Monthly Panorama,* I (May–June, 1810). 2 parts. Uncompleted.

Reprints only the first half of the story.

1059. A REVERIE AT THE BOAR'S-HEAD-TAVERN IN EASTCHEAP. [By Oliver Goldsmith.] *British*(2), I (February–April, 1760). 3 parts (5500).

Reprinted in the *Essays* of 1765. There are numerous differences between the two texts.

1060. The REVIEW, or Three Days' Pleasure. *Children's*, I (January, 1799)–III (February, 1800). 14 parts (27,000).

1061. The REVIEWER, a Literary Tale. Translated from the French of Madame de Genlis. *Entertaining*(1), No. 8 (August, 1802). 1 part (8250).

A translation of "Le Journaliste" (*Nouvelle bibliothèque des romans,* année 4, tom. 3 [1801]).

1062. The RIGID FATHER, or Paternal Authority Too Strictly Enforced. A Novel, in a Series of Letters. Translated from the German of Augustus La Fontaine, *Lady's,* XXXIII (January–December, 1802). 12 parts (38,500).

A translation of "Die väterliche Gewalt" (see *Kleine Romane und moralische Erzählungen, von August Lafontaine,* VI, 3rd edition, 1804).

1063. RINALDO, or the Enchantment, a Tale. [By Johann Carl August Musaeus.] *Edinburgh*(2), XIII (February, 1791). 1 part (5700).

A prefatory note (p. 149) explains that the story is "Abridged from [William Beckford's] *Popular Tales of the Germans,* just published [1791]." The story is a condensation of Beckford's "Books of the Chronicles of the Three Sisters" (*Popular Tales,* I, 74–161). Beckford's source is Musaeus, "Die Bücher der Chronika der Drey Schwestern" (*Volksmährchen der Deutschen,* 1782–1787). For other extracts from *Popular Tales,* see Nos. 163 and 522.

1064. The RING, a Moral Tale, by the Authoress of the "Occasional Essays." *Weekly Entertainer,* XLVII (January 26–October 18, 1807). 36 parts (74,500).

1065. The RIVAL PRINCES, a Novel, Translated from the French, by J. W. O——y. *Lady's,* XXIII (February–Supplement, 1792); XXIV (April–May, 1793). 8 parts (9100). Uncompleted.

The editor of the *Lady's* had difficulties securing continuations of this story, which was resumed by another correspondent ("C.M.") in April, 1793, but abandoned a month later.

1066. The ROBBER-CALIPH, or Adventures of Haroun Al-Raschid with the Princess of Persia and the Fair Zutulbe. *Monthly Extracts,* IV (October, 1792). 1 part (20,000).

Offered as part of a notice of the Heron translation of Chavis and Cazotte, *Suite des Mille et une nuits* (1788–1789), called *Arabian Tales... Translated from the French into English, by Robert Heron* (I, 2–69). For other extracts from the same work, see ARABIAN TALES (Index).

a. Il Bondocani. *Britannic,* IX, Nos. 126–130 (1802). 5 parts.

A slightly abridged version of the same translation, but unacknowledged. Offered as part of the series "Memoirs of Love and Gallantry."

1067. The ROBBERS OF THE FOREST, or the Unfortunate Princess. "Tale 69," *Tell-Tale,* V (1805). 1 part (11,900).

1068. ROBERT M'KENZIE, or the Adventures of a Scotsman. Written by Himself, and Edited by R. Ferrie, Glasgow. *Lady's,* XXXIV (January, June, July, 1803); XXXV (January, May, 1804). 5 parts (13,250). Uncompleted.

The editor of the *Lady's* appealed for further copy in January, March, and August, 1804, with only meager success.

1069. RODOLPH, a Fragment. *Cabinet Mag.,* I (March–May, 1797). 3 parts (6300).

1070. ROLLO AND OTTO, or the Fatal Effects of Ambition, a Tragic Story. *New Universal*(2), II (February–March, 1788). 2 parts (5100).

a. Rollo and Otto, etc. [Same title as above.] *New London,* VII (July–September, 1791). 2 parts.

1071. ROMAN LETTERS. Aristides at Rome, to Thalia, at Athens. *Monthly Mirror,* XVI (October, 1803)–XVII (March, 1804); XVIII (September, 1804). 5 parts (5300). Uncompleted.

a. Roman Letters, etc. [Same title as above.] *Hibernian,* 1803 (December); 1804 (March, April, July, November). 5 parts. Uncompleted.

1072. The ROMANCE OF THE FOUR DERVISHES, a Persian Tale. [Translated by George Swinton.] *British*(3), I (January, 1800)–II (September, 1800). 9 parts (23,000). Uncompleted.

Introductory note (I, 14): "This work was translated from a celebrated Persian work, intituled the *Chehar Derweish,* or Four Dervishes, by George Swinton, Esq., who communicated it for insertion in the 'Oriental Collection'; but as the number of that work now in the press is too far advanced to admit of this tale with the original Persian, Major Ouseley, with consent of the ingenious translator, has transferred it for publication in the *British Magazine.*" The work referred to is Sir William Ouseley's *Oriental Collections,* 3 vols. (1797–1799).

1073. The ROMANCE OF THE PYRENEES. By a Lady. *Lady's,* XXXV (February, 1804)–XXXVII (Supplement, 1806). 38 parts (237,000).

A reprinting of Catherine Cuthbertson, *The Romance of the Pyrenees* (1803), also published by Robinsons. A note at the beginning of the serial explains that almost the whole impression of this novel was destroyed by fire, and readers were therefore offered this "new edition of the work, which is no longer to be procured but in the *Lady's Magazine.*" (XXXV, 87.)

a. The Romance of the Pyrenees. By a Lady. *Hibernian,* 1804 (May)–1808 (December). 52 parts.

1074. ROMEO AND JULIET, a Novel, on Which Shakespeare Founded His Play of That Title. *Lady's,* XXIX (January–June, 1798). 4 parts (9000).

A translation of Luigi da Porto, *Hystoria di due nobili Amanti* (ca. 1525).

a. Romeo and Juliet, a Novel by Luigi da Porto, from Which It Is Plain Shakespeare Took the Subject of His Celebrated Tragedy of the Same Name. *Theatrical Inquisitor,* VI (April–June, 1815). 3 parts. Signed "J.M."

1075. ROSA.... A Moral Tale. *Belfast Monthly,* II (February–May, 1809). 3 parts (12,500). Signed "Maria."

Addressed "To the Editor of the *Belfast Magazine.*"

1076. ROSALIA DE PONT LEON, a Spanish Tale. *Repertory of Arts, etc.,* XII (November–December, 1814). 2 parts (6400).

1077. ROSETTA, a Tale, by M. [Barthelmy] Imbert. *Lady's,* XXII (November–December, 1791). 2 parts (5200).

A translation of "Rosette" (see *Contes moraux, par Imbert,* Vol. II, 1806).

1078. ROSETTA AND CHAMONT, a True Story. *Gentleman's,* XXV (September–October, 1755). 3 parts (7300).

Introduced by a letter (unsigned), addressed to "Mr. Urban."

a. Rosetta and Chamont, a True Story. *Magazine of Magazines,* X (September–October, 1755). 2 parts.

b. Rosetta and Chamont, a True Story. *Newcastle General,* IX (September–October, 1755). 2 parts.

c. Rosetta and Chamont, a True Story. *Gentleman's and London,* 1755 (September, November). 2 parts.

d. Rosetta and Chamont, a True Story. *Weekly Misc.*(Sherborne), VI (July 8–15, 1776). 2 parts.

e. Rosetta and Chamont, a True Story. *Scots Town and Country,* I (September 29–November 10, 1778). 4 parts.

f. Chamont and Rosetta, a True Story. *Lady's,* XII (August–October, 1781); XIII (July, 1782). 4 parts.

Introduced by a letter adapted from that of the *Gentleman's,* but addressed "To the Editor of the *Lady's Magazine,*" and signed "A constant Reader, / And an Old Correspondent, / *Dean-Street, Holborn*" (p. 402). The editor obviously viewed this plagiarism as an original (see his remarks to the "author of the *Letters of Chamont*" in Vol. XII, p. [394]). The long delay between Parts 3 and 4 resulted from the editor's mislaying the MS.

g. Chamont and Rosetta, a True Story. *Hibernian,* 1781 (September–November). 3 parts (5000). Uncompleted.

Reprints only Parts 1–3 of the story as serialized in the *Lady's.*

1079. ROSEVILLE COTTAGE, a Fragment. *Lady's Monthly Museum,* VII (July, 1801)–IX (October, 1802). 9 parts (5700).

1080. The ROUND TOWER. "Tale 8," *Tell-Tale,* I (1803). 1 part (8800).

1081. The RUBY, a Tale from the Italian. *Bon Ton,* I (March–April, 1791). 2 parts (5000).

1082. The RUINS OF ST. OSWALD, a Romance. *Lady's Monthly Museum,* IV (January–June, 1800). 6 parts (23,500).

1083. The RUINS OF THE ABBEY OF FITZ-MARTIN. *New Gleaner,* II (1810), 211–226. 1 part (9100).

Attributed to "Curtis" [i.e., T. J. Horsley Curties(?), author of several celebrated Gothic romances 1801–1806].

1084. SABINA, or Morning Scenes in the Dressing-Room of a Roman Lady. *Belle Assemblée,* I (November, 1806)–III (July, 1807). 7 parts (18,200). Uncompleted.

An unacknowledged translation of C. A. Boettiger, *Sabina, oder Morgenscenen im Putzzimmer einer reichen Römerin* (Leipzig, 1803). Boettinger's original has eight scenes; the *Belle Assemblée* translates only the first six.

1085. The SAD DISASTER, a Tale. By William Shaw. *New Lady's,* V (June–August, 1790). 3 parts (8750).

1086. SADAK AND KALASRADE, an Eastern Tale. *Universal Museum,* n.s. III (April–July, 1767). 4 parts (18,000).

An unacknowledged abridgment of "Tale IX" of *Tales of the Genii* (1764) by the Rev. James Ridley (see No. 1232).

1087. SAILOR'S LOVE-LETTERS. *Westminster,* I (December, 1772–May, 1773). 5 parts (9800).

"For the *Westminster Magazine.*"

1088. SAINCLAIR. Translated from the French of Madame de Genlis. *Belfast Monthly,* III (December, 1809)–IV (April, 1810). 4 parts (13,300).

A translation of "Sainclair, ou la Victime des sciences et des arts" (*Le Comte de Corke,* 1805). "For the *Belfast Monthly Magazine.*" For a reprinting of the same story in the original French, see No. 1089.

1089. SAINCLAIR, ou la Victime des sciences et des arts. Nouvelle, par Mad. de Genlis. *Ambigu,* XXI, No. 181 (April 10, 1808). 1 part (13,250).

Reprinted from *Le Comte de Corke surnommé le Grand, ou la Séduction sans artifice, suivi de six nouvelles, par Mme. de Genlis* (1805). For an English translation of the same story, see No. 1088.

1090. ST. ANTHONY'S GIFT TO CHILDREN, Exemplified in England. *Historical, Biographical, etc.,* I (July–August, 1799). 2 parts (6600).

Part 1 is dated "Moulsey, July 21, 1799."

1091. ST. AUBIN, or Woman Vindicated. A Narrative, from the French. *Lady's Monthly Museum,* n.s. XI (September–October, 1811). 2 parts (7300).

1092. ST. LEGER, a Tale. *Lady's Monthly Museum,* V (September–December, 1800). 3 parts (6200).

1093. SAPPHO, an Historic Romance. *Lady's,* XLII (January, 1811)–XLIII (August, 1812). 19 parts (30,250).

1094. The SCEPTIC. *Biographical and Imperial,* II (November, 1789)–IV (December, 1790). 14 parts (26,500).

The editor appealed in April and May, 1790, for the name and address of the author.

1095. The SCHOOL FOR FATHERS. A Moral Tale. [By Marmontel.] *St. James's*(1), II (July, 1763). 1 part (7400). Signed "D." [i.e., Charles Denis].

The Denis translation of "L'École des pères" (*Contes moraux,* 1761), later collected in their *Moral Tales,* (1764) [see No. 917]. For a competing contemporary translation, see No. 1096.

1096. The SCHOOL FOR FATHERS. A Moral Tale. [By Marmontel.] *Weekly Amusement,* I (May 19–June 30, 1764). 7 parts (6400).

A translation of "L'École des pères" (*Contes moraux,* 1761), extracted from the *Moral Tales* (Becket and De Hondt, 1764) [see No. 917]. For a different contemporary translation, see No. 1095.

1097. The SCHOOL FOR PARENTS, a Tale. By A. K. [*i.e.,* A. Kendall], Author of *Derwent Priory* and of *The Castle on the Rock. Monthly Visitor,* V (October–December, 1798); VII (May–August, 1799). 7 parts (12,600).

Part 3 has appended: "Should this little tale be favourably received by the numerous readers of the *Monthly Visitor,* the writer will, at some future period, again present *George Ormsby* to their future acquaintance." (V, 383.) This part is dated "Isleworth, Dec. 17, 1798." In May, 1799, the story was continued as "School for Parents, Resumed, by A. K./Isleworth."

The story was later republished in a separate volume.

1098. [The Scots Tutor.] [By James Hogg.] *Spy,* Nos. 38, 42, 43 (May 18–July 13, 1811). 3 parts (11,000).

The title is from the table of contents of the collected edition.

1099. The SCOTSMAN'S TALE. From the Fourth Volume of Miss Lee's *Canterbury Tales. Universal,* CIX (September, 1801). 1 part (5750).

Extracted from *Canterbury Tales, Volume IV, by Harriet Lee* (1801). The extract begins with "a short sketch of the preceding part." For another extract, from Vol. III, see No. 300.

a. The Scotsman's Tale, etc. [Same title as above.] *Weekly Entertainer.* XXXVIII (October 12–26, 1801). 3 parts.

A slight abridgment of the above.

1100. [The SCOTTISH MUSES.] [By James Hogg.] *Spy,* Nos. 2, 5, 10 (September 8–November 13, 1810). 3 parts (10,000). Uncompleted.

The title is from Parts 2 and 3. In the table of contents the story is called "Mr. Shuffleton's Allegorical Survey of the Scottish Poets of the Present Day."

1101. SECOND DREAM OF MR. TORPEDO. Being an Imaginary Visit to Terra Conscientiae, or the Lawyer's Purgatory. *Devil,* I, No. 8 (November 18, 1786)–II, No. 2 (January 6, 1787). 8 parts (8500).

Part 8 is signed "ZACKARY TORPEDO." For an earlier dream by the same subject, see No. 328. A third dream of "Mr. Torpedo" in the *Devil* was left uncompleted by the extinction of the magazine.

1102. SECOND LOVE, a Tale. *Lady's Monthly Museum,* n.s. XIII (December, 1812)–XV (August, 1813). 6 parts (6700). Signed "DE COURAYER."

The introductory letter addressed to the editor of the *Museum* presents this story as a translation "from the Spanish."

1103. SECOND-SIGHT. Isle of Sky, North-Britain. *Belle Assemblée,* VI (March–June, 1809). 4 parts (11,600).

1104. The SECRET HISTORY OF VOLATILE, in an Extract of a Letter from a Lady. *Masquerade,* Nos. 5–6 (February–March, 1752). 2 parts (6100).

In the form of a letter signed "D."

1105. The SECRET NUPTIALS, or Beauty in Distress. "Tale 21," *Tell-Tale,* II (1804). 1 part (13,000).

1106. The SECRET OATH, or Blood-Stained Dagger, a Romance. *Marvellous,* I (November 1, 1802). 1 part (28,000).

1107. The SECRET TRIBUNAL, or the Court of Winceslaus, a Mysterious Tale. *Marvellous,* III (May 1, 1803). 1 part (30,000).

1108. The SEDUCER PUNISHED. *Weekly Mirror,* Nos. 16, 18, 20, 21 (January 5–February 9, 1781). 4 parts (7900).

1109. SEDUCTION, a Tale Founded on Fact. *Lady's Monthly Museum,* IX (August–September, 1802). 2 parts (5300).

a. Seduction, a Tale Founded on Fact. *Monthly Pantheon,* II (March–May, 1809). 2 parts.

1110. SEDUCTION, with an Explanation of the Causes Which Gave Rise to It. Founded upon Facts. *Female Preceptor,* III (January–February, 1814). 2 parts (5000).

1111. SELF-CONTROL, a Novel in 2 Volumes (1811). *Glasgow,* I (March–April, 1811). 2 parts (6700).

An epitome of Mary Brunton's novel of the same name, published in 1811.

1112. SELF DENIAL, a Tale. *Lady's Monthly Museum,* 3.s. II (September–November, 1815). 3 parts (6000). Signed "E.T."

1113. The SELF-DISAPPOINTER, Novela Pequeño, or a Novellette. Translated from the Spanish. *Westminster,* II (January, 1774). 1 part (5000).

"For the *Westminster Magazine.*" A note appended to this story says: "From this story Molière formed the fable of *L'Étourdi*; and Dryden borrowed part of the heterogeneous plot of his *Feigned Innocence,* or *Sir Martin Mar-all,* from the French play" (II, 24). The original has not been identified. [See Addenda, p. 647.]

a. The Self-Disappointer, etc. [Same title as above.] *Hibernian,* 1774 (February). 1 part.

1114. The SENTIMENTAL COQUETTE, a Fragment, from the French. *Sentimental,* I (November, 1773)–II (January, 1774). 4 parts (5000).

1115. A SENTIMENTAL JOURNEY, by a Lady. *Lady's,* I (August, 1770)–VIII (April, 1777). 80 parts (270,000). Uncompleted.

Part 44 (Supplement, 1773) is followed by a letter to a reader from the "Author of the *Sentimental Journey*" defending her work, and explaining that her intention is "not to imitate *Sterne,* but to embellish a description of Great Britain with *sentimental reflections,*" adding that "the descriptions will be found to be as accurate as any that have been published." (IV, 676). The work was finally abandoned at the request of many readers (see XIII,]506]).

This story in Robinson and Roberts's *Lady's Magazine* was continued in Wheble's magazine when the periodical geminated in 1771–1772 (see the Note under *Lady's* in the "Register of Periodicals"). There are, therefore, in Wheble's *Lady's* entirely different Parts 10–11 of "A Sentimental Journey" (I, 441–448, 497–504), and probably a further continuation in later copies of his periodical, which were not available for examination.

1116. A SENTIMENTAL JOURNEY, in a Letter to a Friend. *Monthly Visitor,* n.s. I (August–October, 1802). 3 parts (5000). Signed "J.C./July 28, 1802."

1117. A SENTIMENTAL JOURNEY THROUGH FRANCE AND ITALY, by Mr. Yorick. In Two Volumes. By the Rev. Mr. Sterne. *Novelist's,* IX (1782). 1 part (42,000).

First published in 1768. The reprinting in the *Novelist's* includes two engravings, dated June 29 and July 6, 1782.

1118. A SENTIMENTAL JOURNEY THROUGH LIFE. *Sentimental,* I (March–November, 1773). 9 parts (26,500).

A note following Part 9 explains that the work will not be continued, the author and his MS. having both been consumed by fire while he was reading in bed (I, 390).

1119. The SENTIMENTAL RAMBLER, or Sketches of Rural Scenery on a Vernal Day. *Hibernian,* 1792 (July–August). 2 parts (7600).

1120. SENTIMENTAL VAGARIES, by a Rattler. *Fashionable,* I (June–December, 1786). 7 parts (7500).

1121. The SEPARATION OF TITUS AND BERENICE. *Lady's,* V (November, 1774). 1 part (5250). Signed "E——."

1122. The SEQUEL OF THE PERUVIAN PRINCESS, Containing the Letters of Aza. [By Lamarche-Courmont.] *Novelist's,* IX (1782). 1 part (18,000).

A translation by Francis Ashmore of the *Lettres d'Aza ou d'un Péruvien* (1749), printed in the *Novelist's* in conjunction with the "Letters of a Peruvian Princess" by Mme. de Grafigny (No. 764). For an earlier magazine translation of the same work, see No. 766.

a. Letters of Aza. *Smith's Weekly,* I, No. 4 (?February 23, 1793–?). 1 part. *Inc.*

Only a single copy of this magazine is accessible. It contains Letters VIII and IX of the Ashmore translation.

1123. SERAPH, or Vanity Reproved, a Tale for the Ladies. *Belfast Monthly,* VI (April–May, 1811). 2 parts (9900). Signed "D.D."

"For the *Belfast Monthly Magazine.*"

1124. SERAPHINA, a Novel, from the French of M. [Louis Sébastien] Mercier. *Lady's,* XXV (August–September, 1794). 2 parts (5100).

A translation of "Vivonne et Ruyter" (*Fictions morales, par M. Mercier,* Vol. I, 1792).

1125. The SERENADE, or Green Griffin. By a Gentleman Abroad. *Sentinel,* I (November–December, 1804). 2 parts (8800). Uncompleted.

1126. A SERIES OF LETTERS. *Lady's,* X (August, 1779)–XII (March, 1781). 18 parts (9300).

There are 18 letters in the series (misnumbered 19). No author's name is given, but the editor addressed his acknowledgment to "Lavinia" in June, 1779 (p. [282]).

1127. A SERIES OF LETTERS. *Lady's,* XIV (November, 1783)–XV (August, 1784). 10 parts (10,250). Uncompleted.

The prefatory letter is signed "New Correspondent."

1128. A SERIES OF LETTERS. [From Frances Scudamore to Lady Saville.] *Lady's,* IX (April, 1778)–XI (February, 1780). 12 parts (17,400).

There were interruptions in this series between August and November, 1778; March and August, 1779; and October, 1779, and February, 1780. In addition, one letter was lost in the mails, and had to be "recomposed" (X, [58], [116]). There are 11 letters (misnumbered 10). The second part of the title was added in Part 6.

1129. A SERIES OF LETTERS FROM MISS TREVORS TO MISS ROBERTS. *Lady's,* XIII (April, 1782)–XIV (May, 1783). 14 parts (11,500).

In the introductory letter the author calls herself "Angelina."

1130. A SERIES OF ORIGINAL LETTERS. *Lady's,* VII (January–September, 1776). 9 parts (8800). Uncompleted.

The introductory letter to the editor is signed "MATILDA," who offers to "send a letter every month till [the story] is finished" (VII, 43).

1131. The SERVANT. *Belfast Monthly,* V (September–October, 1810). 2 parts (10,500). Signed "S.E."

"For the *Belfast Monthly Magazine.*"

1132. The SEVEN RINGS OF JARCHUS, an Indian Fable. By Joseph Moser, Esq. *European,* XLVII (March, 1805). 1 part (5000).

1133. SEVERN VALE, or the History of Matilda Maden. *Lady's Monthly Museum,* VIII (January–June, 1802). 6 parts (12,000).

1134. SEYMOUR ABBEY, in a Series of Letters. *Lady's,* XVI (December, 1785)–XVIII (January, November, 1787). 12 parts (27,000).

In November, 1787, the magazine printed "Letter IV," unfortunately "Omitted in the Magazine for December, 1785," and also a final letter in the series.

1135. SHABRACO, a Romance. *Lady's Monthly Museum,* I (August–November, 1798). 4 parts (12,500).

This story gave rise to a controversy in the *Museum* (see pp. 264, 350–351, above).

1136. SHAH ABBAS THE GREAT, or the Banian and Ismenia. A Persian Tale, by Joseph Moser, Esq. *European,* LVII (January–February, 1810). 2 parts (5600).

1137. The SHEPHERDESS, a Tale, Written in the Autumn of 1777. Being the First Attempt in This Kind of Writing, by Wm. Sh—w, a Youth of Eleven Years and a Half. *New Lady's,* IV (March–April, 1789). 2 parts (5200). Signed "WM. SH—W."

By William Shaw, author of several other stories in the *New Lady's.*

1138. The SHEPHERDESS OF THE ALPS, a Moral Tale. [By Marmontel.] *Weekly Amusement,* I (January 21–February 18, 1764). 5 parts (8100).

A translation of "La Bergère des Alpes" (*Contes moraux,* 1761); extracted, without acknowledgment, from the *Moral Tales* (Becket and De Hondt, 1764) [see No. 917].

a. The Shepherdess of the Alps, a Moral Tale. *Caledonian Weekly,* I (? June 30, 1773–?). 1 part. *Inc.*

Part 3 of the above, only, appears in this broken run of the *Caledonian.*

b. The Shepherdess of the Alps, a Moral Tale, *Weekly Misc.*(Sherborne), VIII (June 16–July 14, 1777). 4 parts.

c. The Shepherdess of the Alps, a Moral Tale. *Moral and Entertaining,* I (July–August, 1777). 2 parts.

d. The Shepherdess of the Alps, a Moral Tale. *New London,* VI (December, 1790)–VII (April, 1791). 5 parts.

e. The Shepherdess of the Alps, a Moral Tale. *New Lady's,* VIII (October, 1793); IX (February–August, 1794). 7 parts.

f. The Shepherdess of the Alps, a Moral Tale. *Gentleman's and London,* 1793 (December); 1794 (April–July). 4 parts. Uncompleted.

g. The Shepherdess of the Alps. By Marmontel. *New Gleaner,* II (1810), 56–66.

h. The Shepherdess of the Alps. *Entertaining*(2), III (October–December, 1815). 3 parts.

1139. The SHIELD AND SPECTACLES, an Allegorical Romance, by E. F. *Lady's Monthly Museum,* n.s. V (August–December, 1808). 4 parts (7900).

a. The Shield and Spectacles, an Allegorical Romance. *Monthly Pantheon,* I (October, 1808)–II (February, 1809). 4 parts.

1140. The SHIPWRECK AND ADVENTURES OF M. PIERRE VIAUD. *Ipswich,* I (November, 1799–February, 1800). 4 parts (24,000). Uncompleted.

A translation of J. G. Dubois-Fontanelle, *Naufrage et aventures de Monsieur P.V.* (1770), taken without acknowledgment from Mrs. Elizabeth Griffith, *Shipwreck and Adventures of P.V.... Translated from the French by Mrs. Griffith* (1771). For other extracts from the Griffith translation, see Nos. 1141–1143. The version in the *Ipswich,* which reprints the first three-fifths of the English translation, was terminated by the extinction of the magazine.

1141. [The SHIPWRECK AND ADVENTURES OF MONS. PIERRE VIAUD, Translated from the French.] *Literary Register,* III, Nos. 30–32 (1771). 3 parts (7450).

An abridgment of Mrs. Griffith's translations of Dubois-Fontanelle (see No. 1140 above). For two other abridgments of the same, see Nos. 1142–1143. The version in the *Literary Register* is a narrative in the third person. The title is from the introductory note.

1142. The SHIPWRECK AND ADVENTURES OF PIERRE VIAUD, Translated from the French [of Dubois-Fontanelle] by Mrs. [Elizabeth] Griffiths, Who Has Favoured the World with *The School for Rakes,* and Many Other Approved Performances. *London,* XL (April–May, 1771). 2 parts (9000).

A different abridgment of Mrs. Griffith's *Shipwreck and Adventures of P.V....* from Nos. 1140, 1141, and 1143.

1143. SHIPWRECK OF MONSIEUR PIERRE VIAUD. *Harvest Home,* I (1807), 110–132. 1 part (13,400).

An abridgment of Mrs. Griffith's version of J. G. Dubois-Fontanelle. See Nos. 1140–1142.

1144. The SHRUBBERY, a Tale. *European,* II (September, December, 1782); III (April, 1783). 3 parts (6200).

Part 1 is signed "P.R."; Part 2, "N—— G—— / S★★★★★ R★★★★★"; Part 3, "S.R." The correct signature, however, was declared to be "S.R." (III, 242). Written "For the *European Magazine.*"

The story was later collected in *The Moralist, or Portraits of the Human Mind, Exhibited in a Series of Novelettes, Partly Original and Partly Compiled, by the Late T. Potter, Surgeon* (Vol. II, 1785, pp. 117–162).

a. The Shrubbery, a Tale. *General,* III (February–May, 1789). 4 parts.

Attributed to Potter's *Moralist.*

b. The Shrubbery, a Tale. *Universal Mag. and Rev.,* I (March–June, 1789). 4 parts.

Identified as from *The Moralist.*

c. Melmoth, a Tale. *Weekly Misc.* (Glasgow), n.s. I (August 22–September 5, 1792). 3 parts (4750).

An abridgment of the above.

d. The Shrubbery, a Tale. *Strabane,* I (October, December, 1799). 2 parts.

e. Melmoth and Julia. *Britannic,* VII, Nos. 100–101 (1800). 2 parts.

The abridged version of the *Weekly Miscellany.* Included in the series "Memoirs of Love and Gallantry."

f. The Shrubbery, by Mr. Potter. *Gleaner,* I (1805), pp. 114–124. 1 part.

1145. SICILIAN LOVE. *Belle Assemblée,* IV (January–February, 1808). 2 parts (7600).

1146. SIGNE AND HABOR, or Love Stronger than Death. A Gothic Romance, from the Danish of M. Suhm. *Lady's,* XXXIV (January–December, 1803). 10 parts (22,000).

A translation of Peter Frederik Suhm, *Signe og Habor eller Kierlighed stærkere end Døden* (1777), although possibly taken from the German version, *Signe und Habor, oder Liebe stärken als der Tod* (Leipzig, 1778).

a. Signe and Habor, etc. [Same title as above.] *Hibernian,* 1803 (April)–1804 (January, 1804). 10 parts.

1147. SIMOUSTAPHA AND ILSETILSONE. *Britannic,* X, Nos. 137–140 (1803). 4 parts (17,750).

An unacknowledged abridgment of the "Adventures of Simoustapha and the Princess Ilsetilsone" in Volume II of the Heron translation of Chavis and Cazotte, *Suite des Mille et une nuits* (1788–1789), called in English *Arabian Tales* (1792). For other extracts from the same translation, see ARABIAN TALES (Index). Included in the series "Memoirs of Love and Gallantry."

1148. A SIMPLE STORY. *Universal,* LXXXVIII (May–June, 1791). 2 parts (8500). Signed "L."

A résumé of Mrs. Inchbald's *A Simple Story* (1791), offered as a "review."

a. A Simple Story, in Two Volumes 12 mo. By Mrs. Inchbald. *Universal Mag. and Rev.* V (June, 1791)–VI (July, 1791). 2 parts.

A reprinting of the above, but used as a notice for the "Dublin printed" edition.

b. A Simple Story. *Weekly Entertainer,* XVIII (August 15–September 5, 1791). 4 parts. Signed "L."

1149. A SIMPLE TALE OF LOVE, Interspersed with Quotations and Original Verses. *Weekly Entertainer,* XLVI (March 17–May 19, 1806). 8 parts (10,250).

"For the *Weekly Entertainer.*"

1150. The SINCERE HURON, a True History. Translated from the French of M. de Voltaire, by Francis Ashmore, Esq. *Novelist's,* XXI (1786). 1 part (24,500).

A new translation of *L'Ingénu, histoire véritable* (1767), later called *Le Huron.* The first English translation, the *Pupil of Nature,* was published in 1771. The *Novelist's* translation is embellished with an engraving, dated April 29, 1786.

1151. SINGULAR VICISSITUDES IN THE LIFE OF NOOR-JEHAN, Queen of the Emperor Iehangire. A True Story. *Edinburgh*(2), VI (November-December, 1787). 2 parts (7900).

1152. SIR EDWARD SEYMOUR, an English Tale. *Belle Assemblée,* III (September–October, 1807). 2 parts (9400). Signed "E.R."

1153. [SIR GAWEN.] [By Nathan Drake.] *Speculator,* Nos. 10–12 (April 27–May 4, 1790). 3 parts (5000). Signed "N."

No title appears in the original.

a. Sir Gawen, a Tale. *Edinburgh*(2), XII (September, 1790). 1 part.

b. An Interesting Story. *Bon Ton,* I (July–September, 1791). 3 parts.

c. Sir Gawen, a Tale. *Weekly Misc.* (Glasgow), VI, Nos. 148, 151, 152 (April 18–May 16, 1792). 3 parts.

d. Singular Adventures of a Knight. From the *Speculator. Town and Country,* XXIV (May, July, 1792). 2 parts.

e. Singular Adventures of a Knight. *Wonderful,* V, Nos. 51–52 (1794). 1 part.

f. Singular Adventures of a Knight. *Dundee,* II (July–September, 1800). 3 parts.

g. The Story of Sir Gawen. From the *Speculator. Gleaner,* II (1806), Nos. 33–40.

1154. The SISTERS, an Affecting History, with a Perspective View of Reculver Church, in the County of Kent. [By George Keate.] *Universal,* LXXXIX (August, 1791). 1 part (5000).

An introductory paragraph explains that this story was taken from Keate's *Sketches from Nature* (1779; 4th ed., 1790), where it was "extracted... from a Manuscript, which he had the opportunity of perusing in the university of Louvain." (LXXXIX, 97). In the original it bears the title, "The Story of the Two Sisters." The "West View of Reculver Church, Kent," faces p. 97 in the *Universal.*

a. The Sisters, an Affecting History. *Hibernian,* 1791 (September–October). 2 parts.

b. The Sisters, an Affecting History. *Aberdeen*(1), IV (October, 1791). 1 part.

c. The Story of the Two Sisters. *Weekly Entertainer,* XLIII (April 23–30, 1804). 2 parts.

d. The Sisters, an Affecting History. *Gleaner,* I (1805), 310–317.

Attributed in the table of contents to "Keate's *Sketches.*"

1155. The SISTERS, or the History of Lucy and Caroline Sanson, Entrusted to a False Friend. In Two Volumes. By the Rev. Dr. [William] Dodd. *Novelist's,* V (1781). 1 part (120,000).

Probably written by Dodd, but also attributed to William Guthrie (see *DNB,* XV, 155). First published in 1754. The reprinting in the *Novelist's* includes four engravings, dated July 7–28, 1781.

1156. The SISTERS OF ROSE DALE, or Modern Adoption, a Novel. *Lady's Monthly Museum,* n.s. IV (January–June, 1808). 5 parts (9500). Signed "E.F."

1157. A SKETCH OF CHARACTERS Exhibited on a Journey in a Stage Coach. *Matrimonial,* I (April–May, 1775). 2 parts (6250).

1158. SKETCH OF THE GUBBINGS FAMILY. *Entertaining*(2), III (February–September, 1815). 5 parts (11,400). Uncompleted.

1159. SKETCHES FROM NATURE. A Novel in a Series of Letters, by Sophia Troughton. *Lady's,* XXXVIII (July, 1807)–XL (September, 1809). 23 parts (76,000).

1160. The SOLDIER'S DAUGHTER, or the Fair Fugitive, a Pathetick Tale. *Marvellous,* IV (April 2, 1804). 1 part (12,500).

1161. The SOLDIER'S FAREWEL on the Eve of a Battle. By the Translator of "Le Nourrisson." *New Lady's,* III (November–December, 1788). 2 parts (5100).

Signed "Wm. S—w./Westminster."

By William Shaw, the author of several other pieces in the *New Lady's*, including "Le Nourisson" (No. 956). In Part 2 the title was corrected to read "Farewell."

a. The Soldier's Farewell, etc. [Same title as above.] *Hibernian*, 1788 (December–Appendix). 2 parts. Signed "Wm. S—w."

1162. SOLIMAN II. Translated from Marmontel, by a Lady, and Addressed to the Rev. Mr. Madan, and Author of *Thelypthora*. *Lady's*, XII (September, October, Supplement, 1781). 3 parts (5800). Signed "R———."

A translation of "Soliman II," from the *Contes moraux* (1761). For other translations of the same story see Nos. 642, 917, and 1163.

a. Soliman II. Translated from Marmontel, etc. [Same title as above.] *Hibernian*, 1781 (October, November); 1782 (January). 3 parts.

1163. SOLIMAN THE SECOND. A Moral Tale. [By Marmontel.] *St. James's*(1), III (September, 1763). 1 part (6200).

The first English translation of "Soliman II" (*Contes moraux*, 1761), made by Charles Denis (or Robert Lloyd). This version was collected in the *Moral Tales of M. Marmontel, Translated from the French by C. Denis and R. Lloyd* (1764) [see No. 917]. For other translations of the same story, see Nos. 642 and 1162.

a. Soliman the Second. A Moral Tale. *Edinburgh Museum*, I (September, 1763). 1 part.

b. Soliman the Second. A Moral Tale. *Beauties of All the Magazines*, II (October, 1763). 1 part.

"From the *St. James's Magazine*."

c. Solyman the Second. A Moral Tale. *Dublin*(1), II (October, 1763). 1 part.

1164. SOLOMON IN SEARCH OF HAPPINESS. *Universal*, n.s. XIII (April, May, 1810); n.s. XIV (December, 1810). 3 parts (5000). Uncompleted.

1165. SOLYMAN AND ALMENA, an Oriental Tale. By Dr. [John] Langhorne *Novelist's*, II (1780). 1 part (22,500).

First published in 1762. The title-page in the *Novelist's* is dated 1781, but the work preceded Nos. 1306 and 1367, both dated 1780. The engraving that accompanies this reprinting bears the date May 13, 1780.

1166. SOPHIA, or the Advantages of Adversity. *Lady's*, III (Supplement, 1772). 1 part (5000).

"A Letter from a Lady to Her Friend," signed "R."

1167. SOPHIA STEINHEIM, a True Story, Extracted from the Annals or History of the Middle Ages, and Translated from the German Language, by a Young Lady. *Monthly Literary Recreations*, II (May, 1807)–III (November, 1807). 7 parts (31,500).

1168. The SORCERER'S PALACE, or the Princess of Sinadone. By Sarah Wilkinson. "Tale 78," *Tell-Tale,* VI (1805). 1 part (12,000).

1169. The SORROWS OF WERTER, a German Story [by J. W. von Goethe]. Translated from the French Edition of Monsieur Aubry [i.e., Count F. W. K. von Schmettau], by John Gifford, Esq. [i.e., J. R. Green]. *Novelist's,* XXII (1789). 1 part (38,000).

An English rendering of *Les Passions du jeune Werther, Ouvrage traduit de l'allemand de M. Goethe, par M. Aubry* (Paris, 1777). Goethe's original first appeared in 1774; Green's translation of Aubry in 1779. The plates in the *Novelist's* are dated December 1, 1788, and January 1, 1789; the title-page of the novel reads 1789.

1170. The SOUTHERN TOWER, or Conjugal Sacrifice and Retribution. *Marvellous,* II (November 1, 1802). 1 part (30,000).

A disguised redaction of Mrs. Radcliffe, *A Sicilian Romance* (1790).

1171. Extract from *The SPANIARD, OR THE PRIDE OF BIRTH.* A Tale, by M. Rymer. *Lady's,* XXXVIII (June, 1807). 1 part (5300).

From the novel published by Robinson's in 1807. This extract was preceded by an earlier one taken from "the beginning of this ingenious novel" in March, 1807 (4600 words).

a. Extract from *The Spaniard,* etc. [Same title as above.] *Dublin Museum,* I (August, 1807). 1 part.

1172. The SPANISH HERMIT, from *Vanillo Gonzales,* a Novel Just Published, by Le Sage. *Lady's,* XXVIII (Supplement, 1797)–XXXIX (February, 1798). 3 parts (8900).

A translation of the "Histoire du solitaire," Chapter 26 of Le Sage's *Histoire d'Estevanille Gonzalez* (1734); extracted from *The History of Vanillo Gonzales, Surnamed the Merry Bachelor* (1797).

1173. A SPANISH TALE: Bad Example Produces as Many Virtues as Vices. [By Madame de Grafigny.] *Universal,* n.s. XIII (March–June, 1810). 4 parts (12,800).

An introductory letter, signed "W." and dated from London, March 14, 1810, identifies the story as Madame de Grafigny's "Nouvelle espagnole: le mauvais exemple produit autant de vertus que de vices." The original was published in 1745.

a. A Spanish Tale. By Madame de Grafigny, Authoress of the *Letters of a Peruvian Princess.* Bad Example Produces as Many Virtues as Vices. *Weekly Entertainer,* L (July 30–September 10, 1810). 7 parts.

1174. The SPIRIT OF THE RING. Containing Secret Anecdotes of Many Illustrious Personages of This and the Neighbouring Kingdoms. Communicated by Our Old and Valuable Correspondent, C.B.I.A. *Bon Ton,* V (September, 1795–February, 1796). 5 parts (9250).

1175. The SPIRITUAL QUIXOTE, or the Summer's Ramble of Mr. Geoffry Wildgoose. A Comic Romance. *Literary Reg.*, V, Nos. 21–23 (1773). 1 part (5500).

A summary of Richard Graves's novel of the same name (1773), with a long extract.

1176. The SPORTS OF A WEEK. *Irvine Misc.*, I (November, 1814–January, 1815). 3 parts (5100). Signed "SENEX, Irvine."

1177. STORIES OF SEVEN DAYS. *Belle Assemblée*, n.s. IV (August, 1811)–n.s. V (February, 1812). 7 parts (21,500).

The series contains seven "Tales" in a framework of narrative.

a. Stories of Seven Days. *Hibernian*, 1811 (November–December). 2 parts (6000). Uncompleted.

Reprints only through Part 2 of the above.

1178. A STORY FROM THE FRENCH OF VOLTAIRE. *Gentleman's*, XXXV (April, 1765). 1 part (6000).

A translation of "Le Blanc et le noir" (*Contes de Guillaume Vadé*, 1764). For another translation of the same tale, see "The Black and the White" (No. 158).

1179. The STORY OF A NUN. *Sentimental*, III (October–November, 1775). 2 parts (5200).

a. Story of a Nun. *Dumfries Weekly*, XI (December 5, 1775)–XII (December 12, 1775). 2 parts.

1180. [STORY OF ALEXIS AND MATILDA.] [By Eliza Haywood.] *Gentleman's*, XXIV (December, 1754). 1 part (5750).

An extract, greatly condensed, of a story in Mrs. Haywood's *Invisible Spy* (1755; actually 1754). The narrative is included in a review entitled "Some Account of *The Invisible Spy*, Lately Published, in Four Volumes." The title of the story is taken from the index to Volume XXIV of the *Gentleman's*. For a full reprinting of the novel in the *Novelist's Magazine*, see "The Invisible Spy" (No. 711).

a. Some Account of *The Invisible Spy*, Lately Published in Four Volumes. *Gentleman's and London*, 1754 (December). 1 part.

1181. STORY OF AN ECCENTRIC CHARACTER. From Brydge's *Censura Literaria*, Vol. VIII. *Cabinet*, n.s. I (May, 1809)–n.s. II (August, 1809). 4 parts (6400). Uncompleted.

From Samuel Egerton Brydges's "Ruminator," Nos. 37–40, in *Censura Literaria*, Vol. VIII (1808). The series in the *Cabinet* omits "Ruminator," No. 41.

a. Story of an Eccentric character. From Brydge's *Censura Literaria. Monthly Pantheon*, III (September–October, 1809). 2 parts (4900). Uncompleted.

The series in the *Pantheon* includes only "Ruminator," Nos. 37–39.

1182. [STORY OF CLARINDA HARLOWE.] [By Walley Chamberlain Oulton.] *Busy Body,* II, Nos. 16–18 (February 5–10, 1787). 3 parts (7200).

The title is from the table of contents of the collected edition.

1183. [The STORY OF COLONEL CAUSTIC.] [By Henry Mackenzie.] *Lounger,* Nos. 4 (February 26), 6, 14, 31–33 (September 17, 1785). 6 parts (11,750).

There are further extensive references to Colonel Caustic in Nos. 40 (November 5, 1785) and 95 (November 25, 1786). The story bears no title.

1184. The STORY OF DAUBIGNY. *Weekly Entertainer,* LI (May 6–May 20, 1811). 3 parts (5400).

1185. [STORY OF EUGENIO AND HIS AMELIA.] [By William Roberts.] *Looker-On,* Nos. 42–49 (February 16–April 6, 1793). 8 parts (24,500).

The story was further extended by incidents and correspondence in six other numbers of the *Looker-On,* Nos. 8, 12, 18, 27, 64, 67, and 79. The title is from the table of contents of the collected edition.

1186. The STORY OF EUMENIA. *Town and Country,* VI (March–August, 1774). 5 parts (7700). Signed "JUVENIS./W——n, 1774."

Written "For the *Town and Country Magazine.*" An introductory letter declares that this story "has never appeared in print." (VI, 147.) At the end of Part 2 the proprietors of the *Town and Country* request that the author "transmit... the remainder of his story as soon as possible." (VI, 245).

a. The Story of Eumenia. *Bristol,* 1787 (?). 6 parts (5600). Uncompleted.

Reprints only through the first page of Part 5 of the above.

1187. STORY OF HALECHALBE AND THE UNKNOWN LADY. From the *Arabian Tales, or a Continuation of the Arabian Nights Entertainments. Lady's,* XXVI (June–September, 1795). 4 parts (12,700).

Extracted from the Heron translation of Chavis and Cazotte, *Suite des Mille et une nuits* (1788–1789), called *Arabian Tales... Translated from the French into English,* by Robert Heron (I, 176ff.). For other extracts from the same collection, see ARABIAN TALES (Index).

a. Halechalbe and the Unknown Lady. *Britannic,* X, Nos. 133–135 (1802). 3 parts (11,200).

A slight abridgment of the above. Included in the series "Memoirs of Love and Gallantry."

1188. The STORY OF HARRIOT AND SOPHIA. [By Charlotte Lennox.] *Lady's Museum,* I, No. 1–11 (1760–1761). 11 parts (52,500).

This novel was later reprinted in two volumes as *Sophia* (1762).

1189. STORY OF ILLAGE MAHOMET AND HIS SONS, or the Imprudent Man. [From *Arabian Tales, or a Continuation of the Arabian Nights Entertainments...*

Newly Translated from the Original Arabic into French by Dom Chavis... and M. Cazotte... and Translated from the French into English, by Robert Heron.] *General*, VI (1792), 299–310.

An extract from the Heron translation (1792) of the *Suite des Mille et une nuits* (1788–1789); included in the "Impartial Review of British Literature" of the *General Magazine*. For other extracts from the same collection, see ARABIAN TALES (Index).

1190. [STORY OF LA ROCHE.] [By Henry Mackenzie.] *Mirror*, Nos. 42–44 (June 19–26, 1779). 3 parts (5000).

The title is from Parts 2 and 3. The table of contents of the collected edition reads: "Importance of Religion to Minds of Sensibility; Story of La Roche."

a. [La Roche and a Philosopher.] *Scots*, XLI (June, 1779). 1 part.

Attributed to the *Mirror*. The title is from the page headings.

b. Affecting Story of La Roche. *Universal*, LXVIII (March–April, 1781). 2 parts.

Attributed to the "Author of *The Man of Feeling*."

c. Affecting Story of La Roche. *Hibernian*, 1781 (April–May). 2 parts.

d. Affecting Story of La Roche. *Weekly Misc.*(Sherborne), XVI (May 21–28, 1781). 2 parts.

e. The Story of La Roche. *Ulster Rep.*, I, Nos. 13–16 (1785). 4 parts.

f. Story of La Roche. *New Novelist's*, I (1786), 198–204. 1 part.

g. Importance of Religion to Minds of Sensibility. Story of La Roche. *Weekly Misc.* (Glasgow), I, Nos. 20–22 (November 4–18, 1789). 3 parts.

Attributed to the *Mirror*.

h. La Roche. *Gleaner*, I (1805), 289–296.

Attributed to Mackenzie.

1191. [Story of Lady Fanny.] *Court, City and Country*(1), I (May–June, 1762). 2 parts (5200).

The seventh of a series called "Secret History of the Court."

a. [Story of Lady Fanny.] *Edinburgh Museum*, II (March–April, 1764). 2 parts.

No. 6 of the series "Secret History of the Court."

1192. The STORY OF LANDGARTHA, Queen of Norway. *European*, LXVII (March–April, 1815). 2 parts (5600).

1193. [STORY OF LEONORA.] *Court, City and Country*(1), I (November–December, 1761). 2 parts (6100).

No. 3 of the series "Secret History of the Court."

a. [Story of Leonora.] *Edinburgh Museum*, I (December, 1763). 1 part.

No. 5 of the series "Secret History of the Court."

1194. The STORY OF LEONORA. *Literary Reg.*, I, Nos. 32–33 (1769). 2 parts (8300).

The introductory letter, signed "A.C./Newcastle," states that the story is "taken from a book published in the year 1709" (I, 187), but the original has not been identified.

1195. The STORY OF MADAME LA MARQUISE DE ——, as Narrated by Herself to Miss Clifford. (From *Mordaunt,* by the Author of *Zeluco* and *Edward.*) *Universal,* CVI (February–June, 1800). 5 parts (22,000).

From Vol. II, pp. 1–144, of Dr. John Moore's novel, published in 1800.

a. The Story of Madame la Marquise de ——, etc. [Same title as *Universal.*] *Scots,* LXII (March–September, 1800). 5 parts.

1196. [The STORY OF MARIA SCHONING.] [By S. T. Coleridge.] *Friend,* No. 13 (November 16, 1809). 1 part (5100).

The story bears no title of any kind.

1197. The STORY OF MELINDA, by a Lady. *Universal Museum,* I (November–December, 1762). 2 parts (5250).

1198. [The STORY OF MOREDIUS.] [By George Brewer.] *European,* XLII (July–August, 1802). 2 parts (5200). Signed "G.S."

The story is No. 18 in the series "Essays after the Manner of Goldsmith." It bears no other title.

1199. The STORY OF OLD EDWARDS, from *The Man of Feeling* [by Henry Mackenzie]. *Salmon's Mercury,* I, Nos. 2, 4–9 (1778). 6 parts (6600).

Chapters 34–39 of Mackenzie's novel (1771).

a. Old Edwards. Mackenzie. *Harvest Home,* I (1807), 261–269. 1 part (5200).

A shorter version of the above.

b. Old Edwards. *New Magazine of Choice Pieces,* I (1810), 397–409.

The shorter version. Attributed to *The Man of Feeling.*

1200. The STORY OF ROSHANA. *Edinburgh Weekly,* III (February 23–March 16, 1769). 4 parts (6000).

Attributed to *Tales Translated from the Persian of Inatulla of Delhi* [by Alexander Dow] (1768).

a. The Story of Roshana, from Inatulia [in Part 2 corrected to read "Inatulla"]. (*Persian Tales.*) *Universal Museum,* n.s. V (February–March, 1769). 2 parts.

b. Story of Roshana. Translated from the Persian. *Weekly Misc.*(Glasgow), II, Nos. 21–36 (January 20–February 24, 1790). 5 parts.

1201. [STORY OF SABINA.] [By Eliza Haywood.] *Female Spectator,* Book XXI (1745), pp. 137–160. 1 part (5700).

The title is from the index of Volume IV ("Sabina, her character and story").

a. The Folly of Prejudice When Indulged to a Great Excess; or the History of Luellin and Sabina. *Weekly Entertainer,* VIII (August 28–September 4, 1786). 2 parts (5100).

1202. The STORY OF SARAH PHILLIPS, a Novel, by M. de Saint Lambert. *Lady's,* XXIII (September–October, 1792). 2 parts (7600).

A translation of Saint-Lambert's "Sarah Th....," taken, without acknowledgment, from *Tales, Romances, Apologues, Anecdotes, and Novels* (1786), where it appeared under the same English title.

a. Sarah Phillips. From the French of M. Lambert. *Gleaner,* I (1805), 151–163.

1203. [The STORY OF SERAPHINA.] *Literary Leisure,* Nos. 38, 44, 45 (June 12–July 31, 1800). 3 parts (8400).

The title is from the table of contents of the collected edition.

a. Trials of Constancy, or the Singular Story of Seraphina. *Entertaining*(1), I (August, 1802). 1 part.

1204. [STORY OF SOPHIA B——.] *Court, City and Country*(1), I (August, 1762)–II (April, 1763). 8 parts (17,500). Uncompleted.

No. 9 of the series "Secret History of the Court."

1205. The STORY OF THE COUNT DE ST. JULIEN. [By George Keate.] *Westminster,* VII (July–August, 1779). 2 parts (5000).

This story was described as written "For the *Westminster Magazine,*" but it appeared also in Vol. I of Keate's *Sketches from Nature,* reviewed in the August issue of the *Monthly Review* (1779).

a. The Story of the Count Saint Julien. *Weekly Entertainer,* XLII (August 1–15, 1803). 3 parts.

b. The Story of the Count de St. Julien. *Gleaner,* II (1806), 42–50. 1 part.

c. Count Saint Julien. *New Magazine of Choice Pieces,* II (1810), 167–178.

Attributed to Keate.

1206. STORY OF THE COUNTESS OF CHATEAU BRIAND. *London,* n.s. III (October–November, 1784). 2 parts (5250).

"For the *London Magazine.*"

1207. STORY OF THE EXPLOITS AND DEATH OF CAPTAIN RAGGADO AND HIS BRAVOS. From the *Arabian Tales, or a Continuation of the Arabian Nights Entertainments. Lady's,* XXVII (January–June, 1796). 4 parts (11,100).

An extract from the Heron translation of Chavis and Cazotte, *Suite des Mille et une nuits* (1788–1789), called *Arabian Tales... Translated from the French into English, by Robert Heron* (II, 280–317). For another translation of the same story, see No. 1033. A number of other extracts were made from the same collection (see ARABIAN TALES in the Index).

1208. The STORY OF THE LADY OF THE CAVE, in a Letter to Arabella. *Lady's*(2), III (January–February, 1762). 2 parts (5600).

The story is told in three letters addressed to Arabella, and signed "CARICLEA."

1209. STORY OF THE MARCHIONESS DE VALMONT. (From *Memoirs of a Family in Swisserland; Founded on Facts.*) *Universal,* CXI (September–October, 1802). 2 parts (8600).

Extracted from the novel by Anne Ormsby (1802).

1210. The STORY OF THE TAME PIGEON. By the Celebrated Miss Hamilton. *Belle Assemblée,* II (January, 1807). 1 part (5000).

Possibly Miss A. Hamilton, author of several novels between 1806 and 1811; or Miss Emma Hamilton, author of *The Forest of St. Bernardo* (1806), noticed in the *Monthly Review,* n.s. L, 319.

a. The Tame Pigeon, by Miss Hamilton. *Harvest Home,* I (1807), 133–140.

1211. [STORY OF THE YOUNG CRIMINAL.] *Beauties of All the Magazines,* II (December, 1763)–III (January, 1764). 2 parts (6800?). *Inc.*

The title is from Part 2. The copy of Vol. II in the *British Museum* is imperfect.

1212. STORY OF TWO SISTERS. *London,* n.s. III (September, 1784). 1 part (5800).

For an earlier version of the same story, see No. 993.

a. Parental Cruelty, or the History of Two Sisters. *Weekly Entertainer,* V (January 17–31, 1785). 3 parts.

1213. [STORY OF URBAIN GRANDIER.] [By William Roberts.] *Looker-On,* Nos. 69 (August 24), 71 (September 7, 1793). 2 parts (6900).

The title is from the table of contents of the collected edition.

a. Affecting Story of Urbain Grandier. From the *Looker-On,* a Periodical Paper. *Lady's,* XXVI (June–July, 1795). 2 parts.

b. Affecting Story of Urbain Grandier. *Scots,* LVII (August–September, 1795). 2 parts.

"From the *Looker-On.*"

1214. [STORY OF ZULIMA.] *Prater,* Nos. 13 (June 5), 15, 16 (June 26, 1756). 3 parts (5900).

The title is derived from the text of Nos. 13 and 15.

1215. A STORY STRANGE AS TRUE. *Gentleman's,* VII (April, 1737)–VIII (March, 1738). 7 parts (9500).

In Parts 2–7 the story is variously labelled "The Adventures of a Female Correspondent" and "Continuation of the Lady's Adventures." Part 7 is signed "MARIA."

NOTE: The first appearance of this story in the *Gentleman's*, several years before 1740, has been cited because of the story's complicated later history.

a. [A Story Strange as True.] *Wonderful*(1), Nos. 1–4 (September–December, 1764). 4 parts. Uncompleted.

Addressed "To the Authors of the *Wonderful Magazine*" in a letter signed "G.H." This version reprints only Parts 1–6 of the above. The story bears no title.

b. Strange Adventures of a Lady. *Edinburgh Weekly*, XLIX (August 3–31, 1780). 5 parts.

Addressed "To the Publisher, &c."

c. A Story Strange as True. *Berwick Museum*, II (November, 1786)–III (April, 1787). 6 parts. Signed "MARIA."

Addressed "To the Editor of the *Berwick Museum*." Adopts in Parts 2–5 the variant titles of the *Gentleman's*, Parts 2–6.

d. Singular Adventures of a Lady. *Wonderful*(2), I, Nos. 2–6 (1793). 5 parts.

Introduced by a letter to the editor signed "G.H./High-Holborn."

1216. The STORY-TELLER. *Wit's*, I (January–May, 1784). 5 parts (18,400).

Parts 1–4 (signed "E.") are by Thomas Holcroft; Part 5 (signed "H——") is by the editor who replaced him beginning with the May issue of the *Wit's* (see I, 162).

1217. The STRANGER. *Belle Assemblée*, V (November–December, 1808). 2 parts (6100). Signed "F.W."

1218. The STRANGER KNIGHT, an Original Romance. *Theatrical Inquisitor*, I (September–December, 1812); V (July–October, 1814). 8 parts (13,000). Signed "G.S." in black letter.

The seventeen-month's interruption in this story was a source of embarrassment to the editor, but he declined to inform the public of the "circumstances" that dictated it. (IV, 2.)

1219. The STROLLER'S TALE. *Lady's Monthly Museum*, n.s. XI (July, 1811)–n.s. XII (April, 1812). 9 parts (16,350). Signed "C."

1220. SUICIDE, a Novel, in a Series of Letters. By Rosa B——. *New Lady's*, VI (January, 1791)–VII (August, 1792). 13 parts (7700).

The receipt of both this novel and No. 1221 was acknowledged in the supplement of Vol. V (p. [636]).

1221. The SURPRIZE, or the Unexpected Rencontre, a Novel. In a Series of Letters, Written by S. Pure, and Founded on Facts. *New Lady's,* VI (January–December, 1791). 8 parts (9200).

1222. The SYLPH, an Entertaining Story, from the French. *London,* XLIX (November, 1780). 1 part (6400).

a. The Sylph, etc. [Same title as above.] *Hibernian,* 1780 (December–Appendix, 1780). 2 parts.

b. The Sylph, etc. [Same title.] *Weekly Misc.*(Sherborne), XVI (June 11–18, 1781). 2 parts.

1223. The SYLPH, or the History of Sophia Merton. *Weekly Entertainer,* XXXII (November 26, 1798)–XXXIII (April 29, 1799); XXXV (March 10–May 26, 1800). 22 parts (38,000).

Addressed "To the Editor of the *Weekly Entertainer.*"

1224. The SYLPH HUSBAND, a Moral Tale. A New Translation from Marmontel. By Miss Georgiana H——t, a Young Lady between Sixteen and Seventeen. *Lady's,* XI (December, 1780)–XII (February, 1781). 4 parts (9600). Signed "R—."

A translation of "Le Mari sylphe" (*Contes moraux,* Vol. III, 1765). For other translations of the same story, see Nos. 680 and 917.

1225. SYMPATHY. [By Mme. de Genlis.] *Monthly Museum,* II (August–November, 1814). 4 parts (11,000).

An abridged translation of "Les Savinies" (*Le Comte de Corke, surnommé le Grand, ou la Séduction sans artifice, suivi de six nouvelles, par Mme. de Genlis, 1805*). Written "For the *Monthly Museum.*" A note (pp. 172–173) explains that this tale by Mme. de Genlis is little known in English except "through the medium of an indifferent translation" (probably "The Savinias, or the Twins," included in *The Earl of Cork, or Seduction without Artifice,* London, 1808).

1226. The TABLETS, an Eastern Allegory. *Sylph,* Nos. 27 (January 30)–35 (March 26, 1796). 9 parts (13,700).

1227. [A TALE FROM THE FRENCH.] *Yorkshire,* I (May–September, 1786). 5 parts (8750).

Described in a letter "To the Editors of the *Yorkshire Magazine,*" signed "Amicus," as "a Translation of a Pastoral Poem from Gessner, which I believe has never before appeared in English." (I, 138.). The original is Gessner's *Der erste Schiffer* (1762), already known in several French translations. For a later magazine translation of the same poem, see "The First Navigator."

The title is taken from Parts 2–5.

1228. A TALE OF FORMER TIMES. *Belle Assemblée,* II (May, 1807)–III (August, 1807). 4 parts (13,900). Signed "R.E."

1229. The TALE OF GENEURA. From the Italian of Lodovico Ariosto, in the Fifth Book of His *Orlando Furioso. Lady's Museum,* II, No. 10 (1760). 1 part (6250).

Reprinted from Charlotte Lennox, *Shakespear Illustrated,* III (1754), 231–256.

a. The Tale of Geneura, from the Italian of Lodovico Ariosto. *Dublin Library,* I (May 30/June 15–June 15/June 30, 1761). 2 parts.

b. The Tale of Geneura, etc. [Same title as No. 1229a.] *Magazine of Magazines,* XXI (June, 1761). 1 part.

c. The Tale of Geneura, etc. [Same title.] *Repository,* Nos. 3–4 (1763). 2 parts.

d. The Tale of Geneura, on Which the New Tragedy, Entitled *The Law of Lombardy,* Is Founded. From the Italian of Lodovico Ariosto, in the Fifth Book of His *Orlando Furioso. Lady's,* X (February–March, 1779). 2 parts.

e. The Tale of Geneura, etc. [Same title as No. 1229d.] *Gentleman's and London,* 1779 (March–April). 2 parts.

f. The Tale of Geneura, from the Italian of Ariosto. *New Novelist's,* I (1786), 95–102.

1230. A TALE OF MYSTERY, or the Castle of Solitude. Containing the Dreadful Imprisonment of Count L. and the Countess Harmina, His Lady. *Marvellous,* II (January 1, 1803). 1 part (30,000).

1231. [TALE OF ZENAIB AND MUJNOON.] *Medley,* I, Nos. 8–11 (January 29–February 8, 1805). 4 parts (5900).

The story is described as "a tale written by a Bramin in the Persian language, translated by a gentleman in the East Indies." (p. 32.) The title is taken from a reference to the story in No. 12 (p. 89).

1232. The TALES OF THE GENII, or the Delightful Lessons of Horam, the Son of Asmar. Faithfully Translated from the Persian Manuscript, and Compared with the French and Spanish Editions Published at Paris and Madrid. In Two Volumes. By Charles Morell [i.e., the Rev. James Ridley], Formerly Ambassador from the British Settlement in India to the Great Mogul. *Novelist's,* III (1780). 1 part (180,000).

First published in 1764. The reprinting in the *Novelist's* includes five engravings, dated August 19–September 16, 1780. For an earlier extract from the same collection, see No. 1086.

1233. The TALES OF THE TWELVE SOOBAHS OF INDOSTAN. *European,* XLVIII (July, 1805)–L (September, 1806). 13 parts (37,500).

1234. TANT MIEUX POUR ELLE! or the Marriage of Tricolore. Translated from the French [of the Abbé de Voisenon] by T. D———n [i.e., T. Dutton]. *Bon Ton,* V (March–June, 1795). 4 parts (8000). Uncompleted.

A translation of the first eight of the seventeen chapters of Voisenon's *Tant mieux pour elle, conte plaisant* (1760).

1235. TARQUIN THE PROUD, an Historical Romance. *Belle Assemblée,* n.s. VIII (August–October, 1813). 3 parts (9300).

1236. The TARTARIAN PRINCE. "Tale 28," *Tell-Tale,* II (1804). 1 part (13,500).

An unacknowledged translation of Mme. de Gomez, "Le Prince tartare" (*Les Cent nouvelles de Mme. de Gomez,* 1732–1739, Vol. IV).

1237. TARTARIAN TALES, or a Thousand and One Quarters of Hours. Written in French by M. Gueulette. Translated by Thomas Flloyd. *Novelist's,* XIX (1785). 1 part (107,000).

From the translation of *Les Mille et un quarts d'heure, contes tartares* (1712), first published in 1759. The reprinting in the *Novelist's* included four engravings, dated September 10–October 1, 1785.

1238. The TEMPLE OF FAITH. *Protestant Dissenter's,* IV (March, 1797)–V (December, 1798). 12 parts (25,000). Signed "B."

Addressed "To the Editor of the *Protestant Dissenter's Magazine.*"

1239. The TEMPLE OF GNIDUS. By Baron Montesquieu. Translated from the French. *Court, City and Country*(1), II (July–August, 1763). 2 parts (8750).

A translation of *Le Temple de Gnide* (1725).

1240. The TEMPLE OF SENSIBILITY. *Lady's Monthly Museum,* VI (March, 1801). 1 part (5100). Signed "Delius./Stockton, 1800."

1241. The TEMPLE OF VIRTUE, a Dream. *Weekly Amusement,* IV (October 24, 1767). 1 part (5000).

a. The Temple of Virtue, a Vision. *Weekly Misc.*(Sherborne), VI (May 6, 1776). 1 part.

1242. The TENDER MOTHER. *Lady's,* XX (April–June, 1789). 3 parts (6300). Uncompleted.

Nos. 25–27 of the series "The Children's Friend."

1243. The TEST OF HYMEN, a Novel. *Royal*(3), I (January–August, 1788). 9 parts (9000). Uncompleted.

Beginning with Part 5, the label reads "A New Novel."

1244. The TEST OF SINCERITY, an Italian Story. *Selector*(2), Nos. 17–19 (December 18, 1783–January 1, 1784). 3 parts (5000).

1245. THEODORE D'ABLANCOURT, an Original Tale. *Beau Monde*(1), (July–September, 1808). 3 parts (8500). Uncompleted.

a. Theodore D'Ablancourt, an Original Tale. *Monthly Pantheon,* I (September–November, 1808). 3 parts. Uncompleted.

1246. THERE WAS NO HELP FOR IT. A Moral Tale. [By Marmontel.] *General,* VI (1792). 1 part (7100).

A translation of "Il le fallait" (*Mercure,* 1792), taken from *New Moral Tales,* Vol. III (1792), and published in the *General's* "Impartial Review of British Literature," pp. 334–349, as a part of its notice of the *Tales.*

1247. The THOUSAND AND ONE DAYS: PERSIAN TALES. Translated from the French by Mr. Ambrose Philips. In Three Volumes. *Novelist's,* XIII (1783). 1 part (225,000).

A translation of Pétis de la Croix, *Les Mille et un jour, contes persanes* (1710–1712). The Philips translation was first published in 1714–1715. The reprinting in the *Novelist's* was embellished with six engravings, dated November 7–December 13, 1783. For a short magazine extract from the Philips translations, see No. 1318.

1248. TIMUR, an Eastern Tale. *Lady's,* XXIII (October–November, 1792). 2 parts (5000).

1249. TOM CAXON, or Fortune's Buffoon. Related by Himself. *Cyclopaedian,* I (April–August, 1807). 4 parts (7000).

Nos. 2–5 of the series "Narrative Sketches of Men and Manners: Taken, *ad vivium,* in Various Walks of Life."

1250. The TOMB OF AURORA, or the Mysterious Summons. *Weekly Selector,* I, Nos. 3–7, (February 18–March 17, 1812). 5 parts (7200).

1251. TORBOLTON ABBEY, a Gothic Tale. By Mr. S. Wilkinson. *New Gleaner,* II (1810), 30–41. 1 part (6600).

Probably an error for Sarah Wilkinson, the author of many similar magazine pieces.

1252. A Short Account of the TRAGICAL END OF TWO NOBLE FAMILIES of the Tenth Century. An Anglo-Saxon History, Now First Done into English from the Latin of Hugo, Abbot of Brunsbury in the County of Northumberland, Anno Domini circa 1230. With a Commentary by S. D. Y. *European,* XX (October–December, 1791). 3 parts (13,500).

"For the *European Magazine.*"

a. A short Account of the Tragical End of Two Noble Families, etc. [Same title as above, but omitting "by S. D. Y."] *Universal Mag. and Rev.,* VI (December, 1791)–VII (February, 1792). 3 parts.

1253. The TRANSFORMATION OF LOVE, a Real History. *Lady's,* XV (October, 1784)–XVI (February, 1785). 6 parts (7900).

1254. The TRANSGRESSOR THROUGH LOSS OF HONOUR. A Translation from the German of Schiller. *Literary and Masonic,* I (August–September, 1802). 2 parts (7500).

A translation of Schiller's "Der Verbrecher aus verlorener Ehre" (*Thalia,* Vol. II, 1786). For other translations of the same story, see Nos. 266–267.

"For the *Literary and Masonic Magazine.*"

1255. The TRANSMIGRATIONS OF HERMES, a Philosophical Romance. From the French of Madame [Fauques] de Vaucluse. By an English Lady. *Lady's,* V (January–August, 1774). 8 parts (25,500). Uncompleted. Signed "I."

The authority for this attribution is uncertain. The work is unlisted in the catalogues of either the British Museum or the Bibliothèque Nationale. The story was announced in the annual address to the public, in the 1774 volume (p. ii), and thereafter figured frequently in the columns of the editor, who had great difficulty obtaining copy. In February (p. [58]) the magazine's correspondent, who was called *Arbanco,* was described as "transcribing" an original which was in the possession of several "ladies." This text, it is apparent, the editor was having translated, as parcels were received (p. [338]). By August, however, the editor appeared to be in communication with the author herself, for he wrote:

> We are in doubt whether we should thank or blame Madame de Vaucluse, for giving us so much honour, or for plunging us into such an abyss of mortification... the *French* of the Transmigrations of Hermes goes no lower than we have translated [i.e., the "Third Day"]; yet it is in our view to prevent their disappointment... (p. [394]). –

Thus he seemed to hint at a possible continuation. In November and December the author herself was again addressed, and entreated to supply the "sequel," but the story was still left hanging. The parallels between this case and that of Clara Reeve four years later are striking (pp. 312ff., above). Probably Mme. Fauques de Vaucluse, having provided the magazine with an eight-months supply of her story *gratis,* expected something more than a pittance (or mere thanks) for the rest.

1256. The TRANSMIGRATIONS OF INDUR, a Tale. *Edinburgh*(2), n.s. II (October, 1793). 1 part (5500).

1257. The TRAVELLER, an Original Communication. *Aberdeen*(2), I (July–October, 1796). 1 part (6000). Signed "Will. Restless./Abdn. 1796."

Addressed "To the Editors of the *Aberdeen Magazine.*"

1258. The TRAVELLERS, an Allegory. *Youth's,* X (May–July, 1815). 3 parts (5300). Signed "A.B."

1259. TRAVELS INTO SEVERAL REMOTE NATIONS OF THE WORLD. By Lemuel Gulliver, First a Surgeon, and Then a Captain of Several Ships. In Two Volumes. By Dean Swift. *Novelist's,* IX (1782). 1 part (102,000).

First published in 1726. The reprinting in the *Novelist's* included four engravings, dated July 13–August 3, 1782.

a. The Wonderful Travels and Adventures of Mr. Lemuel Gulliver, Written by Himself. *Wonderful*(2), I, No. 3–V, No. 50 (1793–1794). 45 parts.

A full-length reprinting of *Gulliver's Travels,* but without chapter or book divisions. In Volume II of the magazine the editor added to the title: "But, in Reality Written by the Celebrated Dean Swift."

1260. The TRAVELS OF HERACLITUS AND DEMOCRITUS, Translated from the French, by a Lady. *Lady's,* IV (December–Supplement, 1773). 2 parts (7000). Signed "R/Dec. 14th, 1773."

1261. The TRAVELS OF HIMILCO, an Oriental Tale. By the Author of *Chrysal. Universal,* LV (July–August, 1774). 2 parts (8750).

Adapted from Charles Johnstone, *The History of Arsaces, Prince of Betlis* (1774), Books II–III.

1262. The TRAVELS OF REASON. Translated from the French of Voltaire, with a Continuation to the Present Time. [By Leigh Hunt] *Reflector,* I (October, 1810–March, 1811). 1 part (5300).

"Chapter I" is a translation of Voltaire's "Voyage de la raison, discours prononcé dans une académie de province" (*Oeuvres complètes de Voltaire,* Vol. LVIII, 1785). Chapter II is a "Continuation to the Present Time," written by Leigh Hunt, according to the "office copy" preserved in the British Museum.

1263. TRAVELS OF TROPHIMUS. *Youth's,* V (January–December, 1810). 12 parts (15,250).

1264. TRAVELS THROUGH EUROPE. From the French of Voltaire's *Princess of Babylon. Court Misc.,* IV (April–May, 1768). 2 parts (8000).

A translation of Chapters 6–10 of *La Princesse de Babilone* (1768). With a few minor changes the translation is that of *The Princess of Babylon* (London: S. Bladon, 1768), although no acknowledgment is made of the plagiarism.

1265. The TREACHEROUS HUSBAND. *Lady's,* X (August–December, 1779); XI (April–May, 1780); XII (April, 1781); XIII (May, 1782). 8 parts (12,000). Signed "J.L———G./West Lavington, Wilts."

The editor had great difficulty securing continuations of this piece, which was interrupted as a result of "*bad health,* and a multitude of *unexpected incidents.*" (XIII, 257.) The signature also reads "J.L——G., Market-Lavington."

1266. The TRIAL, a Tale, by Augustus Lafontaine. *Universal,* CX (June, 1802). 1 part (7800).

A translation of "Er liebte sie mehr wie sein Leben" (*Die Gewalt der Liebe, in Erzählungen,* Vol. I, 1797). For a later translation of the same tale, see No. 1269.

a. The Trial, a Tale, by Augustus Lafontaine. *Edinburgh*(2), n.s. XX (July–August, 1802). 2 parts.

b. The Trial, a Tale, Written by Augustus Lafontain. *Weekly Entertainer,* XL (August 30–September 20, 1802). 4 parts.

c. The Trial. *Britannic,* XII, Nos. 173–174 (1806). 2 parts.

Part of the series "Memoirs of Love and Gallantry."

1267. The TRIAL OF FRIENDSHIP. A Story Now First Translated from the Third Volume of *Contes moraux,* just published by Marmontel. *Gentleman's,* XXXV (June–July, 1765). 2 parts (11,750).

The earliest translation of "L'Amitié à l'épreuve" (*Contes moraux,* Vol. III, 1765). This story was attacked on the score of improbability in a letter to Mr. Urban in the following August number of the *Gentleman's* (pp. 358–359). For other translations of the same story see Nos. 462–463, and 917.

a. The Trial of Friendship, etc. [Same title as above.] *Scots,* XXVII (June–July, 1765). 2 parts.

Attributed (p. 380) to "*Gent. Mag.*"

b. The Trial of Friendship, a Moral Tale. *Weekly Amusement,* II (November 9–December 21, 1765). 7 parts.

c. The Trial of Friendship, a Moral Tale. *New Universal*(2), I (July–December, 1787). 6 parts.

1268. The TRIAL OF HONOUR, or the Lover's Progress. *New Lady's,* III (November–December, 1788). 2 parts (5750).

a. The Trial of Honour, or Lover's Progress, a Tale. *Hibernian,* 1788 (December). 1 part. Uncompleted.

Reprints Part 1 of the above only.

1269. The TRIAL OF LOVE. From the German of Augustus La Fontaine. *Lady's,* XLII (October, 1811)–XLIII (March, 1812). 5 parts (7150).

A translation of "Er liebte sie mehr wie sein Leben" (*Die Gewalt der Liebe, in Erzählungen,* Vol. I, 1797). For an earlier translation of the same tale, see No. 1266.

1270. TRIALS OCCASIONED BY AN IMPROPER EDUCATION, or the History of Charlotte Clayton. *Lady's Monthly Museum,* XV (October, 1805). 1 part (6000).

1271. TRIALS OF THE HEART. *Lady's Monthly Museum,* n.s. I (October, 1806)–n.s. II (January, 1807). 3 parts (5400).

Nos. 3–4 of the series "Village Tattle."

1272. A TRIP TO MARGATE, by Ansegise Clement, Gentleman. *London,* L (October, 1781)–LI (November, 1782). 12 parts (57,500).

Addressed "To the Editor of the *London Magazine.*"

1273. TRISTRAM AND YSEULT, an Historical Romance. *New Lady's,* IV (June–August, 1789). 3 parts (12,000).

1274. The TRIUMPH OF CONSTANCY. *Westminster,* VII (January–February, 1779). 2 parts (5100).

Possibly by Mrs. Elizabeth Griffith (see the attribution in No. 1274d). Written "For the *Westminster Magazine.*"

a. The Triumph of Constancy. *Hibernian*, 1779 (February–March). 2 parts.

b. The Triumph of Constancy. *Town and Country Weekly*, I, Nos. 26–28 (October 8–22, 1785). 3 parts.

c. William and Anna. *Britannic*, VIII, No. 114 (1801). 1 part.

A slightly abridged version of the above. Part of the series "Memoirs of Love and Gallantry."

d. The Triumph of Constancy. By Mrs. Griffiths. *Harvest Home*, I (1807), 22–28.

1275. The TRIUMPH OF CONSTANCY, A NARRATIVE FOUNDED UPON FACT. *Universal*, LIII (October–December, 1773). 3 parts (12,500).

A note explains that this "little Piece of domestic History" was "written by the Heroine herself, in a Letter to one of her sincere Friends." (LIII, 175.)

a. The Triumph of Constancy, an Interesting Story, Written by the Heroine Herself, in a Letter to One of Her Friends. *Weekly Misc.* (Sherborne), XII (May 3–June 7, 1779). 3 parts.

b. The Triumph of Constancy, etc. [Same title as No. 1275a.] *Moral and Entertaining*, IV (May, 1779)–V (June, 1779). 3 parts.

1276. The TRIUMPH OF FORTITUDE AND PATIENCE OVER BARBARITY AND DECEIT, a True History. [By Eliza Haywood.] *Female Spectator*, Book XXII (1745), pp. 191–250. 1 part (13,500).

The story was prefaced by a letter to the Female Spectator signed "ELISMONDA" (see also No. 741), asserting that "there is not one incident inserted which owes any thing to fiction, but the whole is related with all the exactitude and simplicity of truth."

For a disguised redaction of this story, see No. 558.

a. The Triumph of Fortitude, etc. [Same title as above, but adds "Written by a Lady."] *Weekly Entertainer*, V (February 14–March 28, 1785). 7 parts.

b. The Triumph of Fortitude and Patience over Barbarity and Deceit, a True Story. From the *Female Spectator*. *Glasgow Misc.*, II (1800), 25–50, 74–89. 2 parts.

1277. The TRIUMPH OF TRUTH, a Tale. *Monthly Visitor*, IX (January–April, 1800). 4 parts (5700). Signed "CIVIS/Wolverhampton, April 9, 1800."

1278. The TRIUMPH OF VIRTUE OVER ILLICIT LOVE. *Universal*, XLIX (August, 1771). 1 part (6000).

An introductory note explains that the above title has been prefixed to this historical account, in order to give it "the Air of an instructive Novel" (p. 57). This story is the probable source for Arnaud's "Salisbury" (see No. 343).

a. The Triumph of Virtue over Illicit Love. *Hibernian*, 1771 (September). 1 part.

b. The Triumph of Virtue over Illicit Love, or the History of the Countess of Salisbury. *Weekly Misc.* (Sherborne), VII (October 21, 1776). 1 part.

1279. The TRUE POINT OF HONOR, a Moral History, in a Series of Letters. Translated from the French, by a Lady. *Lady's,* VIII (August, 1777)–XI (Supplement, 1780). 37 parts (82,000).

1280. The TRYING SITUATION, a Moral Tale. *Town and Country,* XI (February, 1779). 1 part (5000).

a. The Trying Situation, a Moral Tale. *Cumberland,* II (March, 1779). 1 part.

1281. The TWIN-BROTHERS, or the Man of Beneficence and the Man of Selfishness. A Moral Tale. *St. James's*(2), I (October, 1774). 1 part (5000). Signed "Sophronius."

Part of the series "The English Marmontel, or the School of Sentiment."

a. The Twin-Brothers, etc. [Same title as above.] *Weekly Misc.*(Sherborne), III (December 5, 1774). 1 part.

b. The Twin-Brothers, etc. [Same title]. *Weekly Misc.*(London), No. 118 (1774). 1 part.

1282. The TWO CASTLES, a Romance. By E. F. *Lady's,* XXVIII (June, 1797)–XXIX (November, 1798). 11 parts (16,250).

a. The Two Castles, a Romance. *Hibernian,* 1797 (August)–1799 (January). 11 parts.

1283. The TWO HERMITS. *Belle Assemblée,* n.s. XII (October–December, 1815). 3 parts (9500).

1284. The TWO HEROINES, or the Sacrifices of Love to Virtue. A Moral Tale. *Universal,* LXVII (Supplement, 1780). 1 part (5000). Signed "R."

a. The Two Heroines, etc. [Same title as above.] *Weekly Misc.*(Sherborne), XVIII (July 29–August 5, 1782). 2 parts.

b. The Two Heroines, etc. [Same title.] *Bristol and Bath,* I, Nos. 12–13 (1782). 2 parts. Signed "R."

1285. [The TWO UNFORTUNATE LADIES. A Moral Tale.] [By Marmontel.] *Weekly Amusement,* I (October 6–20, 1764). 3 parts (5700).

A translation of "Les Deux Infortunées" (*Contes moraux,* 1761), extracted from the *Moral Tales* (Becket and De Hondt, 1764) [see No. 917]. The title in the *Weekly Amusement* appeared on Parts 2 and 3 only.

1286. ULRIC AND GUSTAVUS, or the Unhappy Swedes, a Finland Tale. *Marvellous,* III (September 1, 1803). 1 part (30,000).

1287. The UNCLE AND NEPHEW, a Tale. By Mrs. [Elizabeth?] Hamilton. *Theatrical Inquisitor,* I (December, 1812)–II (March, 1813). 4 parts (8700). Uncompleted.

A continuation was "positively" promised in July, 1813, but never forthcoming.

1288. The UNEXPECTED INTERVIEW, by Eleanor Tatlock. *New Lady's,* VIII (March–December, 1793). 4 parts (6200).

1289. The UNEXPECTED INTERVIEW. *Bon Ton,* II (December, 1792)–III (April, 1793). 4 parts (5750).

A quite different story from No. 1288.

1290. The UNFORCED REPENTANCE, a Moral Tale. *Westminster,* I (September, 1773). 1 part (7000).

Addressed "To the Editor of the *Westminster Magazine.*"

a. The Unforced Repentance, a Moral Tale. *Hibernian,* 1773 (October). 1 part.

Addressed "To the Editor of the *Hibernian Magazine.*"

b. The Unforced Repentance, a Real Story. *Town and Country Weekly,* I, Nos. 28–31 (October 22–November 12, 1785). 4 parts.

1291. The UNFORTUNATE CALEDONIAN, or the Voyages and Adventures of Donald Cameron. "Tale 26," *Tell-Tale,* II (1804). 1 part (11,000).

1292. [The UNFORTUNATE FEMALE.] *Lady's Monthly Museum,* VII (July–October, 1801). 4 parts (7600). Signed "T.B."

Addressed "To the Editor of the *Lady's Monthly Museum.*" The title is from Part 2.

1293. The UNFORTUNATE LOVERS, an Historical Anecdote. (From Mrs. [Ann] Thicknesse's *Sketches of the Lives and Writings of the Ladies of France* [1781].) *Universal,* LXIX (November, 1781). 1 part (6400).

Mrs. Thicknesse's translation of Mlle. Catherine Bernard, *Inès de Cordoue, nouvelle espagnole* (1696).

a. [Inès de Cordova, a Spanish Story.] The Following Very Interesting and No Less Entertaining Spanish Tale, Founded on Facts, Is Taken from the *Sketches of the Lives and Writings of the Ladies of France,* by Mrs. Thicknesse, Just Published. *London,* L (November–December, 1781). 2 parts (7000).

A slightly longer extract from the *Sketches.* The title is taken from the Table of Contents.

b. A Spanish Story, etc. [Rest of title as in No. 1293a.] *Edinburgh Weekly,* LIV (December 27, 1781) – LV (January 10, 1782). 3 parts.

Offered as an example of Mlle. Bernard's writings.

c. The Unfortunate Lovers, etc. [Same title as *Universal.*] *Hibernian,* 1781 (December–Appendix). 2 parts.

d. The Unfortunate Lovers, etc. [Same title.] *Westminster,* IX (Supplement, 1781). 1 part.

Attributed to Mlle. Catherine Bernard.

e. The Unfortunate Lovers, etc. [Same title.] *Weekly Misc.* (Sherborne), XVII (February 25–March 4, 1782). 2 parts.

f. The Unfortunate Lovers. *Lady's,* XX (August–Supplement, 1789). 4 parts (2400). Uncompleted.

Reprints only the first part of the story, with a few changes. Discontinued, possibly, because the editor discovered that it was a plagiarism.

g. Ines de Cordova and the Marquis de Lerma. *Britannic,* VII, No. 98 (1800). 1 part.

Part of the series "Memoirs of Love and Gallantry."

h. The Unfortunate Lovers. *Harvest Home,* II (1808), 365–374. 1 part.

1294. The UNFORTUNATE MARRIAGE, a Novel, from the French of Mons. Le Sage. *Lady's,* VI (January–May, 1775). 4 parts (8800). Signed "ELFRIDA."

A translation of "Le Mariage de vengeance, nouvelle" (*Histoire de Gil Blas,* Book III, Chap. IV). For a complete translation of *Gil Blas,* see No. 45.

1295. The UNFORTUNATE MARRIAGE, or the History of Mr. and Mrs. Hartley. (From a Novel, Recently Published, Called *A Winter in Bath.*) *Weekly Entertainer,* XLVIII (January 4–25, 1808). 4 parts (6800).

From the novel by J. H. James (1807).

1296. UNHAPPY CONSEQUENCES OF AN UNPRINCIPLED EDUCATION. A Narrative by a Lady of Her Own Conduct in Life. *Universal,* LII (April, 1773). 1 part (5000).

a. Unhappy Consequences, etc. [Same title as above.] *Weekly Misc.*(London), II, No. 39 (1773). 1 part.

1297. The UNKNOWN, or the Horrors of Montaldo, a Romance. Written Expressly for This Work. *Compiler,* I, No. 1–6 (1807). 6 parts (7250).

1298. The UNKNOWN GUEST. *Lady's,* XLVI (June–Supplement, 1815). 6 parts (11,100).

1399. The UNWILLING IMPOSTOR, a Tale, Translated from the French. *Lady's Monthly Museum,* n.s. IX (August–October, 1810). 3 parts (7500).

1300. USEFUL INSTRUCTIONS TO NOVICES IN TOWN, Exemplified in the Story of a Country Gentleman. *Edinburgh Weekly,* IV (June 1, 1769)–V (July 13, 1769). 3 parts (6000).

Addressed to the editor in a letter signed "A BROKEN GAMESTER."

1301. The VAGABONDS, or Anecdotes of a Foundling. *Bon Ton,* IV (January, 1795)–V (January, 1796). 9 parts (8750).

1302. VALCE LA COUR, or the Father's Return. Translated from the German of Augustus La Fontaine. *Sentinel,* I (July–October, 1804). 4 parts (9000).

A translation of "Die Rückkehr ins Vaterland" (*Neueste moralische Erzählungen,* 1803).

a. Valce La Cour, or the Father's Return. From the German of Augustus La Fontaine. *New London Gleaner,* I, Nos. 7–8 (1809). 1 part.

The accompanying engraving is dated June 1, 1809.

1303. VALERIA, an Italian Tale. [By M. de Florian.] *Edinburgh*(2), XVI (December, 1792). 1 part (7200).

A translation of "Valérie, nouvelle italienne" (1792), taken without acknowledgment from *New Tales, from the French of M. Florian* (1792).

a. [Valeria.] *General,* VI (1792), 279–294. 1 part.

Extracted from *New Tales,* cited above, and printed in the magazine's "Impartial Review."

1304. VAUXHALL, or the History of Caroline. *Lady's Monthly Museum,* XVI (January–February, 1806). 2 parts (5800).

1305. The VEILED PICTURE, or the Mysteries of Gorgono, the Appennine Castle of Signor Androssi. A Romance of the Sixteenth Century. *Marvellous,* II (December 1, 1802). 1 part (30,000).

A disguised redaction of Mrs. Radcliffe's *Mysteries of Udolpho* (1794). For an epitome of the same novel, see No. 932.

1306. The VICAR OF WAKEFIELD, a Tale. In Two Volumes. By Dr. [Oliver] Goldsmith. *Novelist's,* II (1780). 1 part (65,000).

First published in 1766. The reprinting in the *Novelist's* includes two plates, dated May 20–27, 1780. For a short extract from the same novel, see No. 536.

1307. The VICISSITUDES OF FORTUNE, a True Story. An Original. *Hibernian,* 1793 (June)–1793 (November). 6 parts (11,500).

1308. The VICTIM, by Thomas Bellamy. *General,* II (February–March, 1788). 2 parts (5800).

Later collected in Bellamy's *Miscellanies in Prose and Verse* (1794).

a. The Victim, by the Late Thomas Bellamy. *New Gleaner,* I (1809), 14–24.

1309. The VICTIM OF DESPAIR. *Lady's Monthly Museum,* n.s. XVI (March, 1814)–n.s. XVII (September, 1814). 7 parts (14,000).

1310. The VICTIM OF REVENGE, a Novel, in a Series of Letters, by Rosa B. *New Lady's,* IV (September, 1789)–V (July, 1790). 10 parts (10,700).

The same author, in October, 1789, also submitted "Enigmatical Questions and Solutions" (p. [498]).

1311. The VILLAGE APPRENTICE, an History Founded on Fact. *Watchman,* I, Nos. 10–12 (August–October, 1810). 3 parts (5200).

1312. The VILLAGE CURATE, or As You Like It. A Tale, by Mr. Bacon. *Pocket,* II (February–March, 1795). 2 parts (8400).

Possibly by James or Robert Bacon (see No. 232).

a. The Village Curate, etc. [Same title as above.] *Hibernian,* 1795 (March–April). 2 parts.

b. The Village Curate, etc. [Same title.] *Weekly Entertainer,* XLVIII (December 26, 1808)–XLIX (January 16, 1809). 4 parts.

c. The Village Curate. By Mr. Bacon. *New Gleaner,* II (1810), 7–21.

1313. The VILLAGE GOSSIP. *Lady's Monthly Museum,* V (December, 1800)–VIII (June, 1802). 15 parts (19,000). Uncompleted.

Part 1 is dated from "Tabby Hall, Sept. 29, 1800" (p. 443).

1314. The VILLAGE MAID. "Tale 38," *Tell-Tale,* III (1804). 1 part (13,500).

1315. A VILLAGE TALE. *Lady's Monthly Museum,* XVI (January–February, 1806). 2 parts (5000). Signed "SUSAN."

a. Village Tale. *Hibernian,* 1806 (June–July). 2 parts. Signed "SUSAN."

1316. VIRTUE REWARDED, an African Tale. By Henry Shroeder. *New Lady's,* VIII (September)–IX (May, 1794). 4 parts (6800).

1317. VIRTUE THE GENUINE SOURCE OF NOBLE AND GENEROUS ACTIONS, Illustrated in the History of Valvais, the Bosom Friend of the Great Gustavus Adolphus, King of Sweden. From a Work, Just Published, Intitled *Juliet Grenville, or the History of the Human Heart,* by Mr. [Henry] Brooke. *Universal,* LIV (January, 1774). 1 part (5100).

From the novel published in 1774 (Vol. II, pp. 90–128). Of the seven reprintings of this extract in the miscellanies, the *Universal* alone acknowledged the source.

a. The Triumphs of Friendship, a Swedish Anecdote. *Westminster,* II (January, 1774). 1 part.

b. Virtue the Genuine Source of Noble and Generous Actions, Illustrated in a Swedish History. *Weekly Misc.*(Sherborne), I (February 21–28, 1774). 2 parts.

c. Virtue the Genuine Source, etc. [Same title as No. 1317b.] *Weekly Misc.* (London), II, Nos. 77–78 (1774). 2 parts.

d. Adelaide and Valvaise, a Swedish Tale. *Edinburgh Rep.*(1), No. 1 (March 2, 1774). 1 part.

e. The Triumphs of Friendship, a Swedish Anecdote. *Bristol and Bath,* I, Nos. 2–3 (1782). 2 parts.

f. Triumphs of Friendship. *Britannic,* XI, Nos. 158 (1804). 1 part.

Offered as part of the series "Memoirs of Love and Gallantry."

1318. VIRTUE TRIUMPHANT, or the History of Repsima. An Eastern Tale. *Universal,* XII (February–March, 1753). 2 parts (7300).

A translation of the "Histoire de Repsima" in Pétis de la Croix, *Mille et un jour, contes persans* (1710–1712), taken without acknowledgment from Days 998–1002 in *The Thousand and One Days* (1714–1715), translated by Ambrose Philips. For a complete reprinting of Philips's translation, see No. 1247.

a. Virtue Triumphant, etc. [Same title as above.] *Magazine of Magazines,* V (February–March, 1753). 2 parts.

b. Virtue Triumphant, etc. [Same title.] *Weekly Amusement,* IV (August 29–September 12, 1767). 3 parts.

1319. A VIRTUOUS DOMESTIC, Happy in Her Own Feelings, and a Blessing to Her Employers. *Monthly Monitor,* II (August–September, 1815). 2 parts (6800). Signed "Th. N.R."

1320. VIRTUOUS LOVE REWARDED, a Tale. By Miss Wyndham Foot James. *Lady's,* XL (November, 1809)–XLI (March, 1810). 5 parts (13,200).

The last part is signed at "Lidney, Gloucestershire" (p. 111).

1321. The Virtuous Orphan, or the Life of Marianne, Countess of *****. Translated from the French of Marivaux. In Four Volumes. *Novelist's,* XVI (1784). 1 part (230,000).

A translation of *La Vie de Marianne, ou les Aventures de Mme. la comtesse de ***, par M. Marivaux* (1731–1741). This translation also includes the apochryphal twelfth part of the novel, first published in 1745. The *Novelist's* translation is embellished with ten engravings, dated October 2–December 4, 1784.

1322. The VIRTUOUS TSAMMA, a Fairy Tale. Translated from the German of Rabener. *Edinburgh*(2), IX (January, 1789). 1 part (6500).

A translation of G. W. Rabener, "Das Märchen vom ersten April" (see *Satiren,* 5th ed., Vol. IV, 1759).

1323. The VISION OF FEMALE EXCELLENCE. *Aberdeen,* III, No. 64 (June 17, 1790). 1 part (5000). Signed "JUVENIS./Aberdeen, June 4, 1790."

1324. A VOYAGE TO AND FROM PETERSBURGH. *Tradesman,* IX (July, 1812)–X (June, 1813). 10 parts (24,750). Signed "R.H."

Addressed "To the Editor of the *Tradesman, or Commercial Magazine.*"

1325. WALTER POPMARVEL, an Original Novel. By T. Dutton, Esq. *Bon Ton,* V (July–December, 1795). 5 parts (5000). Uncompleted.

1326. The WANDERING SPIRIT, or Memoirs of the House of Morno. Including the History of Don Pinto D'Antos, a Tale of the 14th Century. *Marvellous,* I (August 1, 1802). 1 part (14,400).

1327. The WANDERINGS AND OPINIONS OF ALGERNON, a Seeker of Wisdom. *Universal,* n.s. XV (June, 1811)–n.s. XVII (February, 1812). 8 parts (21,500). Uncompleted.

1328. WAR, A DREAM. *Belle Assemblée,* III (November–December, 1807). 2 parts (5000). Signed "E.R."

1329. WARBECK, an Historical Novel, from the French of Mr. Arnaud. *Sentimental,* V (August–October, 1777). 3 parts (5000). Uncompleted.

A translation of Baculard D'Arnaud, "Varbeck" (*Oeuvres de M. D'Arnaud,* Vol. VI, 1774). In December, 1776 (XIII, 701–702), the *Oxford Magazine* had published a fragment of the same novel in English, but did not pursue a complete translation.

a. Warbeck, etc. [Same title as above.] *Monthly Misc.,* V (August–September, 1777). 2 parts. Uncompleted.

Reprints Parts 1–2 of the above only. The *Miscellany* seems to have expired in September, 1777.

1330. WARRINGTON GRANGE, or the Victim of Treachery. "Tale 53," *Tell-Tale,* IV (1804). 1 part (5100).

1331. The WARY PRINCESS, or the Adventures of Finette, a Novel. *Universal Spectator,* Nos. 786–788 (October 29–November 12, 1743). 3 parts (5000).

Attributed to "a young Lady in France, who signs her name Mademoiselle L'H***** [i.e., Mlle. Marie-Jeanne L'Héritier]." The story is a translation of "Les Aventures de Finette" in *Oeuvres meslées* (Paris, 1696).

1332. The WATERMAN OF BESONS, a Moral Tale. [By Marmontel.] *Universal,* XCII (January–March, 1793). 3 parts (12,500).

A translation of "Les Bateliers de Besons, conte moral" (*Mercure,* 1792), extracted from *New Moral Tales* (1792). Introducing the above selection, the editor of the *Universal* wrote: "The following beautiful Tale, replete with interesting Incidents, and the most pleasing Delineations of virtuous Sentiment, is selected from a Translation, just published, of a Third Volume of *New Moral Tales,* by the inventive Pen of *Marmontel,* whose former Writings are too well known to our Readers, to need any Eulogy here" (p. 8).

a. The Waterman of Besons. By Marmontel. *Sentimental and Masonic,* II (February–April, 1793). 3 parts.

1333. WAVERLEY, or 'Tis Sixty Years Since. [By Walter Scott.] *Monthly Museum,* II (September–December, 1814). 4 parts (11,000).

A long summary of the novel (1814) with extracts, presented in the form of a review. The editor described it as "a sketch of the tale itself, as far as the scanty limits of our Miscellany permit" (p. 225).

1334. The WEDDING INTERRUPTED, a Novel, Translated from the French. *Universal,* XVII (November, 1765). 1 part (5700).

a. The Wedding Interrupted, etc. [Same title as above.] *Weekly Misc.*(Sherborne), XI (February 15, 1779). 1 part.

b. The Wedding Interrupted, etc. [Same title as *Universal.*] *Moral and Entertaining,* IV (March, 1779). 1 part.

c. The Wedding Interrupted. *Hibernian,* 1779 (May–June, 1779). 2 parts. Signed "PATRICK SCRATCH./College-Green, May 22, 1779."

1335. The WEDDING NIGHT. *Belle Assemblée,* n.s. V (June, 1812)–n.s. VI (July, 1812). 2 parts (6000).

1336. The WELCH COTTAGE, or Adventures of Belinda Beaumont. "Tale 58," *Tell-Tale,* V (1805). 1 part (13,400).

1337. The WELCH PARSON. *Town and Country,* XVII (September–December, 1785). 4 parts (5800).

a. The Welch Parson. *Hibernian,* 1785 (November)–1786 (February). 4 parts.

1338. WESTCOMBE AND EUPHEME. *Britannic,* VI, No. 74 (1798). 1 part (6000). Part of the series "Memoirs of Love and Gallantry."

1339. WHAT FEELINGS! or Charles and Maria. *Belle Assemblée,* n.s. X (December, 1814)–n.s. XI (May, 1815). 6 parts (19,250).

1340. WHAT MIGHT BE. A Tale, by Margaret B. *Lady's,* XLI (July, 1810)–XLIII (May, 1812). 10 parts (24,500).

1341. WHAT WONDERS CANNOT LOVE EFFECT, a Moral Tale. *Oxford,* X (December–Supplement, 1773). 2 parts (5300).

1342. The WHIMSICAL WHIMSICALITIES OF MASTER TRISMEGISTUS AND HIS MAN CRAMBO. With a Full Account of Their Eccentric Equestrianations and Perambulations through the County and City of Cork. And Also Their Observations on Men—Manners—and Things. Their Philosophical Disputations—Philological Dissertations—Physical Operations—Personal Dissections—Religious Animadversions—and Political Disquisitions!!! *Museum,* I, Nos. 8–22 (June 15–November 23, 1796). 12 parts (6800). Uncompleted.

1343. The WHITE CASTLE. "Tale 1," *Tell-Tale,* I (1803). 1 part (7100).

1344. The WHITE OX, a Work Just Published in France by Mons. de Voltaire. *Sentimental,* II (May–December, 1774). 7 parts (7400). Uncompleted.

A translation of *Le Taureau blanc* (1774), omitting the last four chapters of the French original. This is a quite different translation from that published by Bew in the same year (*The White Bull, an Oriental History... by Mr. Voltaire,* 1774).

1345. The WHITE TOWER. By J. Chilton. "Tale 30," *Tell-Tale,* II (1804). 1 part (5300).

1346. The WHITSUN-HOLIDAY, or the Good Uncle. A Moral Tale, Never Before Published. *Universal,* LIV (April, 1774). 1 part (5000). Signed "G."

a. The Whitsun-Holiday, or the Good Uncle, a Moral Tale. *Weekly Misc.*(Sherborne), II (May 30, 1774). 1 part.

b. The Whitsun-Holiday, or the Good Uncle, a Moral Tale. *Weekly Misc.*(London), III, No. 90 (1774). 1 part.

1347. The WIFE AND THE FRIEND, or the Rare Example. An Anecdote Altered from the French of M. [Barthelmy] Imbert. *Lady's Monthly Museum,* 3.s. I (April–June, 1815). 3 parts (5280).

The original has not been identified.

1348. A WIFE OF TEN THOUSAND! A Moral Tale. [By Marmontel.] *Weekly Misc.* (Sherborne), II (September 12–26, 1774). 3 parts (9500).

A translation of "La Femme comme il y en a peu" (*Contes moraux,* Vol. III, 1765), extracted from Vol. III (1766) of the *Moral Tales* of Becket and De Hondt (see "Moral Tales," No. 917). For other magazine translations of the same story, see Nos. 384 and 475.

a. A Wife of Ten Thousand! A Moral Tale. *Weekly Misc.*(London), Nos. 106–107 (1774). 3 parts.

1349. The WIFE OF TWO HUSBANDS, by Sarah Wilkinson. "Tale 17," *Tell-Tale,* II (1804). 1 part (11,500).

1350. The WIFE RECLAIMED, or Rule a Wife and Have a Wife, a Comic Story. *New London,* IV (June–July, 1788). 2 parts (5100).

1351. WILLIAM OF THE WOOD, or the Royal Fugitives. "Tale 50," *Tell-Tale,* IV (1804). 1 part (12,500).

1352. WILLIAM TELL, or the Deliverance of Switzerland. Book the First. A Free Translation from the French of Florian. *Monthly Literary Recreations,* II (January–April, 1807). 4 parts (17,000). Signed "Y."

A translation of *Guillaume Tell, ou la Suisse libre, par M. de Florian... ouvrage postume* (an X [i.e., 1802–1803]). Parts 2–4 translate Books II–IV.

1353. WILLIAM WALLACE, the Hero of the North. "Tale 59," *Tell-Tale,* V (1805). 1 part (13,300).

1354. WISDOM AND FOLLY, a Vision. *Freemason's,* VIII (May, 1797); X (February–May, 1798). 5 parts (12,200). Uncompleted.

1355. WISDOM AND TRUTH, an Allegory, by a Lady. *Lady's,* XXIV (July–August, 1793). 2 parts (7400).

a. Wisdom and Truth, an Allegory in Two Parts. *Strabane,* I (April–July, 1799). 4 parts. Signed "PULCHERIA."

We are informed in the "Correspondence" column for May, 1799, that the "allegory," submitted by "*Eliza* of Dominick-street," has been copied from "the *Columbian Magazine* printed in Philadelphia." The story is found, with the signature "*Pulcheria,* Montgomery County, January 25, 1791," in the *Universal Asylum and Columbian Magazine* (Philadelphia), VI (February–April, 1791), where it must also have been obtained by the *Lady's.*

1356. WOLLMAR AND JACOBINA, a Psychological, Tragi-Comical, Sentimental Novel. Translated from the German by T. Dutton. (Embellished with a Superb Engraving.) *Bon Ton,* V (July, 1795–February, 1796). 8 parts (12,500).

1357. The WOMAN OF FEELING, a Sentimental Fragment. *Town and Country,* VI (December, 1774)–VII (January, 1775). 2 parts (5000).

1358. WONDERFUL DELIVERANCE OF THE SCOTS HEIRESS, and Her Friend Mrs. Dibart, from a Situation of the Most Imminent Danger. With the Interesting History of Donna Emilia de Vidos and Don Carlo de Riva. [From the *Memoirs of a Scots Heiress.*] *Monthly Extracts,* I (October, 1791). 1 part (6750).

From the novel published in 1791—reprinted in the course of review. For another extract in the same review see "Early History of the Heroine."

1359. The WORLD AS IT IS. *Christian Observer,* V (May–November, 1806). 5 parts (13,300).

Addressed "To the Editor of the *Christian Observer*" by "An Anti-Secular Philosopher." (V, 284.)

1360. The WORLD IN A NUTSHELL, or Circumnavigation's *Non Ultra. Devil,* II, Nos. 2–9 (January 6–February 24, 1787). 8 parts (9200).

1361. The YOUNG COTTAGER. [By the Rev. Legh Richmond.] *Christian Guardian,* III (September, 1811)–VI (May, 1814). 6 parts (18,750). Signed "SIMPLEX."

Included in the series "The Poor Man's Friend."

At the end of the last part it was announced: "The Rev. Legh [sic] Richmond has just published a volume, neatly printed in 12mo. containing the foregoing narrative of the Young Cottager complete; together with 'The Dairyman's Daughter,' *considerably enlarged*; and 'The Negro Servant.' The volume is entitled, 'Annals of the Poor.' " (VI, 167.) "The Dairyman's Daughter" and "The Negro Servant" were also first published in the *Christian Guardian* (see Nos. 277 and 948).

An abridged version of "The Young Cottager" was printed in the *Christian Herald* under the title "Some Account of Jane S——, the Young Cottager" (No. 717).

1362. The YOUNG DANE. From a New Publication Entitled *Mental Recreations, Four Danish and German Tales.* [By Andreas Anderson.] *Weekly Entertainer,* XLV (August 26–September 2, 1805). 2 parts (5000).

From the English collection published in 1805.

1363. The YOUNG MOUNTAINEER. *Lady's,* XXXI (March–December, 1800). 10 parts (37,000).

1364. The YOUNG OFFICER, a Tale, by Margaret B. *Lady's,* XLI (May–July, 1810). 3 parts (6400).

1365. A YOUNG PRINCE'S SEARCH AFTER HAPPINESS, or No Fixing on Any Particular Condition of Life upon Incontestable Reasons of Preference. An Eastern Story. *Weekly Amusement,* II (February 2–March 16, 1765). 6 parts (8400).

A disguised redaction of Johnson's *Rasselas,* with the principal proper names expunged. This version was probably based upon the epitome published in the *Universal* in 1759 (see No. 636). For other magazine piracies of Johnson's novel, see Nos. 48 and 633–635.

1366. YOUSOUF AND SAIDA, a Persian Tale. *Universal,* n.s. XV (March–May, 1811). 3 parts (6900). Uncompleted.

1367. ZADIG, or the Book of Fate, an Oriental History. Translated from the French of M. de Voltaire, by Francis Ashmore, Esq. *Novelist's,* II (1780). 1 part (27,000).

A new translation of *Zadig, ou la Destinée, histoire orientale* (1747, 1748). The first English translation of this story appeared in 1749. In the *Novelist's* the accompanying engraving is dated July 15, 1780.

1368. ZARA, or the Adventures of an English Wife. *Belle Assemblée,* n.s. V (January–June, 1812). 6 parts (17,000).

1369. ZELIA IN THE DESERT, or the Female Crusoe, Written by Herself. "Tale 71," *Tell-Tale,* VI (1805). 1 part (13,200).

1370. ZELUCO. Various View of Human Nature, Taken from Life and Manners, Foreign and Domestic. [By Dr. John Moore.] *European,* XVI (October–November, 1789). 2 parts (6600).

A review of Dr. Moore's *Zeluco,* which had just appeared, including an outline of the story and a number of excerpts. For a longer abridgment of the same novel, see No. 1371.

1371. Interesting Extracts from ZELUCO, an Improving and Entertaining Production, Lately Published. *Weekly Entertainer,* XIV (July 27–August 24, 1789). 5 parts (11,300).

A series of excerpts from Dr. Moore's *Zeluco* (1789), enclosed in a summary of the story. For a shorter epitome of the same novel, see No. 1370.

1372. ZELY, or the Difficulty of Being Happy, an Indian Romance. *Sentimental,* V (June–July, 1777). 2 parts (5100). Uncompleted.

a. Zely, etc. [Same title as above.] *Monthly Misc.,* V (June–July, 1777). 2 parts. Uncompleted.

b. Zely, etc. [Same title.] *Gentleman's and London,* 1777 (July–August). 2 parts. Uncompleted.

1373. ZEMIRA, or the Fisherman of Delhi, an Oriental Tale. By Joseph Moser, Esq. *European,* LII (October, 1807)–LIII (April, 1808). 6 parts (20,000).

1374. ZION'S PILGRIM. *Zion's Trumpet,* II (July, 1799)–III (October, 1800). 17 parts (41,000). Signed "CHARLES."

1375. ZULIMAN AND MARINA, a Fairy Tale. *Court Misc.,* I (September, 1765). 1 part (5100).

INDEX OF CATALOGUE REFERENCES

The following Index is strictly supplementary to the foregoing Catalogue of Magazine Novels and Novelettes. Titles listed there under the main headings are not repeated here, except under the author's name or some other secondary classification. In looking for titles like *Sir Launcelot Greaves* and *Grasville Abbey*, therefore, readers may find it necessary to consult both the Catalogue and the Index.

The Index of Catalogue References is confined to:

I. *Authors', editors', and translators' names*, but not pseudonyms, unless they are indistinguishable from real names. For example, "UNDERHILL, Dr. Updike" will refer the reader to "TYLER, Royall," the real author of *The Algerian Captive*. But names and initials like "Amelia Bur——d," "Aspasia," and "D——" have been excluded. The pseudonyms of magazine writers are insufficiently discriminated to warrant indexing, although they are usually cited in the Catalogue entries.

II. *Titles of known English works, exclusive of periodical publications, from which magazine fiction has been derived*—that is novels, collections of essays and stories, travel books, volumes of "miscellanies," and other extramural sources mentioned, but not indexed, in the Catalogue. For example, *The History of Rasselas, Fragments in the Manner of Sterne, Popular Tales of the Germans,* and *New Tales from the French of M. Florian* are duly entered in the Index as sources of miscellany fiction, but not Musaeus's *Volksmärchen der Deutschen* or Florian's *Nouvelles nouvelles*. Similarly, all authors of foreign-language originals have been indexed (see Section I above), but not separate titles like *Gil Blas*, "L'Amitié à l'épreuve," or "Le Blanc et le noir." English periodicals from which magazine fiction was derived will be found listed separately in the Register of Periodicals.

III. *Alternative titles of stories listed in the Catalogue*. The same stories frequently figured under different titles in various magazines, and sometimes in the same magazine. In all such cases the title employed in the first magazine appearance has been taken as standard, but others have been entered in the Index—as, for example, "Melmoth, a Tale" and "Melmoth and Julia," two variant titles of "The Shrubbery," which first appeared in the *European Magazine*.

IV. *Titles of general series* in which magazine stories have been included. Many magazine stories are found gathered in essay-series like "The Children's Friend" or "The Reasoner"; others were published as parts of serial collections, like "Spanish Novels" or "Memoirs of Love and Gallantry," all of which are mentioned in the Index.

In general, items under Classes III and IV above will refer readers to Catalogue entries by number only, but items under Classes I and II include other types of information, in order to give a more readily intelligible picture of the manner in which each author or work is represented. Thus under "VOLTAIRE" the titles of all nine of his magazine reprintings will be cited, together with the names (when known) of his translators, or the English publications from which they were drawn, in square brackets. In addition, in a number of entries an effort has been made to bring related pieces together, as, for example, two or more extracts from the same work, or different translations of the same story.

In the main headings of the Index, definite and indefinite articles have been suppressed in order to provide greater legibility, but elsewhere they have been retained.

Within the entries, items have been arranged in numerical (i.e., alphabetical) order, as they are in the Catalogue of Magazine Novels and Novelettes.

ADDENDA

693. The INDISCREET LOVER.
After the Catalogue had gone to press, this story was discovered to be an unacknowledged reprinting of "The Self-Disappointer" (No. 1113). No. 693, therefore, should properly appear as No. 1113b.

1113. The SELF-DISAPPOINTER.
See the note on No. 693 above.

CHRONOLOGICAL INDEX
(1740–1815)

The Chronological Index is designed to classify stories by calendar years, employing the numbers assigned in the Catalogue. Within any given year, however, the arrangement is strictly alphabetical.

According to the numbering system employed in the Catalogue, arabic numerals without letters represent first magazine appearances of stories, although only a fraction, of course, are genuine originals. Arabic numerals combined with letters represent subsequent magazine appearances, more or less in chronological order—as, for example, "1247b" indicates that the story had already appeared twice, barring simultaneous publication, in which case numbers appear together.

Numbers enclosed in parentheses represent continuations of stories published during two or more calendar years. But when a story was suspended during the whole of any given year, its appearance is not signaled for the period of interruption—as, for example, "The Elville Family Secrets" (No. 358), which is listed for 1804, and 1806–1810, but not for 1805, since no installment of the story appeared during that year.

Users of the Index should remember that magazines normally appeared several days *after* the date they bear, and most December numbers were actually published early in January. For convenience, all such discrepancies have been disregarded, and stories have simply been classified by the dates they bear. Annuals like the *Annual Register* and *Flowers of Literature*, however, have been listed for the year in which they actually appeared, and not for the date they bear.

The distribution of stories by years bears striking witness to the growth of public interest in long prose fiction over this seventy-five year period. Only one long story is recorded for 1740; and for 1741–1742, 1747, and 1757, none are listed at all. The novelty of Mrs. Haywood's efforts in the *Female Spectator* (1744–1746) and Hawkesworth's in the *Adventurer* (1752–1754) is visible in the record of this period. The high-water year for long magazine fiction was 1792, during which a total of eighty-nine novels or novelettes were published, or in the process of publication, in Great Britain and Ireland. If, however, the interest in long fiction seems to slacken after 1792, it is only because of the gradual concentration of this activity in fewer, more widely circulated magazines, which placed more emphasis upon originals, and upon stories of greater length.

A REGISTER OF PERIODICALS CONTAINING LONG PROSE FICTION

The following is an alphabetical list of all the 238 periodicals that figure in the Catalogue of Magazine Novels and Novelettes. The descriptions are made up on the basis of those in the *Union List of Serials,* the *British Union Catalogue of Periodicals,* Crane and Kaye, W. S. Ward's *Index and Finding List of Serials, 1789–1832,* M. E. Craig's *Scottish Periodical Press, 1750–1789,* and the catalogues of the British Museum and the Bodleian Library—subject always to corrections and additions made in the field.

With a few exceptions, the first title under which a given magazine appeared has been accepted as standard, although other titles used between the years 1740 and 1815 are mentioned, and in important cases cross-indexed. The descriptions cover only the period through 1815. Runs which extended beyond this cut-off year are indicated by a (+).

For easy reference each citation is preceded by the short title employed in the Catalogue and in the notes. All of the listed magazines were examined in their entirety, with the exceptions noted in square brackets.

The stories assigned to each magazine, according to Catalogue numbers, are arranged in the order in which they were published in the magazine. As in the Chronological Index, arabic numerals without letters represent first magazine appearances; arabic numerals combined with letters represent subsequent reprintings.

1. *Aberdeen(1)*

ABERDEEN MAGAZINE, LITERARY CHRONICLE, AND REVIEW. Aberdeen. Vols. I–IV (January 17, 1788–December, 1791).

1788 – 459b. *1790* – 1323. *1791* – 619e, 1024a, 1154b, 244c.

2. *Aberdeen(2)*

ABERDEEN MAGAZINE, OR UNIVERSAL REPOSITORY. Aberdeen. Vols. I–III (June 1796–December, 1798).

1796 – 304b, 1257, 75. *1797* – 377c. *1798* – 729a.

3. *Adventurer*

ADVENTURER. London. Nos. 1–140 (November 7, 1752–March 9, 1754).

1752 – 606, 699. *1753* – 106, 442, 404, 511, 899, 791. *1754* – 405.

4. *Adviser*

ADVISER, OR THE MORAL AND LITERARY TRIBUNAL. London. Vols. I–IV, Nos. 1–141 (1803).

1803 – 937, 755.

5. *Alston Misc.*

ALSTON MISCELLANY, OR GENTLEMAN'S MAGAZINE. Alston. Vols. I–II (April, 1799–March?, 1801). [Not examined: I, Nos. 3–4; II, Nos. 2, 4, 5.]

1799 – 423c.

6. *Ambigu*

AMBIGU, VARIÉTÉS ATROCES ET AMUSANTES, JOURNAL DANS LE GENRE ÉGYPTIEN. London. Vols. I+, Nos. 1+ (1803+).

1804 – 369, 416, 723, 93, 279. *1807* – 100. *1808* – 1089, 515, 907. *1809* – 428. *1811* – 770. *1812* – 961. *1813* – 303.

7. *Annual Reg.*

ANNUAL REGISTER, OR A VIEW OF THE HISTORY, POLITICS, AND LITERATURE FOR THE YEAR 1758, etc. London. Vols. I+ (1759+).

1807 – 1000.

8. *Arminian*

ARMINIAN MAGAZINE, CONSISTING OF EXTRACTS AND ORIGINAL TREATISES ON UNIVERSAL REDEMPTION. London. Vols. I+ (January, 1778+). Continued as METHODIST MAGAZINE from January, 1798.

1787 – 469.

Astrologer's Magazine. See *Conjuror's*.

Asylum. See *Weekly Misc.* (Glasgow).

9. *Attic Misc.*

ATTIC MISCELLANY, OR CHARACTERISTIC MIRROR OF MEN AND THINGS. London. Vols. I–III (October, 1789–August, 1792).

1789 – 1040. *1790* – 825, 875. *1791* – 1050f.

10. *Ayrshire*

AYRSHIRE MAGAZINE AND WEST COUNTRY MONTHLY REPOSITORY. Irvine. Vols. I+ (August, 1815+).

1815 – 1035.

11. *Beau Monde*(1)

BEAU MONDE, OR LITERARY AND FASHIONABLE MAGAZINE. London. Vols. I–IV (November, 1806–April, 1809).

1807 – 438. *1808* – 1245.

12. *Beau Monde*(2)

BEAU MONDE AND MONTHLY REGISTER. London. Vols. I–II, Nos. 1–13 (April, 1809–April, 1810).

1809 – 90.

13. *Beauties of All the Magazines*

BEAUTIES OF ALL THE MAGAZINES SELECTED. London. Vols. I–III (February, 1762–December, 1764).

1762 – 105, 902b, 575, 790, 593. *1763* – 701a, 486a, 591a, 1163b, 208c, 1211.

14. *Beauties of Magazines, etc.*

BEAUTIES OF MAGAZINES, REVIEWS, AND OTHER PERIODICAL PUBLICATIONS. Edinburgh. Vols. I–II (January–December, 1788).

1788 – 696a, 423a.

15. *Bee*

BEE, OR LITERARY WEEKLY INTELLIGENCER. Edinburgh. Vols. I–XVIII (December 22, 1790–January 21, 1794).

1791 – 856. *1792* – 713. *1793* – 752, 690, 715, 86.

16. *Belfast Monthly*
BELFAST MONTHLY MAGAZINE. Belfast. Vols. I–XIII, Nos. 1–77 (September, 1808–December, 1814).
1808 – 376. *1809* – 1075, 260, 1088. *1810* – 846, 1131, 830. *1811* – 1123. *1813* – 550. *1814* – 164.

17. *Belle Assemblée*
BELLE ASSEMBLÉE, OR BELL'S COURT AND FASHIONABLE MAGAZINE. London. Vols. I–VII (February, 1806–December, 1809). New Series Vol. I + (January, 1810 +).
1806 – 146, 992, 534, 471, 194, 579, 1084. *1807* – 1052, 1210, 160, 1228, 199, 176, 266a, 329a, 1152, 1328, 317a. *1808* – 1145, 934, 84, 1026, 264, 345, 320, 526, 819, 89, 1217, 820. *1809* – 243, 731a, 681, 1103, 674a, 162, 787, 656, 362. *1810* – 220, 1058, 1048, 1020, 816, 382. *1811* – 818, 967, 539, 743, 209, 570, 1177. *1812* – 1368, 360, 485, 1335, 297, 980, 897, 253, 964, 23. *1813* – 921, 13, 108, 1235, 203, 332, 7, 618. *1814* – 392, 746, 200, 839, 316, 935, 334, 1339. *1815* – 678, 1283, 592.

18. *Berwick Museum*
BERWICK MUSEUM, OR MONTHLY LITERARY INTELLIGENCER. Berwick-upon-Tweed. Vols. I–III (January, 1785–December, 1787).
1785 – 201, 1049. *1786* – 811d, 1215c. *1787* – 694a, 599, 612b.

19. *Biographical and Imperial*
BIOGRAPHICAL AND IMPERIAL MAGAZINE. London. Vols. I–V (January, 1789–1792).
1789 – *1094*.

20. *Bon Ton*
BON TON MAGAZINE, OR MICROSCOPE OF FASHION AND FOLLY. London. Vols. I–V, Nos. 1–61 (March, 1791–March, 1796).
1791 – 1081, 1153b, 273. *1792* – 788, 798, 223a, 793, 795, 1289. *1793* – 453. *1794* – 18, 324, 307, 219, 557, 871. *1795* – 1301, 1234, 724, 1356, 1325, 1174, 823.

21. *Bouquet*
BOUQUET, OR BLOSSOMS OF FANCY. London. Vols. I–II, Nos. 1–12 (August 15, 1795 – July 1?, 1796).

22. *Bristol*
BRISTOL MAGAZINE, SUNDRIES. A VARIETY OF FUGITIVE PIECES, BY VARIOUS AUTHORS, AND ON VARIOUS SUBJECTS. Bristol. 1787[?].
1787 – 1186a.

23. *Bristol and Bath*
BRISTOL AND BATH MAGAZINE, OR INSTRUCTIVE AND ENTERTAINING MISCELLANY. Bristol. Vols. I–III, No. 8 (1782–1783). [Only Vols. I–II, No. 23, were examined.]
1782 – 1317e, 489c, 925a, 1284b. *1783* – 565c, 133b, 642a.

24. *Britannic*
BRITANNIC MAGAZINE, OR ENTERTAINING REPOSITORY OF HEROIC ADVENTURES AND MEMORABLE EXPLOITS. London. Vols. I–XII, Nos. 1–185 (1793–1807). Continued as BRITANNIC MAGAZINE AND CHRONOLOGICAL REPOSITORY. London. New Series I (April, 1807–December, 1809).
1794 – 208e. *1796* – 603e. *1797* – 141b, 835c. *1798* – 691d, 388a, 939c, 1338, 11a, 508b. *1799* – 459h, 736. *1800* – 1293g, 1144e, 797. *1801* – 43h, 1274c, 627e, 1016a. *1802* – 4b, 1066a, 134c, 1187a. *1803* – 1147. *1804* – 1317f, 693. *1805* – 410, 455a. *1806* – 1266c. *1807* – 341.

Britannic Mag. and Chronological Rep. See *Britannic*.

25. *British*(1)
BRITISH MAGAZINE. London. Vols. I–VI (January, 1746–May, 1751).
1749 – 712.

26. *British*(2)
BRITISH MAGAZINE, OR MONTHLY REPOSITORY FOR GENTLEMEN AND LADIES. London. Vols. I–VIII (January, 1760–December, 1767).
1760 – 622, 779, 1059. *1763* – 208b. *1765* – 158, 680. *1766* – 536a, 451a. *1767* – 628.

27. *British*(3)
BRITISH MAGAZINE. London. Vols. I–II (January, 1800–January, 1801).
1800 – 1072.

28. *British* (Edinburgh)
BRITISH MAGAZINE, OR THE LONDON AND EDINBURGH INTELLIGENCER. Edinburgh. Vols. I–II (January, 1747–December, 1748).
1748 – 741b.

29. *British Mag. and Rev.*
BRITISH MAGAZINE AND REVIEW, OR UNIVERSAL MISCELLANY. London. Vols. I–III (July, 1782–December, 1783).
1782 – 986, 966. *1783* – 565, 687, 111.

30. *Busy Body*
BUSY BODY, A COLLECTION OF PERIODICAL ESSAYS, MORAL, WHIMSICAL, COMIC, AND SENTIMENTAL, BY MR. OULTON. London. Vols. I–II, Nos. 1–25 (January 2–February 26, 1787).
1787 – 1182.

31. *Bystander*
BYSTANDER, OR UNIVERSAL WEEKLY EXPOSITOR. London. Nos. 1–26 (August 15, 1789–February 6, 1790).
1789 – 123, 246.

32. *Cabinet*
CABINET, OR MONTHLY REPORT OF POLITE LITERATURE. London. Vols. I–IV (March, 1807–December, 1808). New Series Vol. I (January–August, 1809).
1809 – 767, 1181.

33. *Cabinet Mag.*
CABINET MAGAZINE, OR LITERARY OLIO. London. Vols. I–II, Nos. 1–9 (November, 1796–July, 1797). [Nos. 8–9 were not examined.]
1797 – 1069, 1041.

34. *Caledonian*(1)
CALEDONIAN MAGAZINE, OR ABERDEEN REPOSITORY. Aberdeen. Vol. I (October 6, 1786–October 5, 1787).
1786 – 359b. *1787* – 265a, 245b, 349a, 263a, 1022a.

35. *Caledonian*(2)
CALEDONIAN MAGAZINE, OR ABERDEEN REPOSITORY. Aberdeen. Vols. I–V (January, 1788–December, 1790).
1788 – 1018f, 67d, 700, 945a, 423b, 245c, 423b. *1790* – 838a, 66c, 150.

36. *Caledonian Mag. and Rev.*
CALEDONIAN MAGAZINE AND REVIEW. Perth. Vols. I–III (March 7[?], 1783–August 27, 1784). [Vol. I, No. 8, Vol. II, Nos. 1–2, and Vol. III, No. 1, were not examined in full.]
1783 – 998, 811a, 98, 950a, 153a. *1784* – 118a.

37. *Caledonian Weekly*
CALEDONIAN WEEKLY MAGAZINE, OR EDINBURGH INTELLIGENCER. Edinburgh. Vol. I (June 9, 1773–?). [Only the issues for June 30, July 21, and July 28 were examined.]
1773 – 1138a, 133a, 449a, 474a.

38. *Carlton House*
   CARLTON HOUSE MAGAZINE, OR ANNALS OF TASTE, FASHION, AND POLITENESS. London. Vols. I–V, No. 1 (January, 1792–January, 1797).
   1792 – 1045.
39. *Champion*
   CHAMPION, A WEEKLY POLITICAL AND LITERARY JOURNAL. London. Nos. 1 + (1813 +). Nos. 1–51 (1813) were called DRAKARD'S PAPER. [No. 58 was not examined.]
   1814 – 765.
40. *Cheap*
   CHEAP MAGAZINE, OR POOR MAN'S FIRESIDE COMPANION. Haddington. Vols. I–II (January, 1813–December, 1814). Succeeded by *Monthly Monitor* (q.v.).
   1813 – 145. *1814* – 551, 433.
41. *Children's*
   CHILDREN'S MAGAZINE, OR MONTHLY REPOSITORY OF INSTRUCTION AND DELIGHT. London. Vols. I–IV (January, 1799–December, 1800).
   1799 – 1060, 786.
42. *Christian Guardian*
   CHRISTIAN GUARDIAN, A THEOLOGICAL MISCELLANY. Bristol. Vols. I–X (1802–1806); New Series Vols. I–II (1807–1808). Continued as CHRISTIAN GUARDIAN AND CHURCH OF ENGLAND MAGAZINE. London. Vols. I + (1809 +).
   1809 – 947. *1810* – 277. *1811* – 1361.
43. *Christian Herald*
   CHRISTIAN HERALD FOR 1814, etc. Edinburgh. Vols. I + (January, 1814 +).
   1814 – 717.
44. *Christian Mirror*
   CHRISTIAN MIRROR: EXHIBITING SOME OF THE EXCELLENCES AND DEFECTS OF THE RELIGIOUS WORLD: CONTAINING VARIOUS ESSAYS IN PROSE AND VERSE. London. Nos. 1–27 (1805).
   1805 – 987.
45. *Christian Observer*
   CHRISTIAN OBSERVER, CONDUCTED BY MEMBERS OF THE ESTABLISHED CHURCH. London. Vols. I + (January, 1802 +).
   1802 – 757. *1806* – 1359. *1813* – 256.
46. *Compiler*
   COMPILER, OR LITERARY BANQUET. London. Vols. I–II, Nos. 1–14 (1807–1808).
   1807 – 1297. *1808* – 412, 745, 862.
47. *Conjuror's*
   CONJUROR'S MAGAZINE, OR MAGICAL AND PHYSIOGNOMICAL MIRROR. London. Vols. I–II (August, 1791–July, 1793). Vol. III continued as ASTROLOGER'S MAGAZINE AND PHILOSOPHICAL MISCELLANY. New Series Vol. I (August, 1793–January, 1794).
   1793 – 944.
48. *Cottage*
   COTTAGE MAGAZINE, OR PLAIN CHRISTIAN'S LIBRARY. London. Vols. I + (January, 1812 +).
   1812 – 552. *1814* – 781.
49. *Country Spectator*
   COUNTRY SPECTATOR. Gainsborough. Nos. 1–33 (October 9, 1792–May 21, 1793).
   1793 – 530.

50. *County*

COUNTY MAGAZINE. Salisbury. Vols. I–VI (January, 1786–December, 1792). Continued from 1789 as WESTERN COUNTY MAGAZINE.

1788 – 691.

51. *Court and City*

COURT AND CITY MAGAZINE, OR A FUND OF ENTERTAINMENT FOR THE MAN OF QUALITY. London. Vols. I–II (January, 1770–December, 1771).

1770 – 357, 387, 120.

52. *Court, City and Country*(1)

COURT MAGAZINE, OR ROYAL CHRONICLE. London. Vols. I–III (September, 1761–November, 1765). Continued from March, 1763, as COURT AND CITY MAGAZINE. Continued from February, 1764, as COURT, CITY AND COUNTRY MAGAZINE.

1761 – 1193. *1762* – 1191, 1204. *1763* – 1239. *1765* – 603c.

53. *Court, City and Country*(2)

COURT, CITY AND COUNTRY MAGAZINE, OR GENTLEMAN AND LADY'S UNIVERSAL AND POLITE INSTRUCTOR. London. Vol. I (January–April, 1788).

1788 – 420.

Court Magazine. See *Court, City and Country*(1).

54. *Court Misc.*

COURT MISCELLANY, OR LADIES NEW MAGAZINE. London. Vols. I–VII (July, 1765–December, 1771). Continued from 1766, as COURT MISCELLANY, OR GENTLEMAN AND LADY'S NEW MAGAZINE.

1765 – 596, 1375, 475. *1766* – 576. *1767* – 641. *1768* – 1264, 537a, 642, 408. *1769* – 926. *1771* – 649.

55. *Covent Garden*

COVENT GARDEN MAGAZINE, OR THE AMOROUS REPOSITORY. London. Vols. I–III (July, 1772–1774[?]). [Only Vols. I–II and a fragment for August, 1774, were examined.]

1772 – 535, 229, 533. *1773* – 30, 865, 783, 870.

56. *Culler*

CULLER. Glasgow. Vol. I, Nos. 1–20 (August 12–December 23, 1795).

1795 – 1050h.

57. *Cumberland*

CUMBERLAND MAGAZINE, OR WHITEHAVEN MONTHLY MISCELLANY. Whitehaven. Vols. I–IV (1778?–December, 1781). [Vol. I and the October, 1780, issue were not examined.]

1778 – 602b. *1779* – 1280a, 567a. *1780* – 448a. *1781* – 427b.

58. *Cyclopaedian*

CYCLOPAEDIAN MAGAZINE AND DUBLIN MONTHLY REGISTER. Dublin. Vols. I–III, No. 4 (January, 1807–April, 1809).

1807 – 112a, 1249, 801, 1b. *1808* – 1026a.

59. *Devil*

DEVIL: CONTAINING A REVIEW AND INVESTIGATION OF ALL PUBLIC SUBJECTS WHATEVER, BY A SOCIETY OF LITERARY GENTLEMEN. London. Vols. I–II, No. 9 (October 2, 1786–February 24, 1787).

1786 – 328, 1101. *1787* – 1360.

60. *Dublin*(1)

DUBLIN MAGAZINE. Dublin. Vols. I–IV, No. 1 (January, 1762–January, 1765).

1763 – 1163c.

61. *Dublin*(2)
DUBLIN MAGAZINE, OR MONTHLY MEMORIALIST. Dublin. Vol. I (November, 1812–September, 1813).
1812 – 496a.

62. *Dublin Library*
DUBLIN LIBRARY, OR IRISH MAGAZINE. Dublin. Vol. I (May 1/15–October, 1761).
1761 – 1229a.

63. *Dublin Museum*
DUBLIN MUSEUM, OR ENTERTAINING POCKET COMPANION. Dublin. Vol. I (January–December, 1807).
1807 – 709, 1017a, 1171a.

64. *Dumfries Weekly*
DUMFRIES WEEKLY MAGAZINE. Dumfries. Vols. I–XVIII (March 16, 1773–June 24, 1777). [Only Vols. I–VII, IX–XII, XV, and fragments of the other volumes were examined.]
1773 – 863b, 682a. *1775* – 572a, 1179a.

65. *Dundee*
DUNDEE MAGAZINE AND JOURNAL OF THE TIMES. Dundee. Vols. I–IV (January, 1799–May, 1802). [Only Vols. I, II (February, June–November), and IV were examined.]
1800 – 1153f.

66. *Dundee Rep.*
DUNDEE REPOSITORY OF POLITICAL AND MISCELLANEOUS INFORMATION. Dundee. Vols. I–II (February 15, 1793–February 21, 1794).
1793 – 687e, 647.

67. *Edinburgh*(1)
EDINBURGH MAGAZINE. Edinburgh. Vols. I–V (July, 1757–December, 1762).
1759 – 48.

68. *Edinburgh*(2)
EDINBURGH MAGAZINE, OR LITERARY MISCELLANY. Edinburgh. Vols. I–XVI (January, 1785–December, 1792); New Series Vols. I–XXII (January, 1793–December, 1803).
1785 – 119. *1786* – 77. *1787* – 849, 1022, 451d, 1151. *1788* – 945, 331, 1038. *1789* – 1322, 3, 687d. *1790* – 57a, 1153a, 484, 1050d. *1791* – 143, 1063, 244, 522, 66g, 473, 121d. *1792* – 459g, 222a, 16, 1303. *1793* – 714, 81, 117, 185, 1256, 506b. *1794* – 1033, 346, 963b, 687f, 245d. *1795* – 388, 669, 728. *1796* – 43c. *1797* – 749, 942, 395, 216a. *1798* – 939a, 547b. *1799* – 300c. *1800* – 72, 254. *1801* – 228a, 627b, 134a, 504. *1802* – 455, 1266a, 4c. *1803* – 400a.

69. *Edinburgh Eighth-Day*
EDINBURGH EIGHTH-DAY MAGAZINE, OR SCOTS TOWN AND COUNTRY INTELLIGENCER. Edinburgh. Vols. I–III (September 1, 1779–June 30, 1780). [The issue for June 30, 1780, was not examined.]
1779 – 322.

Edinburgh Magazine. See *Edinburgh Weekly*.

70. *Edinburgh Mag. and Rev.*
EDINBURGH MAGAZINE AND REVIEW. Edinburgh. Vols. I–V (Nov., 1773–August, 1776).
1774 – 57. *1776* – 887a.

71. *Edinburgh Museum*
EDINBURGH MUSEUM, OR NORTH BRITISH MAGAZINE. Edinburgh. Vols. I–II (January, 1763–December, 1764).
1763 – 622a, 1163a, 1193a. *1764* – 1191a.

72. *Edinburgh Rep.*(1)

EDINBURGH REPOSITORY, OR FORTNIGHT'S MAGAZINE. Edinburgh. Nos. 1–?? (March 2, 1774–?). [Only the first number was examined.]

1774 – 1317d.

73. *Edinburgh Rep.*(2)

EDINBURGH REPOSITORY FOR POLITE LITERATURE. Edinburgh. Vol. I, Nos. 1–6[?] (1793).

1793 – 106e, 899c.

74. *Edinburgh Weekly*

WEEKLY MAGAZINE, OR EDINBURGH AMUSEMENT. Edinburgh. Vols. I–LX (July 7, 1768–June 24, 1784). Continued as EDINBURGH MAGAZINE, OR LITERARY AMUSEMENT from December 30, 1779. Continued as EDINBURGH WEEKLY MAGAZINE from July 3, 1783.

1769 – 1200, 1300. *1770* – 138. *1771* – 381. *1778* – 895. *1779* – 29a. *1780* – 1215b. *1781* – 411a, 1293b. *1783* – 565b, 111b. *1784* – 687c.

75. *English Lyceum*

ENGLISH LYCEUM, OR CHOICE OF PIECES IN PROSE AND IN VERSE, SELECTED FROM THE BEST PERIODICAL PAPERS, AND OTHER BRITISH PUBLICATIONS. Hamburg and London. Vols. I–III, No. 9 (July, 1787–June, 1788).

1788 – 451f.

76. *Enquirer*

ENQUIRER, OR LITERARY, MATHEMATICAL, AND PHILOSOPHICAL REPOSITORY. London. Vols. I–III (1811–1813).

1811 – 929.

77. *Entertaining*(1)

ENTERTAINING MAGAZINE, OR POLITE REPOSITORY OF ELEGANT AMUSEMENT, etc. London. Vol. I, Nos. 1–12 (January–December, 1802).

1802 – 702, 565i, 662a, 36, 265b, 1203a, 1061, 188, 245e, 629a, 1028, 966b, 989, 627g, 481.

78. *Entertaining*(2)

ENTERTAINING MAGAZINE, OR REPOSITORY OF GENERAL KNOWLEDGE. London. Vols. I–III (January, 1813–December, 1815).

1813 – 109d. *1815* – 655b, 1158, 1138h, 329b.

79. *European*

EUROPEAN MAGAZINE AND LONDON REVIEW. London. Vols. I + (January, 1782 +).

1782 – 589, 502, 812, 1144. *1783* – 950. *1784* – 406. *1785* – 301. *1787* – 975, 451b, 1018d, 80. *1789* – 1370. *1790* – 66e, 619. *1791* – 1252. *1792* – 223. *1794* – 963, 932. *1797* – 216. *1801* – 228. *1802* – 1198. *1804* – 418, 973. *1805* – 953, 1132, 1233. *1806* – 28. *1807* – 930, 1373. *1808* – 52. *1810* – 1136, 234. *1811* – 505. *1812* – 496. *1814* – 350. *1815* – 1192.

80. *Every Man's*

EVERY MAN'S MAGAZINE, OR MONTHLY REPOSITORY OF SCIENCE, INSTRUCTION, AND AMUSEMENT. London. Vols. I–II (July, 1771–January, 1773).

1772 – 393.

81. *Family*

FAMILY MAGAZINE, OR A REPOSITORY OF RELIGIOUS INSTRUCTION AND RATIONAL AMUSEMENT. London. Vols. I–III (January, 1788–June, 1789).

1788 – 918.

82. *Fashionable*
FASHIONABLE MAGAZINE, OR LADY'S AND GENTLEMAN'S MONTHLY RECORDER OF NEW FASHIONS, etc. London. Vol. I (June–December, 1786).
1786 – 1120, 694, 577, 851.

83. *Female Preceptor*
FEMALE PRECEPTOR. London. Vols. I–III, No. 6 (January, 1813–June, 1814).
1813 – 974, 520a, 891, 940. *1814* – 1110, 312.

84. *Female Spectator*
FEMALE SPECTATOR. London. Books I–XXIV (1744–1746).
1744 – 571. *1745* – 902, 741, 167, 1201, 1276.

85. *Flowers of Literature*
FLOWERS OF LITERATURE FOR 1801 AND 1802, etc. London. Vols. I–VII (1803–1809).
1807 – 340. *1808* – 847, 1031.

86. *Freeholder's*
FREEHOLDER'S MAGAZINE, OR MONTHLY CHRONICLE OF LIBERTY, BY A PATRIOTIC SOCIETY. London. Vols. I–III (September, 1769–August, 1771).
1770 – 821, 467.

87. *Freemason's*
FREEMASON'S MAGAZINE, OR GENERAL AND COMPLETE LIBRARY. London. Vols. I–XI (June, 1793–December, 1798).
1793 – 338. *1795* – 141. *1797* – 1354. *1798* – 230, 274, 547d.

88. *Friend*
FRIEND, A LITERARY, MORAL, AND POLITICAL WEEKLY PAPER... CONDUCTED BY S. T. COLERIDGE. Penrith and London. Nos. 1–27 [actually 28] (June 1, 1809–March 15, 1810).
1809 – 1196.

89. *General*
GENERAL MAGAZINE AND IMPARTIAL REVIEW. London. Vols. I–VI (June, 1787–December, 1792).
1787 – 780, 978, 603d. *1788* – 606d, 1308, 688, 459. *1789* – 835, 1144a, 11, 508, 931. *1790* – 691a, 882, 1014. *1791* – 210, 298, 74, 246a. *1792* – 168, 753e, 222b, 1303a, 1189, 1246.

90. *General Chronicle*
GENERAL CHRONICLE AND LITERARY MAGAZINE. London. Vols. I–VI (January, 1811–December, 1812).
1811 – 440, 840. *1812* – 317b.

91. *Gentleman's*
GENTLEMAN'S MAGAZINE, OR MONTHLY INTELLIGENCER. London. Vols. I +. (January, 1731 +). Continued as GENTLEMAN'S MAGAZINE AND HISTORICAL CHRONICLE from 1736.
1737 – 1215. *1743* – 876. *1751* – 122. *1754* – 1180. *1755* – 1078. *1765* – 1178, 1267. *1766* – 325. *1768* – 774.

92. *Gentleman's and London*
LONDON MAGAZINE AND MONTHLY CHRONICLER. Dublin. 1741–1794. Continued as GENTLEMAN'S AND LONDON MAGAZINE, OR MONTHLY CHRONOLOGER from 1755.
1751 – 122b. *1753* – 37a. *1754* – 1180a. *1755* – 1078c. *1776* – 53b. *1777* – 1372b. *1778* – 602a, 17a. *1779* – 1229e, 29b. *1783* – 565a, 687a. *1785* – 565e, 301a. *1786* – 811c. *1787* – 849a, 1018b, 780a. *1788* – 956a. *1789* – 835b. *1790* – 308. *1791* – 619c. *1792* – 896a, 753a. *1793* – 1138f.

93. *German Miscellany*

GERMAN MISCELLANY, CONSISTING OF DRAMAS, DIALOGUES, TALES, AND NOVELS, TRANSLATED FROM THAT LANGUAGE BY A. THOMSON. Perth. Vol. I (1796).

1796 – 965, 594.

94. *German Museum*

GERMAN MUSEUM, OR MONTHLY REPOSITORY OF THE LITERATURE OF GERMANY, THE NORTH, AND THE CONTINENT IN GENERAL. London. Vols. I–III (January, 1800–June, 1801).

1800 – 317, 329, 674, 731, 266. *1801* – 1016, 415.

95. *Glasgow*

GLASGOW MAGAZINE AND CLYDESDALE MONTHLY REGISTER. Glasgow. Vols. I–III (September, 1810–June, 1812).

1811 – 1111, 497. *1812* – 187.

96. *Glasgow Mag. and Rev.*

GLASGOW MAGAZINE AND REVIEW, OR UNIVERSAL MISCELLANY. Glasgow. Vol. I (October, 1783–May, 1784).

1783 – 286a.

97. *Glasgow Misc.*

GLASGOW MISCELLANY. Glasgow. Vols. I–II (1800–1801). [Only Vol. II was examined.]

1800 – 1276b, 614, 521. *1801* – 627f, 330.

98. *Gleaner*

GLEANER, OR ENTERTAINMENT FOR THE FIRESIDE, CONSISTING OF TALES, etc. Salford. Vols. I–II (1805–1806). Continued as *Harvest Home* in 1807–1808 (q.v.). Continued as *New Gleaner* in 1809–1810 (q.v.).

1805 – 815, 741f, 1144f, 1003a, 1202a, 174, 265c, 399c, 627i, 121e, 1190h, 1154d, 111d, 1050i, 662b. *1806* – 165a, 182a, 1153g, 1205b, 363, 1018j, 68a, 566a, 239a, 289b, 459i.

99. *Grand*(1)

MAGAZINE OF MAGAZINES, OR UNIVERSAL REGISTER. London. Vols. I–III, Nos. 1–18 (July, 1758–December, 1759). Continued from No. 8 as GRAND MAGAZINE OF MAGAZINES.

1759 – 634, 177.

100. *Grand*(2)

GRAND MAGAZINE OF UNIVERSAL INTELLIGENCE AND MONTHLY CHRONICLE OF OUR OWN TIMES. London. Vols. I–III (January, 1758–December, 1760).

1760 – 632.

101. *Harvest Home*

HARVEST HOME, OR INSTRUCTION AND AMUSEMENT FOR THE FIRE-SIDE, etc. Salford. Vols. I–II (1807–1808). A continuation of the *Gleaner* (q.v.). Continued as the *New Gleaner* (q.v.).

1807 – 1274d, 689, 109c, 144a, 1056b, 1143, 1210a, 405d, 945c, 2a, 1199a, 699b, 65. *1808* – 1024c, 463b, 125, 655a, 687g, 348a, 537b, 67f, 589c, 1293h.

102. *Hibernian*

HIBERNIAN MAGAZINE, OR COMPENDIUM OF ENTERTAINING KNOWLEDGE. Dublin. 1771 (February)–1811 (December). Continued as WALKER'S HIBERNIAN MAGAZINE from 1786.

NOTE: During at least nine months in 1772–1773 the *Hibernian* appears to have been published by two rival Dublin agencies, which issued during this period nearly identical periodicals, although there are a few striking divergences. The original *Hibernian* appears to have been published by James Potts, beginning in February, 1771, and continuing through February 1774, after which Walker evidently acquired Potts's interest. The second *Hibernian*, "Printed for R. Marchbank and Peter Seguin, in King's-street, Stephen's Green," was published between October, 1772 – May, 1773, and in July, 1773. These nine numbers have been examined, and there were probably others. Among the items listed below for 1772–1773, Nos. 443 (Part 1) and 863a are found in both magazines; Nos. 638a and 335a are found only in Potts's; and Nos. 443 (Part 2), 829, and 732a only in Marchbank and Seguin's periodical. The last three items, being missing in the copies of the *Hibernian* usually encountered, are therefore starred (★).

1771–1278a. *1772*–443★. *1773*–638a, 829★, 732a★, 863a, 335a, 1290a, 403a. *1774*–1113a. *1775*–1029a, 532a. *1776* – 204, 422, 53a. *1777* – 426a, 378a. *1778* – 858a. *1779* – 1274a, 1334c, 38c. *1780* – 609a, 1222a, 427a. *1781* – 646a, 463a, 1190c, 1078g, 1162a, 1293c. *1782* – 733a, 589a. *1783* – 197a, 281a, 993a, 541a, 597a, 111a. *1784* – 262, 118b. *1785* – 406a, 1025a, 1337a. *1786* – 67a, 506a, 76a. *1787* – 975a, 612a, 35a, 451e. *1788* – 80a, 582a, 459a, 331a, 1161a, 1268a. *1789* – 375a, 1038a, 901a. *1790* – 66b, 691b, 882a, 906a, 659b, 946a, 1050a. *1791* – 981a, 82a, 210a, 1154a, 244b, 945b, 273a, 890a. *1792* – 1119, 223e. *1793* – 1307, 949, 453a. *1794* – 486c, 670a, 957a, 932a, 913a, 64a, 963a. *1795* – 1312a, 141a. *1796* – 304a, 43d, 1009, 673a. *1797* – 1282a, 835d. *1798* – 1056a, 492, 470a. *1799* – 300d, 189a. *1800* – 310a. *1801* – 4a, 627d, 134b, 435a. *1802* – 637a, 683a. *1803* – 1146a, 1071a. *1804* – 1073a. *1805* – 953a. *1806* – 1315a, 28a. *1807* – 127a, 718a, 1057a, 1007a, 176a. *1808* – 84a, 934a. *1809* – 89a, 674b, 892a, 787a. *1810* – 220a, 240, 450. *1811* – 539a, 1048a, 209a, 570a, 716, 142, 1177a.

103. *Hibernian*(2)

HIBERNIAN MAGAZINE AND DUBLIN MONTHLY PANORAMA. Dublin. Vols. I–III (January, 1810–May, 1811). [In Vol. II only the August and December numbers were examined, and in Vol. III only the February, April, and May numbers.]

1810 – 266b.

104. *Historical*

HISTORICAL MAGAZINE, OR CLASSICAL LIBRARY OF PUBLIC EVENTS. London. Vols. I–IV (1789–1792).

1791 – 619f.

105. *Historical, Biographical, etc.*

HISTORICAL, BIOGRAPHICAL, LITERARY, AND SCIENTIFIC MAGAZINE. London. Vols. I–II (February, 1799–December, 1800).

1799 – 1090. *1800* – 310.

106. *Imperial*

IMPERIAL MAGAZINE, OR COMPLETE MONTHLY INTELLIGENCER. London. Vols. I–III, Nos. 1–37 (January, 1760–December, 1762).

1762 – 116.

107. *Intruder*

INTRUDER, A PERIODICAL PAPER. Aberdeen. Nos. 1–26 (January 1–October 22, 1802).

1802 – 69.

108. *Ipswich*

IPSWICH MAGAZINE. Ipswich. Vol. I (February, 1799–February, 1800).

1799 – 622b, 106f, 1140.

109. *Ireland's Mirror*

IRELAND'S MIRROR, OR A CHRONICLE OF THE TIMES. Dublin. Vols. I–II (May, 1804–December, 1805). Continued as IRELAND'S MIRROR, OR THE MASONIC MAGA-

ZINE. Vol. III (January–April, 1806).

1804 – 968. *1805* – 20.

110. *Irvine*

IRVINE AND COUNTY OF AYR MISCELLANY. Irvine. Vol. I (September, 1814–July, 1815).

1814 – 1176.

111. *Jester's*

JESTER'S MAGAZINE, OR THE MONTHLY MERRYMAKER. London. Nos. 1–15 (October, 1765–December, 1766).

1766 – 544.

112. *Juvenal*

JUVENAL, A PERIODICAL PAPER, BY TIMOTHY TARTAR. Edinburgh. Nos. 1–8 (February 4–May 14, 1805).

1805 – 1.

113. *Juvenile*

JUVENILE MAGAZINE, OR AN INSTRUCTIVE AND ENTERTAINING MISCELLANY FOR YOUTH OF BOTH SEXES. London. Vols. I–II (January–December, 1788).

1788 – 806, 692.

114. *Juvenile Library*

MONTHLY PRECEPTOR, OR JUVENILE LIBRARY. London. Vols. I–V, Nos. 1–26 (1800–1802). Vol. I appeared as the JUVENILE ENCYCLOPAEDIA.

1800 – 807.

115. *Ladies*

LADIES MAGAZINE, OR THE UNIVERSAL ENTERTAINER. London. Vols. I–IV (November 18, 1749–November 10, 1753).

1749 – 902a. *1750* – 701. *1752* – 122d, 97a, 799. *1753* – 658, 37b.

116. *Lady's*

LADY'S MAGAZINE, OR ENTERTAINING COMPANION FOR THE FAIR SEX. London. Vol. I+ (August, 1770+).

NOTE: The *Lady's Magazine* was launched in 1770 by John Coote, who published it over the name of John Wheble. But in April, 1771, Coote transferred his interest in the magazine to Robinson and Roberts, who proceeded to publish it in their own name. Wheble refused to be shut out in this manner, and thus from April, 1771, to December, 1772, according to Graham Pollard (*Bodleian Library Record,* V, July, 1955, pp. 149–156), there were *two* magazines, each bearing the same title, issuing from adjoining numbers in Paternoster Row. Of Wheble's continuation of the *Lady's,* I have been able to examine only the first three numbers (April – June, 1771). These three numbers contain a separate continuation of "A Sentimental Journey, by a Lady" (No. 1115), and a different translation of Part 2 of "The Pyrenean Hermits" (No. 1037). They also omit Nos. 873 and 925, which were published in Robertson and Roberts's edition of the *Lady's Magazine* exclusively. Unlike the second *Hibernian* (q.v.), Wheble's magazine was not a piracy. Volume I of the *Lady's,* containing the first three numbers of Wheble's unauthorized continuation, is found in the Newberry Library. It is unlisted in the *Union List of Serials*.

1770 – 115. *1771* – 2, 482, 1037, 873, 925, 373, 314, 698. *1772* – 225, 859, 311, 207, 287, 548, 1166. *1773* – 905, 762, 721, 542, 860, 226, 1260. *1774* – 1255, 903, 40, 549, 560, 1121, 461, 556. *1775* – 1294, 645. *1776* – 1130, 268, 763, 564, 5, 972, 590. *1777* – 523, 796, 323, 1279. *1778* – 1128, 766, 477, 979. *1779* – 894, 1229d, 1126, 1265, 808, 489b. *1780* – 448, 384, 748, 707, 867, 1224. *1781* – 419, 463, 559, 1078f, 1162, 525, 295. *1782* – 280, 1129, 290. *1783* – 281, 872, 447, 1127.

1784 – 543, 960, 155, 1253. *1785* – 922, 12, 759, 1134. *1786* – 421, 685. *1787* – 625, 283, 854, 773. *1788* – 756, 417, 804. *1789* – 901, 1242, 639, 1293f, 613, 805. *1790* – 249, 659, 946. *1791* – 26, 82, 244a, 163, 1077. *1792* – 619g, 1065, 445, 472, 459d, 1202, 1248, 223d. *1793* – 478, 1355, 733c. *1794* – 1124, 913, 64. *1795* – 292, 927, 1213a, 1187, 154, 299, 43a. *1796* – 648, 304, 1207, 769, 128, 958. *1797* – 144, 1282, 545, 109, 394, 1172. *1798* – 1074, 470, 193, 547e. *1799* – 364. *1800* – 1363, 588, 43g. *1801* – 637, 627a, 683, 435, 124, 999. *1802* – 258, 1062, 985, 1027, 990. *1803* – 1068, 1146, 130. *1804* – 358, 83, 1073. *1805* – 710, 352, 278, 466. *1806* – 389, 397, 1017. *1807* – 494, 1159, 102, 1171, 91. *1808* – 916, 457. *1809* – 107, 1055, 152, 1320. *1810* – 439, 1364, 1340, 909, 271, 848, 720, 881. *1811* – 1093, 336, 518, 171, 1269, 1013. *1812* – 296, 908, 14. *1814* – 997. *1815* – 857, 904, 181, 1298, 734, 131.

117. *Lady's(2)*

LADY'S MAGAZINE, OR POLITE COMPANION FOR THE FAIR SEX. London. Vols. I–V (September, 1759–1763[?]). [Vols. IV–V were not examined.]

1759 – 650. *1762* – 1208. [See also Nos. 593 and 902b.]

118. *Lady's Monthly Museum*

LADY'S MONTHLY MUSEUM, OR POLITE REPOSITORY OF AMUSEMENT AND INSTRUCTION. London. Vol. I–XVI (July, 1798–June, 1806). New Series Vols. I–XVII (July, 1806–December, 1814). Improved Series Vol. I + (January, 1815 +).

1798 – 834, 434, 1135, 738. *1799* – 170, 676, 92. *1800* – 1082, 186, 1092, 1313. *1801* – 1240, 1079, 1292, 456, 595. *1802* – 1109, 214, 25, 837, 1133. *1803* – 294, 269. *1804* – 984, 157, 697. *1805* – 995, 261, 1270, 233. *1806* – 1315, 1304, 824, 42, 970, 832, 1271, 247. *1807* – 195, 127, 718, 79, 703. *1808* – 1156, 1046, 850, 1139, 517. *1809* – 139, 892, 396. *1810* – 437, 436, 137, 1299, 179, 671, 914. *1811* – 722, 726, 356, 1219, 136, 212, 1091. *1812* – 1047, 853, 1102. *1813* – 206, 493, 213. *1814* – 101, 1309, 342, 70, 928, 513. *1815* – 213a, 425, 1347, 1112.

119. *Lady's Museum*

LADY'S MUSEUM. London. Vols. I–II, Nos. 1–11 (1760–1761).

1760 – 1188, 646, 562, 1229.

120. *Lady's Pocket*

LADY'S NEW AND ELEGANT POCKET MAGAZINE, OR POLITE AND ENTERTAINING COMPANION FOR THE FAIR SEX. London. Vols. I–IV (1795–1796). [Only Vol. IV (July–November, 1796) was examined.]

1796 – 379, 326.

121. *Literary and Masonic*

LITERARY AND MASONIC MAGAZINE. Dublin. Vol. I (March–December, 1802).

1802 – 310b, 1254, 1009a.

122. *Literary Leisure*

LITERARY LEISURE, OR THE RECREATIONS OF SOLOMON SAUNTER, ESQ. London. Nos. 1–60 (September 26, 1799–December 18, 1800).

1799 – 629. *1800* – 1203.

123. *Literary Reg.*

LITERARY REGISTER, OR WEEKLY MISCELLANY. Newcastle-upon-Tyne. Vols. I–V, No. 52 (1769–1773).

1769 – 1194. *1770* – 257. *1771* – 708, 1141. *1773* – 1175, 276a.

124. *London*

LONDON MAGAZINE, OR GENTLEMAN'S MONTHLY INTELLIGENCER. London. Vols. I–LII (April, 1732–June, 1783). New Series Vols. I–IV (July, 1783–June, 1785). Continued as LONDON MAGAZINE AND MONTHLY CHRONOLOGER from 1736; and as LONDON MAGAZINE ENLARGED AND IMPROVED from 1783.

1751 – 97. *1753* – 37. *1759* – 635. *1763* – 591. *1771* – 1142. *1773* – 638, 863, 936. *1774* – 432, 572. *1777* – 426. *1779* – 29. *1780* – 1222, 427. *1781* – 512, 411, 1272, 1293a. *1782* – 991. *1784* – 1212, 1206. *1785* – 242.

London Magazine and Monthly Chronologer (Dublin). See *Gentleman's and London*.

125. *Looker-On*

LOOKER-ON. London. Nos. 1–86 (March 10, 1792–December 21, 1793).

1792 – 366. *1793* – 1185, 1213.

126. *Lounger*

LOUNGER. Edinburgh. Nos. 1–101 (February 5, 1785–January 6, 1787).

1785 – 1183, 938. *1786* – 1018.

127. *Magazin à la mode*

MAGAZIN À LA MODE, DÉDIÉ AUX DAMES. Dublin. Vols. I–II (May, 1777–April, 1778).

1777 – 524.

128. *Magazine of Magazines*

MAGAZINE OF MAGAZINES. Limerick. Vols. I–XXII (January, 1751–December, 1761). [The issues for January and April, 1761, were not examined.]

1751 – 122a. *1753* – 1318a, 489a, 558a. *1755* – 1078a. *1759* – 208a. *1761* – 1229b.

Magazine of Magazines (London). See *Grand*(1).

129. *Marvellous*

MARVELLOUS MAGAZINE AND COMPENDIUM OF PRODIGIES. London. Vols. I–IV (May 1, 1802–April 2, 1804).

NOTE: The separate numbers of the *Marvellous Magazine* were unnumbered and undated except for the engravings accompanying each issue. In dating the stories of this periodical, these labels have been accepted as accurate.

1802 – 893, 319, 1042, 1326, 196, 1106, 1170, 1305. *1803* – 1230, 318, 519, 73, 414, 1107, 740, 1004, 684, 1286, 159, 293, 750. *1804* – 855, 772, 852, 430, 460, 1160, 933.

130. *Masquerade*

MASQUERADE. London. Vol. I, Nos. 1–6 (October–March, 1752).

1752 – 1104.

131. *Matrimonial*

MATRIMONIAL MAGAZINE, OR MONTHLY ANECDOTES OF LOVE AND MARRIAGE FOR THE COURT, THE CITY, AND THE COUNTRY. London. Vol. I, Nos. 1–6 (January–June, 1775).

1775 – 178, 1157.

132. *Medley*

MEDLEY. London. Vol. I, Nos. 1–12 (January 4–February 12, 1805).

1805 – 1231.

133. *Meteor*

METEOR, OR MONTHLY CENSOR. London. Vols. I–II, No. 2 (November, 1813–July, 1814). [Only Vol. I was examined.]

1813 – 885, 1036.

Methodist Magazine. See *Arminian*.

134. *Minerva*

MINERVA MAGAZINE OF KNOWLEDGE, INSTRUCTION, AND ENTERTAINMENT. Dublin. Vol. I (June–December, 1793).

1793 – 949a, 1018i.

135. *Mirror*
MIRROR. Edinburgh. Nos. 1–110 (January 23, 1779–May 27, 1780).
1779 – 652, 1190.

136. *Monitor*
MONITOR, OR BRITISH FREEHOLDER. London. Nos. 1–504 (August 9, 1755–March 20, 1765).
1756 – 184.

137. *Monthly Epitome*
MONTHLY EPITOME AND CATALOGUE OR NEW PUBLICATIONS. London. Vols. I–V (January, 1797–December, 1801). Continued as MONTHLY EPITOME OR READERS THEIR OWN REVIEWERS. New Series Vols. I–III (January, 1802–December, 1804).
1804 – 479.

138. *Monthly Extracts*
MONTHLY EXTRACTS, OR BEAUTIES OF MODERN AUTHORS. London. Vols. I–IV (September, 1791–November, 1792).
1791 – 890, 337, 1358. *1792* – 706a, 1008a, 665, 371a, 753c, 315, 205, 889, 222, 175, 1066, 1019.

139. *Monthly Literary Recreations*
MONTHLY LITERARY RECREATIONS, OR MAGAZINE OF GENERAL INFORMATION AND AMUSEMENT. London. Vols. I–III (July, 1806–December, 1807).
1806 – 94, 351, 251. *1807* – 1352, 514, 112, 1a, 1167.

140. *Monthly Mirror*
MONTHLY MIRROR, REFLECTING MEN AND MANNERS, WITH STRICTURES ON THEIR EPITOME, THE STAGE. London. Vols. I–XXII (December, 1795–December, 1806). New Series Vols. I–IX (January, 1807–February, 1811).
1795 – 182. *1796* – 1056. *1797* – 71. *1799* – 189. *1803* – 1071.

141. *Monthly Misc.*
MONTHLY MISCELLANY, OR GENTLEMAN AND LADY'S COMPLETE MAGAZINE. London. Vols. I–V (January, 1774–September, 1777).
1775 – 532b. *1777* – 1372a, 1329a.

142. *Monthly Misc.* (Dublin)
MONTHLY MISCELLANY, OR IRISH REVIEW AND REGISTER. Dublin. Vol. I, Nos. 1–4 (April–July, 1796).
1796 – 275.

143. *Monthly Monitor*
MONTHLY MONITOR AND PHILANTHROPIC MUSEUM. Haddington. Vols. I–II (January–December, 1815). A continuation of the *Cheap Magazine* (q.v.).
1815 – 1319.

144. *Monthly Museum*
MONTHLY MUSEUM, OR DUBLIN LITERARY REPERTORY OF ARTS, SCIENCE, LITERATURE, AND MISCELLANEOUS INFORMATION. Dublin. Vols. I–II (October, 1813–December, 1814).
1814 – 1044, 1225, 1333.

145. *Monthly Panorama*
MONTHLY PANORAMA. Dublin. Vol. I (January–June, 1810).
1810 – 90a, 1058a.

146. *Monthly Pantheon*
MONTHLY PANTHEON, OR GENERAL REPERTORY OF POLITICS, ARTS,

SCIENCE, LITERATURE, AND MISCELLANEOUS INFORMATION. Dublin. Vols. I–III (June, 1808–October, 1809).

1808 – 1245a, 320a, 1139a. *1809* – 1109a, 731b, 767a, 383, 1181a.

147. *Monthly Visitor*

MONTHLY VISITOR AND ENTERTAINING POCKET COMPANION, BY A SOCIETY OF GENTLEMEN. London. Vols. I–XV (January, 1797–April, 1802). New Series Vols. I–VIII (May, 1802–1804). From Vol. XII called MONTHLY VISITOR AND NEW FAMILY MAGAZINE. [New Series Vols. III–VII were not examined.]

1798 – 729, 1097. *1799* – 952. *1800* – 1277. *1801* – 409, 150a. *1802* – 1116. *1804* – 651.

148. *Moral and Entertaining*

MORAL AND ENTERTAINING MAGAZINE, OR LITERARY MISCELLANY OF INSTRUCTION AND AMUSEMENT. London. Vols. I–VII (April, 1777–December, 1780).

1777 – 1138. *1778* – 1051a, 241b, 474c. *1779* – 652b, 1334b, 630a, 1275b, 38b.

149. *Moral and Political*

MORAL AND POLITICAL MAGAZINE OF THE LONDON CORRESPONDING SOCIETY. London. Vol. I (June–December, 1796).

1796 – 943.

150. *Museum*

MUSEUM. Cork. Vol. I, Nos. 1–23 (March 9–December 14, 1796).

1796 – 1342.

151. *New Gleaner*

NEW GLEANER, OR ENTERTAINMENT FOR THE FIRE-SIDE. Salford. Vols. I–II (1809–1810). A continuation of the *Gleaner* (q.v.) and *Harvest Home* (q.v.).

1809 – 1308a, 565k, 244d, 225a, 606e, 732d, 688a, 792, 733d, 646d, 47, 207b. *1810* – 1312c, 1251, 1138g, 481a, 751, 57c, 966c, 347, 511c, 1083, 666a, 335d, 510.

152. *New Lady's*

NEW LADY'S MAGAZINE, OR POLITE AND ENTERTAINING COMPANION FOR THE FAIR SEX. London. Vols. I–X (February, 1786–December, 1795).

1786 – 951, 1039. *1787* – 553, 612, 956. *1788* – 925b, 31, 1005, 1161, 1268, 375. *1789* – 735, 568, 601, 1137, 6, 1273, 482c, 1310. *1790* – 906, 1085, 461a, 605. *1791* – 1221, 1220, 452a, 543a, 252. *1792* – 454, 291, 643, 465. *1793* – 861, 1288, 353, 1316, 1138e, 486b. *1794* – 1021, 988a.

153. *New London*

NEW LONDON MAGAZINE, BEING AN UNIVERSAL AND COMPLETE MONTHLY REPOSITORY OF KNOWLEDGE, INSTRUCTION, AND ENTERTAINMENT. London. Vols. I–IX, No. 6 (July, 1785–June, 1793). [Vol. IX was not examined.]

1785 – 565d. *1786* – 811b. *1788* – 202, 1350, 309a, 401a. *1790* – 66a, 1138d. *1791* – 1070a.

154. *New London Gleaner*

NEW LONDON GLEANER, OR GENERAL REPOSITORY. London. Vols. I–II, Nos. 1–29 (1809). [Only Nos. 1–16 were examined.]

1809 – 1302a.

New Magazine (Dublin). See *Strabane*.

155. *New Magazine of Choice Pieces*

NEW MAGAZINE OF CHOICE PIECES, OR LITERARY MUSEUM. London. Vols. I–II, Nos. 1–32 (1810).

1810 – 832a, 981b, 847a, 1031a, 43i, 1199b, 888, 1050k, 1205c.

156. *New Musical*

NEW MUSICAL AND UNIVERSAL MAGAZINE. London. Vols. I–III (September, 1774–

December, 1775[?]). [This magazine was largely devoted to music, but offered a supplement called "The Literary Part of the *Musical Magazine*" in which fiction was published.]

1774 – 390.

157. *New Novelist's*

NEW NOVELIST'S MAGAZINE. London. Vols. I–II (1786–1787).

1786 – 265, 562a, 662, 132, 741d, 532c, 1229f, 359a, 67b, 827, 111c, 1190f, 624, 966a, *1787* – 348, 664, 333, 687d, 245a, 349, 565g, 263, 1003, 503, 859c, 589b, 1018e, 121b, 886, 406b, 646c, 289.

158. *New Town and Country*

NEW TOWN AND COUNTRY MAGAZINE, OR GENERAL MONTHLY REPOSITORY OF KNOWLEDGE AND PLEASURE. London. Vols. I–II (January, 1787–December, 1788).

1787 – 452. *1788* – 976a, 924a.

159. *New Universal*(1)

NEW UNIVERSAL MAGAZINE, OR GENTLEMAN'S AND LADY'S POLITE INSTRUCTOR. London. Vols. I–XVI (September, 1751–1759). [Only Vols. I, IV–VIII, X, XIV, and fragments of II, III, IX, and XVI were examined.

1758 – 800.

160. *New Universal*(2)

NEW UNIVERSAL MAGAZINE OF KNOWLEDGE, PLEASURE, AND AMUSEMENT, OR GENTLEMAN'S GRAND IMPERIAL MUSEUM. London. Vols. I–II (July, 1787–December, 1788. [The numbers of Volume II from July to December, 1788, were not examined.]

1787 – 1267c, 679, 955. *1788* – 1070.

161. *New Wonderful Museum*

NEW, ORIGINAL, AND COMPLETE WONDERFUL MUSEUM AND MAGAZINE EXTRAORDINARY. London. Vols. I–VI, Nos. 1–74 (1802–1808).

1808 – 785.

162. *Newcastle*

NEWCASTLE MAGAZINE, OR MONTHLY JOURNAL. BEING A COMPENDIUM OF THE HISTORY POLITICS, LITERATURE... OF THE TIMES. Newcastle-upon-Tyne. Vols. I–II (January, 1785–February, 1786).

1785 – 565f.

163. *Newcastle General*

NEWCASTLE GENERAL MAGAZINE. Newcastle-upon-Tyne. Vols. I–XIV (January, 1747–1760).

1748 – 741a. *1755* – 1078b. *1759* – 55.

164. *Newry*

NEWRY MAGAZINE, OR LITERARY AND POLITICAL REGISTER. Newry. Vols. I +, Nos. 1 + (March/April, 1815 +).

1815 – 704.

165. *North British*

NORTH BRITISH WEEKLY MAGAZINE, OR CALEDONIAN MISCELLANY. Edinburgh. Vols. I–II, No. 6 (October 16, 1782–October 24, 1783). Continued from No. 4 as NORTH BRITISH MAGAZINE, etc.

1783 – 305.

166. *North British Mag. and Rev.*

NORTH BRITISH MAGAZINE AND REVIEW. Edinburgh. Vols. I–III, Nos. 1–14 (January, 1804–February, 1805).

1804 – 520.

167. *Northern Gazette*

NORTHERN GAZETTE, LITERARY CHRONICLE, AND REVIEW. Aberdeen. Vol. I, Nos. 1–39 (April 6–December 27, 1787).

1787 – 451c.

168. *Novelist's*

NOVELIST'S MAGAZINE. London. Vols. I–XXIII (1780–1789).

1780 – 87, 644, 96, 1165, 1306, 60, 1367, 306, 1232, 661. *1781* – 45, 777, 784, 215, 1155, 58, 917. *1782* – 446, 864, 760, 44, 529, 1117, 1259, 41, 779a, 764, 1122, 586. *1783* – 640, 424, 727, 775, 776, 608, 1247. *1784* – 221, 248, 1321, 63. *1785* – 501, 583, 113, 380, 631, 623, 1237, 988. *1786* – 1002, 61, 528, 1150, 368, 831, 880. *1787* – 633, 500. *1788* – 620, 761, 54, 711. *1789* – 1169.

169. *Oxford*

OXFORD MAGAZINE, OR UNIVERSAL AMUSEMENT. London. Vols. I–XIII (July, 1768–December, 1776).

1768 – 705, 607. *1769* – 158a. *1773* – 276, 1341. *1774* – 491.

170. *Parlour Window*

PARLOUR WINDOW, CONTAINING ORIGINAL ESSAYS, POETRY, AND PART OF AN INSTRUCTIVE TALE. Dublin. Nos. 1–8 (1795–1796).

1795 – 183.

171. *Penny Medley*

PENNY MEDLEY, OR WEEKLY ENTERTAINER, CONTAINING SOMETHING TO SUIT EVERY ONE'S TASTE AND POCKET, BEING A CHOICE COLLECTION OF SHORT AND PLEASANT STORIES, etc. London. Nos. 1–12 (1746).

1746 – 668, 1011, 398.

172. *Perth*

PERTH MAGAZINE OF KNOWLEDGE AND PLEASURE. Perth. Vols. I–VI (July 3, 1772–September 24, 1773).

1772 – 898. *1773* – 335b.

Phoenix, or Weekly Miscellany. See *Weekly Misc.* (Glasgow).

173. *Pic Nic*

PIC NIC. London. Vols. I–II, Nos. 1–14 (January 8–April 9, 1803).

1803 – 836.

174. *Pocket*

POCKET MAGAZINE, OR ELEGANT REPOSITORY OF USEFUL AND POLITE LITERATURE. London. Vols. I–V (August, 1794–December, 1796). [The November, 1796, number of Vol. V was not examined.]

1794 – 498. *1795* – 1312, 232, 971. *1796* – 673, 1053, 302, 429.

175. *Political*

POLITICAL MAGAZINE AND PARLIAMENTARY, NAVAL, MILITARY, AND LITERARY JOURNAL. London. Vols. I–XXI (January, 1780–December, 1791).

1788 – 582.

176. *Prater*

PRATER. London. Nos. 1–35 (March 13–November 6, 1756).

1756 – 1214.

177. *Protestant Dissenter's*

PROTESTANT DISSENTER'S MAGAZINE. London. Vols. I–VI (January, 1794–December, 1799).

1797 – 1238.

178. *Rambler*
RAMBLER. London. Nos. 1–208 (March 20, 1750–March 17, 1752).
1751 – 850.

179. *Rambler's*
RAMBLER'S MAGAZINE, OR THE ANNALS OF GALLANTRY, GLEE, PLEASURE, AND THE BON TON. London. Vol. I–VIII (January, 1783–June, 1790).
1783 – 22, 24, 468, 883, 49, 483. *1784* – 103, 27, 46, 354, 527. *1785* – 686, 874. *1786* – 50, 104, 30a, 95, 32. *1787* – 51, 464, 56. *1788* – 217, 782, 33. *1789* – 828, 238.

180. *Ranger*
THE RANGER, A COLLECTION OF PERIODICAL ESSAYS. Brentford. Vols. I–II, Nos. 1–40 (January 1, 1794–March 21, 1795).
1794 – 43.

181. *Recreations*
RECREATIONS IN AGRICULTURE, NATURAL HISTORY, ARTS, AND MISCELLANEOUS LITERATURE. London. Vols. I–VI (1799–1802).
1799 – 1043.

182. *Reflector*
REFLECTOR, A QUARTERLY MAGAZINE, ON SUBJECTS OF PHILOSOPHY, POLITICS, AND THE LIBERAL ARTS. London. Vols. I–II (October, 1810–September, 1811).
1810 – 1262.

183. *Repository*
REPOSITORY, OR LIBRARY OF FUGITIVE PIECES. Dublin. Nos. 1–8 (1763).
1763 – 1229c.

184. *Repository of Arts, etc.*
REPOSITORY OF ARTS, LITERATURE, COMMERCE, MANUFACTURES, FASHIONS, AND POLITICS. London. Vols. I + (January, 1809 +).
1809 – 99. *1812* – 172. *1814* – 231, 1076. *1815* – 915, 114, 744.

185. *Royal(1)*
ROYAL MAGAZINE, OR QUARTERLY BEE. London. Vols. I–III (October, 1750–June, 1751).
1750 – 603. *1751* – 59.

186. *Royal(2)*
ROYAL MAGAZINE, OR GENTLEMAN'S MONTHLY COMPANION. London. Vols. I–XXI (July, 1759–December, 1771).
1766 – 536b. *1767* – 628a.

187. *Royal(3)*
ROYAL MAGAZINE, OR UNIVERSAL CHRONICLE AND PARLIAMENTARY REGISTER. London. Vol. I (January–November, 1788).
1788 – 372, 211, 1243, 313.

188. *Royal Female*
ROYAL FEMALE MAGAZINE, OR THE LADIES GENERAL REPOSITORY OF PLEASURE AND IMPROVEMENT. London. Vols. I–II (January–December, 1760).
1760 – 449, 546.

189. *St. James's(1)*
ST. JAMES'S MAGAZINE, BY ROBERT LLOYD, A.M. London. Vols. I–IV (September, 1762–June, 1764).
1763 – 486, 1095, 845, 1163.

190. *St. James's*(2)

ST. JAMES'S MAGAZINE, OR MEMOIRS OF OUR OWN TIMES. London. Vols. I–III, Nos. 1–34 (February, 1774–July, 1776). [Only Nos. 1–13, 20, and 25 were examined.]

1774 – 386, 1281. *1775* – 994.

191. *Salmon's Mercury*

SALMON'S MERCURY. Bath. Vol. I, No. 1 (November 1, 1777) – Vol. III, No. 130 (May 11, 1781). Continued as SALMON'S MERCURY AND GENERAL ADVERTISER from Vol. I, No. 4; and as SALMON'S MERCURY, OR ENTERTAINING REPOSITORY from Vol. I, No. 22.

1778 – 1199. *1779* – 719b.

192. *Satirist*

SATIRIST, OR MONTHLY METEOR. London. Vols. I–XV, No. 2 (October, 1807–August, 1814).

1809 – 235. *1810* – 236, 866.

193. *Scotch Cheap Rep.*

SCOTCH CHEAP REPOSITORY, CONTAINING MORAL AND RELIGIOUS TALES. Dumfries. Nos. 1–12 (1808–1809).

1808 – 667, 402, 1032, 156.

194. *Scots*

SCOTS MAGAZINE. Edinburgh. Vol. I + (January, 1739 +). Continued from Vol. LVI (1804) as SCOTS MAGAZINE AND EDINBURGH LITERARY MISCELLANY.

1744 – 843a. *1750* – 603a. *1751* – 122c. *1752* – 606a, 699a. *1754* – 511a. *1761* – 88. *1765* – 1267a. *1767* – 151. *1779* – 1190a. *1790* – 66f. *1792* – 223b. *1794* – 670b, 963c. *1795* – 1213b. *1796* – 299a. 648a, 43f. *1797* – 377b. *1798* – 216b, 109b, 547a. *1799* – 300b. *1800* – 1195a. *1801* – 627c. *1814* – 778.

195. *Scots Town and Country*

SCOTS TOWN AND COUNTRY MAGAZINE. Edinburgh. Vols. I–II (July 7, 1778–May 25, 1779).

1778 – 1078e, 321.

196. *Scourge*

SCOURGE, OR MONTHLY EXPOSITOR OF IMPOSTURE AND FOLLY. London. Vols. I + (January, 1811 +). Continued from Volume VII as SCOURGE, OR LITERARY, THEATRICAL, AND MISCELLANEOUS MAGAZINE.

1813 – 879, 413. *1814* – 868, 39.

197. *Selector*(1)

SELECTOR. London. Nos. 1–5 (November 7(?), 1776–January 2, 1777).

1776 – 224.

198. *Selector*(2)

SELECTOR. Leicester. Nos. 1–23 (August 28, 1783–January 29, 1784).

1783 – 1244.

199. *Sentimental*

SENTIMENTAL MAGAZINE, OR GENERAL ASSEMBLAGE OF SCIENCE, TASTE, AND ENTERTAINMENT. London. Vols. I–V (March, 1773–August, 1777).

1773 – 1118, 900, 682, 1114. *1774* – 1344, 742. *1775* – 1029, 1179, 153. *1777* – 1372, 1329.

200. *Sentimental and Masonic*

SENTIMENTAL AND MASONIC MAGAZINE. Dublin. Vols. I–VII (July, 1792–August, 1795). [The numbers for July and August, 1795, were not examined.]

1792 – 459f, 223c. *1793* – 1332a, 478a, 499, 617. *1794* – 10.

201. *Sentinel*
SENTINEL, OR BRITISH MISCELLANY AND REVIEW. London. Vol. I (July–December, 1804).
1804 – 1125, 1302.

202. *Smith's Weekly*
SMITH'S WEEKLY MAGAZINE AND HISTORICAL REGISTER. Dublin. [Only No. 4 for February 23, 1793, was examined.]
1793 – 1122a.

203. *Speculator*
SPECULATOR. London. Nos. 1–26 (March 27–June 22, 1790).
1790 – 1153.

204. *Spirit of the Public Journals*
SPIRIT OF THE PUBLIC JOURNALS FOR 1797, etc. London. Vols. I–XVIII (1798–1815).
1804 – 129. *1812* – 516.

205. *Sporting*
SPORTING MAGAZINE, OR MONTHLY CALENDAR OF THE TRANSACTIONS OF THE TURF, THE CHACE, &c. London. Vols. I + (October, 1792 +).
1808 – 1015, 1001. *1811* – 531.

206. *Spy*
SPY, A PERIODICAL PAPER OF LITERARY AMUSEMENT AND INSTRUCTION. Edinburgh. Nos. 1–52 (September 1, 1810–August 24, 1811).
1810 – 1100, 282, 789. *1811* – 259, 1098, 654.

207. *Strabane*
NEW MAGAZINE. Dublin. Vols. I–II (January, 1799–December, 1800). Published also as STRABANE MAGAZINE after July, 1800.
1799 – 1355a, 1144d. *1800* – 655, 441a.

208. *Sunderland Literary Misc.*
SUNDERLAND LITERARY MISCELLANY. Sunderland. Vol. I, Nos. 1–12 (January–December, 1815).
1815 – 109e, 1050l.

209. *Sylph*
SYLPH. London and Deptford. Vol. I, Nos. 1–40 (September 22, 1795–April 30, 1796).
1796 – 1226.

210. *Tell-Tale*
TELL-TALE, OR UNIVERSAL MUSEUM, CONSISTING OF A SERIES OF INTERESTING ADVENTURES, VOYAGES, HISTORIES, LIVES, TALES, AND ROMANCES. London. Vols. I–VI (1803–1805).
1803 – 1343, 173, 584a, 62, 192, 844, 1080, 810, 140, 255. *1804* – 982, 1349, 166, 1105, 1291, 1236, 115, 1345, 391, 509, 566, 1314, 802, 190, 169, 370, 833, 1351, 739, 1330, 578, 665a, 339. *1805* – 1336, 1353, 135, 794a, 148, 842, 996, 198, 1067, 1369, 912, 165, 149, 585, 15, 1168, 344, 923.

211. *Theatrical Inquisitor*
THEATRICAL INQUISITOR, OR LITERARY MIRROR. London. Vols. I + (Sept., 1812 +). Continued from Vol. II as THEATRICAL INQUISITOR AND MONTHLY MIRROR.
1812 – 1218, 1287. *1814* – 587. *1815* – 161, 1074a.

212. *Thespian*
THESPIAN MAGAZINE AND LITERARY REPOSITORY. London. Vols. I–III (June, 1792–September, 1794).
1793 – 747a.

213. *Town and Country*

TOWN AND COUNTRY MAGAZINE, OR UNIVERSAL REPOSITORY OF KNOWLEDGE, INSTRUCTION, AND ENTERTAINMENT. London. Vols. I–XXVIII (January, 1769–December, 1796).

1769 – 441. *1770* – 877. *1772* – 538. *1774* – 1186, 1357. *1778* – 602, 17. *1779* – 1280, 567. *1780* – 609. *1781* – 646a. *1783* – 604, 597. *1785* – 1337. *1786* – 76. *1789* – 540, 67e. *1791* – 1050e, 962. *1792* – 1153d. *1793* – 1018h.

214. *Town and Country Weekly*

TOWN AND COUNTRY WEEKLY MAGAZINE. Dublin. Vols. I–II, No. 3 (April 16, 1785–January 21, 1786). [Not examined: Vol. I, Nos. 1, 3, 5, 7, 9–15, 17–18.]

1785 – 732b, 794, 600a, 1274b, 1290b, 110, 335c.

215. *Town Talk*

TOWN TALK, OR LIVING MANNERS. London. Vols. I–VI, No. 1 (July, 1811–March, 1814).

1813 – 34.

216. *Tradesman*

TRADESMAN, OR COMMERCIAL MAGAZINE. London. Vols. I–XV (July, 1808–December, 1815).

1812 – 1324.

217. *Ulster Rep.*

ULSTER REPOSITORY, OR COMPENDIUM OF ENTERTAINMENT AND INFORMATION. Belfast. Vol. I, Nos. 1–26 (1785).

1785 – 910, 1190e.

218. *Universal*

UNIVERSAL MAGAZINE OF KNOWLEDGE AND PLEASURE. London. Vols. I–CXIII (June, 1747–December, 1803). New Series Vols. I–XXI (January, 1804–June, 1814). Third Series Vols. I–III (July, 1814–September, 1815).

1753 – 1318, 489, 558. *1759* – 208, 636. *1763* – 241. *1764* – 611. *1765* – 476, 573, 1334, 385. *1766* – 399, 38. *1767* – 924, 976, 401, 621, 407. *1769* – 555. *1770* – 719, 884. *1771* – 1278. *1773* – 969, 1296, 1275. *1774* – 1317, 1346, 1261, 343. *1775* – 887. *1776* – 53. *1777* – 147, 378, 653. *1780* – 1284. *1781* – 1190b, 983, 1293. *1782* – 733, 9, 811. *1783* – 197, 993, 541. *1784* – 118, 814. *1785* – 1025. *1786* – 245, 67, 506. *1787* – 35, 1018a. *1788* – 696, 423. *1789* – 78, 838, 66. *1790* – 1050, 813. *1791* – 981, 619a, 1024, 126, 1148, 1154, 706. *1792* – 896, 1008, 977, 753, 371, 272. *1793* – 1332. *1794* – 670, 957. *1796* – 43b, 1034, 377. *1798* – 109a, 939, 547, 431. *1799* – 300, 672. *1800* – 1195. *1801* – 627, 4, 134, 1099. *1802* – 615, 1266, 1209, 677, 1006, 8. *1803* – 817, 365, 400, 598, 355. *1807* – 1057, 1007, 941. *1809* – 19, 267, 803. *1810* – 1173, 1164, 361. *1811* – 1366, 737, 1327.

219. *Universal Mag. and Rev.*

UNIVERSAL MAGAZINE AND REVIEW, OR REPOSITORY OF LITERATURE. Dublin. Vols. I–IX, No. 2 (January, 1789–February, 1793).

1789 – 835a, 1144b, 508a, 931a. *1790* – 882b, 691c, 1050b, 374. *1791* – 619b, 298a, 126a, 1148a, 1252a. *1792* – 977a, 753d, 1008b, 168a, 459e, 371b, 222c.

220. *Universal Museum*

UNIVERSAL MUSEUM, OR GENTLEMAN'S AND LADY'S POLITE MAGAZINE, etc. London. Vols. I–III (January, 1762–December, 1764). Continued from Vol. III as UNIVERSAL MUSEUM AND COMPLETE MAGAZINE OF KNOWLEDGE AND PLEASURE. New Series Vols. I–VIII (January, 1765–December, 1772).

1762 – 309, 1197. *1763* – 1023. *1765* – 610, 495. *1766* – 536, 451, 237. *1767* – 1086, 462. *1768* – 537. *1769* – 1200a, 826, 284. *1770* – 1012, 675. *1771* – 444, 649a. *1772* – 106b.

221. *Universal Spectator*

UNIVERSAL SPECTATOR AND WEEKLY JOURNAL. London. Nos. 1–908 (October 12, 1728–March 1, 1746). [Most, but not all, of the issues of 1740–1746 were examined. A few are missing from the collections of the Bodleian and the British Museum.]

1740 – 327. *1743* – 1331. *1744* – 843, 563.

Walker's Hibernian Mgaazine. See *Hibernian*.

222. *Watchman*

WATCHMAN, OR THEOLOGICAL INSPECTOR. London. Vol. I, Nos. 1–12 (November, 1809–October, 1810). Continued in Nos. 11–12 as the CHRISTIAN WATCHMAN, etc.

1810 – 1311.

223. *Weekly Amusement*

WEEKLY AMUSEMENT, OR AN USEFUL AND AGREEABLE MISCELLANY OF LITERARY ENTERTAINMENTS. London. Vols. I–IV (December 24, 1763–December 26, 1767). [The *Union List of Serials* divides these four volumes into eight, but the pagination and indexing indicate four.]

1764 – 1138, 133, 474, 1096, 490, 1285, 106a. *1765* – 85, 1365, 1023a, 250, 405a, 754, 1267b. *1766* – 747, 121, 606b, 404a, 511b, 663, 270. *1767* – 1318b, 1241, 573a.

224. *Weekly Entertainer*

WEEKLY ENTERTAINER, OR AGREEABLE AND INSTRUCTIVE REPOSITORY. Sherbourne. Vol. I + (January 6, 1783 +).

1783 – 733b, 687b. *1784* – 959, 902c, 741c. *1785* – 1212a, 1276a, 574, 732c, 657. *1786* – 569, 1201a, 561. *1787* – 67c, 333a, 1025b, 1018c. *1788* – 121c, 289a. *1789* – 1371, 78a. *1790* – 66d, 659a, 660, 1010, 1050c, 208d. *1791* – 813a, 619d, 507, 1148b, 126b. *1792* – 896b, 706b, 753b, 371c, 1024b, 1008c. *1794* – 581. *1795* – 554. *1796* – 43e, 1034a, 377a. *1797* – 626. *1798* – 939b, 547c, 1223. *1799* – 670c, 300a. *1800* – 919. *1801* – 1099a. *1802* – 627h, 1266b, 989a. *1803* – 8a, 565j, 1205a. *1804* – 355a, 1154c, 651a. *1805* – 1362, 227. *1806* – 1149, 824a, 1050j 616. *1807* – 1064, 1057b, 1007b. *1808* – 1295, 666, 1312b. *1809* – 725, 809. *1810* – 234a, 1173a. *1811* – 1184, 841.

Weekly Magazine (Edinburgh). See *Edinburgh Weekly*.

225. *Weekly Mag. and Literary Rev.*

WEEKLY MAG. AND LITERARY REV. London. Nos. 1–16 (April 15–July 29, 1758). [No. 3 was not examined.]

1758 – 758, 603b, 768, 480.

226. *Weekly Mirror*

WEEKLY MIRROR. Edinburgh. Nos. 1–27 (September 22, 1780–March 23, 1781).

1780 – 285, 286. *1781* – 1108.

227. *Weekly Misc.* (Glasgow)

WEEKLY MISCELLANY OF INSTRUCTION AND ENTERTAINMENT. Glasgow. Vols. I–VI (June 25, 1789–June 13, 1792). Continued as PHOENIX, OR WEEKLY MISCELLANY IMPROVED. New Series Vols. I–IV (July 4, 1792–July 2, 1794). Continued as ASYLUM, OR WEEKLY MISCELLANY. Vols. I–III (July 30, 1794–April 14, 1796).

1789 – 1190g, 1018g. *1790* – 1200b, 1022b. *1791* – 459c, 975b, 68, 522a, 451g. *1792* – 741e, 1153c, 1050g, 1144c, 180, 565h. *1793* – 976b, 573b, 57b. *1794* – 911. *1795* – 239, 1054.

228. *Weekly Misc.* (London)

WEEKLY MISCELLANY, OR AGREEABLE AND INSTRUCTIVE ENTERTAINER. London. Vols. I–IV, Nos. 1–180 (1772–1775).

NOTE: The *Weekly Miscellany* (London) and the *Weekly Miscellany* (Sherborne) were obviously affiliated periodicals, and followed such closely parallel courses between 1773 and 1775 that it is difficult to determine which magazine appeared first, particularly since the weekly numbers of the London publication were undated. Very likely the latter was the leader. But in the Catalogue, when both magazines published the identical story, the Sherborne citation has always been listed first, simply because the Sherborne numbers of the *Weekly Miscellany* bear definite dates.

1772 – 1211a. *1773* – 1296a, 488, 404c, 487a. *1774* – 899b, 1317c, 106d, 405c, 1346b, 1348a, 1281b, 859b, *1775* – 482b.

229. *Weekly Misc.* (Sherborne)

WEEKLY MISCELLANY, OR INSTRUCTIVE ENTERTAINER. Sherborne. Vols. I–XIX (October 4, 1773–December 30, 1782). Succeeded by the *Weekly Entertainer* (q.v.).

See the note under *Weekly Misc.* (London).

1773 – 603c, 404b, 487. *1774* – 899a, 1317b, 106c, 405b, 1346a, 1348, 1281a, 859a. *1775* – 482a. *1776* – 1241a, 1078d, 1278b. *1777* – 1138b. *1778* – 1051, 719a, 241a, 474b. *1779* – 630, 1334a, 652a, 1275a, 38a. *1780* – 399a. *1781* – 207a, 427c, 1190d, 1222b, 512a, 571a. *1782* – 1293e, 458, 1284a, 884a, 584.

230. *Weekly Selector*

WEEKLY SELECTOR, OR SLIGO MISCELLANEOUS MAGAZINE. Sligo. Vol. I, Nos. 1–27 (February 4–August 4, 1812).

1812 – 1250, 948, 191.

Western County Magazine. See *County*.

231. *Westminster*

WESTMINSTER MAGAZINE, OR THE PANTHEON OF TASTE. London. Vols. I–XIII (December, 1772–December, 1785).

1772 – 1087. *1773* – 732, 600, 695, 335, 822, 1290, 359, 403, 367. *1774* – 1113, 1317a, 288, 21, 869. *1775* – 532. *1777* – 1030. *1778* – 858, 653a. *1779* – 1274, 1205. *1781* – 1293d. *1782* – 771. *1783* – 218.

232. *Wit's*

WIT'S MAGAZINE, OR LIBRARY OF MOMUS, BEING A COMPLETE REPOSITORY OF MIRTH, HUMOUR, AND ENTERTAINMENT. London. Vols. I–II (January, 1784–May, 1785).

1784 – 1216, 954.

233. *Wonderful*(1)

WONDERFUL MAGAZINE, OR MARVELLOUS CHRONICLE. London. Nos. 1–? (1764–1766[?]). [Only Nos. 1–4 (September–December, 1764) were examined.]

1764 – 1215a.

234. *Wonderful*(2)

WONDERFUL MAGAZINE AND MARVELLOUS CHRONICLE, OR NEW WEEKLY ENTERTAINER. London. Vols. I–V, Nos. 1–60 (1793–1794).

1793 – 1215d, 1259a, 476a, 920. *1794* – 1153e.

235. *Yorkshire*

YORKSHIRE MAGAZINE, OR UNIVERSAL REPOSITORY. York. Vol. I (January-December, 1786).

1786 – 1227.

236. *Young Gentleman's and Lady's*

YOUNG GENTLEMAN'S AND LADY'S MAGAZINE, OR UNIVERSAL REPOSITORY OF KNOWLEDGE, INSTRUCTION, AND ENTERTAINMENT. London. Vols. I–II (1799–1800).

1799 – 878.

237. *Youth's*

YOUTH'S MAGAZINE, OR EVANGELICAL MISCELLANY. London. Vols. I–X + (September, 1805 +).

1808 – 730. *1810* – 1263. *1815* – 1258.

238. *Zion's Trumpet*

ZION'S TRUMPET, A THEOLOGICAL MISCELLANY. Bristol. Vols. I–IV (1798–1801). Succeeded by the *Christian Guardian* (q.v.).

1799 – 1374.

INDEX

This index includes the names of all authors, editors, printers, and booksellers mentioned in Chapters I–V, the three appendices, and the notes, and also the titles of all books, periodicals, magazine stories, and essays given significant attention in any of the above-named places. It does *not* include authors or works cited in the Catalogue of Magazine Novels and Novelettes (which are covered separately in the Catalogue Index); place names; pseudonyms; or the names of persons unconnected with the history of magazine fiction.

Works of known authorship are always gathered under the author's or translator's name, except for periodicals and works published in periodicals, which are listed under the name of the periodical. Thus references to Mackenzie or his novels will be listed under *Mackenzie,* but references to his magazine stories and critical essays will be listed under *MIRROR* and *LOUNGER*. The authorial entry, however, will call attention to the others.

Owing to limitations of space, only the short titles of periodicals have been included. For the same reason, all definite and indefinite articles at the beginnings of titles have been suppressed.